Mastering™
Microsoft® Windows
Vista™ Home

Mastering™
Microsoft® Windows
Vista™ Home
Premium and Basic

Guy Hart-Davis

BICENTENNIAL
1807
WILEY
2007
BICENTENNIAL

Wiley Publishing, Inc.

Acquisitions Editor: Tom Cirtin

Development Editor: Double Gee Editorial

Technical Editor: James Kelly, Blue Rocket Writing

Production Editor: Rachel Meyers

Copy Editor: Cheryl Hauser

Production Manager: Tim Tate

Vice President and Executive Group Publisher: Richard Swadley

Vice President and Executive Publisher: Joseph B. Wikert

Vice President and Publisher: Neil Edde

Book Designers: Maureen Forys and Judy Fung

Compositor: Laurie Stewart, Happenstance Type-O-Rama

Proofreader: Nancy Hanger

Indexer: Ted Laux

Anniversary Logo Design: Richard Pacifico

Cover Designer: Ryan Sneed

Cover Image © Pete Gardner / Digital Vision / gettyimages

Library of Congress Cataloging-in-Publication Data

Hart-Davis, Guy.
  Mastering Windows Vista home : premium and basic / Guy Hart-Davis.
    p. cm.
  ISBN-13: 978-0-470-04614-2 (paper/website)
  ISBN-10: 0-470-04614-7 (paper/website)
  1. Microsoft Windows (Computer file) 2. Operating systems (Computers) I. Title.
QA76.76.O63H35566 2007
005.4'46--dc22   2006100832

10 9 8 7 6 5 4 3 2 1

To Rhonda

Acknowledgments

My thanks go to the following people for their help with this book:

- Tom Cirtin for acquiring the book
- Double Gee Editorial for developing the book
- Cheryl Hauser for editing the book carefully and lightly
- Jim Kelly for reviewing the manuscript for technical accuracy and offering helpful suggestions and encouragement
- Rachel Meyers for coordinating the book project
- Laurie Stewart at Happenstance Type-O-Rama for typesetting the book
- Nancy Hanger for proofreading the book
- Ted Laux for creating the index

Contents at a Glance

Contents

Introduction

Windows Vista Home Edition is a huge operating system both in the number of features it offers and in the number of ways it improves on its predecessor, Windows XP Home Edition. Microsoft has worked hard to make Windows Vista easy to use, but there's still a lot you need to know about it in order to use it most comfortably and effectively.

This book gives you that information.

Whom Is This Book For?

This book is for beginning, intermediate, and advanced users who want to get the most out of the Home versions of Windows Vista with minimum effort. The book covers both Windows Vista Home Premium (the version that includes Windows Media Center and the graphically intense Windows Aero user interface) and Windows Vista Home Basic (the stripped-down version that still offers all the functionality many users need).

Beginning, intermediate, *and* advanced—that's a wide range. Because any book that covered in detail absolutely everything to do with Windows Vista Home would be several thousand pages long, and this book isn't that long, it assumes that you want to get things done with Windows Vista Home rather than know everything about it. Instead of presenting arcane trivia or every single way of doing something, the book presents useful information and the easiest and most effective ways of getting something done. (There *is* some arcane information in the book, but it's there because you may find it useful or interesting.) This book also presents the background that you need to know in order to make important decisions about how to configure and use Windows Vista. But it doesn't hold your hand every step of the way.

WINDOWS 101 IN APPENDIX A

To present the information you need within its limited number of pages, this book assumes that you have basic knowledge of Windows already. If you're new to Windows, see Appendix A, "Windows Vista Basics," for a quick orientation on the Windows Vista Desktop and graphical user interface.

What Does This Book Cover?

This book concentrates on Windows Vista as you'll typically see it—either as the operating system preinstalled on a computer you buy or the operating system you install manually after buying the software in a store. It discusses how to get the most out of Windows Vista's built-in features, and it touches briefly on some other software you may want to use in order to keep Windows Vista working in tip-top condition. It doesn't discuss software that you may want to run on Windows Vista—office applications, music programs, genealogy programs, and so on. For those, you need other books.

The following sections provide a synopsis of the book's content.

Part 1: Up and Running with Windows Vista

Chapter 1, "Getting Started with Windows Vista," discusses how to log on and off, how to switch from one user session to another, and how to exit Windows. It also discusses how you can find out who else is logged on to the computer when you're working at it and how you can get an idea of which programs the other users are running.

Chapter 2, "Connecting to the Internet and Surfing the Web," covers how to choose an Internet connection, how to connect to the Internet, and how to use Internet Explorer to browse the Web. Internet Explorer 7 is a great improvement on earlier versions of the browser and is much more secure, but you may need to configure it manually. Among many other things, this chapter covers how to control your browsing history and use the Content Advisor to screen out objectionable content.

Chapter 3, "Customizing Your Desktop," discusses how to get your Desktop into shape so that you can work comfortably, effectively, and enjoyably. These changes range from those you should make immediately (such as choosing the best display resolution, configuring the keyboard and mouse, and setting any accessibility options you need) to changes you may want to make before too long (such as choosing a screen saver, changing your Desktop background, customizing the Start menu, and creating custom toolbars).

Chapter 4, "Installing, Removing, and Running Programs," discusses how to install, configure, remove, and run programs—and how to shut them down when they stop responding to your commands.

Chapter 5, "Managing Your Files and Folders," explains how to manage files and folders—everything from what files and folders actually are to what you can do with them and the tools that Windows provides for manipulating them.

Chapter 6, "Making the Most of the Bundled Programs," discusses the bundled programs that come with Windows: WordPad, Notepad, Character Map, Paint, Calculator, and Command Prompt. These programs are deliberately limited—Microsoft would like you to buy extra programs, preferably Microsoft programs—but they're useful for various tasks. This chapter points out the most important features of the bundled programs, including features that most users miss.

Chapter 7, "Finding Help to Solve Your Windows Problems," discusses how to use Windows Help and Support to find the help you need to use Windows most effectively.

Part 2: Administering and Troubleshooting Windows Vista

Chapter 8, "Managing Users and Accounts," discusses how to manage users and accounts to give users their own Desktop and folders and to maintain security. The chapter covers what user accounts are, what they're for, and why you should use them; the three different types of user accounts in Windows Vista Home; and how to create, delete, and modify user accounts.

Chapter 9, "Sharing Files and Working with File Types," shows you how to use Windows Vista's sharing and security features to share folders and keep private those you don't want to share. It also discusses the complex but essential topic of file extensions, file types, and file associations, which allow you to control what happens when you double-click different types of files in Explorer.

Chapter 10, "Managing Your Disks and Drives," discusses how to manage your disks and drives, showing you how to take such actions as formatting a disk, converting a disk's file system to NTFS, using compression to free up disk space, and creating and deleting partitions.

Chapter 11, "Working with the Registry," discusses the Registry, the configuration database that contains most Windows settings, and how you can use the Registry Editor to examine it and change it. The chapter starts by detailing the step you *must* take before you make any changes to the Registry and concludes by showing you how to change the Registry so that you can crash your computer with two keystrokes—for testing purposes only.

Chapter 12, "Installing, Configuring, and Managing Printers and Fonts," shows you how to install printers, configure them, and manage print jobs, including printing offline and printing to a file when necessary. This chapter also covers how to install, remove, and use fonts.

Chapter 13, "Managing Hardware, Drivers, and Power," discusses how to install hardware on your computer and how to install, update, and roll back device drivers, the software that makes hardware function. It also covers how to configure power management on your computer.

Chapter 14, "Using Windows Vista Home Edition on a Portable Computer," outlines the considerations for using Windows Vista Home on a portable computer. Many of these considerations (such as the basics of power management) apply to desktop computers as well and so are covered in other chapters, but this chapter discusses using portable-specific power-management features, choosing Tablet PC settings and Pen and Input settings, connecting an external monitor to a portable, and using different locations for dial-up networking. The chapter also shows you how to transfer files between two computers, including using the Briefcase feature to synchronize files.

Chapter 15, "Optimizing Windows Vista Home Edition," explains how to deal with program hangs and crashes and how to use Event Viewer to identify problems with your software. The chapter discusses how to use the Windows Update feature to keep Windows up to date, how to optimize and monitor performance, how to use the Problem Reports and Solutions feature, and how to set start-up and recovery options.

Chapter 16, "Backup and Disaster Recovery," covers a variety of topics related to when things go wrong. This chapter starts by discussing how to protect your data against disaster by backing it up, and how to restore it when necessary. It explains the Windows File Protection feature, which does its best to prevent you (or malware) from deleting vital system files. It discusses how to use System Restore to save snapshots of your system state, and how to return Windows to one of those snapshots. Then the chapter moves on to heavy-duty recovery, discussing how to restore the Last Known Good Configuration (which you can use to recover when Windows won't start successfully), how to use the new Startup Repair feature to recover from severe problems, and how to troubleshoot boot problems.

Part 3: Using Vista's Communication Tools

Chapter 17, "E-mail with Windows Mail," shows you how to master e-mail with Windows Mail, the powerful e-mail and newsreader program that comes with Windows. The chapter covers setting up e-mail accounts; configuring Windows Mail's many options; creating, sending, reading, and replying to messages; filtering your messages and dealing with spam; and working with both multiple e-mail accounts and multiple identities. This is a long chapter, but the topic is almost guaranteed to be of interest to you.

Chapter 18, "Reading News with Windows Mail," shows you how to use Windows Mail's newsreader features to read messages posted to Internet newsgroups and to post messages yourself. It also covers configuring Windows Mail to access your news server.

Chapter 19, "Publishing Information to the Web," discusses the considerations to keep in mind when publishing information to the Web: the legalities of what you can publish, the options of where to publish it, and how to get it there.

Chapter 20, "Instant Messaging with Windows Live Messenger," shows you how to get up to speed with Microsoft's entry into the IM arena: Windows Live Messenger. Apart from text chat, Windows Live Messenger lets you make voice calls and video calls to your contacts and share files easily with them—even when they're not online.

Chapter 21, "Giving and Getting Remote Assistance," shows you how to use Windows Vista's Remote Assistance feature to request assistance securely across the Internet to solve computer problems—or supply such assistance to someone else.

Part 4: Audio, Video, and Games

Chapter 22, "Windows Media Player and Windows Media Center," covers Windows Media Player, the powerful multimedia player incorporated into Windows Vista, and Windows Media Center, the entertainment center that comes with Windows Vista Home Premium (but not Windows Vista Home Basic). You'll learn how to configure Windows Media Player for optimum performance, copy CDs to your hard drive, play DVDs, and deal with digital rights management, and how to use Windows Media Center to watch and record TV, enjoy DVDs, listen to music, and more. The chapter also shows you how to control audio output and input and how to use Sound Recorder to capture audio.

Chapter 23, "Working with Pictures and Videos," shows you how to use image-manipulation tools that Windows provides. Coverage includes installing scanners and digital cameras, scanning documents, retrieving images from a digital camera, viewing pictures and videos with Windows Photo Gallery, making movies with Windows Movie Maker, and creating DVDs with Windows DVD Maker.

Chapter 24, "Burning CDs and DVDs," walks you through Windows Vista's features for burning CDs and DVDs. You'll learn how to choose suitable media and to use both the Live File System format and the Mastered format.

Chapter 25, "Playing Games on Windows Vista," starts by covering the games included with Windows Vista, including—at last!—a chess game. The chapter then discusses the hardware you need for serious gaming, how to add and configure game controllers, and how to get the best performance on games.

Part 5: Networking Windows Vista Home Edition

Chapter 26, "Understanding Windows Networking," discusses what a network is, why you might want to implement one in your home or home office, and what hardware you'll need to get in order to implement a network. It covers what you need to know about network architectures, network topologies, and network equipment in order to choose a network that's right for your situation.

Chapter 27, "Building a Home or Home-Office Network," discusses how to build an effective network for your home or your home office. You'll learn how to install a wired network, a wireless network, or a network that uses both wired and wireless; how to browse the network and map network drives; and how to connect Mac and Linux computers to the network.

Chapter 28, "Sharing Resources on Your Network," shows you how to configure your network manually if necessary. You'll learn how to connect your network to the Internet, share your Internet connection with other computers, share folders, and share printers. You'll also learn how to configure networking components manually and how to connect two networks via a network bridge.

Chapter 29, "Securing Your Network," discusses the points of weakness on most networks and the ways of securing them. It touches on backing up your network, securing your Internet connection, securing other aspects of your network, and troubleshooting both wired and wireless networks. It includes a special section on the threats to the security of a wireless network and how you can counter them most effectively.

Chapter 30, "Connecting to a Remote Computer or Network," discusses the technologies that Windows offers for controlling a remote computer and for connecting to a remote network. The chapter first covers Remote Desktop Connection, which lets you take control of a computer running Windows Vista Business, Windows Vista Ultimate, or Windows XP Professional and work on it as if you were sitting in front of it. (For example, you might access your work PC from home.) The chapter then moves on to creating a dial-up connection to a remote network before discussing how to use virtual private network (VPN) connections to connect securely to a remote network across an insecure connection. It finishes by discussing how to troubleshoot VPNs.

Appendices

Appendix A, "Windows Vista Basics," is for anyone new to Windows—whether you just bought your first computer or you're coming over from the Macintosh world. This appendix provides a quick introduction to the Windows Desktop and the main elements of the graphical user interface.

Appendix B, "Installing or Upgrading to Windows Vista," discusses how to install Windows Vista Home in each of the three ways you're likely to want to install it: as an upgrade to Windows XP Home Edition, as a dual-booting new installation alongside your current version of Windows, or as a clean installation on a computer with no other operating system installed. If you perform a new installation or a clean installation, you will probably need to use Windows Easy Transfer to transfer your files and settings from your old computer or operating system to your new one.

Terminology and Conventions Used in This Book

To present information concisely and accurately, this book uses a number of conventions:

◆ The menu arrow, ➤, indicates selecting a choice from a menu or submenu. For example, "choose Edit ➤ Preferences" means that you should pull down the Edit menu and select the Preferences item from it.

◆ Plus (+) signs indicate key combinations. For example, "press Ctrl+P" means that you should hold down the Ctrl key and press the P key. Likewise, "Ctrl+click" and "Shift+click" indicate that you should hold down the key indicated and then click.

◆ *Italics* mostly indicate new terms being introduced, but sometimes they simply indicate emphasis.

◆ **Boldface** indicates text that you may need to type letter for letter.

Mastering™
Microsoft® Windows
Vista™ Home

Part 1

Up and Running with Windows Vista

Chapter 1

Getting Started with Windows Vista

- ◆ Understanding the differences among Administrator, Standard, and Guest users
- ◆ Logging on and logging off
- ◆ Using the Desktop and the Start menu
- ◆ Switching to another user without closing your programs
- ◆ Locking the computer
- ◆ Checking which user is currently active
- ◆ Seeing who else is logged on to the computer
- ◆ Seeing which programs the other users are running
- ◆ Logging off another user
- ◆ Sending a message to another user
- ◆ Using the Windows Key
- ◆ Putting your computer to sleep
- ◆ Shutting down Windows

This chapter shows you how to get started with Windows Vista. You'll learn how to log on and log off, how to troubleshoot logon problems, how to switch from one user session to another without closing all your programs, how to use the Desktop and the Start menu, and how to exit Windows. The chapter also shows you how to find out who else is logged on to the computer when you're working at it, how to get an idea of which programs the other users are running, and how to log off another user (or all other users) to reclaim the resources they're using.

If you share your computer with other people, you'll probably log on and off, or switch users, several times a day. Logging on and off and switching users are easy, but having two or more people logged on at the same time, and possibly using the same programs and documents, can cause some complications.

This chapter assumes that you've already installed Windows Vista (or someone else has installed it for you). If not, see Appendix B.

Understanding Administrator, Standard, and Guest Users

For security and administration purposes, Windows Vista Home uses three different types of user accounts:

Administrator User An Administrator user has full power to configure the computer. When you first set up Windows Vista, the first user account you create is an Administrator account. An Administrator user can create further user accounts as needed.

Standard User A Standard user can run programs freely and can customize most aspects of Windows that affect their own user account. To configure aspects of Windows that affect other user accounts, a Standard user must supply an Administrator user's password.

Guest User The Guest user (there's only one) can run most programs but can perform almost no configuration or customization.

Microsoft recommends that you log on with a Standard user account except for when you need to perform computer-wide administrative tasks. In practice, though, you may well normally log on using an Administrator account. This chapter gives instructions for both types of accounts. Chapter 8 discusses how to create and manage user accounts and how to set a password on the main Administrator account for your computer

Logging On and Logging Off

To use Windows, you need to log on to your user account (a Windows identity), usually using a password. Once you've logged on, you can run programs, customize Windows, and generally get things done. When you've finished using Windows, you can log off so that someone else can log on (using their own user account).

When you log off, Windows closes any programs you were running. Instead of logging off, you can *switch user*, leaving your programs running in the background so that you can return to them later. When you switch user, Windows displays the Welcome screen so that another user can log on. After that user has logged off or switched user, you can log straight back into your session and pick up where you left off.

Only one user can be *active*—actually using the computer—at any time. A user who is logged on but not active is said to be *disconnected*.

This means that, for example, Jane and Jack can keep their programs open while Ross is using the computer. When Ross disconnects and ambles off for a cup of coffee, Jane logs back on. Windows resumes Jane's session from where she left off, displaying the programs she had running and the files she had open. Windows reestablishes any of Jane's persistent network connections, including any Internet connection that's set to connect automatically.

Being able to leave multiple users up and running is great—up to a point. But it has serious implications for performance. The sidebar "You May Want to Avoid Using Fast User Switching to Improve Performance" discusses these considerations briefly.

Logging On

To start using Windows, log on from the Welcome screen. Figure 1.1 shows an example of the Welcome screen, which displays a list of the users who have accounts set up on the computer. If a user is logged on, the Welcome screen displays *Logged on* beneath the name.

How Logging On and Off Worked in Windows 95, 98, Me, and Windows 2000

Logging on and off in Windows Vista works in much the same way as in Windows XP. But in versions of Windows before Windows XP, only one user at a time could be logged on to a computer running Windows. For a second user to log on, the first user needed to log off. Logging off involved closing all the open programs and files: Either the user could close the programs and files manually before logging off, or Windows would close them automatically when the user issued the Log Off command and confirmed that they wanted to log off.

Once all the programs and files were closed, and all network and Internet connections were closed as well, Windows displayed the Log On to Windows dialog box or the Enter Network Password dialog box, depending on whether the computer was attached to a network. Another user could then log on to Windows, run programs, open files, establish network and Internet connections, and so on.

 Real World Scenario

You May Want to Avoid Using Fast User Switching to Improve Performance

Having multiple users logged on to Windows at the same time affects performance because each user who's logged on takes up some of the computer's memory. Having a user logged on itself takes up a fair amount of memory, and each program that the user has running, and each file that they have open, adds to the amount being used.

Windows Vista needs a minimum of 512MB of RAM to run at all and runs much better with 1GB (1,024MB) or more. For each light user, figure in another 128MB of RAM; for each moderate user, 256MB; and for each heavy user, 512MB. If your computer has 1GB of RAM or more, you should be able to have two or three users logged on and running several programs each without running short of memory.

Another issue is what the programs in a disconnected session are actually *doing*. A program that's running but waiting for user input consumes very few processor cycles, but one that's actively engaged in a task consumes many—sometimes as many as Windows can give it. For example, if you leave Microsoft Word open with a document that you're composing displayed, Word waits for user input, and if you disconnect your session, it just sits there waiting until you come back. But if you're performing a processor-intensive task such as video rendering in a disconnected session, performance in the active session is poor.

Some programs pretty much suspend themselves when Windows disconnects their session and so do not affect the performance of the active session. Experiment with the programs you and the people with whom you share your computer use and establish which programs you can't reasonably leave running in a disconnected session.

If your computer has only 512MB RAM, avoid using Fast User Switching to reduce the amount of memory needed. Instead of switching user, close your programs and log off.

FIGURE 1.1
The Welcome screen lists the users with accounts on this computer and indicates whether each user is logged on.

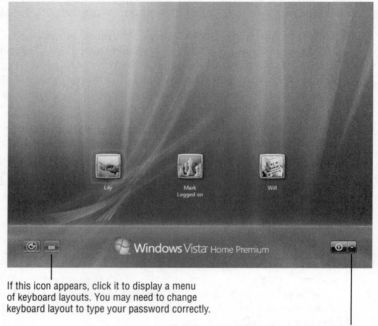

If this icon appears, click it to display a menu of keyboard layouts. You may need to change keyboard layout to type your password correctly.

Click here to display a menu of power-related actions: Restart, Sleep, and Shut Down

To log on, click your username. If Windows prompts you for a password (as shown here), type the password and press Enter or click the arrow button.

Logging on is usually as simple as that, but you may run into any of several complications:

◆ You may have to press Ctrl+Alt+Delete before you can log on. If so, Windows displays a message instructing you to do so. Pressing Ctrl+Alt+Delete is a security measure that ensures that what appears to be the Welcome screen actually *is* the Welcome screen rather than a piece of malware pretending to be the Welcome screen (for example, to capture your username and password). See "Forcing Users to Press Ctrl+Alt+Delete When Logging On" in Chapter 8 for instructions on setting up this security measure.

◆ If you enter the wrong password for the username you chose, Windows tells you "The user name or password is incorrect," as shown here. Click the OK button, and Windows then displays your password hint (if you created one).

◆ Passwords are case sensitive, so you must type your password using the correct case. Windows Vista warns you if Caps Lock is on, as shown here.

◆ You may have to change the keyboard layout so that you can type your password correctly. If the computer has two or more keyboard layouts available (for example, U.S. English and United States – Dvorak), Windows Vista displays a keyboard button in the lower-left part of the Welcome screen. Click the button to display a menu of available keyboard layouts, and then click the keyboard layout you want.

◆ If your keyboard has an embedded keypad (using some letter keys to type numbers when Num Lock is on, as the keyboards on most laptop computers do), having Num Lock switched on may cause you to mistype your password. Windows doesn't warn you about Num Lock being on. So if you find Windows won't accept your password, you've checked the keyboard layout is correct, and your keyboard has an embedded keypad, look to see if Num Lock is causing the problem.

If you've used Windows XP, you'll notice a difference with the Welcome screen. Apart from indicating that a user is logged on, the Windows XP Welcome screen also displays the number of programs the user is running and the number of unread e-mail messages they have.

When you've entered the correct password, Windows displays your Desktop with its current settings. (The section "Using the Desktop and the Start Menu" a little later in this chapter discusses the basics of the Desktop and Start menu. Chapter 3 discusses how to customize the Desktop.)

The first time you log on, Windows creates your folders and sets up program shortcuts for you—so the logon process takes a minute or two. Subsequent logons are much quicker.

 **Real World Scenario**

MAKING WINDOWS LOG YOU ON AUTOMATICALLY

Usually, forcing each user to log on before they can use Windows is a good idea, because it helps to keep your computer secure. However, you may sometimes need to set up a computer so that Windows automatically logs in a particular user account. See the section "Implementing and Preventing Automatic Logons" in Chapter 8 for instructions.

Logging Off

The counterpart to logging on is logging off. When you log off, Windows closes all the programs and files you've been using. If the files contain unsaved changes, Windows prompts you to save them.

To log off, click the Start button, click the right-arrow button to the right of the Lock icon (the padlock icon), and then choose Log Off from the pop-up menu, as shown in Figure 1.2.

If you leave your computer unattended for a while, the screen saver usually starts running—unless you have something open that prevents the screen saver from starting (or you've disabled the screen saver). For example, a dialog box open on screen usually prevents the screen saver from starting. The default setting is for the screen saver to start after 10 minutes and to display the Welcome screen when you interrupt the screen saver. The screen saver gives you some protection against prying eyes (particularly if you're using passwords for logging on), but it also makes it harder to see who's doing what on the computer. Chapter 3 discusses how to choose screen saver settings.

FIGURE 1.2
When you've finished using Windows, log off.

Using the Desktop and the Start Menu

Once you've logged on, Windows displays the Desktop—the background area that Windows provides for you to spread your work across. Figure 1.3 shows what the Desktop looks like the first time you start Windows and start a couple of programs. Because you can customize the Desktop extensively (as discussed in Chapter 3), your Desktop might not look anything like the Desktop shown in the figure: The wallpaper might be different, the Taskbar could be located at a different side of the screen, or various toolbars might be displayed. About the only unchanging thing about the Desktop is the Start menu button—but even this might not be displayed if someone has chosen to hide the Taskbar (of which the Start button is part).

You'll meet the Desktop in more detail in the forthcoming chapters, but these are the basic actions for navigating it:

◆ The Desktop contains one or more shortcuts to items. Usually, there's an icon for the Recycle Bin, if nothing else. Double-click an icon to run the program associated with it.

◆ The Start menu (see Figure 1.4) provides access to the full range of programs and features currently installed on Windows. To display the Start menu, click the Start button, press the Windows key on the keyboard, or press Ctrl+Esc (for example, if your keyboard doesn't have a Windows key). Choose one of the items that appears on it, or click the All Programs button to display a menu containing further items.

FIGURE 1.3
The components of
the Windows Desktop

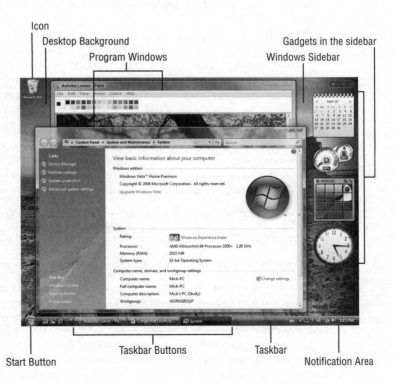

Icon

Desktop Background

Program Windows

Gadgets in the sidebar

Windows Sidebar

Start Button

Taskbar Buttons

Taskbar

Notification Area

FIGURE 1.4

Click the Start button to display the Start menu, then click the item you want on the Start menu itself, on the All Programs menu, or on one of the folders it contains. Click a folder to expand its contents; click again to collapse the contents again. Click the Back link to hide the All Programs menu again.

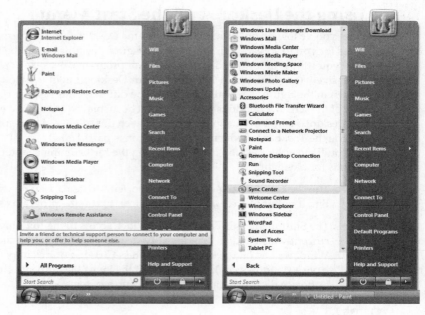

◆ The Taskbar gives you quick access to each program that's currently running. The Taskbar displays a button for each active program window until it runs out of space for reasonable-sized buttons, at which point it groups related windows onto a single button (which expands to show the individual window titles when you click it). To display that window in front of all other windows, click its button. To minimize a program (removing its display from your Desktop, so that only the Taskbar button is left), click its Taskbar button again.

◆ The notification area contains items that are useful to have displayed all the time (such as the clock, which is displayed by default), together with information and alerts (which are displayed at appropriate times). Because the notification area tends to get overstuffed with icons, Windows automatically hides those that are inactive. You can choose which icons to display and which to hide.

◆ The Desktop background is a graphic that you can change at will. From here on, this book uses a white Desktop background, usually without any icons, so that you can see the individual windows more easily.

◆ The Windows Sidebar contains *gadgets*, small programs that display information for you.

Instead of using the Taskbar to switch from one program to another, you can "Windows Flip" by pressing the Alt+Tab key combination. Doing so displays a panel of icons for the program windows currently open (see Figure 1.5). Hold down the Alt key and press the Tab key to move the selection to the program window you want, and then release the Alt key to display that program window. Hold down Alt+Shift and press the Tab key to move backward through the list.

Windows Flip is handy and has been a feature of Windows for many versions now (although it used to be called "coolswitching" or simply "Alt-Tabbing"). Along with the new name, Windows Vista introduces a new version of switching: Press Windows Key+Tab to display the open windows as a rotating stack (see Figure 1.6), and then press Tab repeatedly to bring the window you want to the front. When the window is at the front, release the Windows Key. Press Windows Key+Shift+Tab to move backward through the stack of windows. As with the Alt+Tab version of Windows Flip, the Desktop appears in the stack of windows, so you can use Windows Key+Tab to display the Desktop.

YOU CAN NOW SWITCH TO THE DESKTOP VIA WINDOWS FLIP

In a handy improvement over switching programs in earlier versions of Windows, Windows Vista includes an entry for the Desktop in the Windows Flip list. Selecting this item hides all programs, allowing you to see everything on the Desktop. (In earlier versions of Windows, to get the same effect, you would right-click the notification area or open space in the Taskbar and choose Show the Desktop.)

FIGURE 1.5
Press Alt+Tab to "Windows Flip" (switch) from one open program to another. Select the Desktop item (the rightmost icon shown here) to display the Desktop, hiding all programs.

FIGURE 1.6
Press Windows Key+Tab to display the open windows and the Desktop as a rotating stack. You can also select a window in the stack by clicking it with the mouse. This version of Windows Flip works only with the Vista Aero user interface.

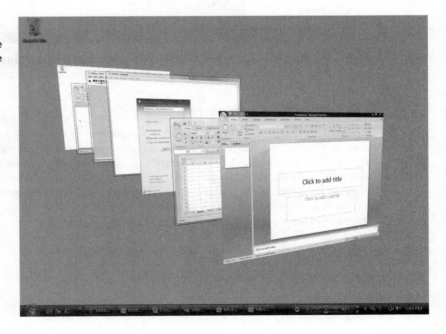

Switching to Another User

Instead of logging off (and closing all the programs you've been using) so that someone else can use the computer, you can switch user, leaving your programs running but letting someone else log on. To switch user, click the Start button, click the right-arrow button to the right of the Lock icon, and then choose Switch User from the pop-up menu, as shown here. Windows then displays the Welcome screen. Your username has the words "Logged on" underneath it to indicate that you're still logged on, even though you've just disconnected.

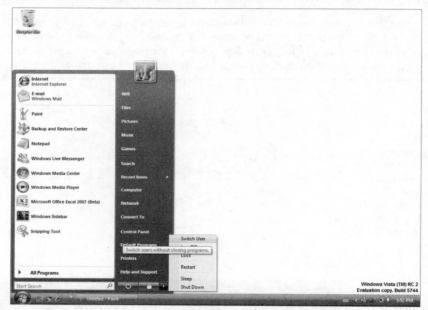

To log back on, click your username, type your password, and press Enter or click the arrow button. Windows displays your session again, with all the programs and windows as you left them.

Locking the Computer

Instead of switching user, you can "lock" your computer. Locking is almost the same as switching user, as it leaves your open programs running, but instead of displaying the Welcome screen with all the user accounts listed, it shows only your user account, together with the information that you're logged on and the computer is locked. You can then log on by clicking your icon and entering your password, or switch user by clicking the Switch User button, clicking the Switch User button again on the resulting screen, and then using the Welcome screen to log on as usual. Figure 1.7 shows an example of Windows in its "locked" state.

FIGURE 1.7
When you've "locked" your computer, Windows displays only your user account, together with the word "Locked" to indicate its status. Click your icon to log on, or click the Switch User button if you need to switch to another user account.

To lock Windows, press Windows Key+L. Alternatively, click the Start button, and then click the Lock button, as shown here. You can also click the right-arrow button to the right of the Lock icon and choose Lock from the pop-up menu, but clicking the Lock icon itself is easier.

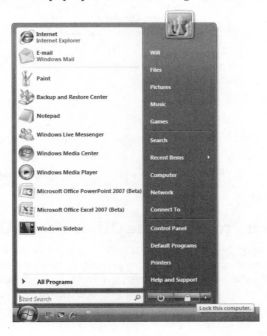

Checking Which User Is Currently Active

Normally, when you log on as yourself, you'll know that you're using your own user account. But if you're switching among user accounts for administration or testing, you may lose track of which account you're using, or you may return to the computer and need to find out whose session is currently connected.

To see which user is currently active, display the Start menu (by clicking the Start button or pressing either the Windows Key or Ctrl+Esc) and check the username displayed at the top, under the picture.

Seeing Who Else Is Logged On to the Computer

You can see who else is logged on to the computer in either of two ways:

◆ Switch user so that Windows displays the Welcome screen, and then look to see which users (apart from you) are marked as being "logged on." The problem with this approach is that you then need to log back on.

◆ Right-click the Taskbar, and then choose Task Manager from the shortcut menu to open Task Manager. Click the Users tab to display the Users page. You can then see the users and their status. Figure 1.8 shows an example.

FIGURE 1.8
The Users page of Task Manager shows you which other users are logged on to the computer. You can send them messages or log them off forcibly.

Seeing Which Programs the Other Users Are Running

It's not easy to see exactly which programs the other users of the computer are running unless you know the names of the executable files for the programs, but you can get an idea by using the Processes page of Task Manager. This page also shows you how much memory each program is using, which can help you establish whether—or why—your computer is running short of memory.

To start Task Manager and display the Processes page, follow these steps:

1. Right-click the Taskbar, and then choose Task Manager from the shortcut menu. Windows displays Task Manager.

2. Click the Processes tab. Windows displays the Processes page, which lists the processes you're running.

3. Click the Show Processes from All Users button, and then authenticate yourself to User Account Control. Task Manager replaces the Show Processes from All Users button with the Show Processes from All Users check box, which it selects, and adds to the list all the processes that the other users are running as well.

Figure 1.9 shows an example of the Processes page. You can sort the list of processes by any column by clicking the column heading; click once to sort in ascending order, and click again to sort in descending order. In the figure, the processes are sorted by the User Name column so that it's easy to see which process belongs to which user.

The figure shows only part of the list, but you can see the users Lily and Mick are both running, and 57 percent of the physical memory is in use. The Mem Usage column lets you see which programs are using more memory than others. See the sidebar called "Finding Out Which Process Belongs to Which Program" for details on how to find out which programs these processes represent.

In the figure, you'll see that Windows also has a number of processes open on its own account: The LOCAL SERVICE account and the NETWORK SERVICE account are each running several instances of the SVCHOST.EXE (service host) process each, together with various other processes. Not shown in the figure is the SYSTEM account, which also various processes, including SVCHOST.EXE and a process called System Idle Process, which indicates what percentage of the available processes are free. (Having a high percentage for System Idle Process indicates that your computer is handling its current workload easily.)

 Real World Scenario

FINDING OUT WHICH PROCESS BELONGS TO WHICH PROGRAM

The Processes page of Task Manager is helpful, but only up to a point. The problem you'll usually face when looking at the list of processes in Task Manager is that you need to identify which program a particular process represents—for example, so that you can decide whether to stop the process (as described later in this chapter).

Some of the other names are readily identifiable. For example, EXPLORER.EXE is the executable for Windows Explorer, and SIDEBAR.EXE is the executable for the Windows Sidebar. You don't need to memorize the mapping of each executable filename to its program, but if you look at Task Manager now and then, you'll learn to scan the list of processes and see which is running. This will help you decide whether you should go ahead and log another user off Windows (as described in the next section) or whether doing so will lose valuable data.

To start finding out which program corresponds to each executable file, click the Applications tab to display Task Manager's Applications page. Right-click a program and choose Go to Process from the shortcut menu. Task Manager displays the Processes page and selects the process for that program.

That's easy enough—but you'll find that there are many more processes running than programs. Try closing all the programs listed on the Applications page of Task Manager, and you'll see that many processes are still running. Turn your attention to the notification area and close as many of the items shown there as you can: Right-click each icon in turn and choose any Close, Quit, or Exit command that appears on the shortcut menu. Try stopping any obvious services that you can temporarily dispense with and see if an associated process disappears. For instance, try closing your Internet connection or stopping your PC Cards. Did either of those actions lose you a process? Then you have an idea of what that process does.

Even after you've done this, you'll find that the Processes page lists many other processes. To find out about these, click the Services tab in Task Manager to view a list of the services that Windows is running. (A *service* is a system process that runs automatically—for example, to provide printing features or network connectivity.) You can right-click a service and choose Go to Process from the context menu to make Task Manager select the process that belongs to the service. (Some services don't allow you to do this.)

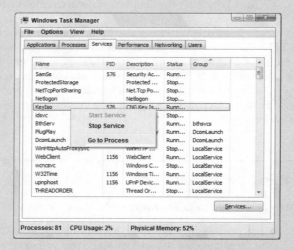

If you still can't identify processes, try searching on the Web. At this writing, one of the best lists is at `http://www.processid.com/processes.html`. Failing that, put the process name and "Windows Vista" into your favorite search engine, and you should turn up plenty of hits.

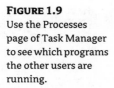

FIGURE 1.9
Use the Processes page of Task Manager to see which programs the other users are running.

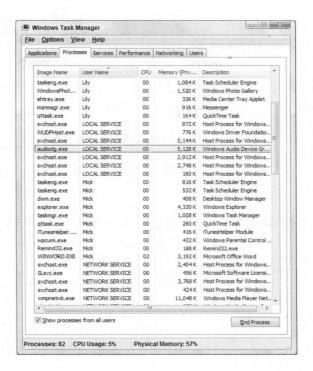

Logging Off Another User

If necessary, any Administrator user can log another user off the computer.

Logging someone else off is something you should do only in a pinch, because while you can use Task Manager to see which processes they're running (as described in the previous section), you can't see whether they have any unsaved work in them. If you don't use passwords to log on to Windows, it's much better to switch to the other user's account, close the programs and documents manually, and then switch back to your own account. If you do use passwords, you'll need to know the other user's password to log on to their account, which largely defeats the point of having passwords in the first place.

Even so, you may need to log off another user if they are running enough programs to affect the computer's performance or if they have open a program that can be used only by a single person at a time or a document that you need to use.

To log off another user, take the following steps:

1. Right-click the Taskbar and choose Task Manager from the shortcut menu to display Task Manager.

2. Click the Users tab. Windows displays the Users page (shown in Figure 1.8, earlier in the chapter).

3. Select the user, and then click the Logoff button. (Alternatively, right-click the user and choose Log Off from the shortcut menu.) Windows displays a confirmation dialog box, as shown here.

4. Click the Log Off User button. The other user's session is ended, and they lose any data that they hadn't saved.

Sending a Message to Another User

Windows provides a feature for sending a message to another user logged on to this computer. Because the other user can't be using the computer at the same time as you, this feature is no use for real-time communication, but it can be useful for making sure a family member or a colleague gets a message the next time they use the computer. (For example, you might ask them not to shut down the computer because you're still using it.) It's also useful for notifying another user that you've had to terminate a program that they were using.

To send a message to another user, take the following steps:

1. Right-click the Taskbar and choose Task Manager from the shortcut menu to display Windows Task Manager.

2. Click the Users tab. Windows displays the Users page.

3. Right-click the user and choose Send Message from the shortcut menu. Windows displays the Send Message dialog box (shown here).

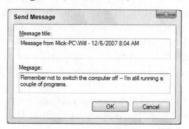

4. Change the message title in the Message Title text box (Windows enters default text that includes the computer's name, your username, and the date and time), and then type the message in the Message text box.

◆ To start a new line, press Ctrl+Enter. (Pressing the Enter key on its own "clicks" the OK button, sending the message.)

◆ To type a tab, press Ctrl+Tab. (Pressing the Tab key on its own moves the focus to the next control.)

5. Click the OK button to send the message.

The next time the user logs on to Windows, they receive the message as a screen pop, as shown here.

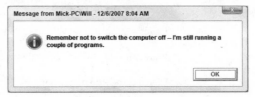

You can send more than one message to the same user, if necessary. When the user logs on, they receive the messages in the order you sent them. Sending multiple messages can be helpful if you need to change or contradict the information you sent it before, but such messages run the risk of being ignored, as the recipient blindly clicks through each pop-up message box in turn in the hope of reaching their Desktop and getting some work done.

Using the Windows Key

Windows provides several keyboard combinations for the Windows Key, the key (or keys) with the Windows logo on the keyboard. If you're comfortable leaving your hands on the keyboard, these combinations are doubly convenient, because not only can you avoid reaching for the mouse but you can also display with a single keystroke a number of windows and dialog boxes that lie several commands deep in the Windows interface.

Table 1.1 lists the Windows Key combinations.

TABLE 1.1:   Windows Key Combinations

WINDOWS KEY COMBINATION	WHAT IT DOES
Windows Key	Toggles the display of the Start menu
Windows Key+Break	Displays the System screen in Control Panel
Windows Key+Tab	Switches (Windows Flip) through the stack of open windows and the Desktop
Windows Key+Shift+Tab	Switches (Windows Flip) backward through the stack of open windows and the Desktop
Windows Key+B	Moves the focus to the notification area
Windows Key+D	Displays the Desktop, hiding all open applications
Windows Key+E	Opens an Explorer window showing Computer
Windows Key+F	Opens a Search window.
Windows Key+Ctrl+F	Opens a Find Computer window
Windows Key+F1	Opens a Windows Help and Support window

TABLE 1.1:   Windows Key Combinations *(CONTINUED)*

WINDOWS KEY COMBINATION	WHAT IT DOES
Windows Key+M	Issues a Minimize All Windows command
Windows Key+Shift+M	Issues an Undo Minimize All command
Windows Key+R	Displays the Run dialog box
Windows Key+U	Displays Ease of Access Center; formerly Utility Manager—hence the shortcut letter
Windows Key+L	Locks the computer

Putting Your Computer to Sleep

When you're not using your computer, you can either put it to sleep (as described here) or shut it down completely (as described in the next section). Putting your computer to sleep lets you keep your programs and documents open so that you can resume work (or play) when you reawaken your computer.

Before you put your computer to sleep, it's a good idea to save all open documents, just in case your computer suffers a problem while asleep or restarting. (For example, the power might go out.)

To put your computer to sleep, click the Start button, and then click the Power button on the Start menu, as shown here.

To wake your computer up again, press its power button. Depending on the computer and its configuration, you may also be able to wake it by moving the mouse or pressing a key on the keyboard.

When Windows resumes, it displays the Locked screen. Type your password and press Enter (or click the arrow button) to log on.

Shutting Down Windows

When you don't need to use your computer for a while—for example, overnight or over the weekend—you can turn it off completely. Rather than just turning off the power, shut down Windows, which will normally turn off the power for you.

When you're logged on, the easiest way to shut down Windows is to click the Start button, click the right-arrow button to the right of the Lock icon, and then choose Shut Down from the menu, as shown here.

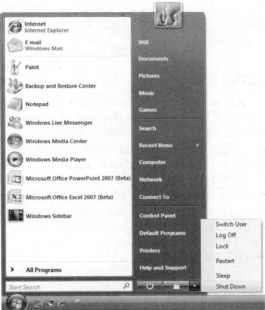

Another way of shutting down Windows when you're logged on is to click the Desktop, press Alt+F4 to display the Shut Down Windows dialog box (shown here), choose Shut Down in the What Do You Want the Computer to Do? drop-down list, and then click the OK button. There's no advantage to shutting down Windows this way unless you happen to enjoy it.

You can also shut Windows down from the Welcome screen by clicking the Power button. If any user (including yourself) is logged on, Windows warns you of the problem, as shown here. Usually, you'll want to click the No button so that you can either log off the other users or have them log themselves off, but you may sometimes need to click the Yes button and shut down their user sessions without saving data.

After you issue the Shut Down command in one of these ways, Windows closes any open files, shuts itself down, and then powers off the computer. If your computer has an unorthodox power setup, you may need to power it off manually.

The Bottom Line

Understanding the differences among Administrator, Standard, and Guest users   An Administrator user can customize Windows freely; a Standard user can customize their own user account; and the Guest user can perform almost no customization.

Logging on and logging off   To use Windows at all, log on using your user account. Click your username on the Welcome screen and then, if you have a password, type it and press Enter. At the end of your Windows session, log off by clicking the Start button, clicking the right-arrow button to the right of the Lock icon, and then choosing Log Off from the pop-up menu.

Using the Desktop and the Start menu   The Desktop contains icons that you can double-click to open Windows items (such as the Recycle Bin), programs, or documents. The Start menu contains links to almost all the programs and features you've installed. Click the Start button or press the Windows Key on the keyboard to display the Start menu. Choose one of the items that appears on the Start menu, or click the All Programs button to display a menu containing further items.

Switching to another user without closing your programs   To stop using Windows so that someone else can log on, but leave your programs running and your documents open, switch user rather than logging off. Click the Start button, click the right-arrow button to the right of the Lock icon, and then choose Switch User from the pop-up menu. Windows then displays the Welcome screen.

Locking the computer   To "lock" your computer, leaving your open programs running, press Windows Key+L or click the Start button, and then click the Lock button. Windows displays a version of the Welcome screen that shows your username, the word "Locked," and a Switch User button for switching to another user.

Checking which user is currently active   To see which user account is active, press the Windows Key or click the Start button, and look at the username at the top of the Start menu, under the picture.

Seeing who else is logged on to the computer   To see who else is logged on to the computer, switch user to the Welcome screen and look to see which accounts are marked as "Logged on." Alternatively, open Task Manager, click the Users tab, and then see which users are listed on the Users page.

Seeing which programs the other users are running   To see which programs the other users are running, open Task Manager, click the Show Processes from All Users button on the Processes page, authenticate yourself to User Account Control, and then see which processes are listed. Some process names are easily identifiable, but you may need to look up others on the Web to identify the programs they represent.

Logging off another user   When necessary, you can log off another user. To do so, open Task Manager, and then click the Users tab. Click the user you want to log off, click the Logoff button, and then click the Log Off User button in the confirmation dialog box that Windows displays.

Sending a message to another user   You can send a message to another user who is currently logged on but disconnected. The user sees this message the next time they log on. Open Task Manager, and then click the Users tab. Right-click the user, choose Send Message from the shortcut menu, type the message in the resulting dialog box, and then click the OK button.

Using the Windows Key   Windows Vista offers various shortcuts using the Windows Key. For example, press Windows Key+D to display the Desktop or press Windows Key+L to lock Windows.

Putting your computer to sleep   To put your computer to sleep, so that you can resume your Windows session later without having to reopen programs and documents, click the Start button, and then click the Power button on the Start menu. Press the power button on your computer to wake Windows again.

Shutting down Windows   To shut down Windows and your computer, click the Start button, click the right-arrow button to the right of the Lock icon, and then choose Shut Down from the menu.

Chapter 2

Connecting to the Internet and Surfing the Web

◆ Connect your computer to the Internet

◆ Surf the Web with Internet Explorer

◆ Configure Internet Explorer for comfort and security

When you set up Windows Vista, it automatically detects any available network and Internet connection—so if you already have a network and an Internet connection, you'll probably find that Windows Vista has established an Internet connection without your intervention. You can then browse the Internet (as described in this chapter), send e-mail (see Chapter 17), read news (Chapter 18), chat via Windows Live Messenger (Chapter 20), use Remote Assistance (Chapter 21), or indeed perform any other online activity.

If you don't have an Internet connection, you'll need to decide which type of connection to get, set it up, and secure it. The first part of this chapter shows you how to do so. The second part shows you how to surf the Web using Internet Explorer. The third part of the chapter shows you how to configure Internet Explorer for ease of use and for security.

Connecting to the Internet

This section discusses how to choose among the various types of Internet connections available and how to set up a connection.

If your computer is already connected to the Internet via a satisfactory connection, skip ahead to the section "Surfing the Web with Internet Explorer."

Choosing an Internet Connection Type and ISP

The Internet is so vital to communication these days that you'll almost certainly want to get the fastest Internet connection available to you at a reasonable price. This section discusses the available connection types in descending order of speed, starting with the type that's by far the fastest but also the one you're least likely to be able to get.

FIBER

Optical fiber Internet connections can deliver speeds of around 100Mbps—the same speed as the Fast Ethernet networks used in many homes and small companies. This bandwidth is typically shared, so you usually won't be able to download at the full 10+MB per second it offers, but you'll find it plenty fast enough for most purposes.

If you can get fiber affordably, forget any other type of Internet connection. Some new housing communities in high-tech areas (such as Silicon Valley, Silicon Island, and Silicon Prairie) are being built with fiber to the home, and some apartment buildings in major cities are being refitted with fiber. But if you live anywhere else, you're apt to be straight out of luck.

An optical fiber connection is "always on," so your computer or network maintains a connection to the network all the time.

DIGITAL SUBSCRIBER LINE

A digital subscriber line (DSL) is a digital telephone line. DSL typically offers between 384Kbps and 6.0Mbps downstream (to the consumer) and slower upstream (to the ISP) speeds. Some short-distance DSL lines can offer up to 24Mbps. With DSL, you computer is continuously connected to the Internet. The telephone line is dedicated to your Internet connection rather than being shared with other people, so you should be able to get the minimum guaranteed rate (sometimes referred to as the *committed information rate*, or *CIR*) any time of the day or night.

DSL works only within a relatively short distance from the telephone company's central office, which means in effect that it's confined to urban locations. Some non-telco DSL providers are more aggressive with the distance than the telcos, but you'll typically have to pay more, and you'll get a lower-speed connection. If you live out in the sticks, you're almost certainly beyond the range of DSL.

CABLE MODEM

Cable modems deliver Internet connectivity across your cable TV connection. The speeds depend on your cable company, the distance of your house from the nearest connection point, and the quality of the hardware used, but are typically from one to several megabits per second.

Cable has three main drawbacks:

◆ First, the bandwidth is usually shared with your neighbors, so if everyone gets online at the same time, the speed drops. Ask the cable company what the network's capacity is, how many people share that capacity, and what minimum bandwidth (if any) they guarantee you. If you find the speed dropping to unacceptable levels, lobby the cable company to add bandwidth to your loop.

◆ Second, many cable companies implement an *upload speed cap*, which limits the amount of data you can upload per second, typically to prevent you from running a web server or FTP server. (Their user agreements usually forbid you to run such servers anyway.) If you're neither going to be running a server nor sharing many files via P2P technologies, this shouldn't be a problem, but make sure that you know what the company's policy is before you sign up.

◆ Third, because the wire is shared, your computer is essentially networked with your neighborhood, so you need to be careful with networking.

INTEGRATED SERVICES DIGITAL NETWORK

If you can't get DSL or cable, your next choice should be Integrated Services Digital Network (ISDN). An ISDN is a digital line that's much slower than a DSL but more widely available, especially for people outside major metropolitan areas. ISDN's *basic rate interface (BRI)* provides two *bearer channels* that deliver 64Kbps each, plus a 16Kbps signaling channel, so it delivers decent speeds when both bearer channels are open. The signaling channel is more formally called a *data channel*, and you'll sometimes hear BRI referred to as *2B+D*—two bearer channels plus one data channel.

Check the prices before you order ISDN: It's traditionally been a business service, and it can be expensive, with most companies levying per-minute charges for each channel. It requires professional installation and extra hardware, and ISDN support at your ISP.

Most ISDN implementations are symmetrical, so you get the same speed upstream as downstream.

SATELLITE SOLUTIONS

If your area is too rural for you to get ISDN, or if ISDN is too slow for you, consider one of the satellite solutions available, such as HughesNet (`http://www.hughesnet.com`) or StarBand (`http://www.starband.com`). These solutions typically offer speeds of around 400Kbps to 500Kbps downstream, so they can be good if you need to download large files.

Satellite solutions used to have one major drawback: The satellite provided only downlink capabilities, so you had to use your phone line to send data to your ISP to tell them which information to deliver by satellite. Less-expensive satellite solutions still use this method, but if you pay more, you can send your outgoing data via satellite as well, which makes satellite much more attractive.

But there are several caveats:

◆ First, the satellite dish and installation can be pricey. (Watch for special offers.)

◆ Second, check the plan or pricing scheme carefully. Make sure it provides enough hours each month so that you don't start incurring expensive extra hours every month on your normal level of usage.

◆ Third, some satellite services have a *fair access policy (FAP)* by which they reserve the right to throttle back your download speed if you continuously run it full bore—in other words, you can have your 400Kbps (or whatever speed the provider offers), but you can't have it all the time. This can put a serious crimp into your ability to download a massive amount every day via a satellite hookup. So read your sign-up agreement carefully for details of the fair access policy, and be especially wary of clauses that allow the service provider to modify the terms of the contract without your explicit consent.

MOBILE CELLULAR SERVICES

Mobile cellular services let you connect to the Internet via your mobile phone, which is great if you need connectivity while you're on the road. However, the services are extremely expensive and the speeds are typically too low (at around 100Kbps) for normal use.

WIRELESS SERVICES

If you're in a city or town, you may be able to find a wireless ISP that you can use from your home or office using a wireless network adapter or wireless access point, either with or without an external antenna.

If you're really lucky, your city may provide free Wi-Fi connectivity for all its residents—but at this writing, few do.

CRITERIA FOR CHOOSING AN ISP

If you have a choice of connection, you may have a choice of ISPs as well. If you're using dial-up, you'll probably have plenty of choices. Use the following criteria to evaluate ISPs' offerings.

How many e-mail accounts do you get? Many ISPs offer five or so e-mail accounts for residential accounts. You may want more than this, particularly if you use your computer for business. The better ISPs give you as many e-mail accounts as you need. Other ISPs charge you for additional mailboxes. You may want to use free e-mail accounts (for example, a Gmail account or a Windows Live Mail account) as well as your regular accounts.

How much connect time are you allowed? (Dial-up connections only.) Some ISPs and some plans allow unlimited connection time. Others allow you a certain number of hours per month and charge extra for each hour or part of an hour beyond that.

Does your ISP provide a full suite of newsgroups? Almost all ISPs provide newsgroups, but some filter out newsgroups they consider offensive or that have exceptionally high volumes of traffic.

How much web space and traffic are you allowed? Make sure that your ISP provides enough space for a personal website: Some ISPs offer 10MB, some 20MB, some 50MB; some provide a certain amount for each of the e-mail addresses. If you plan to get a lot of visitors to your website, check the amount of traffic that the ISP permits before charging you extra. Some ISPs permit unlimited traffic, but others charge beyond a certain limit (usually measured in gigabytes per month).

How many dial-up points of presence does the ISP have? (Dial-up connections only.) First, make sure that the local point of presence (POP) is within your unrestricted calling area. Second, if you're traveling, you'll want to be able to connect at local rates. Make sure that your ISP has POPs in enough geographical areas or the right geographical areas. Your ISP might also have an 800 number that you can use when traveling; it'll probably have a per-minute charge, but it should cost less than calling long distance with hotel surcharges.

Can you use multilink? (Dial-up connections only.) Multilink lets you connect with two or more modems at the same time to get faster throughput. You'll need a second phone line to use multilink, and many ISPs who support multilink charge extra for it.

How good is the service? Ask people who are already using the service. If they report slow browsing and e-mail outages, look elsewhere.

CONNECTING TO THE INTERNET FOR FREE

If you're prepared to have advertising displayed at you the whole time you're connected to the Internet, you may be able to connect to the Internet for free. Check out the list of Cheap and Free ISPs at Freedomlist.com (`http://www.freedomlist.com`) for more information. Downloading the ads steals some of your bandwidth, but usually you need download each only once: After that, it's stored on your computer so that it can be displayed again as needed without being downloaded again.

Does the ISP support Windows Vista?   Some ISPs require you to use their proprietary software, which typically offers a customized front end to the Web but in many cases proves less flexible than using Internet Explorer or another browser.

Can you access your e-mail via the Web?   This feature can be useful when you're traveling without your PC.

Setting Up Your Hardware

Depending on the type of Internet connection you chose, you'll probably need to set up a hardware device for it.

DIAL-UP CONNECTION

For a dial-up connection, follow these general steps:

1. If you're using an external modem, connect it to your computer via USB or via the serial port. Connect a power supply if needed.

2. Connect the modem to your phone line.

3. Run the Connect to a Network Wizard as described in the section "Creating an Internet Connection," later in this chapter.

DSL

To set up a DSL, follow these general steps:

1. Install your DSL "modem" (it's not really a modem, but most people call use that term) and connect it to the telephone line. Depending on the DSL implementation, you may need to install a microfilter (to "clean up" line noise) between the phone socket and your regular telephone.

2. Most DSL modems connect either directly to your computer via USB or Ethernet or to your network switch or router. Connecting to the switch or router is usually better, as it makes sharing the connection with all networked computers easier.

3. If the DSL modem came with installation software, install the software, and then run it to configure the DSL modem with the connection information supplied by your ISP. You may be able to configure the DSL modem directly from a web browser.

CABLE

To set up a cable connection, follow these general steps:

1. Install your cable "modem" (it's not really a modem, but most people call use that term) and connect it to your cable supply.

2. Most cable modems connect either directly to your computer via USB or Ethernet or to your network switch or router. Connecting to the switch or router is usually better, as it makes sharing the connection with all networked computers easier.

3. If the cable modem came with installation software, install the software, and then run it to configure the cable modem with the connection information supplied by your cable company.

4. You may also need to run the Connect to a Network Wizard as described next.

Creating an Internet Connection

If you have an always-on DSL, cable, or fiber connection, your computer should already be connected to the Internet. If you're setting up a dial-up connection or a nonpermanent cable connection, take the following steps:

1. Choose Start ➤ Connect To. Windows launches the Connect to a Network Wizard, which displays its Select a Network to Connect To screen (if it can find a network) or its Windows Cannot Find Any Networks screen (if it can't).

2. At the bottom of the window, click the Set Up a Connection or Network link. The wizard displays the Choose a Connection Option screen, as shown here.

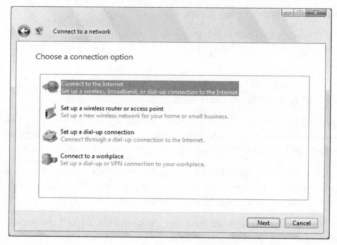

3. Select the Connect to the Internet item, and then click the Next button.

4. If you haven't identified the country (or region) and area code that you're in, or your phone and modem options, Windows displays the Location Information dialog box to prompt you for them.

   ◆ Select your country or region in the What Country/Region Are You in Now? drop-down list.

   ◆ Type your area code in the What Area Code (or City Code) Are You in Now? text box.

   ◆ Type any necessary carrier code in the If You Need to Specify a Carrier Code, What Is It? text box.

   ◆ Type any number needed to get an outside line in the If You Dial a Number to Access an Outside Line, What Is It? text box.

◆ In the Phone System at this Location Uses area, select the Tone Dialing option button unless you know the location uses pulse dialing (in which case, select the Pulse Dialing option button). Tone dialing uses a different note for each key on the telephone keypad; pulse dialing uses a different number of clicks.

◆ Click the OK button. Windows closes the Location Information dialog box, returning you to the wizard.

5. Click the Next button. The wizard displays the How Do You Want to Connect? screen, as shown here.

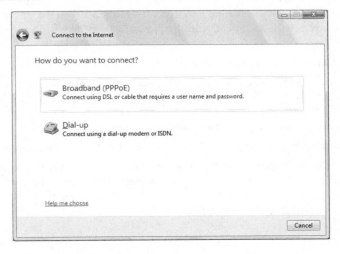

6. Click the appropriate button.

Broadband (PPPoE)   Click this button if you're setting up a broadband connection connected to this computer—for example, a cable modem or a DSL.

Dial-up   Click this button if you're setting up a dial-up connection that uses a standard telephone line or an ISDN line.

7. The wizard displays the Type the Information from Your Internet Service Provider (ISP) screen. The following illustration shows the screen for a dial-up connection, which includes the Dial-up Phone Number text box. The screen for a broadband connection doesn't have this text box but otherwise has the same controls.

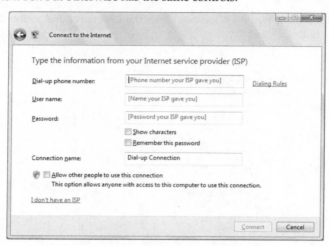

8. Enter the information for the connection:

Dial-up Phone Number   Type the phone number your ISP provided. If you need to set up dialing rules, click the Dialing Rules link, and then work in the Phone and Modem Options dialog box. See the section "Creating a New Location" in Chapter 14 for a discussion of dialing rules.

User Name   Type the username your ISP assigned you.

Password   Type the password for the connection. Select the Show Characters check box if you want to see the characters you're typing rather than the dots that Windows displays for security. Select the Remember This Password check box if you want Windows to store the password so that you don't need to enter it in the future.

Connection Name   Type a descriptive name for this Internet connection.

Allow Other People to Use this Connection   Select this check box if you want to make this connection available to other users of your computer to use the Internet connection. If this is your main Internet connection, you'll probably want to select this check box. Authenticate yourself to User Account Control.

9. Click the Connect button. The wizard attempts to establish the connection, as shown here:

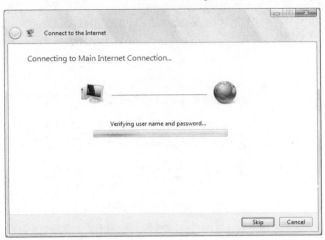

10. When the wizard has established and tested your Internet connection, it displays the You Are Connected to the Internet screen, as shown here.

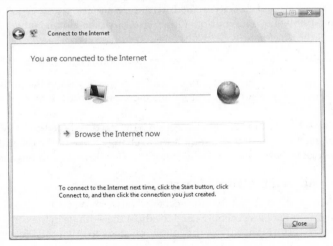

11. Click the Browse the Internet Now button if you want to launch Internet Explorer. Otherwise, click the Close button. Because you've connected to a new network, the Set Network Location Wizard launches and displays the Select a Location screen (see Figure 2.1).

FIGURE 2.1
Use the Set Network Location Wizard to tell Windows whether the network is a home network, a work network, or a public location.

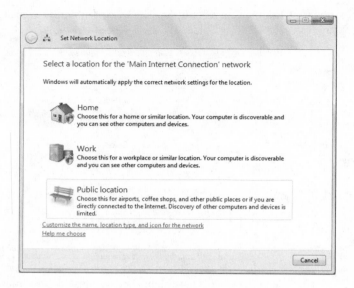

12. If you've connected directly to the Internet via a dial-up connection or a cable connection, click the Public Location button. Otherwise, click the Home Network button. The wizard displays the Successfully Set Network Location screen.

13. Click the Close button. The Set Network Location Wizard closes.

To close the Internet connection, right-click the network icon in the notification area, click the Disconnect From item to display the submenu, and then choose the name you assigned to the Internet connection.

Once you've set up your Internet connection, you can connect as described in the "Establishing a Connection" section. But first you may want to change some of the default settings that the Connect to a Network Wizard applied to the connection, as described in the next section.

CONFIGURING THE CONNECTION MANUALLY

Most of the default settings that the Connect to a Network Wizard applies to Internet connections work well, but in some cases you may need to adjust the settings in the connection's Properties dialog box for better performance. Take the following steps to open the Properties dialog box:

1. Choose Start ➢ Connect To. Windows launches the Connect to a Network Wizard, which displays the Select a Network to Connect To screen.

2. Right-click the connection, choose Properties from the context menu, and then authenticate yourself to User Account Control.

FIGURE 2.2
The General page
of the Properties
dialog box for a
dial-up Internet
connection

GENERAL PAGE OPTIONS

The General page of the Properties dialog box for a dial-up Internet connection (see Figure 2.2) contains the following controls:

Connect Using list box   Select the modem or other device to use for the connection. If you have multiple dial-up devices, select the check box for each that you want to use.

Configure button   Click this button to display the Configuration dialog box for the selected dial-up device. For example, on some modems, you can turn off the speaker on or off.

Phone Number group box   Specify the phone number for the dial-up device to dial and choose whether to use dialing rules.

◆   When you select the Use Dialing Rules check box, Windows enables the Dialing Rules button, the Area Code drop-down list, and the Country/Region Code drop-down list. Click the Dialing Rules button to display the Dialing Rules page of the Phone and Modem Options dialog box, in which you can create dialing rules as discussed in the section "Creating a New Location" in Chapter 14.

◆   If your ISP provides more than one dial-up number for this location, click the Alternates button. Windows displays the Alternate Phone Numbers dialog box (see Figure 2.3). To add a number, click the Add button and work in the resulting Add Alternate Phone Number dialog box. To edit an existing number, select it, click the Edit button, and work in the Edit Alternate Phone Number dialog box. To delete an existing number, select it and click the Delete button. Once you've added the phone numbers, use the up and down buttons to shuffle them into the order in which you want Windows to dial them. Windows automatically selects the If Number Fails, Try Next Number check box, and usually you'll want to leave it selected. If you have no preference among the numbers, you may want to select the Move Successful Number to Top of List check box to allow Windows to promote successful numbers to the top of the list on the basis that they'll be the best ones to try next.

FIGURE 2.3

If your ISP provides multiple dial-up numbers, add them to the list in the Alternate Phone Numbers dialog box.

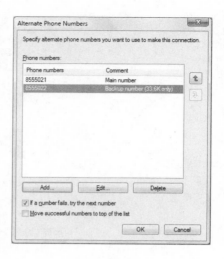

OPTIONS PAGE OPTIONS

The Options page of the Properties dialog box for a dial-up connection (see Figure 2.4) contains the following controls:

Dialing Options group box   This group box lets you specify whether Windows should display message boxes showing its progress as it establishes dial-up connections (the Display Progress while Connecting check box), prompt you for your name and authentication (the Prompt for Name and Password, Certificate, Etc. check box), include the Windows logon domain in the logon information it sends (the Include Windows Logon Domain check box), and prompt you for the phone number for the connection (the Prompt for Phone Number check box). Make sure the Include Windows Logon Domain check box is cleared for a dial-up Internet connection. The other three check boxes are cleared by default, but you may want to experiment with turning off some. If you turn off all these check boxes, when you double-click the connection, Windows dials it without displaying the Connect dialog box.

Redialing Options group box   This group box lets you control how Windows redials the connection if it can't connect at the first attempt or if the line or connection is dropped. Use the Redial Attempts text box to specify the number of times Windows should attempt to establish the connection and the Time between Redial Attempts drop-down list to specify the pause between attempts. (You can set values between 1 second and 10 minutes.) In the Idle Time before Hanging Up drop-down list, specify what length of inactivity Windows should allow before dropping the connection automatically. (You can set values from 1 minute to 24 hours, or you can choose Never to maintain the connection as long as possible.) Select the Redial if Line Is Dropped check box if you want Windows to automatically redial the connection if it's dropped at the other end.

FIGURE 2.4
Set up dialing options
and redialing options
on the Options page
of the Properties
dialog box for a
dial-up connection.

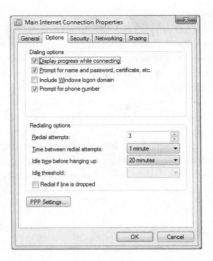

Real World Scenario

MAINTAINING A DIAL-UP CONNECTION TO THE INTERNET

To maintain as permanent a connection as your phone line and ISP permit, select the Redial if Line Is Dropped check box on the Options page and select Never in the Idle Time before Hanging Up drop-down list.

SECURITY PAGE OPTIONS

The Security page of the Properties dialog box for a dial-up connection (see Figure 2.5) contains controls for specifying how to authenticate and secure the connections you made.

In the Security Options group box, you have a choice of two option buttons for specifying a category of security settings: the Typical (Recommended Settings) option button and the Advanced (Custom Settings) option button.

By default, Windows selects the Typical option button for a dial-up Internet connection and selects the Allow Unsecured Password item in the Validate My Identity As Follows drop-down list. This setting allows Windows to validate your identity by using an unsecured password if it's not able to validate it by using a secured password. (Windows tries the secured password first, then drops back to the unsecured password if necessary.)

For increased security, select the Require Secured Password item in the Validate My Identity As Follows drop-down list to prevent Windows from using the unsecured password. For this to work, your ISP must support secured passwords for your connection—if your ISP doesn't, Windows won't be able to establish the connection. Once you select the Require Secured Password item, Windows makes available the Automatically Use My Windows Logon Name and Password (and Domain if Any) check box and the Require Data Encryption (Disconnect if None) check box. Select the former check box only if your dial-up account uses the same username and password as your Windows user account. Select the Require Data Encryption (Disconnect if None) check box if your ISP supports encryption and you need a secure connection.

If you have a smart card for the connection, select the Use Smart Card item in the Validate My Identity As Follows drop-down list. When you select the Use Smart Card item, Windows makes available the Require Data Encryption (Disconnect if None) check box. Select this check box if you need encryption.

If you know which security protocols you can (or must) use for your Internet connection, select the Advanced (Custom Settings) option button, click the Settings button, and work in the Advanced Security Settings dialog box. Chapter 30 discusses these options, which are typically used for connecting to company networks.

FIGURE 2.5
The Security page of the Properties dialog box for a dial-up Internet connection

NETWORKING PAGE OPTIONS

The Networking page of the Properties dialog box for a dial-up connection lets you choose which networking protocols and features to use for a dial-up connection. Normally, the Internet Protocol Version 6 (TCP/IPv6) check box, the Internet Protocol Version 4 (TCP/IPv4) check box, and the QoS Packet Scheduler check box should be selected.

Make sure that the File and Printer Sharing for Microsoft Networks item is *not* selected, because you don't want to be sharing your files and printers automatically with everyone on the Internet.

ADVANCED PAGE OPTIONS

The Advanced page of the Properties dialog box for a dial-up connection lets you share an Internet connection via Internet Connection Sharing (ICS). See Chapter 28 for coverage of ICS.

ESTABLISHING A CONNECTION

To establish a connection, take the following steps:

1. If not, choose Start ➤ Connect To. Windows launches the Connect to a Network Wizard, which displays the Select a Network to Connect To screen.

2. Click the connection, and then click the Connect button. Windows displays the Connect dialog box for the connection (see Figure 2.6).

3. If necessary, type your username in the User Name text box and your password in the Password text box. You won't need to enter these if the person who set up the connection chose to store the username and password in the connection.

4. If you want Windows to store the username and password, make sure the Save This User Name and Password for the Following Users check box is selected. Then select the Me Only option button or the Anyone Who Uses This Computer option button as appropriate. If you click the Anyone Who Uses This Computer option button, authenticate yourself to User Account Control.

5. Click the Dial button (for a dial-up connection) or the Connect button (for a broadband connection). Windows dials the connection or attempts to connect and displays the Connecting dialog box to keep you informed of its progress. If it receives an answer, it checks your username and password and, all being well, logs you on.

Windows displays a status icon for the connection in the notification area.

FIGURE 2.6
The Connect dialog box lets you save a connection's username and password for all users of the computer.

VIEWING THE STATUS OF A CONNECTION

To see the status of your Internet connection, follow these steps:

1. Click the Network icon in the notification area, and then click the Network and Sharing Center link. Windows displays a Network and Sharing Center window (see Figure 2.7).

FIGURE 2.7
Network and
Sharing Center lets
you see whether
your computer is
connected to a
network and to
the Internet.

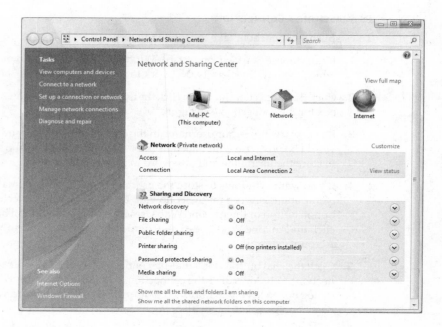

2. Click the View Status link for the connection. Windows displays the Status dialog box (see Figure 2.8), which gives the connection status, duration, speed, and details including the number of bytes of information sent and received and the number of errors.

The General page of the Status dialog box for a dial-up connection contains five buttons:

Details   Click this button to display the Network Connection Details dialog box, which shows you more detail about the connection and its TCP/IP settings.

FIGURE 2.8
The Status dialog
box for a connection
lets you see the
connection speed
and the amount of
data transferred.

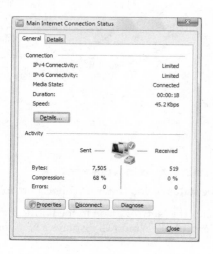

Properties   Click this button and then authenticate yourself to User Account Control to display the Properties dialog box for the connection.

Disconnect   Click this button to disconnect the connection.

Diagnose   Click this button to diagnose problems with the connection.

Close   Click this button to close the Status dialog box without disconnecting the connection.

DISCONNECTING A CONNECTION

To disconnect a network connection, take one of the following actions:

◆   If you have the Status dialog box for the connection open, click the Disconnect button.

◆   If you have Network and Sharing Center open, click the Disconnect link.

◆   Choose Start ➢ Connect To, select the connection, and then click the Disconnect button.

◆   Right-click the network icon in the notification area, click the Disconnect From item to display the submenu, and then choose the name you assigned to the Internet connection.

CONNECTING AUTOMATICALLY TO THE INTERNET

If you set any of your Internet-enabled programs to connect to the Internet automatically (or they set themselves to do so), Windows displays the Dial-up Connection dialog box (as shown next) when a program tries to connect via a connection that's not open.

Click the Connect button to let the program connect. If you want the program to be able to use the connection without your intervention, select the Connect Automatically check box first.

SWITCHING EASILY BETWEEN DIFFERENT DIAL-UP NUMBERS FOR THE SAME ISP

If your ISP provides you with multiple numbers that you'll need to use frequently (for example, if the ISP has multiple different local numbers in your area code, or if you need to call different numbers when you travel), create an entry for the ISP as described earlier in this chapter, then copy it by right-clicking it and choosing Create Copy from the context menu in the Network Connections window. Click the copy, press F2, type a new name, and then press Enter. Edit the copy's properties and change the phone number to the alternate number you want to use.

Securing Your Internet Connection

Windows Vista includes a *firewall*, a device used to secure the connection between one computer or network and another computer or network. This firewall is called Windows Firewall. To protect your computer, Windows Vista automatically uses Windows Firewall on each network connection, adjusting its settings to suit the type of network and the connectivity needs that you specify. For example:

◆ When you tell Windows that your network is a "home" network, Windows Firewall allows the computers on the network to discover each other.

◆ When you tell Windows to share files and printers on your computer, Windows Firewall allows the computers on the network to access the files and printers you've designated for sharing.

◆ When you tell Windows that you've connected to a "public" network, Windows prevents other computers on the network from discovering your computer at all.

You may sometimes need to configure Windows Firewall manually for special purposes. The section "Configuring Windows Firewall Manually" in Chapter 28 shows you how to do so.

WHAT DOES A FIREWALL DO?

A firewall monitors the packets of information being sent and received from the computers inside the network. Depending on the configuration of the firewall, it may pass all the packets it receives (both ingoing and outgoing) to a proxy server that checks whether the packets are allowed to pass the firewall. If the packets are allowed, it passes them on. If they're not allowed, it stops them.

Surfing the Web with Internet Explorer

Once you've established an Internet connection, you're ready to surf the Web with Internet Explorer. This section shows you how to surf and how to configure Internet Explorer's most important settings, including the security settings.

Starting Internet Explorer

These are the easiest ways of starting Internet Explorer:

◆ Choose Start ➢ Internet.

◆ Click the Launch Internet Explorer Browser shortcut on your Quick Launch toolbar (the toolbar that appears by default to the right of the Start button).

◆ Double-click a URL or another file type associated with Internet Explorer.

The Internet Explorer Interface

Figure 2.9 shows the main features of the Internet Explorer window.

The status bar shows information on the current operation (for example, *Connecting to site www.sybex.com*) or information on any hyperlink the mouse pointer is currently pointing to.

FIGURE 2.9

The main features of the Internet Explorer window

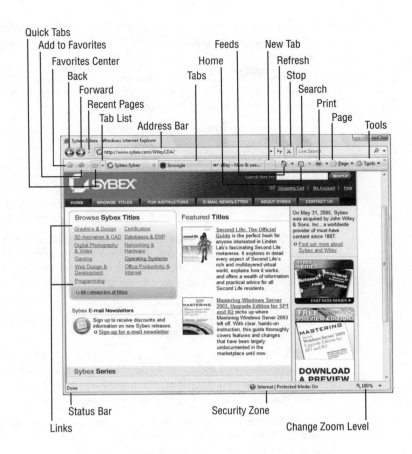

SEE MORE OF THE WEB WITH FULL SCREEN VIEW

Internet Explorer 7 provides more window area than Internet Explorer 6 and earlier versions by suppressing the menu bar and putting several different types of controls (buttons, tabs, and drop-down menus) on the same row. To see even more of the current web page, use Full Screen view.

To enter Full Screen view, choose Tools ➤ Full Screen or press the F11 key. To turn Full Screen off again, press the F11 key.

USING THE COMMAND BAR BUTTONS

Here's how to use the main controls in Internet Explorer:

◆ Click the Back button to move to the previous page you were on.

◆ Click the Forward button to move forward to a page you were on before you clicked the Back button.

◆ Click the Stop button to stop Internet Explorer from pursuing a jump that's in progress. (For example, if the jump has stalled or if the page is loading very slowly, you might want to stop it.)

◆ Click the Refresh button to have Internet Explorer reload the current page. You might want to do this if part of the page fails to transfer properly, or if you think the page may have changed since you loaded this instance of it.

◆ Click the Home button to jump to your home page (the page that Internet Explorer displays when you start it).

◆ To search using the Windows Live search engine, click in the search box, type your search term, and then press Enter or click the search button.

◆ Click the Favorites Center button to display Favorites Center. (The section "Creating and Using Favorites," later in this chapter, discusses favorites.)

◆ To go to a page you've visited recently, click the Recent Pages button, and then choose the page from the drop-down list. To go to a page you've visited but that doesn't appear on the Recent Pages list, click the History item at the bottom of the Recent Pages list. Internet Explorer displays the History feature in Favorites Center.

◆ Click the Feeds button to display available RSS feeds. RSS is the abbreviation for Really Simple Syndication, a means of publishing items on the Web. RSS is typically used for subscribing to web logs (also called *blogs*) or news sites.

◆ Click the Print button to print the current page. (Internet Explorer doesn't display the Print dialog box—it goes right ahead and prints the page.) Click the drop-down button next to the Print button to issue the Print command (which displays the Print dialog box), the Print Preview command, or the Page Setup command.

◆ Click the Page button to display a menu of page-related commands that include opening a new window; cutting, copying, and pasting; saving a web page or sending it by e-mail; and changing the zoom level and text size.

◆ Click the Tools button to display a menu of other commands for configuring Internet Explorer.

USING KEYBOARD SHORTCUTS

You can use the keyboard shortcuts shown in Table 2.1 to navigate in Internet Explorer.

TABLE 2.1:   Keyboard Shortcuts for Internet Explorer

ACTION	KEYBOARD SHORTCUT
Back	Alt+ ← or Backspace
Forward	Alt+ →

TABLE 2.1:   Keyboard Shortcuts for Internet Explorer *(CONTINUED)*

ACTION	KEYBOARD SHORTCUT
Home Page	Alt+Home
Display the Address bar drop-down list	F4
Refresh	F5
Select the contents of the Address box in the Address bar	Alt+D

Using Internet Explorer to Access Web Pages

Each website or web page is identified by an address called a *Uniform Resource Locator*, or *URL* for short. (URL is usually pronounced as "U-R-L," but it's sometimes pronounced "earl.") For example, the URL for the Microsoft website is `http://www.microsoft.com`. By pointing your browser at this URL, you can access the Microsoft website.

To open a URL, click in the Address box, type in the URL, and press Enter to accept it. You don't need to include the `http://` prefix: Internet Explorer adds that automatically if you enter a valid URL. Similarly, to access an FTP site, you don't need to enter the `ftp://` prefix: Just enter the address, and Internet Explorer adds the prefix. (Occasionally this prefix adding doesn't work. In that case, enter the prefix manually.)

If the URL starts with `www.` (after the `http://` prefix) and ends with `.com`, you can enter those parts of the address automatically by pressing Ctrl+Enter. For example, to access the Sybex website, `www.sybex.com`, you could type **sybex** and press Ctrl+Enter to have Internet Explorer enter `http://www.sybex.com`.

If the address you're typing matches an address you've visited within Internet Explorer's memory, Internet Explorer displays a drop-down list of URLs. If one of them is right, use the ↓ key to select it, and then press the Enter key. If not, finish typing the new URL and then press the Enter key or click the Go button.

Internet Explorer includes built-in support for a large number of file formats, including HTML pages, text files, and several types of graphics files (such as GIF, JPEG, and PNG). When you encounter a file type that needs an add-on program or a plug-in, Internet Explorer warns you and seeks permission to download and install the add-on or plug-in.

AUTOCOMPLETE AND ITS DANGERS

Internet Explorer's AutoComplete feature does its best to make a complete URL out of whatever you enter. If you enter part of a URL, AutoComplete adds `http://www` to it and then tries the `.com`, `.edu`, and `.org` domain suffixes (in that order). Be warned that if you give Internet Explorer this much latitude in constructing URLs, you may get some sites you didn't bargain for.

If you don't like the AutoComplete feature, turn it off. Choose Tools ➤ Internet Options and clear the Use Inline AutoComplete check box on the Advanced page of the Internet Options dialog box.

TROUBLESHOOTING: SOLVING PROBLEMS ACCESSING WEB PAGES

This sidebar discusses some of the most common reasons for not being able to access web pages.

"SERVER TOO BUSY" ERROR

The "Server Too Busy" message typically means that the web server the browser contacted was too busy right then handling other requests to deal with your request for information. Click the Refresh button on the toolbar to try the link again. Often, you'll get straight through on the second attempt, but if the server is truly busy, you may need to retry a number of times, or wait until later.

HTTP ERROR 404: "PAGE NOT AVAILABLE"

When you receive HTTP Error 404: "Page Not Available," the page may in fact not be available, but try refreshing it by clicking the Refresh button or pressing the F5 key in case the request simply timed out.

HTTP ERROR 403: "YOU ARE NOT AUTHORIZED TO VIEW THIS PAGE"

The error message HTTP Error 403: "You Are Not Authorized to View This Page" typically means either that you've requested a page that you're really not allowed to access or that you haven't authenticated yourself enough for the website to recognize that you are in fact authorized to view the page. If you think you *have* authenticated yourself, check that the page isn't on a subscription website to which you don't have access because you haven't paid (or because the website has started charging for content).

"THE PAGE CANNOT BE DISPLAYED - CANNOT FIND SERVER OR DNS ERROR"

The error message "The Page Cannot Be Displayed - Cannot Find Server or DNS Error" typically means that the page isn't at the URL anymore. It may also mean that the website that contained the page is no longer available. Try reducing the URL to the domain name and see if the website is still there. If it is, try to navigate to the page you want by using whatever search or navigation mechanisms the site provides.

If you know that the address exists, try it later, when the server may be back online. If not, and if you typed in the URL, double-check each character to make sure you didn't miss or add anything. Then try it again.

Failing the previous suggestions, this error may indicate simply that your Internet connection isn't working. Check the connection manually if you're not certain it's functional.

CHECK YOUR SECURITY SETTINGS

If the website you're trying to reach is secure, make sure that your security settings match its requirements. In the Security section of the Advanced page of the Internet Options dialog box, choose settings for SSL 2.0, SSL 3.0, or TLS 1.0 as necessary. (See the "Security Category" section near the end of this chapter for a discussion of SSL and TLS.)

Jumping to a Hyperlink

Many web documents contain *hyperlinks*, which are jumps to other locations. Hyperlinks are typically displayed as underlined text, graphical objects, or pictures, and are often referred to simply as *links*.

When you move the mouse pointer over a hyperlink, the mouse pointer takes on the shape of a hand with a finger pointing upward. To jump to the hyperlinked location, click the hyperlink. If the hyperlink involves another program, Windows activates that program. For example, a hyperlink in an e-mail message may launch Internet Explorer (or your default browser), or a hyperlink on a web page to a PDF file may launch Adobe Acrobat.

Turning Off Internet Explorer's Clicks

By default, Internet Explorer makes a clicking sound when you click a link, to give you audio feedback that you've clicked it. To turn this clicking off, or to change the sound played, work with the Start Navigation event in the Program Events list box on the Sounds page of the Sound dialog box. See the section "Choosing System Sounds" in Chapter 3 for step-by-step instructions. (There's also a Complete Navigation event that you can configure if you like having sound cues.)

Returning to a Previous Document

Because you'll often access dead ends or pages that don't offer the information you need, you'll often want to return to the previous document you accessed. There are several ways to move back to a document you've visited before:

◆ Click the Back button or press Alt+← to move back one page in the sequence of pages on the current tab. (To move forward, use the Forward button or press Alt+→.)

◆ Click the down arrow at the right end of the Address box and choose the document from the drop-down list. This drop-down list gives you quick access to a good number of the sites you've visited.

◆ Choose one of the items listed in the Recent Pages menu.

◆ Click the Recent Pages button, and then click History on the menu to display the History list in Favorites Center (see Figure 2.10). This list contains a complete list of the pages you've visited and the documents you've opened recently, organized into folders by day and site. Use the drop-down menu on the History button to sort the history sites by date, site, or most visited, or by order visited today; or choose Search History to search the history sites by keyword. Then click the shortcut for the item you want to return to. You can also copy the shortcut to another folder, create a favorite from it, or delete it.

FIGURE 2.10
Use the History list in Favorites Center to return to a previous document.

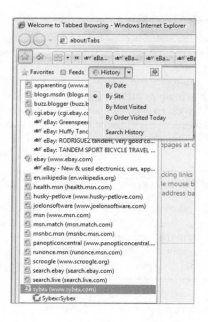

WORKING WITH MULTIPLE TABS

Given the amount of information on the Web, you'll often want to have several or many pages open at the same time. To do so, you can either open further tabs in the same Internet Explorer window or open another Internet Explorer window. Tabs are usually more convenient, but you can display only one tab at a time—so if you need to view two web pages side by side, you should open them in separate Internet Explorer windows.

You can open another tab in either of the following ways:

◆ Click the New Tab button at the right end of the tab bar, or press Ctrl+T. Internet Explorer opens a new tab and displays it.

◆ Right-click a link in a web page open in an existing tab, and then choose Open in New Tab from the context menu. Alternatively, Ctrl-click a link in a page. Internet Explorer opens the linked page in a new tab, but still displays the previous tab.

To display another tab, click it in the tab bar. When the tab bar gets too full to display all the tabs at a useful size, Internet Explorer displays a Previous Tab button (with << on it) at the beginning of the tabs and a Next Tab button (with >> on it) at the end of the tabs. You can click these buttons to navigate to tabs that don't appear.

Internet Explorer offers two other ways of displaying another tab:

◆ Click the Quick Tabs button to display a preview of each tab (see Figure 2.11). From here, you can click a tab to display it, click a tab's Close button (the × button) to close it, or right-click a tab to access the Open, Close, Close Other Tabs, Refresh, and Refresh All Commands.

◆ Click the Tab List button to display a drop-down list showing tab names. Click the tab you want to display.

FIGURE 2.11
The Quick Tabs feature lets you get an overview of the tabs you have open and close those you no longer need.

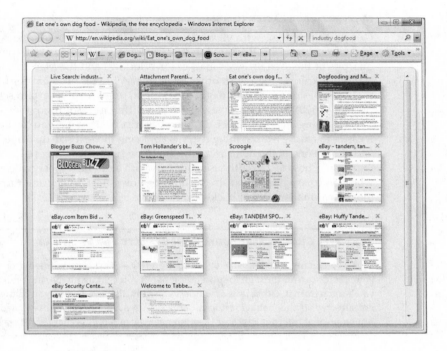

To close a tab, click it, and then click the Close button (the × button) button on the tab. You can also right-click a tab and then choose Close from the context menu, or right-click and choose Close Other Tabs from the context menu to leave open only the tab you clicked.

WORKING WITH MULTIPLE WINDOWS

You can open multiple windows in the following ways:

- To open another copy of the page displayed in the current window, press Ctrl+N or choose Page ➢ New Window.

- To open a hyperlinked location in a new browser window, so that the current window still displays the current page, right-click the hyperlink and choose Open in New Window from the context menu.

- To start a new instance of Internet Explorer, click its shortcut on the Quick Launch toolbar or choose Start ➢ Internet.

- Some websites will open a new browser window for you. This tends to happen when you've chosen to display a page that doesn't involve their site. Keep an eye on the number of browser windows you have open, because there may be more than you have opened yourself—and some of them may be showing items that you haven't specifically chosen to see.

To close a window, click its Close button (the × button) or press either Alt+F4 or Ctrl+W.

MAKING A PAGE EASIER TO READ

One of the problems with viewing web pages is that they tend to look different when displayed in different browsers. Because Internet Explorer is so widely used, commanding more than three-quarters of the total browser market for Windows and the Mac, this is less of a problem with Internet Explorer than with other browsers. A bigger problem for Internet Explorer users is that web designers design pages for optimal viewing at a certain screen resolution (for example, 800 × 600). When you view them at a different resolution, they can be hard to read.

Depending on how the web designer has created the page, you can do a couple of things to make it easier to read. The first thing to try is adjusting the text size displayed. Choose Page ≻ Text Size and choose one of the items from the Text Size submenu: Largest, Larger, Medium, Smaller, or Smallest. (The size currently used appears with a dot next to it on the menu.) If your mouse has a wheel, you can change text size by holding down the Ctrl key and turning the wheel forward (to move to a smaller size) or backward (to move to a larger size).

TEXT-SIZE CHANGE AND ZOOM ARE SEPARATE FOR EACH TAB

When you change the text size by using the View ≻ Text Size submenu, or when you zoom the view, your choice carries through to subsequent pages you visit using the same tab or other tabs (or windows) you launch from it. Other tabs or windows already displayed when you change the text size or zoom are not affected. If this behavior doesn't suit you, see the "Accessibility" heading in the "Changing the Appearance of Internet Explorer" section near the end of this chapter for ways to change it.

SAVING A DOCUMENT

Although you cannot create new documents in Internet Explorer, the program lets you choose Page ≻ Save As and use the Save Webpage dialog box to save documents to your computer. For example, you might want to save a copy of a web page or intranet page to your hard disk so that you can examine it in detail when your computer is offline.

Internet Explorer can save pages in four formats, which you choose from the Save As Type drop-down list in the Save Webpage dialog box:

◆ The Web Page, Complete (*.htm, *.html) format saves all the information on the page, creating a file with the .htm or .html extension containing the page itself and a folder with the page's name and the suffix _files for the other files (such as graphics) that make up the page. Windows manages these pairs of pages and folders as individual objects; for example, if you move a page file, Windows automatically moves the paired folder as well so that the page can still find its supporting files. If you rename a page file, Windows warns you that you'll need to rename the folder as well.

◆ The Web Archive, Single File (*.mht) format creates a single file that contains both the web page and its supporting information. This format is the most convenient if you want to store an entire web page.

◆ The Web Page, HTML Only (*.htm, *.html) format saves only the HTML content of the page (with formatting).

◆ The Text File (*.txt) item saves only the text from the web page without any graphics or formatting.

Choose a location for the file as usual, specify a filename, choose the format in the Save As Type drop-down list, and click the Save button. Internet Explorer closes the Save Webpage dialog box and saves the file.

SAVING, PRINTING, OR E-MAILING A PICTURE

Sometimes you'll want to save a picture from a web page rather than save the entire page—or you may want to e-mail the picture, print it, or use it as your desktop background. Right-click the picture, and then choose Save Picture As, E-mail Picture, Print Picture, or Set As Desktop Background from the context menu.

PRINTING A DOCUMENT

To print the web page you're viewing without choosing any printing options, click the Print button on the toolbar.

To display the Print dialog box so that you can choose printing options, click the drop-down button on the Print button, and then choose Print from the menu. Choose options in the Print dialog box—for example, the Options page offers options for printing frames (layout areas of web pages), printing all linked documents, and printing a table of links—and then click the Print button.

DOWNLOADING FILES

Apart from surfing the Internet, you'll probably find yourself using Internet Explorer for downloading many files: drivers, patches, updates, programs, games, screen savers, audio, video, or other content. Internet Explorer lets you download files seamlessly via both HTTP and FTP. Most of the time, you don't need to worry about whether the download is happening via HTTP or FTP. (The exception is when you're accessing a password-protected FTP server. More on this in a minute.)

Here's what usually happens when you download a file:

1. You click a link on a web page to download a file. Internet Explorer displays a File Download dialog box containing buttons for taking actions on the file. The next illustration shows an example for a program file. If the file's extension indicates a file type that's not a program but is registered on your computer, Internet Explorer displays an Open button instead of a Run button. If the extension indicates a file type not registered on your computer, Internet Explorer displays a Find button instead of a Run button.

2. You choose what to do with the file:

   ◆ For any file, click the Save button if you want to save the file to a folder on your computer. Normally, this is the best choice, as it enables you to try to run the program or open the file again, if the first try is unsuccessful, without needing to download the file again. Use the Save As dialog box to choose a drive, folder, and filename for the file.

◆ For a program file, you can click the Run button if you want to run the program without saving it to a folder on your computer. Running the program usually works, but sometimes it may not.

◆ For a document file whose type is registered on your computer, you can click the Open button to open the file with the associated program.

◆ For a document file whose type isn't registered on your computer, you can click the Find button to find a program suitable for opening that file type.

◆ If the file you're downloading is of a file type registered to play, Internet Explorer starts it playing rather than giving you the opportunity to save it to disk. For example, if you click a link for an audio stream, Internet Explorer starts it playing. For copyright reasons, most companies and individuals that stream audio and video try to prevent the listener or viewer from saving the file. This is because streaming a file is legally analogous to broadcasting, whereas distributing savable files is legally analogous to copying them.

3. If you chose to download the file, when the download finishes, Internet Explorer changes the Download window title to Download Complete and provides three command buttons, as shown here.

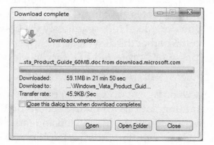

Open Click this button to open the downloaded file in the associated program, if there is one.

Open Folder Click this button to open an Explorer window showing the folder containing the downloaded file. You can then double-click the file to open it.

Close Click this button to close the Download Complete window. You can then run or open the downloaded file manually whenever suits you. If you regularly find yourself clicking the Close button, select the Close This Dialog Box When Download Completes check box if you want Internet Explorer to close the Download window automatically when it has received the whole file.

You can download multiple files at the same time by setting multiple downloads in motion. All downloads share your Internet connection, so running multiple downloads will make each take longer than it would if it were the only download running—unless you have a fast Internet connection that is being held back by slow (or busy) servers at the other end *and* each of your downloads is coming from a different server. On the other hand, you may want to run multiple downloads concurrently if you're planning to take a break from your computer.

USE A DOWNLOAD MANAGER WHEN DOWNLOADING MANY FILES OR LARGE FILES

If you download many files over an unreliable dial-up connection, consider getting a download manager that can resume downloads from the point at which they get broken off. Download managers include GetRight (`http://www.getright.com`) and Go!Zilla (`http://www.gozilla.com`).

CREATING AND USING FAVORITES

Internet Explorer lets you designate URLs as *favorites*, which allows you to access them quickly using Favorites Center. (Other web browsers such as Netscape call favorites *bookmarks*.) To use favorites, you create them as described in the next section, then access them from Favorites Center.

SUPPLYING AN FTP USERNAME AND PASSWORD IN INTERNET EXPLORER

Internet Explorer handles accessing FTP servers via anonymous logon transparently. But if the FTP server requires you to supply a username and password, you need to enter it in the Address bar as follows:

`ftp://username:password@ftpserver/url`

As you can see, this makes for tricky typing. If you access password-protected FTP servers frequently, consider getting a dedicated graphical FTP client such as WS_FTP Pro (`http://www.ipswitch.com`) or CuteFTP (`http://www.globalscape.com`).

ADDING A PAGE TO YOUR FAVORITES

To add the current URL (the page that Internet Explorer is currently displaying) to your list of favorites, follow these steps:

1. Press Ctrl+D, or click the Add to Favorites button and then choose Add to Favorites from the drop-down menu. Internet Explorer displays the Add a Favorite dialog box, as shown here.

2. In the Name text box, enter the name by which to identify the favorite. You often need to change the default name, which is the page's title, to something shorter, more descriptive, or more memorable.

3. Choose where you want to create the favorite. You can create the favorite either at the top level, so that it appears directly in Favorites Center, or in a folder.

   ◆ To create the favorite in a different folder within Favorites, click the Create In drop-down list, and then choose the folder.

◆ To create the favorite in a new folder, click the New Folder button. Internet Explorer displays the Create a Folder dialog box, as shown here. Type the folder name in the Folder Name text box, select the parent folder (the folder that will contain the new folder) in the Create In drop-down list, and then click the Create button. Internet Explorer creates the folder and selects it in the Create In download in the Add a Favorite dialog box.

4. Click the OK button. Internet Explorer closes the Add a Favorite dialog box and creates the favorite.

ORGANIZING YOUR FAVORITES INTO FOLDERS

Favorites Center presents your favorites in the folders you create, which works well until you create a large number of folders. When you do, you'll need to organize these favorites into folders. Take the following steps:

1. Press Alt+Z or click the Add to Favorites button, and then choose Organize Favorites from the menu. Internet Explorer displays the Organize Favorites dialog box (shown in Figure 2.12).

2. Organize your favorites into folders by using the following techniques:

◆ To move a favorite to a folder, either drag it to the folder in the list, or select the favorite and then click the Move button. Internet Explorer displays the Browse for Folder dialog box. Select the folder, and click the OK button. Internet Explorer closes the Browse for Folder dialog box and moves the favorite.

FIGURE 2.12
Use the Organize
Favorites dialog
box to organize your
favorites into folders.

◆ To change the order of the list, drag a favorite or a folder up or down the list box.

◆ To rename a favorite or a folder, select it, and then click the Rename button. Type the new name over the existing name, and then press the Enter key.

◆ To delete a favorite or a folder, select it, and then click the Delete button. Internet Explorer displays the Delete File dialog box or the Delete Folder dialog box. Click the Yes button. Internet Explorer closes the dialog box and deletes the favorite or folder.

◆ To create a new folder, select the folder within which you want to create it, and then click the Create Folder button. Internet Explorer creates a new folder called New Folder and selects its name. Type in the new name for the folder, and then press the Enter key.

3. Click the Close button. Internet Explorer closes the Organize Favorites dialog box.

Customizing Internet Explorer

Apart from favorites, Internet Explorer provides several features for quickly accessing particular sites. These features include your home page, your search page, the links bar, and the command bar. You also can configure Internet Explorer to control how it looks and how it runs.

CUSTOMIZING YOUR HOME PAGE

Your *home page* is the page or set of pages that Internet Explorer automatically opens when you start Internet Explorer and when you click the Home button on the toolbar. You'll usually want to change your home page from Internet Explorer's default (MSN.com) to the site you want to see first in every Internet Explorer session. Normally, having one home page is easiest, but you may want to create a whole set of home pages if you have a fast Internet connection.

To change your home page, take the following steps:

1. Navigate to your target page or the page you want to add to your existing set of home pages. If you want to create a set of home pages, open them all on tabs in the same Internet Explorer window. Close any tabs that contain pages you don't want to include in the set of home pages.

2. Click the drop-down button to the right of the Home Page button, and then choose Add or Change Home Page from the menu. Internet Explorer displays the Add or Change Home Page dialog box, as shown here.

3. Select the appropriate option button:

Use This Webpage As Your Only Home Page   Select this option button if you want to have a single home page.

Add This Webpage to Your Home Page Tabs Select this option button if you want to add the current web page to your existing web pages.

Use the Current Tab Set As Your Home Page Select this option button if you want to use all the web pages you have open in tabs as your home pages.

4. Click the Yes button. Internet Explorer closes the Add or Change Home Page dialog box and applies your choice.

 Real World Scenario

AUTOMATIC UPDATES MAY CHANGE YOUR HOME PAGE

Installing or updating Microsoft programs, including Automatic Updates provided via Windows Update, may reset your home page to its default setting without warning you. In case this happens, create a favorite for your start page so that you will be able to access it quickly in order to restore it as your home page.

CREATING A CUSTOM HOME PAGE LOCALLY

One of the problems with most home pages is that, even with the fastest of connections, they take a few seconds to load. If you want to see what's new on the home page, that may be well and good. But if you just want to use the home page as a jumping-off point for sites further afield, the delay may be annoying.

To avoid this delay, create a custom home page and store it on your hard drive. It needs to contain no more than a little HTML—though you can make it as complex as you like. Alternatively, start with a blank page, which will load immediately and won't automatically connect to the Internet (which is useful if you don't have a permanent Internet connection).

DISPLAYING AND CUSTOMIZING THE LINKS BAR

Your home page or pages let you load one or more pages automatically each time you launch Internet Explorer, and favorites provide a handy way of accessing all the sites you're most interested in. But you'll probably have a handful or two of sites that you want to be able to access instantly without going through Favorites Center. For these sites, you can put sites on the Links bar.

To display the Links bar, choose Tools ➢ Toolbars ➢ Links. Internet Explorer displays the Links bar above the Commands bar. At first, the Links bar is normally empty except for a Customize Links button that you can click to display a tab of instructions for customizing the Links bar.

Once you've read those instructions, put into practice the instructions for deleting a button: Right-click the Customize Links button, choose Delete from the context menu, and then click the Yes button in the Delete File dialog box.

To add a site to the Links bar, navigate to a page you want to add, and then drag the page icon from the beginning of the Address box to the Links bar. Drop the icon in an open space on the bar. Internet Explorer creates a link for it.

To rearrange the buttons on the Links bar, click a button and drag it to where you want it to appear.

To rename a button, right-click it, choose Rename from the context menu, type the new name in the Rename dialog box, and then click the OK button. Use short names to pack more buttons onto the Links bar.

CUSTOMIZING THE COMMAND BAR

You can customize the Command bar by adding, removing, or rearranging buttons, and changing the presentation of the labels on the buttons you display. Take the following steps:

1. Right-click one of the buttons on the Command bar (for example, click the Favorites Center button), and then choose Customize Command Bar from the context menu to display the Customize Command Bar submenu.

2. To choose how the buttons on the Command bar appear, select one of the top three items:

    Show All Text Labels   Makes Internet Explorer display a text description as well as an icon for each button. This setting is useful if you find it hard to remember what the icons do, but it can make the Command bar too long for normal-sized windows.

    Show Selective Text   Makes Internet Explorer displays a text description on the Page button, the Tools button, and the Help button, but not on the other buttons. This is the default setting.

    Show Only Icons   Makes Internet Explorer display only an icon for each button, suppressing all text descriptions. The effect is compact and graphical but harder to interpret.

3. To change the buttons that appear on the Command bar, click the Add or Remove Commands item. Internet Explorer displays the Customize Toolbar dialog box, as shown here.

4. Add, remove, or rearrange buttons as needed:

    Add a Button   In the Current Toolbar Buttons list box, click the existing button before which you want to add the button. Click the button in the Available Toolbar Buttons list box, and then click the Add button.

    Remove a Button   Click the button in the Current Toolbar Buttons list box, and then click the Remove button.

    Rearrange the Buttons   In the Current Toolbar Buttons list box, click the button you want to move, and then click the Move Up button or the Move Down button.

    Reset the Toolbar   To reset the toolbar to the default set of buttons, click the Reset button.

5. Click the Close button. Internet Explorer closes the Customize Toolbar dialog box.

Going Offline

If you have a dial-up Internet connection, you may want to open various web pages in different tabs while you're online, and then go offline to read the pages. Once offline, you can choose Tools ➢ Work Offline to tell Internet Explorer that you're working offline and that it should prompt you before trying to connect to the Internet.

When you go offline, Internet Explorer displays an indicator on the status bar—a network cable with a red cross on it and a gray cloud above it—to show that you're currently offline.

To go back online, choose File ➢ Work Offline again. Alternatively, click a link on one of the web pages you have open (or click a favorite, or the Home button), and then click the Connect button in the Webpage Unavailable while Offline dialog box that Internet Explorer displays (as shown here).

Configuring Internet Explorer

This section discusses the most important options that Internet Explorer offers for controlling how it runs. You can configure most aspects of its behavior—everything from the font size Internet Explorer uses to display text, to security, to improving performance over a slow Internet connection.

Internet Explorer has a huge number of options, so this section doesn't discuss all of them. Instead, it concentrates on the options that will make the most difference in your daily surfing.

You'll find all these options in the Internet Options dialog box. Start by choosing Tools ➢ Internet Options to open this dialog box (see Figure 2.13).

FIGURE 2.13
The Internet Options dialog box lets you configure many aspects of Internet Explorer's behavior.

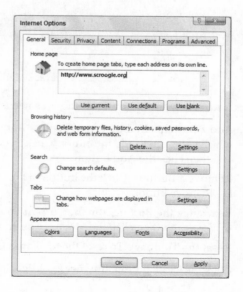

Controlling Your Temporary Internet Files and History

Every time you view a web page, Internet Explorer downloads the files that make up the page and stores it in temporary files on your hard drive. Storing the information lets you view the information more quickly the next time you access the page, as Internet Explorer has to download only new items if the page has changed. Over a high-speed network, that may not make a big difference, but over the average Internet connection, it can save anything from a few seconds to a minute or two.

The disadvantages to having the files on your hard drive are that they take up space and that you can have embarrassing or dangerous information stored on your computer without your knowledge. So it's a good idea to clear out your temporary files periodically. You may also want to get rid of your browsing history so that other people can't see which sites and pages you've visited.

CHOOSING HOW MANY TEMPORARY FILES AND HOW MUCH HISTORY TO KEEP

To control how long Internet Explorer keeps temporary Internet files and history, click the Settings button in the Browsing History group box on the General page of the Internet Options dialog box. Internet Explorer displays the Temporary Internet Files and History Settings dialog box (shown in Figure 2.14).

FIGURE 2.14
Use the Temporary Internet Files and History Settings dialog box to keep your temporary Internet files under control and to decide how long to keep history.

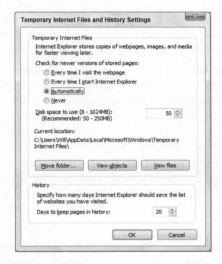

In the Check for Newer Versions of Stored Pages list, select an option button to determine how frequently Internet Explorer should check for newer versions of stored pages:

Every Time I Visit the Webpage　Internet Explorer checks for a new version of the page each time you browse to the page, even if your last visit was only moments ago.

Every Time I Start Internet Explorer　Internet Explorer checks for a new version of the page in each new Internet Explorer session but not necessarily each time you go back to the page within the same session.

Automatically　Internet Explorer builds its own schedule for updating each stored page. If you return to a page the same day and during the same Internet Explorer session as your previous visit, Internet Explorer doesn't check for a new version of the page (unless you issue a Refresh command). If your last visit was in an earlier session or on an earlier day, Internet Explorer updates the page. Subsequently Internet Explorer monitors the page and tries to establish a schedule that approximately reflects the page's frequency of change. The schedule Internet Explorer establishes may result in your seeing an out-of-date version of the page.

Never Internet Explorer never checks for a new version of a stored page.

In the Disk Space to Use box, check the amount of disk space Internet Explorer is using for temporary files. The readout shows the minimum and maximum amount of data you can store. If you're not concerned about having potentially embarrassing information stored, store more information to speed up browsing.

The Current Location readout shows the folder Windows is using to store temporary Internet files. You can use the three buttons below this readout to take the following actions:

◆ Move the folder to another folder or drive if necessary by clicking the Move Folder button and using the resulting Browse for Folder dialog box to designate the folder. If you do this, you need to restart Internet Explorer.

◆ Display an Explorer window listing the objects installed—for example, ActiveX controls or Java Runtime Environments—by clicking the View Objects button.

◆ Display an Explorer window showing your temporary files by clicking the View Files button. You probably won't need to do this unless you want to delete an objectionable item (for example, a graphics file) that you know Internet Explorer has downloaded.

To control how long Internet Explorer stores your browsing history, set the Days to Keep Pages in History number. The default setting is 20 days.

When you've chosen suitable settings, click the OK button. Internet Explorer closes the Temporary Internet Files and History Settings dialog box.

DELETING TEMPORARY FILES, COOKIES, HISTORY, FORM DATA, AND PASSWORDS

To clear out your current temporary files, history, and other items, click the Delete button in the Browsing History area on the General page of the Internet Options dialog box. Internet Explorer displays the Delete Browsing History dialog box (see Figure 2.15).

FIGURE 2.15
Use the Delete Browsing History dialog box to delete your temporary Internet files, cookies, history, form data, or passwords.

To delete all your offline content, select the Delete All check box, and then click the Yes button in the confirmation dialog box that Internet Explorer displays (shown next). You can select the Also Delete Files and Settings Stored by Add-Ons check box if you want to delete information stored by Internet Explorer add-on (helper) programs too.

To delete one of the items, click the Delete button in its area, and then click the Yes button in the confirmation dialog box that Internet Explorer displays. For example, to delete all your temporary Internet files, click the Delete Files button, and then click the Yes button in the Delete Files dialog box (shown here).

When you've finished deleting items, click the Close button. Internet Explorer closes the Delete Browsing History dialog box. If you chose to delete all items or delete cookies, close Internet Explorer and then restart it to clear any cookies from the current Internet Explorer session.

Changing Your Search Engine

To change the search engine that Internet Explorer uses, take the following steps:

1. Click the Settings button in the Search area on the General page of the Internet Options dialog box. Internet Explorer displays the Change Search Defaults dialog box, as shown here.

2. If the search engine you want appears in the Search Providers list, select it, and then click the Set Default button. Otherwise, follow these steps to add the search engine:

   ◆ Click the Find More Providers link. Internet Explorer opens a browser window to a list of providers on the Microsoft website.

◆ Click the provider you want. Internet Explorer displays the Add Search Provider dialog box, as shown here.

◆ If you want to make this search engine the default, select the Make This My Default Search Provider check box.

◆ Click the Add provider button. Internet Explorer adds the provider.

Changing Your Settings for Using Tabs

Most people find tabbed browsing a great addition to Internet Explorer, but you may prefer to turn tabbed browsing off or configure it to behave differently. To do so, click the Settings button in the Tabs area. Internet Explorer displays the Tabbed Browsing Settings dialog box (see Figure 2.16). The dialog box offers the following settings:

Enabled Tabbed Browsing   Clear this check box if you want to turn off tabbed browsing. Internet Explorer makes all the other settings unavailable. You then need to restart Internet Explorer.

Warn Me When Closing Multiple Tabs   Select this check box if you want Internet Explorer to warn you when you're closing a window that contains two or more tabs. This setting helpful when you're getting used to tabs after using older versions of Internet Explorer that open each page in a separate window.

FIGURE 2.16
The Tabbed Browsing Settings dialog box lets you change how Internet Explorer handles tabs—or turn off the use of tabs altogether.

Always Switch to New Tabs When They Are Created   Select this check box if you want Internet Explorer to display each new tab you open. Usually it's handier to navigate to new tabs manually when you're ready.

Enable Quick Tabs   Select this check box if you want to use the Quick Tabs feature. Most people find this feature useful, but if you don't, you may be able to improve your computer's performance by turning it off and restarting Internet Explorer.

Open Only the First Home Page When Internet Explorer Starts   Select this check box if you've set up multiple home pages and you want to open only the first of them when you launch Internet Explorer. Normally, you'll want to open all your home pages, but if you have a slow Internet connection, you may prefer to open only the first automatically.

Open New Tabs Next to the Current Tab   Select this check box if you want Internet Explorer to open each new tab next to the tab from which you launched the new tab rather than after all existing tabs.

Open Home Page for New Tabs instead of a Blank Page   Select this check box if you want Internet Explorer to load your home page instead of the blank page when you create a new tab without specifying content (for example, by clicking the New Tab button rather than opening a link in a new tab).

When a Pop-Up Is Encountered   In this group box, select the Let Internet Explorer Decide How Pop-Ups Should Opens option button if you want Internet Explorer to decide whether to open pop-up windows as new windows or as new tabs. If you prefer to take control, select the Always Open Pop-Ups in a New Window option button or the Always Open Pop-Ups in a New Tab option button, as appropriate.

Open Links from Other Programs In   In this group box, select the A New Window option button if you want to open links you click in other programs (for example, Windows Mail) in new windows. Select the A New Tab in the Current Window option button if you want such links to open on new tabs in the current window (this is usually the best option). Select to the Current Tab or Window option button if you want the linked page to replace the page you were previously viewing.

Restore Defaults   Click this button if you want to restore Internet Explorer's default settings for tabs.

When you've finished choosing settings for tabbed browsing, click the Close button.

Changing the Appearance of Internet Explorer

The four buttons in the Appearance area of the General page of the Internet Options dialog box let you change the appearance of web pages to make them more readable.

Colors   To change the colors Internet Explorer uses, click this button and then work in the Colors dialog box. Clear the Use Windows Colors check box, and then choose a suitable color for text, background, visited links, unvisited links, and items over which you hover the mouse.

Languages   If you need to be able to view web pages in other languages, click the Languages button, and then use the Language Preference dialog box to add languages and set an order of preference. You can also select the Do Not Add 'www' to the Beginning of Typed Web Addresses check box if you want to prevent Internet Explorer from adding the www designation to the beginning of partial URLs you type that appear to lack it.

Fonts   To change the fonts Internet Explorer uses, click the Fonts button, and then work in the Fonts dialog box. For example, you might choose a font that you find easier to read.

Accessibility   To make pages easier to read, you can click the Accessibility button, and then choose settings in the Accessibility dialog box. You can tell Internet Explorer to ignore the colors, font styles, and font sizes that web pages specify, or apply a custom style sheet of your own to web pages. The results may look peculiar.

Choosing Security Options

The Security page in the Internet Options dialog box (see Figure 2.17) lets you control the amount of protection that Internet Explorer provides.

The Select a Web Content Zone to Specify Its Security Settings box at the top of the page contains four categories of sites. The easiest way to explain them is in reverse order:

Restricted Sites   Sites you've specifically designated as potentially dangerous

Trusted Sites   Sites you've specifically designated as trusted not to damage your computer or your data

Local Intranet   Local sites not specifically designated as restricted or trusted

Internet   All other sites

The security zone for the current site appears in the status bar.

You can set a different level of security for each category by selecting the category, and then dragging the Security Level for this Zone slider up or down. If you understand the specifics of security, you can also specify a custom level for a zone by selecting the category and clicking the Custom Level button. Internet Explorer displays the Security Settings dialog box (see Figure 2.18). Select settings for the different categories, and then click the OK button. Internet Explorer closes the Security Settings dialog box and implements your settings.

FIGURE 2.17

Choose canned security options on the Security page of the Internet Options dialog box.

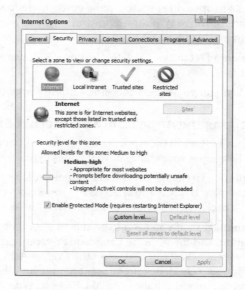

FIGURE 2.18
You can use the Security Settings dialog box to implement custom security settings.

By default, the Internet category has a Medium-High security level designed to let you browse effectively while protecting you from harmful content. Local Intranet has a Medium-Low level, Trusted Sites has a Medium level, and Restricted Sites has a High level.

To change your list of Local Intranet sites, Trusted Sites, or Restricted Sites, select the category and click the Sites button. Internet Explorer displays the Local Intranet dialog box, the Trusted Sites dialog box, or the Restricted Sites dialog box (see Figure 2.19). To add a site to the list, enter its URL in the Add This Website to the Zone text box and click the Add button; to remove a site from the list, select it in the Websites list box and click the Remove button. Click the OK button to close the dialog box.

CHOOSING A LEVEL OF PRIVACY

For the Internet zone, use the Privacy page of the Internet Options dialog box (see Figure 2.20) to set the level of privacy to use.

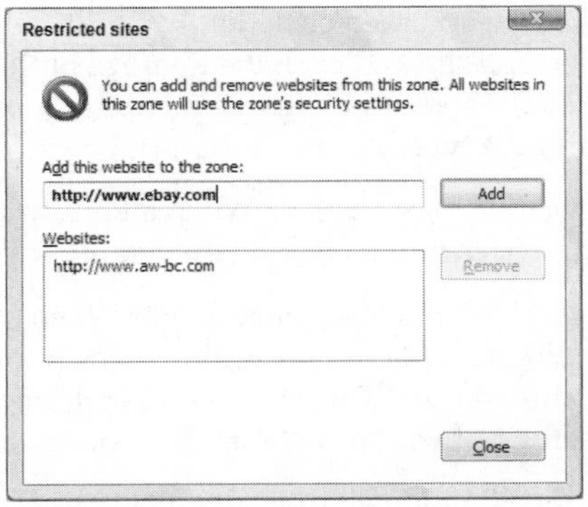

FIGURE 2.19
Use the Restricted Sites dialog box (shown here), the Trusted Sites dialog box (not shown), or the Local Intranet dialog box (not shown) to adjust your list of restricted sites, trusted sites, or local intranet sites.

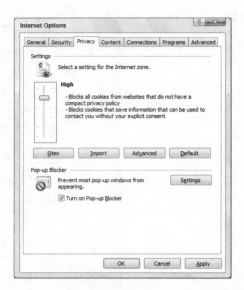

Drag the slider in the Settings group box to specify the level of security to use. Beside the slider, Internet Explorer displays specifics for that level of privacy.

If you prefer to have the boundaries of your privacy designed by other people, you can download privacy settings files from privacy organizations. Then click the Import button and use the resulting Privacy Import dialog box to import the file, which applies the preferences it contains.

BLOCKING POP-UPS

To prevent websites from displaying pop-up windows via scripts, select the Turn on Pop-up Blocker check box in the Pop-up Blocker group box on the Privacy page of the Internet Options dialog box.

With default settings, the Pop-up Blocker takes care of most pop-up windows. To fine-tune the Pop-up Blocker, click the Settings button and work in the Pop-up Blocker Settings dialog box (see Figure 2.21).

To allow specific sites to display pop-ups, type each address into the Address of Website to Allow text box, and then click the Add button. To remove a site from the Allowed Sites list you build, select the site and click the Remove button.

The Notifications and Filter Level group box lets you control the sensitivity of the Pop-up Blocker and the types of notifications it gives you:

◆ Select the Play a Sound When a Pop-up Is Blocked check box to receive an aural warning. This check box is enabled by default. If you find this sound annoying, clear the check box.

◆ Select the Show Information Bar When a Pop-up Is Blocked check box to have Internet Explorer display a notification in the Information bar, which appears temporarily below the Command bar. This check box is selected by default. In most cases, the Information bar is useful, but you may choose to suppress it if you find it annoying.

◆ In the Filter Level drop-down list, select High: Block All Pop-ups (Ctrl to Override), Medium: Block Most Automatic Pop-ups, or Low: Allow Pop-ups from Secure Sites, as appropriate.

FIGURE 2.21
You can change the
sensitivity of the
Pop-up Blocker by
using the controls in
the Pop-up Blocker
Settings dialog box.

Click the Close button to close the Pop-up Blocker Settings dialog box and return to the Internet
Options dialog box.

HANDLING COOKIES

A key aspect of privacy is handling *cookies*, the text files that websites place on your computer in
order to track your dealings with their site. For example, if you visit an e-commerce site and fill out
a form to buy a product, the information you enter in the form is typically stored in a cookie so that
the website can maintain the information in the fields if you need to go back to a previous page.
Only the website that creates a cookie can read it; other websites cannot. Most cookies are *persistent*,
lasting from one session to another so that their information can be used when you revisit a site in
a later session, but there are also *temporary cookies* or *session cookies* that last only until the end of the
current Internet Explorer session.

To specify custom cookie handling, take the following steps:

1. Click the Advanced button on the Privacy page of the Internet Options dialog box. Internet
   Explorer displays the Advanced Privacy Settings dialog box (shown in Figure 2.22 with
   some settings chosen).

2. Select the Override Automatic Cookie Handling check box.

FIGURE 2.22
Use the Advanced
Privacy Settings
dialog box to specify
custom handling of
cookies.

3. In the First-Party Cookies list, choose the Accept option button, the Block option button, or the Prompt option button as appropriate. *First-party cookies* are those that come from the website you're viewing. These are the cookies you're most likely to want to accept.

4. In the Third-Party Cookies list, choose the Accept option button, the Block option button, or the Prompt option button as appropriate. *Third-party cookies* are those that come from websites associated with the one you're viewing. They're often used for advertising or marketing, so you might want to block them.

5. If you want to use session cookies no matter what your settings in the First-Party Cookies list and the Third-Party Cookies list, select the Always Allow Session Cookies check box. Session cookies are temporary cookies maintained during a session to facilitate communication with websites. Internet Explorer deletes session cookies when you close it.

6. Click the OK button. Internet Explorer closes the Advanced Privacy Settings dialog box and applies your choices.

That custom cookie handling you just set applies to all websites. If you want to be more specific about which sites can and cannot place cookies on your computer, click the Sites button on the Privacy page. Internet Explorer displays the Per Site Privacy Actions dialog box (see Figure 2.23).

To allow or block cookies from a website, enter the domain name in the Address of Website text box and then click the Allow button or the Block button as appropriate. Use the Remove button to remove a blocked or allowed site from the Managed Web Sites list box, or use the Remove All button to clear the list.

Click the OK button. Internet Explorer closes the Per Site Privacy Actions dialog box and applies your choices.

When a blocked site tries to set a cookie, Internet Explorer displays the Privacy Report icon, an eye with a no-entry sign overlapping it, in the middle of the status bar. Double-click the Privacy Report icon to display the Privacy Report dialog box (see Figure 2.24). Use the Show drop-down list to toggle between Restricted Websites and All Websites. Click the Settings button if you want to move to the Privacy page of the Internet Options dialog box (for example, to block a new offender). Or click the Close button to close the Privacy Report dialog box.

FIGURE 2.23
You can use the Per Site Privacy Actions dialog box to specify which websites may use cookies and which websites are blocked.

FIGURE 2.24

In the Privacy Report dialog box, you can see which sites are being blocked from sending you cookies.

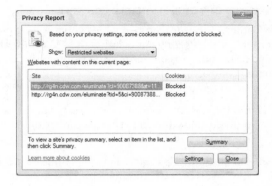

Choosing Content Options

The Content page of the Internet Options dialog box (see Figure 2.25) lets you implement parental controls, use ratings to control the content that Internet Explorer can access, manage certificates, and configure AutoComplete and RSS feeds.

SETTING UP PARENTAL CONTROLS

To set up parental controls for Windows Vista and Internet Explorer, click the Parental Controls button on the Content page, and then authenticate yourself to User Account Control. Windows displays the Parental Controls window. Work as described in the section "Implementing Parental Controls" in Chapter 8.

FIGURE 2.25

The Content page of the Internet Options dialog box

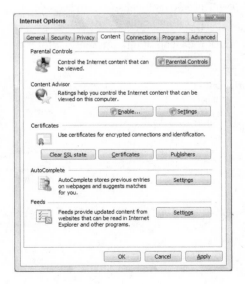

SCREENING OUT OBJECTIONABLE CONTENT

The Content Advisor feature enables you to set up content screening based on the ratings of the Internet Content Rating Association (ICRA). Content Advisor is useful if children or easily offended friends or relatives may be using your computer. (You may also want to implement parental controls.)

To set up Content Advisor, take the following steps:

1. On the Content page, click the Enable button in the Content Advisor group box, and then authenticate yourself to User Account Control. Internet Explorer displays the Content Advisor dialog box.

2. On the Ratings page (see Figure 2.26), select the item in the Select a Category to View the Rating Levels list box, and then drag the Adjust the Slider to Specify What Users Are Allowed to See slider to a suitable level. The Description text box explains what the current setting permits.

3. Click the Approved Sites tab. Internet Explorer displays the Approved Sites page (see Figure 2.27).

4. Set up your list of approved and disapproved sites by taking the following steps:

    ◆ In the Allow This Website text box, type the URL of the website you want to make always viewable or never viewable.

    ◆ Click the Always button or the Never button as appropriate. Internet Explorer adds the site to the List of Approved and Disapproved Websites list box and marks it with the corresponding icon.

    ◆ To remove a website from the List of Approved and Disapproved Websites list box, select it and click the Remove button.

5. Click the General tab. Internet Explorer displays the General page (see Figure 2.28).

FIGURE 2.26

Choose rating levels on the Ratings page of the Content Advisor dialog box.

FIGURE 2.27
Use the Approved Sites page to specify sites that should be always viewable or never viewable regardless of their rating.

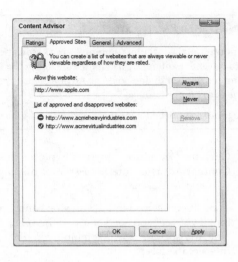

FIGURE 2.28
Choose general options on the General page of the Content Advisor dialog box.

6. Choose options as appropriate:

◆ Select the Users Can See Websites That Have No Rating check box if you want users to be able to view websites that don't use ratings. This check box is cleared by default, because unrated websites may well have offensive content.

◆ Leave the Supervisor Can Type a Password to Allow Users to View Restricted Content check box selected (as it is by default) if you want to be able to let other users view restricted sites by your entering a password. If not, clear this check box.

◆ To change the supervisor password, click the Create Password button and specify the new password in the resulting Change Supervisor Password dialog box.

ADDING OTHER RATING SYSTEMS

If you don't find the Internet Content Rating Association (ICRA) adequate, you can add other rating systems to Internet Explorer by using the controls in the Rating Systems group box on the General page of the Content Advisor dialog box. The Advanced page contains controls for adding a ratings bureau and PICSRules to Content Advisor.

You're unlikely to need to use these options for home or home-office computing.

7. Click the OK button. Internet Explorer closes Content Advisor. The first time you close Content Advisor, Internet Explorer displays the Create Supervisor Password dialog box (see Figure 2.29).

8. Type the password in the Password and Confirm Password text boxes, create a password hint if you feel you need one, and then click the OK button. Internet Explorer displays a Content Advisor message box telling you that Content Advisor has been installed and to close Internet Explorer.

9. Click the OK button. Internet Explorer closes the Content Advisor dialog box and returns you to the Internet Options dialog box, where the Enable button has changed to the Disable button.

10. Click the OK button. Internet Explorer closes the Internet Options dialog box.

11. Close Internet Explorer, and then reopen it.

FIGURE 2.29

Create a supervisor password in the Create Supervisor Password dialog box. Even though Internet Explorer prompts you to enter a password hint, don't do so—it compromises your security.

To adjust the settings for Content Advisor, click the Settings button in the Content Advisor group box on the Content page of the Internet Options dialog box. Internet Explorer displays the Supervisor Password Required dialog box. Enter your password and click the OK button to display the Content Advisor dialog box, then change the settings and click the OK button.

To disable ratings again, click the Disable button in the Content Advisor group box on the Content page of the Internet Options dialog box. Internet Explorer displays the Supervisor Password Required dialog box. Enter your password and click the OK button. Internet Explorer displays a Content Advisor message box telling you that Content Advisor has been turned off.

When users hit a site that contains unapproved content, they see a Content Advisor dialog box (see Figure 2.30). If you're the user, you can enter the supervisor password and choose the Always Allow This Website to Be Viewed option button (to make a lasting exception for the site), the Always Allow This Webpage to Be Viewed option button (to make a lasting exception for the page but not the site), or the Allow Viewing Only This Time option button (to make a temporary exception). Then click the OK button. Internet Explorer closes the Content Advisor dialog box and displays the site. (A user without the supervisor password will need to click the Cancel button and will not be able to reach the site.)

FIGURE 2.30
Content Advisor in action. If you've applied a password hint, anybody can use it to guess your password.

CLEARING YOUR CERTIFICATES INFORMATION

The Certificates area of the Content page lets you display the list of certificates installed on the computer (click the Certificates button) or the list of trusted software publishers (click the Publishers button). You can also clear your personal security information by clicking the Clear SSL State button. You'll normally need to do this only if you've been using someone else's computer—for example, a public computer or a friend's computer—and have provided your credentials on a smart card.

MANAGING YOUR AUTOCOMPLETE INFORMATION

AutoComplete is a great feature that can save you a lot of fuss with passwords and often-repeated information. But it can also severely compromise your digital persona and your finances, so you need to understand what it does and how it works so that you can use it appropriately.

AutoComplete automatically fills in URLs and entries on forms for you. To do so, it needs to watch as you enter URLs and information on forms, and store that information. Then, when you start typing a URL or access a form it recognizes, it can fill in the information for you. For example, the first time you access your Windows Live Mail account via Internet Explorer, AutoComplete can learn your username and password, and offer to fill them in for you in the future.

The downside to AutoComplete is that Internet Explorer is storing sensitive or secret information, which means that other people who use your computer can more easily masquerade as you. There's also a risk that your computer could be hacked to give up this information, though this risk is less severe than the direct risk from people who can physically access your computer.

To configure AutoComplete, follow these steps:

1. Click the AutoComplete button in the Personal Information group box on the Content page of the Internet Options dialog box. Internet Explorer displays the AutoComplete Settings dialog box (see Figure 2.31).

FIGURE 2.31
Choose AutoComplete options in the Auto-Complete Settings dialog box.

2. In the Use AutoComplete For group box, specify the items for which you want to use AutoComplete:

Web Addresses   Select this check box to have AutoComplete track the URLs you access and suggest matching URLs in the Open dialog box and the Address box.

Forms   Select this check box to have AutoComplete track your entries in forms (other than usernames and passwords).

User Names and Passwords on Forms   Select this check box to make AutoComplete track the usernames and passwords you enter in forms. This is the most sensitive information, so you may want to clear this check box. If you select it, leave the Prompt Me to Save Passwords check box selected so that Internet Explorer gets your consent each time it's about to store a password of yours. (These settings let you use AutoComplete for less sensitive passwords but not for high-security passwords.)

3. Click the OK button. Internet Explorer closes the AutoComplete Settings dialog box.

CHOOSING SETTINGS FOR FEEDS

To control how Internet Explorer handles feeds, click the Settings button in the Feeds area of the Content tab of the Internet Options dialog box, and then work in the Feed Settings dialog box (see Figure 2.32).

Default Schedule   In this group box, select the Automatically Check Feeds for Updates check box if you want Internet Explorer to look for updates for you. Use the Every drop-down list to specify the frequency—anything from 15 minutes to 1 week.

Automatically Mark Feed As Read When Reading a Feed   Select this check box if you want Internet Explorer to mark a feed as read once you've started reading it.

Turn On Feed Reading View   Select this check box if you want Internet Explorer to switch automatically to feed-reading view.

Play a Sound When a Feed Is Found for a Webpage   Select this check box if you want Internet Explorer to give you an aural heads-up when it finds a feed on a web page.

Click the OK button to close the Feed Settings dialog box.

FIGURE 2.32
The Feed Settings dialog box lets you choose whether to check automatically for feeds.

Specifying Programs for Internet Services

The Programs page of the Internet Options dialog box (see Figure 2.33) lets you see which web browser is your default, manage add-ons, and set programs for HTML editing and accessing the Internet.

CHECKING YOUR DEFAULT WEB BROWSER

The Default Web Browser area shows your default web browser—for example, Internet Explorer.

Select the Tell Me if Internet Explorer Is Not the Default Web Browser check box if you want Internet Explorer to warn you should some other web browser supplant it.

FIGURE 2.33
On the Programs page of the Internet Options dialog box, you can manually configure the programs that you want Windows to use for Internet services.

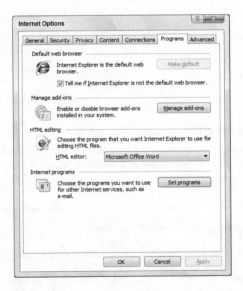

MANAGING ADD-ONS

To manage the add-on programs used to extend Internet Explorer's capabilities, click the Manage Add-ons button on the Programs page of the Internet Options dialog box. Internet Explorer displays the Manage Add-ons dialog box (shown in Figure 2.34).

In the Show drop-down list, make sure that Add-ons That Have Been Used by Internet Explorer is selected. You can then disable an add-on by selecting it in the list box and selecting the Disable option button, or reenable a disabled add-on by selecting the Enable option button. If the add-on is an ActiveX control rather than a toolbar, a browser helper object, or a browser extension, you can delete it by clicking the Delete button.

After making your choices for add-ons, click the OK button to close the Manage Add-ons dialog box.

FIGURE 2.34

Use the Manage Add-ons dialog box to enable, disable, or update the add-ons that Internet Explorer is using.

Choosing Advanced Options

The Advanced page of the Internet Options dialog box (see Figure 2.35) contains a formidable number of options organized in a number of categories. The following sections discuss the most important options.

 Real World Scenario

YOU PROBABLY DON'T NEED TO CHANGE MANY ADVANCED SETTINGS

Because many of the options on the Advanced page control important behavior on the part of Internet Explorer, don't change them unless you understand exactly what they do and what the results can be. For most people, the default settings work well.

If you think you've chosen some unwise settings, you can click the Restore Advanced Settings button to restore the default settings.

FIGURE 2.35
On the Advanced page of the Internet Options dialog box, you can choose a wide variety of settings.

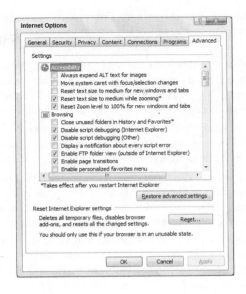

ACCESSIBILITY CATEGORY

The Accessibility category contains the following options:

Always Expand ALT Text for Images   This check box controls whether Internet Explorer displays alternative text for images. Normally, you'll need to see the alternative text only if the image fails to load.

Move System Caret with Focus/Selection Change   This check box controls whether Internet Explorer moves the oddly named *system caret* (the insertion point or cursor) to the new focus or selection. Select this check box if you're using Magnifier to magnify the area around the cursor.

Reset Text Size to Medium for New Windows and Tabs   This check box controls whether Internet Explorer displays each new window or tab with the Medium text size or whether it carries your current text size through to each new window or tab.

Reset Text Size to Medium while Zooming   This check box controls whether Internet Explorer resets the text size to medium when you zoom in or out. This behavior is usually helpful.

Reset Zoom Level to 100% for New Windows and Tabs   This check box controls whether Internet Explorer resets the zoom level to 100 percent when you open a new window or tab. If you find yourself having to zoom each new window or tab, clear this check box.

BROWSING CATEGORY

These are the key options in the Browsing category:

Enable FTP Folder View (outside of Internet Explorer)   Select this check box if you want to be able to open FTP folders in Windows Explorer windows so that you can upload files as well as download them.

Enable Personalized Favorites Menu   Clear this check box unless you want Internet Explorer to automatically hide those parts of your Favorites menu that you don't visit often enough for its liking.

Notify When Downloads Complete   Leave this check box selected (as it is by default) if you want Internet Explorer to prompt you when it finishes downloading a file. Clear this check box if you find the notification annoying.

Reuse Windows for Launching Shortcuts (When Tabbed Browsing Is Off)   Applies only when tabbed browsing is turned off. When selected, this check box causes Internet Explorer to display the page for a hyperlink you click in the current window. Clear this check box if you want Internet Explorer to display the linked page in a new window by default.

Underline Links   Select the Always option button (the default), the Hover option button, or the Never option button to specify whether and when Internet Explorer should underline links. (*Hover* means that you position the mouse pointer over the link.)

Use Inline AutoComplete   This check box controls whether Internet Explorer offers Auto-Complete suggestions when you're typing an address or URL in the Address box or in Explorer. Most people find AutoComplete helpful, but its suggestions can be embarrassing if you've been visiting URLs or viewing documents you shouldn't have.

Use Passive FTP (for Firewall and DSL Modem Compatibility)   Select this check box if you want to use passive FTP—FTP in which your computer does not need to supply its IP address. Because of this, passive FTP is normally more secure than regular FTP. Depending on your network settings, you may need to use passive FTP—for example, if you have a vigilant firewall. Generally speaking, stick with regular FTP unless you find it doesn't work, in which case, try passive FTP.

Use Smooth Scrolling   This check box (which is selected by default) controls whether Internet Explorer scrolls the contents of its window in a smooth and gentle fashion or in jerks (as most Windows programs do). If you're used to regular Windows behavior, or if you find the smooth scrolling sick making, try clearing this check box.

MULTIMEDIA CATEGORY

These are the key options in the Multimedia category:

Enable Automatic Image Resizing   This check box controls whether Internet Explorer automatically resizes images that are too large to fit in the browser window. Usually, this resizing is a good idea, as it enables you to see the whole image without scrolling right or down.

Play Animations in Webpages   This check box controls whether Internet Explorer plays animations. If your computer or connection is slow, you may want to turn off animations.

Play Sounds in Webpages   This check box controls whether Internet Explorer plays sounds. Because sound files can be big, consider clearing this check box to speed up your downloads.

Show Pictures   This check box controls whether Internet Explorer displays pictures. If your Internet connection is really slow (for example, if you're surfing via a cell-phone hookup), you may want to turn off pictures—but the Web is so graphical nowadays that some pages may be hard to read without their pictures. If you have a slow connection but use pictures, consider selecting the Show Image Download Placeholders check box, which causes Internet Explorer to display placeholder boxes for the images it's downloading. The placeholder boxes enable you to immediately see the page correctly laid out (but without the images).

SECURITY CATEGORY

Most of the items in the Security category are worth understanding:

Allow Active Content from CDs to Run on My Computer   Clear this check box unless you want active content from CDs you insert in your CD drive to be able to run on your computer. *Active content* means ActiveX controls, ActiveX scripts, and Java programs.

Allow Active Content to Run in Files on My Computer   Clear this check box unless you want active content from files to be able to run on your computer.

Allow Software to Run or Install Even if the Signature Is Invalid   Leave this check box clear unless you have a good reason to want to install unsigned or incorrectly signed software.

Check for Publisher's Certificate Revocation   Select this check box to have Internet Explorer verify that a software publisher's digital certificate is still valid before accepting it. Checking a certificate slows down the installation of add-on software but offers you a little extra protection against bad software.

Check for Server Certificate Revocation   This check box controls whether Internet Explorer checks an Internet site's certificate to make sure it hasn't been revoked.

Check for Signatures on Downloaded Programs   Select this check box to ensure that Internet Explorer verifies the digital signatures on the software you download. You should install only software that has a digital signature from a software publisher that you trust. If the software appears to be from a software publisher that you trust, but it doesn't have a digital signature, don't install it. Likewise, don't install any software from any software publisher that you don't trust, no matter whether it has a digital signature or not.

Do Not Save Encrypted Pages to Disk   Select this check box if you want to prevent Internet Explorer from saving encrypted web pages to disk.

Empty Temporary Internet Files Folder When Browser Is Closed   This check box controls whether Internet Explorer deletes all temporary files each time you close Internet Explorer. If you're concerned about security, select this check box.

Enable Integrated Windows Authentication   Leave this check box selected if you want to use Integrated Windows Authentication, a form of authentication that avoids sending the logon name and password across the network.

Enable Memory Protection to Help Mitigate Online Attacks   This check box is available only if you clear the Enable Protected Mode check box on the Security page. Turning off Protected Mode is not a good idea.

 Real World Scenario

EVEN MAJOR SOFTWARE PUBLISHERS SOMETIMES LET CERTIFICATES LAPSE

Surprisingly, even some major software publishers have been known to let their certificates lapse. If you select the Check for Publisher's Certificate Revocation check box, you may occasionally have to override warnings that a certificate is out of date in order to install add-ons you need.

Enable Native XMLHTTP Support   Select this check box if you want to be able to use XMLHTTP, which is used for some web applications. (This setting is usually helpful.)

Phishing Filter   In this area, select the Turn On Automatic Website Checking option button.

Use SSL 2.0 and Use SSL 3.0   Leave these check boxes selected (as they are by default) if you want to use the Secure Sockets Layer Level 2 (SSL 2) and Secure Sockets Layer Level 3 (SSL 3) protocols for securing the transmission of information. SSL 3 is supposed to be more secure than SSL 2 and is starting to supplant it.

Use TLS 1.0   Leave this check box selected (as it is by default) if you want to use Transport Layer Security (TLS) to secure the transmission of information. TLS is not widely used.

Warn about Certificate Address Mismatch   This check box (which is selected by default) controls whether Internet Explorer warns you if a digital certificate is invalid. Keep this check box selected.

Warn if Changing between Secure and Not Secure Mode   Select this check box if you want Internet Explorer to warn you when you are switched from a secure (encrypted) connection to a server to an insecure connection. Keep this check box selected until you've got the hang of secure connections. When the warnings become an irritant, clear this check box.

Warn if POST Submittal Is Being Redirected to a Zone That Does Not Permit Posts   This check box (which is selected by default) controls whether Internet Explorer warns you when a form you've submitted is being redirected to a different destination than its apparent destination. Many forms contain sensitive information, so keep this check box selected.

The Bottom Line

Connect your computer to the Internet   If you don't have an existing Internet connection, you'll need to get one. Optical fiber Internet connections are the fastest, but they're hard to get. Cable and DSL connections give satisfactory speeds in urban areas, but if you're in a rural area, you may have to settle for satellite, ISDN, or regular dial-up. After you set up the hardware for the Internet connection, Windows may simply identify the connection and configure itself. If not, run the Connect to a Network Wizard to set up your Internet connection.

Surf the Web with Internet Explorer   Choose Start ➤ Internet to launch Internet Explorer. You can then go to a web address (or URL) by typing it in the Address box and pressing Enter or by clicking the link on a page that's displayed. Choose a home page (or set of pages) for the start of each Internet Explorer session, and create favorites or links of pages that you want to be able to access easily.

Configure Internet Explorer for comfort and security   Internet Explorer is highly customizable, offering many options that you can set in the Internet Options dialog box. Internet Explorer's default configuration works well for many people, so you may not need to change any settings. If you choose unsuitable settings, you can reset Internet Explorer to its default settings to start again.

Chapter 3

Customizing Your Desktop

- ◆ Choosing the best display resolution
- ◆ Configuring the keyboard and mouse
- ◆ Choosing ease-of-access options
- ◆ Choosing a screen saver
- ◆ Changing the look and feel of Windows
- ◆ Configuring the Taskbar, Start menu, and Desktop toolbars
- ◆ Using the Sidebar

This chapter discusses how to get your Desktop into shape so that you can work comfortably, effectively, and enjoyably. Some of these changes are so important to working (or playing) ergonomically in Windows that you should perform them right away. These include choosing the best display resolution, configuring the keyboard and mouse, and setting accessibility options (if you need them).

This chapter covers these topics first. After that, it discusses changes that you don't *need* to implement right away, but that you may well want to make before too long. These changes include choosing a screen saver, changing your Desktop background, customizing the Start menu, creating custom toolbars, choosing system sounds, configuring the Start menu and the Taskbar, and using the new Windows Sidebar.

Choosing the Best Display Resolution

How do you set the best display resolution for you and your computer? If you're squinting at the screen, or if it's flickering at you, or if the display slops over the edges of the monitor, you won't be productive or happy. Choosing the best display resolution involves three things: your eyesight, your monitor, and your graphics card. The first is up to you and your optometrist. The second and third are discussed below.

RESOLUTION AND REFRESH RATE

The *resolution* is the number of pixels that the screen displays. The resolution consists of a horizontal measurement and a vertical measurement. For example, the widely used resolution 1024 × 768 uses 1024 pixels across the screen and 768 pixels from top to bottom. This resolution is called Extended Graphics Array, or XGA.

The *refresh rate* is the number of times that the graphics card redraws the picture on the monitor. Typical refresh rates run from 60 times a second, or 60 hertz (Hz), to more than 100 Hz.

Pixel is short for *picture element* and means one of the elements that make up the display you see on your screen.

Your Monitor

There are two widely used types of computer monitors: liquid crystal display (LCD) panels, which are thin and light in form, and cathode-ray tube (CRT) monitors, which are much bulkier and heavier. All laptop computers use LCDs, as do most modern desktops, now that LCD prices have dropped to within easy commuting distance of CRT prices.

LCDs USUALLY DISPLAY ONLY ONE RESOLUTION WELL

Most LCD panels and some other monitors are designed to deliver optimal quality at only one resolution and only one refresh rate. By contrast, almost all CRTs can display multiple resolutions at a variety of refresh rates.

Some LCD panels will display lesser resolutions as well as their optimum resolution, but the result is jagged and awkward to look at. Some LCD panels—usually on laptops—can display a *higher* resolution than their normal resolution. This can be useful for special effects, but it means that you can't see all of the screen at once, so you usually have to use your keyboard or mouse to scroll down and right to see the southern and eastern regions.

Your Graphics Card

The graphics card in your computer sends information to the monitor. The resolutions and refresh rates that the graphics card supports depend on the amount of video memory it contains. If you want to play games at high resolutions and fast frame rates, you need to make sure that your graphics card is powerful enough (rather than that your processor speed is fast enough).

Choosing Video Settings

To choose video settings, you use the Display Settings dialog box. To open the Display Settings dialog box, follow these steps:

1. Right-click the Desktop, and then choose Personalize. Windows displays the Personalization window in Control Panel (see Figure 3.1).

2. Click the Display Settings link. Windows opens the Display Settings window (see Figure 3.2).

FIGURE 3.1
The Personalization window in Control Panel gives you access to the display settings and to most of the other settings for personalizing your Desktop.

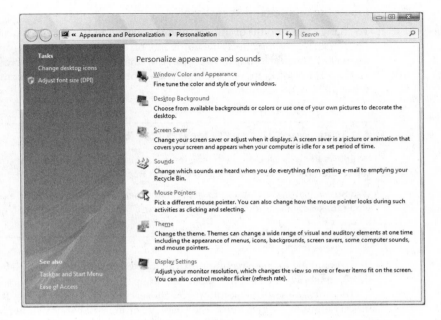

FIGURE 3.2
Use the Display Settings dialog box to set the screen resolution and the number of colors Windows uses.

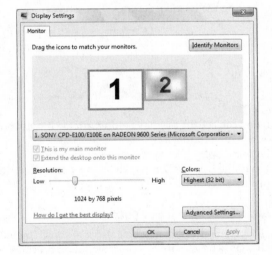

USING MULTIPLE MONITORS IN WINDOWS

Windows supports multiple monitors—you can use up to 10 monitors on a single computer so that you can see a larger amount of information at once. See the section "Setting Up and Using Multiple Monitors" in Chapter 13 for coverage of this feature.

CHANGING THE SCREEN RESOLUTION

To change the amount of information displayed on the screen, you change the *screen resolution*. The screen resolution affects the number of pixels Windows displays on the screen. The more pixels displayed, the more you can see—but the smaller everything on screen appears. For example, at 1280×1024 resolution, you see more of a word processing document or a spreadsheet than you see at 1024×768 resolution.

ALL USERS MUST USE THE SAME DESKTOP RESOLUTION

Windows Vista's Fast User Switching feature requires that all users of the computer use the same Desktop resolution. The Welcome screen also uses this resolution.

If some users of your computer have much sharper eyes than others, find a compromise resolution that won't make anyone suffer unduly. Any user can change the resolution, but in doing so, they change it for all other users as well.

To change the screen resolution, drag the Resolution slider to the left or right. The readout under the slider shows the next available resolution.

To apply the screen resolution you chose, click the Apply button. If you haven't used this resolution before, Windows opens the Display Settings dialog box shown next to make sure that you can see the display properly. (If you have used this resolution before, Windows may apply it without opening the Display Settings dialog box.)

If you can see the Display Settings dialog box, all is probably well. Click the Yes button to apply the screen resolution.

If your display becomes garbled or faded, or if you don't like what you see, either click the No button in the Display Settings dialog box or wait the 15 seconds until Windows restores your previous video settings.

CHANGING THE NUMBER OF COLORS

The Display Settings dialog box also lets you change the number of colors that Windows uses for the display. The Windows Vista installation routine sets your system to use the highest color quality that your monitor and graphics card support at a reasonable refresh rate, so you shouldn't normally need to change the number of colors.

If your computer has a powerful enough graphics card and enough graphics memory, Windows automatically uses the Vista Aero user interface. Vista Aero has the graduated colors in the title bars and borders of windows (as in the screens in this book) and, if you turn on its Glass option, displays the desktop background through the title bars and borders. Vista Aero requires 32-bit color—so if you want to keep using Vista Aero, you can't reduce the number of colors used.

If you're using the Vista Basic user interface (with solid color in the title bars and borders of windows), you can change the number of colors. Click the Colors drop-down list and choose a different setting in it. For example, you might choose Medium (16 Bit) instead of Highest (32 Bit) if Windows is running slowly and you want to try to improve graphics performance.

CHANGING THE REFRESH RATE

When you install Windows, the installation routine tries to apply a suitable refresh rate for your monitor so that it produces a good image without flickering. But if your screen flickers noticeably, you may need to adjust the refresh rate.

LCDs SUFFER FLICKER MUCH LESS THAN CRTs

Flicker is produced by the video card redrawing the image on the monitor slowly enough for you to be able to notice. As a result, your eyes have to work a bit harder to decode what they're seeing, which tends to lead to eyestrain and headaches, particularly if you don't take those ergonomically recommended breaks from staring at the screen.

Flicker shows more on large monitors than small monitors. This is not just because there's more of the screen to look at, but also because most people notice flicker more out of the corner of their eye than straight on, and you see more of a larger screen in your peripheral vision.

Some people are much more sensitive to flicker than others. At 60Hz (60 cycles per second) most people find flicker very noticeable on CRT monitors. At 70Hz, many people don't see it. By 75Hz, things look good to most people. At 85Hz, few people can detect flicker. Above that, you're entering the hypochondriac zone—though if your hardware supports a very high refresh rate, there's no reason why you shouldn't use it.

LCD screens flicker far less than CRTs, so they don't need such high refresh rates. Many LCD screens are designed for optimal performance at a refresh rate of 60Hz and produce a beautifully stable picture at this rate, which would produce very pronounced flicker on a CRT. Other LCDs support refresh rates of 72Hz or 75Hz. Most LCDs don't support refresh rates faster than 75Hz.

Which refresh rates are available to you depends on your graphics card and your monitor. For you to be able to use a refresh rate, both the graphics card and the monitor must support the rate. To set the refresh rate, take the following steps:

1. Click the Advanced Settings button in the Display Settings dialog box. Windows displays the dialog box for the monitor and the graphics card. This dialog box's title bar shows the name of the monitor model and the graphics card model.

2. Click the Monitor tab. Windows displays the Monitor page (shown in Figure 3.3).

3. In the Screen Refresh Rate drop-down list, choose one of the settings. As long as Windows has correctly identified your monitor and graphics card, you should be safe choosing the fastest refresh rate listed.

FIGURE 3.3
Set the refresh rate
on the Monitor page
of the dialog box for
the monitor and
graphics card.

4. Click the Apply button. If you haven't used this refresh rate before, Windows displays a
    Display Settings dialog box, as shown here, asking you whether you want to keep the set-
    tings. (If you have used this refresh rate, Windows may simply apply the settings.)

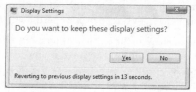

5. If you click the Yes button, Windows keeps the settings. If you click the No button, or if you
    wait 15 seconds, Windows reapplies your previous settings.

Adjusting Your Monitor If Necessary

Once you've settled on a display resolution, color depth, and refresh rate, you may need to adjust
your monitor to maximize the image area so that you're seeing the whole image as large as possible.
(It's amazing how many people leave an inchwide band of unused space at each edge of the monitor and then complain that they have to peer closely at the image.)

Monitor controls vary, but almost all CRTs and some LCDs let you adjust the height, width, and
vertical and horizontal positions of the image. Open a program and maximize its window so that
you can clearly see where the edges of the screen are. Then use the monitor controls to make your
Desktop fills the display area of your monitor at the resolution you set.

FORCING WINDOWS TO APPLY A DIFFERENT REFRESH RATE

As you can see in Figure 3.3, the Monitor Settings group box on the Monitor page also contains the Hide Modes That This Monitor Cannot Display check box. Windows Vista normally makes this check box unavailable, so that you cannot select it (if it is cleared) or clear it (if it is selected).

If the Hide Modes That This Monitor Cannot Display check box is available, you *can* clear this check box to force Windows to list in the Screen Refresh Rate drop-down list refresh rates that Windows thinks your monitor doesn't support. You *can* apply these refresh rates—but doing so may be a bad idea, because you can permanently damage a monitor by setting a refresh rate higher than it supports. The only reason to try this is if you are unable to get Windows to recognize your monitor correctly and you need to trick Windows into applying a refresh rate that you know from the monitor's documentation is supported.

If your screen settings still aren't satisfactory, you may need to take further steps, such as changing hardware acceleration, changing the video driver, or making Windows correctly identify the monitor you're using. Turn to Chapter 13 for details on how to take these actions.

Configuring the Keyboard and Mouse

Both these input devices—the keyboard and the mouse—are vital to getting information into and out of your computer. Both devices can cause you great discomfort if you don't configure them correctly.

YOU MAY NEED TO USE EASE-OF-ACCESS OPTIONS

If configuring the keyboard and mouse doesn't give you the control you need, try the ease-of-access options (which used to be called accessibility options in Windows XP). The section "Choosing Ease-of-Access Options," later in this chapter, discusses these options.

Configuring the Keyboard

Windows offers three keyboard configuration options:

- The *repeat delay* (the length of time that Windows waits before repeating a key when you hold it down)
- The *repeat rate* (the speed with which a key repeats its character once the repeat delay is over)
- The rate at which the cursor blinks

The repeat delay and repeat rate are vital to comfortable and accurate typing. The cursor blink rate is a matter of visual preference.

To configure your keyboard, follow these steps:

1. Choose Start ➢ Control Panel. Windows displays a Control Panel window.

2. If Control Panel is in Classic view, with a dot next to Classic View in the left panel, click the Control Panel Home link to switch to Control Panel Home view. Figure 3.4 shows the two views.

3. Click the Hardware and Sound link. Windows displays the Hardware and Sound window.

4. Click the Keyboard link. Windows displays the Keyboard Properties dialog box. If the Speed page (see Figure 3.5) isn't foremost, click its tab to bring it to the front.

5. Choose settings by adjusting the Repeat Delay slider, the Repeat Rate slider, and the Cursor Blink Rate slider. Use the Click Here and Hold Down a Key to Test Repeat Rate text box for testing your repeat rate.

6. Click the OK button. Windows closes the Keyboard Properties dialog box.

FIGURE 3.4

Control Panel provides two ways to view its contents. Control Panel Home view shows the items divided into categories, whereas Classic view shows an icon for each item in Control Panel.

FIGURE 3.5
You can adjust the repeat rate, repeat delay, and the cursor blink rate of your keyboard on the Speed page of the Keyboard Properties dialog box.

The Hardware page of the Keyboard Properties dialog box lets you see which type of keyboard Windows thinks you're using. From here, you can access the Properties dialog box for this type of keyboard so that you can change the driver that it's using.

Configuring the Mouse

To configure your mouse, follow these steps:

1. Choose Start ➤ Control Panel. Windows displays a Control Panel window.

2. In Control Panel Home view, click the Mouse link in the Hardware and Sound Category. Windows displays the Mouse Properties dialog box.

YOUR MOUSE PROPERTIES DIALOG BOX MAY HAVE OTHER PAGES

The Mouse Properties dialog box in these figures has the standard controls. If your mouse has extra features or custom software, you may see other pages of options in the Mouse Properties dialog box. For example, if your mouse has a wheel, the Mouse Properties dialog box also contains a Wheel page.

---

3. The Buttons page (see Figure 3.6) offers these options:

   Switch Primary and Secondary Buttons check box   Select this check box if you want to swap the functions of the primary and secondary mouse buttons. This setting is most useful for changing a mouse from right-hand configuration to left-hand configuration.

   Double-Click Speed slider   Drag this slider toward its Fast end or its Slow end to set the double-click speed of your mouse. Double-click the box to the right to see if Windows is registering your double-clicks properly. When the area registers a double-click, the graphic changes.

FIGURE 3.6

Choose button options on the Buttons page of the Mouse Properties dialog box.

Turn on ClickLock check box   Select this check box to turn on the ClickLock feature, which lets you drag without holding down the mouse button all the time. (You click the mouse button again to release the locked item after dragging it.) ClickLock can be useful if you get the hang of it, but it can be an annoyance if you find yourself setting the lock unintentionally when clicking. If you turn ClickLock on, click the Settings button and use the Settings for ClickLock dialog box (shown here) to specify how long you must hold down the mouse button to trigger the lock.

4. If you want to use different pointers for your mouse, click the Pointers tab. Windows displays the Pointers page (see Figure 3.7). This page offers a variety of mouse pointer schemes, some of them fun (for example, the Dinosaur scheme) and others more useful (such as the various large, extra large, and inverted schemes, which can make the mouse pointers much easier to see).

◆ In the Scheme drop-down list, select the scheme you want to use.

◆ To customize the scheme, select a pointer in the Customize list box. Click the Browse button, use the resulting Browse dialog box to select the pointer you want to use instead, and then click the Open button. (Windows displays the \Windows\Cursors\ folder in the Browse dialog box, but you can navigate to other folders in which you have placed custom mouse pointers.) You can also click the Use Default button to use the standard Windows pointer in place of the selected pointer.

◆ To turn off pointer shadows, clear the Enable Pointer Shadow check box.

◆ To save your customized scheme, click the Save As button, enter the name for the scheme in the Save Scheme dialog box, and click the OK button. Custom pointer schemes are stored in the Registry (in the HKEY_CURRENT_USER key) and are not available to other users.

5. Click the Pointer Options tab to display the Pointer Options page (see Figure 3.8). This page offers the options discussed in the following list. Windows applies the settings on the Pointer Options page of the Mouse Properties dialog box immediately, so you can see them in action without needing to click the Apply button.

Select a Pointer Speed slider Drag the slider toward its Slow end or its Fast end to adjust the speed at which the pointer moves.

FIGURE 3.7
Choose a pointer scheme—or create a custom pointer scheme—on the Pointers page of the Mouse Properties dialog box.

FIGURE 3.8
Change the speed and behavior of the mouse on the Pointer Options page.

Enhance Pointer Precision check box   Select this check box if you want to make the mouse pointer decelerate more quickly on screen as you stop moving the mouse. This behavior sounds strange, but many people find it helpful for controlling the mouse swiftly and accurately. To use more gradual deceleration, clear this check box.

Automatically Move Pointer to the Default Button in a Dialog Box check box   Select this check box if you want Windows to automatically position the mouse pointer over the default button in each dialog box you display. This automatic movement can save you time, but it can also be confusing because when you or Windows open a dialog box the mouse pointer is no longer where you left it.

Display Pointer Trails check box and slider   Select this check box if you want the mouse pointer to display a contrasting trail of phantom pointers when you move it. This option is most useful for low-contrast LCD screens or viewing in bright sunlight, when making out the mouse pointer can be hard. If you turn this feature on, adjust the slider to give yourself the length of pointer trails that suits you.

Hide Pointer While Typing check box   Select this check box if you want Windows to hide the mouse pointer when you're typing, so that you can see the text more easily. (In some programs, Windows hides the pointer when you're typing even if this check box isn't selected.)

Show Location of Pointer When I Press the Ctrl Key check box   Select this check box if you want to be able to make Windows identify the mouse key by zooming in a circle on it when you press the Ctrl key. This feature is useful for LCD screens on which the mouse pointer tends to disappear.

Choosing Ease-of-Access Options

For users with disabilities, Windows offers a good selection of ease-of-access options. To reach these options, choose Start ➤ All Programs ➤ Accessories ➤ Ease of Access ➤ Ease of Access Center. Windows opens the Ease of Access Center (see Figure 3.9).

If you don't know which settings to adjust, click the Get Recommendations to Make Your Computer Easier to Use Link. Windows then walks you through a questionnaire to determine which of the ease-of-access options may be helpful. Figure 3.10 shows the first of the screens of questions, which deals with eyesight problems.

When you've answered all the questions, Windows displays the Recommended Settings window (see Figure 3.11), which lets you choose the settings you want and apply them.

You may also want to set individual settings one by one to see if you find them helpful. The rest of this section discusses the ease-of-access options that Windows offers.

FIGURE 3.9
Ease of Access Center lets you optimize the visual display, set up alternative input devices (such as the On-Screen Keyboard or Speech Recognition), and make the keyboard and mouse easier to use.

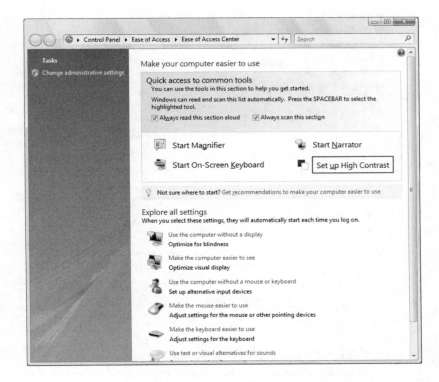

FIGURE 3.10
To get recommendations on which ease-of-access options may help you use Windows, tell Windows about any eyesight, hearing, or other computer-use problems you have.

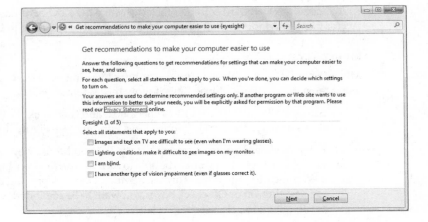

FIGURE 3.11
In the Recommended Settings window, select the check box for each ease-of-access setting you want to apply, and then click the Apply button.

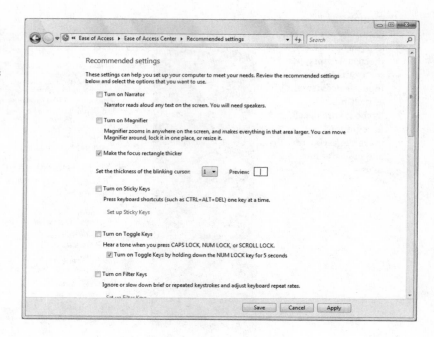

Keyboard Accessibility Options

To make the keyboard more accessible, Windows offers keyboard accessibility options, an On-Screen Keyboard, and Speech Recognition.

To access the keyboard settings, click the Make the Keyboard Easier to Use link in the Ease of Access Center. Windows displays the Make the Keyboard Easier to Use window (see Figure 3.12).

MOUSE KEYS

Mouse Keys lets you control the mouse pointer by using your keyboard's numeric keys instead of using the mouse. To use Mouse Keys, follow these steps:

1. Select the Turn on Mouse Keys check box, and then click the Set Up Mouse Keys link. Windows displays the Set Up Mouse Keys window (see Figure 3.13).

2. In the Keyboard Shortcut area, select the Turn on Mouse Keys with Left Alt+Left Shift+Num Lock check box if you want to be able to turn Mouse Keys on and off easily. Select the Display a Warning Message When Turning a Setting On check box and the Make a Sound When Turning a Setting On or Off check box if you want to be reminded when you turn Mouse Keys on or off; otherwise, clear these check boxes.

FIGURE 3.12
The Make the Keyboard Easier to Use window lets you turn on Mouse Keys, Sticky Keys, Toggle Keys, Filter Keys, and keyboard shortcuts.

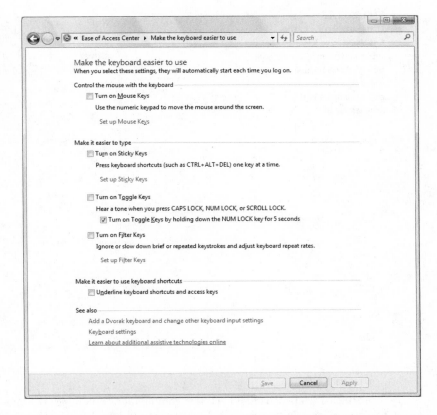

3. In the Pointer Speed area, drag the Top Speed slider and the Acceleration slider to suitable positions. Test the mouse pointer's movement by using the arrow keys. Select the Hold Down Ctrl to Speed Up and Shift to Slow Down check box if you want to be able to use the modifier keys to change the speed.

4. In the Other Settings area, select the On option button if you want Mouse Keys to be active when Num Lock is on; select the Off button if you want Mouse Keys active when Num Lock is off. Select the Display the Mouse Keys Icon on the Taskbar check box if you want the notification area to display an icon for turning Mouse Keys on and off.

5. Click the Save button to save your settings and apply them.

FIGURE 3.13
Use the controls in the
Set Up Mouse Keys
window to configure
how fast the mouse
pointer moves
and how quickly it
accelerates.

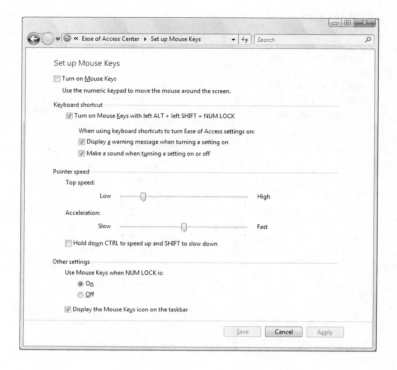

STICKY KEYS

Sticky Keys lets you enter keyboard combinations involving the Shift, Ctrl, or Alt key one key at a
time rather than needing to hold down the modifier key while you press subsequent keys. To use
Sticky Keys, follow these steps:

1. Select the Turn on Sticky Keys check box, and then click the Set Up Sticky Keys link. Windows
   displays the Set Up Sticky Keys window (see Figure 3.14).

2. In the Keyboard Shortcut area, select the Turn on Sticky Keys When Shift Is Pressed Five
   Times check box if you want to be able to use repeated presses of Shift to turn on Sticky Keys.
   Select the Display a Warning Message When Turning a Setting On check box and the Make
   a Sound When Turning a Setting On or Off check box if you want to be reminded when you
   turn Sticky Keys on or off; otherwise, clear these check boxes.

3. In the Options area, select the Lock Modifier Keys When Pressed Twice in a Row check box
   if you want to be able to "stick" a modifier key on by pressing it twice. For example, you
   would press Alt twice to "stick" it on. Select the Turn off Sticky Keys When Two Keys Are
   Pressed at Once check box if you want Windows to turn off Sticky Keys when the user uses
   keyboard shortcuts normally—for example, if someone else starts using your computer.

FIGURE 3.14
Configure Sticky Keys
in the Set Up Sticky
Keys window.

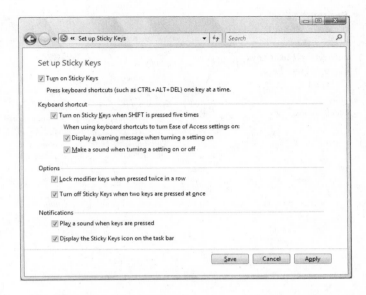

FIGURE 3.14
Configure Sticky Keys
in the Set Up Sticky
Keys window.

4. In the Notifications area, select the Play a Sound When Keys Are Pressed check box if you want Windows to beep when you press a modifier key with Sticky Keys on. This aural reminder can be helpful, but it may also prove an irritant. Select the Display the Sticky Keys Icon on the Taskbar check box if you want the notification area to display an icon for turning Sticky Keys on and off.

5. Click the Save button to save your settings and apply them.

TOGGLE KEYS

Toggle Keys makes Windows sound a tone when you press the Caps Lock key, the Num Lock key, or the Scroll Lock key. Select the Turn on Toggle Keys check box if you want to use Toggle Keys. Select the Turn on Toggle Keys by Holding Down the Num Lock Key for 5 Seconds check box if you want to be able to turn Toggle Keys on and off using the Num Lock key.

FILTER KEYS

Filter Keys lets you tell Windows to ignore either repeated keystrokes (such as those caused by holding down a key for longer than a single key press) or quick keystrokes (such as those caused by accidentally blipping a key while trying to press another key).

To set up Filter Keys, follow these steps:

1. Select the Turn on Filter Keys check box, and then click the Set Up Filter Keys link. Windows displays the Set Up Filter Keys window (see Figure 3.15).

FIGURE 3.15
If you find it hard to press the keys accurately, Filter Keys can be a great help.

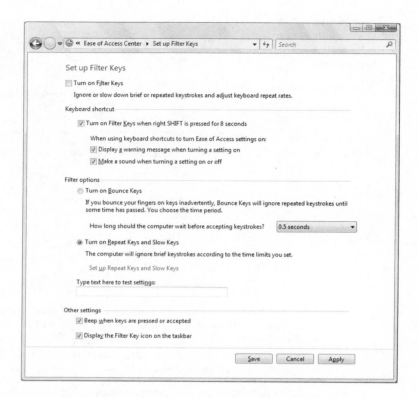

2. In the Keyboard Shortcut area, select the Turn on Filter Keys When Right Shift Is Pressed for 8 Seconds check box if you want to be able to turn on Filter Keys with a sustained press of the Shift key. Select the Display a Warning Message When Turning a Setting On check box and the Make a Sound When Turning a Setting On or Off check box if you want to be reminded when you turn Sticky Keys on or off; otherwise, clear these check boxes.

3. In the Filter Options area, choose between using Bounce Keys and using Repeat Keys and Slow Keys (together). You'll probably need to experiment with your settings by typing in the Type Text Here to Test Settings text box.

   ◆ If you tend to bounce your fingers on the keys accidentally, Select the Turn on Bounce Keys option. In the How Long Should the Computer Wait before Accepting Keystrokes? drop-down list, select a suitable length of time.

   ◆ If you find you get repeat keystrokes unintentionally, select the Turn on Repeat Keys and Slow Keys option button, and then click the Set up Repeat Keys and Slow Keys link. Windows displays the Set up Repeat Keys and Slow Keys window, which lets you set a delay for avoiding accidental keystrokes and either ignore all repeated keystrokes or slow down the rate at which the computer registers repeated keystrokes. When you've found settings that suit you, click the Save button to apply them and to return to the Set up Filter Keys window.

4. In the Other Settings area, select the Beep When Keys Are Pressed or Accepted check box if you want Windows to beep to confirm each key press that it accepts. Select the Display the Filter Key Icon on the Taskbar you want the notification area to display an icon for turning Filter Keys on and off.

5. Click the Save button to save your settings and apply them.

DISPLAYING KEYBOARD SHORTCUTS AND ACCESS KEYS

If you want to be able to issues commands from the keyboard, select the Underline Keyboard Shortcuts and Access Keys check box. Windows then displays an underline under the letter that you can press to click a button or other control or issue a menu command. This setting also makes Windows Explorer windows display the menu bar when you press the Alt key.

USING THE ON-SCREEN KEYBOARD

The On-Screen Keyboard displays a keyboard in a window on screen so that you can enter keyboard commands with a mouse or other pointing device. To start the On-Screen Keyboard, follow these steps:

1. Click the Use the Computer without a Mouse or Keyboard link in the Ease of Access Center window. Windows displays the Use the Computer without a Mouse or Keyboard window.

2. Select the Use On-Screen Keyboard check box, and then click the Save button. Windows displays the On-Screen Keyboard, as shown here.

The options for On-Screen Keyboard include the following:

◆ To make the keyboard click when you press a key, choose Settings ➢ Use Click Sound. (The click sound makes it easier to notice when you've mis-clicked or clicked twice.)

◆ To make the keyboard enter a key when you hover the pointer over it (so that you don't need to click), choose Settings ➢ Typing Mode. In the resulting Typing Mode dialog box, select the Hover to Select option button and specify the reaction time in the Minimum Time to Hover text box. Click the OK button.

◆ To display a standard keyboard rather than an enhanced keyboard, or to use a block layout rather than the regular offset layout, or to use a 102-key or 106-key keyboard instead of a 101-key keyboard, choose the appropriate command from the Keyboard menu.

Once you've displayed the On-Screen Keyboard, Windows displays it automatically each time you log on, so that you can use it immediately. To turn off the On-Screen Keyboard, open the Ease of Access Center window.

USING SPEECH RECOGNITION

Windows Vista includes speech-recognition capabilities that allow you to control your computer by speaking into a microphone. You can even dictate into programs such as Word with impressive accuracy, provided that you spend some time training the speech-recognition feature.

To use speech recognition, follow these steps:

1. Click the Use the Computer without a Mouse or Keyboard link in the Ease of Access Center window. Windows displays the Use the Computer without a Mouse or Keyboard window.

2. Click the Use Speech Recognition link. Windows displays the Speech Recognition Options window in Control Panel (see Figure 3.16).

3. Click the Start Speech Recognition link to set up speech recognition. These are the main steps of the setup process:

   ◆ If you haven't already set up a microphone, Windows launches the Microphone Setup Wizard, which walks you through the steps of setting up a microphone.

   ◆ In the Improve Speech Recognition Accuracy window, it's a good idea to select the Enable Document Review option button. Document Review lets Windows read your documents and e-mail messages to identify words you use frequently, on the basis that you'll likely use them in documents you dictate.

   ◆ Windows offers you the opportunity to view or print the Speech Reference Card, which lists the commands you can use to control Windows and programs. You'll probably want to keep this card handy until you've memorized all the commands you need.

   ◆ Choose whether to run Speech Recognition automatically every time you start your computer. If you plan to use Speech Recognition each session, automatic starting is a good idea.

   ◆ Take the interactive speech recognition tutorial to get the hang of Speech Recognition.

FIGURE 3.16
Speech Recognition allows you to control Windows and most programs via a microphone.

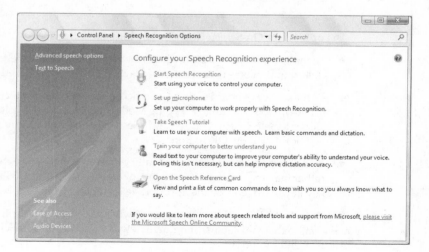

Once you've set up Speech Recognition, the Speech Recognition window appears, as shown here. Issue the "Start Listening" command to start it listening to you, and you're ready to start using the commands from the Speech Reference Card or to dictate into a program.

Using Display Accessibility Options

To make the screen easier to read or interpret, Windows provides a High Contrast display option, Narrator and Audio Description features, and several other features.

To access these options, click the Make the Computer Easier to See link in the Ease of Access Center window. Windows displays the Make the Computer Easier to See window (see Figure 3.17).

FIGURE 3.17

The options in the Make the Computer Easier to See window include letting you apply high contrast, have Narrator read text on screen, or use Magnifier to zoom in on an area.

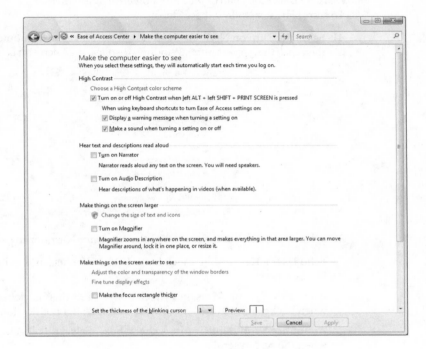

HIGH CONTRAST

The High Contrast display option makes Windows use fonts and colors that are designed to be easy to read rather than look good. To use this option, follow these steps:

1. Click the Choose a High Contrast Color Scheme link. Windows displays the Appearance Settings dialog box. In the Color Scheme list box, select one of the high-contrast schemes (High Contrast White, High Contrast Black, High Contrast #2, or High Contrast #1), and then click the OK button. Windows closes the Appearance Settings dialog box and applies the high-contrast scheme.

2. If you want to be able to turn High Contrast on and off easily from the keyboard, select the Turn On or Off High Contrast When Left Alt + Left Shift + Print Screen is Pressed check box.

3. Select the Display a Warning Message When Turning a Setting On check box and the Make a Sound When Turning a Setting On or Off check box if you want to be reminded when you turn Sticky Keys on or off; otherwise, clear these check boxes.

4. Click the Save button to save your settings and apply them.

NARRATOR AND AUDIO DESCRIPTION

The Narrator program can read aloud a variety of things from the screen: menu commands, dialog box controls, and characters you type. The voice is synthesized, and its phrasing and cadence make it hard to understand. It's usable in a pinch, but for sustained use you may want to check `http://www.microsoft.com/enable` for more powerful alternatives.

To start Narrator, follow these steps:

1. Select the Turn on Narrator check box in the Make the Computer Easier to See window, and then click the Apply button. Windows displays the Microsoft Narrator window, as shown here.

2. Select the check boxes for the actions you want Narrator to perform:

Echo User's Keystrokes check box   Select this check box to make Narrator announce each key you press.

Announce System Messages check box   Select this check box to make Narrator tell you when background events occur—for example, if a notification-area pop-up appears.

Announce Scroll Notifications check box   Select this check box to make Narrator tell you when the screen scrolls.

Start Narrator Minimized check box   Select this check box to make Narrator start minimized rather than in a normal-size window.

3. If you want to adjust the voice used and the pitch, speed, and volume, click the Voice Settings button, and then use the options in the Voice Settings dialog box.

To stop using Narrator, select the Exit button in the Narrator window, and then choose the Yes button in the Exit Narrator dialog box that makes sure you didn't hit the button by accident.

MAGNIFIER

Magnifier displays a magnified version of the section of the screen around the mouse pointer, the keyboard focus, or the section of text you're editing. This section appears in a panel at the top of the screen. You can resize this panel so that it takes up as much as half of the screen. To use Magnifier, follow these steps:

1. Select the Turn on Magnifier check box in the Make the Computer Easier to See window, and then click the Apply button. Windows splits the screen horizontally about three-quarters of the way up. The lower pane shows the screen at normal size, and the upper pane shows an enlarged version of the area the mouse pointer is currently in.

2. To configure Magnifier, click the Magnifier button on the Taskbar, and then work in the Magnifier window (see Figure 3.18).

3. When you've finished choosing settings, minimize the Magnifier Settings window to get it out of your way.

4. To stop using Magnifier, click the Exit button in the Magnifier Settings window.

FIGURE 3.18
To configure Magnifier, choose your desired magnification level in the Scale Factor drop-down list, decide whether to invert colors, and whether (and where) to dock Magnifier. You can also specify which items Magnifier should track: the mouse cursor, the keyboard focus, or text editing.

CHOOSING OTHER VISUAL SETTINGS

The Make the Computer Easier to See window offers three more settings:

Make the Focus Rectangle Thicker check box If you find the normal Windows cursor hard to see, select this check box, and then choose the width of the cursor in the Set the Thickness of the Blinking Cursor drop-down list.

Turn off All Unnecessary Animations (When Possible) check box Select this check box to tell Windows to suppress animations whenever possible.

Remove Background Images (Where Available) check box Select this check box to make Windows remove background images from windows over which it has control.

Using Text or Visual Alternatives for Sounds

If you have a hearing problem, you may want to use visual alternatives for system sounds. To do so, follow these steps:

1. Click the Use Text or Visual Alternatives for Sounds link in the Ease of Access Center. Windows displays the Use Text or Visual Alternatives for Sounds window (see Figure 3.19).

2. Select the Turn on Visual Notifications for Sounds (Sound Sentry) check box.

3. In the Choose Visual Warning area, select the Flash Active Caption Bar option button, the Flash Active Window option button, or the Flash Desktop option button.

4. If you want Windows to make programs display captions when they make sounds or convey information via spoken words, select the Turn on Text Captions for Spoken Dialog (When Available) check box. This setting works for only some programs.

5. Click the Save button. Windows applies your settings, and then displays the Ease of Access Center window.

FIGURE 3.19
Sound Sentry lets you use a flash as a visual notification of a sound.

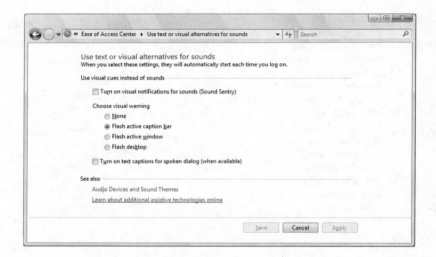

Applying Your Ease-of-Access Settings to the Logon Desktop

If you want to apply the ease-of-access settings to the Windows logon screen so that the settings are in effect for the next time you log on to Windows, follow these steps:

1. In the Ease of Access Center window, click the Change Administrative Settings link in the left panel. Windows displays the Change Administrative Settings screen.

2. For safety, in case any of the ease-of-access settings have unexpected results, it's a good idea to click the Create a Restore Point for Backup link and use System Restore to create a restore point. If something goes wrong, you can then restore your system to this point. See Chapter 16 for details.

3. Select the Apply All Settings to the Logon Desktop check box.

4. Click the Save button.

5. Restart Windows, and verify that all the settings are working as you expect.

Choosing a Screen Saver

A *screen saver* is a program that blanks out your monitor or displays a moving pattern over it when you haven't used the keyboard or mouse for a specified period of time. Windows comes with a variety of screen savers built in. You can also buy commercial screen savers or download them for free from philanthropists, egomaniacs, and advertisers (but see the nearby sidebar).

Screen savers used to be important in the 1970s and 1980s, because they would save your screen—literally. In those days, text-based displays would burn into the phosphors of a CRT monitor, creating a ghost image that then overlaid whatever else was being displayed. These days, most monitors aren't susceptible to phosphor burn-in, and in any case, graphical displays pose fewer problems with burn-in than text-based displays. LCDs don't suffer from phosphor burn-in, but they can exhibit *image persistence*, in which liquid crystals that have been displaying the same image for a long time don't show exactly the right color when the image changes. Image persistence is temporary rather than permanent.

Nowadays, there are only two reasons to use a screen saver:

◆ First, to hide your work (or play) from prying eyes when you've left your computer idle for more than a certain length of time. When you use a screen saver to hide your work, apply a password to the screen saver so that only you can turn off the screen saver. A better alternative is to lock your computer manually rather than wait for a screen saver to start.

◆ Second, to have your monitor display something pretty or intriguing to amuse you when you're not actively using the computer. Most screen savers, true to their phosphor-protecting heritage, display moving patterns that can be entertaining to look at, but some display trivia, quizzes, or educational flashcards. Windows includes a screen saver called Photos that displays the pictures in a designated folder or selection one by one, turning your computer into a slide show when it's not being used.

 Real World Scenario

AVOID SCREEN SAVERS IF POSSIBLE

Screen savers are notorious for causing trouble, some through malice and some through incompetence.

Malice: Free, downloadable screen savers are a favorite tool of the writers of viruses and malware. When they create a screen saver of something diverting or of a celebrity, the writer can be almost certain of achieving widespread distribution. They can then use the screen saver as a Trojan horse to get a virus onto the downloader's system, and the virus is free to execute at a time of the writer's choosing.

Incompetence: Because they kick in and interrupt normal operations on the computer, screen savers can cause software conflicts and crashes. The screen savers that Microsoft supplies with Windows are robust and safe, but *any* screen saver might destabilize your system.

To avoid security threats, never download a third-party screen saver, however attractive it may seem.

If your Windows computer is part of a home network and provides services such as file sharing, printer sharing, or Internet connectivity to the other computers, there's another good reason not to use a screen saver: Many screen savers give the processor quite a workout in order to produce their intricate patterns. This not only wastes energy but also prevents the computer from responding promptly to requests for services. (You can also configure many screen savers to use less energy by selecting their lowest settings, but doing so tends to make them so much less entertaining that it's better not to use them in the first place.)

Even worse, having a vigorous screen saver kick in can ruin a CD or DVD burn if the recorder doesn't have protective features. So if you burn CDs or DVDs and you feel you *must* use a screen saver, configure the screen saver with a long enough delay that any burn you leave running will be long finished before the screen saver starts.

One exception worth mentioning is screen savers used to implement distributed-computing projects, such as SETI@home, the Search for Extraterrestrial Intelligence at Home project (`http://setiathome.ssl.berkeley.edu`). Such projects actively grab your available processor cycles (so don't run them on a computer providing services) and use them to compute part of a much greater whole.

To apply a screen saver, follow these steps:

1. Right-click the Desktop and choose Personalize from the context menu. Windows displays the Personalization window.

2. Click the Screen Saver link. Windows displays the Screen Saver Settings dialog box (see Figure 3.20).

FIGURE 3.20
Use the Screen Saver Settings dialog box to configure a screen saver.

3. In the Screen Saver drop-down list, select the screen saver to use.

♦ To see how a screen saver looks full screen, click the Preview button.

♦ Move the mouse or press any key on the keyboard to stop the preview.

4. To choose settings for the screen saver, click the Settings button and work in the resulting Settings dialog box.

♦ Which settings are available depends on the type of screen saver you choose. Some screen savers have no settings; others have a dozen or more.

♦ Figure 3.21 shows the Photos Screen Saver Settings dialog box, which offers a variety of settings for customizing the slide show, including the following: which pictures to use, the speed at which to run the slide show, which slideshow theme to use, and whether to shuffle the order of the pictures.

♦ Use the Preview button again after choosing settings to see if the settings you chose meet your liking.

5. In the Wait text box, enter the number of minutes of inactivity that you want before the screen saver kicks in.

6. If you want Windows to display the logon screen when a user reactivates the computer after the screen saver has been running, select the On Resume, Display Logon Screen check box.

7. Click the OK button. Windows applies your screen saver preferences and closes the Screen Saver Settings dialog box.

From the Screen Saver page of the Display Properties dialog box, you can click the Change Power Settings link in the Power Management group box to display the Power Options window in Control Panel. Power management is an involved topic and is discussed in Chapter 13.

FIGURE 3.21
Most screen savers have some configurable settings.

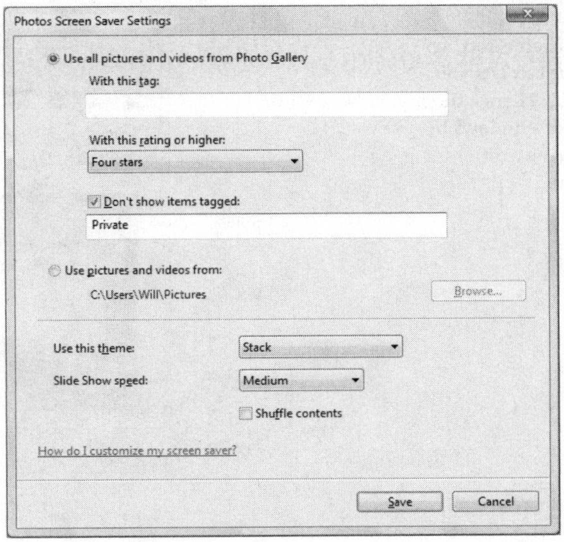

Changing the Look and Feel of Windows

You can change the look and feel of Windows by applying a different theme, or suite of settings; changing the background; choosing which items appear on the Desktop; adjusting the appearance of individual components of the user interface; choosing sounds for system events; or rearranging the items on your Desktop. This section shows you how to perform all these actions.

Applying a Theme

A *theme* is a coordinated look for various different aspects of the Windows screen: the Desktop background, colors, font styles and sizes, window sizes, sound events, mouse pointers, icons, and even the screen saver. By applying a different theme, you can change the way Windows looks.

To apply a theme, take the following steps:

1. Right-click the Desktop and choose Personalize from the context menu. Windows displays the Personalization window.

2. Click the Theme link. Windows displays the Theme Settings dialog box (see Figure 3.22).

3. In the Theme drop-down list, select the theme to apply. Watch the Sample box to see how the different themes look. To select a theme that doesn't appear in the Theme drop-down list, select the Browse item. Windows displays the Open Theme dialog box. Navigate to and select the theme file, and then click the Open button.

4. Click the Apply button. Windows applies the theme without closing the window (allowing you to change it again if you don't like the appearance).

To create a custom theme, select a theme to start with and modify it to suit your taste by changing the background, window colors, or other elements as described in the following section. When the theme is as you want it, open the Theme Settings dialog box again, click the Save As button, and use the Save As dialog box to save the theme. You can then apply the theme at will.

FIGURE 3.22
The Theme Settings dialog box lets you quickly change the look of Windows by applying a different theme.

Changing the Background

To give your Desktop a different look, you can change its background picture or pattern. Follow these steps:

1. Right-click the Desktop and choose Personalize from the context menu. Windows displays the Personalization window.

2. Click the Desktop Background link. Windows displays the Desktop Background dialog box (see Figure 3.23).

3. In the drop-down list, choose the category of pictures:

   ◆ Windows Wallpapers contains several different descriptive categories of wallpaper images, including Vistas, Black and White, Textures, Paintings, Widescreen, and Light Auras.

   ◆ Pictures lets you use pictures in your Pictures folder.

   ◆ Sample Pictures shows pictures in the Sample Pictures folder, which appears (via a link) to be inside your Pictures folder.

   ◆ Public Pictures shows pictures in the Public folder.

   ◆ Solid Colors lets you pick a solid color for the whole desktop.

   ◆ To use an image that's not listed, click the Browse button and use the resulting Browse dialog box to navigate to and select the file. (From an Explorer window, you can also right-click a picture file and choose Set as Desktop Background from the context menu.)

FIGURE 3.23
Changing the Desktop background can make a dramatic difference to how Windows looks.

4. Once you've chosen the category, select the picture (unless you browsed, in which case you've selected the picture already). Windows applies it to the Desktop so that you can preview the effect.

5. If the image you choose is smaller than the screen, select one of the How Should the Picture Be Positioned? option buttons: Fit to Screen (the left option button), Tile (the center option button), or Center (the right option button).

   ◆ If the image doesn't have the same proportions as the screen, the Fit to Screen option distorts the image. If you want to have a full-screen picture without distortion, open the image in a graphics program (for example, Paint), crop it to the right proportions, and then save the cropped version under a different name for use on your Desktop.

   ◆ If the image you want to use is a picture from a high-resolution digital camera, it may be *bigger* than the screen. In this case, the Tile option isn't much use. The Center option centers the center of the picture on the screen, so you'll see only part of it. The Stretch option shrinks the picture to fit the screen.

6. Click the OK button. Windows closes the Desktop Background window.

Changing Desktop Items

Windows displays some items on your Desktop by default, such as the Recycle Bin. You can't get rid of these by conventional means such as deleting them. But you can remove them and, if you wish, add other items by using the Desktop Items dialog box.

To change the items displayed on the Desktop, follow these steps:

1. Right-click the Desktop and choose Personalize from the context menu. Windows displays the Personalization window.

2. Click the Change Desktop Icons link in the left pane of the Personalization window. Windows displays the Desktop Icon Settings dialog box (see Figure 3.24).

FIGURE 3.24

The Desktop Icon Settings dialog box lets you decide which icons appear on the Desktop—if any.

3. In the Desktop Icons group box, select the check box for each icon you want to appear on the Desktop. Clear the check box for each icon you want to hide.

4. To change the icon displayed for one of the icons shown in the list box, click the icon, and then click the Change Icon button. Windows displays the Change Icon dialog box. In the Select an Icon from the List Below list box, choose the icon you want to use, and then click the OK button to apply it. You can reapply the default icon for an item by selecting the item and clicking the Restore Default button in the Desktop Items dialog box.

5. Click the OK button. Windows closes the Desktop Icon Settings dialog box and applies your choices.

FINDING ICONS

If you don't see an icon you like in the Change Icon dialog box, click the Browse button and use the resulting Change Icon dialog box (a common Open dialog box in disguise) to select a file that contains icons. The file SHELL32.DLL in the \Windows\System32\ folder contains a wide variety of icons, and the file MORICONS.DLL (in the same folder) contains a selection of older icons, some of which have amusement value.

You can also find a wide variety of icons on the Web, or create your own icons with icon-editor programs.

Changing the Appearance of Windows Items

A theme gives you a way to apply an overall look to your Desktop, but you can take far finer control of the elements of the user interface if you want. For example, you may want to use different fonts or change the width of window borders. To do so, follow these steps:

1. Right-click the Desktop and choose Personalize from the context menu. Windows displays the Personalization window.

2. Click the Window Color and Appearance link. Windows displays the Window Color and Appearance window (see Figure 3.25).

3. At the top of the window, select the color scheme to use as the basis for Windows' look.

4. If you want to use the Aero Glass transparency effect, which makes the desktop background show through window title bars and frames, select the Enable Transparency check box.

5. To change the color intensity, drag the Color Intensity slider to the left or right.

6. If you want to adjust the hue, saturation, and brightness, click the Show Color Mixer button, and then use the three sliders (shown in the figure) to produce an effect you like.

7. To adjust individual window elements, click the Open Classic Appearance Properties for More Color Options link. Windows displays the Appearance Settings dialog box (see Figure 3.26).

FIGURE 3.25
The Window Color and Appearance window lets you apply a color scheme; adjust hue, saturation, and brightness; and turn transparency on and off.

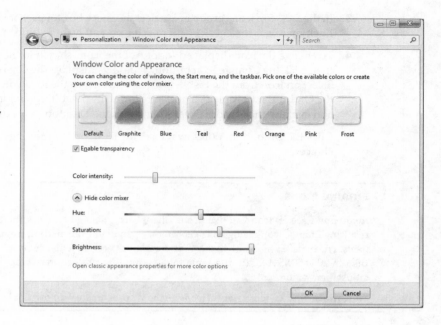

FIGURE 3.26
The Appearance Settings dialog box lets you switch among "color schemes," or overall visual effects. Normally, you'll want to keep the Windows Vista Aero color scheme selected if it's available, and use the Effects button or the Advanced button to make adjustments to specific items.

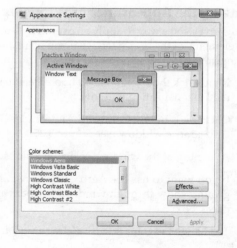

8. To change Desktop effects, click the Effects button. Windows displays the Effects dialog box, shown here.

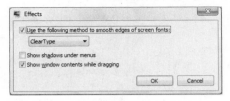

9. Choose effects (explained in the following list), and then click the OK button.

Use the Following Method to Smooth Edges of Screen Fonts check box and drop-down list Select this check box if you want to have Windows smooth the edges of screen fonts so that they look less jagged and are easier to read. (Smoothing is usually a good idea.) Then choose one of the options from the drop-down list: Standard or ClearType. ClearType is a Microsoft font-rendering technology that uses subpixel rendering to smooth the edges of fonts, making them easier to read. (Instead of turning on a whole pixel, or turning it off, ClearType can turn on *part* of a pixel to achieve a more graduated, less blocky effect.) ClearType is most effective on LCD screens, though it also has some effect on CRT screens as well. If you're used to reading on screen, ClearType may make you rub your eyes at first, as its effect is to blur the edges of the letters.

Show Shadows under Menus check box Select this check box to have Windows display shadows at the bottom and right edge of menus to give a 3-D effect. Clear this check box if you prefer your menus plain.

Show Window Contents while Dragging check box Select this check box to have Windows display the contents of a window when you're moving it or resizing it. If your video card struggles to display the window's contents, try clearing this check box. Windows then displays only the window's frame when you move or resize it, then displays the contents when you've finished the maneuver.

10. If you want to adjust the appearance of individual items, click the Advanced button in the Appearance Settings dialog box. Windows displays the Advanced Appearance dialog box (see Figure 3.27).

11. To adjust an item, follow these general steps:

- In the Item drop-down list, select the item.

- Use the Size, Color 1, and Color 2 controls to change how the item looks. Watch the preview at the top of the dialog box.

- If the item includes text, choose the font in the Font drop-down list, and then use the Size, Color, Bold, and Italic controls to specify how the font looks.

- In the Item drop-down list, select the next item you want to change. (You don't need to save the settings you applied to the first item—Windows saves them automatically.)

FIGURE 3.27
The Advanced
Appearance dialog
box gives you fine
control over the
colors, sizes, and fonts
Windows uses for
different interface
items, such as title
bars, window frames,
and icons.

12. When you've finished choosing settings, click the OK button. Windows closes the Advanced Appearance dialog box, returning you to the Appearance Settings dialog box.

13. Click the OK button. Windows closes the Appearance Settings dialog box and applies the visual choices you made.

Choosing System Sounds

If you've got speakers or headphones attached to your computer, you'll have noticed by now that by default Windows plays sounds when you log on or off or when you take an action Windows considers unwise.

You may want to change these sounds. You can even create sound schemes so that you can keep multiple sets of system sounds and switch from one set to another as the fancy takes you.

To assign system sounds, follow these steps:

1. Right-click the Desktop and choose Personalize from the context menu. Windows displays the Personalization window.

2. Click the Sounds link. Windows displays the Sounds page of the Sound dialog box (see Figure 3.28).

3. To apply an existing sound scheme, select it in the Sound Scheme drop-down list. (To apply peace and quiet, select the No Sounds scheme.) If you were using a custom sound scheme before, but you haven't saved it, Windows displays the Save Previous Scheme dialog box prompting you to save it. Choose the Yes button or the No button as appropriate.

4. To customize the current sound scheme, take the following steps:

◆ Select an event in the Program Events list box.

◆ In the Sounds drop-down list, select the sound you want to assign to the event. To find out how a sound sounds, click the Play button with the sound selected.

FIGURE 3.28
The Sounds page of
the Sound dialog
box lets you change
either an entire sound
scheme or just the
sound associated with
a particular event.

The Sounds list box lists all the WAV files in the \Windows\Media\ folder. To make your own WAV files available in the Sounds list box, copy or move them to this folder before-hand. Alternatively, use the Browse button to locate individual files you want to assign to events.

To save the customized scheme, click the Save As button. Windows displays the Save Scheme As dialog box. Enter the name for the scheme and click the OK button. Once you've saved a scheme, it's available from the Sound Scheme drop-down list. If you tire of it, you can delete it by clicking the Delete button.

5. To turn off the Windows startup sound, clear the Play Windows Startup Sound check box.

6. Click the OK button. Windows applies your new sound scheme and closes the Sound dialog box.

Arranging Icons on Your Desktop

Depending on your installation of Windows, you may start off with just the Recycle Bin icon on the Desktop or a variety of icons. As you saw earlier in the chapter, you can show or hide icons for your User Files folder, Computer, Network, Control Panel, and Internet Explorer by selecting or clearing the check boxes in the Desktop Icon Settings dialog box. You can save files to the Desktop and create shortcuts there as you need them (more on this later in the chapter). And many programs place one or more shortcuts on the Desktop when you install them.

One way or another, your Desktop normally gathers icons rapidly. To keep things in order, you can arrange the icons on your Desktop by dragging them to wherever you want them to appear or by right-clicking the Desktop and using the commands on the context menu.

First, choose options on the View submenu:

Specify the icon size by choosing View ➢ Large Icons, View ➢ Medium Icons, or View ➢ Classic Icons.

◆ The Auto Arrange command controls whether Windows automatically arranges the icons into neat columns and rows, starting with a column beginning at the upper-left corner of the screen. You can toggle this command on and off. When it's on, the menu displays a check mark next to it.

◆ The Align to Grid command controls whether Windows aligns icons on an invisible grid or lets you place them wherever you want them. You can toggle this command on and off by selecting it; again, it displays a check mark when it's on. This command is supposedly independent of the Auto Arrange command, but in practice the Auto Arrange command essentially overrules it: When you let Windows arrange your icons, it parks them according to the grid whether the Align to Grid command is on or off.

◆ The Show Desktop Icons command lets you choose whether to show the icons or hide them. When a check mark appears next to this item, the icons are visible.

Next, choose how to sort the icons. Right-click the Desktop, display the Sort By submenu on the context menu, and then choose Name, Size, Type, or Date Modified. Windows sorts the icons by the attribute you choose. Windows displays a dot next to the currently selected item on the menu when the Auto Arrange command is active.

Configuring the Taskbar, Start Menu, and Desktop Toolbars

To make your work easier, you can control how the Taskbar and Start menu behave and which items appear on them. You can also use Desktop toolbars to keep important items close to hand.

Configuring the Taskbar

Both the Taskbar and the Start menu have changed considerably in Windows from the way they were in its predecessors, and you may want to restore some of their old behavior. This section discusses how to configure the Taskbar to meet your needs. The section after this discusses how to configure the Start menu.

RESIZING AND REPOSITIONING THE TASKBAR

By default, the Taskbar appears at the bottom of the Desktop and is locked so that you cannot expand, shrink, or reposition it. To unlock the Taskbar, right-click open space on it or in the notification area and select the Lock the Taskbar item from the context menu. Windows removes the check mark from the Lock the Taskbar item. (To lock the Taskbar again, repeat this command.)

You can also unlock the Taskbar by clearing the Lock the Taskbar check box on the Taskbar page of the Taskbar and Start Menu Properties dialog box, but this technique is handy only if you have this dialog box displayed already.

Once you've unlocked the Taskbar, you can resize it or reposition it:

◆ To reposition the Taskbar, click open space in it and drag it toward (or to) one of the edges of the screen so that the Taskbar snaps to it.

◆ To resize the Taskbar, drag its inside edge to expand or shrink the Taskbar. The inside edge is the edge nearest to the center of the screen. For example, in the Taskbar's default position at the bottom of the screen, the top edge is the inside edge.

When the Taskbar is positioned at the top or bottom of the screen, it grows and shrinks in increments of its original depth rather than gradually, so you can drag it to one-button depth, two-button depth, and so on. When the Taskbar is positioned at the side of the screen, it grows and shrinks gradually, so you can get exactly the width you want.

POSITION THE TASKBAR LEFT OR RIGHT WHEN YOU HAVE MANY WINDOWS OPEN

Unless you have a lot of windows open, placing the Taskbar at the side of the screen tends to waste space, because the buttons have a standard depth, leaving the lower part of the Taskbar unused.

If you do have a lot of windows open, placing the Taskbar at the side of the screen lets you read the button titles quickly in a column—and you can drag the column width to display more or less of each title as you need.

USING THE TASKBAR TO NAVIGATE BETWEEN PROGRAMS

The Taskbar lets you see which programs are open, navigate quickly to a program, and maximize, minimize, restore, or close programs easily.

The Taskbar displays a button for each open program window. That's *program window* rather than just *program*: If a program displays multiple separate program windows, the Taskbar shows one button for each window. If the program uses only one program window (including if the program has several document windows open within a program window), the Taskbar typically shows only one button for it.

For example, Word 2007 normally displays each document in a separate window, so Windows displays a separate Taskbar button for each document window. If you have Word set to display only one window, the Taskbar displays only one button for Word.

When the Taskbar has taken up all the available space with buttons, it groups any related buttons into a single button for the category. For example, if you have five Excel workbooks open, it groups their five buttons into a single group button that contains a menu of the buttons. While the individual buttons bear the names of the document windows, the group button bears the program name and the number of windows the program has open—in this case, 5 Microsoft Excel. Similarly, the Taskbar will display an Explorer button named 4 Windows Explorer containing a Control Panel button, a Network button, a Computer button, and a Recycle Bin button.

To display a program, click its button on the Taskbar. If the button is grouped into a group button, click the group button to display the menu of buttons, and then choose the button from the menu, as shown here.

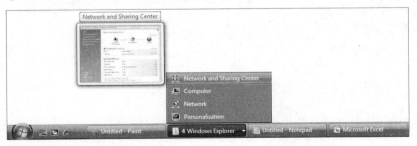

To resize, move, or close a program window, right-click its Taskbar button and choose Restore, Move, Size, Minimize, Maximize, or Close from the context menu.

To arrange all the program windows, right-click open space in the Taskbar or in the notification area and choose the appropriate command from the context menu. This offers the Cascade Windows command, the Show Windows Stacked command, the Show Windows Side by Side command, and the Show the Desktop command. When you've issued a Show the Desktop command, the context menu contains the Show Open Windows command instead of the Show the Desktop command.

WORKING QUICKLY WITH MULTIPLE WINDOWS

You can right-click a group button to manipulate all its windows at once. The context menu offers Cascade, Show Windows Stacked, Show Windows Side by Side, Minimize Group, and Close Group commands.

To work with multiple windows at once, hold down the Ctrl key and select the Taskbar button for each window. Then right-click one of the windows and choose the action from the context menu.

CONFIGURING THE TASKBAR'S BEHAVIOR

To configure the Taskbar, right-click open space in it or in the notification area and choose Properties from the context menu. Windows displays the Taskbar page of the Taskbar and Start Menu Properties dialog box (see Figure 3.29).

The Taskbar Appearance group box offers these six options:

Lock the Taskbar   Select this check box to prevent the Taskbar from being moved to another edge of the screen or resized. Clear the check box if you want to move or resize the Taskbar. It's usually easier to lock or unlock the Taskbar from its context menu.

Auto-Hide the Taskbar   Select this check box to make the Taskbar hide itself until you move the pointer over its edge of the screen. This option is useful for maximizing the amount of the screen available to you, especially when you've increased the size of the Taskbar to accommodate more programs. The disadvantage is that you can't use the Taskbar to see your other windows unless you force it to appear.

FIGURE 3.29
Use the Taskbar page of the Taskbar and Start Menu Properties dialog box to configure the Taskbar to your liking.

Keep the Taskbar on Top of Other Windows   Select this check box to have the Taskbar appear on top of any window. Instead of using the Auto-Hide feature to hide the Taskbar, you can clear this check box so that the Taskbar remains on screen. You can then display another window on top of the Taskbar if you want.

Group Similar Taskbar Buttons   Select this check box to have Windows group similar buttons when the Taskbar starts to get full. (See the previous section for further explanation and an example.) Individual buttons can make it easy to find the window you want, but the buttons take up a lot of space, or each button on the Taskbar gets shrunk to a tiny size to fit them all in.

Show Quick Launch   Select this check box to display the Quick Launch toolbar on the Taskbar. See "Using the Desktop Toolbars" later in this chapter for a discussion of the Quick Launch toolbar.

Show Window Previews (Thumbnails)   Select this check box to make Windows display a preview of the window when you hover the mouse pointer over a Taskbar button. This feature is usually helpful, but it may prove distracting if you tend to park your mouse pointer over the Taskbar to get it out of the way of a document window.

CONFIGURING THE NOTIFICATION AREA

The Taskbar is one of the busiest parts of the Windows user interface, but the notification area is far busier yet. To control what appears in the notification area, click the Notification Area tab of the Taskbar and Start Menu Properties dialog box, and then work on the Notification Area page (see Figure 3.30).

In the Icons group box, select the Hide Inactive Icons check box if you want Windows automatically to remove from the notification area any items that you haven't used recently. Windows hides the items and displays a Show Hidden Icons button that you can use to display them. This option can be useful for keeping your notification area uncluttered. If you find it unsettling to have icons disappear, clear this check box.

FIGURE 3.30
The Notification Area page of the Taskbar and Start Menu Properties dialog box lets you choose which items appear in the notification area.

You can also customize how Windows handles notification-area icons by clicking the Customize button and working in the Customize Notification Icons dialog box (see Figure 3.31). Select the item in the Current Items list or the Past Items list, and then choose Hide When Inactive, Hide, or Show from the context menu. (If you mess up, click the Default Settings button to restore Windows' default behavior with the notification area.) Click the OK button to return to the Taskbar and Start Menu Properties dialog box.

In the System Icons group box, select or clear the Clock check box, the Volume check box, the Network check box, and the Power check box to tell Windows which icons to display permanently. The Power check box is available only if your computer can run on battery power—for example, if it's a laptop. (The Power icon lets you see whether the computer is running on battery power or AC power and whether the battery is charging.)

MAKING THE CLOCK DISPLAY THE DAY AND DATE

When the Taskbar is displayed as only one row at the top or bottom of the screen, the clock displays only the time. To display the day and date as well, increase the Taskbar depth to two rows or more.

FIGURE 3.31
The Customize Notification Icons dialog box lets you decide which notification-area icons to display and which to hide.

Customizing the Start Menu

Windows Vista introduces a new-look Start menu (see Figure 3.32) that's different from Windows XP's Start menu, which in turn differed from the Start menu in earlier versions of Windows. The Start menu automatically adjusts its contents to show your most recently used and most used programs. You can also configure the Start menu to make your computing easier.

If you prefer the "classic" Start menu used in Windows 9x, Windows NT 4, and Windows 2000, you can easily restore it: Select the Classic Start Menu option button on the Start Menu page of the Taskbar and Start Menu Properties dialog box, and then click the Apply button. This book assumes that you're using the Windows Vista–style Start menu, so if you choose the classic Start menu, you'll need to choose Start menu commands a little differently. The section after next discusses how to customize the classic Start menu, but after that, all coverage uses the Windows Vista Start menu.

FIGURE 3.32
The new-look Start menu appears as a two-column panel with the current user's name at the top.

CUSTOMIZING THE WINDOWS START MENU

To customize the Windows Vista Start menu, take the following steps:

1. Right-click the Start button, and then choose Properties from the context menu. Windows displays the Start Menu page of the Taskbar and Start Menu Properties dialog box (see Figure 3.33).

FIGURE 3.33
On the Start Menu page of the Taskbar and Start Menu Properties dialog box, choose between the (Windows Vista) Start Menu and the Classic Start Menu.

2. In the Privacy group box, select or clear the Store and Display a List of Recently Opened Files check box and the Store and Display a List of Recently Opened Programs check box, as appropriate. Having these lists can be handy, but it may allow someone else to see which files and programs you've been using.

3. Click the upper Customize button to display the Customize Start Menu dialog box (see Figure 3.34).

4. In the main list box, choose which items to display and (for some) whether to display them as links or as menus:

   ◆ For example, the Computer item initially appears as a link, so that clicking it opens a Windows Explorer window showing the Computer folder. Instead, you can display the Computer item as a menu that cascades off the Start menu.

   ◆ The items you can display as links, menus, or not at all are Computer, Control Panel, Documents, Games, Music, Personal Folder (the folder with your username), and Pictures.

   ◆ Other items you can turn on or off. These include Connect To, Default Programs, Favorites Menu, Help, Network, Printers, Run Command, and Search.

   ◆ You can configure search further. In the Search Files area, select the Search This User's Files option button, the Don't Search for Files option button, or the Search Entire Index option button, as appropriate. You can also restrict searching by selecting or clearing the Search Communications check box, the Search Favorites and History check box, and the Search Programs check box.

5. Choose other settings for the Start menu:

   Enable Context Menus and Dragging and Dropping check box   Select this check box if you want to be able to right-click items on the Start menu to produce a context menu of commands. Selecting this check box also lets you drag items from one place on the Start menu to another, which is usually helpful.

FIGURE 3.34
The Customize Start Menu dialog box lets you choose which items appear on the Start menu and whether they appear as links or menus.

Highlight Newly Installed Programs check box   Leave this check box selected if you want Windows to display a yellow highlight on the Start menu and its submenus to show you the path to newly installed programs. Windows removes the highlighting once you've used the program. This highlighting can be useful, but because Windows applies it to each new shortcut the freshly installed program has created, the highlighted path persists until you've used each shortcut—which may be awhile for shortcuts to uninstall features, Help files, and documentation. If you don't like the highlighting, clear this check box.

Open Submenus When I Pause on Them with My Mouse check box   Leave this check box selected (as it is by default) if you want the Start menu to display its submenus when you hover the mouse pointer over them for more than a few milliseconds. Clear this check box if you prefer to have the submenus appear only when you click them.

Sort All Programs Menu by Name   Select this check box if you want Windows to sort the items on the All Programs menu by name. Alphabetical sorting makes for an easy way to find programs, but you may prefer to turn this setting off so that you can use drag-and-drop to rearrange the All Programs menu into an order you prefer—for example, your most used programs first.

Use Large Icons check box   Select this check box if you want to use large icons on the Start menu.

Start Menu Size group box   In the Number of Recent Programs to Display text box, specify how many programs the Start menu should display. You can set any number from 0 to 30.

Show on Start Menu group box   To display an Internet item on the Start menu, select the Internet Link check box; to remove this item, clear the check box. If you leave the check box selected, use the drop-down list to select the program used for browsing the Internet. Similarly, to display an e-mail item on the Start menu, select the E-mail check box and specify the program in the drop-down list.

6. Click the OK button. Windows closes the Customize Start Menu dialog box.

7. Click the OK button. Windows closes the Taskbar and Start Menu Properties dialog box.

Besides customizing the Start menu using the Taskbar and Start Menu Properties dialog box, you can also customize it in the following ways:

◆   To prevent Windows from moving an item on the Start menu, *pin* it in place. Right-click the item in the Start menu and choose Pin to Start Menu from the context menu.

◆   You can also pin an item to the Start menu by dragging it to the Start button and dropping it there.

◆   To unpin an item, right-click it in the Start menu and choose Unpin from Start Menu from the context menu.

◆   To remove an item from the most-used section of the Start menu, right-click the item and choose Remove from this List from the context menu.

◆   To add an item to the All Programs menu or one of its submenus, drag the item to the Start button, hover the mouse pointer there until Windows displays the Start menu, drag the item to the All Programs button and hover there, then drag to the location on the menu where you want the item to appear.

CUSTOMIZING THE CLASSIC START MENU

You can customize the classic Start menu so that it contains exactly the items you want. To do so, you add items to the menu, remove existing items, and sort the menu if necessary.

To customize the classic Start menu, follow these steps:

1. Right-click the Start button and choose Properties from the context menu to open the Taskbar and Start Menu Properties dialog box.

2. Select the Classic Start Menu option button (it should already be selected).

3. In the Privacy group box, select or clear the Store and Display a List of Recently Opened Files check box and the Store and Display a List of Recently Opened Programs check box, as appropriate. These lists give you quick access to the files and programs you've used recently, but they can be a security concern.

4. Click the lower Customize button. Windows displays the Customize Classic Start Menu dialog box (shown in Figure 3.35).

5. Add items to the Start menu and remove items from it:

   ◆ To add an item to the Start menu, click the Add button and follow the steps in the Create Shortcut Wizard that Windows displays.

   ◆ To remove an item from the Start menu, click the Remove button. Windows displays the Remove Shortcuts/Folders dialog box. Select the item you want to remove, and then click the Remove button.

   ◆ To add and remove items freely, click the Advanced button. Windows opens an Explorer window showing the Start menu. You can then create and delete shortcuts as you see fit by using standard Explorer techniques.

   ◆ To sort the Start menu alphabetically, click the Sort button.

   ◆ To clear the details of recently used documents, programs, and websites, click the Clear button.

FIGURE 3.35
The Customize Classic Start Menu dialog box lets you customize the classic Start menu extensively to put the items you need most right at hand.

MANIPULATING THE START MENU VIA EXPLORER

Your Start menu folder is stored in the `\Users\`*Username*`\AppData\Roaming\Microsoft\Windows\`
`Start Menu\` folder, where *Username* is your username. You can navigate to it by using Explorer and
manipulate it without opening the Customize Classic Start Menu dialog box.

---

6. In the Advanced Start Menu Options list box, choose settings for the following options:

Display Administrative Tools check box Select this check box to have Windows display
the Administrative Tools menu on the Programs menu. You can also access these tools
through the Administrative Tools page of Control Panel, but using the menu is quicker for
frequent access.

Display Favorites check box Select this check box to have Windows display the Favorites
menu on the Start menu. This menu lets you quickly access your favorites, but it can become
unwieldy if you have a large number of favorites.

Display Log Off Select this check box to make Windows display a Log Off button on the
Start menu.

Display Run check box Select this check box to have the Start menu include the Run
item, which you can use for running a program. Clear this check box to remove the Run
item. You might want to remove Run to help discourage users from running programs not
on the Start menu.

Enable Context Menus and Dragging and Dropping check box Select this check box if
you want to be able to right-click items on the Start menu to produce a context menu of commands. Selecting this check box also lets you drag items from one place on the Start menu
to another, which is usually helpful.

Expand Control Panel check box Select this check box if you want Windows to display a
menu of Control Panel items instead of opening a Control Panel window when you select
Start ➢ Settings ➢ Control Panel. This menu gives you faster access to the Control Panel
items than does opening a Control Panel window.

Expand Documents check box Select this check box if you want Windows to display a
menu listing the items in the Documents folder instead of displaying a window when you
choose Start ➢ Documents. This menu gives you quick access, but it can be hard to navigate
if you accumulate many documents and folders in the Documents folder.

Expand Network Connections check box Select this check box if you want Windows to
display a menu of network connections instead of displaying a window when you choose
Start ➢ Settings ➢ Network Connections.

Expand Pictures check box Select this check box if you want Windows to display a menu
listing the items in the Pictures folder when you choose Start ➢ Documents ➢ Pictures.

Expand Printers check box Select this check box if you want Windows to display a menu
of printers instead of displaying a window when you choose Start ➢ Settings ➢ Printers and
Faxes.

Scroll Programs check box Select this check box if you want Windows to display the Programs menu as a scrolling menu when it is too tall to fit on the screen. With this check box
cleared, Windows displays the Programs menu as two or more columns.

Show Small Icons in Start Menu check box   Select this check box to have Windows display small icons instead of large icons in the Start menu. Small icons let you pack more items on the Start menu but make it harder to read.

Use Personalized Menus check box   Select this check box to have Windows automatically tailor the Start menu to what it thinks are your needs. For example, if you don't use a program for a long time, Windows removes its item from the Start menu on the assumption that you don't need it. When Windows has removed items like this, it displays a button at the foot of the menu with a double arrow pointing downward to indicate that more items are available. Click this button to display the items that have been removed.

7. Click the OK button. Windows closes the Customize Classic Start Menu dialog box, returning you to the Taskbar and Start Menu Properties dialog box.

8. Click the OK button. Windows closes the Taskbar and Start Menu Properties dialog box and applies your choices.

Using the Desktop Toolbars

Windows offers several built-in toolbars that you can display on the Desktop. You can also create custom toolbars of your own to give you quick access to folders and web pages of your choice. The main toolbars are as follows:

Address toolbar   This toolbar works in the same way as the Address bar in Internet Explorer. Enter a URL and click the Go button (or press the Enter key) to open a web page in Internet Explorer. Enter a drive letter or folder name to open it in an Explorer window. Enter a filename and path to open the file in the program associated with its file type.

Windows Media Player   This toolbar displays a miniature version of Windows Media Player in the Taskbar, allowing you to control your music without having a Windows Media Player window taking up valuable working space.

Desktop toolbar   This toolbar displays an icon for each item on your Desktop and menus for key folders (for example, the Computer folder and the Network folder). By displaying this toolbar, you can save yourself having to display the Desktop to access a program, a folder, or a file. Many people find this toolbar most useful reduced to a button. You can then click the toolbar's expansion arrow to get a menu of the items on your Desktop.

Links toolbar   This toolbar is the Links toolbar from Internet Explorer. You can use it to provide quick access to websites you want to be able to access frequently.

Quick Launch toolbar   This toolbar provides quick access to programs and documents you designate. The Quick Launch toolbar initially contains four icons and appears to the right of the Start button (when the Taskbar is at the bottom of the screen): Launch Internet Explorer Browser, Launch Outlook Express, MSN Explorer, and Show Desktop (which brings the Desktop to the foreground, in front of all open windows). You can add other icons to suit your needs, as discussed in the section after next.

Tablet PC Input Panel   This toolbar provides quick access to the Tablet PC input panel, the panel for writing with a tablet.

You may also see other toolbars, such as the Language Bar, on the Toolbars context menu. Some third-party applications can also install themselves in the Quick Launch area.

DISPLAYING AND HIDING THE DESKTOP TOOLBARS

To display or hide a toolbar, right-click the notification area, choose Toolbars from the context menu, and select the toolbar from the submenu, as shown here.

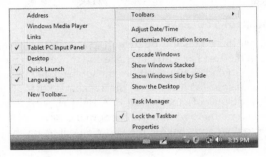

CUSTOMIZING THE QUICK LAUNCH TOOLBAR

As you've seen, the Start menu tries to put your most-used programs within easy reach by juggling the Start menu items and letting you pin items to the Start menu. But you may find it even easier to put the programs and documents you use most often on the Quick Launch toolbar and not have to worry about pinning them (or having Windows remove them to make room for another program).

There are two easy ways to add a shortcut to the Quick Launch toolbar:

◆ Drag the target file from an Explorer window (or from the Desktop) to the Quick Launch toolbar. Windows creates a shortcut to the file (the document or the program) there. You can also drag Control Panel items to the Quick Launch toolbar by displaying Control Panel in Classic view (choose Start ➢ Control Panel to open Control Panel, and then click the Classic View link in the left pane). Shortcuts on the Quick Launch toolbar don't show the usual shortcut arrow, though if you look at the Quick Launch folder, you'll see that the shortcut arrows are there.

◆ Right-click open space in the Quick Launch toolbar and choose Open Folder from the context menu. Windows displays the Quick Launch folder. Create shortcuts by right-dragging any file or folder to this folder and choosing Create Shortcuts Here from the context menu.

Once you have the shortcuts you need on the Quick Launch toolbar, drag their icons into the order in which you need them, left to right. This way, if only part of the Quick Launch toolbar is displayed on screen, you'll be able to access your most-needed icons without needing to display the hidden portion of the toolbar.

CREATING AND USING CUSTOM TOOLBARS

In addition to using the four ready-made toolbars, you can create custom toolbars to display the contents of any folder. A custom toolbar can be a great way of giving yourself access to the documents you use frequently.

To create a custom toolbar, take the following steps:

1. Right-click open space in the Taskbar or anywhere in the notification area, and then choose Toolbars ➢ New Toolbar from the context menu. Windows displays the New Toolbar—Choose a Folder dialog box.

2. Navigate to and select the folder in the list box.

3. Click the Select Folder button. Windows creates a toolbar for the folder or web page, and then displays the toolbar on the Taskbar.

Managing Your Desktop Toolbars

If you have the Taskbar locked (as it is by default), you can't resize or move the toolbars you display. But if you unlock the Taskbar, you can resize and move them by dragging their sizing handles (the dotted area at the left end or upper end of the toolbar). For example, you can give the Quick Launch toolbar as much space as it needs on the Taskbar so that all its icons are visible.

You can turn off the display of a toolbar's text by right-clicking the toolbar and clicking the Show Text item on the context menu to remove its check mark, or turn off the display of a toolbar's title by right-clicking the toolbar and clicking the Show Title item on the context menu to remove its check mark.

Using the Sidebar

The Sidebar is a new feature in Windows Vista that enables you to place live content, such as stock tickers or RSS feeds, on your Desktop. Each item that you place on the Sidebar is called a *gadget*. Figure 3.36 shows the Sidebar.

Launching and Closing the Sidebar

Windows Vista normally launches the Sidebar automatically until you prevent it—so the Sidebar may already be running. If not, to launch the Sidebar, choose Start ➢ All Programs ➢ Accessories ➢ Windows Sidebar.

Figure 3.36
The Sidebar appears on the right side of the screen by default, in a graduated shaded area, but you can move it to the left side if you prefer. You can also turn the Sidebar off if you prefer not to use it.

To close the Sidebar, right-click anywhere in the shaded area, and then choose Close Sidebar from the shortcut menu. Alternatively, right-click the Windows Sidebar icon in the notification area, and then choose Exit from the context menu.

Configuring the Sidebar

To configure the Sidebar, follow these steps:

1. Right-click anywhere in the shaded area, and then choose Properties from the context menu. Windows displays the Windows Sidebar Properties dialog box (see Figure 3.37).

2. Select the Start Sidebar When Windows Starts check box if you want Windows to launch the Sidebar when you log on.

3. In the Arrangement group box, choose where to display the Sidebar by selecting the Right option button or the Left option button. If you have two or more monitors, use the Display Sidebar on Monitor drop-down list to specify which monitor the Sidebar appears on. If you want the Sidebar to appear on top of any other window (like the Taskbar does by default), select the Sidebar Is Always on Top of Other Windows check box.

4. Click the OK button. Windows closes the Windows Sidebar Properties dialog box and applies your choices.

FIGURE 3.37
You can configure the Windows Sidebar to show exactly the content you want—or turn the Sidebar off to reclaim your Desktop.

Adding, Removing, and Configuring Gadgets

To change the selection of gadgets on the Sidebar, follow these steps:

1. To add a gadget, click the + button at the top of the Sidebar. Windows displays a window showing available gadgets (see Figure 3.38). You can then double-click a gadget to add it to the Sidebar or drag it to the position you want. Close the window when you've finished adding gadgets.

FIGURE 3.38
You can add any available gadget to the Sidebar, or get more gadgets online.

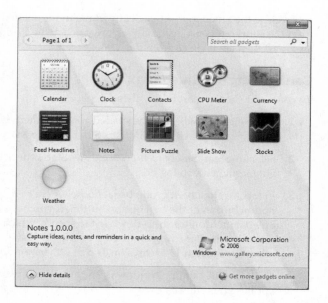

2. To remove a gadget, move the mouse pointer over it in the Sidebar, and then click the Close button (the × button) that appears beside it.

3. To rearrange gadgets in the Sidebar, drag a gadget to the position in which you want it. The other gadgets move to accommodate the gadget your drag.

4. To detach a gadget from the Sidebar, right-click it, and then choose Detach from Sidebar from the context menu. Windows displays the gadget on your Desktop. To reattach the gadget to the Sidebar, right-click it, and then choose Attach to Sidebar.

5. To change the opacity of a gadget, so that it stands out more or less from the Sidebar's shading, right-click the gadget, choose Opacity from the context menu, and then choose the value you want. A lower value (such as 20 percent) makes the Sidebar's shading show through more.

6. To configure a gadget, right-click it and choose Options from the context menu. Windows displays a window containing options for the gadget. Choose settings, and then click the OK button.

The Bottom Line

Choosing the best display resolution   To use Windows comfortably, choose a display resolution that suits you and your monitor. Right-click the Desktop, choose Personalize, and then click the Display Settings link. In the Display Settings dialog box, drag the Resolution slider, and then click the Apply button. You may also need to adjust your monitor so that the picture fills the screen.

Configuring the keyboard and mouse   To configure the keyboard, choose Start ➢ Control Panel, click the Hardware and Sound link, and then click the Keyboard link. To configure the mouse, choose Start ➢ Control Panel, and then click the Mouse link.

Choosing ease-of-access options   To choose ease-of-access options, such as special key settings, a high-contrast color scheme, or Speech Recognition, choose Start ➤ All Programs ➤ Accessories ➤ Ease of Access ➤ Ease of Access Center.

Choosing a screen saver   To choose a screen saver, right-click the Desktop, choose Personalize, and then click the Screen Saver link.

Changing the look and feel of Windows   You can change the look and feel of Windows by applying a different theme, or suite of settings; changing the background; choosing which items appear on the desktop; adjusting the appearance of individual components of the user interface; choosing sounds for system events; or rearranging the items on your Desktop. You access most of these settings from the Personalization window, which you display by right-clicking the Desktop and choosing Personalize from the context menu.

Configuring the Taskbar, Start menu, and Desktop toolbars   To configure the Taskbar, right-click open space in the Taskbar (or anywhere in the notification area), choose Properties from the context menu, and then work on the Taskbar page of the Taskbar and Start Menu Properties dialog box. Use the controls on the Notification Area page of this dialog box to customize the notification area and those on the Start Menu page to customize the Start menu. To control which Desktop toolbars appear, right-click the notification area and use the options on the Toolbars submenu.

Using the Sidebar   The Sidebar lets you display useful gadgets that you want to keep to hand. To add gadgets to the Sidebar, click the + button at the top, and then work in the resulting window. To remove a gadget, move the mouse pointer over it, and then click the Close button (the × button) that appears.

Chapter 4

Installing, Removing, and Running Programs

◆ Choose programs that will run well on Windows Vista

◆ Prepare to install a program

◆ Install a program

◆ Remove a program that you no longer need

◆ Run programs normally, using Compatibility mode, or automatically at startup

◆ Choose default programs for browsing the Web, e-mail and IM, and audio and video

Windows Vista comes with bundled programs (most of which are discussed in Chapter 6) that let you perform various everyday tasks from creating simple documents to playing music and video, or from performing calculations to creating video movies of your own. But sooner or later you're going to want to install a third-party program and run it so that you can carry on with your business and your life.

This chapter discusses how to install, configure, remove, and run programs—and how to shut them down when they stop responding. It also uses various programs as examples, ranging from programs specially designed for Windows Vista to much older programs, to show you the issues you'll encounter with installing, running, and removing programs.

If you performed an in-place upgrade of your previous version of Windows to Windows Vista, the upgrade process should have configured all your programs for use already, so you shouldn't need to reinstall them. However, if you have old programs that you find don't run properly on Windows Vista, you may need to run them in Compatibility mode. If so, turn to the section "Running Programs in Compatibility Mode," later in this chapter.

Choosing Programs to Run on Windows Vista

Before you install a program on Windows Vista, make sure that it's suitable to run on Windows Vista. Windows Vista can run a wide variety of programs, but some programs you shouldn't even try to install on it, because they won't run and the installation process may cause trouble.

Looking for Programs Designed for Windows Vista

Windows is the market-leading operating system, so most software companies design their programs to run on Windows Vista. Use the following criteria when choosing software to run on your Vista installation:

◆ **Buying new software** If you're buying software, make sure you get a version designed for Windows Vista rather than for an earlier version of Windows.

◆ **Windows XP programs** If you already have a program designed for Windows XP, it will almost certainly run on Windows Vista as well. (See "Avoiding Programs That May Cause Trouble on Windows Vista," later in this chapter, for details of some exceptions.) You may need to apply an update or a patch to make the program run well on Windows Vista.

◆ **Windows 2000 or Windows 98/Me programs** If you already have a program designed for Windows 2000, Windows 98, or Windows Me, it may run on Windows Vista. Programs designed for Windows 2000 are more likely to run well than programs designed for Windows 98 or Windows Me, because Windows 2000 was based on the same operating system core as Windows Vista. (Windows 98 and Windows Me use a different operating system basis.) You may need to use compatibility mode to make these programs run well in Windows Vista. If you're lucky, Windows Vista will apply the required compatibility options for you automatically when you install or run the program.

◆ **DOS programs** If you still need old programs designed for DOS (the Disk Operating System that preceded Windows), you may be able to run them on Windows Vista. Generally, it's best to avoid DOS programs unless they perform a vital purpose that no Windows program can. For example, you might have an old accounting program that you need to run—or perhaps custom software that you developed yourself at an earlier time.

 **Real World Scenario**

EVALUATE SOFTWARE LICENSES BEFORE BUYING PROGRAMS

When you buy software you usually receive an item protected by a license, which means an item that you cannot use freely, unlike when you buy (say) a stick of butter or a car. Most software licenses set strict limits on what you can do with the software. Some software companies also enforce their software licenses strictly, while other companies are more tolerant and reasonable.

When choosing software, evaluate the licenses to make sure that they suit your needs and that you won't have to pay for extra copies. Here are two examples:

◆ If you have two computers (for example, a desktop and a laptop), make sure that the license allows you to install the software on both, on the basis that, since you're the only person who will use these computers, you'll be able to use only one of them at a time. Avoid licenses that insist that you buy a separate copy for each computer on which you install the software, even if there's no way you could use more than one copy at a time.

◆ Unless you're sure you won't upgrade your computer within the software's lifetime, ensure that the license allows you to transfer software from one computer to another. Avoid licenses that restrict the software to one computer. Normally, you'll want to be able to upgrade your computer freely. But with some software, such as tax-preparation software that you use only once and then have to buy the new version the next year, upgrading is not an issue.

If possible, learn about any activation procedure that applies to the software. For example, when you install Microsoft Office, you have to activate it after you have run its programs 50 times or used it for a certain length of time (depending on the version). Having to jump through activation hoops can be awkward when you're testing a new computer or if you tend to tinker with your computer, giving it upgrades that may cause the activation mechanism to believe that it is running on a new computer.

For the greatest freedom, you may prefer to use open-source software rather than closed-source (proprietary software). For example, you may prefer to use the free, open-source OpenOffice.org suite rather than the costly, closed-source Microsoft Office. Most open-source software is freely available, and if you have programming skills, you can even modify the software's code to change its functionality to suit your needs.

Avoiding Programs That May Cause Trouble on Windows Vista

Windows Vista includes compatibility modes for running programs designed for earlier versions of Windows (or even for some DOS programs). Even so, you should avoid the following types of program, which are likely to cause problems with Windows Vista:

Operating systems You can't install another operating system—for example, another version of Windows, a version of Linux, or a version of Unix—directly on top of Windows Vista. If you need to run another operating system on the same computer, you have two options:

◆ Set up a dual-boot or multi-boot system (see Chapter 1). At startup, your computer shows you a list of the operating systems available, and you can choose which to launch. To switch to another operating system, you must restart your computer.

◆ Use PC-emulation software such as Virtual PC or Virtual Server (both from Microsoft) or VMWare Workstation or VMWare Server (both from VMWare, Inc.). These programs create an emulated PC (a pretend one) on which you can install operating systems. For example, your PC itself may run Windows Vista. On top of Windows Vista, you run the VMWare Workstation product, inside VMWare Workstation, you run Linux.

It may be possible in the future to use a hypervisor program. This type of program lets two or more operating systems run at the same time on the same hardware. At this writing, no hypervisor program is available for Windows Vista—but one may be by the time you read this.

Old antivirus programs Antivirus programs designed for previous versions of Windows don't know how to deal with Windows Vista. You may be able to update the program so that it'll be able to work with Windows Vista. More likely, you'll need to get a whole new version. If in doubt, consult the manufacturer's website to find out whether the program runs on Windows Vista.

Old troubleshooting and cleanup utilities Most troubleshooting and cleanup utilities designed for earlier versions of Windows will cause Windows Vista problems. So will disk utilities (for example, Norton Utilities) designed for earlier Windows versions. Instead of running an old utility, invest in a new utility specifically designed for Windows Vista.

Some programs that may cause trouble on Windows Vista are smart enough to check which operating system you're using and refuse to install. The next illustration shows the Incorrect Operating System dialog box that an old version of Network Associates' VirusScan displays if you try to install it on Windows Vista. When you click the OK button, the installation ends.

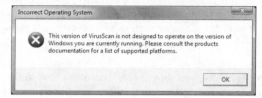

Getting Ready to Install a Program

Before you install a program, make sure you have a copy of the program itself, an Administrator password, and enough disk space to contain the program. You may also want to set a restore point manually in case the installation fails and you need to return Windows Vista to its previous state.

Getting a Copy of the Program

If the program you want to install is on a CD, DVD, or other removable medium, load it into the appropriate drive on your computer. If the program is on a network drive, establish a connection to that drive. If the program is on the Internet, download a copy of it.

Making Sure You Have an Administrator Password

To help protect your computer against malware (malevolent software), Windows Vista lets only Administrator users install software. If you log on as an Administrator user, you're all set. If you log on as a Standard user or the Guest user, you need to enter an Administrator password when you start the installation. If you're not sure whether you have a Standard account or an Administrator account, see the sidebar "Find Out What Kind of User Account You Have."

If you administer your computer, but as a security measure use a Standard account for non-administrative work, you'll know your Administrator password. Otherwise, get an Administrator to enter his or her password for you—assuming he or she agrees to your installing the program.

FIND OUT WHAT KIND OF USER ACCOUNT YOU HAVE

If you're not sure whether you have a Standard account or an Administrator account, take the following steps to find out:

1. Choose Start ➤ Control Panel to open a Control Panel window.

2. If Control Panel is in Classic view (a dot appears next to "Classic View" in the left pane), click Control Panel Home.

3. Click the Add or Remove User Accounts link. The User Account Control window appears.

4. If the User Account Control window includes the prompt "To continue, type an administrator password," you have a Standard account. Otherwise, you have an Administrator account.

5. Click the Cancel button to cancel the User Account Control authorization, and then click the Close button (the × button) to close the Control Panel window.

Making Sure You Have Enough Disk Space

Usually, the setup routine checks to make sure that you've got enough disk space to install the program; if you haven't, the setup routine warns you about the problem. Even so, it's a good idea to check the program's requirements before installing it. You'll find the requirements on the packaging, in the readme file, or on the program's website.

Consider doing the following:

◆ Delete any surplus files that have been hanging around.

◆ Empty the Recycle Bin.

◆ Defragment your hard disk manually to make sure it's in good order. See Chapter 15 for instructions on defragmenting.

If the program requires more disk space than you have free, you have three main options:

◆ Install the program on a different disk. It's easiest to keep all your program files together in the Program Files folder, as Windows recommends you do (and assumes you will do). But most setup routines let you specify another disk—for example, a second hard drive in a desktop computer.

◆ Clear more space by deleting data files you no longer need, moving old files to another disk or a CD or DVD, or using Disk Cleanup (see Chapter 15) to get rid of unnecessary files and compress old files.

◆ Add an extra hard disk.

Setting a Restore Point

The setup routines used for many programs, including all the latest Microsoft programs, automatically create a restore point. This is done so that, if setup has bad results, you can use Windows' System Restore feature to restore Windows to the way it was before you ran the setup routine. But to be sure that a suitable restore point exists, it's a good idea to create one yourself. You can also give the restore point an explicit name—for example, "Restore point before installing iTunes"—that enables you to identify the restore point later. See Chapter 16 for details on using System Restore.

Closing All Other Programs

Windows can install most programs while other programs are still running, but it's best to close all open programs before you start the installation just in case something goes wrong with the installation. Some setup routines require you to restart your computer afterward. If you're not running any programs, you can accept the setup routine's automated restarting of Windows.

Installing a Program

At this point, you should be ready to launch the setup routine and follow through its steps. This section discusses the steps typically involved in installing programs, shows examples of the types of screens you're likely to see, and explains how to deal with problems.

Starting the Setup Routine

To begin the installation, start the setup routine running. You can do this in several ways:

◆ If the program is on a CD or DVD, insert the disc into your optical drive. AutoPlay may prompt you to start the installation (see Figure 4.1) or simply start the setup routine automatically and display its opening screen. What you do from here depends on the program, but usually you confirm which program you want to install (if there's any doubt) and then click the Next button to start installing it.

◆ If the program is on a USB key or similar drive, AutoPlay usually runs and displays the opening screen of the setup routine.

◆ If the program is in a file on your hard disk or a network drive, open an Explorer window to the installation file, and then double-click the installation file to start the installation. Typical names for installation files include SETUP.EXE, *PROGRAM_NAME*_SETUP.EXE (for example, ITUNESSETUP.EXE), or INSTALL.EXE

◆ When you download a file, the File Download – Security Warning dialog box gives you the option of running the file or saving it. Click the Save button, specify the name, and then allow the download to complete. In the Download Complete dialog box, click the Run button. Figure 4.2 shows these two dialog boxes.

FIGURE 4.1

If AutoPlay is enabled on your computer, you may see an AutoPlay dialog box when you insert a disc or drive that contains software. Click the Install or Run Program link for the program if you want to start the installation running, or click the Open Folder to View Files if you prefer to investigate the contents of the CD first. You can click the Set AutoPlay Defaults in Control Panel link to open the AutoPlay feature in Control Panel.

FIGURE 4.2

Usually, it's best to click the Save button in the File Download – Security Warning dialog box and save the download to your hard disk rather than installing it across the Internet by clicking the Run button. When the File Download dialog box changes to the Download Complete dialog box, click the Run button to launch the setup routine.

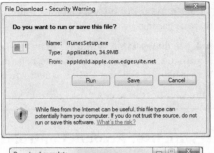

Real World Scenario

SETTING AUTOPLAY DEFAULTS

Windows Vista's AutoPlay feature is convenient for installing software and for connecting devices such as USB drives to your computer. However, you may prefer to turn AutoPlay off so that you can choose exactly when to run software. Or, if you've already turned AutoPlay off, you may need to turn it on.

To configure AutoPlay, follow these steps:

1. Choose Start ➢ Control Panel to open a Control Panel window.

2. If the Control Panel window uses Control Panel Home view, click the Hardware and Sound link, and then click the AutoPlay link. If the Control Panel window uses Classic view, double-click the AutoPlay icon.

3. In the Software and Games list box, choose the setting you want:

   ◆ **Install or Run Program** Windows Vista starts the setup routine automatically.

   ◆ **Open Folder to View Files Using Windows Explorer** Windows Vista opens a Windows Explorer window showing the disc's contents. From there, you can double-click the setup program (which is usually called setup.exe) to start the setup routine automatically.

◆ **Take No Action** Windows Vista does not use AutoPlay when you insert a disc containing software or games.

◆ **Ask Me Every Time** Windows Vista displays an AutoPlay dialog box like that shown in Figure 4.2, asking you whether to run the software or open a Windows Explorer window. This is usually the best choice unless you mind the extra step of approving each installation.

4. Click the Save button to close the Control Panel window and apply your changes.

Dealing with User Account Control If Necessary

When you start a setup routine running, you may see a User Account Control dialog box like the one shown in Figure 4.3. Windows displays this dialog box to make sure that it's you who has set the routine running rather than someone remote or some malware.

FIGURE 4.3
Whenever Windows detects an attempt to install a program that it can't identify, it displays the User Account Control dialog box to warn you.

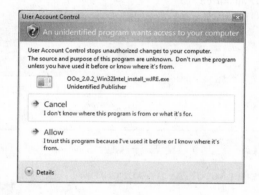

Choose what to do:

◆ If you've launched the setup routine yourself, you'll know what the file is. Click the Allow button to proceed. But sometimes the setup routine for one program may launch the installation for another. If in doubt, make certain of the program's identity before proceeding with the installation.

◆ If you're not sure about what the file is, click the Details button to display the file's name and location, which may help you identify it, as shown here:

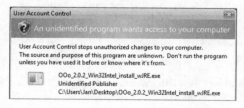

◆ If you don't want to proceed, click the Cancel button. If you wait for several minutes without clicking any button, Windows figures that you don't want to proceed with the installation and cancels it for you. This automatic cancellation helps to protect your computer if an automated process (rather than a live person) has set the setup routine running.

The Splash Screen and License Agreement

The setup routine often begins with a splash screen that gives the product's name and explains the basics of the installation procedure, as in the example here. If you've inserted a disc that contains several related programs, the splash screen may let you choose which program to install. (In other cases, you may have to install all the applications in a prescribed order.)

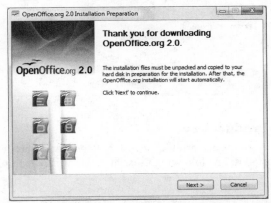

After the splash screen, you typically see a license agreement. You must select the acceptance option button or check box to enable the Next button, which you then click to continue the installation, as in this example:

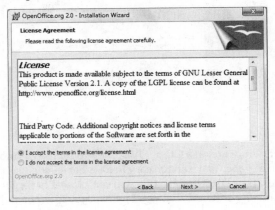

Entering Your Name and Organization Name

If the program or its registration needs to know your name and that of your organization (if any), the setup routine prompts you to enter them, as in this example:

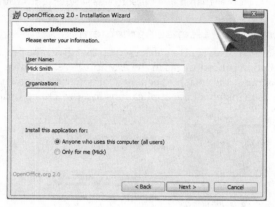

Entering Your Product Key

Most commercial programs use product keys to help ensure that only the person who has bought the program can install it. The following illustration shows an example of such a screen.

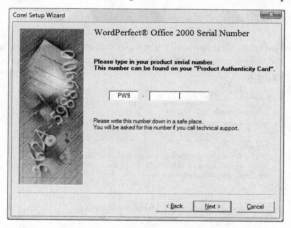

If you bought the software on a CD or DVD, the product key is most likely on the packaging—or perhaps in a slip of paper that's all too easy to lose. For safety, use a CD marker pen to write the product key on the CD or DVD itself so that you can't lose it or forget which product key belongs with which program. For software that you buy over the Internet and download, print out the product key and keep it safe, or keep a simple document (for example, a text file) of program names and product keys on your computer or on an online storage site.

Choosing the Setup Type

Many programs let you choose among two or more types of setup, such as Complete or Custom. Some programs offer a minimal installation (which is sometimes named Compact), which is useful when you need only some of the features or when your computer's hard disk is short of space. The following illustration shows an example of a setup type screen.

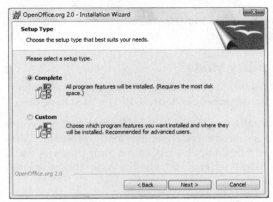

If you choose a Custom installation, you see a Custom Setup screen such as the one shown next. You can expand any of the items that have a plus (+) sign next to it to see a list of its components. For each component that has a box with a picture of a drive, you can click the drop-down arrow and choose from the resulting menu whether to install the component, install the component and all its subcomponents (if it has any), or make it unavailable (in other words, not install it).

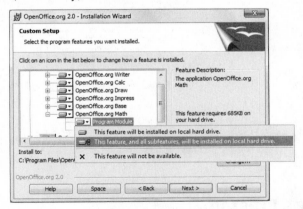

Most setup routines automatically install the program for all users of the computer, including the Guest user. Some setup routines let you choose between installing the program just for yourself (in other words, for the user account under which you're currently logged on) and installing it for all users. This choice is useful when you want to prevent other users from running the program you're installing—for example, because you don't want them to be able to open your files or because the program has very strict license terms.

Letting the Setup Routine Run, and Restarting Windows If Necessary

After you've clicked the final Next button or the Install Now button, let the setup routine complete the installation. While this is happening, it's best not to run other programs on your computer if you can help it. Giving the setup routine free rein and as many processor cycles and memory as it needs also help it to finish the installation as quickly as possible.

At the end of the setup routine, you usually get a message box telling you that setup completed successfully. This message box may also tell you that you need to restart Windows to complete the installation. If so, close any programs that you have been running, and then restart.

Using Compatibility Mode

If Windows Vista detects that a program fails to install because of compatibility issues, the Program Compatibility Assistant opens (see Figure 4.4). You then have three choices:

◆ Click the Reinstall Using Recommended Settings button if you want to retry installation, using Windows Vista's recommended settings for the program. (Windows Vista has a compatibility database called AppCompat—application compatibility—that contains settings for thousands of programs.) The Program Compatibility Assistant applies the settings and restarts the setup routine automatically.

◆ Click the This Program Installed Correctly button if the program actually did install and you don't need the Program Compatibility Assistant's help.

◆ Click the Cancel button if you don't want to proceed with the installation after all.

FIGURE 4.4
The Program Compatibility Assistant offers to apply recommended compatibility settings to help install a program whose installation has failed.

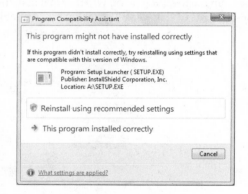

Removing a Program

Removing a program is typically easier and faster than installing a program, because you don't usually have to have the setup medium (CD, floppy, or whatever) or installation file, and you have to make even fewer decisions.

To remove a program, follow these steps:

1. Choose Start ➢ Control Panel. Windows displays Control Panel.

2. In Control Panel Home, click the Uninstall a Program link in the Programs topic. In Classic view, double-click the Programs and Features icon. Windows displays the Programs and Features window (see Figure 4.5).

3. Click the program you want to remove. The bar at the top of the window displays buttons that show the options available for the program—for example, an Uninstall button, a Change button (or an Uninstall/Change button), and a Repair button, as in Figure 4.6. Different programs have different sets of buttons; for example, some have only an Uninstall button, and others have an Uninstall button and a Change button.

4. If you need to make sure you've got the right program, look at the panel at the bottom of the window, which shows details about the program selected in the list.

FIGURE 4.5

The Programs and Features window lets you see which programs are installed on your computer, which company published them, when you installed them, and how much space they're occupying.

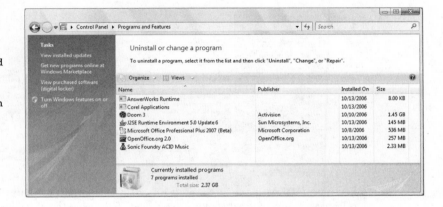

FIGURE 4.6

Click the program to display buttons such as Uninstall, Change, and Repair in the bar above the list.

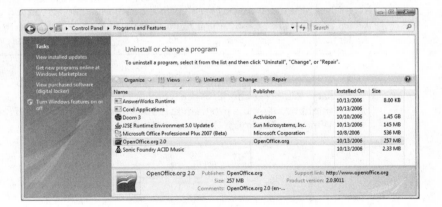

SORT THE PROGRAMS DIFFERENTLY TO FIND THE ONE YOU WANT TO REMOVE

The Installed Programs list displays the programs sorted by program name at first. If you have a lot of programs installed, you may find another sort order better. Click a column heading once to sort the programs in ascending order by that column; click the same column heading again to sort them in descending order by that column.

You can also click the drop-down arrow at the right end of the selected column heading and use the resulting panel to divide the programs into groups. For example, the drop-down panel on the Publisher column lets you group the programs by publisher, and the drop-down panel on the Size column lets you group by size.

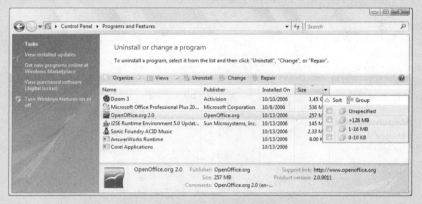

To view more information about the programs, right-click any of the column headings, and then choose More from the drop-down panel. Windows displays the Choose Details dialog box, which lets add any of about 15 other categories of details to the list by selecting the appropriate check boxes. For example, you might select the Last Used On check box to add a column that lets you sort the programs by the date on which they were last used. Or you could select the Location check box to add a column showing the folder in which each program is installed.

5. Click the Uninstall button, and then authenticate yourself to User Account Control if necessary. Windows checks to see whether other users are using the computer (because they might be using the program that you're about to remove). If any other user is logged on, Windows displays a Warning dialog box, as shown here.

◆ At this point, you can click the Switch User button to display the login screen, then log on as each user from there and log them off. You'll need to know each user's password in order to log in under that username. Usually you'll find it easier to use the Users page of Task Manager to either switch to the other users or simply log them off.

◆ When you're ready, click the Continue button. (You can also simply click the Continue button without logging off the other users, but Windows may not be able to remove the program completely if another user is running it.)

6. Windows starts the uninstall routine for the program. Windows then confirms the uninstallation, as shown here.

7. Click the Yes button. If you want to skip this check whenever you remove a program from now on, select the In the Future, Do Not Show Me This Dialog Box check box before clicking the Yes button.

8. If the uninstall routine tells you that it was unable to remove some parts of the program that you've asked to uninstall completely, it usually lets you know which parts are left. You will then need to delete these folders manually by using Explorer (unless you want to leave them lying around).

Running Programs

You can start a program either directly by opening it or indirectly by opening a file whose file type is associated with the program. (Chapter 5 explains file types and how you can associate them with programs.)

You can start a program directly in any of the following ways:

◆ Click its shortcut on the Start menu or on the All Programs menu.

◆ Click a shortcut on the Quick Launch toolbar or another Desktop toolbar. (Chapter 3 discusses the Desktop toolbars and how to customize them.)

◆ Double-click a shortcut on the Desktop or in an Explorer window. (Chapter 5 discusses how to create shortcuts wherever you want.)

◆ Double-click the icon or listing for the program in an Explorer window (or on the Desktop). You can also use the Search feature (discussed in Chapter 5) to locate the program you want to run.

 **Real World Scenario**

RUNNING PROGRAMS THAT DON'T APPEAR ON THE START MENU OR QUICK LAUNCH TOOLBAR

When you install a program, the setup routine usually creates one or more ways to run it. For example, most setup routines put a shortcut for the program on the Start menu; some setup routines place a shortcut directly on the Desktop or in the notification area, or both. The better setup routines let you choose where the routine creates shortcuts, but others just create them without consulting you.

But some programs, especially the more specialized utilities built into Windows, have no shortcuts. In this case, the easiest way to run the program is to use the Run dialog box. Follow these steps:

1. Press Windows Key+R or choose Start ➤ All Programs ➤ Accessories ➤ Run. Windows displays the Run dialog box (shown here).

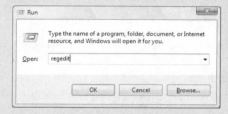

2. Enter the name of the program in the Open text box, either by typing it or by browsing for it. To browse, click the Browse button. Windows displays the Browse dialog box. Navigate to and select the file, then click the Open button.

3. Press Enter or click the OK button to run the program.

You can use the Run dialog box to run any program (even ones that have icons everywhere), but it's usually convenient only for programs that don't have icons.

If you need to use such a program frequently, create a shortcut for it somewhere convenient—for example, on the Quick Launch toolbar.

Running Programs in Compatibility Mode

If a program won't run normally on Windows Vista, try running it in Compatibility mode because the program might be better suited for a legacy version of Windows. Compatibility mode lets you tell Windows to emulate earlier versions of Windows so that a program thinks it's running on the operating system it requires. Windows Vista lets you emulate the following operating systems:

- ◆ Windows 95
- ◆ Windows 98 and Windows Me (together, as they're very similar)
- ◆ Windows NT 4 with Service Pack 5
- ◆ Windows 2000
- ◆ Windows XP with Service Pack 2
- ◆ Windows Server 2003 with Service Pack 1

You can set Compatibility mode only on files on local drives.

Windows provides two ways of setting up a program to run in Compatibility mode: by using the Program Compatibility Wizard, and by changing the properties of a shortcut for the program. The Program Compatibility Wizard is usually a better option, as it allows you to test Compatibility mode on the program.

SETTING COMPATIBILITY MODE USING THE PROGRAM COMPATIBILITY WIZARD

To set up a program to use Compatibility mode using the Program Compatibility Wizard, follow these steps:

1. Choose Start ➢ Control Panel. Windows display Control Panel.

2. If Control Panel is in Classic view, click Control Panel Home in the left panel to switch to Control Panel Home view.

3. Click the Programs heading in the list. Windows displays the Programs window.

4. In the Default Programs list, click the Use an Older Program with This Version of Windows link. Windows displays the first screen of the Program Compatibility Wizard.

5. Read the information and cautions on the Welcome to the Program Compatibility Wizard screen, and then click the Next button. Windows displays the How Do You Want to Locate the Program That You Would Like to Run with Compatibility Settings? screen (shown in Figure 4.7).

6. Use one of the following three ways to locate the program:

    ◆ To set Compatibility mode for a program that's already installed, select the I Want to Choose from a List of Programs option button, and then click the Next button. The wizard scans your hard drive and displays a list of programs. Select the program and click the Next button.

    ◆ To set Compatibility mode for a program you're installing from CD or DVD, insert the disc, select the I Want to Use the Program in the CD-ROM Drive option button, and then click the Next button.

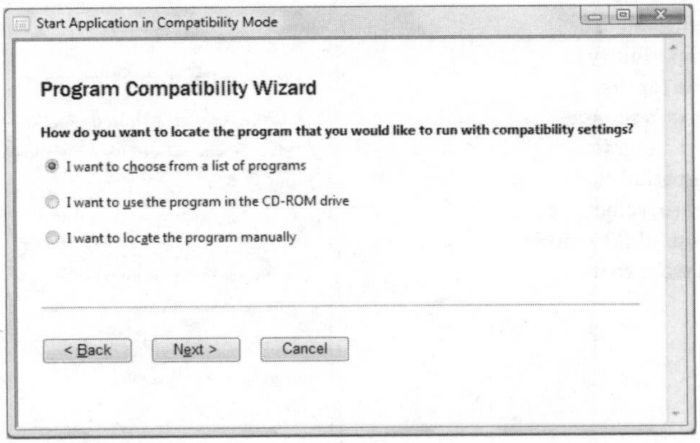

FIGURE 4.7
The Program Compatibility Wizard walks you through the process of setting up a program to use one of Windows Vista's compatibility modes. You can use this Wizard both to install programs that won't install normally and to run programs that install successfully but won't run.

◆ To set Compatibility mode for a program that isn't installed and whose installation medium isn't on CD or DVD, select the I Want to Locate the Program Manually option button and click the Next button. The wizard displays the Which Program Do You Want to Run with Compatibility Settings? screen. Enter the path in the text box either by typing or by clicking the Browse button and using the resulting Please Select Application dialog box (an Open dialog box with a different name) to select the program. Click the Next button.

7. The wizard displays the Select a Compatibility Mode for the Program screen (shown in Figure 4.8).

8. Select the option button for the operating system you think the program needs: Windows 95, Windows NT 4.0 (Service Pack 5), Windows 98/Windows Me, Windows 2000, or Windows XP (Service Pack 2). To use Windows Server 2003 with Service Pack 1, use the Properties dialog box as described in the next section.

9. Click the Next button. The wizard displays the Select Display Settings for the Program screen (shown in Figure 4.9).

10. If necessary, select the check box for any display limitation you want to apply. (See the list below for explanations of what these check boxes do.) You won't normally need to apply these display limitations at this stage of setting compatibility mode unless you're aware of a problem with running the program. Most likely, you'll need to apply these limitations later, once you've got the program running and found that the display looks wrong.

256 Colors Select this check box if you want to restrict the program to using 256 colors instead of the thousands or millions of colors that Windows is using.

640 × 480 Screen Resolution Select this check box if you need to force the program to use this resolution (which is also called VGA resolution) rather than the higher resolution that Windows is using. This setting enables some games to run that do not run at higher resolutions.

Disable Visual Themes If the title bar appears to be too big for the program's title bar or button bar, select this check box to make Windows use "classic"-style window frames rather than themed-style windows. Classic-style windows have square corners instead of rounded corners and a shallower title bar than themed-style windows.

FIGURE 4.8
On the Select a Compatibility Mode for the Program screen of the Program Compatibility Wizard, select the Compatibility mode you want to use.

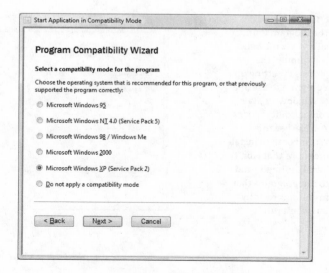

FIGURE 4.9
On the Select Display Settings for the Program screen of the Program Compatibility Wizard, you can apply limitations to the display settings used for the program.

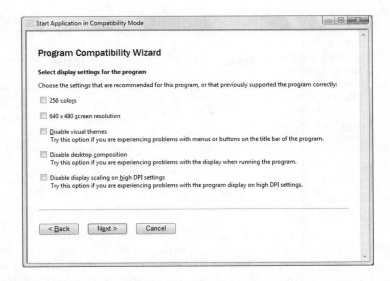

Disable Desktop Composition   If the program's display seems garbled, select this check box to turn off desktop composition.

Disable Display Scaling on High DPI Settings   If you're using a display that has many dots per inch (DPI) and using display scaling to make icons, menus, and buttons a suitable size for viewing on screen, you may find that some of an older program's display elements are the wrong size. Select this check box to disable display scaling for the program.

11. Click the Next button. The wizard displays the Does the Program Require Administrator Privileges? screen.

12. If the program requires administrator privileges, select the Run This Program as an Administrator check box. If you're not an Administrator user, you'll need to provide an Administrator user's password (or have an Administrator user provide it). Normally, you should leave this check box cleared until you find that the program won't run because it needs administrator privileges.

13. Click the Next button. The wizard displays the Test Your Compatibility Settings screen, which lists the settings you've chosen.

14. Check the settings you've chosen, then click the Next button. The wizard launches the program with the compatibility settings you specified and displays the Did the Program Work Correctly? screen (shown in Figure 4.10).

15. Choose the appropriate option button:

    ◆ If the program ran okay, select the Yes, Set This Program to Always Use These Compatibility Settings option button. Click the Next button. The wizard displays the Program Compatibility Data screen, on which you can choose whether to send Microsoft information on the program, the settings you chose, and whether they solved the problem.

    ◆ If the program didn't run correctly, but you want to try other settings, select the No, Try Different Compatibility Settings option button. Click the Next button. The wizard returns to the Select a Compatibility Mode for the Program screen. Return to step 5 and try again.

FIGURE 4.10
On the Did the Program Work Correctly? screen, tell the Program Compatibility Wizard whether the program launched correctly with the computer settings.

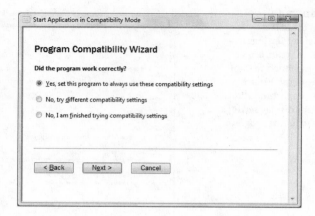

- When no compatibility settings seem to work, select the No, I Am Finished Trying Compatibility Settings option button. Click the Next button. The wizard displays the Program Compatibility Data screen (discussed in the first bulleted paragraph above). In this case, you have more incentive for sending Microsoft information, as it may help them fix the problem with this program in the future.

16. On the Program Compatibility Data screen, choose the Yes button or the No button as appropriate.

17. Click the Next button. If you chose the Yes button, the wizard sends the compatibility data. Either way, it displays the Completing the Program Compatibility Wizard page.

18. Click the Finish button. The wizard closes itself.

You can now run the program from the Start menu or from a shortcut on the Desktop or the Quick Launch toolbar.

ADJUSTING COMPATIBILITY MODE USING THE PROPERTIES DIALOG BOX

You can also set Compatibility mode by using the Properties dialog box for a shortcut to the program. This method is normally most useful for adjusting the Compatibility mode you've already applied to a program, but if you know which settings you want, you can also use it as an alternative to the Program Compatibility Wizard.

1. Right-click the shortcut for the program and select Properties from the context menu. Windows displays the Properties dialog box for the shortcut.

2. Click the Compatibility tab. Windows displays the Compatibility page. Figure 4.11 shows an example of this page.

3. Select the Run This Program in Compatibility Mode For check box if it's not already selected.

4. In the drop-down list, select the mode you want to use.

5. In the Settings group box, select the check box for any display limitation you want to apply. (See step 10 of the list in the previous section for an explanation of these options.)

FIGURE 4.11
You can also choose Compatibility mode settings on the Compatibility page of the Properties dialog box for the shortcut.

6. If you need to run the program with Administrator privileges, select the Run This Program as an Administrator check box.

7. Click the OK button. Windows applies your choice and closes the Properties dialog box.

 Real World Scenario

EVEN WITH COMPATIBILITY MODE, SOME PROGRAMS DON'T WORK

Some programs don't work even when you use Compatibility mode. If you can't get a program to run by using the Program Compatibility Wizard, try the Application Compatibility Toolkit, which you can download from http://www.microsoft.com/technet/prodtechnol/windows/appcompatibility/default.mspx. The Toolkit provides advanced tools for checking which compatibility fixes are required for a particular application and applying them.

Making Programs Run at Startup

If you want a program to start every time you log on to Windows, place a shortcut to it in your Startup folder. Starting programs automatically like this can save you a few seconds each time you start Windows if you always need to use the same programs.

To open your startup folder, follow these steps:

1. Choose Start ➢ All Programs. Windows displays the All Programs menu.

2. Right-click the Startup folder, and choose Open from the shortcut menu. Windows opens a Windows Explorer window showing your Startup folder.

You can now drag a shortcut to the Startup folder. For example, click the Start button (or choose Start ➤ All Programs), and then drag a shortcut from the Start menu (or the All Programs menu) to the Startup folder.

To prevent a program from running at startup, open the Startup folder as described above, click the shortcut to the program, and then press the Delete button.

Specifying the Size at Which a Program Runs

By default, most programs start in a "normal" window—one that's not maximized and not minimized. If you'd like the program to start up in a maximized or minimized window, right-click its shortcut and choose Properties from the context menu. In the Properties dialog box that Windows displays, choose Maximized or Minimized in the Run drop-down list on the Shortcut page, and click the OK button.

You can do this for any shortcut to a program or to a file—so if you want, you can have shortcuts open different-sized windows for files of the same file type.

Killing a Program That's Not Responding

Programs run pretty well on Windows Vista—but not all programs run well all the time. Sooner or later, a program will *hang* (stop responding) or *crash* (close unexpectedly) when you're using it.

When a program hangs, first make sure the program doesn't have an open dialog box that you can't see. When you're working with multiple programs, you can easily get an open dialog box stuck behind another open window. If the dialog box is *application modal*, it prevents you from doing anything else in the program until you dismiss it. (Dialog boxes can also be *system modal*, in which case they prevent you from doing anything else on your computer until you deal with them.)

Minimize all other open windows (right-click the Taskbar and choose Show the Desktop from the context menu), and see whether the dialog box appears. If not, you'll probably have the program that's not responding still displayed on your screen, probably with only some parts of the window correctly drawn. For example, typically the areas of the program that were covered by other programs or windows will not be redrawn (or not redrawn correctly).

Next, try using Windows Flip (press Alt+Tab or Windows Key+Tab) to switch to the program and bring out from behind it any dialog box that's hiding. Chances are that this won't work either, but it's worth a try. If the dialog box appears, deal with it as usual, and the program should come back to life.

If that didn't work, try using Task Manager to switch to the program. Follow these steps:

1. Right-click the Taskbar and choose Task Manager from the context menu. Windows displays Task Manager.

2. If the Applications page isn't displayed, click the Applications tab. Windows displays the Applications page, which lists each running program and its status (see Figure 4.12). The status can be either Running (all is well with the program, as far as Windows knows) or Not Responding (Windows believes that the program is not responding to commands).

3. Click the program that's not responding.

4. Click the Switch To button. Task Manager attempts to switch to the program and minimizes itself in the process.

If that didn't work either, it's probably time to kill the program. Take the following steps:

1. Restore Task Manager by clicking its button on the Taskbar.

FIGURE 4.12
When a program stops responding, open the Applications page of Task Manager and try to switch to the program.

2. Decide whether the program has hung or crashed. (See the nearby sidebar "'Not Responding' Status Isn't Always Terminal" for advice on determining whether the program is still viable.)

3. Click the task in the Task list.

4. Click the End Task button. Windows displays available options for ending the program.

◆ For many programs, Windows displays the End Program dialog box (shown here). Click the End Now button. Windows terminates the program and frees up the memory it contained.

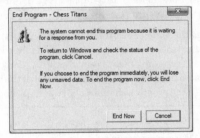

◆ For programs with more sophisticated error handling, such as the Microsoft Office programs, Windows displays a dialog box such as the one shown here (for Excel). You can choose among restarting the program, closing the program, and waiting for the program to respond.

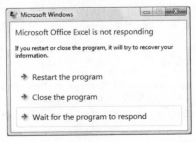

5. If killing the program like this doesn't work, you have several options. Here they are, in descending order of preference:

♦ Close all other programs that are responding. Then log off Windows. Doing this should shut down any programs you're running.

♦ If you can't close the program and can't log off Windows, but Task Manager is still working (apart from not being able to kill the program), use Task Manager to switch to another user, then log off the user session that contains the crashed program.

♦ At this point, you're pretty much out of options. Press the Reset button or the Power button on your computer.

 Real World Scenario

"NOT RESPONDING" STATUS ISN'T ALWAYS TERMINAL

When you see a program listed as Not Responding on the Applications page of Task Manager, you may want to kill it off right away. But wait a minute or two before killing it, because Not Responding doesn't necessarily mean that a program has hung:

♦ First, Not Responding may mean only that a program is responding more slowly than Windows expects. If you give it a few seconds, or perhaps a few minutes, it may start responding normally again. If your computer seems unresponsive overall (perhaps because you're running many programs or using some huge files), give it a few minutes to sort itself out.

♦ Second, Not Responding may mean that Windows is struggling to allocate enough memory to the program. Reallocating memory often causes the program to run slowly.

♦ Third, programs that use the Visual Basic for Applications (VBA) programming language (for example, Microsoft Word and Microsoft PowerPoint) often appear Not Responding when they're running a macro. In this case, Not Responding means only that VBA temporarily has control over the program. When the routine or macro ends and VBA releases control of the program, Task Manager lists the program as Running again. (If the program shouldn't be running a macro, try pressing Ctrl+Break to stop it.)

Setting Default Programs

In a standard configuration, Windows uses Internet Explorer as its web browser, Windows Mail as its e-mail program, Windows Media Player as its media player, and Windows Messenger as its instant messaging program. Your computer's manufacturer may have installed other programs for one or more of these functions and configured Windows to use them. If not, you can do so—or you can go back to Microsoft's offerings if you prefer.

To set default programs, follow these steps:

1. Choose Start ≻ Default Programs. Windows opens a Windows Explorer window to the Default Programs folder.

2. Click the Set Program Access and Computer Defaults item, and then authenticate yourself to User Account Control. Windows displays the Set Program Access and Computer Defaults window (shown in Figure 4.13 with the Non-Microsoft option button selected).

3. Click one of the option buttons to display the options for that configuration. Figure 4.14 shows the options for the Custom set.

4. For each program type (web browser, e-mail program, media player, instant messaging program, and virtual machine for Java), select the appropriate option button. To prevent access to a program, clear the Enable Access to This Program check box.

5. Click the OK button to close the Computer Defaults window, and then click the Close button (the × button) to close the Control Panel window.

FIGURE 4.13
The Computer Defaults window lets you choose which programs to use as defaults. The choice is among a Microsoft Windows configuration, a Non-Microsoft configuration that your computer manufacturer may have installed, and a Custom configuration.

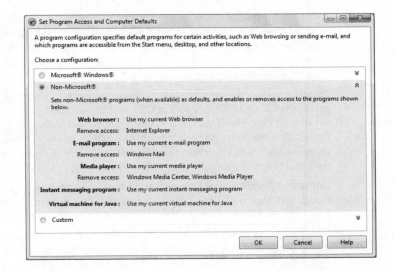

FIGURE 4.14
Use the Custom configuration to choose which web browser, e-mail program, media player, instant messaging program, and Java virtual machine.

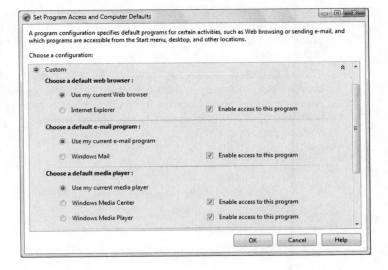

The Bottom Line

Choose programs that will run well on Windows Vista When buying new programs, choose ones designed for Windows Vista. Programs designed for earlier versions of Windows will probably run, although you may have to use Compatibility mode. Avoid antivirus programs and troubleshooting and cleanup programs for earlier versions of Windows, because these are likely to cause trouble on Windows Vista. Evaluate software licenses before you buy programs to make sure that you can use the programs as you need—for example, on both a desktop and a laptop.

Prepare to install a program Apart from the program itself, you'll need to have an Administrator password (or an Administrator prepared to provide one) and enough disk space to contain the program. Deleting surplus files, emptying the Recycle Bin, and defragmenting your hard disk are usually a good idea. You may also want to use System Restore to set a restore point to which you can return Windows if the installation goes wrong. It's best to close all other programs before starting the installation.

Install a program Windows' AutoPlay feature may start a program's setup routine when you insert the CD or DVD or attach a USB device containing the program. If not, you can start the setup routine manually from a Windows Explorer window. After dealing with User Account Control, follow through the setup routine, which usually includes accepting a license agreement, entering a product key, choosing where to install the program, and choosing whether to install all its features or only some of them. You may need to restart Windows at the end of the installation.

Remove a program that you no longer need To remove a program, choose Start ➤ Control Panel, and then click the Uninstall a Program link in the Programs topic. Windows displays the Programs and Features. Click the program you want to remove, and then click the Remove button.

Run programs normally, using Compatibility mode, or automatically at startup You can start a program from the Start menu or a shortcut, or by opening a file associated with the program. To start a program that doesn't have a shortcut, press Windows Key+R, type the program's name in the Run dialog box, and then press Enter. If a program won't run normally, choose Start ➤ Control Panel, click the Programs heading, and then click the Use an Older Program with This Version of Windows link. Work through the Program Compatibility Wizard to set compatibility options. To make a program launch automatically when you log on to Windows, place a shortcut to the program in your Startup folder.

Choose default programs for browsing the Web, e-mail and IM, and audio and video To choose default programs, choose Start ➤ Default Programs, and then click the Set Program Access and Computer Defaults item. Click the Microsoft Windows option button, the Non-Microsoft option button, or the Custom option button, as appropriate, and then work with the options that appear.

Chapter 5

Managing Your Files and Folders

- ◆ Understand what files and folders are and what you can name them
- ◆ Launch Windows Explorer and navigate to the files you need
- ◆ Choose folder options to control how Windows Explorer behaves
- ◆ Copy and move files and folders
- ◆ Delete and rename files and folders
- ◆ Search to find the files and folders you need
- ◆ Use compressed folders and shortcuts
- ◆ Configure AutoPlay and customize Windows Explorer's columns

This chapter shows you how to manage files and folders. It starts off by discussing what files and folders *are* before explaining what you can do with them and how to use Windows Explorer, Windows' primary file-management tool.

Windows Explorer is vital to using Windows effectively. You can use Windows Explorer to search for files and folders, to manipulate them, to view them in different ways, and to delete them, either temporarily or permanently. You can also use Windows Explorer to compress and uncompress files and folders, either to save space or to make archive files that are easy to handle.

At the end of the chapter, you'll find a section on how to configure AutoPlay's behavior and how to customize folders in Windows Explorer.

Understanding the Basics of Files and Folders

If you've used computers at all, you'll know that a *file* is a named object containing information that's stored on a disk. The disk can be a local hard drive; a networked drive (including a web server); a CD, DVD, or other removable drive; a tape drive; or even a humble floppy drive.

Each file has a name so that you and the computer can distinguish it. In Windows, each filename can be up to 255 characters long. Filenames can include letters, numbers, and some punctuation, such as commas (,), periods (.), semicolons (;), single quotation marks (' '), or apostrophes ('). Filenames cannot contain forward slashes (/), backslashes (\), colons (:), asterisks (*), question marks (?), double quotation marks ("), less-than (<) and greater-than (>) signs, or pipe characters (|), because Windows either uses those characters literally or assigns special meanings to them. For example, a colon is used to denote a drive (for instance, C: refers to the C: drive), and an asterisk is a wildcard character that represents one or more characters in searches and commands.

The 255 characters include the path to the file. The *path* (also sometimes called the *directory path*) gives the sequence of drive and folders that describes the location of the file and folders. For example, if a file is in the `Documents` folder in the `\Will\` folder of the `\Users\` folder on the C: drive, the path to that file is `C:\Users\Will\Documents`. That path is 23 characters long, including the backslashes and the spaces, so any file stored in that folder can have a filename of up to 232 characters (255 minus the 23 characters in the path).

A *folder* is a file that can contain other files or folders. By using folders, you can organize your files into categories. Folder names can be up to 255 characters long, but you'll need to keep them shorter than this if you want to use long filenames within the folders. The possible length of a folder name also includes the path to the folder and the length of any filenames that the folder already contains. (If you rename a folder so that the path and filename of a file it contains add up to more than 255 characters, you can no longer access the file.)

When working in a graphical environment such as Windows, you don't normally need to type paths to files the way you often had to in DOS and similar text-based operating systems. Instead, you use graphical representations of folders and files to navigate to the folders and files you need, and then manipulate them in graphical windows. Some of this you do with Windows Explorer (discussed in the next section), and some via dialog boxes in the individual programs.

Using Windows Explorer

Windows Explorer is Windows' built-in utility for managing files and folders—all kinds of files and folders, including the files and folders that make up the Start menu, those that make up Control Panel, and so forth. Windows Explorer is a separate program from Internet Explorer, the web browser that you use for browsing the Internet.

This book uses *Windows Explorer* to refer to Windows Explorer (including those for Computer, Network Connections, Control Panel, and so on), *Internet Explorer* to refer to any Explorer window that calls itself Internet Explorer, and descriptive terms such as *the Desktop*, *the Taskbar*, and *the notification area* to refer to the named components of the shell.

TROUBLESHOOTING: CLOSE AND RESTART WINDOWS EXPLORER IF YOUR DESKTOP STOPS RESPONDING

As well as letting you manage files and folders, Windows Explorer is also the *shell* for Windows—a logical layer that provides a graphical interface that lets you interact with Windows without talking code. Windows Explorer runs the Desktop, the Taskbar, the notification area, and the other components of the Windows interface.

Normally, this fact is just a curiosity, but if the Desktop stops responding, you may be able to bring it back under control by closing and restarting Windows Explorer. To do so, follow these steps:

1. Right-click open space on the Taskbar and choose Task Manager from the context menu. Windows displays Task Manager.

2. Click the Processes tab. Windows displays the Processes page.

3. Select the process named EXPLORER.EXE.

4. Click the End Process button. Task Manager displays a Task Manager Warning dialog box warning that terminating the process could lose your data or cause your system to be unstable.

5. Click the Yes button. Task Manager terminates Windows Explorer. The Taskbar and notification area disappear, together with the Start button and all your Desktop icons. Task Manager keeps running.

6. Still in Task Manager, choose File ➤ New Task (Run). Windows displays the Create New Task dialog box.

7. Type **Explorer** in the Open text box.

8. Click the OK button. Windows closes the Create New Task dialog box and runs Windows Explorer. Back come your icons, the Start button, the Taskbar, and the notification area, together with all their functionality.

Starting Windows Explorer

The easiest way to start Windows Explorer is to click the Start button so that Windows displays the Start menu, and then choose one of the shortcuts associated with Windows Explorer: Documents, Pictures, Music, Computer, or Network (if this shortcut appears on the Start menu). Each of these opens a Windows Explorer window to the specified folder.

You can also run Windows Explorer by choosing Start ➤ All Programs ➤ Accessories ➤ Windows Explorer. Doing so opens a Documents window in Explore mode.

EXPLORING MY COMPUTER

If you choose Start ➤ Computer, Windows displays an Windows Explorer window showing the contents of the Computer folder, as in the example shown in Figure 5.1.

Here's a quick tour of what you see in Figure 5.1:

Forward button and Back button When you've navigated from one folder to another in the Windows Explorer window, you can click the Back button to go back to each previous folder in turn. After using the Back button, you can click the Forward button to go forward again. When you first open an Windows Explorer window, as in the figure, there's no folder path for you to move along.

Recent Pages drop-down list Click the Recent Pages drop-down list to display a list of the folders you've used recently. To jump to a folder, select it in the list.

Address bar The Address bar indicates which folder the Windows Explorer window is displaying. You can click one of the triangle buttons to display a list of contents in the folder named before the button. For example, in Figure 5.1, you can click the triangle button to the right of Computer to display a list of the folders and objects contained in the Computer folder.

Toolbar The Toolbar contains buttons for taking widely used actions in Windows Explorer. The Organize button and the Views button display drop-down menus of commands.

Search box To search for a file or folder, click in the Search box, and then type the search term or terms. Windows searches as you type.

Favorite Links area The Favorite Links area in the left panel contains links to frequently used folders, such as Documents, Pictures, and Music. The set of links changes depending on which folder is displayed in the Windows Explorer window. When the Folders pane is displayed, you may need to click the More item at the bottom of the Favorite Links list to access the links at the bottom of the list.

Folders bar Click the Folders bar to toggle the display of the Folders pane on and off. The Folders pane lets you navigate through drives and folders by using a hierarchical arrangement of icons: Each drive appears as an expandable item, with the folders it contains appearing below it when you expand it; similarly, you can expand those folders to reveal their subfolders beneath them.

Document window The document window displays the contents of the folder shown in the Address bar. Windows Explorer provides several different views for the document window, as you'll see later in this chapter. Figure 5.1 shows the folder's contents sorted into groups: Hard Disk Drives, Devices with Removable Storage (floppy disk drives, optical drives, and removable disks such as USB drives), Network Location (network folders to which this computer is connected), and Other (which contains items such as My Sharing Folders, folders shared using the Windows Live Messenger instant-messaging software).

FIGURE 5.1

The Computer folder open in a Windows Explorer window

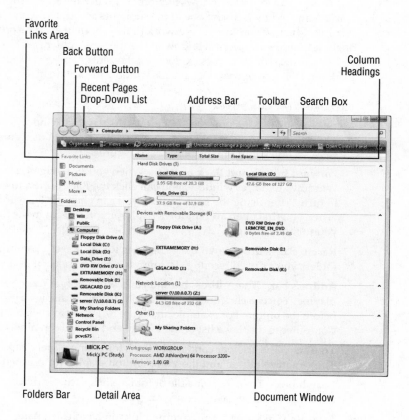

Favorite Links Area

Back Button

Forward Button

Recent Pages Drop-Down List

Address Bar

Toolbar

Search Box

Column Headings

Folders Bar

Detail Area

Document Window

ADDING THE MENU BAR TO WINDOWS EXPLORER WINDOWS

If you've used an earlier version of Windows, you'll notice that one of the big differences in Windows Explorer windows in Windows Vista is that there's no menu bar. Instead, the main commands appear as command buttons and drop-down buttons on the toolbar.

If you want to add the menu bar to Windows Explorer windows so that you can give commands much as you used to in earlier versions of Windows, click the Organize button, choose the Layout item on the menu, and then choose Menu Bar from the submenu.

If you prefer to display the menu bar only momentarily when you need it, press the Alt key. You can then issue menu commands using either the keyboard or the mouse.

UNDERSTANDING LINKS, OBJECTS, AND PROPERTIES

Windows presents information and folders to you in a variety of formats, including links, objects, and properties:

◆ The Favorite Links area contains links to folders. When you click a link once, Windows displays the linked folder.

◆ The items displayed on the right side of the screen are objects. An *object* is a general descriptor for a distinct entity on a computer—a file, a folder, a computer, and so on. Everything that you see in Windows Explorer is an object. A file is an object; a folder is an object; a computer you can see across the network is an object. Even the links displayed in the Favorite Links area are objects.

◆ Each object has *properties*—attributes—that you can view and, in some cases, set. For example, most objects have a name property that contains the name of the object. Many also have a read-only property that can be turned on and off and that determines whether a user can change the object (if the property is off) or not (if the property is on). Most objects also have *methods*—actions associated with the object. For example, many objects have a click method that determines what takes place when you click the object. Link objects execute when you click them, whereas objects such as files and folders become selected when you click them and execute when you double-click them.

EXPLORE MODE

The Computer window you opened in the previous section is pretty straightforward, but there's one complication: You can open Windows Explorer windows in two different modes: Open mode and Explore mode. Open mode is the standard mode and doesn't display the folders in the Folders bar in the left pane of the window; you can click the Folders bar to display the folders. Explore mode displays the folders, making moving up and down the directory tree easy.

To open a Computer window in Explore mode, click the Start button, right-click the Computer item, and then choose Explore from the context menu. Figure 5.2 shows a Computer window in Explore mode.

FIGURE 5.2

Viewed in Explore mode, the Computer window displays the Folders bar on the left side for quick navigation. An empty triangle pointing to the right indicates an item you can expand to reveal its contents. A filled triangle pointing down and to the right indicates an item that's already expanded.

Explore mode is easy to use, but the following details are worth knowing:

◆ Click a drive or folder in the Folders bar to display its contents in the right pane.

◆ You can select only one drive or folder at a time in the Folders bar, whereas you can select multiple drives or folders in the right pane.

◆ When you move the mouse pointer into the area of the Folders bar, Windows displays a little triangle next to each expandable item. Click the triangle to expand the item. Click the resulting triangle to collapse the item again.

◆ You can move folders by dragging them about in the left pane or the right pane.

◆ To move an item to a folder that's currently collapsed, drag the item to the parent and hover the mouse pointer there until Windows Explorer expands the collapsed folder.

◆ If you accidentally move a folder by dragging it when you intended only to select it, choose Organize ➢ Undo to put the folder back where it belongs.

Understanding Windows' Folder Structure

This section discusses the folder structure that Windows creates on your hard drive. You don't *need* to understand the folder structure in order to use Windows effectively, because the Favorite Links list provides an easy way to navigate among the folders that Windows wants you to use for the files you install, create, and use. But if you want to administer the computer and make the best use of Windows' management features, understanding the folder structure is helpful.

Windows places all these folders on the same drive on which Windows itself is installed.

YOUR FOLDER STRUCTURE MAY BE DIFFERENT THAN THAT SHOWN HERE

The folder structure discussed in this section is the one you get when you install a fresh copy of Windows on your computer without changing any settings. If anyone has customized your computer, or if you've upgraded from a Windows XP installation that was itself an upgrade from an earlier version of Windows, your folder structure may be different.

To start looking at the folder structure, follow these steps:

1. Choose Start ➢ Computer. Windows opens a Computer window showing your computer's drives.

2. Double-click the hard disk drive that contains Windows. This drive's icon includes a Windows symbol, as on the C: drive shown here.

Local Disk (C:)   Local Disk (D:)

3. Windows displays a Local Disk window containing folders named Program Files, Users, and Windows, as shown in Figure 5.3. Depending on your computer manufacturer and administrator, you may see other folders too.

But that's not all the folders. By default, Windows hides what it calls *protected operating system files*—translation, any files or folders it would prefer you not to see or mess with. It also hides hidden files and folders—files and folders marked with the Hidden attribute. Windows and some programs mark some files with the Hidden attribute automatically to keep them out of your view, but you can also mark files as Hidden yourself if you feel you'll benefit from doing so.

FIGURE 5.3
Your computer's system drive appears to contain a simple folder structure because Windows hides protected system files and hidden files.

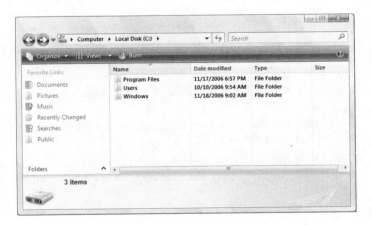

To display hidden files and protected operating system files, follow these steps:

1. Choose Organize ➤ Folder and Search Options. Windows displays the Folder Options dialog box.

2. Click the View tab. Windows displays the View page (see Figure 5.4).

FIGURE 5.4
Use the View page of the Folder Options dialog box to display hidden files and protected operating system files.

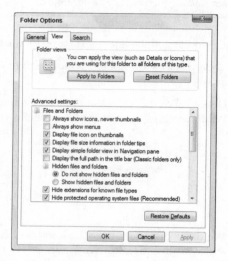

3. In the Advanced Settings list box, select the Show Hidden Files and Folders option button. (By default, the Do Not Show Hidden Files and Folders option button is selected.)

4. A little further down the Advanced Settings list box, clear the Hide Protected Operating System Files check box. Windows displays the Warning dialog box shown next when you clear this check box.

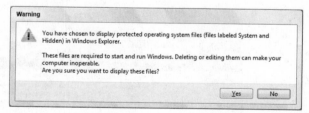

5. Click the Yes button. Windows closes the Warning dialog box and returns you to the Folder Options dialog box.

6. Click the OK button. Windows closes the Folder Options dialog box and applies the changes. You should now see a list of folders similar to that in Figure 5.5.

The folder structure contains the Windows folder, the Program Files folder, the ProgramData folder, and the Users folder. The following sections discuss these folders. There's also the $Recycle.Bin folder, which controls the Recycle Bin, and the System Volume Information folder, which Windows keeps locked against user intrusion to protect its contents. If Microsoft Office is installed on your computer, you may also see an MSOCache folder, which contains installation files for the Office applications.

You'll also see several files, including autoexec, config.sys, hiberfil.sys, and pagefile.sys. You'll learn about these files later in this chapter.

FIGURE 5.5

When you display hidden files and system files, the system drive looks much busier.

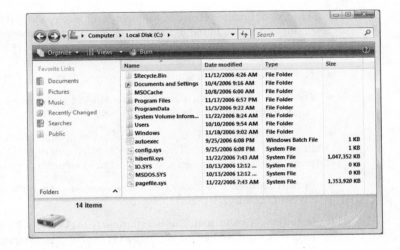

THE *WINDOWS* FOLDER

The Windows folder contains most of the files needed to keep Windows running. If you open this folder, you'll see dozens of subfolders and files. You'll seldom need to use any of these folders or files directly, as Windows manages them for you.

THE *PROGRAM FILES* FOLDER

The Program Files folder is designed to hold (almost) all the files for all the programs on the computer. The setup routines for most programs know that they're supposed to install the programs in the Program Files folder, and do so unless you explicitly specify a different location. There are some exceptions to this rule. For example, Microsoft puts some applications, including Notepad (a limited text-editor program included with Windows) in the Windows folder rather than in the Program Files folder.

You'll need to work with the contents of the Program Files folder only seldom—for example, when something goes wrong with an uninstall routine, or when you're trying to perform a special tweak on a program. But you may well want to look through this folder to see what it contains.

THE *USERS* FOLDER

The Users folder contains the documents and settings for each user for whom you create an account on the computer and who has logged on at least once, together with a Guest folder for the Guest user if you've enabled the Guest account and a user has logged on to it. Windows recommends that each user put his or her own files and folders in the folders in his or her user account, which the user can access quickly via the links on the Start menu. For example, the Documents link on the Start menu takes the user to the Documents folder in his or her user account.

Double-click the icon for the Users folder. You'll see something like the window shown in Figure 5.6.

The number of folders you see in your Users folder depends on the number of user accounts you set up on the computer. In the figure, you see the following folders:

◆ **User folders.** Lily, Mick, and Will each have a folder.

◆ **Guest folder.** The Guest user has its own folder.

◆ **Public folder.** Windows provides the Public folder for sharing files and folders among users of this computer or on the network.

◆ **All Users shortcut.** This is a shortcut to the ProgramData folder. ProgramData contains items that are used for all users, such as Microsoft digital rights management (DRM) settings, user account pictures, and Windows Defender definitions and quarantine files.

◆ **Default folder.** This folder contains settings that are applied to all new users created (until the user customizes them).

◆ **Default User shortcut.** This is a shortcut to the Default folder and is there for compatibility with programs that look for a Default User folder. (Windows XP used a Default User folder.)

Each user's folder contains the same folder structure until the user changes it. Figure 5.7 shows an example.

Table 5.1 provides a quick breakdown of the folder structure. The next section examines the Documents, Music, Pictures, and Videos folders. You'll meet the other folders as needed later in the book.

FIGURE 5.6
The Users folder contains the user profile for each user (including the Guest), together with a Public folder, and links to the All Users folder and the Default User folder.

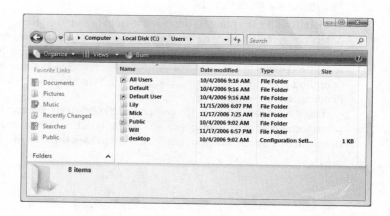

FIGURE 5.7

Each user's folder contains this folder structure at first.

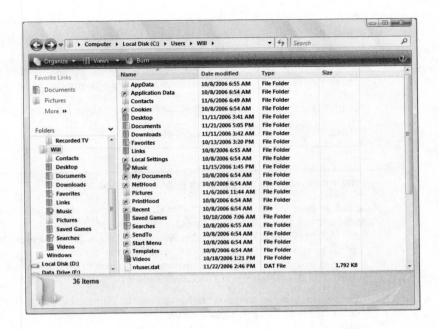

TABLE 5.1: Folders in Each User's Folder Structure

FOLDER NAME	CONTENTS
AppData	Your settings for programs.
Contacts	Your contacts (people in your address book).
Desktop	Your Desktop shortcuts (apart from the standard Desktop shortcuts that Windows provides, such as Computer and the Recycle Bin) and any files or folders you've placed on the Desktop.
Documents	Your documents, including the My Music folder, the My Pictures folder, and the My Videos folder
Downloads	Files you download (for example, by using Internet Windows Explorer or Windows Live Messenger).
Favorites	Your Internet Windows Explorer favorites
Links	The links that appear in the Favorite Links list.
Music	Your music files.
Pictures	Your graphics files.

TABLE 5.1: Folders in Each User's Folder Structure *(CONTINUED)*

FOLDER NAME	CONTENTS
Saved Games	Games you've saved while playing them—for example, a Chess Titans game.
Searches	Details of standard searches built into Windows and custom searches you create.
Videos	Your video files.

WHAT ARE ALL THE SHORTCUTS IN MY USER FOLDER?

As well as the folders explained in Table 5.1, your user folder also contains various shortcuts, such as Application Data, Cookies, Local Settings, My Documents, NetHood, PrintHood, Recent, SendTo, Start Menu, and Templates. Windows Vista includes these shortcuts for compatibility with applications designed for Windows XP, which used folders with these names. (For example, NetHood contained information about the computer's mappings to network drives, and PrintHood contained information about mappings to network printers.)

These shortcuts are for programs rather than users. Windows Vista doesn't let you access the folders to which these shortcuts are mapped via the shortcuts. If you double-click one of these shortcuts, you see a Location Is Not Available message box such as this:

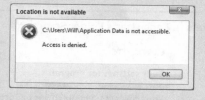

THE *DOCUMENTS, MUSIC, PICTURES,* AND *VIDEOS* FOLDERS

The Documents, Music, Pictures, and Videos folders are where Windows suggests you keep all your data files, music files, pictures, and video files except those that you share with other people. You can rename any of these folders if you choose. There are two main advantages to using these folders:

- ◆ You have a central point of administration that you can protect or back up easily.

- ◆ All Windows Vista–aware programs know where to look for files.

The Documents link, Pictures link, and Music link on the Start menu displays the Documents, Pictures, or Music folder (respectively) for the user who is currently active. For example, when Paula is logged on and active, choosing Start ➢ Documents causes Windows Explorer to display the Users\Paula\Documents folder rather than any other user's Documents folder.

Each user's Documents folder contains three shortcuts mapped as follows:

Documents Folder Shortcut	Mapped To
My Music	The Music folder in the user's folder
My Pictures	The Pictures folder in the user's folder
My Videos	The Videos folder in the user's folder

As with the shortcuts in the user's folder, these shortcuts are for the use of programs rather than users.

Moving Your Documents, Music, Pictures, or Videos Folder

You can move your Documents, Music, Pictures, or Videos folder from its default location. For example, you may need to move a folder to another drive that has more space available or gives better performance; or you may want to place a folder on a networked drive so that you can access your files from any computer connected to the network.

To move one of these folders, take the following steps:

1. Click the Start button, and then click your username on the Start menu. Windows opens an Windows Explorer window showing your user account.

2. Right-click the Documents folder, the Music folder, the Pictures folder, or the Videos folder, and then choose Properties from the shortcut menu. Windows displays the Properties dialog box.

3. Click the Location tab. Windows displays the Location page. Figure 5.8 shows the Location page of the Properties dialog box for the Documents folder. The text box shows the current folder that contains the folder.

FIGURE 5.8
Use the Location page of the Properties dialog box to move your Documents, Music, Pictures, or Videos folder to a different folder or drive.

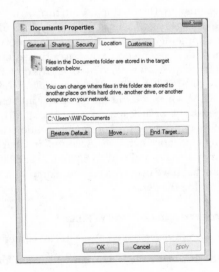

4. Click the Move button. Windows displays the Select a Destination dialog box.

5. Select the folder, and then click the Select Folder button. Windows displays the Move Folder dialog box, as shown here asking if you want to move all the files from the old location to the new location. It's best to move all the items; if you don't, your user folder displays two folders of this type, one for the new folder and one for the old one—for example, two Documents folders. Having two folders can be confusing.

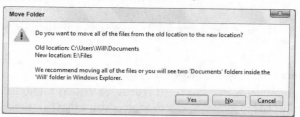

6. Click the Yes button if you want to move the documents; otherwise, click the No button.

Putting Your Documents, Music, Pictures, or Videos Folder back in Its Original Location

To restore your Documents, Music, Pictures, or Videos folder to its original location, click the Restore Default button on the Location page of the Properties dialog box for the folder.

PAGEFILE.SYS AND HIBERFIL.SYS

As mentioned a page or two ago, not *all* the files needed to keep Windows running reside in the Windows folder. There are a couple of massive exceptions: the paging file and the hibernation file.

If you look at the root of the drive on which Windows is installed, you should see a large file named PAGEFILE or PAGEFILE.SYS, depending on whether Windows Explorer is hiding or displaying file extensions. (If you don't see it, turn on the display of protected and hidden files as discussed a couple of pages ago.) This is the *paging file*, a file in which Windows stores information temporarily to supplement the RAM (physical memory) in your computer. (Chapter 15 discusses what the paging file does and how you can optimize and move it.) Windows keeps the paging file locked, so don't try to access it from Windows Explorer. You may also see another large file, this one called HIBERFIL or HIBERFIL.SYS. This is the *hibernation file*, the file in which Windows stores the contents of RAM when you put the computer into Hibernation mode. The hibernation file takes up as many megabytes of disk space as you have RAM. Don't mess with this file either. If you don't need hibernation, you can get rid of the hibernation file and reclaim the space it takes. See the section "Cleaning Up Your Own User Account" in Chapter 10.

You may also see a file called ERRORLOG or ERRORLOG.TXT. As its name suggests, it is a log of critical errors that have occurred on your computer. If you haven't had any critical errors, there won't be an error log file yet.

THE AUTOEXEC AND CONFIG.SYS FILES

On your system drive, you'll also find two other files:

◆ The autoexec file is a dummy file used for command prompt sessions.

◆ The config.sys file is a configuration file provided for compatibility with programs that expect to be running on earlier versions of Windows.

HIDING HIDDEN FILES AND PROTECTED OPERATING SYSTEM FILES

Now that you've seen the folder structure, you might want to hide the program folders, system folders, and hidden files again so that you see Windows as Microsoft intended. To do so, follow these steps:

1. Choose Organize ➤ Folder and Search Options. Windows displays the Folder Options dialog box.

2. Click the View tab. Windows displays the View page.

3. In the Advanced Settings list box, select the Do Not Show Hidden Files and Folders option button and the Hide Protected Operating System Files check box.

4. Click the OK button. Windows closes the Folder Options dialog box and applies the changes.

Using Views

Windows Explorer supports a number of views to let you browse folders and files comfortably and be able to tell what you're looking at:

Icons view   This view displays an icon for each file or folder. If the file contains a preview, Windows displays the preview as the icon, together with an icon indicating the program associated with the file. If the file doesn't contain a preview, Windows displays just the icon for the associated program. You can change the icon size by choosing Extra Large Icons, Large Icons, Medium Icons, or Small Icons from the View drop-down menu or by dragging the slider to one of these positions or an intermediate position.

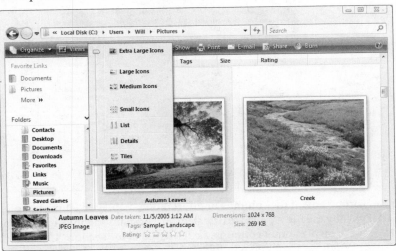

List view   This view displays a list of folders and files, showing only the filename or folder name and a small icon for each. List view is good for sorting through folders that contain a large number of files or folders.

Details   This view displays a list of files and folders, showing the filename or folder name, a small icon, the file size, the file type, and the date on which it was modified. (You can customize the details displayed for a folder. See the end of the chapter for instructions.) Details view is good for sorting files and folders by different types of information to quickly locate the file or folder you need.

Tiles view   This view displays a medium-sized icon for each file or folder. Windows Explorer displays icons rather than miniatures for graphics files. Tiles view is good for sorting through folders that contain relatively few files or folders.

You can apply a view in any of these ways:

◆ Click the View button on the toolbar, and then choose from the drop-down menu.

◆ Right-click in an Windows Explorer window, choose View from the context menu, and choose from the submenu.

Arranging Icons

Once you've applied a view, you can choose how to arrange the icons displayed in the view. Windows Explorer lets you sort icons, group them, and stack them.

SORTING ICONS

To sort icons, right-click empty space in the folder, select Sort By on the context menu, and then choose the sort item on the submenu, as shown here.

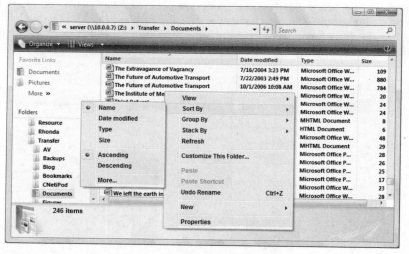

You can sort by any of the columns of information displayed—for example, by Name, Date Modified, Type (by the file type), Size (file size), or Tags (any tag information applied to the file). You may want to display other columns, as discussed in the section "Choosing Which Columns to Display in Windows Explorer Windows" at the end of this chapter, so that you can sort by them.

As well as choosing the means of arranging the icons, you can choose either the Ascending item (to sort in alphabetical and ascending order) or Descending (to sort in reverse order).

For Icon view and Tiles view, you can toggle on and off two further options as suits you:

Auto Arrange   This option tells Windows Explorer to arrange the icons into the specified order automatically. This option is good for keeping the icons in order.

Align to Grid   This option tells Windows Explorer to snap the icons back to an invisible grid, thus tidying up the window.

GROUPING ICONS

In Icons view, Tiles view, or Details view, you can group icons as well as sorting them. To group icons, right-click empty space in the folder, select Group By on the context menu, and then choose the grouping item on the submenu. You can group by any of the columns of information displayed, and you can choose between ascending and descending grouping. Figure 5.9 shows documents grouped by type.

STACKING ICONS

Windows offers a further way of arranging icons: stacking. Stacking creates stacks, or search groups, arranged by the attribute you chose.

To stack icons, right-click in open space in the folder, select Stack By on the context menu, and then choose the stack item on the submenu. You can stack by any of the columns of information displayed, and you can choose between ascending and descending order. Figure 5.10 shows a folder's worth of icons stacked by file type.

Windows treats stacking as a form of searching, so when you issue a Stack By command, the Address bar of the Windows Explorer window switches to "Search Results in" and the name of the folder. To return to the folder itself from the stacks, click the Back button. Alternatively, you can also remove stacking but continue using the Search Results view. To do so, right-click in open space in the window, and then choose Stack By ➤ (None) from the context menu. (The parentheses appear around the "None" item on the submenu.)

FIGURE 5.9

Grouping icons by type lets you quickly find all the documents of a particular type— for example, Power-Point presentations.

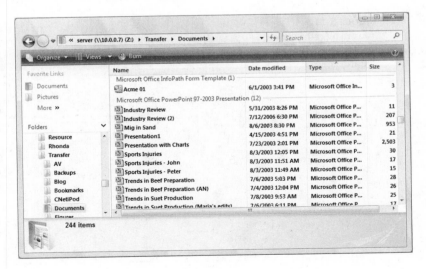

FIGURE 5.10
Stacking icons lets you create stacks of icons that share a particular attribute. You can then double-click a stack to see the contents of the stack.

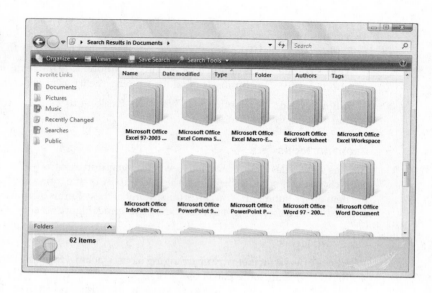

SORTING AND FILTERING USING COLUMN HEADINGS

You can click any column heading to sort by that column in ascending order, or click again to sort in descending order. The column button displays an upward-pointing arrow to indicate a sort in ascending order or a downward-pointing arrow to indicate a sort in descending order.

To filter the items shown, click the drop-down arrow that appears when you hover the mouse pointer over a column heading, and then choose filtering options from the panel that appears. For example, you can click the Authors drop-down arrow and then select the check boxes for the authors whose documents you want to view (see Figure 5.11). The column heading displays a check mark on its drop-down button to indicate that a filter is in place.

FIGURE 5.11
You can filter the view by the contents of any column.

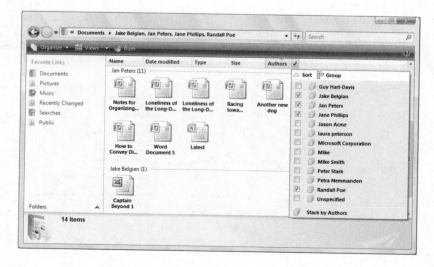

Navigating among Folders

To navigate among the folders you've used recently, use the three buttons in the upper-left corner of the Windows Explorer window:

Back button   Click this button to move back to the previous folder or view that was displayed.

Forward button   This is the counterpart to the Back button, and becomes available only when you've used the Back button. After you've moved back along the path of folders you've browsed through, you can use the Forward button to move forward through them again.

Recent Pages button   Click this button to display a list of folders and views you've used recently. Choose a folder or view from the list to display it.

USING THE ADDRESS BAR

The Address bar lets you navigate quickly among the drives and folders on your computer. Figure 5.12 shows you how to use the Address bar.

FIGURE 5.12
You can use the Address bar to choose drives or folders from a list, or click the icon at the left end and then type an address in the text box.

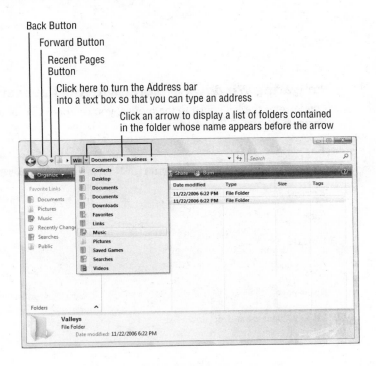

Back Button

Forward Button

Recent Pages Button

Click here to turn the Address bar into a text box so that you can type an address

Click an arrow to display a list of folders contained in the folder whose name appears before the arrow

Rearranging the Panes in the Windows Explorer Window

Windows Explorer window normally display the Navigation pane (the pane containing the Favorite Links list and the Folders bar) and the Details pane (the pane at the bottom that shows details of the selected item). You can also display a Search pane, the Preview pane, and the menu bar (see Figure 5.13).

To control which items an Windows Explorer window displays, choose Organize ➤ Layout, and then click an item on the submenu to display it (if it's hidden) or hide it (if it's already displayed).

FIGURE 5.13

You can toggle the Navigation pane, Details pane, Search pane, Preview pane, and menu bar on and off.

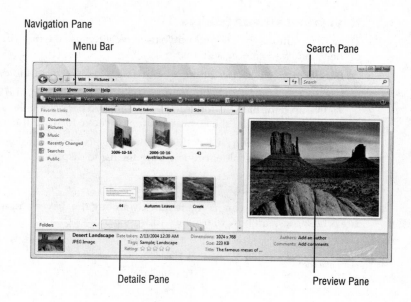

Navigating Windows Explorer with the Keyboard

If you prefer the keyboard to the mouse, you can perform some basic navigation with keyboard shortcuts. Table 5.2 lists these keyboard shortcuts.

TABLE 5.2: Keyboard Shortcuts for Navigating Windows Explorer

ACTION	KEYBOARD SHORTCUT
Back	Alt+ ← *or* Backspace
Forward	Alt+ →
Up one level	Alt+↑
Home page	Alt+Home
Display Address bar drop-down list	F4
Refresh	F5
Select the contents of the Address box in the Address bar	Alt+D

Navigating by Using Type-Down Addressing

Instead of navigating with the mouse, you can navigate through folders by using the keyboard and type-down addressing. This technique works best for accessing a file or folder whose name and location you know, but you can also use it for browsing through folders or files if you find it fast and comfortable.

Type-down addressing sounds forbidding, but it's easy and intuitive—and a great saver of time and effort. To use type-down addressing, you put the focus in the appropriate area—for example, in an Windows Explorer window or in the Address bar. You can then type down through the contents of the folder. As you type each letter, Windows Explorer selects the files or folders that match what you've typed, progressively narrowing down the possibilities until you reach the file or folder you want. At that point (or before), you can select it as usual.

Here's an example of using type-down addressing:

1. Choose Start ➢ Computer. Windows displays a Computer window.

2. Click the Address bar, or press Alt+D, to select the current entry (Computer).

3. Type the letter of the hard drive on which Windows is installed, followed by a colon and a backslash. For example,

   ```
   C:\
   ```

4. Windows Explorer displays a drop-down list of the matching folders and files.

5. Type **u**. Windows narrows down the selection to the files and folders that start with the letter *u*—typically, the Users folder.

6. Press the ↓ key to select the Users folder, and then type a backslash (\).

7. You can then type down through the Users folder to reach the folder or file you want.

Refreshing the Listing in a Folder

If you take an action in an Windows Explorer window that causes the contents of the folder displayed to change, Windows Explorer automatically refreshes the display. For example, if you create a new folder within the folder, Windows Explorer updates the display to show the new folder along with the previous contents. If you delete a file from the folder, Windows Explorer removes the file from the display.

But if the contents of the folder displayed in an Windows Explorer window change because of an action *not* taken in the window, Windows Explorer doesn't usually notice right away. Periodically, it will reread the contents of the folder and update the display. But if you don't want to wait, you can refresh the display manually. To do so, press the F5 key, or right-click empty space in the folder and choose Refresh from the context menu.

Choosing Folder Options

The View page of the Folder Options dialog box offers you the following options, some of which you've already met earlier in this chapter:

Always Show Icons, Never Thumbnails   Select this check box if you want to prevent Windows Explorer from displaying thumbnails for files and folders.

Always Show Menus   Select this check box if you want the menus to appear in every Windows Explorer window. If you're used to an earlier version of Windows that includes the menus, you may find this option useful.

Display File Icon on Thumbnails   Select this check box if you want Windows Explorer to display an icon indicating the associated program on each thumbnail. (*Thumbnails* are the larger sizes of icons.) For example, if you select this check box, Windows Explorer displays icon previews of Excel 2007 workbooks together with an Excel program icon. Usually, the program icon is helpful for visually identifying the file type.

Display File Size Information in Folder Tips Select this check box to control whether or not Windows Explorer displays an information pop-up when you hover the mouse pointer over a folder. As its name implies, this option doesn't apply to files—just to folders. So when you've cleared this check box, Windows still displays file information when you hover the mouse pointer over a file in an Windows Explorer window.

Display Simple Folder View in Navigation Pane Select this check box if you want to hide the dotted lines used to connect the folders and subfolders in the Navigation pane.

Display the Full Path in the Title Bar (Classic Folders Only) Select this check box if you want Windows Explorer to display the full path in the title bar of Windows Explorer windows when you're using "classic" folders.

Show/Do Not Show Hidden Files and Folders Select the Show Hidden Files and Folders option button to make Windows Explorer display hidden files and folders. By default, the Do Not Show Hidden Files and Folders option button is selected.

Hide Extensions for Known File Types Clear this check box if you want to make Windows Explorer display file extensions, the last section of each file's name. (For example, in the filename MYBOOK.DOC, the extension is .DOC.) By default, this check box is selected, so Windows Explorer hides extensions. But as discussed in "Working with File Associations, File Extensions, and File Types" in Chapter 9, you may find displaying file extensions helpful at least sometimes.

Hide Protected Operating System Files Select this check box to make Windows Explorer hide operating-system files. Hiding these files is usually a good idea, because it helps you avoid deleting them accidentally. But for some special purposes, you'll need to display these files temporarily.

Launch Folder Windows in a Separate Process Select this check box if you want to make Windows Explorer open each separate folder window in a separate area of memory rather than sharing a single area of memory among the folder windows displayed. Using separate folders theoretically increases the stability of Windows, because if one instance of Windows Explorer crashes, the others shouldn't be affected. However, using separate folders consumes more memory and processor cycles. This option is turned off by default. Turn it on only if you find that Windows seems to be crashing when you're working in Windows Explorer windows.

Remember Each Folder's View Settings Select this check box if you want Windows Explorer to use the same view for a folder when you reopen it. Clear this check box if you want Windows Explorer to revert to the default view for each window you open.

Restore Previous Folder Windows at Logon Select this check box if you want Windows to reopen Windows Explorer and Internet Windows Explorer windows to the folders and addresses at which they were open when you logged off. This option can be useful for helping you pick up work where you left off.

Show Drive Letters Clear this check box if you want to see only descriptive names (also called *friendly* names) for drives rather than drive letters (such as C: or D:). Windows displays drive letters by default.

Show Encrypted or Compressed NTFS Files in Color Select this check box if you want Windows Explorer to display compressed files on NTFS partitions in blue instead of black (in the default color scheme). Windows Vista Home doesn't support encryption, but in Windows Vista Business and Windows Vista Ultimate (which do support encryption) encrypted files appear in green when you select this option. This option is off by default. Normally, you don't need to know whether files are compressed.

Show Pop-up Description for Folder and Desktop Items   Select this check box if you want Windows Explorer to display a descriptive pop-up when you hover the mouse pointer over a folder or an item on the Desktop. This option is on by default and is usually helpful. Clear this check box if you find the pop-ups distracting.

Show Preview Handlers in Preview Pane   If you don't use the Preview pane, you can clear this check box to prevent Windows from using the handlers (programs) that display previews in Windows Explorer windows. Turning off the handlers may improve performance a little.

Use Check Boxes to Select Items   Select this check box if you want Windows to display a check box next to each file or folder you highlight in an Windows Explorer window. You can then use these check boxes to make a selection of multiple files and folders—for example, if you find it uncomfortable to hold down Shift or Ctrl while making a selection.

Use Sharing Wizard   Select this check box if you want to use the Sharing Wizard for sharing files and folders. Clear this check box if you prefer to set up sharing for files and folders manually.

When Typing in List View Options   Select the Automatically Type into the Search Box option button if you want Windows to treat text you type into an Windows Explorer window in List view as search text. Normally, you'll want to leave the Select the Typed Item in the View option button selected, so that Windows lets you "type down" to select an item.

Creating a New Folder

To create a new folder, right-click open space in the folder in which you want to create the new folder and choose New ➤ Folder from the context menu. Alternatively, choose Organize ➤ New Folder. Windows creates a new folder, assigns it a default name based on New Folder (New Folder, New Folder (2), and so on), and displays an edit box around the name. Type the name for the folder and press the Enter key or click elsewhere in the window.

You can create a new folder in any folder for which you have permission to make changes. If you're not able to create a folder, the folder you're working in probably belongs to someone else who has chosen not to give you permission to make changes in it.

Copying a File or Folder

Windows gives you several ways to copy a file or folder. Because copying is an action you'll need to perform often, this section shows you most of the convenient ways to copy a file or folder. You may end up using only one or two of these ways, but you should try them all out and see which you find easiest in which circumstances.

Some of the ways of copying a file involve opening multiple Windows Explorer windows (or having the Desktop visible). For others, you need have only one Windows Explorer window open (or the Desktop).

This section says "a file or folder," but most of the techniques work just as well for multiple files or folders.

If the folder to which you're copying or moving a file already contains a file with the same name, Windows displays the Copy File dialog box shown in Figure 5.14. You then have three choices:

Copy and Replace Click this button to replace the existing file in the folder with the new file.

Don't Copy Click this button to cancel the copy operation. You can also click the Cancel button at the bottom of the dialog box.

Copy, but Keep Both Files Click this button to copy the new file into the folder but give it a new name. The button shows the name the file will receive. This option is useful when you're not sure whether the file you're copying contains newer data than the existing file.

FIGURE 5.14
Windows displays the Copy File dialog box when a copy operation is about to overwrite a file that has the same name.

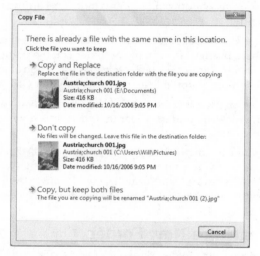

Similarly, if you go to paste a folder into a folder that already contains a folder with the same name, Windows displays the Confirm Folder Replace dialog box (see Figure 5.15). Look at the details carefully to make sure you're clear which folder you will replace if you proceed, and then click the Yes button or the No button as appropriate.

 Real World Scenario

WHAT IF YOU'RE COPYING SEVERAL FILES THAT WILL REPLACE OTHER FILES?

If you're copying two or more files that will replace other files with the same names, the Copy File dialog box includes a Skip button and a Do This for the Next *N* Conflicts check box (where *N* is the number—for example, Do This for the Next 2 Conflicts). Click the Skip button to skip the current question. Select the check box and then click the appropriate button if you want to apply the same action to all the conflicts. For example, you might select the check box, and then click the Copy, But Keep Both Files button.

FIGURE 5.15
Windows displays
the Confirm Folder
Replace dialog box
when you're about
to replace a folder in
a copy operation.

Copying a File or Folder by Using Drag-and-Drop

When you're copying a file or folder, Windows distinguishes between copying it to another folder on the same drive or to a folder on a different drive:

Same drive   Windows assumes that you mean to move the file or folder rather than copy it.

Different drive   Windows assumes that you mean to copy the file or folder.

Because of this assumption, you need to use different techniques for copy operations depending on the drives you're using.

COPYING A FILE OR FOLDER TO THE SAME DRIVE

To copy a file or folder to another folder on the same drive, take the following steps:

1. Open an Windows Explorer window to the folder that contains the source file or folder.

2. Open another Windows Explorer window to the destination folder.

3. Select the file or folder in the source folder.

4. Hold down the Ctrl key, and then drag the file or folder to the destination folder. Windows displays a plus (+) sign on the mouse pointer to indicate that the file or folder will be copied to the destination.

5. Release the mouse button and the Ctrl key. Windows copies the file or folder. While it does so, it displays the Copying dialog box (shown here), which lists the file or folder being copied and

an estimate of how long the whole Copy operation will take. You can click the More Information button or Less Information button to change the amount of detail displayed.

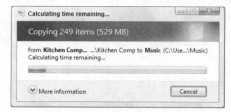

COPYING A FILE OR FOLDER TO A DIFFERENT DRIVE

To copy a file or folder to a folder on a different drive, use the technique described in the previous list, but don't hold down the Ctrl key. When you drag a file to another drive, Windows automatically copies the file rather than moving it.

Because it's easy to get confused about which drive a folder is on, you may prefer to use the right-drag-and-drop technique described in the next section instead of the plain drag-and-drop technique.

Copying a File or Folder by Using Right-Drag-and-Drop

You can also copy a file or folder by using the right-drag-and-drop technique. Follow these steps:

1. Open an Windows Explorer window to the folder that contains the source file or folder.

2. Open another Windows Explorer window to the destination folder.

3. Right-click the file or folder in the source folder and right-drag it to the destination folder. Windows displays a context menu of options, as shown below.

4. Select the Copy Here item. Windows copies the file or folder.

The advantage of this technique over the plain drag-and-drop technique is that you can always choose whether to copy the file or move it.

Copying a File or Folder by Using the Copy and Paste Commands

You can also copy a file or folder by using the Copy and Paste commands. Follow these steps:

1. Open an Windows Explorer window to the source folder.

2. Select the file or folder.

3. Issue a Copy command by right-clicking and then choosing Copy from the context menu, or by pressing Ctrl+C.

4. Navigate to the destination folder, either in the same Windows Explorer window or in another Windows Explorer window.

5. Select the destination folder.

6. Issue a Paste command by choosing Organize ➢ Paste, right-clicking and choosing Paste from the context menu, or pressing Ctrl+V. Windows pastes the copy of the file or folder into the destination folder.

Copying a File or Folder by Using the Copy to Folder Command

If you've chosen to display the Windows Explorer menus, you have another way of copying a file or folder: by using the Copy to Folder command. Take the following steps:

1. Select the file or folder you want to copy.

2. Choose Edit ➢ Copy to Folder. Windows displays the Copy Items dialog box, as shown here.

3. Navigate to the folder in which you want to create the copy of the file or folder. To create a new folder in the currently selected folder, click the Make New Folder button. Windows creates a folder named `New Folder` and displays an edit box around it. Type the name for the folder, and then press Enter. Windows renames the folder and leaves it selected.

4. Click the Copy button. Windows copies the file, and then closes the Copy Items dialog box.

Copying a File or Folder by Using the Send To Command

If you frequently need to copy files or folders to a particular location, using the Send To menu is usually the quickest and most convenient way to do so. For example, you might need to copy files or folders to another folder in order to burn backups of them to CD.

To copy a file or folder via the Send To menu, right-click the file or folder, choose Send To from the context menu, and then select the location from the submenu, as shown here.

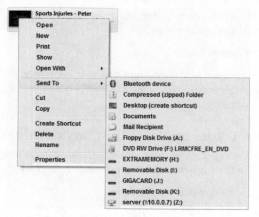

Moving a File or Folder

Windows' drag-and-drop techniques for moving a file depend on whether the source folder (the folder the file is currently in) and the destination folder (the folder to which you want to move the file) are on the same drive or on different drives. The techniques for moving are closely related to the techniques for copying a file.

Moving a File or Folder to a Folder on the Same Drive

To move a file or folder to a folder on the same drive, take the following steps:

1. Arrange one or two Windows Explorer windows so that you can see the source folder and the destination.

2. Drag the file or folder from the source folder to the destination folder, and drop it there. Windows moves the file or folder.

Moving a File or Folder to a Folder on a Different Drive

To move a file or folder to a folder on a different drive, take the following steps:

1. Arrange one or two Windows Explorer windows so that you can see the source folder and the destination.

2. Select the file or folder.

3. Hold down the Shift key.

4. Drag the file or folder to the destination folder.

5. Release the Shift key and the mouse button. Windows moves the file.

This technique doesn't work well for multiple files or folders, because holding down the Shift key and clicking the selected files or folders (in preparation for dragging them) changes the selection.

Moving a File or Folder by Using Right-Drag-and-Drop

You can also move a file or folder by using the right-drag-and-drop technique. Follow these steps:

1. Open an Windows Explorer window to the folder that contains the source file or folder.

2. Open another Windows Explorer window to the destination folder.

3. Right-click the file or folder in the source folder and right-drag it to the destination folder. Windows displays a context menu of options.

4. Select the Move Here item. Windows moves the file or folder.

The advantage of the right-drag technique is that it always produces a move operation, no matter whether the destination folder is on the same drive as the source folder.

Moving a File or Folder by Using the Move to Folder Command

If you've chosen to display the Windows Explorer menus, you have another way of moving a file or folder: by using the Move to Folder command. Take the following steps:

1. Select the file or folder you want to move.

2. Choose Edit ➢ Move to Folder. Windows displays the Move Items dialog box, shown here.

3. Navigate to the destination folder. To create a new folder in the currently selected folder, click the Make New Folder button. Windows creates a folder named New Folder and displays an edit box around it. Type the name for the folder, and then press Enter. Windows renames the folder and leaves it selected.

4. Click the Move button. Windows copies the file and closes the Move Items dialog box.

Moving a File or Folder by Using Cut and Paste

You can also move a file or folder by using Cut and Paste commands. Follow these steps:

1. Open an Windows Explorer window to the source folder.

2. Select the file or folder.

3. Issue a Cut command by pressing Ctrl+X or by right-clicking and then choosing Cut from the context menu.

4. Navigate to the destination folder, either in the same Windows Explorer window or in another Windows Explorer window.

5. Select the destination folder.

6. Issue a Paste command by pressing Ctrl+V or right-clicking and then choosing Paste from the context menu. Windows pastes the cut file or folder into the destination folder.

 Real World Scenario

UNABLE TO COPY OR MOVE A FILE OR FOLDER

If you find you can't copy or move a file or folder, especially one on a network drive, you probably don't have the necessary permission. Because moving a file involves deleting its original from the folder it's in, you need permission to change a folder in order to move a file from it. (You may be able to create a copy instead, because copying doesn't involve deleting the original.) Likewise, you need permission to create a file in the destination folder; if you don't have this permission, neither moving nor copying will work.

Deleting a File or Folder

Deleting a file or folder is easy once you understand the two-stage process that Windows uses to help prevent you from deleting any files or folders unintentionally.

Windows has a holding area called the Recycle Bin for files or folders that you've deleted. (If you're familiar with Mac OS, you'll find similarities between the Recycle Bin and the Trash.) When you tell Windows to delete a file or folder that's stored on a local drive, Windows confirms that you're sure about the deletion, and then moves the file or folder from its current folder to the Recycle Bin. When a file or folder is in the Recycle Bin, it hasn't been deleted yet, and you can retrieve it easily. Windows calls this *restoring* a file or folder—restoring it from the Recycle Bin to its previous folder.

Files or folders stay in the Recycle Bin until either you empty it or the Recycle Bin grows to occupy its full allocation of disk space, at which point Windows starts discarding the oldest files or folders in the Recycle Bin without consultation to make space for further files or folders you delete.

When you tell Windows to delete a file or folder on a network drive, Windows deletes it immediately without moving the file to the Recycle Bin. Unless you work strictly with files or folders on local drives, it's a bad idea to rely on the Recycle Bin to rescue you from careless Delete operations.

If you want, you can turn off the confirmation of deletion, and you can stop Windows from using the Recycle Bin. That way, when you delete a file or folder, it's deleted instantly without confirmation, and there's no easy way of restoring it. (You can sometimes restore deleted files or folders with third-party undelete utilities, but you shouldn't rely on being able to do so.)

Moving a File or Folder to the Recycle Bin

To move a file or folder to the Recycle Bin, take any of the following actions:

◆ Select the file or folder, and then press the Delete key.

◆ Right-click the file or folder, and then choose Delete from the context menu.

◆ Select the file in an Windows Explorer window, and then choose Organize ➤ Delete.

◆ Select the file or folder, and then drag it to the Recycle Bin on the Desktop.

Once you've issued a Delete command, Windows displays the Delete File dialog box, shown here, or the Delete Folder dialog box (which is similar).

Click the Yes button if you're sure you want to send the file to the Recycle Bin.

If you accidentally delete a file or folder in an Windows Explorer window, you can recover it by choosing Organize ➤ Undo Delete or by pressing Ctrl+Z before taking any other actions in Windows Explorer.

Deleting a File or Folder without Moving It to the Recycle Bin

To delete a file or folder without moving it to the Recycle Bin, hold down the Shift key as you issue the Delete command:

◆ Select the file or folder, hold down the Shift key, and then press the Delete key.

◆ Right-click the file or folder, hold down the Shift key, and choose the Delete item on the context menu.

◆ Select the file or folder in an Windows Explorer window, hold down the Shift key, click the Organize button, and then click Delete.

Windows displays the Delete File dialog box (shown here) or the Delete Folder dialog box with different wording.

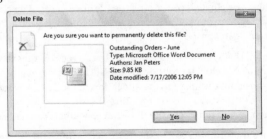

Click the Yes button to delete the file or folder.

Recovering a File or Folder from the Recycle Bin

To recover a file or folder from the Recycle Bin, follow these steps:

1. Double-click the Recycle Bin icon on the Desktop. Windows opens a Recycle Bin window.

2. Click the file or folder you want to restore.

3. Click the Restore This Item button on the toolbar. To restore all items, select no item, and then click the Restore All Items button on the toolbar. Windows restores the item to its previous folder.

If you've created another file with the same name in the folder the file to be restored previously occupied, Windows displays the Move File dialog box (see Figure 5.16) to let you decide whether to overwrite the newer file with the one you're restoring.

If you restore a folder from the Recycle Bin after you've created another folder with the same name in the folder into which it'll return, Windows displays the Confirm Folder Replace dialog box (see Figure 5.17), which lets you choose whether to merge the folder you're restoring with the existing folder. If any of the files you're restoring have the same names as files in the folder, you can choose whether to replace the existing files. Click the Yes button to merge the folders.

 Real World Scenario

FILE DELETION AND RESTORATION

Each file is stored in a number of clusters on your hard disk. The file system—NTFS or FAT—maintains an allocation table of which sectors each file is stored in. When a program goes to open a file, Windows gets from the file system the location of the clusters that contain the file and instructs the hard disk to retrieve the information. These clusters may be located pretty much anywhere on the disk partition that contains the drive. If they're located near each other, the hard disk can retrieve them faster, but if your drive is fragmented, they may be scattered all over the disk. Either way, the file system assembles the data they contain so that Windows can present them as a single file in the correct order.

When you delete a file (when you perform a real Delete operation, that is—not when you put a file in the Recycle Bin), Windows tells the file system to get rid of the file. The file system does so by deleting the entry that tells it where the clusters containing the file are located. The clusters that the file is actually stored in remain intact but are marked as being available for storing data, so they may be overwritten by another Save operation at any point.

This method of deletion is why some undelete utilities can recover files that have been "deleted" by the operating system. Before the clusters containing the file have been overwritten, the information can be reassembled by synthesizing the entry in the allocation table. This may not work perfectly—often, the result is a bit rough—but it works surprisingly often. After the clusters containing the file have been overwritten, it's much harder to restore the file—but specialists can usually do it.

If you want to be sure that nobody can easily restore the files you delete, get a shredder utility that overwrites the clusters in which the file's data is stored as soon as you delete the file. (Norton's WipeInfo comes highly recommended.) But if you want to be entirely sure that nobody will ever be able to read the data on your hard disk again, destroy the hard disk. A sledgehammer, an oxy-acetylene lamp, or strong acid might be needed.

FIGURE 5.16
When restoring a file from the Recycle Bin, Windows lets you decide how to deal with any files that have the same name as existing files.

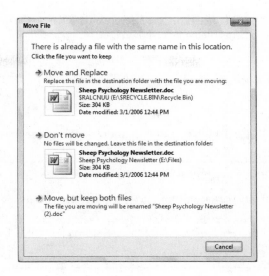

FIGURE 5.17
Windows displays the Confirm Folder Replace dialog box when restoring a folder from the Recycle Bin will replace an existing folder.

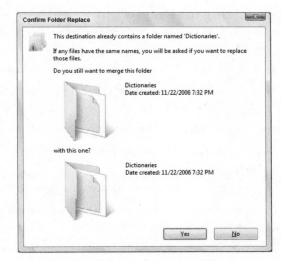

Emptying the Recycle Bin

Under normal usage, your Recycle Bin gradually fills up with files and folders you delete. Windows lets the Recycle Bin fill, and then automatically deletes the oldest files or folders in it when it needs space for newer files or folders you delete, so you don't *need* to empty the Recycle Bin. But for security, it's a good idea to clear out old files you wouldn't want others to see. So every now and then, visit the Recycle Bin, look through it, restore any files or folders you want to keep, and empty out the rest.

To empty the Recycle Bin, follow these steps:

1. Double-click the Recycle Bin icon on your Desktop. Windows opens the Recycle Bin window.

2. Restore any files or folders you want to keep.

3. Click the Empty the Recycle Bin button on the toolbar. Windows displays the Delete Multiple Items dialog box, shown here.

4. Click the Yes button. Windows deletes the files from the Recycle Bin.

QUICKLY EMPTY THE RECYCLE BIN

To empty the Recycle Bin quickly without checking its contents, follow these steps:

1. Right-click the Recycle Bin icon on your Desktop, and then choose Empty Recycle Bin from the context menu. Windows displays the Delete Multiple Items dialog box.

2. Click the Yes button.

Customizing the Recycle Bin

The Recycle Bin's standard behavior works well for many people, but you can change the way the Recycle Bin behaves:

◆ You can make Windows delete items immediately without using the Recycle Bin.

◆ You can turn off confirmation of deletion, so that files go directly to the Recycle Bin (if you're using it) or to oblivion.

◆ You can change the amount of space set aside for the Recycle Bin.

To customize the Recycle Bin, follow these steps:

1. Right-click the Recycle Bin icon on your Desktop, and then choose Properties from the context menu. Windows displays the Recycle Bin Properties dialog box (see Figure 5.18).

2. In the Recycle Bin Location list box, select the drive you want to affect. You can choose different settings for each hard drive.

3. In the Settings for Selected Location group box, select the "Do Not Move Files to the Recycle Bin. Remove Files Immediately When Deleted" option button if you want to stop using the Recycle Bin for this drive. Otherwise, leave the Custom Size option button selected, and change the size in the Maximum Size box if necessary. For example, you might want to reduce the amount of space that the Recycle Bin can take up.

4. If you want to turn off confirmation of deletion, clear the Display Delete Confirmation Dialog check box. This setting affects all drives at once: you can't choose different confirmation settings for different drives. If you chose in the previous step to stop using the Recycle Bin for a drive, clearing this check box as well means that items you delete get deleted permanently without confirmation.

5. Click the OK button. Windows closes the Recycle Bin Properties dialog box.

FIGURE 5.18
The Recycle Bin
Properties dialog
box lets you turn
off confirmation of
delete, change the
amount of space the
Recycle Bin uses, or
stop using the Recycle
Bin altogether.

EXPERT KNOWLEDGE: PERFORMING FILE OPERATIONS IN COMMON DIALOG BOXES

You can perform file operations such as Copy, Paste, Rename, and Delete in many common dialog boxes used by Windows programs. Just right-click the listing for a file to display a context menu of the actions you can take, as in the illustration below.

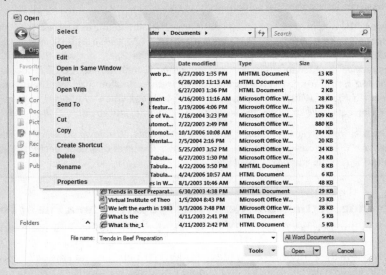

Doing this can save you time because you don't need to open an Windows Explorer window. For example, say you're working in Word and you need to save the active document under a name that another document in the same folder already has without overwriting that document. Instead of opening an Windows Explorer window, you can right-click the filename, choose Rename to display an edit box, and rename it there.

Renaming a File or Folder

To rename a file or folder, follow these steps:

1. Open an edit box for the file's name by taking one of these actions:

   ◆ Right-click the file or folder, and then choose Rename from the context menu.

   ◆ Click the file or folder, and then choose Organize ➢ Rename.

   ◆ Click the file's or folder's name, wait a moment, and then click again.

2. Type the name in the edit box, and then press Enter or click in open space outside the edit box.

RENAMING MULTIPLE FILES OR FOLDERS AT ONCE

Windows lets you rename multiple files or folders at the same time by selecting the files, pressing the F2 key, entering the base filename, and then pressing Enter, but the feature is useful only in certain specialized circumstances that seldom occur in real life.

Because the renamed files or folders can't have the same name as each other, Windows adds ascending numbers in parentheses to all files after the first: (1), (2), and so on. So if you rename the files Letter to Jane.doc, Letter to Fred.doc, and Letter to the Bank.doc with the name Correspondence, the files receive the filenames Correspondence.doc, Correspondence (1).doc, and Correspondence (2).doc. Counterintuitively, it's the *last* file in the selection that gets the unadorned name, because this is the file for which Windows displays the edit box when you press the F2 key. The first file in the selection gets the (1) name, the second the (2) name, and so on.

If the files you're renaming have different extensions, Windows preserves those extensions—even if you have file extensions displayed in Windows Explorer *and* you specify the extension for the file around which the edit box is displayed.

Viewing, Setting, and Removing Properties for a File or Folder

As you'll remember from earlier in the chapter, files and folders are objects, and objects have properties.

To view the properties for a file or folder, right-click it and choose Properties from the context menu. (Alternatively, select it and choose Organize ➢ Properties.) Windows displays the Properties dialog box for the file or folder.

Figure 5.19 shows an example of the General page of the Properties dialog box for a file. The General page shows the following information:

◆ File name (in the title bar and in the text box at the top).

◆ File type—for instance, Microsoft Office Word Document (.docx).

◆ Program set to open the file—for example, Microsoft Office Word. You can change the associated program by clicking the Change button. Chapter 9 discusses the implications of doing so.

◆ Location (the folder that contains the file).

◆ The size and size on disk. The size on disk may be different if the drive uses compression.

◆ The dates on which the file was created, last modified, and last accessed.

◆ The Read-Only status, which controls whether users can only view the file or can save changes to it. You can select or clear this check box.

◆ The Hidden status, which controls whether Windows displays the file when Windows Explorer is set to hide hidden files. You can select or clear this check box.

You can set advanced attributes for the file or folder by clicking the Advanced button and then working in the Advanced Attributes dialog box that Windows displays. (Chapter 9 discusses these options.)

The Details page of the Properties dialog box contains information about the file or folder. Figure 5.20 shows two examples. Depending on the file type, you may be able to edit some of the properties.

FIGURE 5.19
The General page of the Properties dialog box for a file

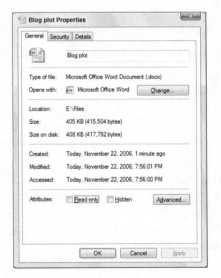

FIGURE 5.20
The Details page of the
Properties dialog box
for a file lets you view
properties. For some
file types, you can edit
properties, as shown
on the right here.

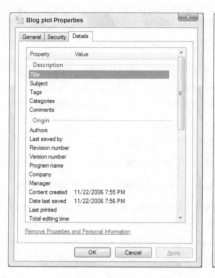

When you're planning to distribute a file, you may want to remove certain properties from it so that people who receive the file can't view potentially sensitive information. You can either remove properties from the file itself or create a copy without those properties, leaving the original file with its properties intact.

To remove properties, follow these steps:

1. Click the Remove Properties and Personal Information link on the Details page. Windows displays the Remove Properties dialog box (see Figure 5.21).

2. Choose whether to make a copy or remove properties from the original file:

   ◆ To make a copy, select the Create a Copy with All Possible Properties Removed option button.

   ◆ To remove properties from the original file, select the Remove the Following Properties from This File option button. You can then click the Select All button to select the check box for each removable property or select the check boxes individually.

3. Click the OK button. Windows closes the dialog box, removes the properties, and returns you to the Properties dialog box. If you chose to create a copy, Windows creates a new file named with the original filename and – Copy. For example, the copy of Lake.wmv is named Lake – Copy.wmv.

When you've finished examining or changing properties, click the OK button. Windows closes the Properties dialog box.

FIGURE 5.21
Windows Vista
makes it easy for
you to remove select-
ed properties from a
file itself or to make
a copy with the prop-
erties removed.

Finding a File or Folder

Unless you're incredibly well organized, have a great memory, or never create any files, you'll
probably forget where a particular file or folder is located. Windows provides powerful searching
that you can use to find files by their name, their size, the date they were created, or even by a word
or phrase contained in the body of the file.

You can start a search directly from the Start menu, from an Windows Explorer window you've
already opened, or by opening a Search Results window.

Searching from the Start Menu

Searching from the Start menu is handy when you don't have an Windows Explorer window open
and when you want to be able to start searching the Internet as well as your computer.

To search from the Start menu, follow these steps:

1. Click the Start button. Windows displays the Start menu and displays an insertion point in
   the Search box just above the Start button.

2. Type your search term. As you type, Windows searches and displays a list of hits in the left
   part of the Start menu (see Figure 5.22).

3. If the item you want appears in the list, click it to open it. Otherwise:

   ◆ To see the full list of results, click the See All Results link. Windows opens a Search
   Results window showing the results. Double-click an item to open it.

   ◆ Click the Search the Internet link if you want to start searching the Internet for the search
   term. Windows opens Internet Windows Explorer and searches using your current
   search engine.

FIGURE 5.22
To search from the
Start menu, type in
the Search box, and
then click the item you
want to open. You can
also display all search
results or start search-
ing the Internet for the
search term.

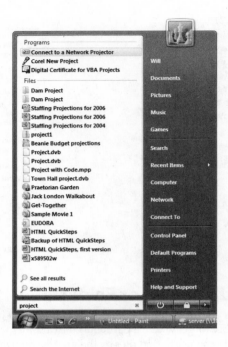

Searching from an Open Windows Explorer Window

If you've already opened an Windows Explorer window, you can start searching by typing in the Search box in its upper-right corner. Windows searches within the current folder and displays the results it finds. Double-click an item to open it.

Searching from a Search Results Window

For the most powerful and flexible searching, use a Search Results window. Follow these steps:

1. Choose Start ➤ Search. Windows opens a Search Results window with the basic Search features displayed, as shown here.

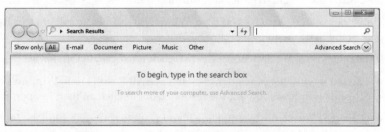

2. For a simple search, type in the Search box. Windows searches the entire index and returns results. You can double-click an item to open it, or click one of the buttons on the Show Only bar to view only those items. For example, you can click the Picture button to restrict the list of search results to pictures.

3. For an advanced search, click the Advanced Search button at the right end of the Search bar. Windows displays the Advanced Search bar, as shown here.

4. In the Location drop-down list, choose where you want to search:

◆ Choose Everywhere to search through your entire file system. The search may be slow because some of the folders are not indexed for searching.

◆ Choose Indexed Locations to search through the index of all the folders Windows is set to index for searching. The search will be quick, because searching the index is much faster than searching through folders.

◆ Choose one of the drives in the list to search only that drive.

◆ To search only one or more specified folders, click the Choose Search Locations item. Windows displays the Choose Search Locations folder (see Figure 5.23).

◆ In the Change Selected Locations box, select the check box for each folder you want to search. Windows adds the folders to the Included Locations list in the Summary of Selected Locations box. You can exclude a subfolder of a selected folder by clearing the subfolder's check box. Windows then adds the subfolder to the Exclusions list in the Summary of Selected Locations box.

◆ Click the OK button. Windows closes the Choose Search Locations dialog box and adds the details to the Location drop-down list.

5. Use the Date line of controls to specify any date criteria by which you want to search. You can choose Date, Date Modified, Date Created, or Date Accessed in the first drop-down list; Any, Is, Is Before, or Is After in the second drop-down list; and the date in the third drop-down list. For example, you might choose Date Modified Is after 9/10/2007 to find only files modified after September 10, 2007.

6. Use the Size line of controls to set any size criteria you want to use. In the drop-down list, you can choose Any, Equals, Is Less Than, or Is Greater Than. For any choice except Any, type the size in the Add a File Size box. For example, you might choose Size (KB) Is Greater than 1,024 to find only files of more than 1MB (1,024KB).

7. Select the Include Non-Indexed, Hidden, and System Files check box if you want to broaden the search to include files that Windows isn't set to index, including hidden files and system files. Searching these files slows down the search, so select this check box only when you need the most thorough search for files you've lost.

FIGURE 5.23
Use the Choose Search
Locations dialog
box to tell Windows
exactly which folders
to search.

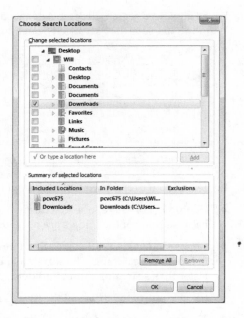

8. In the Filename text box, type the entire filename or part of the filename:

◆ Enter only as much of the name as you're sure of. Usually, it's better to get multiple results from a search using part of the name than to get no results from using search criteria that are too specific and not quite right.

◆ If you know the extension of the file, include it. If you're not sure of the extension, omit it.

◆ You can use the wildcards asterisk (*) and question mark (?) to increase the scope of your search. The wildcard * represents any number of characters, while ? represents just one character. For example, searching for `Letter*` returns a list of all files whose names include the word *Letter* and have one or more characters after it, while searching for `Letter?` returns a list of all files whose names start with *Letter* followed by another character.

9. In the Tags text box, type any tag information by which you want to search.

10. In the Authors text box, type any author name you want to use in the search.

11. Click the Search button. Windows returns any matching results. You can click one of the buttons on the Show Only bar to view only those items.

From the Search Results window, you can perform most actions that you can from any Windows Explorer window:

◆ Select a file to display its information in the Details pane.

◆ Double-click a file to open it.

- Press the Delete key to move the selected file to the Recycle Bin.

- Drag a file to another folder.

- To open the folder that contains a file you've found, right-click the file, and then choose Open File Location from the context menu.

Saving a Search

After you've performed a successful search, you can save the search criteria so that you can repeat the search easily in the future. To save the search, click the Save Search button in the Search pane, type a name in the Save As dialog box, and then click the Save button. Windows saves your searches in the Searches folder in your user account, which is normally a handy place to keep them.

To open a saved search, click your Searches folder in the Navigation pane, and then double-click the search.

Configuring Searching

Windows' standard search options can be effective, but you may need to tune them to your needs before you can get the best search results.

To configure searching, follow these steps:

1. Choose Start ➢ Computer. Windows opens a Computer window.

2. Choose Organize ➢ Folder and Search Options. Windows displays the Folder Options dialog box.

3. Click the Search tab. Windows displays the Search page (see Figure 5.24).

FIGURE 5.24
Choose search options on the Search page of the Folder Options dialog box.

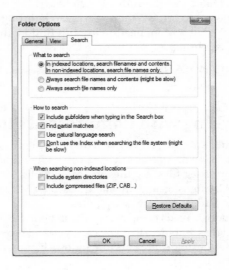

4. In the What to Search group box, choose what to search:

   In Indexed Locations, Search Filenames and Contents. In Non-Indexed Locations, Search Filenames Only   Select this option button for Windows' standard searching behavior: When searching an indexed folder, include the contents; otherwise, don't. This search behavior produces good results fast, but you may need to change the list of folders that Windows indexes. See the section "Changing the List of Folders That Windows Indexes" in Chapter 10 for details.

   Always Search File Names and Contents   Select this option button to force Windows always to search file contents even in folders that aren't indexed. Your searches will be slower but more thorough. If you find you need content searches to find the right files, consider adding more folders to Windows' indexing list.

   Always Search File Names Only   Select this option button to make Windows confine searching to filenames. Your searches will be faster than if you search contents, but you forego the benefit of content matches.

5. In the How to Search group box, select or clear these check boxes as needed:

   Include Subfolders When Typing in the Search Box   Select this check box if you want to search subfolders as well as the current folder when you search using the Search box.

   Find Partial Matches   Select this check box if you want to find partial matches as well as complete matches.

   Use Natural Language Search   Select this check box if you want to use "natural language" searches—ones in which you specify a search phrase such as "document created last week." Natural language searches can be effective, but you may get better results by putting your requests into computer terms.

   Don't Use the Index When Searching the File System   Select this check box if you want to force Windows to search through the file system rather than using the index. You'll seldom need to use this option unless you suspect your index has become corrupted.

6. Click the OK button. Windows closes the Folder Options dialog box, and you're ready to search.

Working with Compressed Files

As you'll know if you've needed to transfer files or store them on limited-capacity media, file-compression programs can save you a lot of time and trouble. There are two widely used forms of compressed files: Zip files and cabinet files. Zip files have the ZIP extension. Cabinet files have the CAB extension and are mainly used by Microsoft for distributing files. Windows lets you create Zip folders but not cabinet files.

Windows reads compressed files in both ZIP and CAB formats and displays both Zip files and cabinet files as folders that you can open and browse in Windows Explorer as you would any other folder. A Zip folder appears in Windows Explorer as a closed folder icon with a zipper across it, and a cabinet folder appears as a filing cabinet with an open drawer busy consuming a document, as shown here.

data2.cab   Storage.zip

You can create compressed folders in the Zip format from one or more files or folders as follows:

◆ To create a compressed folder containing one or more files or folders, right-click the file or folder in an Windows Explorer window, and then choose Send To ➤ Compressed (Zipped) Folder from the context menu. Windows creates the file, gives it a default name based on its contents, and then selects the name. Type a new name if needed, and then press Enter to apply it.

◆ To create a new compressed folder, right-click in empty space in an Windows Explorer window, and then choose New ➤ Compressed (Zipped) Folder from the context menu. Windows creates a new compressed folder named `New Compressed (zipped) Folder` (or `New Compressed (zipped) Folder.ZIP`, if you've displayed extensions) and selects the name so that you can enter a new name. Type the new name, and then press the Enter key (or click elsewhere in the window) to apply it.

Once you've created a compressed folder, you can add files to it by dragging them to the folder and dropping them in or on it.

Creating and Organizing Shortcuts

A *shortcut* is a pointer to a file or folder. (If you're used to the Mac, a shortcut is like an alias.) By placing shortcuts in convenient places, you can give yourself quick access to files and folders stored in remote locations. For example, you could create a shortcut on your Desktop to a WordPerfect document stored in the nethermost subfolder of a network drive. By double-clicking the shortcut from the comfort of your Desktop, you could open the document without browsing through the drives and folders to reach it.

You can create as many shortcuts as you want for any file or folder. You can even create a shortcut to a shortcut to make an item really easy to reach. Each shortcut is typically less than 1KB in size, so you don't need to worry about the amount of disk space they take up.

Shortcuts have been around for many versions of Windows, but Microsoft has been improving them along the way. In the old days, if you renamed or moved the target file or folder to which a shortcut referred, Windows would be unable to find the target file when you double-clicked the shortcut. Nowadays, Windows can almost always find the target file unless you move it to somewhere truly inaccessible or delete it. (When you rename or move a file, Windows doesn't immediately update any shortcuts that refer to the file to reflect the new name or new location. Instead, it updates a shortcut when you use it to access the file.)

You can tell a shortcut icon on the Desktop or in an Windows Explorer window by the small white box containing an upward-curling black arrow in its lower-left corner. Figure 5.25 shows a text file (on the left) and a renamed shortcut to it. When you let Windows name a shortcut, it creates a name consisting of the filename and – Shortcut, but you can change the name to anything you want by using standard Windows renaming techniques. (Renaming is discussed earlier in this chapter.)

It's always safe to delete a shortcut, because deleting a shortcut never deletes the file that it's associated with. And as you saw in Chapter 3, you can customize a shortcut so that it launches the associated program in Compatibility mode or in a window of a specified size.

FIGURE 5.25
A shortcut icon (on the right) bears an upward-curling black arrow in its lower-left corner but can have the same name and icon as the file it leads to.

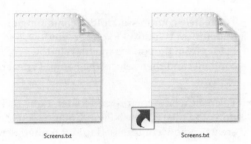

Screens.txt   Screens.txt

Creating a Shortcut

You can create a shortcut in several easy ways. The setup routines of most programs install shortcuts automatically for you, so you should already be equipped with shortcuts to your programs. Most of these shortcuts will be on the Start menu. Some programs place shortcuts on the Desktop or in the notification area, despite Microsoft's guidelines telling program designers not to do either. Better-designed programs are courteous enough to consult you before placing shortcuts like this. Other programs go right ahead and please themselves.

CREATING A SHORTCUT THE QUICK WAY

To create a shortcut the quick way, follow these steps:

1. Right-click the file on your Desktop or in an Windows Explorer window and drag it (holding down that right mouse button) to where you want the shortcut to be.

2. Release the mouse button, and then choose Create Shortcuts Here from the context menu. Windows creates a shortcut named with the name of the file and – Shortcut. For example, the shortcut for Industry.xlsx is named Industry.xlsx – Shortcut.

3. If you want to rename the shortcut, right-click it, and then choose Rename from the context menu. Type the new name in the resulting edit box, and then press the Enter key.

CREATING A SHORTCUT ON THE DESKTOP OR IN AN WINDOWS EXPLORER WINDOW

To create a shortcut on the Desktop or in an Windows Explorer window (the more formal way), follow these steps:

1. Right-click open space on the Desktop or in an Windows Explorer window and choose New ➤ Shortcut from the context menu. (Alternatively, choose File ➤ New ➤ Shortcut.) Windows displays the Create Shortcut Wizard (see Figure 5.26).

FIGURE 5.26
The Create Shortcut Wizard is the formal way of creating a shortcut to a file or folder.

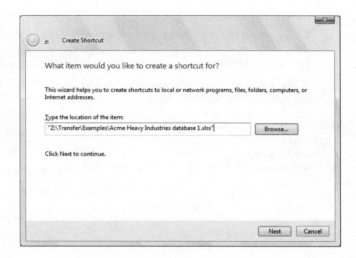

2. Enter the location of the file or folder to which you want to create the shortcut. Either type it in, or click the Browse button, use the resulting Browse for Files or Folders dialog box to navigate to and select the file or folder, and then click the OK button.

3. Click the Next button. The wizard displays the What Would You Like to Name the Shortcut? screen.

4. Type the name that you want the shortcut to have. This can be just about anything, so make it descriptive and memorable.

5. Click the Finish button. The wizard closes and creates the shortcut.

Setting Properties for a Shortcut

To set properties for a shortcut, right-click it, and then and choose Properties from the context menu. Windows displays the Properties dialog box. For a shortcut to a document, this dialog box contains four pages: a General page, a Shortcut page, a Security page, and a Details page. For a shortcut to a program, this dialog box contains a Compatibility page as well.

The General page is just like the one you saw earlier in this chapter, while the Shortcut page (of which Figure 5.27 shows an example) contains a number of items of interest.

Target text box This contains the path and filename of the target file (or folder). To open an Windows Explorer window showing the target in its folder, click the Open File Location button.

Start In text box This text box contains the path to the target file. You may need to change this setting occasionally, but not regularly.

Shortcut Key text box To set a shortcut key to run the shortcut, click in this text box and press the letter you want to use. By default, Windows creates a shortcut using the Ctrl key and the Alt key, so if you press **P**, it creates the shortcut Ctrl+Alt+P. You can override this default by pressing Ctrl+Shift or Alt+Shift as you enter the letter.

Run drop-down list As discussed in the section "Specifying the Size at Which a Program Runs" in Chapter 4, you can use this drop-down list to make the program (or the program associated with the file) run minimized, maximized, or in a "normal" window.

Comment text box In this text box, you can enter a comment associated with the shortcut.

Change Icon button To change the icon displayed for the shortcut, click this button and use the Change Icon dialog box to select an icon you like. As mentioned in Chapter 3, SHELL32.DLL and MORICONS.DLL (both in the Windows\System32 folder) contain a selection of icons.

When you've finished adjusting the shortcut, click the OK button. Windows closes the Properties dialog box and applies your changes.

FIGURE 5.27
The Shortcut page of the Properties dialog box for a shortcut

SETTING ADVANCED PROPERTIES FOR A SHORTCUT

You can set two advanced properties for shortcuts that lead to program files. To do so, click the Advanced button on the Shortcut page of the Properties dialog box for the shortcut. Windows displays the Advanced Properties dialog box (shown in Figure 5.28).

Run as Administrator check box Select this check box to have Windows run this program using an Administrator account. Running a program as Administrator is sometimes necessary when the program requires administrator-level permission but the user has only a Standard account. When you double-click the shortcut, you must authenticate yourself to User Account Control. (A standard user may need to have an administrator enter a password.)

Run in Separate Memory Space check box You can change this setting only for 16-bit programs, which you can choose *not* to run in a separate memory space. (Windows always runs all 32-bit programs in separate memory spaces to prevent them from corrupting each other.) By default, Windows runs all 16-bit programs in separate memory spaces, but you may sometimes need to run two or more 16-bit programs in the same memory space so that they can communicate directly with each other (for example, via DDE, Dynamic Data Exchange).

Click the OK button. Windows closes the Advanced Properties dialog box and applies the settings you chose.

FIGURE 5.28

The Advanced
Properties dialog
box for a shortcut
to a program lets
you specify whether
to run the program as
an administrator. If
the program is 16 bit,
you can also choose
not to run it in sepa-
rate memory space.

Customizing Windows Explorer

This section discusses the main ways in which to customize Windows Explorer: AutoPlay, customizing folders, customizing the toolbar, and choosing which columns Windows Explorer displays in
Details view.

Customizing and Turning Off AutoPlay

By default, Windows is set to use its AutoPlay feature, which tries to automatically run any CD or
DVD that you insert in your computer's optical drive and examine the contents of any removable
disk or memory card you attach to your computer.

What *run* means for a CD or DVD depends on the disc's contents and the action that the disc's
developer has specified in the disc's AUTORUN.INF initialization file, a hidden file stored at the root
of the disc's file system. If the initialization file doesn't contain specific instructions, or if there's no
initialization file, Windows may pop up a dialog box offering you a choice of possible actions to
take with the disc.

These are the usual actions for AutoPlay:

◆ For a music CD, AutoPlay activates the default player for files of the CD Audio Track
   type. Usually, this means that Windows Media Player (or whichever program has ousted
   Windows Media Player as the default player) starts playing the CD.

◆ For a software installation disc, AutoPlay usually activates the setup routine, unless
   Windows detects that you've installed the software already.

◆ For a game disc, AutoPlay usually starts playing the game.

◆ For a CD containing video files, AutoPlay may start playing a file.

◆ For a DVD containing a video, AutoPlay may start playing the video.

AutoPlay also manifests itself in other ways, such as the AutoPlay dialog box, which lets you
specify an action to take when you insert a disc that contains a specific type of file. Figure 5.29
shows an example of the AutoPlay dialog box.

FIGURE 5.29
The AutoPlay dialog box asks you which action to take for pictures.

SUPPRESSING AUTOPLAY TEMPORARILY

To suppress AutoPlay temporarily, hold down the left Shift key as you close the optical drive after inserting a disc. Release the Shift key when Windows has loaded the disc (for example, when you see the disc's name and contents appear in an Windows Explorer window).

Use the left Shift key because, by default, holding down the right Shift key for 8 seconds turns on the FilterKeys accessibility feature. (Alternatively, clear the Turn On Filter Keys When Right Shift Is Pressed for 8 Seconds check box in the Set Up Filter Keys window, which you can access from the Ease of Access Center in Control Panel.)

 Real World Scenario

BENEFITS OF SUPPRESSING AUTOPLAY WHEN LOADING A DISC

Some copyright protection schemes for audio discs use AutoPlay to install a special driver that prevents you from copying the audio from the disc to your computer. This driver is installed the first time you insert such a disc in your optical drive and is then used each time you load a disc that's protected in this way.

If you don't want your Windows configuration to be changed by this surreptitious installation of unapproved software, suppress AutoPlay by holding down the Shift key when you load audio discs.

CUSTOMIZING AUTOPLAY—AND TURNING IT OFF

Windows Vista lets you customize AutoPlay for a wide variety of media and devices. To customize AutoPlay, follow these steps:

1. Choose Start ➢ Control Panel. Windows displays a Control Panel window.

2. Click the Hardware and Sound link. Windows displays the Hardware and Sound window.

3. Click the AutoPlay link. Windows displays the AutoPlay window (see Figure 5.30).

4. If you want to turn off AutoPlay completely for all items, clear the Use AutoPlay for All Media and Devices check box. If you want to use AutoPlay, leave this check box selected.

5. If you leave AutoPlay on, open each drop-down list in the Media area in turn, and then choose an option in the list. Here are examples of what you can choose:

◆ For an Audio CD, you can choose Play Audio CD, Rip Music from CD, Open Folder to View Files, Take No Action, or Ask Me Every Time. The Ask Me Every Time option makes Windows displays the AutoPlay dialog box.

◆ For a DVD Movie, you can choose Play DVD Movie, Open Folder to View Files, Take No Action, or Ask Me Every Time.

◆ For a Blank CD, you can choose Burn an Audio CD, Burn Files to Disc, Take No Action, or Ask Me Every Time.

6. If any devices appear in the Devices section of the window, choose a setting for each device.

7. Click the Save button. Windows saves your choices and closes the AutoPlay window.

FIGURE 5.30
The AutoPlay window lets you choose what Windows should do when you insert CDs, DVDs, and other media or connect devices.

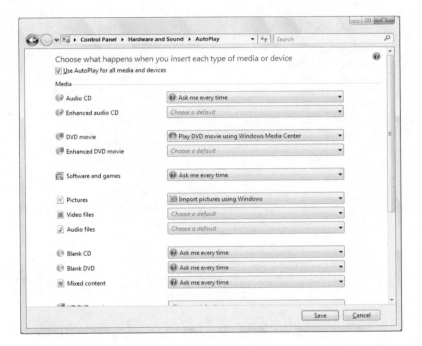

Customizing a Folder

You can customize a folder by designating a particular type of role for it, by applying a picture to it (for Thumbnails view), and by changing the icon displayed for it (for all views other than Thumbnails).

To customize a folder, take the following steps:

1. Right-click the folder, and then choose Properties from the context menu. Windows displays the Properties dialog box for the folder.

2. Click the Customize tab. Windows displays the Customize page (see Figure 5.31).

3. In the Use This Folder Type as a Template list box, you can select a template for the folder. Windows offers assorted templates for Documents, Pictures and Videos, Music Details, and Music Icons. If you'll be creating subfolders of this folder and putting the same type of content in them, select the Also Apply This Template to All Subfolders check box.

4. To specify the picture that Windows displays on the folder in Thumbnails view, click the Choose File button. Windows displays the Browse dialog box. Navigate to the picture you want to use, select it, and click the Open button. To reapply the default picture to the folder, click the Restore Default button.

5. To specify the icon that Windows displays for the folder in all views other than Thumbnails view, click the Change Icon button. Windows displays the Change Icon dialog box. Select an icon, and then click the OK button.

6. Click the OK button. Windows closes the Properties dialog box and applies your choices to the folder.

FIGURE 5.31
Use the Customize page of a folder's Properties dialog box to customize the folder.

Choosing Which Columns to Display in Windows Explorer Windows

You can customize Windows Explorer windows to display the columns you want in any given folder. For example, you might want to add the artist, album, track name, and bitrate to a folder containing MP3 files. Similarly, you might want to display the title and subject for office documents so that you have another means of identifying them apart from their names.

To choose which columns appear, follow these steps:

1. Right-click a column heading in the window. Windows displays a list of commonly used columns for the template currently applied to the folder.

2. If the column you want appears on the list, select its check box. Alternatively, clear the check box for any existing column you want to remove.

3. To add a column that's not listed, choose the More item from the list. Windows displays the Choose Details dialog box (see Figure 5.32).

4. In the list box, select the check boxes for the columns you want Windows Explorer to display. Clear the check boxes for any currently displayed columns that you want to hide.

5. Use the Move Up button and Move Down button to arrange the columns into the order in which you want them to appear from left to right.

6. To specify the width for a column, select the column, and then enter the width in the Width of Selected Column (in Pixels) text box. (Usually it's easier to resize a column manually when you have information displayed and can see how much space it needs.)

7. Click the OK button. Windows closes the Choose Details dialog box. Windows Explorer displays the columns you selected.

FIGURE 5.32
Use the Choose Details dialog box to select the columns you want to have in an Windows Explorer window.

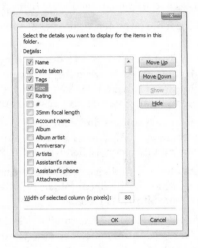

The Bottom Line

Understand what files and folders are and what you can name them   A *file* is a named object containing information that's stored on a disk. A *folder* is a file that can contain other files or folders. Folders enable you to organize your files into categories. A file's name, including the full *path* to it through the drive and folders that contain it, can be up to 255 characters long. Filenames can include letters, numbers, spaces, underscores, commas, periods, semicolons, and single quotation marks.

Launch Windows Explorer and navigate to the files you need   Windows Explorer runs all the time you're using Windows, because it manages the Windows desktop. To work in an Windows Explorer window, click the Start button, and then click one of the items in the upper-right part of the Start menu. For example, choose Documents to open your Documents folder, or Pictures to open your Pictures folder. You can navigate to folders by clicking links in the Favorite Links area of the Windows Explorer window or by double-clicking folders in the document area.

Choose folder options to control how Windows Explorer behaves   To control how Windows Explorer behaves, choose Organize ➤ Folder and Search Options, and then choose options on the View page of the Folder Options dialog box. For example, you can choose always to display menus, which is useful if you've come to Windows Vista from a version of Windows in which Windows Explorer always displays menus.

Copy and move files and folders   You can copy files and folders by using drag-and-drop techniques or by using menu commands. Drag-and-drop can be confusing because Windows interprets the action differently depending on whether the source and destination folders are on the same drive or different drives. One handy technique is right-drag-and-drop, which always lets you choose whether to copy the items or move them.

Delete and rename files and folders   When you delete files and folders, Windows places them in the Recycle Bin rather than deleting them outright. You can open the Recycle Bin and restore files and folders if you find you need them again. You can also configure Windows to delete files and folders immediately instead of putting them in the Recycle Bin if you prefer.

To rename a file or folder, right-click it, choose Rename, type the new name, and then press Enter.

Search to find the files and folders you need   To find the files (which are in effect special folders), you can search from the Start menu, from any Windows Explorer window open to a folder you want to search, or by opening a Search Results window (choose Start ➤ Search). Simple search can give effective results, but Advanced Search lets you specify exact criteria.

Use compressed folders and shortcuts   Windows can read both Zip files and cabinet files, but lets you create only Zip files. To create a Zip file, right-click the item or items you want the file to contain, and then choose Send To ➤ Compressed (Zipped) Folder.

To access files and folders easily, you can create as many shortcuts as you need. To create a shortcut, right-click the file or folder, right-drag to where you want the shortcut to be, and then choose Create Shortcuts Here.

Configure AutoPlay and Customize Windows Explorer's Columns   To configure AutoPlay, choose Start ➤ Control Panel, click the Hardware and Sound link, and then click the AutoPlay link. The AutoPlay window lets you either turn off AutoPlay completely or choose a default AutoPlay action for each media type (for example, audio CDs or blank DVDs).

To choose which columns appear in an Windows Explorer window, right-click any column heading. You can then either select or clear check boxes for the short list of frequently used columns, or click More, and then use the Choose Details dialog box to select columns and customize them.

Chapter 6

Making the Most of the Bundled Programs

- ◆ Creating simple word-processing documents with WordPad
- ◆ Creating text files with Notepad
- ◆ Inserting special characters with Character Map
- ◆ Manipulating graphics with Paint
- ◆ Making the most of Calculator
- ◆ Working from the command line with Command Prompt

Windows Vista includes a wide range of programs to help you with your work and play. These programs come in all shapes and sizes, from monsters such as Windows Mail (see Chapter 17) and Windows Media Player (see Chapter 22) to much smaller programs generally called "applets" (little applications) or "accessories."

This chapter shows you how to use the following accessories: WordPad, Notepad, Character Map, Paint, Calculator, and Command Prompt. You'll find coverage of other accessories in chapters that cover related topics. For example, Chapter 22 (the Windows Media Player chapter) also covers Sound Recorder, an applet for recording audio.

These programs have relatively limited functionality: They're intended to take care of some basic tasks, but not to discourage you from buying fuller programs from either Microsoft or its competitors. Because they're limited, most of these programs are relatively small and easy to use. This chapter discusses only the most important features of the programs, leaving you to work out the easy stuff on your own.

YOUR COMPUTER MAY INCLUDE DIFFERENT PROGRAMS

Where the operating system stops and where other programs begin has long been a source of contention between Microsoft, the U.S. Department of Justice, and (more recently) the European Commission. For example, the European Commission forced Microsoft to release a version of Windows XP that didn't include Windows Media Player (this was for competitive reasons—so that computer manufacturers could include other companies' media players).

If your copy of Windows Vista doesn't include some or all of the programs discussed in this chapter or other chapters, the reason may be that the computer's manufacturer has decided to include other programs that offer similar functionality. Consult your computer's documentation for details, or hunt through the Start menu to see what you can uncover.

WordPad

WordPad (see Figure 6.1) is a lightweight word-processing program. It provides rudimentary features including font formatting, bulleted lists, paragraph alignment, margin placement, and support for different sizes of paper. It also lets you insert objects such as graphics and parts of other documents, so in a pinch you can create attractive documents with it. WordPad's Print Preview feature (File ➤ Print Preview) lets you make sure your documents look okay before you commit them to paper. But WordPad has no advanced features; for example, it doesn't offer style formatting, tables, or macros. It also lacks a spelling checker or grammar checker, so you'll need to proof and check your documents visually.

FIGURE 6.1

WordPad is good for creating and editing documents that don't need styles or other complex formatting.

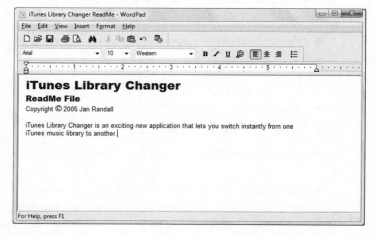

Because of these limitations, if you have Microsoft Word, Corel WordPerfect, Sun StarOffice, OpenOffice.org's OpenOffice, or another full-fledged word processor, you'll probably have little use for WordPad. But if you don't have another word processor, and if you need to create only simple documents, you may find WordPad useful.

WordPad can open documents in Rich Text format (RTF) and text formats. If you have font-formatted documents created in another word processing program, RTF may prove the best format for getting them into WordPad. This is because RTF supports a wide range of formatting, and most word processors can create and read RTF files.

Each instance of WordPad can have only one document open at once, but you can run multiple instances of WordPad if you need to have two or more documents open at the same time. Simply choose Start ➤ All Programs ➤ Accessories ➤ WordPad again to open a second or subsequent instance of WordPad. You can also open a new instance of WordPad by right-clicking the document you want to open in an Explorer window (or on the Desktop) and choosing Open With ➤ WordPad from the shortcut menu. If you already have an Explorer window open, this option tends to be quicker and more convenient than opening WordPad from the Start menu.

Most of WordPad's commands are easily found on its six short menus and two toolbars. For example, click the Open button or choose File ➤ Open to open a document, and click the Save button or choose File ➤ Save to save a document. The following are also worth mentioning:

◆ If you're using WordPad simply to create text, you may want to maximize your workspace by stripping down the interface to the bone. The View menu lets you hide the Toolbar, the Format bar, the ruler, and the status bar, which gives you a good amount more space.

◆ WordPad doesn't have a command for inserting symbols. Instead, run Character Map (see "Character Map," later in this chapter), copy the character you need, and paste it into your WordPad document.

◆ As well as using the Tabs dialog box (Format ➤ Tabs) to set and clear tabs, you can set and clear tabs for the currently selected paragraph or paragraphs by working in the ruler. Click in the ruler to place a tab where you click. Drag an existing tab to move it to a different location. Or drag an existing tab downward into the document area to get rid of it.

◆ If you need to create Windows documentation, you can copy a full screen by pressing Print Screen or capture the active window by pressing Alt+Print Screen. Windows places the resulting graphic on the Clipboard. You can then paste the graphic into a WordPad document. Alternatively, you can paste the graphic into a Paint picture, and then save it as a file for use later.

The most complex part of WordPad is the Options dialog box (View ➤ Options), which has four pages: Options, Text, Rich Text, and Embedded:

◆ The Options page of the Options dialog box (shown at the top of Figure 6.2) lets you choose measurement units: Inches, Centimeters, Points, or Picas. (Points and picas are typesetting measurements. A *point* is $1/72$ inch, and a *pica* is $1/6$ inch, so there are 12 points to the pica.) It also contains the Automatic Word Selection check box, which controls whether WordPad selects the whole of each second and subsequent word when you click and drag to select from one word to the next. If Automatic Word Selection is turned off, WordPad lets you select character by character. (If you've used Word, you're probably familiar with this behavior.)

◆ The Text, Rich Text, and Embedded pages contain options for the different document types that WordPad can handle. For each, you can choose word-wrap settings (No Wrap, Wrap to Window, or Wrap to Ruler) and whether you want to display the toolbar, the Format bar, the ruler, and the status bar. The lower part of Figure 6.2 shows the Rich Text page.

FIGURE 6.2
If you use WordPad more than a little, choose suitable options for your needs. You can set different options for the different types of files: Text, Rich Text (shown here), and Embedded.

Notepad

Notepad (see Figure 6.3) is a *text editor*, a program designed for working with text files. A *text file* is a file that contains only text (characters); it has no formatting and no graphical objects. You may also hear text files described as ASCII files. *ASCII* is the acronym for American Standard Code for Information Interchange.

Rather than force you to use a monospaced font such as Courier, Notepad lets you select a font for the display of text on-screen (choose Format ≻ Font). It has a word-wrap option (choose Format ≻ Word Wrap) so that lines of text don't reach past the border of the window to the horizon on your right. And you can insert the time and date in a Notepad file by choosing Edit ≻ Time/Date or pressing the F5 key.

AVOIDING NOTEPAD'S DEFAULT TXT EXTENSION

Notepad automatically adds the TXT extension to files you save. To save a file under a different extension, enter the filename and extension in double quotation marks in the File Name text box in the Save As dialog box—for example, "**boot.ini**".

Generally speaking, you shouldn't spend any more time using Notepad than you need to, because Notepad is a very limited program. But it's good for several tasks:

◆ Notepad is small and simple, so you can keep it running without worrying about it slowing your computer down. Because Notepad takes up little memory, you can run multiple instances without affecting your computer's performance appreciably. This can be useful for taking a variety of notes. Notepad lets you open only a single file at a time, but by opening multiple instances of Notepad, you can open as many files as you need.

◆ Notepad is good for editing Windows programs' configuration files. But if you're editing any of the standard Windows configuration files that remain in Windows Vista for compatibility with older programs (for example, WIN.INI), use the System Configuration Editor instead. The System Configuration Editor is essentially Notepad after a couple of doses of steroids and customizations for editing system files. (To run the System Configuration Editor, choose Start ≻ Accessories ≻ Run or press Windows Key+R, enter **sysedit** in the Open text box in the Run dialog box, and click the OK button.)

FIGURE 6.3
Notepad is a text editor that you can use for creating text-only files and reading text files such as readme files.

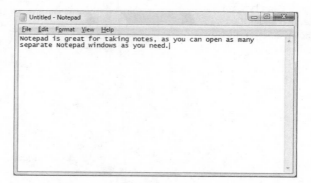

◆ By default, Notepad prints documents with a header that consists of the file name and a footer that consists of "Page" and the page number. This default header and footer can help you tell one document from another, but you'll sometimes want to either omit the header or footer or use text of your own. To do so, choose File ➢ Page Setup and change the text in the Header text box and the Footer text box. Table 6.1 lists the codes you can use in these text boxes.

◆ Apart from working with text files that use regular text-file formats (such as those with the TXT file extension), Notepad is good for creating and editing other text-only files. For example, it's good for editing playlists for programs such as MP3 players. These are text files, though they use extensions such as M3U and PLS to give them file-type functionality. If you create such a file using Notepad, remember to use double quotation marks around the filename when saving it.

◆ You can use Notepad to open documents other than text files. (Select the All Files item in the Files of Type drop-down list in the Open dialog box.) For example, if Word for Windows crashes, you may end up with a corrupted file that Word itself cannot open. By opening up the file in Notepad, you may be able to rescue part of the text. You'll see a lot of nonalphanumeric characters that represent things like Word formatting (for example, styles), but you'll also find readable text. If the document has been saved using Word's Fast Save feature, you'll even find deleted parts of the document still in the file—which can be intriguing or embarrassing, depending on whether you wrote the document.

TABLE 6.1:   Header and Footer Codes in Notepad

CODE	MEANING
&f	Insert the file name
&p	Insert the page number
&d	Insert the date
&t	Insert the time
&l	Align the header or footer left
&c	Center the header or footer
&r	Align the header or footer right
&&	Insert an ampersand (&)

Character Map

Character Map is a small utility that lets you insert characters and symbols that don't appear on your keyboard in your documents. Figure 6.4 shows Character Map in its Standard view with the Arial font displayed.

FIGURE 6.4

Character Map lets you select any character in any font installed on your computer. For example, you can use it to insert symbols such as copyright characters in WordPad files.

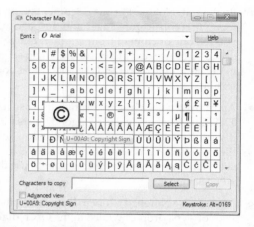

Windows Vista hides Character Map on the System Tools menu (Start ➤ All Programs ➤ Accessories ➤ System Tools ➤ Character Map). If you don't find it there but think it's installed on your computer, choose Start ➤ All Programs ➤ Accessories ➤ Run (or press Windows Key+R) to display the Run dialog box, enter **charmap** in the Open text box, and click the Open button.

Inserting a Character

To insert a character with Character Map, take the following steps:

1. Select the font in the Font drop-down list.

2. Scroll the list box until the character is visible:

   ◆ To display a magnified view of a character, click it. Alternatively, use the arrow keys (↑, ↓, ← and →) to select it, and then press the spacebar.

   ◆ Once you've displayed a magnified view, you can use the arrow keys to move the magnifier around the grid of characters.

   ◆ To remove the magnified view, click the magnified character or press the spacebar.

3. Select the character and click the Select button. Character Map copies it into the Characters to Copy text box.

4. Select other characters as necessary, then click the Copy button to copy the character or characters to the Clipboard.

5. Activate the program and paste the characters into it.

GRAPHICAL CHARACTERS MAY CHANGE IN TEXT-BASED PROGRAMS

Some text-based programs cannot accept characters, so they convert them to the nearest character they support. For example, if you paste a Wingdings telephone character into Notepad, Notepad converts it to a mutated parenthesis. If you paste the same telephone character into WordPad, WordPad displays it correctly. Similarly, some e-mail programs strip incoming messages down to text, so it's a waste of time to send messages that contain unusual characters to people who use such programs.

Inserting a Character in Advanced View

Character Map's Standard view is fine for inserting many weird and wonderful characters in your documents. But if you want to work with a particular character set, you need to use the Advanced view. (Character sets are discussed in the next sidebar.) Select the Advanced View check box to display Character Map in Advanced view (shown in Figure 6.5).

As you can see in the figure, Character Map in Advanced view has several extra controls:

Character Set drop-down list   Use this drop-down list to select the character set you want to work with. The default selection is Unicode.

Group By drop-down list   When necessary, choose a grouping for the character set. Depending on the character sets installed on your computer, you'll see options such as All, Ideographs by Radicals, Japanese Kanji by Hiragana, Japanese Kanji by Radical, Japanese Shift-JIS Subrange, and Unicode Subrange.

Go to Unicode text box   Use this text box to display the Unicode character associated with a character code. Type the code into this text box. When you type the fourth character of the code, Character Map displays the associated Unicode character.

Search For text box and Search button   Use this text box and button to search for a character by its description. For example, to find the inverted question mark character (¿), enter text such as **question inverted** or **inverted question** and click the Search button. Character Map displays all characters that match the criteria.

EXPERT KNOWLEDGE: ASCII, UNICODE, AND CODE PAGES

ASCII, Unicode, and code pages are all ways of mapping the binary codes that computers use to store characters to (a) the characters on whichever keyboard you happen to be using and (b) what you see on-screen.

ASCII and Unicode are both standard character-encoding schemes for text-based data. If you have information that can be represented in characters (such as this paragraph, for example), you can encode it in ASCII or in Unicode so that a computer can store it.

In ASCII, each character is represented by one byte. There are two forms of ASCII: *Standard ASCII* uses a 7-bit binary number combination to represent each character, which gives enough combinations for 128 characters. *Extended ASCII*, which is also known as *high ASCII*, uses an 8-bit number combination for each character, which gives enough combinations for 256 characters.

Given that the English alphabet uses 26 uppercase letters, 26 lowercase letters, 10 numbers, some punctuation (comma, period, parentheses, and so on), and control characters, standard ASCII's capacity for 128 characters starts to look paltry. Extended ASCII doubles the ante and adds some foreign characters (for example, accented characters), graphic symbols, and symbol characters to standard ASCII's set.

Extended ASCII works pretty well provided you're satisfied with 256 characters. But even 256 characters are far too few if you want anything beyond the main European languages.

The solution to the limitations of ASCII is Unicode. In Unicode, each character is represented by two bytes (16 bits), which gives 65,536 character combinations (256 × 256)—enough to cover most of the characters in the world's many languages. As of the year 2000, about 39,000 of those 65,536 combinations had been assigned, with Chinese alone accounting for about 21,000 of them. (Japanese, with its borrowed and mutated kanji, is another of the greedier languages for Unicode combinations.)

When do you have to worry about ASCII and Unicode? Windows Vista is pretty smart about Unicode, so usually you don't have to worry about whether you're using Unicode or ASCII, because Windows uses Unicode almost exclusively.

For programs that don't support Unicode, you can use code pages to enable the programs to communicate effectively with the user. A *code page* is a table that maps a program's character codes (which are binary) to the keys on the keyboard, the characters on the display, or (preferably) both. Previous versions of Windows used code pages.

If you need to use a program that can't handle Unicode, assign a code page for it as follows:

1. Choose Start ➢ Control Panel. Windows displays Control Panel.

2. In the Clock, Language, and Region category, click the Change Keyboards or Other Input Method link. If you're using Classic view, double-click the Regional and Language icon. Windows displays the Regional and Language Options dialog box.

3. Click the Administrative tab. Windows displays the Administrative page.

4. Click the Change Settings button. Windows displays the Regional and Language Settings dialog box.

5. In the Select a Language for Non-Unicode Programs drop-down list, select the language to use.

6. Click the OK button to close the Regional and Language Settings dialog box.

7. If you want to copy these settings you're applying to the system accounts or the default user account (which controls any new user accounts that you or other Computer Administrator users create on this computer), click the Reserved Account Settings button. Windows displays another Regional and Language Settings dialog box.

8. Select the Default User Account check box if you want to apply the changes to the default user account.

9. Select the System Accounts check box if you want to apply the changes to the system accounts.

10. Click the OK button to close the Regional and Language Settings dialog box.

11. Click the OK button to close the Regional and Language Options dialog box.

Here's an example of inserting a Japanese kanji using Advanced view:

1. In the Character Set drop-down list, select the Windows: Japanese item.

2. In the Group By drop-down list, select the grouping you want. In the example, this is Japanese Kanji by Hiragana. Character Map opens a window displaying the kanji.

3. In the Japanese Kanji by Hiragana window, select the hiragana (phonetic character) that represents the sound of the kanji character. The main Character Map window (shown in Figure 6.6 with the Japanese Kanji by Hiragana window) displays a scrolling list of kanji that can be pronounced with that sound.

4. Select and copy the character as usual, then paste it into the document.

If you need to enter a particular character frequently in your documents and don't want to have to access Character Map each time, select the character in Character Map and memorize the Alt code displayed in the status bar. (Only some characters have these Alt codes.) To enter the character at the insertion point in a document, make sure that Num Lock is on, then hold down the Alt key and type the code for the character.

EXPERT KNOWLEDGE: USING PRIVATE CHARACTER EDITOR TO CREATE YOUR OWN CHARACTERS

Windows includes a hidden applet called Private Character Editor that you can use for creating your own characters and logos. To run Private Character Editor, choose Start ➤ Run or press Windows Key+R. Windows displays the Run dialog box. Enter **eudcedit** in the Open text box and click the OK button.

FIGURE 6.5
Select the Advanced View check box to work with a particular character set in Character Map.

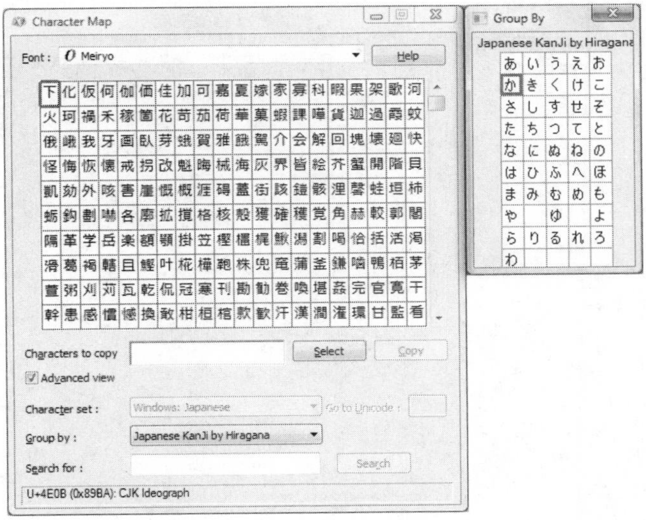

FIGURE 6.6
Using Character Map's Advanced view to select Japanese kanji

Paint

Paint (Start ➤ All Programs ➤ Accessories ➤ Paint) is a basic illustration program that's been included with almost all known desktop versions of Windows. Windows Vista's version of Paint (see Figure 6.7) lets you create bitmap files (BMP, DIB), GIF files, JPEG files (JPG and JPEG), Portable Network Graphic files (PNG), and TIFF files (TIF)—enough to make it useful for basic illustration needs, and significantly better than the versions of Paint in most versions of Windows 9*x*, which could work only with bitmaps.

If you're into creating drawings or paintings on the computer, you'll find that Paint's limitations present more challenges than its capabilities do. Paint's Image menu provides tools for flipping and rotating images, stretching and skewing images, changing their attributes (for example, changing a color file to black and white), and inverting colors—but that's about it. If you want to do serious image-editing work, consider a heavy-duty image-editing program such as Paint Shop Pro or Adobe Photoshop. If you want to do serious illustration work, investigate programs such as Adobe Illustrator, Procreate Painter, or CorelDRAW.

If you're *not* into creating drawings or paintings on the computer, you'll probably find Paint quite useful for some basic graphical tasks such as the following:

Creating background images for your Desktop   If you want to use a digital photo or a scan as a background image for your Desktop, you may need to rotate it from a portrait orientation to a landscape orientation or crop it down to size.

Capturing images directly from a web camera   You can capture images directly from a web camera by using the File ➤ From Scanner or Camera command. Chapter 23 discusses how to work with pictures.

FIGURE 6.7
Paint is useful for capturing images from a scanner or camera, cleaning up images, and saving screen captures.

Cleaning up scanned images   Images you scan can easily pick up dots from specks of dirt on the scanner or from damage to the picture. You can use Paint to edit pictures and remove small defects such as these.

Capturing screens   If you're preparing documentation on how to use software, you may want to capture the screen or a window. To capture the whole screen to the Clipboard, press the Print-Screen (PrtScn) key. To capture only the active window to the Clipboard, press Alt+PrintScreen. (These keystrokes are from Windows itself rather than from Paint, so you don't need to have Paint running while you issue them.) Then activate Paint and choose Edit ➤ Paste to paste in the screen or window, where you can work with it as you would any other graphic.

Calculator

Though useful, Calculator (Start ➤ All Programs ➤ Accessories ➤ Calculator) seems such a basic program that it barely deserves mention. But there are several things you should know about it:

◆ Calculator displays itself by default in its Standard view, but it also has a Scientific view that's useful if you need to work in hexadecimal, binary, or octal; calculate degrees or radians; or perform similar tasks. To switch Calculator to Scientific view, choose View ➤ Scientific. (To switch Calculator back to Standard view, choose View ➤ Standard.) Figure 6.8 shows Calculator in Scientific view calculating hex. For hex, octal, and binary, you can choose from four display sizes: Byte (8-bit representation), Word (16-bit representation), Dword (32-bit representation), and Qword (64-bit representation).

◆ When you switch Calculator from Standard view to Scientific view, or switch it back, it wipes the display. To take the current number from one view to the other view, use the MS button to store it, switch view, and then use the MR button to retrieve it. Binary, octal, or hex numbers get converted to decimal when you move them to Standard view by using this technique.

◆ You can operate Calculator entirely from the keyboard if you want to. Choose Help ➤ Help Topics to open the Help file, then investigate the "Using Keyboard Equivalents of Calculator Functions" topic.

◆ You can use key sequences as functions. For example, the sequence :p performs the equivalent of clicking the M+ key. Check the "Using Key Sequences as Functions" topic in the Help file for more information.

FIGURE 6.8
Calculator offers a
Scientific view in
addition to its
Standard view.

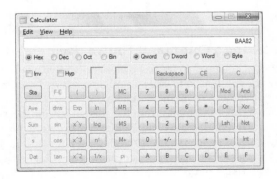

◆ If you're working with long numbers, you may want to choose View ≻ Digit Grouping to have Calculator group the digits into threes separated by commas. For example, with digit grouping, 44444444444 appears as 44,444,444,444, making it easier to read.

◆ Press Esc to clear the Calculator.

Command Prompt

Command Prompt (Start ≻ All Programs ≻ Accessories ≻ Command Prompt) gives you a command prompt window that you can use to run character-mode (text-only) programs or to issue commands. To run a program, you type its name (and its path, if needed) at the prompt, and then press the Enter key.

Command Prompt is especially useful for command-line utilities such as ping and tracert, which you use for checking network connectivity. Figure 6.9 shows ping running in a Command Prompt window.

If you've been using computers for a few years, you may remember DOS, the text-only operating system on which early versions of Windows (for example, Windows 3.1) ran. The Command Prompt window looks like DOS, but in fact it's not DOS. Windows Vista doesn't include DOS; instead, it includes a Virtual DOS Machine (VDM). A VDM runs within Windows and synthesizes a computer running DOS so that Windows can run programs that require DOS. You can customize the way a Command Prompt window looks or even make it run full screen (which gives it a very DOS-like look).

For most purposes, there's no advantage in using Command Prompt to issue commands instead of using the Run dialog box (choose Start ≻ All Programs ≻ Accessories ≻ Run, or press Windows Key+R) except that in Command Prompt you can see the history of the commands you've issued in this session.

FIGURE 6.9

Running ping in a Command Prompt window

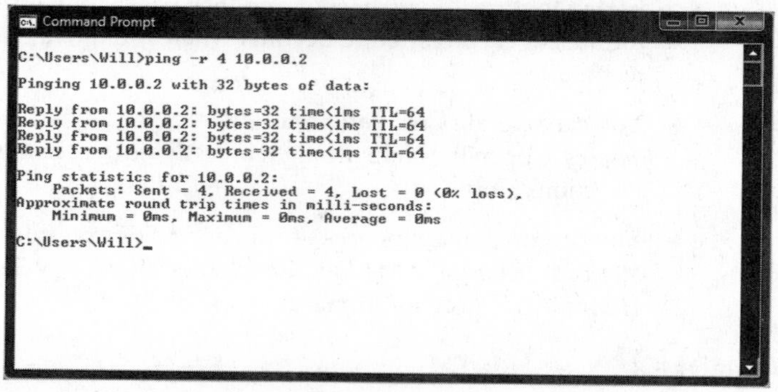

Recalling a Command You've Used

Often, you'll need to reuse a command you've used earlier in the current Command Prompt window, or you'll need to issue a similar command. Command Prompt stores your recent commands so that you can recall them quickly.

To recall a command from the current session, press the ↑ key. The first press displays the previous command, the second the command before that, and so on. If you go too far back in the list, press the ↓ key to go back through the list toward the later commands.

Once you've reached the command you want to use, you can edit it or add to it, or simply press the Enter key to run it.

Selecting, Copying, and Pasting in Command Prompt

Selecting, copying, and pasting in Command Prompt windows is much clumsier than in graphical windows, but it works well enough once you know how. To use the mouse to select text in Command Prompt, you need to turn on QuickEdit mode. You can turn it on either temporarily or permanently:

Turn on QuickEdit temporarily   Click the control-menu box at the left end of the title bar and choose Edit ➢ Mark.

Turn on QuickEdit permanently   Select the QuickEdit Mode check box on the Options page of the Console Windows Properties dialog box or the Command Prompt Properties dialog box.

Once you've turned on QuickEdit, click to place an insertion point, or drag to select a block of text.

To copy, right-click after making a selection. (Alternatively, press Enter, or choose Edit ➢ Copy from the control menu.) Issuing a Copy command in any of these ways collapses the selection, so that it looks as though the Copy operation has failed, but in fact Windows has copied the selection to the Clipboard, from which you can paste it into another program or back into the Command Prompt window.

You can also copy information from another program and paste it into Command Prompt by placing the insertion point, then choosing Edit ➢ Paste from the control menu.

Customizing Command Prompt

By default, Command Prompt uses a white system font on a black background, but you can change the look by using the Properties dialog box.

CUSTOMIZING THE CURRENT COMMAND PROMPT WINDOW

To customize the current Command Prompt window, click the control-menu box at the left end of the window's menu bar and choose Properties. Command Prompt displays the Properties dialog box.

TROUBLESHOOTING: COMMAND PROMPT ERRORS INVOLVING SPECIAL CHARACTERS

If Command Prompt gives you the error "<name> is not recognized as an internal or external command, operable program or batch file" when you try to run a program, or the error "The system cannot find the path specified" when you try to create, delete, or change a directory, chances are that the program or directory name includes a special character such as an ampersand (&), a space, parentheses (( )), a caret (^), a semicolon (;), a comma (,), or a vertical bar (|). For example, if you have a folder named Bits&Bobs and issue the command **cd bits&bobs** to change directory to it, Command Prompt will tell you that "The system cannot find the path specified" and that "'bobs' is not recognized as an internal or external command, operable program or batch file"—which is true, but not helpful.

To get around this problem, either put double quotation marks around the name of the item that contains the special character (in the example, cd "bits&bobs"), or put a caret immediately before the special character to notify Command Prompt that it's there (for example, cd bits^&bobs).

Options Page

The Options page of the Command Prompt Properties dialog box (shown on the left in Figure 6.10) contains three group boxes of options:

Cursor Size group box   Choose the Small option button, the Medium option button, or the Large option button to specify which cursor size to use. The Small cursor (the default) looks like a flashing underline; the Medium cursor looks like a flashing block half the character height; and the Large cursor looks like a flashing block the full character height.

Command History group box   In the Buffer Size text box, you can adjust the number of commands that Command Prompt stores in its buffer. (Storing more commands needs a little more memory, but not enough to worry about.) In the Number of Buffers text box, you can adjust the number of processes allowed to have distinct history buffers. Select the Discard Old Duplicates check box if you want the buffered list to omit repeated commands. Omitting them reduces the list and can make it more manageable.

Edit Options group box   Select the QuickEdit Mode check box if you want to be able to use the mouse for cutting and pasting in Command Prompt. Leave the Insert Mode check box selected (as it is by default) if you like the standard way of inserting text at the cursor, moving along any characters to the right of the cursor instead of typing over them. If you prefer typeover, clear the Insert Mode check box.

Font Page

On the Font page of the Command Prompt Properties dialog box, select the font and font size you want to use for the Command Prompt window.

Layout Page

On the Layout page of the Command Prompt Properties dialog box (shown on the right in Figure 6.10), specify how the Command Prompt window should look, where it should appear on the screen, and how many commands it should retain:

Screen Buffer Size group box   In the Width text box, specify the number of characters that you want each line in the buffer to contain. (Note that this is the buffer, not the window.) In the Height text box, specify the number of lines of data that you want to store.

Window Size group box   In the Width text box, specify the number of characters for the width of the window. Usually it's best to set this to the same value as the width of the screen buffer. (You can set it to a smaller value and have the window display scroll bars, but you can't set it to a larger value.) In the Height text box, specify the number of lines for the height of the window.

Window Position group box   Use the Left text box and the Top text box to specify the position of the left side and the top of the window. Alternatively, select the Let System Position Window check box if you want to allow Windows to decide where to put the window.

Colors Page

On the Colors page of the Command Prompt Properties dialog box, you can choose colors for the screen text, the screen background, the pop-up text, and the pop-up background. Use the preview boxes to get an idea of the effect you're creating.

Click the OK button to close the Command Prompt Properties dialog box and apply the changes you've made.

FIGURE 6.10
On the Options page (left) of the Command Prompt Properties dialog box, specify cursor size, command history, and editing options. On the Layout page (right), specify how you want the Command Prompt window to appear.

The Bottom Line

Creating simple word-processing documents with WordPad   WordPad is a lightweight word-processing program that supports font formatting, bulleted lists, paragraph alignment, margin placement, and inserted objects, but not styles or spell checking. WordPad is good for creating simple word- processing documents, but if you need to create complex documents, you'll probably need a dedicated word-processing application, such as Microsoft Word.

Creating text files with Notepad   Notepad is a text editor that you can use to edit text files or system files. You can run multiple instances of Notepad at the same time, so it's great for taking notes. But Notepad is text-only, so you can't apply formatting or insert objects (such as pictures).

Inserting special characters with Character Map   Character Map (choose Start ➢ All Programs ➢ Accessories ➢ System Tools ➢ Character Map) lets you insert into documents characters and symbols that don't appear on your keyboard.

Manipulating graphics with Paint   Paint is a basic illustration program that lets you create bitmap files (BMP, DIB), GIF files, JPEG files (JPG and JPEG), Portable Network Graphic files (PNG), and TIFF files (TIF). You can use Paint to create background images for your desktop, capture images from a webcam, clean up scanned images, or save screens or windows captured using Print Screen or Alt+Print Screen.

Making the most of Calculator   Calculator is an essential utility for performing both basic and scientific calculations. Choose View ➢ Scientific to switch Calculator to Scientific mode, in which you can work in hexadecimal, binary, and octal instead of decimal.

Working from the command line with Command Prompt   If you need to run character-mode programs or issue text commands, choose Start ➢ All Programs ➢ Accessories ➢ Command Prompt, and then work in the Command Prompt window. You can recall a command from the current session by pressing the ↑ key one or more times. You can customize the Command Prompt window by clicking the control-menu box at the left end of the window's menu bar, choosing Properties, and then working in the Properties dialog box.

Chapter 7

Finding Help to Solve Your Windows Problems

◆ Using Help and Support to find the help information you need

◆ Finding help on the Internet and Web

This chapter shows you how to find the help you need to use Windows Vista most effectively. Windows Vista includes a wide range of help resources, both online and off, that you can access through the built-in Windows Help and Support program. This chapter describes how to use Help and Support and the various areas it offers, including access to the Knowledge Base on Microsoft Support Services. It also mentions other resources that you may need to turn to when you run into less tractable problems.

You may also want to use Windows' Remote Assistance feature to get help. Chapter 21 explains how to use Remote Assistance both to receive help from others and to provide help to others.

Using Help and Support

Windows Vista's Help and Support program is the latest in Microsoft's efforts to provide computer-based help resources powerful enough to silence the ringing of the phones on its costly support lines. Help and Support lets you use a single window to search for help both on your computer and on the Internet. Better yet, many hardware manufacturers are now providing product-support information that's accessible through Help and Support.

HELP AND SUPPORT IS MUCH DIFFERENT THAN WINDOWS XP'S HELP AND SUPPORT CENTER

If you've used Help and Support Center in Windows XP, you'll notice a huge difference in Windows Vista. Where Windows XP's Help and Support Center had a busy window loaded with options (too many for most people, perhaps), Windows Vista's Help and Support keeps its interface as simple as possible. But the help information is still there, and you can access it in several ways.

One disappointment in Help and Support is that you can open only a single window at a time. By contrast, Help and Support Center in Windows XP let you open two or more windows. You could then pursue a different line of inquiry in each window, which gave you a better chance of finding useful information without running into a dead end and having to retrace your steps using the Back button.

Starting Help and Support

Choose Start ➤ Help and Support to open Help and Support at the home page. You should see something like Figure 7.1, except that it may contain some updated information. Your hardware manufacturer may also have customized Help and Support by adding content to it or by adapting its interface. For example, if you have a Dell PC, you may see some Dell support resources; if you have a Lenovo PC, you may see resources for accessing Lenovo support; and if you have an HP PC, you may see resources for shifting your troubles onto HP.

As you can see in Figure 7.1, the Help and Support window has a toolbar (at the top, starting with the Back button) for primary navigation rather than a menu bar. This toolbar is called the *navigation bar*. Below the navigation bar appears the Search bar.

Configuring Help and Support

Before you start plowing through help in Help and Support, you may need to change the text to a comfortable size, choose whether to use online help or offline help, and choose Help settings.

FIGURE 7.1
The home page in Help and Support provides links to the many different areas of Help and Support.

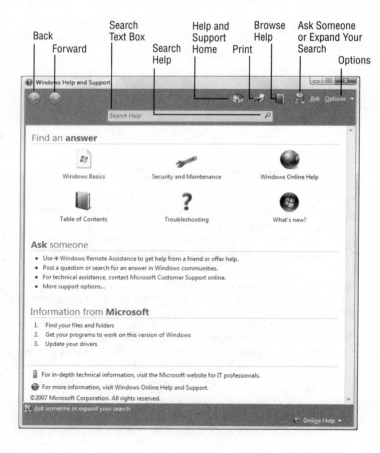

CHANGING THE TEXT SIZE

If you find the text size Help and Support is using too small or too large, click the Options button in the upper-right corner and choose a different size (Largest, Larger, Medium, Smaller, or Smallest) from the Text Size menu, as shown here.

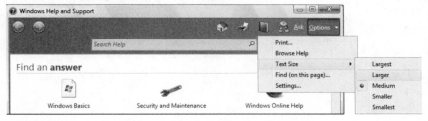

CHOOSING WHETHER TO USE ONLINE HELP

Help and Support lets you choose whether to use offline help or online help. If you have an Internet connection, online help gives you a wider range of help information, including the latest help available.

The easiest way to choose whether to get online help is to click the Offline Help drop-down list in the lower-right corner of the Help and Support window. (The drop-down list's name changes depending on whether you're currently using online help or offline help.) Choose Get Online Help or Get Offline Help from the shortcut menu, as shown here.

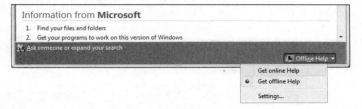

You can also use the Help Settings dialog box (see Figure 7.2) to specify whether to use online help. The Help Settings dialog box also lets you choose to participate anonymously in the Help Experience Improvement Program, which gradually improves Microsoft's help mechanisms by collecting details of user searches. To open the Help Settings dialog box, click the Options button and choose Settings from the drop-down list. Select or clear the Include Windows Online Help and Support When You Search for Help check box, and then click the OK button.

Finding Your Way around Help and Support

Help and Support has access to a large amount of information in Help files that Windows installs on your hard drive, together with troubleshooters for stepping you through the process of finding solutions to common problems and links for running Windows programs (such as Remote Assistance and the System Configuration Utility) that may help you solve or eliminate problems. But Help and Support's strongest feature is that it also provides a gateway to information resources on the Web and Internet.

Because of the amount of information and resources that Help and Support offers, you may find that it takes you a while to get the hang of navigating around Help and Support. This section highlights the main ways of finding the information you need.

FIGURE 7.2
The Help Settings
dialog box provides
another way of
choosing whether
to use online help
(Windows Assistance
Online).

Searching for Help

If the Help and Support home page shows a link that seems to be related to the topic on which you need help, click the link and see whether it takes you to useful information. If you see no related link on the home page, the easiest way to find information on a particular topic is to search for it.

To search, type the search term or terms in the Search text box and click the Search Online Help button. Help and Support displays a list of results, with a brief description of each; click a result to display the full topic. The left screen in Figure 7.3 shows an example of search results. The right screen in Figure 7.3 shows a Help topic.

FIGURE 7.3
Help and Support
displays a list of search
results (left). Click
one of the results to
display the full topic
(right).

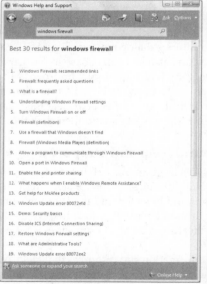

EXPERT KNOWLEDGE: MAKING THE MOST OF THE MICROSOFT KNOWLEDGE BASE

The Microsoft Knowledge Base is an online repository of knowledge and wisdom accumulated by Microsoft about its products. Given that the Knowledge Base is one of the main tools that Microsoft's support engineers use for troubleshooting customer problems with Windows, it's a great resource for searching for solutions to problems that Vista's local help resources don't know about.

The disadvantage to the Knowledge Base, and the reason perhaps why it's not more heavily emphasized in Microsoft's battery of help solutions, is the way it's arranged and the necessarily scattershot nature of its coverage. The Knowledge Base consists of a large number of answers that Microsoft's support engineers and other experts have written to questions that frustrated users and developers have submitted. The answers vary greatly in length, depending on the complexity of the problem and user level, ranging from beginner to super-advanced (developer-level) topics. Coverage is patchy, because the questions tend to be answered only when they're not covered in the Help files and other more accessible resources.

Each article in the Knowledge Base is identified by a six-digit Article ID number. Each article has a title that describes the problem it covers, information on which products and versions it covers, a summary that you can scan to get an idea of the contents, and the full text of the article. Beyond this, each article is tagged with keywords describing the main areas of its content. By searching for keywords, you can avoid passing references to words you might have included in the search, thus producing a more focused set of results.

To reach the Knowledge Base from Help and Support, click the More Support Options link on the home page, and then click the Knowledge Base link in the Other Resources section. Windows opens a browser window to the Knowledge Base. Click in the Search Support box, type your search terms, and then press Enter to start searching.

For power use, you'll probably find it easier to access the Knowledge Base directly from Internet Explorer (or your favorite browser) rather than go through Help and Support. To go to the Knowledge Base directly, point your browser at `http://support.microsoft.com/`. Click in the Search Support (KB) text box, type your search term, and then press Enter.

If you know the number of a particular article, enter it in the Search Support (KB) text box. For example, if you read newsgroups on Microsoft-related subjects, you'll often see references to particular articles mentioned as the place to find a fix for a given problem.

Browsing for Help

To browse for help, click the Options drop-down button and choose Browse Help from the menu. Help and Support displays a list of its contents, showing major topics—such as Getting Started, Security and Privacy, Maintenance and Performance—as shown in Figure 7.4.

Click one of the major topics to display the topics available for it (see Figure 7.5), and then click the topic you want to open.

Some of the Help topics provide only information, but most provide links that enable you to open the tools you need or connect to other help resources. For example, the screen shown in Figure 7.6 includes a link you can click to open the Performance Rating and Tools screen.

FIGURE 7.4
Click a major topic on
the Contents page to
go to that topic.

FIGURE 7.5
Click one of the topics
to display its contents.

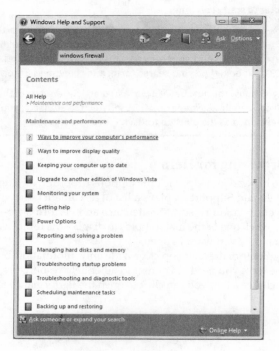

FIGURE 7.6
The Help system provides links to enable you to reach the tools you need to fix specific problems.

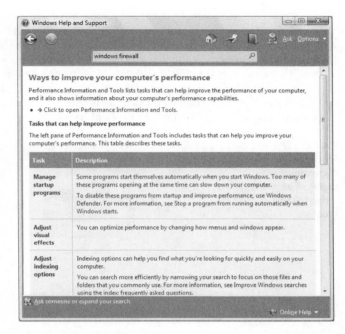

To search for a particular word or phrase within the Help page that's currently open, click the Options button, and then choose Find (on This Page) from the drop-down menu. Windows displays the Find dialog box, as shown here.

Type the word or phrase in the Find text box, and then click the Next button to find the next instance or the Previous button to find the previous instance. You can select the Match Whole Word Only check box to restrict matches to whole words rather than partial words (so that you find only "print" rather than "printer" or "printing," for example). You can select the Match Case check box to find only matches for the capitalization you use.

When you've finished searching, click the Close button (the × button). Windows closes the Find dialog box.

Navigating with Help History

You can navigate backward and forward in the chain of pages you've browsed by using the Back button and Forward button on the toolbar. Unlike in earlier versions of Windows Help, you can't click and hold one of these buttons to display a list of pages in the Back list or Forward list. There's also no Help history for finding pages you've visited in the past.

Printing Out Help Information

You may want to print out Help information so that you can refer to it more easily—for example, when the steps for solving a problem require you to restart Windows (and thus close Help and Support).

To print the current topic, click the Print button. Help and Support displays the Print dialog box. The General page offers standard printing options: You can choose which printer to use, decide whether to print all the pages or just some of them, print a single copy or multiple copies, or even "print to file," creating a file that you can then print from another computer. (You won't usually need to use the "print to file" capability when printing Help information.)

The Options page of the Print dialog box (see Figure 7.7) lets you print a whole section of help by selecting the Print All Linked Documents check box. You can also select the Print Table of Links check box if you want to print a table of linked pages.

FIGURE 7.7
Printing all linked documents can be useful when you're trying to solve a problem.

Using the "Ask Someone" Options

The Ask Someone section of the Help and Support home page directs you to Remote Assistance, the Windows Communities, Microsoft Customer Support, and further support options. You can also access this information at any time by clicking the Ask button on the navigation bar.

REMOTE ASSISTANCE

The most direct way in which you can get help is by using Windows' Remote Assistance feature to let someone else connect to your computer from a remote computer so that they can see what's happening and offer advice via text-based chat. If you trust your helper enough, you can even let them take control of your computer so that they can take actions to fix the problem.

Chapter 21 discusses how to configure and use Remote Assistance, both for getting help and for providing help to others.

WINDOWS COMMUNITIES

The Windows Communities are an assortment of Windows Vista–related online newsgroups that you can access through Internet Explorer or another web browser. Microsoft organizes the Windows Communities, but most of the content is written by Windows users rather than by people who work for Microsoft. You'll find a lot of useful information in the Windows Communities, but the quality of information and advice is variable.

You Need a Windows Live ID to Sign In to the Windows Communities

Anyone can browse the Microsoft Communities freely, but to ask questions, post replies, or request notifications of replies on a topic, you must sign in with a Windows Live ID. "Windows Live ID" is Microsoft's new name for what it formerly called "Microsoft Passport." If you have a Hotmail account or an MSN account, you already have a Windows Live ID that you can use; likewise if you've signed up for a Microsoft Passport separately (without getting a Hotmail account or MSN account).

If you don't have a Windows Live ID, you can get one easily by going to the Windows Live website (http://www.live.com) or the Hotmail website (http://www.hotmail.com), clicking the Sign Up link, and then filling in a form.

Once you've signed in to Windows Communities (or another site, such as Microsoft Customer Support) using your Windows Live ID, any searches you run and any questions or replies you post are associated with your ID. The ID helps Microsoft deliver information to you (for example, by notifying you of new posts on a topic), but it does mean that your actions are monitored. If you're sensitive to privacy issues, you may sometimes prefer to search for information without signing in.

To use the Windows Communities, follow these steps:

1. Click the Windows Communities link in the Ask Someone section of the Help and Support home page. Windows opens Internet Explorer (or your default web browser, if you're not using Internet Explorer) to the Microsoft Windows Vista Newsgroups page (see Figure 7.8).

2. To search for information, type your search terms in the Search For box, choose the newsgroups to search in the In drop-down list (for example, choose Windows Vista Newsgroups), and then click the Go button. Your browser displays a list of results (see Figure 7.9).

3. To browse the topics available, use the navigation links on the left side of the window.

Figure 7.8

Windows Communities lets you search Internet discussion groups for Windows Vista–related advice and information.

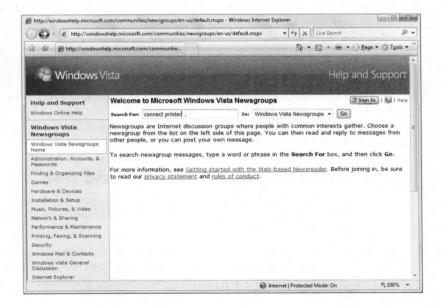

FIGURE 7.9
You can expand and collapse the list of search results to see posts that interest you. To receive notification of replies, click the Notify Me of Replies drop-down button and choose From Microsoft or From Anyone in the drop-down list.

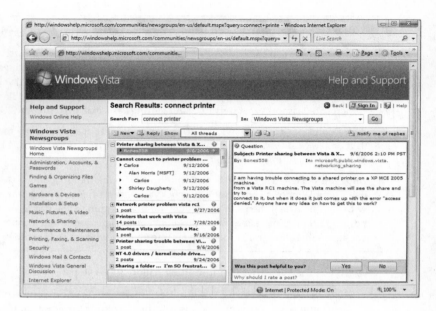

EVALUATE WINDOWS NEWSGROUPS ADVICE CAREFULLY BEFORE FOLLOWING IT

You're probably familiar with the disclaimer "this information comes without guarantee"—in other words, you try whatever is described at your own risk. The advice you encounter on the Windows newsgroups should probably have this disclaimer attached. While some of the postings contain high-quality advice from people who know what they're talking about, other postings are wrong or dangerous, and following the advice supplied (with whatever good intent) can threaten or damage your data or your computer. Proceed with caution.

MICROSOFT CUSTOMER SUPPORT

Click the Microsoft Customer Support link in the Ask Someone area of the home page to open a browser window to a page on Microsoft Support that explains the support options available for Windows Vista. This page includes links to pages where you can learn about contacting Microsoft via e-mail or telephone and the cost of support.

Finding Help on the Internet and Web

Help and Support provides many links to the Microsoft website and related websites (such as the Windows Communities). But if you don't find the help you need on these sites, search for help on the Web or look in newsgroups:

◆ **General searches** For a general search, take your web browser to a search engine such as Google (http://www.google.com) or Yahoo! (http://www.yahoo.com). Use advanced search options to specify exactly what you're looking for and limit the number of results you get.

◆ **Hardware and software manufacturers' sites** If you're having problems with a particular hardware device, check the manufacturer's website for solutions. Similarly, if you're having trouble with software, see if the manufacturer's website contains the answer.

◆ **Newsgroups** The many computer-related public newsgroups (such as the comp.sys hierarchy) and the Microsoft public newsgroups (in the microsoft.public hierarchy) can be a great source of specific information. Chapter 18 discusses how to read news.

The Bottom Line

Using Help and Support to find the help information you need   Choose Start ➤ Help and Support to open the Help and Support window, and then use the links and controls inside it to find the information you need. You can search for information by entering keywords and clicking the Search button or browse through major topics to specific topics. The Ask Someone links let you launch Remote Assistance, open a browser window to the Windows Communities newsgroups, or find contact information for Microsoft Customer Support.

Finding help on the Internet and Web   If Help and Support doesn't provide the information to solve a problem, search for a solution by using an Internet search engine (such as Google or Yahoo!) or by visiting a hardware or software manufacturer's website. You may also want to search through computer-related public newsgroups.

Part 2

Administering and Troubleshooting Windows Vista

Chapter 8

Managing Users and Accounts

- ◆ Understand what user accounts are and what they're for
- ◆ Know when to use the three types of user accounts and what user profiles are
- ◆ Create a user account
- ◆ Delete a user account
- ◆ Change a user account
- ◆ Use the Guest account, automatic logon, and secure logon
- ◆ Restrict and monitor users with Parental Controls

As you've seen by now, Windows Vista is a multiuser operating system. To help you keep each user's files and settings separate, you should create a separate user account for each person who regularly uses the computer.

This chapter shows you manage users and accounts. First, it explains what user accounts are and what they're for. Then it details the three different types of user account that Windows Vista supports, together with their capabilities and limitations. After that, it tells you how to create, delete, and modify user accounts; how to require passwords for them; and how to make Windows automatically log on a particular account at startup. You'll also learn how to use Windows Vista's new Parental Control features to limit what users can do.

If you're the only person who ever uses your computer, you hardly need to worry about user accounts. But if you share your computer with anybody else, you should use user accounts to the fullest extent, because they offer great benefits and require minimal setup and administration. Read on.

What Are User Accounts and What Are They For?

A *user account* is a group of settings that lets you tailor the Windows environment to each regular user. By using user accounts, you can let each user set different preferences on the computer, so that each user can maintain a custom Desktop that provides the look they like and the shortcuts and information they need. Each user can also keep separate favorites and histories in Internet Explorer. (Chapter 2 discusses Internet Explorer's History and Favorites features.) Each user can protect their user account with a password if they choose, and they can choose to share folders with other users via the network. (Chapter 9 discusses how to share folders with other users.)

By using accounts effectively and setting passwords, you can control access to your computer, and you can allow different privileges to different users. For example, you could prevent the less responsible members of the household from accessing critical files by storing them in secure folders. User accounts are particularly useful when your computer is networked (including always-on connections to the Internet).

Each user account is identified by a username that Windows uses to manage it. The account has a full-name field that typically contains the full name of the user (which appears on the Welcome screen and at the top of the Start menu) and a comment field that can be used for storing a comment about the user. Each user account has an account type that defines its permissions and a set of folders in which the user's details and preferences are stored.

Understanding the Three Types of User Accounts and User Profiles

Windows Vista lets you use three types of user accounts: Administrator, Standard, and Guest. The following sections discuss what each account can do and which type of account is suitable for which type of user.

Administrator Accounts

Administrator accounts are intended for power users who administer the computer. An Administrator account can perform just about any action on the computer, including installing programs and hardware on the computer and creating, modifying, and deleting user accounts. By default, an Administrator account can access all the files on the computer.

When you first set up Windows Vista, the first account you create is an Administrator account. After that, you can create Administrator accounts and Standard accounts as needed.

Standard Accounts

A Standard account can take any action needed for day-to-day work or play but cannot configure computerwide settings without providing the password for an Administrator account.

A Standard user can:

◆ Change their picture, Desktop background, or screen saver.

◆ Change their password, or remove their password (so that they don't need to enter a password to log on to Windows).

◆ Create, edit, and delete their own files.

A Standard user cannot:

◆ Read other users' files that aren't explicitly shared with the Standard user.

◆ Install most hardware (except for reinserting Plug and Play hardware that has already been installed on the computer).

◆ Install or remove most programs.

◆ Create, modify, or delete user accounts.

◆ Log off another user who's locked the computer.

🌐 Real World Scenario

GOOD SECURITY PRACTICES VERSUS REALITY

Microsoft recommends that everyone who has Windows Vista should log on as a Standard user for normal use and use an Administrator account only on those (supposedly rare) occasions when they actually need to install hardware or software, set up users, or otherwise configure the computer in ways a Standard user cannot. By not using an Administrator account all the time, you get the greatest possible protection from the User Account Control feature and Windows Vista's other security mechanisms: Each time Windows receives a request to run a potentially sensitive program, it double-checks that you're the one who issued the request (rather than malware issuing it in your name).

If you're used to logging on to Windows XP as a Computer Administrator user (as Windows XP called Administrator users), or you're used to using Windows 98/Me (in which every user had full privileges), you'll probably find User Account Control irritating at first even if you log on as an Administrator user. Even so, create a Standard account for your day-to-day work and try using it. Chances are, you'll get used to working with reduced privileges and authenticating yourself to User Account Control when you do need to configure the computer.

The Guest Account

The Guest account is a special account for use by guests—either literally guests of your household or company, or figuratively in the sense that the user will need to use the computer only briefly. For longer-term use, create a Standard account for the user so that they can maintain their preferred settings.

You can't require a password for the Guest account. That's to prevent one guest from locking out another guest. And you can have only one Guest account on an installation of Windows, so the account needs to be shared among guests. You can't create or delete the Guest account, but you can turn it off and on. (For instructions, see the section "Turning On and Off the Guest Account," later in this chapter.) By default, the Guest account is off until you turn it on.

The Guest account cannot access password-protected folders. It can change only supposedly harmless settings. For example, the Guest account can change screen resolution and color schemes, but the only user-account option it can change is the picture displayed for Guest.

ALL USERS SHARE THE SAME SCREEN RESOLUTION

Because Windows Vista always uses Fast User Switching (explained in Chapter 1), each user has to use the same screen resolution. So does the Welcome screen.

If one of the other users of your computer changes the resolution, you'll find the Welcome screen and your user session using the new resolution. When you change the resolution back to your preferred setting, the resolution changes for all other users as well.

Understanding User Profiles

Information for each user account is kept in what Microsoft calls the *user profile*, which is stored in the user's folder under the `\Documents and Settings\` folder. This information includes the contents of your Start menu and Desktop, information about your network settings and printers, and so on—all the information listed in Table 5.1 and discussed at some length in Chapter 5.

To move a user profile from one computer to another, use the Files and Settings Transfer Wizard, discussed in Appendix B.

You may sometimes need to copy a user profile—for example, so that you have a backup of it for safekeeping. You can copy a user profile only for a user who is not logged on (even in a disconnected session).

To copy a user profile, follow these steps:

1. Press Windows Key+Break. Windows displays the System window in Control Panel.

2. Click the Advanced System Settings link in the left panel, and then authenticate yourself to User Account Control. Windows displays the System Properties dialog box.

3. Click the Advanced tab. Windows displays the Advanced page.

4. In the User Profiles group box, click the Settings button. Windows displays the User Profiles dialog box (see Figure 8.1).

5. Click the Copy To button. Windows displays the Copy To dialog box, as shown here.

FIGURE 8.1
The User Profiles dialog box enables you to copy a user profile to a folder.

6. In the Copy Profile To text box, type the folder to which you want to copy the profile. Use a folder that has no contents, as Windows will overwrite any contents. Alternatively, click the Browse button, use the Browse for Folder dialog box to select the folder, and then click the OK button.

7. Click the OK button. Windows copies the user profile.

Creating a User Account

When you first install Windows Vista, the OS makes you create a single Administrator account, which it encourages you to protect with a password. Once you've logged on to that account, you can create such other accounts as needed.

Windows provides two tools for working with user accounts: the User Accounts window in Control Panel (which you'll meet in this section) and the User Accounts dialog box (which you'll meet later in this chapter). The User Accounts dialog box is also known as the Advanced User Accounts Control Panel.

To create a user account, log on as an Administrator user and take the following steps:

1. Choose Start ➤ Control Panel. Windows displays Control Panel.

2. If Control Panel is in Classic view, click the Control Panel Home link to switch to Control Panel Home view.

3. In the User Accounts and Family Safety list, click the Add or Remove User Accounts link, and then authenticate yourself to User Account Control. Windows displays the Manage Accounts window (see Figure 8.2).

4. Click the Create a New Account link. Windows displays the first Create New Account screen (see Figure 8.3).

FIGURE 8.2
From the Manage Accounts screen in Control Panel, you can create, delete, and modify user accounts.

FIGURE 8.3
On the Create New
Account screen,
enter the name for
the new user account
and choose whether
to make it a Standard
account or an Admin-
istrator account.

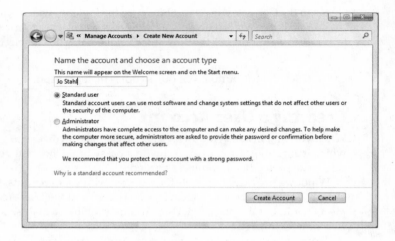

5. Type a name for the account:

   ◆ Usernames can be up to 20 characters long and are not case sensitive.

   ◆ Windows automatically assigns the username you enter as the full name for the user account. You can change this, and add a comment to the user account, by using the User Accounts dialog box (discussed later in this chapter).

   ◆ Names can contain letters, numbers, and most symbols. They cannot contain any of these characters: *, ?, +, =, , (comma), : (colon), ; (semicolon), <, >, | (pipe character), " (double quotation marks), [,], /, or \.

   ◆ Names can start with letters, numbers, or symbols. Names can even consist of nothing but underscores.

   ◆ It can be amusing to create idiosyncratic names, but consider using a naming convention if you're creating more than a few user accounts and want to keep things formal and organized.

6. By default, Windows selects the Standard User option button. Select the Administrator option button if you want the account to be an Administrator instead.

7. Click the Create Account button. Windows creates the account, assigns it a picture at random, and displays the User Accounts screen again, with the new user listed.

As soon as you've created a new account, you should assign a password to it. See "Requiring a Password for an Account," later in this chapter, for instructions.

Deleting a User Account

You may need to delete a user account—for example, if someone who has been using the computer gets a computer of their own. Deleting the user account is easy, but you need to decide whether to keep the user's Desktop configuration files and their Documents folder.

To delete a user account, log on as an Administrator user and take the following steps:

1. Check whether the user is logged on to the computer in a disconnected session and, if so, log them off:

   ◆ Right-click the notification area, and then choose Task Manager from the shortcut menu. Windows displays Task Manager.

   ◆ Click the Users tab. Windows displays the Users page.

   ◆ If the user appears in the list, select their entry, and then click the Logoff button. Windows displays a Windows Task Manager dialog box warning you that the user might lose unsaved data.

   ◆ Click the Log Off User button.

2. Choose Start ➢ Control Panel. Windows displays Control Panel.

3. If Control Panel is in Classic view, click the Control Panel Home link to switch to Control Panel Home view.

4. In the User Accounts and Family Safety list, click the Add or Remove User Accounts link, and then authenticate yourself to User Account Control. Windows displays the Manage Accounts window.

5. Click the user's icon. Windows displays the Change an Account window (shown in Figure 8.4).

6. Click the Delete the Account link. Windows displays the Do You Want to Keep *Username*'s Files? window (shown in Figure 8.5), where *Username* is the user's name.

FIGURE 8.4
The Change an Account window lets you delete a user account as well as make less drastic changes, such as changing the picture or setting up Parental Controls.

FIGURE 8.5
When you delete a user, you get to choose whether to keep the user's files.

7. Click the Keep Files button or the Delete Files button as appropriate. Windows displays the Are You Sure You Want to Delete *Username*'s Account? window (see Figure 8.6) to make sure you've thought about what you're doing.

8. Click the Delete Account button if you're sure you want to proceed. Windows deletes the account and displays the Manage Accounts window again.

FIGURE 8.6
If you choose to keep the files, Windows tells you that it will save the user's files to a folder on your Desktop.

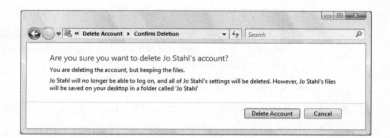

Real World Scenario

DELETING YOUR OWN ACCOUNT

Sometimes, you'll need to delete your own account from a computer. For example, you might buy a new computer, so you no longer need to use the computer you've been using before.

The best way to delete your own account is by using another Administrator account. If yours is the only Administrator account on the computer, create a new Administrator account (either from scratch or by promoting a Standard account to Administrator status), and then use it to delete your account.

Alternatively, you can use the User Accounts dialog box (press Windows Key+R, type `control userpasswords2`, and click the OK button) to delete your account while you're logged on to it. This isn't a great idea, as you'll see in the section "Performing Other Management Actions from the User Accounts Dialog Box," later in this chapter, but it does work. Log off immediately after deleting your account like this.

Changing a User Account

If you set up a user account but don't quite get it right, you can change it easily. You can change a user account from Standard to Administrator or vice versa, change the account name, change the picture, add a password to the account, or apply Parental Controls.

To change an account, open the Change an Account window as follows:

1. Choose Start ➤ Control Panel. Windows displays Control Panel.

2. If Control Panel is in Classic view, click the Control Panel Home link to switch to Control Panel Home view.

3. In the User Accounts and Family Safety list, click the Add or Remove User Accounts link, and then authenticate yourself to User Account Control. Windows displays the Manage Accounts window.

4. Click the user's icon. Windows displays the Change an Account window.

You can then change the account by taking one or more of the actions detailed in the next sections.

Assigning a Picture to a User Account

You can personalize your account by assigning a picture to it. The picture appears on the Welcome screen (so all users of the computer see it) and on the Start menu. Even the Guest user can change their picture.

The picture for a user's account can be of the BMP, GIF, JPG, PNG, or TIF file type. Windows shrinks the picture down to the appropriate size, but you'll need to take care of any cropping or rotating first. (Windows Photo Gallery can handle the rotation. Paint can handle both rotation and cropping, together with capturing a still picture from a webcam. See Chapter 6 for a brief discussion of Paint, and Chapter 23 for a discussion of Windows Photo Gallery.)

To change the picture for a user, follow these steps from the Change an Account window:

1. Click the Change the Picture link. Windows displays the Choose a New Picture for *Username*'s Account window (shown in Figure 8.7), where *Username* is the user's name.

2. Choose the picture you want:

- ◆ To use a built-in picture, click it in the list box, and then click the Change Picture button.

- ◆ To use a picture of your own, click the Browse for More Pictures link. Windows displays an Open dialog box. Navigate to the picture you want to use, select it, and then click the Open button. Windows applies the picture to your account.

Click the Start button to check out how your picture looks on the Start menu. Now disconnect your session so that you can see how the picture looks on the Welcome screen.

FIGURE 8.7
Any user can change the picture shown for them on the Welcome screen and on their Start menu.

CHANGING YOUR OWN ACCOUNT'S PICTURE QUICKLY

To change the picture for your user account, click the picture at the top of the Start menu. Windows displays the User Accounts window with the Make Changes to Your User Account screen showing. Click the Change Your Picture link.

Applying a Password to an Account

Windows Vista encourages you to create a password for the Administrator account that you create during setup, but after that you're free to create Administrator accounts or Standard accounts without a password. For security, you should require a password for each account (except for the Guest account, which can't have a password, but which you can turn off).

If you don't require a password for an account, anyone can log on to that account. If it's an Administrator account, whoever logs on can make major changes to Windows, such as creating other user accounts.

To make Windows require passwords, take these steps from the Change an Account window:

1. Click the Create a Password link. Windows displays the Create a Password for *Username*'s Account window (shown in Figure 8.8), where *Username* is the user's name. If you're creating a password for your own account, you get the same text boxes but not the warnings.

2. Type the password in the New Password text box and the Confirm New Password text box. For security (is someone looking over your shoulder?), Windows displays each character as an asterisk (*).

FIGURE 8.8
Use the Create Password window to create a password and (if necessary) a password hint for the account.

3. If you think it appropriate, enter a password hint in the Type a Password Hint text box. Anybody trying to log on to the computer can display the password hint, so you need to tailor it carefully to the person. The password hint must mean something to the user without meaning anything to anyone else. It's much easier to get this wrong than right. For security, do not use password hints, but create a password reset disk for each user.

4. Click the Create Password button. Windows applies the password to the account. (If the two instances of the password didn't match, Windows tells you so and returns you to the Create Password window.)

When you require passwords, Windows prompts the user for a password when they click their name on the Welcome screen. The user can click the Password Hint link to display the hint for the password.

When a user account is password protected, Windows displays *Password protected* under the account type on the User Accounts screens.

One problem that can occur with passwords is having the Caps Lock feature switched on, either when you're creating the password or when you're subsequently entering it. Windows does its best to warn you if the Caps Lock key is on when you're entering a password, but if you miss the warnings, double-check Caps Lock first if Windows won't accept your password. On keyboards with an embedded numeric keypad, such as those on most notebooks, you can give yourself a similar problem by having the Num Lock feature on while typing the password. Windows won't warn you about this.

 Real World Scenario

PASSWORDS ARE A MUST

Passwords are more or less mandatory in any serious business setting, and they can be a good idea in many family or dorm situations as well. Even if everybody who can directly access your computer is above suspicion, you should also protect it against attack by remote malefactors across the Internet. Passwords are a major element in such protection, as is Windows Firewall.

Unfortunately, Windows doesn't have a high-security arrangement for implementing passwords. Ideally, there'd be a setting that you (the Administrator user) could set that would make each user apart from the Guest user create a password for their account the next time they used the computer. Each user would then create a password that only they would know, and the computer would be secure against unauthorized users logging on. Each user would be able to change their password whenever they wanted to (or, better, would be made to change the password frequently) and wouldn't be able to remove password protection from the account. The Business versions of Windows Vista work somewhat like this, but the Home versions are less well protected.

Given that Windows doesn't have this ideal security arrangement, here's what you should do:

1. As soon as you create a user account, assign a password to it. Write the password down, and give it to the user who will use the account. Tell the user to change the password immediately, so that you don't know the password. Don't use a password hint.

2. If your computer already has a user account that doesn't use a password, persuade the user to add a password immediately. Stress the benefits of having a strong password that only the user knows.

3. If you suspect that your password has been compromised, change it immediately. Have all other users do the same.

4. Disable the Guest account. If a visitor needs to use the computer once, turn on the Guest account for as short a time as possible, and then turn it off again.

Instead of making users create their own passwords, it's possible to create passwords for a user yourself from an Administrator account. This method has two disadvantages. First, you know the passwords (so the user will need to change the password as soon as possible). Second, and much worse, *the user loses all the personal certificates they've stored, together with any passwords they've saved for network resources (such as folders and printers) and for websites.* To avoid losing this information, it's best to create the password before the user has used their account.

Removing Password Protection from an Account

Any user can remove the password protection from their own user account as follows:

1. Click the Start button, and then click your picture at the top of the Start menu. Windows opens the User Accounts window.

2. In the Make Changes to Your User Account list, click the Remove Your Password link. Windows displays the Remove Your Password window (shown here).

3. In the Current Password text box, type your current password to verify your identity.

4. Click the Remove Password button. Windows removes the password and displays the User Accounts window again.

Encourage all users of your computer never to remove their passwords, because even one user account without a password opens the whole computer to attack.

Just as an Administrator user can apply password protection to another user's account, so they can remove it. But the same problem applies to removal as to application: The user loses all the personal certificates they've stored, together with any passwords they've saved for network resources (such as folders and printers) and for websites. So if you need to remove password protection from an account, it's far better to have the users do it themselves.

⊕ Real World Scenario

HOW—AND WHY—TO CREATE SECURE PASSWORDS

If you use passwords—and you should, if you value your data—it's vital to make sure that they're effective. You wouldn't believe the number of people who don't understand why passwords are important and who see them as an irritant.

Actually, you *might* believe that. But would you believe that between 90 and 95 percent of *all* passwords are the same 100 words? This is what some security experts estimate based on the passwords they see in daily use. Crackers (malevolent hackers) try these popular passwords first when trying to guess a password because they work so often.

To create a secure password, it helps to understand how crackers go about breaking a password. The most common method is to use a *dictionary attack*. The attacker runs a script that tries to match each word in a specified "dictionary" with your password until it gets a hit. The dictionary can be in any language or a mixture of languages, and will usually contain all popular passwords in all major languages at its beginning. The dictionary isn't so much a dictionary in the conventional sense as a list of words arranged in some kind of descending order of probability—most likely words first.

Dictionary attacks are often effective. But if the would-be victim has created a tough password (by using the methods described below), the cracker may resort to *social engineering*—the art of extracting passwords from the unsuspecting by posing as someone in authority (for example, as a system administrator or a troubleshooter for your ISP). Again, security experts tend to be amazed by how freely many users give up their passwords over the phone. (Even worse, in an April 2004 survey of office workers in the UK, 71 percent traded what they claimed was their computer password for a chocolate egg. You have to hope that most of them lied.)

To keep your password secure, *never* write it down (and if you must write it down, don't stick the paper containing it onto your computer or monitor) and *never* tell anyone else what it is. You are the only person who ever needs to know your password. No ISP and no system administrator should need to be given your password, over the phone or in person. ISP personnel and system administrators may need to reset your password or assign you a new password—for example, if you forget your password. In this case, *they'll* give *you* the new password. You then log on with it and create a new, secure password for yourself immediately. (At least, that's the theory.)

Follow these rules to create a secure password:

◆ Create a password of an appropriate length. Windows, many ISPs, and most services will let you create passwords of any length between 6 characters and 15 characters. Treat 6 characters as the absolute minimum. Aim for a password of at least 8 characters, and more like 12 if you're feeling insecure. Passwords of 5 characters or fewer are relatively easy to crack by brute force; passwords of 6 characters are much harder; and longer passwords are much harder yet. If you're allowed to create a password of any length, be sensible and limit the password to a length that you can remember and type without undue stumbling.

◆ Never use a real word in any language for a password. Real words can be broken easily by a dictionary attack.

◆ Instead, use symbols (@, $, %, ^, !, &, and so on) as substitute characters in a word or phrase, or reduce a phrase or sentence to its initial letters or key letters. Mix letters and numbers. Use uppercase and lowercase creatively (passwords are case sensitive). Alternatively, open a text editor, close your eyes, and type randomly for a few seconds, making sure to hold down the Shift key at intervals. Then pick a particularly cryptic part of the result to use as a password.

◆ Never use any example password that you see, no matter how compelling it may seem. For example, books on security provide example passwords. These may look wonderfully cryptic, but you should assume that they're all known to crackers and included in cracking dictionaries.

◆ Never use information of personal relevance or importance—your pet's name, a family member's name, your birthday, your driver's license number, your social security number, or (perhaps the ultimate no-no) your credit-card number. Most of these pieces of information can be obtained by trivial searches or the mildest of social engineering, making them near useless as passwords.

◆ Never use any option that offers to save a password for you. For example, Windows offers to store your dial-up passwords so that you can access your dial-up accounts more easily. These passwords not only let unauthorized users of your computer access your dial-up accounts effortlessly, but also can be cracked easily by commonly available programs.

◆ Use a different password for each account or program that requires one. That way, if one password is compromised, the others will still be secure.

◆ As soon as you suspect that a password may have been compromised, change it. Also change any associated passwords.

◆ Never repeat a password you've used in the past. Create an entirely new password each time you change a password.

◆ Memorize your passwords. Never write them down. If you write a password down, you've compromised it. If you must write a password down, keep it in the safest of places. If that place is virtual rather than physical, protect your password stash with another password—a good one.

◆ Never tell anybody any of your passwords—not even the ones you've stopped using. (They might be able to use these passwords to guess at your newer passwords.)

If you can follow the simple advice in this list, you'll be ahead of 99 percent of the computer-using population—and much more secure than any of them.

That said, be warned that no password is totally secure. Any password can be broken by an attacker who has sufficient time, determination, and computer operations. But most crackers will not be prepared to spend more than a few minutes (or, at the most, hours) on any given password, and will swiftly move on to other targets. So your goal is to keep your passwords secure against random attackers, not against the NSA. If the NSA is on your case, you'll have much worse things to worry about than whether your passwords are strong enough.

To remove password protection from an account, follow these steps:

1. On the Change an Account screen, click the Remove Password link. Windows displays the Remove Password window (shown here), which warns you of what the user will lose.

2. Click the Remove Password button. Windows removes the password, and then returns you to the Change an Account screen.

Creating a New Password for a User

If a user forgets their password, they won't be able to log on to Windows. They'll need to get an Administrator user to create a replacement password for them. But again, as with applying and removing passwords, the user loses all the personal certificates they've stored, together with any passwords they've saved for network resources (such as folders and printers) and for websites.

To create a replacement password for another user, log on as an Administrator user and follow these steps:

1. On the Change an Account screen, click the Change Password link. Windows displays the Change *Username's* Password window (see Figure 8.9).

FIGURE 8.9

Changing a user's existing password loses their encrypted files, personal certificates, and stored passwords—so you should do it only when the user has forgotten the password and doesn't have a password reset disk.

2. Type the password in the New Password text box, type it again in the Confirm New Password text box, and type a password hint if you must.

3. Click the Change Password button. Windows applies the new password and displays the Change an Account window again.

You're probably thinking that all this losing of the user's personal certificates and passwords should be avoidable, even if the user is unwise enough to forget their password. And it is avoidable. Read on.

Using Password Reset Disks to Recover from Lost Passwords

If a Standard user forgets their password, they need to get an Administrator user to create a new password for them or remove the password from the account. That's easy enough—but if there's no Administrator user around, it could prove a big waste of time. And the user loses any personal certificates and passwords they have stored.

If any Administrator user forgets their password, they'll need to have another Administrator user create a new password for them (because they won't be able to log on to their own account). That too is easy enough—provided that there's another Administrator user and that they're handy. Again, though, those personal certificates and passwords go overboard.

But if all available Administrator users forget their passwords, you may need to reinstall Windows to get it working again.

To avoid these problems, each Administrator and Standard user should create a password reset disk. Each user can do this only for their own account. You can use either a floppy disk or a removable memory card (for example, a CompactFlash card or an SD card).

CREATING YOUR PASSWORD RESET DISK

To create a password reset disk, follow these steps:

1. Click the Start button, and then click your picture at the top of the Start menu. Windows opens the User Accounts window.

2. In the left panel, click the Prepare for a Forgotten Password link. Windows launches the Forgotten Password Wizard, which displays the Welcome to the Forgotten Password Wizard page.

3. Click the Next button. The wizard displays the Create a Password Reset Disk page (see Figure 8.10), which lets you choose which drive to use.

4. Choose the drive in the drop-down list. If you choose to use your computer's floppy drive, insert a blank, formatted disk.

   ◆ If you have multiple floppy drives, choose the option button for the one you put the floppy in.

   ◆ The floppy doesn't actually have to be blank. The wizard creates only one file, USERKEY.PSW, which is typically only a couple of kilobytes large. So unless the floppy is completely full, the file will usually fit. Even so, it's a good idea to use a blank disk that you're not using for other purposes.

FIGURE 8.10
On the Create a Password Reset Disk page of the Forgotten Password Wizard, choose the drive to use. If your computer doesn't have a removable disk drive, this page prompts you to insert a blank, formatted floppy disk.

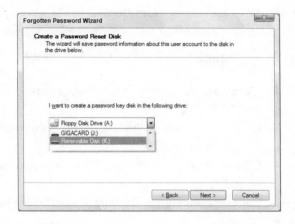

FIGURE 8.11
Type the account's current password (if it has one) on the Current User Account Password page of the Forgotten Password Wizard.

5. Click the Next button. The wizard displays the Current User Account Password page (see Figure 8.11).

6. Type your password in the Current User Account Password text box.

7. Click the Next button. The wizard displays the Creating Password Reset Disk page asking you to wait while it creates the disk. When it has finished, it makes the Next button available.

8. Click the Next button. The wizard displays the Completing the Forgotten Password Wizard page.

9. Click the Finish button. The wizard closes itself. Remove the disk, label it, and put it somewhere safe; anyone who can access this disk can use it to get into your user account. You can't create another password reset disk without invalidating this disk, so don't try making multiple disks—only the last one will work.

This disk doesn't store your password as such. Instead, it stores encrypted information that enables you to create a new password.

USING YOUR PASSWORD RESET DISK

To use the password reset disk, take the following steps:

1. When you get stuck at the Welcome screen and can't remember your password, insert the disk.

2. Click the green arrow button without entering your password. Windows tells you that "the user name or password is incorrect."

3. Click the OK button. Windows displays the Reset Password link under the Password text box on the logon screen.

4. Click the Reset Password link. Windows starts the Password Reset Wizard, which displays its Welcome page.

5. Click the Next button. The wizard displays the Insert the Password Reset Disk page.

6. Insert the disk, specify the drive if necessary, and click the Next button. The wizard displays the Reset the User Account Password page.

7. Enter your new password twice, and enter a hint if you think it wise.

8. Click the Next button. The wizard displays the Completing the Password Reset Wizard page.

9. Click the Finish button. The wizard closes itself and returns you to the logon screen.

10. Log on using the new password. Remove the password reset disk and put it away somewhere safe. (You don't need to update it.)

Removing a Windows Live ID from an Account

Many of Windows's communications features (such as Windows Live Messenger's text, audio, and video messaging capabilities) require you to have and use a Windows Live ID, a digital persona that's used to identify you online. When you tell Windows Live Messenger or another program to store your Windows Live ID, Windows saves the ID inside your user account. You may sometimes need to remove a Windows Live ID from your user account—for example, so that you can use another ID instead.

To remove a Windows Live ID from your user account, take the following steps:

1. Close Windows Live Messenger and any other programs that use your Windows Live ID.

2. Click the Start button, and then click your picture at the top of the Start menu. Windows opens the User Accounts window.

3. In the left panel, click the Manage Your Network Passwords link. Windows displays the Stored User Names and Passwords dialog box (see Figure 8.12).

4. Click the username in the list box, and then click the Remove button. Windows displays the dialog box shown next.

FIGURE 8.12
Use the Stored User
Names and Passwords
dialog box to remove
a Windows Live ID
that you no longer
want to use from
your Windows user
account.

5. Click the OK button. Windows removes the username and password.

6. Click the Close button to close the Stored User Names and Passwords dialog box.

Using the Guest Account, Automatic Logon, and Secure Logon

If you want your computer to be moderately secure, it's a good idea to leave the Guest account turned off until you need it. You may also sometimes need to make a particular user account log on automatically when Windows starts, or ensure that users press the Ctrl+Alt+Delete security keystroke before logging on. This section shows you how to do these three things.

Turning On and Off the Guest Account

In a family setting, the Guest account can be a good idea, particularly if nobody keeps private or secret information on the computer. In an office, dorm, or just about any other setting, the Guest account is a bad idea because it compromises the security of your computer. The Guest account is more limited in what it can do than Administrator accounts and Standard accounts, but even so, it has the potential to cause trouble, either with local files or via a network or Internet connection.

The Guest account is disabled by default in Windows Vista Home. To turn on the Guest account, follow these steps:

1. Choose Start ➤ Control Panel. Windows displays Control Panel.

2. If Control Panel is in Classic view, click the Control Panel Home link to switch to Control Panel Home view.

3. In the User Accounts and Family Safety list, click the Add or Remove User Accounts link, and then authenticate yourself to User Account Control. Windows displays the Manage Accounts window.

4. Click the Guest link. Windows displays the Do You Want to Turn On the Guest Account? screen (shown here).

5. Click the Turn On button. Windows turns on the Guest account and displays the Manage Accounts window again.

To disable the Guest account, click the Guest link in the User Accounts window. Windows displays the What Do You Want to Change about the Guest Account? window. Click the Turn Off the Guest Account link.

Implementing and Preventing Automatic Logons

Sometimes, you may need to make Windows automatically log on a particular user when you start the computer. Having a user logged on automatically can be useful when multiple people need to share a user identity that you want to have available all the time. For example, some institutions (such as libraries) use this capability for their public terminals.

SUPPRESSING THE AUTOMATIC LOGON

When you've set up a computer to log on a user automatically, you can suppress the automatic logon by holding down the Shift key while the computer is starting up. Windows displays the Welcome screen as usual.

IMPLEMENTING AN AUTOMATIC LOGON

To implement an automatic logon, take the following steps:

1. Press Windows Key+R. Windows displays the Run dialog box.

2. Type `control userpasswords2` in the Open text box, click the OK button, and then authenticate yourself to User Account Control. Windows displays the User Accounts dialog box, with the Users page (see Figure 8.13) foremost.

3. Clear the Users Must Enter a User Name and Password to Use This Computer check box.

FIGURE 8.13
The User Accounts
dialog box lets you
set up Windows to log
on a particular user
automatically.

4. Click the OK button. Windows displays the Automatically Log On dialog box (shown next).

5. Enter the username and password (twice), and then click the OK button. Windows closes the Automatically Log On dialog box and the User Accounts dialog box and sets the specified user account to automatically log on.

Windows doesn't verify the password when you enter it, so it's possible to enter the wrong one. For this reason, it's a good idea to test straightaway that the automatic logon works.

PREVENTING AUTOMATIC LOGONS

If your computer is set up to automatically log on a user, you can prevent it from doing so by displaying the User Accounts dialog box as described in the previous section, selecting the Users Must Enter a User Name and Password to Use This Computer check box, and then clicking the OK button.

Incidentally, that check box is poorly named, because it implies that when the check box is selected, each user must use a password. That's not the case. The check box means that Windows isn't set up to log on one particular user automatically.

Forcing Users to Press Ctrl+Alt+Delete When Logging On

For security, you can force users to press the Ctrl+Alt+Delete key combination in order to bring up the Welcome screen so that they can log on. To do so, select the Require Users to Press Ctrl+Alt+Delete check box in the Secure Logon group box on the Advanced page of the User Accounts dialog box (see Figure 8.14).

The advantage of pressing Ctrl+Alt+Delete (which is also known as the Vulcan Nerve Pinch, the Triple Bucky, and other humorous names) is that it sends an interrupt to Windows that causes Windows to display the Welcome screen. This interrupt helps to ensure that a malicious hacker can't create a fake Welcome screen that would capture the user's username and password rather than (or as well as) logging them on.

FIGURE 8.14
The Advanced page of the User Accounts dialog box lets you manage passwords and implement secure logons.

PERFORMING OTHER MANAGEMENT ACTIONS FROM THE USER ACCOUNTS DIALOG BOX

The User Accounts dialog box offers various options for managing user accounts. Most of these options are functional, but you're usually better off using the user-management tools in Control Panel, which usher you through each account-management process and steer you toward the choices likely to be most suitable for normal needs. Here are brief notes on what you can do—and why you shouldn't:

Add Click the Add button and use the Add New User Wizard to specify the user's name, description, and password. You also specify the group to which the user belongs. Standard users belong to the Users group, and Administrators belong to the Administrators group, but beyond these groups there are other groups (such as Debugger Users or Performance Monitor Users) that the User Accounts tool doesn't offer. However, you run the risk of creating users that do not appear on the Welcome screen or in the User Accounts tool. Normally, it's best to use the User Accounts tool to create new user accounts.

Remove Click the user account you want to remove, and then click the Remove button to remove it. This method of deleting an account doesn't let you save the user's files the way the User Accounts tool does.

Properties   Click the Properties button to display the Properties dialog box for the selected user. On the General page of the Properties dialog box, you can change the user's username (the name that appears on the Welcome screen and most places in the user interface), assign a full name, and assign a description. On the Group Membership page of the Properties dialog box, you can change the group to which the user belongs. As with Add, assigning a user to any group other than those the User Accounts tool lets you use may make the user account disappear from the Welcome screen and the User Accounts tool.

Reset Password   You can reset the selected user's password by clicking the Reset Password button, entering the new password in the Reset Password dialog box, and clicking the OK button. To reset your own password, you must press Ctrl+Alt+Delete, which takes you to a Welcome-like screen. On it, click the Change a Password link, enter your old password and new password (twice), and then press Enter. Click the OK button to resume your session.

Advanced User Management   If you look at the Advanced User Management group box on the Advanced page of the User Accounts dialog box, you'll see it says "Local Users and Groups can be used to perform advanced user management tasks." But if you click the Advanced button, you'll find that the word "can" there should really have been "can't," because Microsoft has chosen to disable the Local Users and Groups snap-in for Microsoft Management Console in Windows Vista Home.

USING THE *NET USER* AND *NET LOCALGROUP* COMMANDS

In Windows XP, you could perform some advanced administration by opening a command-prompt window and using the `net user` and `net localgroup` commands. For example, by using the `net user` command, you could limit a user to logging on during certain hours (for example, Monday to Friday, 6 AM to 6 PM) or even deactivate their user account temporarily. By using the `net localgroup` command, you could create custom user groups.

Windows Vista severely restricts what you can do with these commands. You can run the `net user` command with a user's name (for example, **`net user chris`** or **`net user "John Adams"`**—use quotes around any name that contains a space) to display a screenful of details on what the user may do, including nuggets of useful information such as when the user last set their password. And you can run the `net localgroup` command to see which groups the computer knows (just type **`net localgroup`** and press Enter) or to see who the members of a group are (for example, type **`net localgroup administrators`** to see who the Administrators group contains). But that's about all. To implement restrictions on a user, use Parental Controls instead, as discussed in a moment.

Turning On or Off User Account Control

Windows Vista comes with the User Account Control feature enabled, so that each time a program asks to change a potentially sensitive part of Windows, you receive a notification. User Account Control is usually helpful, but you may sometimes want to disable it—for example, if you are performing some complex administrative tasks that seem to summon a User Account Control dialog box every other minute.

To turn off User Account Control, follow these steps:

1. Close all the programs you're running. You'll need to restart Windows to apply the change.

2. Click the Start button, and then click your picture at the top of the Start menu. Windows opens the User Accounts window.

3. Click the Turn User Account Control On or Off link, and then authenticate yourself to User Account Control. Windows displays the Turn User Account Control On or Off window (see Figure 8.15).

4. Clear the Use User Account Control (UAC) to Help Protect Your Computer check box.

5. Click the OK button. Windows warns you that will need to restart your computer to apply the changes, as shown here.

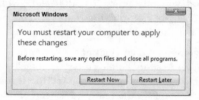

6. Click the Restart Now button if you want to restart Windows now. Otherwise, click the Restart Later button, and then restart Windows when you're ready.

FIGURE 8.15
You can turn off User Account Control if you find its frequent interventions annoying.

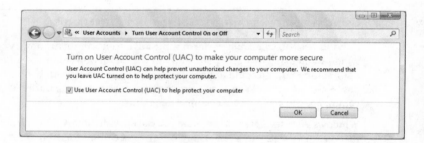

Implementing Parental Controls

For controlling your children (or your parents, if you so choose), you can use Windows Vista's Parental Controls. Parental Controls let you impose some restrictions on what a Standard user can do. For example, you can restrict a user to logging on between certain times, prevent a user from accessing specific websites or from downloading files, and prevent a user from running certain programs or playing some games. You can also collect information about what the user does with the computer, so that you can check whether they're accessing inappropriate sites.

You can't use Parental Controls on an Administrator account, because the user would have the authority to remove the controls (or perhaps apply them to a deserving parent's user account instead). So your first step is to create a Standard user account for each child who needs Parental Controls.

Setting Up Parental Controls

To set up Parental Controls, follow these steps:

1. Choose Start ➤ Control Panel. Windows displays a Control Panel window.

2. Under the User Accounts and Family Safety heading, click the Set Up Parental Controls for Any User link, and then authenticate yourself to User Account Control. Windows displays the Parental Controls window (see Figure 8.16).

3. Click the user's name. Windows displays the User Controls window (Figure 8.17).

FIGURE 8.16
Parental Controls let you impose restrictions on a Standard user.

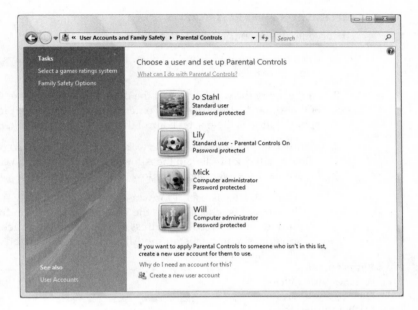

FIGURE 8.17
The User Controls window lets you turn on and off Parental Controls, decide whether to collect information about how the user uses the computer, and access the different types of restrictions you can apply. The readouts on the right side summarize the current settings.

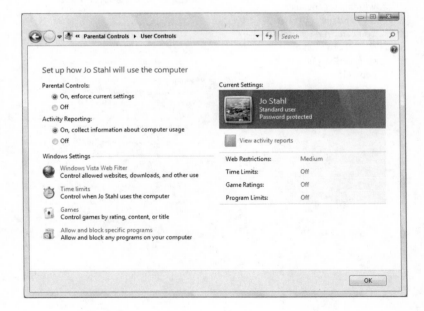

4. In the Parental Controls area at the upper-left corner of the window, select the On, Enforce Current Settings option button to turn on Parental Controls.

5. In the Activity Reporting area, select the On, Collect Information about Computer Usage option button if you want to collect data. Otherwise, select the Off option button.

IMPLEMENTING WEB RESTRICTIONS

To implement web restrictions, follow these steps:

1. Click the Windows Vista Web Filter link. Windows displays the Web Restrictions window (see Figure 8.18).

2. At the top of the window, select the Block Some Websites or Content option button instead of the Allow All Websites and Content option button. The Block Some Websites or Content option button is the master control that turns on all the other controls in the window.

3. If you want to designate specific websites as being allowed or blocked, click the Edit the Allow and Block List link in the Allow and Block Specific Websites area. Windows displays the Allow Block Webpages window (see Figure 8.19).

   ◆ Allowing sites is useful for when you select the Only Allow Websites Which Are on the Allow List check box in the Web Restrictions window. To allow a site, type its address in the Website Address text box, and then click the Allow button. Windows adds the site to the list in the Allowed Websites list box.

FIGURE 8.18
Windows Vista's Web Filter gives you a lot of flexibility in deciding which sites the user may and may not visit. You can even restrict the user to a list of sites you've chosen yourself.

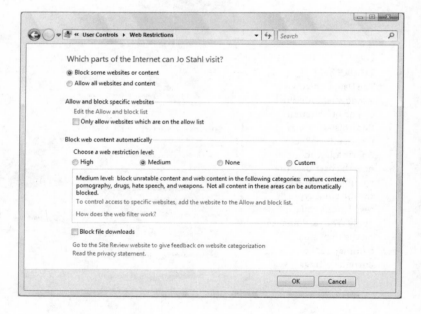

◆ Blocking sites is useful when you identify a particular site you don't want the user to access, even if the other settings you choose allow the user to access that site. To block a site, type its address in the Website Address text box, and then click the Block button. Windows adds the site to the list in the Blocked Websites list box.

◆ To remove a site from one of the lists, click it in the list box, and then click the Remove button.

◆ Once you've built up a list of sites that you want to use on another computer, you can click the Export button, and then use the Save As dialog box to save the list.

◆ To import an existing list of sites (either a list you've created or a list that you've obtained from someone else), click the Import button, use the resulting Open dialog box to select the file that contains the list, and then click the Open button.

◆ When you've finished creating your lists of sites, click the OK button to close the Allow Block Webpages window and return to the Web Restrictions window.

◆ If you want to allow only websites on the Allow list, select the Only Allow Websites Which Are on the Allow List check box.

4. In the Block Web Content Automatically area, select the option button for the level of restriction you want (see the following list).

◆ **High** Select this option button if you want the user to be able to access only the children's websites on Windows' built-in list.

◆ **Medium** Select this option button if you want to block mature content, drugs, pornography, hate speech, weapons, and unrated content.

FIGURE 8.19
Use the controls in the Allow Block Webpages window to build a list of Allowed Websites and a list of Blocked Websites.

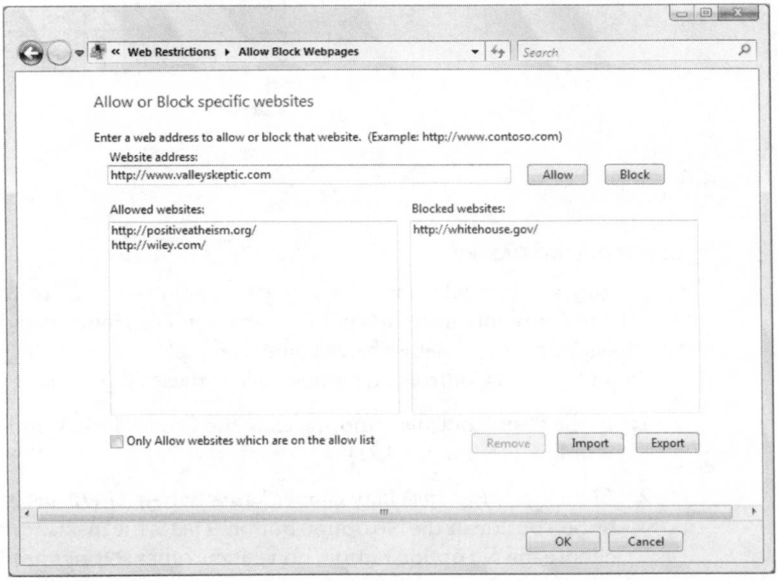

◆ **None** Select this option button if you want to implement no automatic blocking.

◆ **Custom** To implement a custom level of restriction, select the Custom option button, and then select the check boxes of your choice in the Check the Content You Want to Block list. The check boxes include Pornography, Mature Content, Sex Education, Hate Speech, Bomb Making, Weapons, Drugs, Alcohol, Tobacco, Gambling, and Unratable Content.

5. Select the Block File Downloads check box if you want to prevent the user from downloading files. Files on the Internet can contain all kinds of threats, so there's plenty of reason to block them—but if you do, you may prevent the user from accessing beneficial information.

6. Click the OK button. Windows closes the Web Restrictions window and returns you to the User Controls window.

SETTING TIME LIMITS WHEN THE USER CAN USE THE COMPUTER

To limit the user to using the computer only at certain times, click the Time Limits link. Windows displays the Time Restrictions window (see Figure 8.20). Drag through the hours you want to block, and then click the OK button to apply the restriction.

FIGURE 8.20
The Time Restrictions window gives you hour-by-hour control of when the user may use the computer.

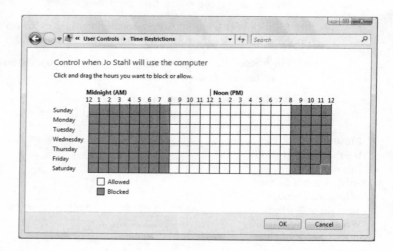

CONTROLLING GAMES

Games can be a particular source of worry for parents—games can be great for keeping children entertained, but may contain all sorts of unsuitable content, from violence to profanity to sexual situations. Windows Vista lets you either block games completely or control which types of games a user can play.

To set Parental Controls on games, follow these steps:

1. In the User Controls window, click the Games link. Windows displays the Game Controls window (see Figure 8.21).

2. In the Can *Username* Play Games? area (where *Username* is the user's name), select the Yes option button or the No option button. This is the master control for the games settings. If you choose the No option button, none of the other settings apply, so you can click the OK button to return to the User Controls window. Normally, you'll want to choose the Yes option button so that you can specify which games to allow and which to block.

FIGURE 8.21

The Game Controls window lets you turn off games altogether or access the settings for controlling which games the user can play.

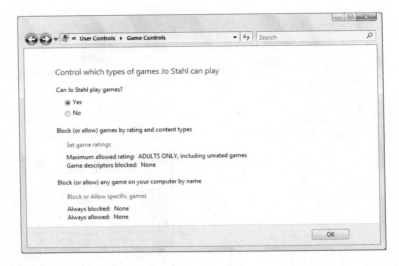

3. Click the Set Game Ratings link. Windows displays the Game Restrictions window (see Figure 8.22).

4. In the If a Game Has No Rating, Can *Username* Play It? area (where *Username* is the user's name), select the Allow Games with No Rating option button or the Block Games with No Rating option button, as appropriate. Normally, you'll want to block games that don't have a rating, because various adult-oriented games don't carry ratings.

5. In the Which Ratings Are OK for *Username* to Play? list, select the appropriate option button: Early Childhood, Everyone, Everyone 10+, Teen, Mature, or Adults Only. Each option button has an explanation of the contents that the rating permits.

6. In the Block These Types of Content list further down the window, select the check box for each content type you want to block. These check boxes allow you to screen out specific content types that are permitted by the ESRB rating you chose in the previous step. The next illustration shows a section of this list.

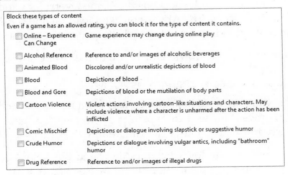

7. Click the OK button. Windows closes the Game Restrictions window and returns you to the Game Controls window.

FIGURE 8.22

In the Game Restrictions window, choose the Entertainment Software Ratings Board rating by which to screen games, and then choose which specific types of content to block.

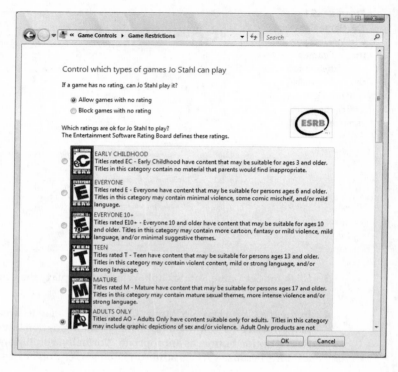

8. In the Block (or Allow) Any Game on Your Computer by Name area, click the Block or Allow Specific Games link if you want to allow or block specific games that are already loaded on the computer. Windows displays the Game Overrides window (see Figure 8.23).

9. For each game, select the Always Allow option button if you want to ensure that the game is allowed, or the Always Block option button if you want to block the game. If you want to let the game's rating control whether the user can play it, select the User Rating Setting option button.

10. Click the OK button. Windows closes the Game Overrides window and returns you to the Game Controls window. The Always Blocked readout and the Always Allowed readout at the bottom of the window now show which games you just blocked and allowed.

11. Click the OK button. Windows returns you to the User Controls window.

ALLOWING OR BLOCKING SPECIFIC PROGRAMS

Apart from games, you may need to prevent a user from running specific programs. For example, you may choose to prevent the user from using peer-to-peer (P2P) file-sharing software.

To control which programs the user can run, follow these steps:

1. In the User Controls window, click the Allow and Block Specific Programs link. Windows displays the Application Restrictions window (see Figure 8.24).

FIGURE 8.23
Use the Game Over-rides window to control whether the user may or may not play specific games installed on your computer.

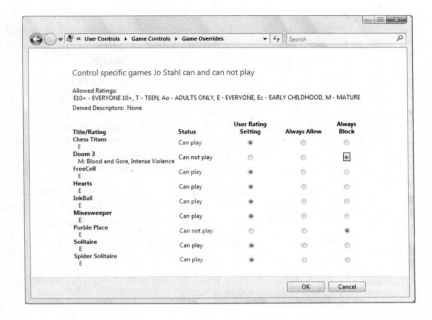

FIGURE 8.24
The Application Restrictions window lets you restrict the user to running a list of approved programs.

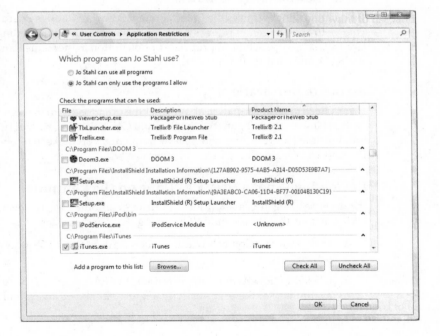

2. In the Which Programs Can *Username* Use? area (where *Username* is the user's name), select the *Username* Can Use Only the Programs I Allow option button if you want to restrict the user. Otherwise, select the *Username* Can Use All Programs option button, which turns off all the other controls in the window.

3. In the Check the Programs That Can Be Used list, select the check box for each program you want to allow the user to use. The list of programs is extensive even if you've installed only a few programs, because Windows' built-in components appear in the list. Being able to allow some components while blocking others gives you lots of flexibility, but it means you'll need to take care constructing the list of programs. Normally the best way to proceed is to click the Check All button to select each check box, and then clear the check box for each program you want to block.

4. If a program doesn't appear on the list, click the Browse button, use the resulting Open dialog box to find the program, and then click the Open button. Windows adds the program to the list, where you can select or clear its check box.

5. Click the OK button. Windows closes the Application Restrictions window and returns you to the User Controls window.

6. Click the OK button. Windows closes the User Controls window and applies the restrictions to the user's account.

SELECTING A GAME RATING SYSTEM

By default, Windows uses the Entertainment Software Ratings Board rating system for games. To change to another games rating system, click the Select a Games Rating System link on the Parental Controls screen, select the appropriate option button in the Game Rating Systems window (see Figure 8.25), and then click the OK button.

SETTING UP NOTIFICATIONS

If you chose to log information about what the user does with the computer, click the Family Safety Options link in the left panel of the Parental Controls window and use the Family Safety Options window (see Figure 8.26) to choose how frequently you'd like to receive reminders of reading activity reports: Weekly, Every Day, or Never.

Reviewing What a User Has Done on the Computer

If you chose to log information about the user's computer use, review it periodically to see if they're taking actions that they shouldn't be taking. Follow these steps:

1. In the Parental Controls window, click the user's name. Windows displays the User Controls screen.

2. Click the View Activity Reports link. Windows displays the Activity Viewer window with a summary of the user's activity. Figure 8.27 shows an example.

3. To see more detail, click the plus (+) sign next to the user's name, and then expand the category in which you're interested. Click an item to display its details. Figure 8.28 shows an example.

4. Click the Close button (the × button). Windows closes the Activity Viewer window.

FIGURE 8.25
Windows offers a choice of games rating systems. The system you select applies to all users—you can't use different rating systems for different users.

FIGURE 8.26
If you've chosen to read activity reports, use the Family Safety Options window to tell Windows how frequently you'd like reminders about them.

FIGURE 8.27
The Summary page in Activity Viewer gives you an overview of the websites the user has visited, their logon times, the programs they've run, and more.

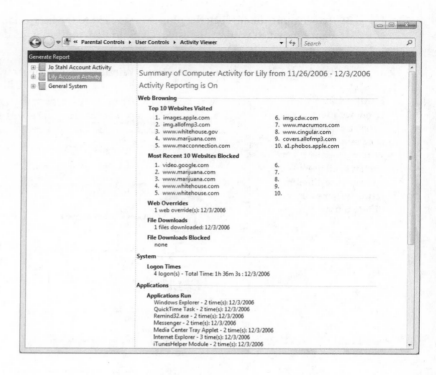

FIGURE 8.28
You can "drill down" to view the specific actions the user has taken. Click the Generate Report button if you want to create a report of the information collected.

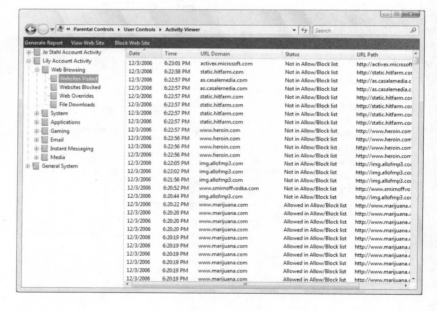

Real World Scenario

DISCUSS PARENTAL CONTROLS WITH THE USERS YOU'RE AFFECTING

Before implementing Parental Controls on a user, discuss with the user which controls you're implementing and your reasons for doing so. If you choose to log information about the user's activities, explain to the user what you'll be able to see—the websites they've visited, the people with whom they've chatted (and whether they've used a webcam), and even which songs and videos they've played.

The Parental Controls icon in the notification area servers to remind the user that Parental Controls are on and gives them an easy way to open the Parental Controls window so that they can see what they're allowed to do and what they're not. They'll also see the effect of any restrictions you apply—for example, preventing them from accessing a website, as shown here.

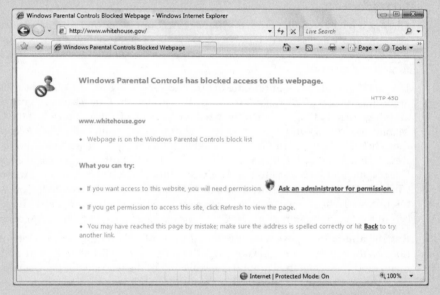

Knowing that Parental Controls are on may encourage the user to be more responsible. Finding out that they're under surveillance without any warning is likely to provoke a strong negative reaction.

The Bottom Line

Understand what user accounts are and what they're for   Windows Vista lets you easily create a separate user account for each user of the computer so that each can keep their files and settings separately.

Know when to use the three types of user accounts and what user profiles are   Windows Vista Home lets you create Administrator accounts and Standard accounts. There's also a built-in Guest account that you can switch on and off as needed. You must always have at least one Administrator account so that one account can administer the computer. Beyond that, create an Administrator account for each user who needs administrative privileges. For each other user, create a Standard account. Microsoft recommends that even administration-level users use a Standard account for day-to-day computing, but many such users find a Standard account awkwardly limiting.

Create a user account   To create a user account, choose Start ➤ Control Panel, click the Add or Remove User Accounts link, and then click the Create a New Account link. Type the username, choose the account type (Standard or Administrator), and then click the Create Account button.

Delete a user account   To delete a user account, log on as an Administrator user and use Task Manager to make sure that the your victim is not logged on. Choose Start ➤ Control Panel, click the Add or Remove User Accounts link, and then click the user's icon. In the Change an Account window, click the Delete the Account link. Choose whether to keep the user's files, and then confirm the deletion.

Change a user account   From the Manage Accounts window, you can apply a picture to a user account, apply a password, remove a password, or create a new password for a user who's forgotten theirs. Every user should create a password reset disk so as to be able to recover from a forgotten password.

Use the Guest account, automatic logon, and secure logon   In Windows Vista, the Guest account is turned off by default for security. Turn on the Guest account only when you need it, and then turn it off again when the need has passed. (To turn it on, click the Guest link in the Manage Accounts window. To turn it off, click the Guest link in the User Accounts window, and then click the Turn Off the Guest Account link.) To implement automatic logon, press Windows Key+R, type control userpasswords2, click the OK button, and clear the Users Must Enter a User Name and Password to Use This Computer check box in the User Accounts dialog box. Click the OK button, enter the username and password of the user to log on, and then click the OK button. To implement secure logon, select the Require Users to Press Ctrl+Alt+Delete check box in the Secure Logon group box on the Advanced page of the User Accounts dialog box.

Restrict and monitor users with Parental Controls   Parental Controls let you define restrictions on the actions users can take. Click the Start button, click your picture at the top of the Start menu, and then click the Parental Controls link in the left pane of the User Accounts window. Click the user's name to open the User Controls window, which provides access to all the Parental Control settings for the user.

Chapter 9

Sharing Files and Working with File Types

- ◆ Understanding how Windows Vista's sharing works
- ◆ Setting up sharing and discovery
- ◆ Sharing files and folders
- ◆ Seeing which files and folders you're sharing
- ◆ Working with file associations, file extensions, and file types

Chances are that you have some files that you need to keep private and other files that you want to share with other people—perhaps with people who use your computer, or with people who use computers connected to the same network.

Windows Vista lets you secure your files or share them with other people. Windows makes sharing as simple as possible, but it's a good idea to understand how the system works so as to avoid inadvertently sharing files or folders with people who shouldn't see them.

This chapter starts by giving you an overview of Windows Vista's security and sharing features. After that, it discusses how to share folders with other users of the computer or other users of your network, and how to see which files and folders you're sharing—for example, in case you want to stop sharing one or more of them.

After that, this chapter tackles the subject of file extensions, file types, and file associations. If you've ever become confused about why different things happen when you double-click different types of files in Explorer, if you wish you could change the program in which a particular file type opens, or if you want to see extensions for your files, read this section.

Understanding How Windows Vista's Sharing Works

The Business versions of Windows Vista, which let you connect your computer to a network running Windows Server, have extremely fine-grained permissions. For example, with the right settings, you can allow one user to open files in a particular folder but not change them. Or you can prevent another user from seeing those files in that folder, but allow them to navigate through that folder to a subfolder it contains and then allow them to work with just one of the files in that subfolder.

Setting such permissions is intricate and tricky—and in any case, most home users don't need such complex permissions. So, the Home versions of Windows Vista provide a simplified set of permissions and set up sharing as follows:

◆ Windows encourages you to create a separate user account for each person who uses your computer and to protect each user account with a password. Windows keeps each user account's files separately.

◆ Windows Vista creates a folder named Users on the system drive—for example, C:\Users. This folder contains each user's user account and a separate collection of settings for each user. By contrast, Windows XP stores the user accounts in the Documents and Settings folder (for example, C:\Documents and Settings).

◆ The Users folder contains a folder for each user account you've created, together with a Public folder, which Windows Vista creates so that you can share files and folders with other users of the computer and the network.

◆ Windows Vista automatically protects files and folders in each user account from Standard users and the Guest user. However, any Administrator user can access the contents of any user's user account folders.

◆ Windows Vista assumes that you'll want to share some files and folders with other users of your computer, but not with other computers on the network. For such sharing, Windows Vista provides folders that are automatically shared with all users of your computer (the Public folder structure). You can't stop Windows from sharing these folders.

◆ Windows Vista lets you choose whether to let other computers on the network see your computer and whether to share files, the Public folder, and printers from your computer. You can choose whether to limit the sharing of the Public folder and printers to people who have a user account on your computer or whether to let anyone access these items.

◆ Windows Vista lets you share your media library—your music, pictures, and videos—with other users on the network.

◆ For any folder apart from folders owned and protected by the operating system, you can choose to share the folder on the network. You can even share your Documents folder (but it's not usually a good idea).

◆ You can share either a folder or individual files. Normally, it's best to set up folders for sharing and then place in them the files you want to share. If you share a file and let other users modify it, they can also create new files in the folder that contains the file.

WHO ARE THE ADMINISTRATOR USERS?

The user who set up Windows Vista on your computer becomes an Administrator user. That user can create other Administrator users as needed. The computer must always have at least one Administrator user so that there's someone to administer it if a problem occurs.

EXPERT KNOWLEDGE: MANIPULATING PERMISSIONS WITH *CACLS* AND *XCACLS*

If you find the file sharing arrangements in Home versions of Windows Vista too simple, you may be glad to know that Windows Vista includes a tool that lets you manipulate permissions on individual files. It's called `cacls`, it's a command-line utility, and it's awkward to use because you need to understand permissions in order to make it do what you want.

`cacls` stands for "change access control lists," and there's a more powerful version of `cacls` called `xcacls` ("extended change access control lists") that you can download for free from the Microsoft website (search for "`xcacls.exe`"). In Windows, an *access control list* (ACL) is used to store the permissions for an object, such as a file, a folder, a printer, or another resource.

Because `cacls` and `xcacls` are highly esoteric, this book leaves you to explore them on your own if you decide you need them. Use the /? switch from the command line (for example, `cacls /?`) to display the help available.

Setting Up Sharing and Discovery

Sharing and discovery is the group of Windows settings that control how your computer can communicate with other computers on your network. These settings are part of Windows Firewall, a software-based form of protection for your computer.

To set up sharing and discovery, you must be an Administrator user or know an Administrator user's password. Your computer should be connected to a private network rather than a public network—for example, connected to your home network (where you do want to share files) rather than to a public network at your local airport or coffee shop (where you don't want to share files).

Opening a Network and Sharing Center Window

To set up sharing and discovery, first open a Network and Sharing Center window (see Figure 9.1). Click the Start button, right-click the Network item, and then choose Properties from the context menu.

FIGURE 9.1
The Sharing and Discovery settings in the Network and Sharing Center control whether other computers on the network can access files, folders, and printers your computer is sharing.

Making Sure Your Computer Is on a Private Network

In the Network area, make sure that Windows Vista knows your computer is connected to a private network. If the Network readout says "Public network," follow these steps:

1. Click the Customize link. Windows launches the Set Network Location Wizard, which displays the Customize Network Settings screen (see Figure 9.2).

2. In the Network Name text box, check the name that's entered. If Windows Vista is still using "Network," consider giving the network a more descriptive name—for example, "Home Network" or "Our Network."

3. In the Location Type area, select the Private option button.

4. If you want to change the network icon used, click the Change button, select a different icon in the Change Network Icon dialog box, and then click the OK button.

5. Click the Next button and then authenticate yourself to User Account Control if necessary. The wizard displays the Successfully Set Network Settings screen.

6. Click the Close button.

FIGURE 9.2
Before setting up file sharing, ensure that your computer is connected to a private network—and that Windows Vista knows that it is.

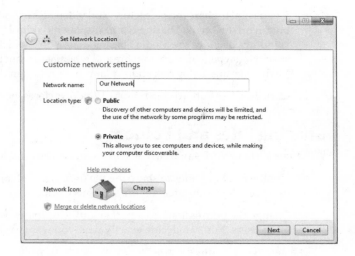

Choose Sharing and Discovery Settings

Next, arrange the sharing you need by choosing suitable sharing and discovery settings. You need to authenticate yourself to User Account Control for most of these settings. Follow these steps:

1. To enable your computer to see and be seen by other computers on the network, click the drop-down button on the Sharing and Discovery bar to display its controls, select the Turn on Network Discovery option button, and then click the Apply button.

2. If you want to share files and folders within folders other than the `Public` folder, click the drop-down button on the File Sharing bar to display its controls, select the Turn on File Sharing option button, and then click the Apply button.

3. If you want to share items in your computer's `Public` folder with other computers on the network, click the drop-down button on the Public Folder Sharing bar to display its controls. If you want to share items so that others can open them but not change them, select the Turn on Sharing So Anyone with Network Access Can Open Files option button. If you want others to be able to change the files you're sharing or create new files in the folders you're sharing, select the Turn on Sharing So Anyone with Network Access Can Open, Change, and Create Files option button. Click the Apply button.

4. If you want to share a printer attached to your computer, click the drop-down button on the Printer Sharing bar to display its controls, select the Turn on Printer Sharing option button, and then click the Apply button.

5. If you shared the `Public` folder in step 3 or a printer in step 4, but you want to restrict access to the folder or printer to those people who have user accounts on your computer (but are accessing the folder or printer from another computer), click the drop-down button on the Password Protected Sharing bar to display its controls, select the Turn on Password Protected Sharing option button, and then click the Apply button.

6. If you want to share music, picture, and video files in your media library, click the drop-down button on the Media Sharing bar to display its controls, and then click the Change button. Windows displays the Media Sharing dialog box, which walks you through the process of specifying what you want to share and whom you want to share it with. Chapter 22 shows the Media Sharing dialog box and explains the process in detail.

7. Click the Close button (the × button). Windows closes the Network and Sharing Center window.

Sharing Files and Folders

Windows Vista provides two easy ways of sharing files and folders:

◆ Use the Public folder to share the file or folder with all other users of the computer and users of other computers on the same network.

◆ Change the permissions on a particular file or folder so that it's shared with one or more other users. You can decide exactly who you want to share the file or folder with.

The next two sections discuss these ways of sharing a folder.

Sharing Files and Folders with All Other Users of Your Computer and Network

To share a file or a folder with all the other users of your computer and the network to which it is connected, put the file or folder in the Users\Public folder.

If you've turned on Public Folder Sharing in the Network and Sharing Center, as described in "Choose Sharing and Discovery Settings," earlier in this chapter, Windows makes the file or folder available to all other users of the network; if you allowed others to change items, they can edit or delete a file or folder, or create new files within a folder. If you allowed others only to open the file, they can open it but not save changes to it within the Public folder.

If you've turned off Public Folder Sharing, items you place in the Public folder are available to other users of your computer but not to users of other computers on the network.

Sharing a File or Folder with Specific Users

Sharing a file or folder with everyone can be useful, especially for items such as music files that everyone needs to access. But often you'll want to share a file or folder with some people but not with others.

To share a file or folder with specific users, follow these steps:

1. Open an Explorer window to the folder that contains the file or folder you want to share. For example, choose Start ➢ Computer to open a Computer window, and then navigate to the folder.

2. Select the file or folder, and then click the Share button on the toolbar. You can also right-click the file or folder, and then choose Share from the shortcut menu. Windows displays the File Sharing dialog box (see Figure 9.3).

3. In the drop-down list, select the user with whom you want to share the file or folder. Select the Everyone (All Users in This List) item if you want to share it with everyone. Your own username appears in the list, but you already have access to the file or folder. You can also choose the Create a New User item in the drop-down list and create a new user, but normally it's best to share only with the existing users.

FIGURE 9.3
Use the File Sharing dialog box to specify the users with whom you want to share a file or folder and what you want them to be able to do with the file or folder.

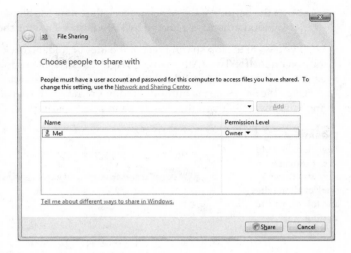

4. Click the Add button to add the selected user or group to the list in the list box. Windows assigns the user or group the Reader permission level. This permission level allows the user or group to open the file or folder, but not change it.

5. If you want to give the user or group a different level of permission for this file or folder, click the drop-down button next to the Reader item, and then choose Contributor or Co-Owner from the drop-down list:

   Contributor   The user or group can open all the files in the folder, add new files, and change or delete files they add. They cannot change or delete files you've created.

   Co-Owner   The user or group can work freely with all the files in the folder, changing or deleting them as needed, or adding new files.

6. Click the Share button to apply the sharing you've set up, and then authenticate yourself to User Account Control. Windows Vista applies the permissions, and then displays a File Sharing window telling you that the items are shared. The window may include a link that lets you automatically send details of the shared file or folder to the user or users with whom you have shared it.

7. Click the Done button. Windows closes the File Sharing window.

Seeing the Files and Folders You're Sharing

When you share a file or folder, Windows Vista adds to the file or folder's icon a little square icon showing the heads and shoulders of a couple of regular folks. If you're using Extra Large Icons or Large Icons in Explorer, and you're sharing only a few files and folders, you may be able to use these squares to keep track of the items you're sharing—but more likely, you could use an easier way of tracking these items.

To see which files and folders you're sharing, follow these steps:

1. Click the Start button, right-click the Network item, and then choose Properties from the context menu. Windows displays a Network and Sharing Center window.

2. At the bottom of the window, click the Show Me all the Files and Folders I Am Sharing link. Windows displays a Shared by Me window showing the items you're sharing (see Figure 9.4).

If you want to stop sharing one of the files or folders, click it in the list, and then click the Share button on the toolbar. (Alternatively, right-click the file or folder, and then choose Share from the shortcut menu.) Windows displays the File Sharing window shown in Figure 9.5.

Click the Stop Sharing button. Windows removes the permissions, and then displays a File Sharing window telling you that you have stopped sharing the file or folder. Click the Done button.

FIGURE 9.4
The Shared by Me folder provides an easy way to keep track of all the files and folders you're sharing.

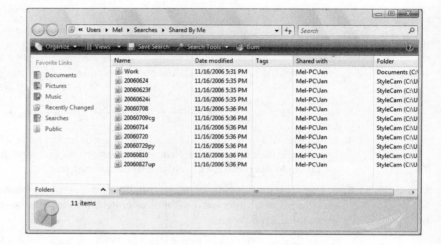

FIGURE 9.5
Use the File Sharing window to stop sharing a file or folder.

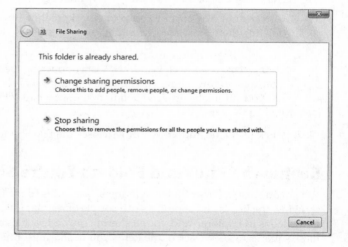

Working with File Associations, File Extensions, and File Types

If you double-click a file with an `.exe` extension, Windows runs the file. If you double-click a file with a `.txt` extension, Windows opens the file in Notepad (or your default text editor). If you double-click a file with an `.mp3` extension, Windows starts it playing in Windows Media Player (or your default audio player for MP3 files).

In each of these examples, your double-click triggers a different action keyed by the file type with which the file extension is associated. This section discusses file extensions, file types, and file associations, how they interact, and how you can customize them to suit your work needs.

What Are File Extensions?

The *extension* is that part of the filename that appears after the last period in the filename. For example, in a file named `September 2008 Report.doc`, the extension is `.doc`. In a file named `September 2008 Report. Edited by Bill.doc`, the extension is still `.doc`, even though there's an earlier period in the filename. A filename doesn't have to have an extension, but almost all files do, because the extension identifies the file type associated with the file, and the file type contains information on the program and action to use for the file. (More on this in a minute.) If a file doesn't have an extension, Windows doesn't know what to do with it—unless the file is one of the file types designed to have no extension, such as a folder or a DVD.

Most extensions are three characters (for example, `.exe`, `.doc`, or `.avi`), but some are four characters (for example, `.jpeg`, `.mpeg`, or `.html`). Extensions can be up to 200 characters long, but this length is impractical and unnecessary for all but the most specialized purposes. Despite the proliferation of programs and file types, many three-character extensions remain unused and available, though developers who need to create a new file type may prefer a distinctive four-character extension to an unmemorable three-character extension. Users—particularly those who grew up using DOS—tend to be familiar with three-character extensions, so four-character extensions seem strange or a bit wrong. With the Office 2007 programs, Microsoft is gradually transitioning to four-character extensions. For example, Word 2007 documents use the `.docx` file extension, and Excel 2007 workbooks use the `.xlsx` file extension.

What Are File Types?

Ideally, each file extension is linked to a *file type*, a descriptive category with which actions can be associated. For example, the `.bmp` extension is linked by default to the Bitmap Image file type. The default action associated with the Bitmap Image file type is Open. So when you double-click a file with the `.bmp` extension, Windows opens the file in the default program (Windows Photo Gallery). Other actions associated by default with the Bitmap Image file type are Edit, Print, and PrintTo.

Windows comes with preset associations for file types of which it's already aware, and programs you install add further associations for their file types. Unlike Windows XP, which lets you edit the action associated with a file type, Windows Vista does not let you edit the action.

Each extension can be linked to only one file type at a time. If an extension isn't linked to a file type, when you double-click the file, Windows opens a dialog box telling you the problem and letting you choose between using a Web service to find the correct program or choosing the program from a list of installed programs.

Multiple extensions can be linked to a given file type. For example, by default the extensions .mpa, .mpe, .mpeg, .mpg, and .mpv2 are linked to the Movie Clip file type. So when you double-click a file with any one of those five extensions, Windows performs the default action for the Movie Clip file type, which is to open it and play it.

Registering File Types and Associations

Windows stores its file types and associations in the Registry. You can dig at them there (by using the techniques described in Chapter 11), but it's seldom a good idea unless you know exactly what you're doing. Windows provides tools for viewing and changing file types and associations, so you don't need to visit the Registry unless you're trying to create very special effects.

When you install a program, the setup routine typically handles the registration of any file types associated with the program. The better setup routines check with you before registering the file types, because they may already be registered to other programs. But more aggressive programs monitor the file types associated with them and try to reclaim them each time you run the program. Audio players (particularly MP3 players) and video players tend to be the worst offenders on this front, but they're by no means the only ones; productivity programs can be greedy too. The better programs let you specify whether they should reclaim file types automatically and, if so, which file types.

Specifying the File Type of a File

Typically, you specify the file type of a file by adding the appropriate extension (or one of the appropriate extensions) to it. Most Windows programs use common dialog boxes for Save operations. These common dialog boxes include a Save As Type drop-down list that you use to specify the file type for the file.

By default, the program displays the most likely file type in the Save As dialog box. If you don't explicitly specify the extension for the file, the program adds it. For example, if you save a workbook file in Excel 2007, Excel suggests the Microsoft Excel Workbook file type in the Save As Type drop-down list. If you don't add an extension to the filename, Excel automatically adds the extension .xlsx, which is linked to the Microsoft Excel Workbook file type.

Finding Out Which File Type a File Is

Your first clue to which file type a file is should be the icon that Windows uses for the file. For example, if Windows shows a stylized Word icon for the file, it's probably some form of Word document. But icons can be hard to identify, especially when they're small—and in any case, Windows often uses the same icon for several file types (for example, different types of Word documents).

To find out which file type a file is, right-click the file in an Explorer window or on the Desktop, and then choose Properties from the context menu. The General page of the Properties dialog box for the file displays its file type. Figure 9.6 shows an example.

Alternatively, switch the Explorer window to Details view, and then look at the Type column.

FIGURE 9.6

If you can't identify a file's file type by its icon, display the General page of the Properties dialog box.

Displaying all File Extensions

Windows has an engrossing love/hate relationship with file extensions. It can't live without them, but it'd sure like to keep them out of sight.

Windows needs file extensions so that it knows the actions it can take with a particular file. But Microsoft seems to feel that extensions look ugly, so it makes Windows hide them for as long as possible. This improves the cosmetic look of long filenames and a few other things, but it also has some undesirable consequences.

So by default, Windows hides file extensions for registered file types, relying on icons in their various forms (thumbnails, tiles, and icons) to identify the file type and the extension. In Details view, the Type column in the Explorer windows and dialog boxes displays the file type. And because most every file type is registered either by Windows itself or by the program you install that creates that type of file, all file extensions remain hidden until you change the settings.

If you're comfortable with icons, this is more or less okay. But if not, you can display most file extensions as follows:

1. Choose Organize ➤ Folder and Search Options to display the Folder Options dialog box.

2. Click the View tab to display the View page.

3. Clear the Hide File Extensions for Known File Types check box.

4. Click the OK button to close the dialog box.

 **Real World Scenario**

UNDERSTANDING THE DANGERS OF HIDDEN FILE EXTENSIONS

Clearing the Hide File Extensions for Known File Types on the View page of the Folder Options dialog box displays *most* file extensions—but not all of them. Windows still hides the following file extensions:

.url	Internet shortcut or URL	.job	Task Scheduler Task Object file
.jse	JScript Encoded Script file	.vbe	VBScript Encoded Script file
.js	JScript Script file	.vbs	VBScript Script file
.shs	Scrap object	.scf	Explorer command file
.lnk	Shortcut	.wsf	Windows Script file
.shb	Shortcut to section of a document		

As you can see in the list, the LNK file type is used for shortcuts. So if you make Windows display the extension for LNK files, you'll see a .lnk extension popping up for shortcuts on your Desktop, for shortcuts on your Start menu, and for shortcuts in Explorer windows. The .lnk extensions on the Desktop are entirely harmless, but the extensions on the Start menu *are* ugly and make it a little more awkward to use. For one thing, the four extra characters—the period and *LNK*—make each of the cascading menus wider than it would otherwise be. And apart from the visual distraction, it's conceptually a little distracting to realize that many of the items on the Start menu are plain old shortcuts. It's not quite like pulling aside the wizard's curtain, but it gives a feeling that the Start menu is held together by virtual string and sealing wax.

Similarly, the URL file type is for Internet shortcuts and URLs. So if you make Windows display the .url extension, it appears on all Internet shortcuts, including those on your Favorites menus. This too looks ugly, and you can see why Microsoft doesn't want these extensions displayed.

The problem with not displaying extensions is that some file types can be used to deliver viruses. All the scripting file types—VBE and VBS files, JSE and JS files, WSF files, even SCF files—can perform a wide variety of actions on your computer without consulting you.

No savvy user will run a script that arrives unsolicited: It could be just about anything, and the chances of it doing anything pleasant are small. But, because Windows hides these extensions, a script file can easily masquerade as another file type. For example, say a malefactor creates a script file and names it Latest Britney Clip.mp3.vbs. Because the .vbs extension is hidden, this file shows up as Latest Britney Clip.mp3. If the user double-clicks it, thinking that doing so will start the file playing in their default MP3 player (for example, Windows Media Player), the script executes instead. The icon for the script will be wrong, but people often miss this, particularly in Details view in Explorer or when opening an attachment from e-mail. Any antivirus program worth using will catch such scripts, but many people forget to check every file they receive, especially if a file seems to have appealing contents.

Windows Vista doesn't let you display these always-hidden extensions, so keep using your antivirus program, and check the source of any files you receive that appear suspicious.

Changing the File Type Linked to an Extension

As mentioned earlier, some programs grab file types without asking, either during their setup routines or each time you run them. Other programs ask for permission before grabbing. Either way, you'll sometimes need to change file types so that they're associated with the program you want rather than with the greediest program around.

To change the file type linked to a particular extension, follow these steps:

1. Right-click a file with that extension, and then choose Properties from the context menu. Windows displays the Properties dialog box for the file. (See Figure 9.6, earlier in the chapter, for an example of the Properties dialog box.) The General page displays information including the type of file (the Type of File readout) and the program associated with it (the Opens With readout).

2. Click the Change button. Windows displays the Open With dialog box (shown in Figure 9.7).

3. In the Programs list box, select the program with which to open the file:

    ◆ Windows breaks down the programs it offers into two categories: *Recommended Programs* and *Other Programs*.

    ◆ If neither category lists the program you want to use, click the Browse button. Windows displays a second Open With dialog box. This dialog box is an Open dialog box in disguise. Navigate to and select the program, and then click the Open button. Windows closes the second Open With dialog box and returns you to the first Open With dialog box.

4. Click the OK button. Windows closes the first Open With dialog box and links the extension to the file type you selected.

5. Click the OK button. Windows closes the Properties dialog box for the file.

FIGURE 9.7
Use this Open With dialog box to specify the program with which you want to open the file.

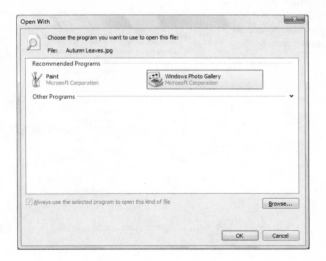

Changing the Program Associated with a File Type

If you find that one program grabs another program's file types, you may need to change the program associated with a file type. To do so, follow these steps:

1. Choose Start ➢ Default Programs to open a Default Programs window.

2. Click the Associate a File Type or Protocol with a Specific Program link to open the Set Associations window (see Figure 9.8).

3. In the list box, select the file type you want to change. By default, this list is sorted alphabetically by file extension name, but you can sort by the Description column or the Current Default column by clicking the appropriate column heading.

4. Click the Change Program button to display the Open With dialog box (see Figure 9.9).

5. If the program you want to use appears in the Recommended Programs list or the Other Programs list, select it. Otherwise, click the Browse button to display a second Open With dialog box, which is a standard Windows Open dialog box given a new name. Navigate to the folder that contains the program you want, select the program, and then click the Open button. Windows returns you to the first Open With dialog box, in which it selects the program you chose.

6. Click the OK button to close the Open With dialog box and apply your choice.

FIGURE 9.8

The Set Associations window lets you see which program is currently set to open a particular file type— and change that file type to another program if need be.

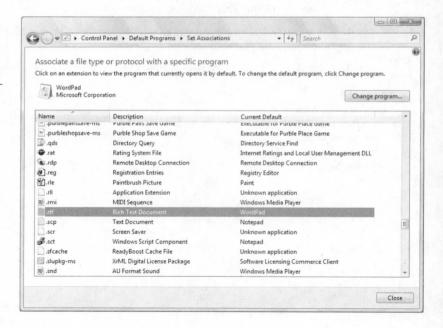

FIGURE 9.9

In the Open With dialog box, choose the program you want to use to open this file type. The Recommended Programs area shows programs that Windows knows can open this file type, but you'll often need to browse to find the program you actually want.

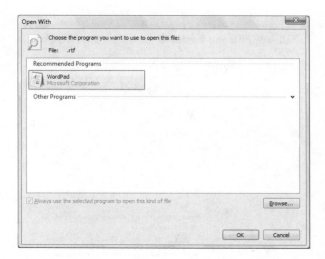

Real World Scenario

CREATING AND REGISTERING A NEW FILE TYPE

If you want, you can create a file of an unregistered file type simply by specifying an extension that hasn't been used. You won't normally need to do this, because any program you install on Windows should automatically register its own file types. But you may sometimes need to use this technique for a program that was designed for an earlier version of Windows and that can't install itself successfully on Windows Vista. You may be able to get the program running by copying an existing installation across to your Windows Vista computer—but that probably won't include details of the file types.

To create and register a new file type, open Notepad, enter a space, and save the new document it automatically creates under a name that uses the extension you want—for example, `"Example.888"` if you need to use the 888 extension. You must enter the filename and extension within double quotation marks, because otherwise Notepad automatically assigns the `.txt` extension, which is associated with the TXT file type. Exit Notepad once you've created the file.

Now open an Explorer window to the folder in which you created the file, change to Details view, and you'll see the `.888` extension (or whatever extension you chose) displayed. Explorer decides that the file type for this file is "888 File"; you've created a new file type.

Now you need to tell Windows which program to use for opening this file type.

1. Double-click the file in Explorer. Wait while Windows consults the Registry about the file type and comes up dry. Windows then displays the Windows Cannot Open This File dialog box.

2. Choose the Select a Program from a List of Installed Programs option button. Windows displays a slightly different version of the Open With dialog box, as shown here.

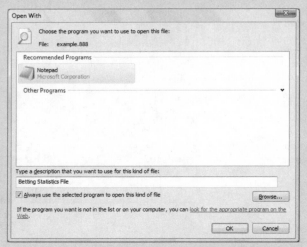

3. In the Type a Description That You Want to Use for This Kind of File text box, enter the name you want to assign to the file type. Make it as concise and descriptive as possible.

4. In the Programs list box, select the program you want to associate with the file type. If the program isn't listed, click the Browse button and use the resulting Open With dialog box to identify it.

5. Select the Always Use the Selected Program to Open This Kind of File check box.

6. Click the OK button. Windows creates the file type, creates Registry entries for it, and opens the file in the specified program.

Now, when you double-click a file of your new file type, Windows opens the file using the program you chose.

Opening a File with a Program Other than the Associated Program

Once you have the correct file association in place, double-clicking a file opens it in the associated program. Sometimes you may want to open the file in a different program. For example, you might want to use the Word Viewer (which you can download from the Microsoft website) instead of Word to open a DOC file just in case the file contains malware that your antivirus program has missed.

To open a file with a program other than the associated program, take the following steps:

1. Right-click the file and choose Open With from the context menu. Windows displays the Open With dialog box. If Windows displays an Open With submenu (see Figure 9.10), you can simply select the program if it's listed; if not, select the Choose Default Program item.

2. In the list box, select the program with which to open the file. If the program you want to use does not appear in either the Recommended Programs list or the Other Programs list, click the Browse button, use the second Open With dialog box to choose the program, and then click the OK button.

FIGURE 9.10
The Open With command lets you open a file with a different program than the default program.

3. If you want Windows to create an Open With submenu for this file type and place an item for this program and the default program for this file type on the submenu, select the Always Use the Selected Program to Open This Kind of File check box.

4. Click the OK button. Windows closes the Open With dialog box and opens the file with the program you chose.

If you selected the Always Use the Selected Program to Open This Kind of File check box in step 3, Windows adds an Open With submenu to the context menu for the file type.

The Bottom Line

Understanding how Windows Vista's sharing works   Windows Vista encourages you to create a separate user account for each person who uses the computer. Windows keeps each user's folder separate from other users' and protects the contents of each user's folder. An Administrator user can view any user's folder. You can share files or folders by placing them in the Public folder (which is always shared) or by setting up sharing on individual files or folders.

Setting up sharing and discovery   To let users of other computers see the files and folders your computer is sharing, you must enable discovery. You can then choose whether to share files and folders, your computer's Public folder, your computer's printer, and your media library. You can also decide whether to limit sharing to people who have a user account on your computer.

Sharing files and folders   To share a file or folder with all other users of your computer or network, place the file or folder in your computer's Public folder. To share a file or folder only with specific users, select the file or folder, click the Share button on the toolbar, and then use the File Sharing dialog box to select the users and specify which level of permissions to give them.

Seeing which files and folders you're sharing To see which files and folders you're sharing, choose Start ➤ Network, click the Network and Sharing Center button on the toolbar, and then click the Show Me All the Files and Folders I Am Sharing link. In the Shared by Me window that Windows Vista displays, you can choose to stop sharing files or folders.

Working with file associations, file extensions, and file types Windows normally manages file types, file extensions, and their associations with programs for you, but if you find that the wrong program opens when you double-click a file in an Explorer window, you may need to change the program associated with a file type. To do so, choose Start ➤ Default Programs, click the Associate a File Type or Protocol with a Program link, select the file type, select the program, and then click the OK button.

Chapter 10

Managing Your Disks and Drives

◆ Format a disk so that Windows can use it

◆ Change your computer's name, description, and workgroup

◆ Convert a disk to NTFS for efficiency and stability

◆ Free up space on your disk using compression

◆ Tell Windows which folders to index

◆ Keep your hard disks defragmented and cleaned up

◆ Change your disk volumes or mount them in folders for easy access

This chapter discusses how to manage your disks and drives, showing you how to understand and undertake the key actions you'll need to perform with them. These actions range from formatting a disk to using compression to free up disk space on an NTFS disk and from defragmenting your disks to creating and deleting volumes (or partitions).

Formatting a Disk to Make It Usable

Be it hard, removable, or floppy, a disk needs to be formatted before it's usable. *Formatting* imposes a file system on the disk's physical sectors, arranging them into logical clusters that Windows can access and manipulate.

You use the same procedure for formatting hard, removable, and floppy disks. By contrast, recordable and rewritable CDs and DVDs need a different kind of formatting because they use different file systems.

WINDOWS CAN READ 720KB FLOPPIES BUT NOT FORMAT THEM

Windows can format only 1.44MB floppies. It can't format 720KB floppies—neither from the Format dialog box nor from the command-line FORMAT command—though it can read 720KB floppies formatted using other operating systems.

You'll find it hard to buy 720KB floppies these days, but if you have a box of old media, some may be lurking there. If you find you can't format a floppy, check its capacity.

To format a disk, follow these steps:

1. Choose Start ➤ Computer. Windows displays a Computer window, showing the disks on your computer.

2. Right-click the disk, and then choose Format from the context menu. Windows displays the appropriate Format dialog box for the disk:

   ◆ For a local hard disk, Windows displays the Format Local Disk dialog box (shown in Figure 10.1). You need to go through User Account Control to format a local hard disk.

   ◆ For a floppy disk, Windows displays the Format Floppy Disk Drive dialog box.

   ◆ For a removable disk, Windows displays the Format Removable Disk dialog box.

3. When formatting a hard disk, make sure that the Capacity drop-down list is showing approximately the right size for the disk. You shouldn't be able to change this setting, but you should check it in case Windows is having trouble reading the disk, which could indicate a physical problem with the disk.

4. In the File System drop-down list, choose the file system with which to format the disk:

   ◆ For a hard disk, you can choose between NTFS and FAT32. NTFS (the New Technology File System) is more secure and more stable than FAT32 (the 32-bit File Allocation Table file system), so you should normally choose NTFS. Choose FAT32 only if you need an operating system that cannot read NTFS (for example, Windows 9x) to be able to access the disk.

   ◆ For a floppy disk, you can choose only FAT.

   ◆ For most removable disks, you can choose among NTFS, FAT32, and FAT. Use NTFS unless you need to be able to read the disk using a computer or other device (for example, a portable music player) that requires FAT32 or FAT. Use FAT only for low-capacity disks, because this file system is far less efficient than FAT32 or NTFS.

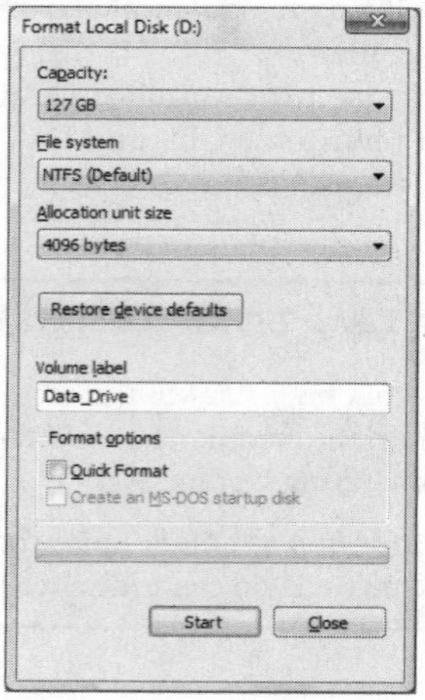

FIGURE 10.1
In the Format Local
Disk dialog box,
specify the file system
to use for the disk.

5. In the Allocation Unit Size drop-down list, you can specify the cluster size for the disk. By default, Windows selects the Default Allocation Size item. Typically the options for NTFS are 512 bytes, 1,024 bytes, 2,048 bytes, and 4,096 bytes. You shouldn't need to specify the cluster size, but see the sidebar "What Is the Cluster Size, and Should You Specify It?" if you're curious as to why not.

6. In the Volume Label text box, you can enter a name for the volume. (A *volume* is an area of storage on a hard disk—typically a partition.) FAT and FAT32 volume names can be up to 11 characters long, while NTFS volume names can be up to 32 characters long. There's no obligation to enter a volume label, but doing so makes the volume easier to identify. (This tends to be less important for a floppy disk than for a small removable disk or a hard disk volume, especially if you label the outside of the floppy.)

7. In the Format Options group box, select the Quick Format check box if you want to skip scanning the disk for bad sectors. Skipping the scan speeds up the format significantly, because it means that all Windows has to do is mark the files on the disk as being deleted. But it's best to perform the scan by running a standard format unless you've recently scanned the disk for bad sectors and found it clean.

WHAT'S THE "CREATE AN MS-DOS STARTUP DISK" CHECK BOX FOR?

The Create an MS-DOS Startup Disk check box lets you create a floppy disk that boots to a DOS prompt. (DOS is the acronym for Disk Operating System, an old operating system for PCs. MS-DOS was Microsoft's version of DOS.) You can't do much from DOS to a Windows computer, so you probably won't need to use this capability.

---

8. Click the Start button. Windows displays a warning dialog box (shown in Figure 10.2) checking that you're sure you want to format the disk.

9. If you *are* sure, click the OK button. Windows starts the formatting operation.

10. When Windows has finished formatting the disk, it displays a Formatting Local Disk dialog box (or a Formatting Floppy Disk dialog box, or a Formatting Removable dialog box, or whatever) to tell you that the format is complete.

11. Click the OK button. Windows closes the dialog box and returns you to the Format dialog box that was previously displayed.

12. Click the Close button. Windows closes the Format dialog box.

You can now use the formatted disk to store files.

FIGURE 10.2
Because you're about to wipe the contents of the disk, Windows double-checks with this warning dialog box to make sure you know what you're doing.

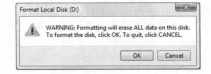

EXPERT KNOWLEDGE: WHAT IS THE CLUSTER SIZE, AND SHOULD YOU SPECIFY IT?

The *cluster size* is the smallest amount of disk space that you can allocate for storing a file. Windows uses clusters as a logical overlay to let it get at the physical sectors on the disk in which the information is actually stored. Most files take up multiple clusters; the smaller the cluster size, the more clusters a file of any given size takes up.

In the days when both disks and files were smaller than they are today, cluster size used to be more of an issue than it is now. Operating systems that used the FAT16 file allocation table, such as DOS and Windows 95, weren't able to create enough clusters to handle large disks efficiently: For a drive of 120MB, FAT16 uses a 2KB cluster size, which is fine; for a 512MB drive, 16KB, which is lavish; and for a 3GB drive, 64KB, which is prodigal. Any space not used in the cluster is wasted, so if you stored a 1KB file on that 3GB drive under FAT16, you were wasting 63KB.

Unlike FAT16, FAT32 and NTFS *can* create enough clusters to handle even large disks, so cluster size shouldn't be an issue with Windows. As mentioned a moment ago, you can specify cluster sizes of 512 bytes (0.5KB), 1KB, 2KB, and 4KB: all good, small sizes. If you're creating files smaller than 4KB these days, you're doing well—and in any case, hard disks have grown so much that occasionally wasting a few KB seldom causes much pain anymore.

The best cluster size depends on the size of the disk in question. If you're familiar with the cluster size recommended for the size of disk you have, you *can* specify the cluster size you want to use. But because Windows is preloaded with information about cluster sizes, it's usually best to let Windows allocate the cluster size automatically. To do so, leave the Default Allocation Size entry (the default) selected in the Allocation Unit Size drop-down list.

Normally you set the cluster size, either explicitly or implicitly, when you format a disk. However, some partitioning utilities, such as PartitionMagic, let you change cluster sizes without reformatting, which can save you a huge amount of time and effort.

Changing the Computer's Name, Description, and Workgroup

Each computer has a name and a description, and belongs to a workgroup:

Name   The computer's *name* isn't the name for the Computer item, which shows you the drives and devices on your computer (and which you can rename without affecting anything more than the user interface): It's the name by which the computer appears on any network to which it's attached. The name is partly for your benefit, partly for the benefit of other users, partly for that of Windows, and partly for that of other computers on the network: It enables you, other users, Windows, and the other computers to identify your computer.

Description   The *description* is entirely for your and other users' benefit: It's a text field that lets you describe the computer identified by the name. Windows doesn't assign a description by default, so the computer doesn't have a description until you enter one.

Workgroup   The *workgroup* is a logical collection of computers intended to work together. By default, the Windows Vista Home setup routine adds your computer to a workgroup named WORKGROUP. It's a good idea to change the workgroup name, especially if you connect to the Internet via a cable modem, which can lead to your sharing the workgroup inadvertently with your neighbors on the same cable loop.

You can change the computer's name, description, and workgroup easily enough. To do so, follow these steps:

1. Press Windows Key+Break. (Alternatively, click the Start button, right-click the Computer item, and then choose Properties from the context menu.) Windows displays a System window (see Figure 10.3).

2. In the Computer Name, Domain, and Workgroup Settings area, click the Change Settings link and then authenticate yourself to User Account Control. Windows displays the Computer Name page of the System Properties dialog box (see Figure 10.4).

3. In the Computer Description text box, type the description for the computer.

4. To change the computer name or workgroup, click the Change button. Windows displays the Computer Name Changes dialog box (see Figure 10.5).

5. Change the name in the Computer Name text box if necessary.

  ◆ You can use letters, numbers, and hyphens, but not any of the characters in the following list. (Technically, you *can* use some of these characters, such as the underscore, but they create "nonstandard" names that may cause problems, so it's best to avoid them.)

     ` ~ ! @ # $ % ^ & * ( ) = + _ [ ] { } \ | ; : . ' " , < > / ?

  ◆ For compatibility with older computers, limit the name to 15 characters maximum.

FIGURE 10.3
The Computer Name, Domain, and Workgroup Settings area in the System window shows your computer's name, description (if any), and workgroup.

FIGURE 10.4
The Computer Name
page of the System
Properties dialog box
shows the description,
computer name, and
workgroup name.

FIGURE 10.5
If you need to change
the computer's name,
type it in the Comput-
er Name text box in
the Computer Name
Changes dialog box.
Here, you can also
change the workgroup
of which your com-
puter is part.

6. Change the name in the Workgroup text box if necessary.

7. Click the OK button. Windows assesses the changes you've made and displays a Computer Name/Domain Changes dialog box if there's a problem or an action you must take:

   ◆ If you used nonstandard characters, Windows tells you that the name won't work, as shown here.

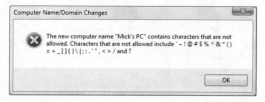

FINDING OUT THE COMPUTER'S NETBIOS NAME

If your network includes computers running older operating systems, you may need to know the Net-BIOS name for your Windows Vista computer in order to enable the older computers to communicate with it on the network. The NetBIOS name is normally the same as the name that appears in the Computer Name text box in the Computer Name Changes dialog box, but to make sure, click the More button in this dialog box, and then look at the NetBIOS Computer Name readout in the DNS Suffix and NetBIOS Computer Name dialog box (shown here).

You can't change the NetBIOS name here, and you shouldn't need to change the computer's primary DNS suffix for a computer running Windows Vista Home, so after verifying the NetBIOS name, click the Cancel button to close the DNS Suffix and NetBIOS Computer Name dialog box. DNS is the abbreviation for Domain Name System, the system that translates computer names (such as sybex.com) to IP addresses (such as 208.215.179.220).

◆ If you used a computer name more than 15 characters long, Windows warns you that the NetBIOS name will be a shorter version of the name, as shown here.

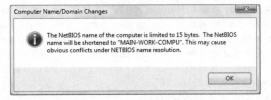

◆ If you used a nonstandard name by including a nonstandard character (for example, an underscore), Windows tells you about the issue and lets you decide whether to use the nonstandard name or change it, as shown here.

◆ If all is well with the name, Windows tells you that you need to restart the computer to apply the change, as shown here.

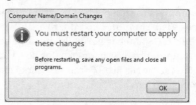

8. Click the OK button. Windows closes the second Computer Name Changes dialog box, returning you to the System Properties dialog box. The Computer Name page now displays a warning telling you that changes will take effect after you restart the computer.

9. Click the OK button. Windows closes the System Properties dialog box. If you need to restart your computer, Windows displays a dialog box offering to restart it.

10. Choose the Restart Now button if you want Windows to restart your computer straight away. Choose the Restart Later button if you want to take any other actions (for example, closing other programs and saving your documents) and then restart the computer yourself.

Converting a Disk to NTFS

If you need to use Windows's security features or compression (discussed next), your volumes need to be NTFS rather than FAT. Windows provides a tool for converting a disk from FAT or FAT32 to NTFS, so you can convert your volumes at any time. This is a one-way process, in that you can't convert the disk back to FAT unless you reformat it (which involves removing all the data from the disk), so it's not something to try idly or on a whim.

The best time to convert a disk from FAT to NTFS is when you install Windows. The second-best time is when you need to format the disk, because formatting overwrites all the contents of the drive anyway. But if you want to maintain a dual-boot system with Windows 9*x* until you're sure that Windows Vista suits you, you'll need to keep one or more drives formatted with FAT, which means that neither of these options is viable—unless you're prepared to blow away the contents of the FAT disk when you decide to commit to NTFS.

To convert a FAT disk to NTFS without affecting the data on it (other than the file system on which the data is stored), follow these steps:

1. Close any other programs you're running. This step is optional, but it allows the conversion to run unhindered. Also, you'll need to reboot your computer twice during the conversion.

2. Choose Start ➢ All Programs ➢ Accessories ➢ Command Prompt. Windows opens a Command Prompt window.

3. Issue a convert command for the appropriate drive. The syntax for the convert command for converting a drive to NTFS is convert *drive:* /FS:NTFS, where *drive:* is the letter of the drive to convert. For example, the following command converts the D: drive:

```
convert d: /FS:NTFS
```

4. Give your computer some time to perform the conversion, and reboot it when Windows asks you to.

The `convert` command takes a while to run, depending on how big the drive is and how much it contains. You should know a couple of other things about it:

◆ `convert` needs a modest amount of space for the conversion, so the disk can't be stuffed to the gills with files when you convert it. (If the disk *is* stuffed—which isn't a great idea anyway—you just need to move some of the files off the drive temporarily while you perform the conversion. You can then move the files back onto the drive, and Windows will store the moved files using NTFS.)

◆ If you want the files and folders on the converted drive to have no security on them, add the `/NoSecurity` flag to the command. You won't usually want to do this, but it may be useful in special circumstances.

◆ Converting the system volume to NTFS requires two reboots. The conversion happens after the first reboot, and Windows then reboots itself again.

Using Compression to Free Up Space

To save disk space, you can *compress* files, folders, or even an entire drive that uses NTFS. (You can't compress a FAT32 drive using Windows.) How much disk space you save depends on the types of file you're compressing. Anything that's already compressed—for example, a Zip file or a compressed multimedia file such as an MP3 music file or an MPEG movie—won't compress much, if at all. Files such as Word documents or Excel spreadsheets compress nicely. Uncompressed graphics—for example, Windows Bitmap (BMP) files—compress very well.

Compression saves space so that you can pack more information on your drives, but it has two main disadvantages:

◆ First, your computer takes longer to access a compressed file, folder, or drive. If your computer can run Windows Vista at a decent speed, the extra effort required for compression shouldn't matter unless you need every ounce of performance (for example, for games).

◆ Second, you cannot encrypt a compressed file or folder. However, Windows Vista Home doesn't offer encryption, so this concern applies only to the Business and Ultimate versions of Windows Vista.

Compressing a File or Folder

To compress a file or a folder, take the following steps:

1. Right-click the file or folder and choose Properties from the context menu. Windows displays the Properties dialog box for the file or folder.

2. On the General page, click the Advanced button. Windows displays the Advanced Attributes dialog box (shown in Figure 10.6).

3. Select the Compress Contents to Save Disk Space check box.

4. Click the OK button. Windows closes the Advanced Attributes dialog box.

5. Click the OK button. Windows closes the Properties dialog box.

To uncompress a file or folder, repeat this procedure but clear the Compress Contents to Save Disk Space check box.

FIGURE 10.6

To save space, you can compress a file or folder by selecting the Compress Contents to Save Disk Space check box in the Advanced Attributes dialog box.

 Real World Scenario

SOME FILES AND FOLDERS AREN'T WORTH COMPRESSING

When deciding whether to compress a folder, consider the files it will contain. If the files are already in a highly compressed format, compressing the folder will save no further space. For example, files such as MP3 and WMA audio files and MPEG video files are already compressed as far as they will go, so there's no point in compressing a folder that will contain them.

Compressing a Drive

Compressing individual folders (let alone individual files) is a slow business, and may not save you a large amount of space. You'll usually get better results from compressing a whole drive.

To compress an NTFS drive, take the following steps:

1. Choose Start ➤ Computer. Windows open a Computer window.

2. Right-click the drive, and then choose Properties from the context menu. Windows displays the Properties dialog box for the drive (see Figure 10.7).

3. On the General page, select the Compress This Drive to Save Disk Space check box.

4. Click the Apply button. Windows displays the Confirm Attribute Changes dialog box (shown in Figure 10.8), asking if you want to apply this change only to the root of the drive or to its subfolders and files as well.

5. Select the Apply Changes to *drive*:\, Subfolders and Files option button (where *drive* is the drive letter).

FIGURE 10.7

To compress a drive and all the folders and files it contains, select the Compress This Drive to Save Disk Space check box on the General page of the Properties dialog box.

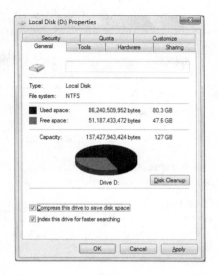

FIGURE 10.8

To compress a drive and its contents, select the Apply Changes to Drive:\, Subfolders and Files option button in the Confirm Attribute Changes dialog box.

6. Click the OK button. Windows closes the Confirm Attribute Changes dialog box and displays the Access Denied dialog box, as shown here, saying that you will need to provide administrator permission to change the drive's attributes.

7. Click the Continue button, and then authenticate yourself to User Account Control.

8. Once you're authenticated, Windows displays the Applying Attributes dialog box, and starts compressing the drive, as shown here.

9. When compression is complete, click the OK button in the Properties dialog box for the drive. Windows closes the dialog box.

If you find that compressing the drive seems to have reduced your computer's performance, you can uncompress it easily enough. Repeat the steps in the above list, but this time, clear the Compress This Drive to Save Disk Space check box. You need to authenticate yourself for decompression as well.

WINDOWS MAY BE UNABLE TO COMPRESS FILES THAT ARE IN USE

While compressing a drive, Windows may display the Error Applying Attributes dialog box telling you that an error occurred applying the attribute to (in other words, compressing) a file because the file is being used by another process. This dialog box offers you an Ignore button, an Ignore All button, a Try Again button, and a Cancel button, as shown here.

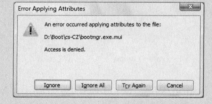

Usually, the best approach is to click the Retry button to retry the operation. If the dialog box reappears, click the Ignore button. If Windows keeps producing the Error Applying Attributes dialog box, click the Ignore All button to ignore all the errors and continue with the compression, or click the Cancel button to cancel applying the compression for now so that you can try the operation again later.

Setting Archiving and Indexing for a File or Folder

Apart from compression, the Advanced Attributes dialog box (shown in Figure 10.6, earlier in the chapter) for a file or folder offers two other options:

File/Folder Is Ready for Archiving check box   Select this check box (or leave it selected) to specify that the file or folder can be archived. Nothing will happen to the folder until you use a program that checks the archiving status of files.

Index This Folder for Fast Searching check box   Select this check box (or leave it selected) to include this folder in any indexing operations you tell Windows to perform. By indexing your folders, Windows creates a database that lets you search more quickly for files matching specified criteria.

When you've finished choosing settings in the Advanced Attributes dialog box, click the OK button. Windows closes the Advanced Attributes dialog box. Then click the OK button. Windows closes the Properties dialog box for the file or folder.

Configuring Indexing and Search Options

Windows Vista automatically creates indexes of all the files and folders on your computer that are marked for indexing. Windows marks most of your data files and folders for indexing by default, so it indexes these items unless you specifically tell it not to (by clearing the Index This File for Fast Searching check box or the Index This Folder for Fast Searching check box in the Advanced Attributes dialog box for the file or folder). Windows doesn't index your system files and program files, because normally you won't store data in your system folders and program folders, so you won't need to search through them.

Unlike Windows XP, which let you turn off indexing if you found it slowed your computer down at inconvenient times, Windows Vista doesn't let you turn off indexing. However, you can choose which files and folders Windows indexes and tell Windows how to index any given file type.

To configure indexing and search options, open the Indexing Options dialog box. You can then modify the list of folders that Windows indexes, choose advanced settings for particular categories and types of files, rebuild your index, or move the index to a different disk drive.

OPENING THE INDEXING OPTIONS DIALOG BOX

To open the Indexing Options dialog box, follow these steps:

1. Choose Start ➢ Control Panel. Windows open a Control Panel window.

2. In Control Panel Home view, click the System and Maintenance link. Windows displays the System and Maintenance window.

3. Click the Indexing Options link. Windows displays the Indexing Options dialog box (see Figure 10.9).

FIGURE 10.9
The Indexing Options dialog box shows you which folders Windows is currently indexing and how many items have been indexed. If you're using the computer, you may also see the message "Indexing speed is reduced due to user activity."

CHANGING THE LIST OF FOLDERS THAT WINDOWS INDEXES

To change the list of folders that Windows indexes, follow these steps:

1. In the Indexing Options dialog box, click the Modify button. Windows displays the Indexed Locations dialog box (see Figure 10.10).

2. In the Change Selected Locations list box, select the check box for each folder you want to index. Windows adds each folder to the Included Locations side of the Summary of Selected Locations list box.

3. If you want to include a folder and most but not all of its subfolders, select the check box for the folder, and then clear the check box for each subfolder you don't want to include. Windows adds the subfolder's name to the Exclude side of the Summary of Selected Locations list box.

4. Click the OK button. Windows closes the Indexed Locations dialog box and returns you to the Indexing Options dialog box.

FIGURE 10.10

The Indexed Locations dialog box lets you choose exactly which folders to index. When you first display this dialog box, it may be empty. If so, click the Show All Locations button and authenticate yourself to User Account Control to make Windows display items in the list boxes.

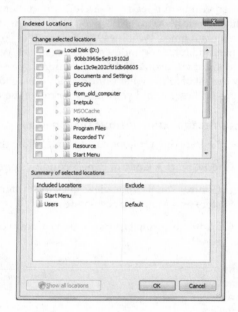

CHOOSING ADVANCED INDEXING OPTIONS OR MOVING THE INDEX

Normally, Window's default indexing settings work well for most computers, so you may need to do no more than change the list of folders that Windows indexes, as described in the previous section. However, Windows also provides advanced settings with which you may want to experiment. To do so, follow these steps:

1. In the Indexing Options dialog box, click the Advanced button, and then authenticate yourself to User Account Control. Windows displays the Advanced Options dialog box, which has two pages of settings: the Index Settings page and the File Types page. Figure 10.11 shows the Index Settings page.

FIGURE 10.11

The Index Settings page of the Advanced Options dialog box includes controls for rebuilding your index after it gets damaged and moving your index to a different drive.

2. In the File Settings group box on the Index Settings page, ignore the Index Encrypted Files check box, which applies only to versions of Windows Vista that include encryption (which Windows Vista Home doesn't). Select the Treat Similar Words with Diacritics as Different Words check box if you want Windows to use diacritics to distinguish words instead of ignoring them (and treating, say, Motörhead the same as Motorhead).

3. In the Troubleshooting group box, you can click the Rebuild button to rebuild your index if you suspect that it has become corrupted—for example, because Search now doesn't find files in folders that Windows is set to index. You can click the Restore Defaults button to restore your index to its default settings if you've made changes that appear to have had a negative effect.

4. The Index Location group box shows you the current location of the index file. You can move the file to a different location by clicking the Select New button, choosing the drive and folder in the Browse for Folder dialog box, and then clicking the OK button. The only reason for moving the index is if your computer has two or more hard disks and you can move the index to a faster disk than it is currently on. (Having the index on a faster disk will give you somewhat faster indexing and searching.)

5. The File Types page of the Advanced Options dialog box (see Figure 10.12) lets you choose which file types Windows indexes and whether it indexes only the properties or the properties and the file contents. Follow these steps:

   ◆ In the list box, select the file extension associated with the file type you want to affect. For example, select the DOCX file extension to affect Word 2007 documents.

   ◆ Select the check box to make Windows index the file type. (Windows automatically selects the check boxes for file types that you can create.)

   ◆ In the How Should This File Be Indexed? group box, select the Index Properties and File Contents option button if you want Windows to index the document's content as well as its properties. Otherwise, select the Index Properties Only option button.

◆ If you need to add a file extension to the list, click in the text box near the bottom of the File Types page, type the extension, and then click the Add New Extension button. Windows adds it to the list and selects its check box and the Index Properties Only option button. You can then select the Index Properties and File Contents option button if appropriate.

6. When you've finished choosing advanced options, click the OK button. Windows closes the Advanced Options dialog box and returns you to the Indexing Options dialog box.

7. Click the Close button. Windows closes the Indexing Options dialog box.

FIGURE 10.12
If you need to be able to search within the contents of a particular file type, click it on the File Types page of the Advanced Options dialog box and make sure that the Index Properties and File Contents option button is selected in the How Should this File Be Indexed? group box.

WHY NOT INDEX ALL FILE CONTENTS?

There are three reasons not to index all file contents:

1. Indexing file contents as well as file properties takes Windows much longer to complete the indexing process.

2. Your index file quickly becomes larger than it needs to be.

3. Searching tends to become less efficient, as you get more unrelated hits.

For these reasons, it's best to index file contents only for data files that you might need to be able to identify by their contents. For example, you might need to be able to pick out a Word document by a particular phrase it contains.

Maintaining Your Hard Disks

The better you treat your hard disks, the better performance they give you and the longer they last—with any luck. This section details the steps you can take to keep your disks in good order.

Defragmenting Your Disks

Data is stored on your hard disk in physical areas called *sectors* that are mapped into logical areas called *clusters*. Each cluster contains a relatively small amount of information so that Windows can use the clusters efficiently. As a result, most files occupy more than one cluster. These clusters can be located just about anywhere on the partition of the drive that contains the volume. Ideally, all the data in a file is stored in contiguous clusters, so that the hard disk's heads can read the data without having to move too far. The further the hard disk's actuator arm has to move to allow the heads to read the clusters that make up the file, the slower the file is to load.

When files are stored in widely spread-out clusters, the volume is said to be *fragmented*. To improve disk performance, you *defragment* (or *defrag*) it using a disk *defragmenter* (or *defragger*). A defragmenter rearranges the data on the disk so that each file occupies contiguous clusters wherever possible. Windows Vista includes a disk defragmenter called "Disk Defragmenter" that's adequate for most home and small-business purposes. (You can also buy third-party disk defragmenters that have extra capabilities.)

ANOTHER TYPE OF PERFORMANCE IMPROVEMENT

Related to defragmenters but more specialized are tools such as the Microsoft Office optimizer, which defragments a specific set of files and arranges them in a location on the hard drive that the disk heads can quickly access.

Depending on how fragmented a volume is, and how big it is, defragmentation can take anything from a few minutes to a few hours. You *can* work on your computer while defragmentation is going on, but you'll find the computer responding more slowly than usual, and any files that you create, move, or copy may slow down the defragmentation process. Because of this, the best time to defragment a volume is when you're not using your computer. For this reason, Windows comes set to defragment your hard disk automatically in the early hours of the morning one day a week. This works well if you leave your computer running, but if you switch it off at night, you may do better to defragment your disk manually when you're going to leave your computer for a few hours.

You can start Disk Defragmenter in several ways. Here are the two easiest ways:

◆ Choose Start ➢ All Programs ➢ Accessories ➢ System Tools ➢ Disk Defragmenter, and then authenticate yourself to User Account Control.

◆ Choose Start ➢ Computer, right-click any hard disk icon (it doesn't matter which), and then choose Properties from the context menu. In the Properties dialog box, click the Tools tab, click the Defragment Now button, and then authenticate yourself to User Account Control.

Figure 10.13 shows Disk Defragmenter.

FIGURE 10.13
Use Disk Defrag-
menter to defragment
your drives either on
a schedule or on
the spot.

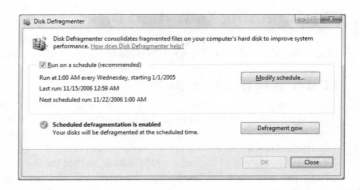

DEFRAGMENTING THE DISK IMMEDIATELY

To defragment the hard disk now, click the Defragment Now button. Disk Defragmenter starts defragmenting your hard disks. For best effect, leave your computer now so you don't slow down the defragmentation process. If Disk Defragmenter is still running when you return, you can click the Cancel Defragmentation button to end the defragmentation.

HOW DISK DEFRAGMENTER IN WINDOWS VISTA IS DIFFERENT THAN DISK DEFRAGMENTER IN WINDOWS XP

If you've used Disk Defragmenter in Windows XP, you'll notice several major differences in Disk Defragmenter in Windows Vista:

◆ Disk Defragmenter comes set to run on a schedule.

◆ When you run Disk Defragmenter, it defragments all your hard disks. You can't tell it to defragment one disk but not another.

◆ Disk Defragmenter no longer lets you analyze a disk and get a report about how fragmented it is and which files are suffering particularly badly. Instead, you simply set it running and let it do its job.

◆ Disk Defragmenter no longer gives you a readout of its progress. All you get is the laconic message "Defragmenting hard disks... This may take from a few minutes to a few hours."

CHANGING THE DEFRAGMENTATION SCHEDULE

If you want to run Disk Defragmenter on a schedule, select the Run on a Schedule check box in the Disk Defragmenter dialog box. The readout shows the details of the schedule—for example, "Run at 1:00 AM every Wednesday"—and details of the last run and the next run.

To modify the schedule, click the Modify Schedule button, and then choose settings in the Disk Defragmenter: Modify Schedule dialog box (see Figure 10.14). Early in the morning is a good time for defragmentation if you leave your computer running; if you switch your computer off at night, choose, instead, a time when you normally will be busy away from your computer but the computer will be on.

FIGURE 10.14

The Disk Defragmenter: Modify Schedule dialog box lets you run Disk Defragmenter daily, weekly, or monthly. For weekly and monthly schedules, you can specify the day; for all schedules, you can specify the hour at which to start.

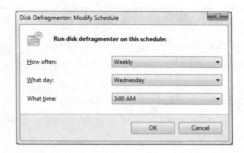

Cleaning Up Your Disks with Disk Cleanup

Most Windows programs create temporary files that they use to store information temporarily when you're running them. Some programs remember to get rid of these files when you exit them. Others forget. And if your computer loses power or crashes, even the well-behaved programs don't have a chance to get rid of temporary files.

Windows' Disk Cleanup feature provides an effective way to remove from local drives not only these temporary files but also temporary Internet files, downloaded program files, offline web pages, and the contents of the Recycle Bin. (Disk Cleanup doesn't work on network drives.) A standard user can clean up their own user account, and an administrator can clean up system-wide items as well.

CLEANING UP YOUR OWN USER ACCOUNT

To clean up your own user account using Disk Cleanup, follow these steps:

1. Close all programs you're running. (This step is optional, but it's usually a good idea.)

2. Choose Start ➢ All Programs ➢ Accessories ➢ System Tools ➢ Disk Cleanup. Windows displays the Disk Cleanup Options dialog box, as shown here, asking which files you want to clean up:

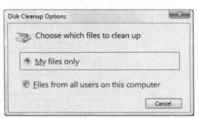

3. Click the My Files Only button if you want to clean up your own files. You'll probably want to start by cleaning up your own files, so this section shows you this path first. If you're an administrator and want to clean up everyone's files, click the Files from All Users on This Computer button, and follow the path in the next section.

ANOTHER WAY TO LAUNCH DISK CLEANUP

You can also launch Disk Cleanup by following these steps:

1. Choose Start ➢ Computer. Windows displays a Computer window.

2. Right-click the icon for the hard disk you want to clean up, and then choose Properties from the context menu. Windows displays the Local Disk Properties dialog box for that disk.

3. On the General page, click the Disk Cleanup button. Windows displays the Disk Cleanup Options dialog box.

When you launch Disk Cleanup this way, Windows doesn't display the Select Drive dialog box, because you've already told it which drive you want to clean up.

---

4. If your computer has multiple hard disk drives, Disk Cleanup displays the Disk Cleanup: Drive Selection dialog box, as shown here. (If your computer has only one hard disk drive, Disk Cleanup doesn't need to ask you which disk to clean up.)

5. Select the disk in the Drives drop-down list, and then click the OK button. Disk Cleanup examines the disk, and then displays the Disk Cleanup dialog box for that disk. Figure 10.15 shows you an example of what you may see in this dialog box (depending on which disk you choose and which software you have installed).

FIGURE 10.15
Disk Cleanup presents a list of the items you can remove to clean up your disk.

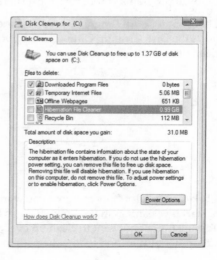

6. Select the check box for each item you want to delete. Here is an explanation of the items.

Downloaded Program Files   ActiveX controls and Java applets downloaded by Internet Explorer so that it could display pages that needed them. If you delete these files, Internet Explorer may need to download the controls and applets again when you next access pages that need them, which may slow down your browsing a bit. You can click the View Files button to make Windows display an Explorer window containing the files.

Temporary Internet Files   These files are the components of web pages that Internet Explorer has downloaded and has stored on your hard drive so that it can retrieve them quickly when you access the same sites again. Deleting these files means that Internet Explorer will need to download them again the next time you access one of the sites, which will slow down your browsing. Again, you can click the View Files button to have Windows display an Explorer window containing these files—but be warned that there are usually thousands of them, and that the format in which they appear is less than informative.

Hibernation File Cleaner   Select this check box if you want to delete the hibernation file on your computer *and disable hibernation*. Disabling hibernation on a desktop computer is a fair enough idea, but you probably don't want to disable it on a notebook computer. Your computer's hibernation file is the same size as the computer's RAM (when the computer hibernates, it writes the contents of RAM to disk to preserve it), so you can recover a fair amount of disk space by deleting the hibernation file.

Microsoft Office Temporary Files   Select this check box to delete any temporary data files or log files left behind by the Microsoft Office applications.

Offline Web Pages   This item appears only if you use offline favorites in Internet Explorer. These files hold the information for the cached copies of your offline favorites. If you use offline favorites extensively, these files may take up a lot of space. If you delete these files, you won't be able to view your offline favorites until you synchronize them again—and synchronizing them will probably reclaim most of the disk space that deleting these files freed up.

Recycle Bin   These files are the contents of the Recycle Bin. As usual, make sure that you want to get rid of these files before you tell Disk Cleanup to delete them. You can click the View Files button to have Windows display an Explorer window showing the contents of the Recycle Bin.

Temporary Remote Desktop Files   These files are temporary picture files used to display information more quickly when you're using Remote Desktop Connection. You can safely get rid of them, but your subsequent Remote Desktop Connection sessions may run a bit more slowly.

Temporary Files   These files are temporary storage files that should have been deleted by the program that created them. You can delete with impunity any temporary files that aren't currently being used. (Disk Cleanup leaves alone any temporary files still in use.)

Thumbnails   Select this check box to make Windows delete the thumbnail images it maintains of your picture files. Windows will then recreate the thumbnails as needed when you open each folder containing picture files, but displaying the thumbnails will take longer. Unless you're desperate for disk space, you'll probably find it easier to keep the thumbnail files.

Per User Queued Windows Error Reporting Files   Select this check box to make Windows delete the error-report files that are in the queue for reporting. Normally, you'll want to keep these files until they've been reported.

Per User Archived Windows Error Reporting Files   Select this check box to make Windows delete the error-report files it keeps. Normally, these files take up only a minimal amount of space, but you might as well get rid of them unless you need to be able to track back through problems your computer is experiencing.

7. Click the OK button. Windows displays a Disk Cleanup dialog box confirming that you want to get rid of the files, as shown here.

8. Click the Delete Files button. Windows closes the Disk Cleanup dialog box and disposes of the items you chose.

CLEANING UP SYSTEM-WIDE ITEMS

Depending on what you chose to delete, you may have been able to reclaim a useful amount of disk space by deleting items in your own user account. For a full cleanup, run Disk Cleanup again and use the Administrator-only options, which let you remove system-wide items, including surplus programs and unneeded System Restore points.

To clean up files for all users of your computer, follow these steps:

1. Choose Start ➢ All Programs ➢ Accessories ➢ System Tools ➢ Disk Cleanup. Windows displays the Disk Cleanup Options dialog box.

2. Click the Files from All Users on this Computer button, and then authenticate yourself to User Account Control. Windows displays the Disk Cleanup: Drive Selection dialog box.

3. Select the drive you want to clean up, and then click the OK button. Windows displays the Disk Cleanup dialog box, which offers the options listed in step 6 of the previous list, together with the following additional items:

    System Archived Windows Error Reporting Files   Select this check box to delete these archived error reports, which are similar to the per-user archived reports but apply to errors experienced by the system rather than by applications run by a particular user.

    System Queued Windows Error Reporting Files   Select this check box if you want to delete these error reports that are queued but not yet archived. Unless you're desperate for disk space, it's probably best to keep these reports in case you need to examine them.

4. If you need to reclaim more space, click the More Options tab to display the More Options page of the Disk Cleanup dialog box (see Figure 10.16).

FIGURE 10.16
The More Options page of the Disk Cleanup dialog box lets you open the Programs and Features window (so that you can remove unneeded programs) and discard all but the last system restore point.

5. To remove programs you no longer need, click the Clean Up button in the Programs and Features group box. Windows displays a Programs and Features window, which you can use to delete programs. (See the section "Removing a Program" in Chapter 4 for instructions on how to remove programs using the Programs and Features window.)

6. To remove all System Restore restore points, except the latest one, click the Clean Up button in the System Restore and Shadow Copies group box, and then click the Delete button in the next Disk Cleanup dialog box (shown here). Chapter 16 shows you how to use System Restore.

7. Click the OK button. Windows displays a Disk Cleanup dialog box confirming that you want to get rid of the files, as shown here.

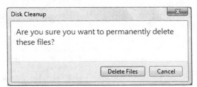

8. Click the Delete Files button. Windows closes the Disk Cleanup dialog box and disposes of the items you chose.

Checking a Disk for Errors

Once you've cleaned unnecessary files off your hard disk, it's a good idea to check it for errors. Errors typically occur when sectors go bad, which can happen through natural selection (some disks age more quickly in parts) or unnatural intervention (such as physical damage resulting from the disk being bumped or receiving an electrical spike).

To check a disk for errors, follow these steps:

1. Close all programs that are on the disk or that might be accessing the disk. (In practice, it's best to close all programs for the time being.) Close any files open from the disk.

2. Choose Start ➤ Computer. Windows opens a Computer window.

3. Right-click the drive you want to check, and then choose Properties from the context menu. Windows displays the Properties dialog box for the drive.

4. Click the Tools tab. Windows displays the Tools page of the Properties dialog box.

5. Click the Check Now button, and then authenticate yourself to User Account Control. Windows displays the Check Disk dialog box (shown in Figure 10.17).

6. If you want Windows to repair file-system errors, select the Automatically Fix File System Errors check box.

7. If you want Windows to scan for bad sectors and attempt to recover information from them, *and* repair file-system errors, select the Scan for and Attempt Recovery of Bad Sectors check box.

8. Click the Start button to run Check Disk. Windows displays the Checking Disk dialog box while it performs the checks.

   If you see a dialog box like the one shown in Figure 10.18 telling you that "Windows can't check the disk while it's in use" and asking whether you want to schedule the disk check to take place the next time you restart the computer, click the Schedule Disk Check button. This dialog box typically appears when you're checking a system volume: Because Windows is constantly using the volume, Check Disk can't get exclusive access to it.

9. When Check Disk has finished, it displays a message box telling you that the disk check is complete.

10. Click the OK button. Check Disk closes and returns you to the Properties dialog box.

11. Click the OK button. Windows closes the Properties dialog box.

FIGURE 10.17
In the Check Disk dialog box, specify whether to automatically fix errors in the file system and whether to detect bad sectors and attempt to recover their contents.

FIGURE 10.18
This dialog box tells you that it can't check the disk while it's in use and asks whether you want to run the check the next time you restart the computer.

Managing Disks and Volumes

Formatting disks and converting their file system is all very well—but what if you need to create or delete a partition or volume? For these tasks, Windows provides a tool called Disk Management.

Starting Disk Management

Take the following steps to start Disk Management:

1. Choose Start ➤ Control Panel. Windows displays Control Panel.

2. In Control Panel Home view, click the System and Maintenance link. Windows displays the System and Maintenance window.

3. In the Administrative Tools list, click the Create and Format Hard Disk Partitions link, and then authenticate yourself to User Account Control. Windows displays the Disk Management window (see Figure 10.19).

FIGURE 10.19
Disk Management is Windows' tool for creating and deleting disk partitions. Disk Management shows local hard disks, removable disks, and optical disks.

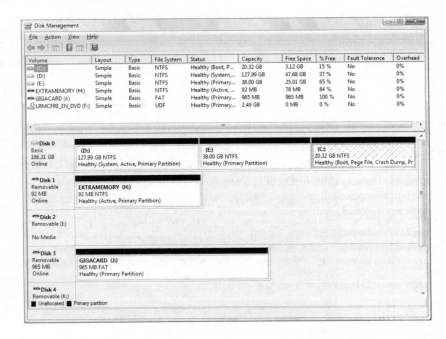

START DISK MANAGEMENT USING THE *RUN* COMMAND

If you prefer not to go through the Control Panel, you can start Disk Management via the Run command:

1. Press Windows Key+R. Windows displays the Run dialog box.

2. Type `diskmgmt.msc` in the Run dialog box, and then press Enter.

As you can see in the figure, the top section of the Disk Management window lists the volumes currently defined on the system, giving the following information about each volume:

Column	Explanation
Volume	The letter for the volume (for example, C:) and any name assigned to the volume (for example, in the figure, a memory card is named EXTRAMEMORY).
Layout	The volume's layout—whether it's a full disk or a partition.
Type	The volume type (basic or dynamic).
File System	The file system (FAT, FAT32, NTFS, CDFS, UDF, and so on).
Status	The volume's status—for example, Healthy (Boot, Page File, Crash Dump, Primary Partition) for a boot volume in good condition containing a page file and a crash dump.
Capacity	The capacity in megabytes, gigabytes, or larger units.
Free Space	The amount of free space, in megabytes, gigabytes, or larger units.
% Free	The percentage of the volume free.
Fault Tolerance	Whether fault tolerance is used on the volume.
Overhead	The overhead consumed by fault tolerance (if it's used).

Below this list, Disk Management shows a graphical representation of each physical disk attached to the computer and how it's broken down. Here's what you see in the figure:

◆ Disk 0 is the first hard disk (because computer counting begins at 0 rather than 1). It contains a 127.99GB NTFS D: drive, a 38.00GB NTFS E: drive, and a 20.32GB NTFS C: drive.

◆ Disk 1 contains EXTRAMEMORY (F:), a removable disk containing a 92MB FAT partition. (This is a CompactFlash card with a nominal capacity of 96MB.)

◆ Disks 2 and 4 (drives G: and I:) are removable disk drives that are currently empty.

◆ Disk 3 contains GIGACARD (H:), a removable disk containing a 965MB FAT partition. (This is an SD card with a nominal capacity of 1GB.)

◆ CDROM 0 (which appears too far down the window to be visible in the figure) contains a DVD that is assigned to drive E:.

EXPERT KNOWLEDGE: DYNAMIC DISKS AND FAULT TOLERANCE

That bit about basic disks and dynamic disks may have raised your eyebrows a bit—especially since Disk Management shows that your computer has basic disks. But don't worry—the term refers to the disk's configuration rather than to its capabilities. If you bought the largest and fastest hard drive on the block, it'll still be the largest and fastest until the engineers release something better, no matter that it uses the basic disk configuration.

A *basic disk* is one configured to support primary partitions, an extended partition, and logical drives (within that extended partition). A *dynamic disk* is one configured so that you can use fault tolerance or create multidisk volumes on the fly. You can't create dynamic disks in Windows Vista Home Edition, but because Windows Vista Home Edition borrows the Disk Management tool from Windows Vista's Business editions and from Windows Server, Disk Management shows the disk type for Windows Vista Home Edition too.

Fault tolerance is a feature typically implemented only in servers or high-end workstations. It uses multiple disks to avoid the possible loss of information when disk problems occur. Windows Server 2003 and Windows Vista Ultimate Edition implement software fault tolerance through a redundant array of inexpensive disks (RAID). Fault tolerance involves *overhead*—extra space used to keep extra copies of information so that it isn't lost if hardware fails.

Creating a Volume

If you have free space available, you can create a volume in it, as in the following example. The options available to you depend on your disk configuration.

1. Right-click the free space and choose New Simple Volume from the context menu. Disk Management starts the New Simple Volume Wizard, which displays its Welcome page.

2. Click the Next button. The wizard displays the Specify Volume Size page (see Figure 10.20).

FIGURE 10.20
On the Specify Volume Size page of the New Simple Volume Wizard, specify the size of the new volume.

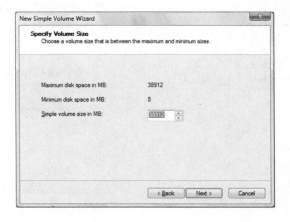

3. In the Simple Volume Size in MB text box, enter the size of volume you want to create. The wizard suggests using all the space available, which you may not want to do. The readout above the text box shows the minimum and maximum sizes possible.

4. Click the Next button. The wizard displays the Assign Drive Letter or Path page (see Figure 10.21).

5. Leave the Assign the Following Drive Letter option button selected and specify the letter in the drop-down list.

   ◆ Instead of assigning a drive letter, you can select the Mount in the Following Empty NTFS Folder option button and specify the folder in the text box. See the next sidebar for a discussion of this option.

   ◆ Instead of doing either of the above, you *can* avoid assigning a drive letter or path by selecting the Do Not Assign a Drive Letter or Drive Path option button. The only reason to do this is if you're planning to assign letters (or paths) later after creating other partitions. To access the partition through the Windows interface (for example, from Explorer or from an application), you'll need to assign a drive letter or path to it sooner or later—and it may as well be sooner.

6. Click the Next button. The wizard displays the Format Partition page (see Figure 10.22).

7. Leave the Format This Volume with the Following Settings option button selected and choose settings:

   ◆ Choose the file system (preferably NTFS, but FAT32 or FAT if necessary) in the File System drop-down list.

   ◆ Leave the Allocation Unit Size drop-down list set to Default unless you've got a very good reason to change it.

FIGURE 10.21
On the Assign Drive Letter or Path page of the New Simple Volume Wizard, specify the drive letter to use.

FIGURE 10.22
On the Format
Partition page of the
New Simple Volume
Wizard, specify the
file system and label
for the new volume.

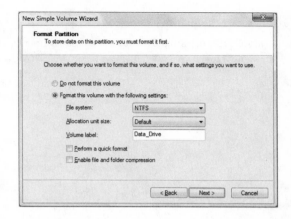

♦ Type the label for the volume in the Volume Label text box. (The wizard suggests New Volume, but you should be able to come up with something more descriptive. You can use up to 20 characters for the label on an NTFS volume and 11 characters for that on a FAT or FAT32 volume.)

♦ Select the Perform a Quick Format check box if you've checked the disk for errors recently and found none. If not, it's better to perform a full format, including the check for errors.

♦ Select the Enable File and Folder Compression check box if you want to use compression on the volume. Compression lets you pack more files onto the volume (assuming that the files aren't already fully compressed) but degrades performance a little.

8. Click the Next button. The wizard displays the Completing the New Simple Volume Wizard page, which summarizes the choices you've made.

9. Click the Finish button. The wizard closes, creates the volume, formats it, and displays an Explorer window showing the volume's contents (nothing).

EXPERT KNOWLEDGE: MOUNTING A VOLUME IN AN EMPTY NTFS FOLDER

Instead of assigning a drive letter to a volume, you can mount the volume in an empty NTFS folder. Doing so has a couple of advantages:

♦ You can connect more drives to your computer than the 26 letters of the alphabet would let you.

♦ You can make files appear to be more readily available or appear to be available in multiple locations. For example, you could keep your videos in a central location but create a subfolder in each user's Videos folder and assign it to the appropriate drive path.

To do this, take the following steps:

1. Right-click the drive in the list box in Disk Management and choose Change Drive Letter and Paths from the context menu. Windows displays the Change Drive Letter and Paths dialog box, as shown here.

2. Click the Add button. Windows displays the Add Drive Letter or Path dialog box, as shown here.

3. Make sure the Mount in the Following Empty NTFS Folder option button is selected. (This option button should be selected by default.)

4. Click the Browse button and use the resulting Browse for Drive Path dialog box to specify the folder. Alternatively, type the path in the text box.

5. Click the OK button. Windows assigns the path and closes the Add Drive Letter or Path dialog box.

You'll then be able to access the drive through the folder you assigned.

To see if a folder is really a mounted volume, display the Properties dialog box for the folder and see if the Type readout on the General page says *Mounted Volume*.

To check which drives are mounted as which folders, choose View ➤ Drive Paths from Disk Management. Windows displays the Drive Paths dialog box (shown next), which lists the drive paths and their volume mapping and which includes a Remove button for removing drive mappings.

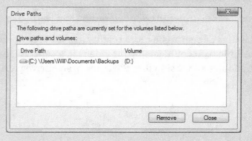

Extending and Shrinking Volumes

Windows Vista reduces the problems associated with managing volumes by allowing you to extend volumes with available free space or shrink volumes to create free space.

EXTENDING A VOLUME

If there is unallocated space outside the boundaries of a volume, you can extend the volume into that space. To extend a volume, follow these steps:

1. Right-click the volume, and then choose Extend Volume from the context menu. Windows launches the Extend Volume Wizard, which displays its Welcome screen.

2. Click the Next button. The wizard displays its Select Disks screen (see Figure 10.23).

3. In the Available list box, select the space to use to extend the volume, and then click the Add button. The wizard adds the space to the Selected list box. (If there's only one space you can use, the wizard adds it to the Selected list box automatically.)

4. In the Select the Amount of Space in MB box, enter the amount of space to use. The wizard suggests using all the available space, which is a good choice unless you have another use for part of the space.

5. Click the Next button. The wizard displays its Completing the Extend Volume Wizard screen, which summarizes the changes you've decided to make.

6. Click the Finish button. The wizard extends the volume and closes itself.

FIGURE 10.23
On the Select Disks screen of the Extend Volume Wizard, choose which space to use to extend the volume, and then specify the amount of space to use.

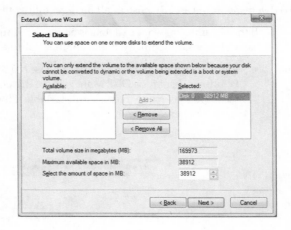

SHRINKING A VOLUME

To shrink a volume, follow these steps:

1. Right-click the volume, and then choose Shrink Volume from the context menu. Windows displays the Shrink dialog box, as shown here.

2. In the Enter the Amount of Space to Shrink in MB box, enter the amount of space by which you want to shrink the volume. The Size of Available Shrink in MB box shows you the maximum amount by which you can shrink the volume, and Windows sets this value in the Enter the Amount of Space to Shrink in MB box automatically.

3. Click the Shrink button. Windows shrinks the volume by the specified amount and creates unallocated space after it.

Deleting a Volume

To delete a volume and dispose of all its data, follow these steps:

1. If the volume you want to delete is active, you must make another volume active before you can delete your victim. To make another volume active:

   ◆ Right-click that volume, and then choose Mark Partition as Active from the context menu. Windows displays a Disk Management dialog box warning you that changing the active partition may make the disk not startable if the partition doesn't have valid system files, as shown here.

   ◆ If you're sure the volume you're making active does contain system files, click the Yes button. Windows makes the volume active.

2. Right-click the volume you want to delete, and then choose Delete Volume from the context menu. Disk Management displays the Delete Volume dialog box—for example, for a Simple layout, Disk Management displays the Delete Simple Volume dialog box shown here.

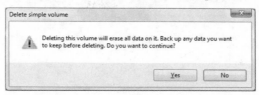

3. Click the Yes button. If the volume isn't being used, Disk Management simply deletes it. If an application is using the volume, Disk Management displays a dialog box such as the one shown here:

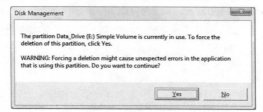

4. Close any applications that may be using the volume, and then click the Yes button. Disk Management deletes the volume and marks it as unallocated space.

Changing the Drive Letter

Disk Management also lets you change the drive letter for a volume other than your system volume or boot volume. This capability comes in handy if you get your drive letters in a tangle. Be aware, though, that changing the drive letter will confuse any program that has learned the path to files on this drive.

To change the drive letter, follow these steps:

1. Right-click the drive whose letter you want to change and choose Change Drive Letter and Paths from the context menu. Disk Management displays the Change Drive Letter and Paths dialog box, as shown here.

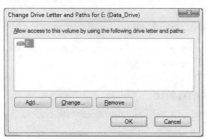

2. To change the drive letter, select it, and then click the Change button. Disk Management displays the Change Drive Letter or Path dialog box, shown here.

3. Make sure the Assign the Following Drive Letter option button is selected, and then select the letter in the drop-down list.

4. Click the OK button. Disk Management displays the following dialog box, warning you that changing the drive letter might prevent programs from running.

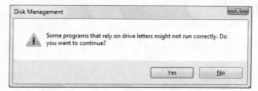

5. Click the Yes button. If files on the drive are open, Disk Management displays the Disk Management dialog box shown next, telling you that you can continue to use the old drive letter until you reboot and asking if you want to continue.

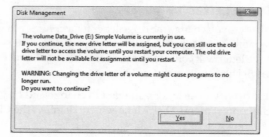

6. Click the Yes button. Disk Management makes the change.

7. Change other drive letters if necessary, and then restart your computer so that you can start using the new drive letter assignments.

Exiting Disk Management

When you've finished working in Disk Management, choose File ➤ Exit to close Disk Management.

The Bottom Line

Format a disk so that Windows can use it   You must format a disk before Windows can use it. Choose Start ➢ Computer, right-click the disk, and then choose the Format command from the context menu.

Change your computer's name, description, and workgroup   Your computer's name is the name by which other computers on the network know it. The description is to help humans identify the computer, and the workgroup is the name for the group of computers to which your computer is connected. To change the name, description, or workgroup, press Windows Key+Break, and then click the Change Settings link in the Computer Name, Domain, and Workgroup area of the System window.

Convert a disk to NTFS for efficiency and stability   NTFS is not only more efficient and more stable than FAT32, but it also provides security features. You can convert a disk from FAT or FAT32 to NTFS without losing data by choosing Start ➢ All Programs ➢ Accessories ➢ Command Prompt and then issuing a `convert` command: `convert drive: /FS:NTFS`, where `drive:` is the letter of the drive to convert.

Free up space on your disk using compression   To pack more data on a disk, you can compress files, folders, or whole disks.

- ◆ To compress a file or folder, right-click it, choose Properties, and then click the Advanced button. In the Advanced Attributes dialog box, select the Compress Contents to Save Disk Space check box, and then click the OK button in each dialog box.

- ◆ To compress a whole drive, choose Start ➢ Computer, right-click the drive, and then choose Properties. Select the Compress Drive to Save Disk Space check box on the General page, click the Apply button, choose Apply Changes to *drive*:\, Subfolders and Files option button, and then click the OK button.

Tell Windows which folders to index   To configure indexing, choose Start ➢ Control Panel, click the System and Maintenance link, and then click the Indexing Options link. Click the Modify button in the Indexing Options dialog box to display the Indexed Locations dialog box, which lets you choose which folders to index.

Keep your hard disks defragmented and cleaned up   To defragment your hard disks, choose Start ➢ All Programs ➢ Accessories ➢ System Tools ➢ Disk Defragmenter, and then click the Defragment Now button. To clean up your disks, choose Start ➢ All Programs ➢ Accessories ➢ System Tools ➢ Disk Cleanup, click the My Files Only button in the Disk Cleanup Options dialog box, choose the drive, select the items to clean up, and then click the OK button.

Change your disk volumes or mount them in folders for easy access   To work with disk volumes, choose Start ➢ Control Panel, click the System and Maintenance link, and then click the Create and Format Hard Disk Partitions link. You can then use the Disk Management window to create new disk volumes, shrink or expand existing volumes, or mount a volume in a folder so that you can access it more easily through the file system.

Chapter 11

Working with the Registry

◆ Understand what the Registry is, what it's for, and why you may need to work with it

◆ Back up your Registry and learn how to restore it

◆ Navigate the Registry and create, edit, and delete keys and value entries

◆ Understand the Registry data types and what they contain

◆ Work with examples of making changes to the Registry

◆ Use Registry favorites to store and access the keys you need most

This chapter shows you how to work with one of the most mentioned but least understood components of Windows—the Registry, the huge database of Windows' settings for your computer's hardware and software.

The chapter starts by discussing what the Registry is, what it does, why you might want to work with it, and what the dangers are of making changes to the Registry. It then explains the step you *must* take before you make any changes to the Registry: backing up the Registry so that you can restore it if something goes wrong. After that, the chapter shows you how to use Registry Editor to examine the contents of the Registry, find what you're looking for, and make changes. It mentions several Registry changes that you may want to make to change how Windows Vista behaves. It concludes by showing you how to goose the Registry so that you can crash your computer with two keystrokes.

What Is the Registry and What Does It Do?

In Windows, the *Registry* is a hierarchical database of all the settings required by your installation of Windows and the programs you've installed. These settings include information on the hardware installed on your computer and how it's configured, all the programs and their file associations, profiles for each user and group, and property settings for folders and files.

The Registry stores the information needed to keep your computer running. Windows itself stores a huge amount of information in the Registry, and each program you install stores information there too. You can store information in the Registry yourself if you want to, although unless you're creating programs, there's not much reason to do so.

The number of entries in the Registry depends on the number of users of the computer and the software installed, but between 50,000 and 100,000 entries is normal. This multitude of entries makes browsing through the Registry practical only for those with serious amounts of time weighing on their hands. Even searching through the Registry can be a slow process, because many of the entries contain similar information.

Windows 95 introduced the Registry, and all 32-bit and 64-bit desktop versions of Windows since then have used the Registry. In Windows 3.*x*, information was stored in initialization files—INI files for short. For example, Windows configuration information was stored in files such as WIN.INI and SYSTEM.INI. Most programs typically created configuration files of their own.

Centralizing all the information in the Registry has two main advantages. First, all the information is in a single location. Second, you can back up the Registry (though most users forget or fail to do so) and restore it. This centralization also has a disadvantage: damage to the Registry can cripple Windows completely.

Why Work with the Registry?

Normally, you *don't* work directly with the Registry—most of the time. In theory, you should never need to mess with the Registry.

That's why Windows provides no direct way from the user interface to view the Registry and change its contents. If you want to explore and change the Registry, you need to deliberately run the Registry Editor program, which is tucked away in a safe place where no casual user should stumble across it.

Most of the information that's stored in the Registry you'll never need to change. Those relatively few pieces of information that Windows is happy for you to change are accessible through the Windows user interface, which provides you with an easier—if more restrictive—way of changing them than working in the Registry. For example, the settings in Control Panel applets store most of their information in the Registry, so you *could* edit the Registry and change the information there. But for all normal purposes, you'll do better to work through those Control Panel applets and let them set the values in the Registry for you. Control Panel is designed to be easy to use, while the Registry isn't. Control Panel shows you your options in mostly intelligible ways; the information in the Registry is arcane when not incomprehensible. And Control Panel seldom makes mistakes in translating your choices into hexadecimal and binary, whereas the Registry will happily accept input that will instruct Windows to disable itself.

That said, sometimes you may need to access the Registry to change a vital piece of information that you cannot change through the user interface. Sometimes you'll need to access the Registry because something has gone wrong, and you need to change an entry manually. But more often, you'll hear about a cool tweak that you can perform by entering a new value in the Registry or by changing an existing value.

You can also use the Registry to store information of your own that you want to have available to Windows or to the programs you use. You might want to do this if you write your own programs, or if you use a macro language to create automated procedures in a program—for example, if you use VBA to automate tasks in Word, Excel, or Outlook. (You *could* also use the Registry to store odd information, such as names and addresses—but there are far better ways of spending your time.)

Preparing to Access the Registry

Before you do anything to the Registry, you need to understand this:

> *If you mess up the Registry, you may disable parts of Windows' functionality. You may even disable Windows itself so that it cannot boot.*

So before you do *anything* to the Registry, back it up by exporting it as discussed in the section after next. In fact, even if you don't make any changes to the Registry, it's a good idea to keep a backup of your Registry in case a program, Windows itself, or (more likely) a piece of malware makes a change for the worse.

SYSTEM RESTORE MAY BE ABLE TO UNDO REGISTRY DAMAGE

System Restore (discussed in detail in Chapter 16) rolls back Registry entries to their state when the restore point was created, so you can use System Restore to recover from damage to the Registry. Because System Restore also changes other settings, however, it's a clumsy solution that's best avoided unless you've failed to back up your Registry before mangling it. However, you may want to create a new restore point as insurance before making changes to the Registry.

Running Registry Editor

To work with the Registry, you use the program called Registry Editor. Windows provides no Start menu item for Registry Editor, but you can create your own Start menu item or Desktop shortcut if you want.

Unless you create a Start menu item or shortcut, the easiest way to run Registry Editor is as follows:

1. Press Windows Key+R. Windows displays the Run dialog box.

2. Type **regedit** in the Open text box, press Enter or click the OK button, and then authenticate yourself to User Account Control. Windows starts Registry Editor (shown in Figure 11.1).

FIGURE 11.1
Registry Editor
is your tool for
making changes
to the Registry.

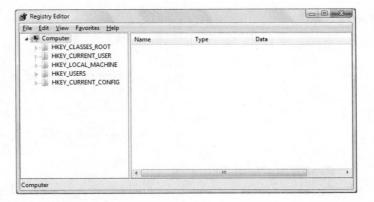

Backing Up Your Registry

Before you do anything else with Registry Editor—and that includes exploring the subtrees and keys of the Registry, let alone changing any values—back up your Registry. Depending on what's installed on your computer, a full backup of the Registry may be 100–200MB altogether, so you'll normally want to back up the Registry to a file on your computer. You can then burn the file to a recordable CD or DVD, store it on a secure network drive, or put it on a USB keychain or USB drive.

To back up the Registry, export it by taking the following steps from Registry Editor:

1. Select the Computer item in Registry Editor if you want to back up your whole Registry (as you should do at first). If you want to back up only a subtree of the Registry, select the subtree instead of the Computer item.

2. Choose File ➤ Export. Registry Editor displays the Export Registry File dialog box (shown in Figure 11.2). As you can see in the figure, this dialog box is a common Save As dialog box with an extra section tacked on at the bottom to house the Export Range group box.

3. In the Export Range group box, make sure the All option button is selected. If you chose a subtree in step 1, the Export Registry File dialog box appears with the Selected Branch option button selected and the subtree's name entered in the Selected Branch text box.

4. Specify the filename and location for the file as usual.

5. Click the Save button. Registry Editor closes the Export Registry File dialog box and saves the Registry file.

FIGURE 11.2
In the Export Registry File dialog box, specify that you want to export all of the Registry.

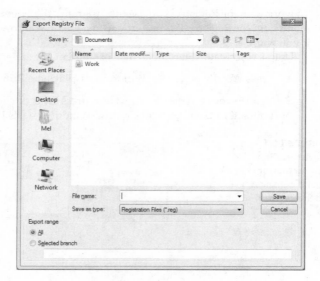

Restoring Your Registry

To restore your Registry (or part of it) from a Registry file you've exported, follow these steps:

1. From Registry Editor, choose File ➤ Import. Registry Editor displays the Import Registry File dialog box (see Figure 11.3).

2. In the drop-down list above the Open button, select the Registration Files item if you're restoring your entire Registry. If you're restoring a hive file, select the Registry Hive Files item.

FIGURE 11.3

The Import Registry File dialog box is a standard Windows Open dialog box given another name. Choose whether to display Registration Files (entire Registry files) or Registry Hive Files (partial Registry files).

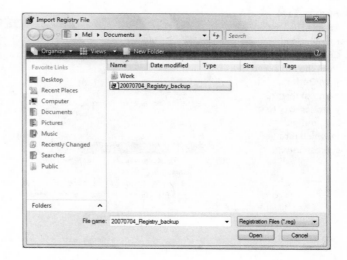

3. Select the Registry file to import.

4. Click the Open button. Registry Editor imports the Registry file and adds it to the Registry.

Restoring the Registry to Its Last Known Good Configuration

If you damage the Registry so badly that Windows won't boot anymore, you may need to restore the Registry to its Last Known Good Configuration in order to get Windows running again. The *Last Known Good Configuration* is the one with which Windows last booted successfully. Restoring the Last Known Good Configuration loses any changes you've made to your Windows configuration since the last boot—including whichever change has disabled Windows.

To restore the Registry to the Last Known Good Configuration, take the following steps:

1. Restart or start your computer:

   ◆ If Windows is still running, restart it: click the Start button, click the right-arrow button to the right of the Lock button, and then choose Restart.

   ◆ If Windows isn't running, power up your computer as usual.

2. As Windows restarts or starts, or when (in a multiboot configuration) it displays the Windows Boot Manager, press the F8 key. Windows displays the Advanced Boot Options menu (see Figure 11.4).

3. Select the Last Known Good Configuration item and press the Enter key. Windows starts and displays the Welcome screen.

FIGURE 11.4

Choose the Last Known Good Configuration item from the Advanced Boot Options menu to restore your Registry to its last configuration in which it ran successfully.

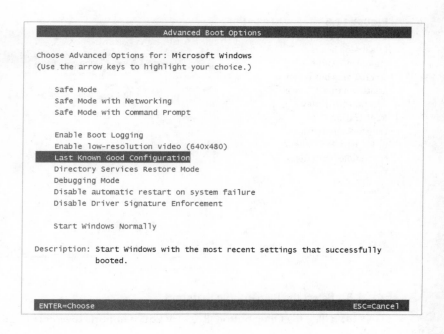

```
                          Advanced Boot Options

Choose Advanced Options for: Microsoft Windows
(Use the arrow keys to highlight your choice.)

    Safe Mode
    Safe Mode with Networking
    Safe Mode with Command Prompt

    Enable Boot Logging
    Enable low-resolution video (640x480)
    Last Known Good Configuration
    Directory Services Restore Mode
    Debugging Mode
    Disable automatic restart on system failure
    Disable Driver Signature Enforcement

    Start Windows Normally

Description: Start Windows with the most recent settings that successfully
             booted.


ENTER=Choose                                          ESC=Cancel
```

Working in the Registry

Now that your Registry is safely backed up, it's time to examine how the Registry works and how you can change it.

The Registry is a hierarchical database, with its contents arranged into a hierarchy of folders that are organized into five main areas called *subtrees* or *root keys*. You'll also sometimes hear them called *predefined keys*, though the term tends to be confusing because the Registry contains thousands of keys that are predefined—at least, from the user's point of view. As you can see in Figure 11.1 (earlier in this chapter), each subtree's name begins with the letters HKEY.

The Five Subtrees of the Registry

These are the five subtrees and the types of information they contain:

HKEY_CLASSES_ROOT   This subtree contains an exhaustive list of the file types that Windows recognizes, the programs associated with them, and more.

HKEY_CURRENT_USER   This subtree contains information on the current user and their setup. For example, when you're logged on, all your Desktop preferences are listed in this subtree.

HKEY_LOCAL_MACHINE   This subtree contains information on the hardware and software setup of the computer.

HKEY_USERS   This subtree contains information on the users who are set up to use the computer, together with a DEFAULT profile that's used when no user is logged on to the computer.

HKEY_CURRENT_CONFIG   This subtree contains information on the current configuration of the computer—the hardware with which the computer booted.

Keys, Subkeys, and Value Entries

In Registry Editor, expand the HKEY_CURRENT_USER subtree by clicking the plus (+) sign next to it or by double-clicking its name. Registry Editor displays the items contained within the subtree— an apparently endless list of folderlike objects, many of them containing further objects. Figure 11.5 shows the HKEY_CURRENT_USER subtree with some of its subkeys expanded and the \Control Panel\ Desktop\WindowMetrics key displayed.

FIGURE 11.5
Each subtree contains keys, subkeys, and value entries.

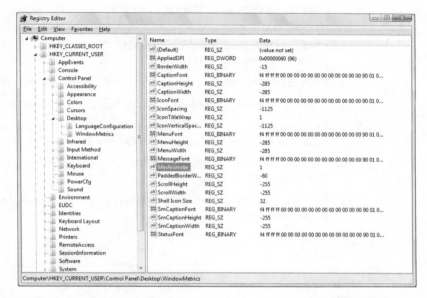

Within each subtree are keys, subkeys, and value entries. A *key* is one of the folders within the subtree. Just as a subfolder is a folder within a folder, a *subkey* is a key within a key. Also as with "folder" and "subfolder," many people say "key" rather than "subkey" except when they need to be specific; this chapter does the same.

Each key or subkey can contain subkeys and value entries. The term *value entry* sounds like a management-consultant way of saying "value," but in fact it's not: A value entry is the current definition of a key and consists of a name, a data type, and the value assigned to the key.

For example, consider the MinAnimate key and value entry that you can see in Figure 11.5 in the HKEY_CURRENT_USER\Control Panel\Desktop\WindowMetrics\ subkey. As you can see in the Data column, the value of MinAnimate is 1. This value entry controls whether Windows animates windows when you minimize, maximize, or restore them. (The animation zooms the window from its displayed size and position down to its button on the Taskbar, and vice versa, instead of popping it off or back on the screen instantly.) A value of 0 indicates that the animation is off; a value of 1 that the animation is on.

Try this example of changing a setting both via Windows' user interface and via Registry Editor. Follow these steps:

1. In Registry Editor, expand the HKEY_CURRENT_USER\Control Panel\Desktop\ WindowMetrics key so that you can see the MinAnimate key. Its value should be 1, the default value for a computer that's fast enough to run Windows Vista without struggling.

2. Press Windows Key+Break. Windows displays the System window of Control Panel.

3. In the left panel, click the Advanced System Settings link, and then authenticate yourself to User Account Control. Windows displays the System Properties dialog box with its Advanced page at the front.

4. In the Performance group box, click the Settings button. Windows displays the Performance Options dialog box with the Visual Effects page at the front (see Figure 11.6).

5. In the list box, clear the Animate Windows When Minimizing and Maximizing check box. Windows selects the Custom option button above the list box (if another option button was selected).

6. Click the OK button. Windows closes the Performance Options dialog box, returning you to the System Properties dialog box.

7. Click the OK button. Windows closes the System Properties dialog box.

8. Click the Registry Editor button on the Taskbar to activate Registry Editor.

9. Press F5 or choose View ➤ Refresh to refresh the Registry listing. Notice that the `MinAnimate` value has changed to 0 because you cleared the check box.

10. Click the Minimize button on Registry Editor to minimize the window. Notice that Windows doesn't animate the minimization.

11. Click the Registry Editor Taskbar button to restore the window. Again, Windows doesn't use an animation.

FIGURE 11.6

The Animate Windows When Minimizing and Maximizing check box on the Visual Effects page of the Performance Options dialog box is the UI control that affects the MinAnimate Registry setting.

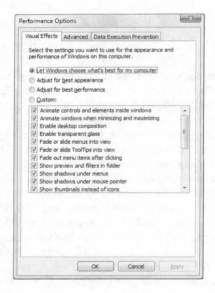

12. In Registry Editor, double-click the `MinAnimate` key. Registry Editor displays the Edit String dialog box, as shown here, which lists the value name and the current value data.

13. In the Value Data text box, type **1** (replacing the 0), and then press Enter or click the OK button. Registry Editor closes the dialog box and applies the value.

14. Click the Minimize button on Registry Editor to minimize the window. Notice that Windows again doesn't animate the minimization. This is because many changes you make via Registry Editor require you to log out and then log in again before they take effect.

15. Log off, and then log on again.

16. Open a window, and then minimize it. Windows uses the animation again. If you open the Performance Options dialog box again, you'll find that the Animate Windows When Minimizing and Maximizing check box is now selected.

Registry Data Types

As you can see in Figure 11.5, the `MinAnimate` value entry is of type `REG_SZ`. REG means Registry; SZ means string, indicating that the value entry contains a string of text (text characters, as opposed to, say, binary data). The `\WindowMetrics\` key also contains value entries of two other data types, `REG_BINARY` (binary data) and `REG_DWORD` (the double-word data type).

Strings and binary data are the most widely used of the data types in the Registry. Double-word data comes third, followed by `REG_MULTI_SZ` (multistring entries), and `REG_EXPAND_SZ` (expandable strings). Table 11.1 provides a roundup of the five most widely used data types.

TABLE 11.1:   The Five Most Widely Used Registry Data Types

TYPE	TYPE DISPLAYED	EXPLANATION
String	REG_SZ	Text
Multistring	REG_MULTI_SZ	Text, but with multiple text values
Expandable String	REG_EXPAND_SZ	Text, but expandable
Binary	REG_BINARY	A binary value, displayed as hexadecimal
DWORD	REG_DWORD	Double-word: a 32-bit binary value displayed as an 8-digit hexadecimal value

---

OTHER REGISTRY DATA TYPES YOU'LL SELDOM NEED TO USE

Beyond the five widely used data types listed in Table 11.1, the Registry can contain many different data types, such as REG_DWORD_BIG_ENDIAN (a value stored in reverse order of double-word value), REG_DWORD_LITTLE_ENDIAN (another type of double-word value), REG_FULL_RESOURCE_DESCRIPTOR (a hardware-resource list), REG_QWORD (a quadruple-word value), and REG_FILE_NAME (a filename). You shouldn't need to mess with any of these unless you get into programming Windows—in which case you'll need a book more specialized than this one.

You can create and edit value entries with any of these data types. We'll get to that a bit later in the chapter, after discussing where the Registry is stored and how to find information in it.

Where the Registry Is Stored

Most of the Registry is stored in several different files on your hard drive. (Part of the Registry is created automatically when Windows boots and discovers which devices are attached to your computer.) These files are binary and are called *hives* (think bees, not allergies) or *hive files*.

Perhaps surprisingly, some of the hives aren't hidden files, so you don't even need to tell Windows to display hidden files before you can see them. But you do have to go through Windows's veil of secrecy over the files by clicking the Show the Contents of This Folder link.

Hive files containing computer-related information are stored in the *Windows**system32*\\ *config*\\ folder, where *Windows*\\ is your Windows folder. Hive files containing user-specific information are stored in the \\Users*Username*\\ folder for each user.

These are the main hive files:

SYSTEM   This file contains information about the computer's hardware and about Windows. This information goes into the HKEY_LOCAL_MACHINE\\SYSTEM\\ key.

NTUSER.DAT   This file contains information about the user's preferences. Windows keeps an NTUSER.DAT file for each user in the \\Users*Username*\\ folder. This information goes into the HKEY_CURRENT_USER subtree.

SAM   This file contains the user database. This information goes into the HKEY_LOCAL_MACHINE\\ SAM\\ key.

SECURITY   This file contains information on security settings. This information goes into the HKEY_LOCALMACHINE\\SECURITY\\ key.

SOFTWARE   This file contains information on the software installed on the computer. This information goes into the HKEY_LOCAL_MACHINE\\SOFTWARE\\ key.

DEFAULT   This file contains information about the default user setup. This information goes into the HKEY_USERS\\DEFAULT\\ key.

Each of the hive files has a log file named after it: DEFAULT.LOG, SOFTWARE.LOG, NTUSER.DAT.LOG, and so on. These log files note the changes to the hive files so that, if a change is applied that crashes the system, Windows can read the log, identify the problem change, and undo it.

Windows doesn't let you open the hive files directly (other than by using Registry Editor). But you can find keys and value entries or information in the Registry, change values, and create (and delete) keys and value entries of your own.

Finding Information in the Registry

There are two ways to find information in the Registry: by digging through the Registry looking for it, or by using the Find function.

Digging through the Registry takes minimal explanation, because it's very similar to browsing in Explorer in Explore mode. You can expand and collapse keys as you would drives and folders in Explorer, and you can use type-down addressing to reach the next key or entry matching the letters you type. But because of the number of keys and value entries the Registry contains, you'll usually do better by searching through it rather than browsing.

If you know the name of a key, the name of a value entry, or the data contained in a value entry, you can search for it. For example, if you wanted to find where FTP sites were listed, you might search for **FTP Sites**. If you wanted to find out what the entry for the Microsoft Office AutoCorrect file was called, you might search for **.ACL**, the extension of the AutoCorrect file.

To search the Registry, follow these steps:

1. In Registry Editor, choose Edit ➤ Find or press Ctrl+F. Registry Editor displays the Find dialog box (shown here).

2. In the Find What text box, type the term for which you want to search.

3. If you want to restrict the search, select only the check boxes for the items you're looking at— Keys, Values, or Data—in the Look At group box.

4. If you want to search for only the entire string, select the Match Whole String Only check box. Selecting this check box prevents Find from finding the string you're looking for inside other strings—it makes Find locate only whole strings that match the string in the Find What text box.

5. Click the Find Next button to start the search.

Because of the volume of information that Windows stores in the Registry, the first match you find may not be the key (or value entry, or value) you need. For example, if you use your company's name as the Find item when looking for the RegisteredOrganization key for Windows, you may find another key, such as the registered organization for Internet Explorer. Close examination of the key will usually tell you whether you've found the key you were looking for. If not, press the F3 key or choose Edit ➤ Find Next to find the next instance.

Editing a Value Entry

To edit a value entry in the Registry, navigate to it or find it, and then double-click it. (Alternatively, select it and choose Edit ➤ Modify or right-click it and choose Modify from the shortcut menu.) Windows displays the Edit dialog box for the type of data the value entry contains.

String values and expandable string values are the easiest values to edit. In the Edit String dialog box (shown in Figure 11.7), enter the text of the string in the Value Data text box, and then click the OK button.

Multistring values are relatively simple to edit. In the Edit Multi-String dialog box (shown in Figure 11.8), enter all the data for the value entry on separate lines, and then click the OK button.

Double-word values are the next easiest values to edit. In the Edit DWORD (32-bit) Value dialog box (shown in Figure 11.9), enter the data in the Value Data text box, then choose the Hexadecimal option button or the Decimal option button as appropriate in the Base group box. (When you're editing a built-in double-word value, you shouldn't need to change the existing Base setting.) Click the OK button.

Binary values are difficult to change, and you probably won't want to mess with them for fun. In the Edit Binary Value dialog box (shown in Figure 11.10), edit the data in the Value Data text box with great care, and then click the OK button.

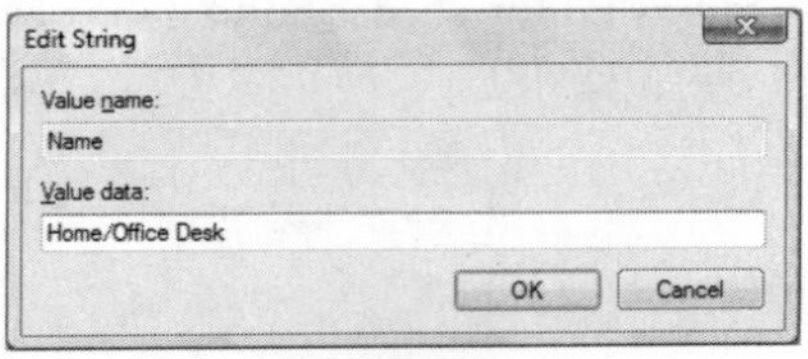

FIGURE 11.7
You can edit both string values and expandable string values in the Edit String dialog box.

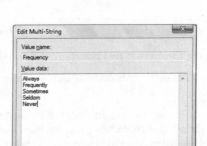

FIGURE 11.8
Editing a multistring value in the Edit Multi-String dialog box

FIGURE 11.9
Editing a double-word value in the Edit DWORD (32-bit) Value dialog box

FIGURE 11.10

Editing a binary
value in the Edit
Binary Value dialog
box is hard work.

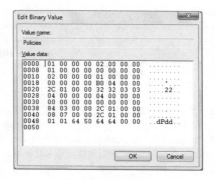

Adding a Key or a Value Entry

You can add a key or a value entry to the Registry either automatically or manually.

To add a key or value entry to the Registry automatically, double-click a `.reg` file that you've received. For example, some programs sold via download use Registry keys to implement a license: You pay for the program and download it. The company then e-mails you a license and a .reg file. To add the registration data to your Registry, double-click the `.reg` file. Windows adds the necessary keys and value entries to the Registry.

To add a key or a value entry to the Registry manually, follow these steps:

1. Right-click the key in which you want to create the new key or value entry, choose New from the context menu, and choose the appropriate item from the submenu: Key, String Value, Binary Value, DWORD (32-Bit) Value, QWORD (64-Bit) Value, Multi-String Value, or Expandable String Value. Registry Editor creates a new key named `New Key #1` or a new value entry named `New Value #1` (or the next available number) and displays an edit box around it.

2. Type the name for the key or value entry.

3. Press the Enter key or click elsewhere in the Registry Editor window. Registry Editor assigns the name you specified to the key or value entry.

If you created a value entry, double-click it. Registry Editor displays the Edit dialog box for the value entry's data type. Enter the data for the value entry as described in the previous section.

Deleting a Key or a Value Entry

Just as you can create keys and value entries, you can delete them. Generally speaking, it's a bad idea to delete any keys other than those you've created. Windows itself and Windows programs protect some keys in the Registry, but you'll find a surprising number that aren't protected and that you can therefore delete freely.

To delete a value entry, right-click it and choose Delete from the context menu. Registry Editor displays the Confirm Value Delete dialog box (shown here). Click the Yes button to confirm the deletion.

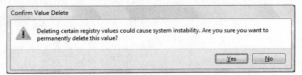

To delete a key, right-click it and choose Delete from the shortcut menu. Registry Editor displays the Confirm Key Delete dialog box (shown here) to make sure you want to get rid of the key and all its subkeys (and value entries). Click the Yes button to delete the key.

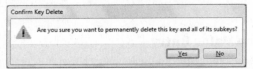

If the key or value entry is locked against deletion, Registry Editor displays an error message box.

Copying a Key Name

If you're describing to someone how to find particular information in the Registry, you'll need to get the key name right. But you don't need to type it painstakingly—you can copy it instead.

To copy a Registry key name, select it in the left pane in Registry Editor and choose Edit ➤ Copy Key Name. You can then paste it from the Clipboard into a program.

Examples of Working with the Registry

As mentioned at the beginning of the chapter, Microsoft reckons you should seldom (or preferably never) need to make changes to the Registry directly. But you'll probably run into tips and tweaks, online or in magazines, that promise to improve Windows' performance, compatibility, or behavior with a judicious change or two. This section presents some examples of working with the Registry to customize your system.

Remember that tinkering with the Registry isn't recommended, because it can have unexpected results. Before you try any of these examples, back up your Registry (as described earlier in this chapter) and make sure that you know how to restore it.

 Real World Scenario

EVALUATE ANY REGISTRY CHANGES CAREFULLY BEFORE TRYING THEM

Before you try applying any Registry change that you read about online, think carefully about how much you trust the source of the information and whether you're likely to realize the benefits promised by the change. Changes recommended by print magazines and by reputable online magazines are likely to be okay, but changes posted by supposedly friendly parties in newsgroups or on websites might be malicious rather than helpful.

If you have any doubts, spend a few minutes searching for corroboration of the Registry change rather than applying it blindly and suffering the consequences. If you can't find confirmation of what the change does, don't try it.

Removing Spyware

Spyware is malicious software that installs itself automatically without your consent and monitors your actions, either to learn what you do (for example, to find out which websites you visit and send lists of them back to base) or to try to glean sensitive information (such as passwords or credit card numbers). You can remove much spyware by using tools such as Spybot Search&Destroy (http://www.safer-networking.org/en/index.html), but you may have to remove determined pieces of spyware manually.

Many pieces of spyware install themselves in the HKEY_LOCAL_MACHINE\SOFTWARE\Microsoft\ Windows\CurrentVersion\Run key, so this is a good place to look for spyware. After deleting the entries and using Windows Explorer to delete any matching executable files that are the actual spyware, you'll need to restart Windows—and then check that the spyware hasn't managed to reinstall the Registry entry by using another trick. (If it has, search for instructions online on how to remove the spyware.)

Changing Your Windows Name and Organization

If you misspelled your name or your organization's name during setup, or if you've bought a computer loaded with Windows from someone else, you may need to change the name or organization that appears on the General page of the System Properties dialog box.

There's no way to make this change through the Windows user interface, but by navigating to the HKEY_LOCAL_MACHINE\SOFTWARE\Microsoft\WindowsNT\CurrentVersion\ key and changing the RegisteredOwner and RegisteredOrganization value entries, you can fix the problem in a minute or two.

Changing Your *Program Files\ Folder*

If you want to prevent a Windows installation routine from installing a program to your \Program Files\ folder (for example, because you're running out of space on the drive that contains the folder), change the location of your \Program Files\ folder by navigating to the HKEY_ LOCAL_MACHINE\SOFTWARE\Microsoft\Windows\CurrentVersion subkey and changing the ProgramFilesDir value entry to the appropriate drive and folder.

Restart your computer to make the change take effect, and then run the installation routine to install the program there. Change the ProgramFilesDir value entry back again to its normal value if you want to install future programs in the \Program Files\ folder.

Change the Name for a Removable Drive

When you insert a media item (such as a CD, DVD, or CompactFlash card) in a removable drive, Windows displays the item's name. But when there's no media item in a removable drive, Windows displays the drive's default name. If you have many removable drives attached to your computer, telling one from the other can be hard when they're empty.

To change the default name for a removable drive, navigate to the HKEY_LOCAL_MACHINE\ SOFTWARE\Microsoft\Windows\CurrentVersion\Explorer key and create a new key named DriveIcons within it. Within the DriveIcons key, create a new key with the drive's name— for example, E. Within this new key, create a new key named DefaultLabel. Double-click the (Default) value entry, type the name you want Explorer to display for the drive when it's empty, and press Enter.

You may need to restart Windows to make Explorer notice the change.

Clearing the Paging File at Shutdown

If you're concerned about your system's security—well, you ought really to be using Windows Professional rather than Windows Home. But here's a technique that you can use with both OSes to clear the paging file when you shut down Windows. Chapter 15 discusses the paging file in detail; but briefly, it's a huge file on your hard disk that Windows uses to store information temporarily so as to spare physical memory (RAM). So the paging file can contain sensitive information that a malicious hacker or a federal agency could recover.

To clear the paging file when you shut down Windows, navigate to the HKEY_LOCAL_MACHINE\ SYSTEM\CurrentControlSet\Control\Session Manager\Memory Management key and change the value of the value entry ClearPageFileAtShutdown to 1. Then restart your computer.

FOR TESTING ONLY: CRASHING YOUR COMPUTER ON CUE

Most people want their computer to crash seldom or (preferably) never. But if you want to test what happens when it crashes (for example, to see how memory dumping works), you'll be relieved to know that you don't have to wait for Windows to crash: Windows includes a built-in way of crashing itself. You just have to add the right Registry entry, set the appropriate value, and then press a couple of keys.

Here's what to do:

1. Back up your Registry. (Yes, really back it up this time.)

2. Open Registry Editor (for example, choose Start ➢ Run, enter **regedit,** and press the Enter key).

3. Navigate to the HKEY_LOCAL_MACHINE\SYSTEM\CurrentControlSet\Services\i8042prt\ Parameters\ key.

4. Right-click in the right pane and choose New ➢ DWORD Value from the context menu. Registry Editor creates a new value called New Value #1 and displays an edit box around the new value's name.

5. Enter the name **CrashOnCtrlScroll** and press the Enter key.

6. Double-click the CrashOnCtrlScroll value. Registry Editor displays the Edit DWORD Value dialog box.

7. Enter 1 in the Value Data text box. In the Base group box, leave the Hexadecimal option button selected.

8. Click the OK button. Registry Editor closes the Edit DWORD Value dialog box.

9. Close Registry Editor.

10. Restart your computer and log back on.

11. Hold down the Ctrl key on the right side of the keyboard and press the Scroll Lock key twice. Windows goes down as if sandbagged, and any memory dumping you've set occurs.

Using Registry Favorites to Quickly Access Keys

If you find yourself using the Registry a lot, there's another feature you should know about: Registry favorites. To access the keys you need to work with frequently, you can create favorites in Registry Editor much as you can in Explorer and Internet Explorer.

To create a favorite, follow these steps:

1. Select the key to which you want the favorite to refer.

2. Choose Favorites ➤ Add to Favorites. Registry Editor displays the Add to Favorites dialog box (shown here).

3. In the Favorite Name text box, enter the name for the favorite. (By default, Registry Editor suggests the key name, but you may well want to change this to more descriptive text.)

4. Click the OK button. Registry Editor adds the favorite to your Favorites menu.

To access a favorite, display the Favorites menu and choose the favorite from the list, as shown here.

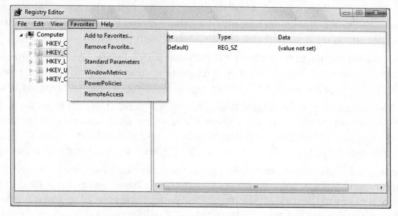

To remove a favorite from the Favorites menu, choose Favorites ➤ Remove Favorite. Windows displays the Remove Favorites dialog box, shown here. Choose the favorite in the Select Favorite list box (or select multiple favorites if you want to delete them), and then click the OK button.

The Bottom Line

Understand what the Registry is, what it's for, and why you may need to work with it   The *Registry* is a hierarchical database of all the settings for all the hardware, software, and users on your computer. Normally, you change the Registry only by working through the Windows user interface—for example, by making a change in Control Panel, or by installing hardware or software. But sometimes you may need to edit the Registry directly to solve a problem or implement a tweak.

Back up your Registry and learn how to restore it   Before you edit the Registry, you should back it up in case your changes cause trouble. Launch Registry Editor by pressing Windows Key+R, typing **regedit**, and pressing Enter. Back up the Registry by clicking the Computer item, choosing File ➢ Export, and specifying the filename and folder. Restore the Registry by choosing File ➢ Import, selecting the backup file, and clicking the Open button. To repair severe damage, you may need to restart (or start) your computer, press F8, and select Last Known Good Configuration from the Windows Advanced Options menu.

Navigate the Registry and create, edit, and delete keys and value entries   To navigate the Registry, expand the subtree and the keys it contains just as you would the folder listing in an Explorer window. You can also choose Edit ➢ Find and use the Find dialog box to find a key or data. To create a key, right-click the key that will contain the new key, choose New ➢ Key from the shortcut menu, type the name, and then press Enter. To create a new value entry, right-click the key that will contain it, choose New from the shortcut menu, and then choose the data type from the submenu. Type the name for the value entry, and then press Enter to apply the name. Double-click the value entry to open a dialog box for setting its value. To delete a key or value entry, right-click it and choose Delete from the shortcut menu.

Understand the Registry data types and what they contain   Most of the Registry data consists of five data types: String (text data), Binary (binary values), DWORD (double-word values), Multi-Strings (multiple pieces of text), and Expandable String (text whose length can expand).

Make changes to the Registry   Books, magazines, and above all websites will shower you with advice on changes you can make to the Registry. Evaluate any change carefully before you make it, because it might destabilize Windows, and always keep a recent backup of your Registry for recovery. You may need to restart Windows to make some changes take effect.

Use Registry favorites to store and access the keys you need most   Registry favorites help you navigate quickly to keys you need to change. Choose Favorites ➢ Add to Favorites to add the current key to the list at the bottom of the Favorites menu. To go to a favorite, open the Favorites menu and select the favorite from the list. To delete a favorite, choose Favorites ➢ Remove Favorites, and then work in the Remove Favorites dialog box.

Chapter 12

Installing, Configuring, and Managing Printers and Fonts

◆ Understand printing terminology and how printing works in Windows

◆ Install a printer on your computer

◆ Configure a printer's behavior to suit your needs

◆ Print documents and manage print jobs

◆ Learn advanced printing techniques and print to a file

◆ View, install, and delete fonts

With the promise of the paperless office seemingly destined to remain unfulfilled, printing continues to be vital to the average home office, and only marginally less vital to the average home.

This chapter discusses how to install, configure, and manage printers and fonts. Chapter 28 discusses how to share a printer via your network and how to connect to a shared printer.

Understanding the Basics of Windows Printing

Windows makes the process of installing a printer as straightforward as possible. But before you start, it helps to understand the basics of printing in Windows. First, some of the terminology is confusing. Second, Windows offers three ways of installing a printer; this chapter discusses the first of those ways, and Chapter 28 discusses the other two. Third, you should know the essentials of how an item you print makes its way from the program to the printer.

The Terminology of Windows Printing

Just as the windows in Windows are most likely substantially different from those in your home, Windows terminology for printing is a little different from regular terminology. Here are the terms that you need to know before you consult the Help files or call for tech support:

◆ A *printer* is the hardware device that actually prints the page—in other words, what people normally mean when they say "printer." This doesn't go without saying because Microsoft sometimes refers to a printer as a *print device*. If so, what does Microsoft mean by *printer* at those times? Read on.

◆ When the hardware device is called a *print device*, a *printer* is the software that controls the *print device*. Normally, it's clearer to call this software a printer driver, even if this isn't technically 100 percent accurate.

◆ A *print job* (or just plain *job*) is an item sent to a printer for printing. For example, if you print the first spreadsheet in an Excel workbook, that's a print job. If you then print three pages of a Word document, that's another print job.

◆ A *network printer*, *shared printer*, or *printer connection* is a printer that's being shared by another computer or by a print server and that you can connect to across the network.

◆ A *print server* is a device (typically a hardware device) that relays print jobs to a printer. Windows also has print server software built in for managing print jobs.

This book uses the terms *printer* for the hardware device and *printer driver* for the software that drives it.

Three Ways of Installing a Printer

Windows supports three ways of installing a printer:

Local printer attached to the computer   The simplest way of installing a printer is to install it *locally*—in other words, attach it directly to the computer. The printer is usually attached directly to the computer with a cable to the parallel port or USB port. There are also more specialized arrangements, such as wireless printer connections or infrared printer connections.

Networked printer attached to a server   The next way of installing a printer is to install it as a *networked*—shared—printer attached to a server. The server in this case doesn't have to be a server in the sense of a computer *dedicated* to providing services to other computers. It can be just a peer computer that's sharing a printer directly attached to it and so providing printing services to other computers. Alternatively, it can be a dedicated server running a server operating system. The client computer connects to the networked printer through a network (cabled, wireless, or—rarely—infrared). The network can be the Internet, as Windows supports the Internet Printing Protocol (IPP). Chapter 28 discusses how to print to a printer across the Internet.

Networked printer attached to a print server or containing a print server   You can also share a printer attached to a print server. A print server is typically a specialized computer designed for sharing and managing printers. The advantage of using a print server over a networked computer is that you don't need to keep a computer running all the time in order to use the printer. Print servers can be either wired to the network or wireless. Some printers have their own print servers built in.

Figure 12.1 illustrates these printer configurations.

How Does a Print Job Get Printed?

Provided your printer works as it should, you don't need to know how the printing process works. But if anything goes wrong with printing, understanding the basic process can be a great help in troubleshooting the problem.

FIGURE 12.1

The three basic configurations for printers: a local printer attached directly to the computer, a networked printer shared by another computer, and a networked printer attached to a print server

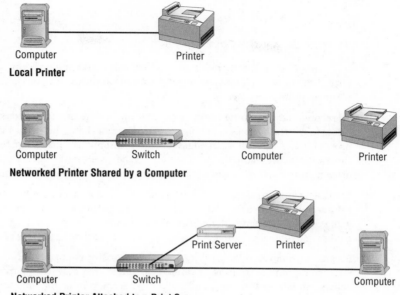

Computer   Printer

Local Printer

Computer   Switch   Computer   Printer

Networked Printer Shared by a Computer

Print Server   Printer

Computer   Switch   Computer

Networked Printer Attached to a Print Server

Here's what typically happens in the print process:

1. You issue a Print command for a document you've got open in a program. For example, you're working on a workbook in Excel and you get a worksheet into shape to print. You press Ctrl+P, choose options in the Print dialog box, and click the OK button.

2. The program tells Windows that it needs to print the document.

3. The printer driver (the print software, or what Microsoft sometimes calls the *printer*) grabs the information that the program is sending about what needs to be printed. The printer driver *spools* the printing information; that is, it saves it to disk all at once and then feeds it to the printer (the hardware print device) at a speed the printer and its cable can handle. Older parallel printer cables transfer data very slowly compared to the wiring inside the computer, and if the printer didn't spool the data, the program would be stuck transferring the information to the printer bit by bit. High-speed parallel cables and USB 2.0 cables are much faster.

Some programs are intelligent enough to print in the background while allowing you to continue working in the foreground. But generally speaking, spooling lets you continue your work much more quickly.

There's one other part to this: Each print job is typically spooled into a *print queue* rather than just fed into the printer. Documents in the print queue are normally printed in the order in which they are submitted, but you can assign different priorities to different users' print jobs if you want. If you have Administrator privileges, you can also manage the print queue, promoting, demoting, pausing, and deleting print jobs.

KEEPING DOWN THE COST OF PRINTING

Chances are you're familiar with the axiom about marketing razors and razor blades: The manufacturers sell the razor itself at a low price to get you committed to buying the blades, on which they make plenty of profit.

The economics of printing works in a similar way. Printer manufacturers sell printers at temptingly low prices to get you hooked on buying ink cartridges for them, then they sting you on the cartridges. If you print a lot, the cost of the cartridges for your printer will probably run to between 5 times and 20 times the printer's cost before the printer gives up the ghost—so it's well worth evaluating the cost per page of each printer you're considering rather than just the printer's price and features.

Because color cartridges tend to be much more expensive than black cartridges, consider getting a printer that uses separate color and black cartridges rather than one that essentially forces you to print using color all the time. (If you print many documents in grayscale, and your color printer uses high-quality and high-cost media, it may even be worth getting a separate printer for your grayscale work.)

Because printer cartridges are expensive, enterprising companies provide less expensive alternatives. First, some companies provide refilled cartridges that cost less than new cartridges but supposedly deliver similar performance and reliability. Some printer manufacturers have made their printers respond negatively to printer cartridges that don't include the manufacturer's identifying technology—for example, by claiming that third-party cartridges are empty long before they actually are—and by claiming that third-party cartridge manufacturers are infringing the provisions of the Digital Millennium Copyright Act (DMCA).

Second, other companies sell kits that let you refill ink cartridges, usually with a syringe and needle and a trusty hand. Some people swear by these kits, which have the potential not only to save you money but also to distribute ink where you don't want it, but rather more people swear *at* them. Further adding to the problem is the fact that, because the manufacturers don't design the nozzles in most ink cartridges to be reused, the output quality is likely to degrade if you refill a cartridge.

Another possibility is to print most of your documents in draft mode, which uses lower resolution but is plenty readable enough for everyday use, and save high-quality mode for documents that need the extra resolution (for example, pictures, or text documents that you're going to give to clients rather than use yourself). An extra bonus of this approach is that draft mode may print more quickly than high-quality mode.

If you print a lot, or if you can afford to take a long-term view, buy a laser printer. Laser printers have much lower per-page running costs than inkjet printers, particularly for standard-quality monochrome printing. The disadvantage is that laser printers tend to be more expensive than inkjets, so you need to make more of an investment up front.

Unfortunately, there's no printer equivalent of an electric razor—except for viewing documents on screen rather than printing them out on paper. In any case, you should use Print Preview to check that your documents look approximately okay before you print them.

Printers Window

Windows Vista's central location for working with printers is the Printers window in Control Panel. To display the Printers window, follow these steps:

1. Choose Start ➤ Control Panel. Windows displays a Control Panel window.

2. In Control Panel Home view, click the Printer link under the Hardware and Sound heading. Windows displays a Printers window (see Figure 12.2).

FIGURE 12.2

The Printers window is your central location for adding and managing printers.

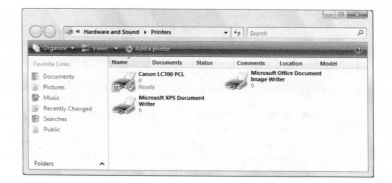

PUTTING A PRINTERS ITEM ON YOUR START MENU

If you find yourself working often in the Printers window, put a link to it on your Start menu. Follow these steps:

1. Right-click the Start button, and then choose Properties from the context menu. Windows displays the Start Menu page of the Taskbar and Start Menu Properties dialog box.

2. Click the Customize button. Windows displays the Customize Start Menu dialog box.

3. Select the Printers check box.

4. Click the OK button to close each dialog box.

Installing a Local Printer

If your printer was connected to the computer when you installed Windows, Setup should have set it up for you. If you connect it afterward, you'll need to set it up by using the hardware wizards.

Installing a USB Printer via Automated Installation

These days, most consumer printers connect to your computer via USB. Normally, Windows' automated procedures take care of installing USB printers for you, although you may need to intervene at some points.

Here's an example of the steps you'll probably follow:

1. Set the printer up and connect its power cord.

2. Connect the printer to your computer's USB port.

3. If the printer has an on/off switch, turn it on. Windows notices the printer and launches the Add Printer Wizard.

4. What happens next depends on the printer and on Windows' configuration:

   ◆ The wizard may simply install the printer, displaying a balloon in the notification area to let you know that it is doing so, as shown here. Go to the end of this list.

   ◆ With other printers, you may see a screen such as that in Figure 12.3, which tells you that Windows needs to install driver software for your Generic IEEE 1284.4 printing support. This message appears for some USB-connected printers, because IEEE 1284.4 is a USB standard. Click the Locate and Install Driver Software button, and then authenticate yourself to User Account Control.

5. If Windows can find a driver for the printer, it installs the driver automatically. If not, it prompts you for the driver, as shown in Figure 12.4.

6. If you have the disc, insert it, and then either click the Next button or wait while AutoPlay identifies the disc and restarts the installation process. The wizard displays the Please Select the Best Match for Your Hardware from the List Below screen (see Figure 12.5). If you don't have the disc, click the "I Don't Have the Disc. Show Me Other Options" button, and follow through the procedure for searching for a suitable driver.

FIGURE 12.3
Windows may tell you that it needs to install driver software for your Generic IEEE 1284.4 printing support. This is fine.

FIGURE 12.4
Windows prompts
you for the printer
driver if it can't find
a suitable driver of
its own.

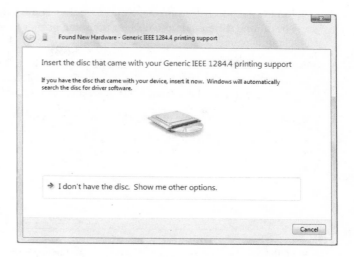

FIGURE 12.5
On the Please Select
the Best Match for
Your Hardware from
the List Below screen
of the Add Printer
Wizard, choose the
make and model of
your printer.

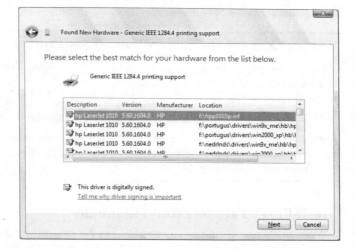

MAKE SURE THE DRIVER IS DIGITALLY SIGNED

After you select a driver on the Please Select the Best Match for Your Hardware from the List Below screen of the Add Printer Wizard, make sure that the This Driver Is Digitally Signed readout appears.

A digital signature is an encrypted identifier placed on a file using a digital certificate that's unique to the company, organization, or individual who holds it. A digital signature lets you be sure that the driver has come from the holder shown rather than from someone masquerading as them. A digital signature doesn't prevent the driver from containing poorly written or even malevolent code, but it does provide an audit trail about where the code came from.

7. In the list box, select the make and model. In some cases, as in the figure, your choice may be among different languages for the same printer model; if so, make sure you choose the language you want.

8. Click the Next button. The wizard displays the Installing Driver Software screen while it installs the software. It then displays the Driver Software Installation dialog box shown here, telling you that the software has been successfully installed.

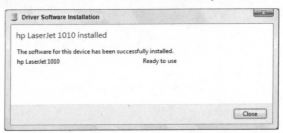

9. Click the OK button. Windows closes the Driver Software Installation dialog box, and the printer appears in the Printers window.

OTHER TIMES YOU MAY NEED TO RUN THE ADD PRINTER WIZARD MANUALLY

Even though Windows adds USB printers automatically when you connect them, you may need to run the Add Printer Wizard manually to add a printer.

◆ You may want to add a new printer configuration for a printer that Windows already knows about. See the section "Creating Multiple Entries for the Same Printer," later in this chapter.

◆ You may want to add an entry for a printer to which your computer won't actually connect, so that you can print documents to files formatted for that type of printer (and then print the files later, perhaps from another computer).

Installing a Parallel Printer Manually

When installing a printer that connects to your computer via the parallel port, you'll normally need to install it manually. However, depending on your computer's hardware, Windows may also notice when you connect a parallel printer and start the installation automatically; if so, follow the procedure described in the previous section.

To install a printer by running the Add Printer Wizard manually, take the following steps:

1. In the Printers window, click the Add a Printer button on the toolbar. Windows starts the Add Printer Wizard, which displays the Choose a Local or Network Printer screen (shown in Figure 12.6).

2. Click the Add a Local Printer button. The wizard displays the Choose a Printer Port screen (see Figure 12.7).

FIGURE 12.6
On the Choose a Local or Network Printer screen of the Add Printer Wizard, click the Add a Local Printer button.

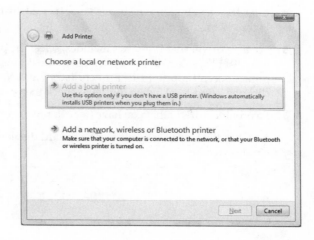

FIGURE 12.7
On the Choose a Printer Port screen of the Add Printer Wizard, select the port to which the printer is connected.

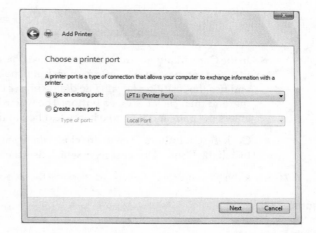

3. Make sure the Use an Existing Port option button is selected, and then select the port in the drop-down list.

♦ The default setting is LPT1, which is typically the port for the parallel port on your computer. If your computer has multiple parallel ports, you may need to use LTP2 or LPT3 instead.

♦ The COM ports (COM1, COM2, and so on) are serial ports. Very few printers connect to serial ports, because they are very slow.

♦ The FILE port is for printing to a file. See the section "Printing to a File," later in this chapter.

♦ The XPSPort port is for printing to an XML Paper Specification file. See the section "Printing to an XPS File," later in this chapter.

4. Click the Next button. The wizard displays the Install the Printer Driver screen (shown in Figure 12.8).

5. To use a driver that Windows includes, select the printer's manufacturer in the Manufacturer list box, select the printer model in the Printers list box, and then go to step 7. If your printer doesn't appear in the Printers list box and your computer is connected to the Internet, click the Windows Update button to check the Windows Update site for a driver.

6. To provide a driver that you have (for example, on a CD or a floppy disc), follow these steps:

   ◆ Click the Have Disk button. The wizard displays the Install from Disk dialog box, as shown here.

   ◆ In the Copy Manufacturer's Files From text box, enter the path and filename of the driver file. You can type in this information, but usually it's easier to click the Browse button and use the resulting Locate File dialog box (a common Open dialog box) to select the file, and then click the Open button. The wizard closes the Locate File dialog box and enters the path and filename in the text box in the Install from Disk dialog box.

   ◆ Click the OK button. The wizard closes the Install from Disk dialog box and displays the Install the Printer Driver screen, which lists the printer for which the driver is designed.

7. Click the Next button. The wizard displays the Type a Printer Name screen (see Figure 12.9).

FIGURE 12.8
On the Install the Printer Driver screen of the Add Printer Wizard, choose the printer's manufacturer and model if you want to use a driver included with Windows. You can also check Windows Update for a driver, or provide a driver yourself.

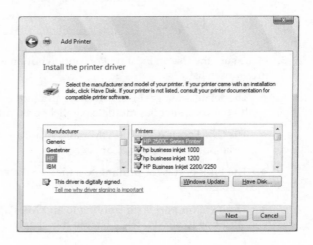

FIGURE 12.9
On the Type a Printer Name screen of the Add Printer Wizard, name your printer and decide whether to make it your computer's default printer.

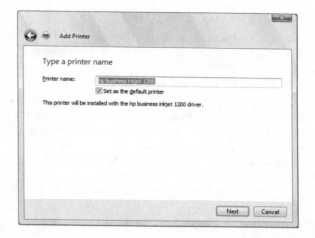

8. In the Printer Name text box, adjust the default name that the wizard suggests for the printer. Keep the name relatively short, because some programs have problems with printer names that are longer than 31 characters. If you share this printer with other computers, those 31 characters must include your computer's name.

9. Select the Set As the Default Printer check box if you want to use this printer as your computer's default printer.

10. Click the Next button. The wizard installs the printer driver, and then displays a screen telling you that you've successfully added the printer.

11. If you want to print a test page on the printer to make sure the printer driver is working, click the Print a Test Page button. The wizard sends a test page to the printer and displays a dialog box such as the one shown here. Click the Close button if the page prints correctly; if it doesn't, click the Troubleshoot Printer Problems link, and then follow through the troubleshooter that the wizard displays.

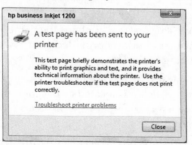

12. After printing a test page, or if you decide not to, click the Finish button. The Add Printer Wizard closes, and the printer you added appears in the Printers window.

Configuring a Printer

This section discusses how to configure a printer—everything from setting a printer as your default to telling it what kind of separator pages to print.

Setting a Printer as Your Default

Your default printer is the one that Windows assumes you want to print to unless you specify another printer. Windows displays a green circle with a white check mark on the default printer in the Printers window and in the Select Printer box in most Print dialog boxes so that you can identify your default printer at a glance.

To set a printer as your default, right-click it in the Printers window, and then choose Set as Default Printer from the context menu.

To set properties for a printer, display its Properties dialog box by taking either of the following actions:

◆ Right-click the printer in the Printers window, and then choose Properties from the context menu.

◆ Select the printer in the Printers window, and then click the Set Printer Properties button on the toolbar. Normally, this button appears on the hidden section of the toolbar, so you'll need to click the Display Additional Commands button (the button with the two chevrons, >>), and then click Set Printer Properties on the drop-down menu.

The following sections discuss the standard options in the Properties dialog box for a printer. Depending on the type of printer you're using and the printer driver you installed for it, you may see other pages than these. For example, for a color printer you'll see a Color Management page, on which you can associate color profiles with the printer so that you get approximately the colors you want. For an inkjet printer, you may see a Utilities page or a Maintenance page that offers options such as Nozzle Check and Head Cleaning.

Setting General Page Options

The General page of the Properties dialog box (see Figure 12.10) for a printer contains the following options:

Printer Name text box This text box contains the name you entered for the printer during setup or a default name that Windows provided on the basis of the printer driver used. You can change the name by typing in the text box.

Location text box In this text box, you can enter any location information about the printer—for example, the room in which it is located or the computer to which it is attached. This information is more useful when you're sharing a printer on the network than when the printer is used only by your computer.

Comment text box In this text box, you can enter further information about the printer—for example, which kind of print jobs to use it for and which to avoid. This information too is primarily useful when you're sharing the printer on the network, but you might also use it to note that the printer is loaded with a special type of paper.

Features list box This list box provides information about the printer's capabilities, such as whether it can print in color, print double-sided, staple, and so on.

Printing Preferences button   Click this button to display the Printing Preferences dialog box, on whose pages you can choose options for layout, paper selection, and print quality. Different settings are available for different printers. The settings are implemented through the printer driver, so updating the driver may make more settings available to you.

Print Test Page button   Click this button to print a test page to the printer to make sure it's handling text and graphics correctly.

FIGURE 12.10

The General page of the Properties dialog box for a printer lets you re-name the printer, add its location or a comment, set print-ing preferences, and print a test page.

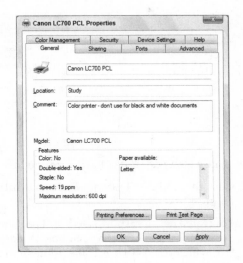

Setting Sharing Page Options

The Sharing page of the Properties dialog box for a printer contains options for sharing the printer on the network. Chapter 27 discusses how to use these options.

Setting Ports Page Options

The Ports page of the Properties dialog box for a printer (see Figure 12.11) contains options for creating, deleting, and configuring ports. Normally, you won't need to change the port the printer uses, but you may want to implement printer pooling if you have two printers.

CREATING A PRINTER PORT

Windows automatically provides you with three printer ports (LPT1 through LPT3), four serial ports (COM1 through COM4), and several other types of ports, so normally you'd add a port only in these circumstances:

◆   When your printer or other output device requires a specialized port setup. In this case, you need an initialization file (a file with an INF extension) from the manufacturer of the printer or device.

◆   When you need to use a TCP/IP port. In this case, you need to know the details of the port you're creating.

FIGURE 12.11
The Ports page of
the Properties dialog
box for a printer lets
you create ports for
specialized printing
needs.

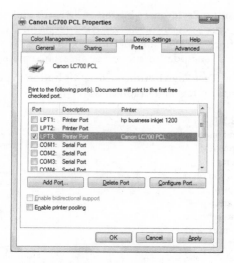

To create a new port, install the device and take the following steps:

1. Click the Add Port button. Windows displays the Printer Ports dialog box (shown in Figure 12.12).

2. To create a new local port, select the Local Port item in the Available Port Types list box, and then click the New Port Type button. Windows displays the Installing Print Monitor dialog box, which you use to select the printer initialization file containing the port monitor installation information. Windows then installs the port.

3. To create a new standard TCP/IP port for a network printer, select the Standard TCP/IP Port item in the Available Port Types list box, and then click the New Port button. Windows starts the Add Standard TCP/IP Printer Port Wizard, which walks you through the process of adding a TCP/IP port and then returns you to the Printer Ports dialog box. You will need to know the IP address of the printer.

4. Click the Close button. Windows closes the Printer Ports dialog box, returning you to the Ports page of the Properties dialog box for the printer.

FIGURE 12.12
For specialized printer
needs, use the Printer
Ports dialog box to
create a new local
port or TCP/IP port.

DELETING A PRINTER PORT

Windows doesn't let you delete any of the system ports that come built in, but you can delete any custom ports that you create. To delete a port, take the following steps:

1. Select the port in the Print to the Following Ports list box.

2. Click the Delete Port button. Windows displays the Delete Port dialog box.

3. Click the Yes button.

CONFIGURING A PRINTER PORT

Windows offers only one configuration setting for a parallel port: the number of seconds allowed to elapse before Windows decides the printer has taken a hike. To set this timeout, follow these steps:

1. Select the port in the Print to the Following Ports list.

2. Click the Configure Port button. Windows displays the Configure LPT Port dialog box, shown here.

3. In the Transmission Retry text box, enter the number of seconds you wish Vista to continue retrying to submit the print job before canceling the print operation.

4. Click the OK button. Windows closes the Configure LPT Port dialog box.

For TCP/IP port monitors, Windows offers further configuration options.

USING BIDIRECTIONAL SUPPORT

If the Enable Bidirectional Support check box is available, you can select it to allow the printer to send status information back to the computer. For example, the printer can notify you that it's running out of ink or paper.

USING PRINTER POOLING

If you have two or more identical printers, you can *pool* them to create a single logical printer capable of twice the throughput. Set up the printers as usual, and then select the Enable Printer Pooling check box for each printer. In the Print to the Following Ports list box, select the appropriate ports. You can then print to the printer pool, and Windows will use the first printer that's available. Printer pooling is widely used in offices, but it tends to be overkill for most home printing.

Setting Advanced Page Options

The Advanced page of the Properties dialog box (see Figure 12.13) for a printer contains a slew of options for everything from setting availability times for printers to adding separator pages between print jobs.

FIGURE 12.13

The Advanced page of the Properties dialog box for a printer lets you control the printer's availability, change spooling options, or add separator pages between print jobs.

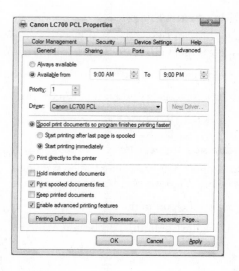

SETTING AVAILABILITY OPTIONS

By default, Windows sets the printer to be always available, selecting the Always Available option button. This setting is useful for many home or office situations, but you may want to limit availability in some situations. For example, you might want to prevent people from printing at night if that might disturb the household.

To limit availability, select the Available From option button, and then use the "two time" text boxes to specify the range of time the printer should be available.

SETTING THE PRIORITY

You need set the priority for the printer only when you're using multiple *printer entries*—software entities that represent the printer. Printer entries are a way of managing the printer. See "Creating Multiple Entries for the Same Printer," later in this chapter.

To set the priority for the printer, adjust the setting in the Priority text box. You can set priorities from 1 (the lowest priority) to 99 (the highest priority). Each job printed by this printer entry gets the same priority, so by setting one printer entry to a higher priority than another, you can give priority to the computers or jobs that use that printer entry.

CHANGING THE DRIVER

You can change the printer driver to another currently installed printer driver by using the Driver drop-down list. To install a new printer driver, click the New Driver button. Windows starts the Add Printer Driver Wizard, which walks you through the process of installing the driver.

CHOOSING SPOOLING OPTIONS

As you'll remember from the section "How Does a Print Job Get Printed?" earlier in this chapter, the print driver saves information to the hard disk and from there sends it along to the printer. This process, *spooling*, lets you continue your work without having to wait while the program you're working in sends every byte of the print job down the cable to the printer.

By default, Windows selects the Spool Print Documents so Program Finishes Printing Faster option button and its suboption, the Start Printing Immediately option button. If starting printing immediately seems to be causing problems, you can try selecting the Start Printing after Last Page Is Spooled option button to give the printer more time to process the information. If this doesn't help, you can cut out spooling by selecting the Print Directly to the Printer option button—but be warned that printing this way can be very slow. Even if the printer is connected to your computer via a high-speed USB connection, the printer's memory buffer may not be able to hold an entire print job at once.

CHOOSING OTHER OPTIONS

The next four options defy easy grouping:

Hold Mismatched Documents   Select this check box if you want Windows to make sure the spooled document matches the printer setup before sending the document to the printer. If the document doesn't match the printer setup, Windows holds the document in the print queue.

Print Spooled Documents First   Select this check box if you want spooled documents to print before partially spooled documents that carry a higher priority. This setting improves printer efficiency but is relevant only if you use printer priorities.

Keep Printed Documents   Select this check box if you want to keep the spooled files on disk so that you can resend them to the printer from the print queue if necessary. Use this option only if you're having difficulty printing documents correctly—for example, if you're reconfiguring your printer and don't want to waste time and effort by resending the print job from the program. The spooled files consume disk space, so you won't normally want to keep them.

Enable Advanced Printing Features   Clear this check box if you want to disable advanced printing features (such as booklet printing) in order to troubleshoot printing problems.

SETTING PRINTING DEFAULTS

To set default properties for the printer, click the Printing Defaults button and choose options in the resulting Printing Defaults dialog box. For example, you might want to change the printer from printing in portrait orientation to printing in landscape orientation, or make it print in back-to-front order instead of in front-to-back order.

CHANGING THE PRINT PROCESSOR

To use a different print processor or a different data type, click the Print Processor button, and then choose settings in the resulting Print Processor dialog box. Don't mess with this setting unless you're sure you know what you're doing.

USING SEPARATOR PAGES

To make Windows print a *separator page* between print jobs, click the Separator Page button. Windows displays the Separator Page dialog box, as shown here.

Click the Browse button, use the resulting Separator Page dialog box (a common Open dialog box) to locate the separator page file, and then click the OK button. Windows closes the Separator Page dialog box.

Windows includes several separator page files, which have the SEP extension. You can also create custom separator files of your own by using a text editor such as Notepad.

Device Settings Page Options

The Device Settings page of the Properties dialog box contains settings specific to your printer. For example, for many printers you can change the paper assigned to the paper trays or choose options for manual feed. Figure 12.14 shows an example of the settings for a modest color printer.

FIGURE 12.14

The choice of settings on the Device Settings page of the Properties dialog box varies greatly depending on the printer.

Color Management Page Options

If your printer supports color printing, its Properties dialog box should include a Color Management page. This page contains a Color Management button that you can click to open Windows Vista's Color Management application.

Color management lets you adjust the way that colors look on different devices. For example, you may find that colors in photos look different on screen than they look when they print. If that bothers you (and many people either don't notice or don't care, or simply curse the printer), you can use color management to try to make the colors match.

The basic color management adjustment is to make a different color profile the default profile for a device (for example, for a printer). To do so, take the following steps:

1. On the Color Management page of the printer's Properties dialog box, click the Color Management button. Windows displays the Color Management application.

2. On the Devices page (see Figure 12.15), select the printer in the Device drop-down list.

3. Select the Use My Settings for this Device check box.

FIGURE 12.15
Color management lets you change the color profile used for the printer—for example, to make the printer's colors look the way you want them to.

4. In the Profile Selection drop-down list, choose the Manual item.

5. In the Profiles Associated with This Device list box, click the profile you want to use, and then click the Set as Default Profile button.

6. Click the Close button. Windows closes the Color Management dialog box and returns you to the Properties dialog box for the printer.

Removing a Printer

To remove a printer, take the following steps:

1. In the Printers window, right-click the printer, and then choose Delete from the context menu. Alternatively, click the printer, and then click the Delete this Printer button on the toolbar (or, if necessary, click the Display Additional Commands button, and then click Delete this Printer on the drop-down menu). Windows displays a Printers dialog box asking if you're sure, as shown here.

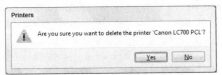

2. Click the Yes button. Windows closes the Printers dialog box and removes the printer, but it leaves the printer driver on your computer so that you can create the printer again easily if you need to.

Printing a Document

The conventional way of printing a document is as follows:

1. Issue a Print command from the program that created the document or from a program designed to handle its file type.

2. Choose any relevant options (which pages to print, or the resolution to use) in the Print dialog box.

3. Click the Print button or the OK button.

Windows also lets you print directly to the printer from Explorer. You can print a document from Explorer by dragging it and dropping it on the printer in the Printers window (or on a shortcut to the printer). Windows prints the document with default settings, so you don't get to choose any of the usual printing options. But usually you won't have the printer (or a shortcut to it) handy enough for this technique to be useful, although you can create shortcuts to a printer wherever you need them, such as on the Desktop. For this technique to work, the file must include the extension linked to the appropriate file type and program; otherwise, Windows doesn't know which program to use to print the file.

Many programs support printing directly from Explorer and so include a Print command on the context menu for the document. To print a document, right-click it, and then choose Print from the context menu.

Managing Your Print Jobs

Once you've sent a document to the printer, you can just wait for Windows to print it. If you're the only person using this printer, and if there's no problem with the printer (such as being out of paper, ink, or toner), it should print more or less right away. But if you're printing many documents, or if you're sharing one or more printers with people who are printing many documents, you may find yourself needing to manage print jobs. This section discusses how to do so.

 Real World Scenario

DEALING WITH A PRINT JOB GONE WRONG

It's much easier, neater, and cleaner to cancel a job before it starts printing than after it starts printing—but often you'll only realize that you need to cancel a particular print job when the printer starts spewing out garbage—sheets of paper with only a single column of letters, or with mangled graphics, or page after page of PostScript codes instead of the layout of ink they're supposed to represent.

When you cancel a print job that's being printed, the printer may get confused. Give it a minute or two (depending on the printer's speed) to clear its memory of the interrupted job. If that doesn't work, you may need to reset the printer, by pressing a hardware reset button, by issuing a software reset command supported by the printer's custom software, or by turning the printer off and then back on again.

Pausing and Resuming Printing

To pause printing of all documents on the printer, right-click the printer in the Printers window, and then choose Pause Printing from the context menu. Alternatively, click the printer, and then click the Pause Printing button on the toolbar.

To resume printing, right-click the printer and choose Resume Printing from the context menu. Alternatively, click the printer, and then click the Resume Printing button on the toolbar.

On a network printer, you have only the privileges of a Guest user on that computer. This means that you can pause, restart, and delete only your own print jobs; you can't affect other people's print jobs.

Managing Print Jobs by Using the Print Queue

To cancel print jobs, or rearrange the order in which they print, use the print queue. To open the print queue by using one of the following methods:

◆ If the notification area is displaying a printer icon for the printer, double-click the icon.

◆ Double-click the printer in the Printers window, or click the printer, and then click the See What's Printing button on the toolbar.

Figure 12.16 shows an example of the print queue for a printer.
From the print queue, you can take the following actions:

Cancel a print job Right-click the job in the print queue and choose Cancel from the context menu. Alternatively, choose Document ➤ Cancel.

Pause a print job Right-click the job in the print queue and choose Pause from the context menu. Alternatively, choose Document ➤ Pause.

Resume a paused print job Right-click the paused job in the print queue and choose Resume from the context menu. Alternatively, choose Document ➤ Resume.

Restart a paused or failed print job Right-click the paused or failed job in the print queue and choose Restart from the context menu. Alternatively, choose Document ➤ Restart.

Change priorities or time restrictions for a print job Right-click the job and choose Properties from the context menu. Windows displays the Document Properties dialog box for the print job. On the General page (shown in Figure 12.17), drag the Priority slider to set the priority for the job, or use the controls in the Schedule text box to set or remove time scheduling. Click the OK button. Windows closes the Document Properties dialog box.

FIGURE 12.16

Use the print queue to see what's printing, to cancel a print job, or to manage print jobs.

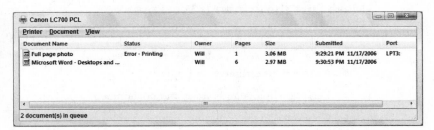

FIGURE 12.17
On the General page of the Document Properties dialog box for a print job, you can change the priority and schedule for the print job.

Troubleshooting Printing Problems

This section presents a general approach to troubleshooting printing problems. Given that there are about as many types of printers as there are types of cars, and that the drivers for those printers vary in quality even more widely than the drivers you'll encounter in a trip the length of Interstate 40, the information in this section is just a start—but if you persevere, you should find it can help you solve many problems.

Check Which Printer You're Printing To

If your computer is configured to connect to more than one printer, make sure that you're printing to the printer you think you're printing to. Few things are more irritating than wasting time troubleshooting an innocent and fully functional printer only to find that you've printed out five copies of the same secret document on another printer—and your colleagues have found them.

Given that the Print dialog box shows you which printer you're using, this problem is most likely to occur when you issue a Print command that starts the print job without displaying the Print dialog box.

Make Sure the Printer Is Working

Next, make sure the printer is working. Check that it's

- ◆ Powered on.

- ◆ Not set to be offline or paused.

- ◆ Loaded with ink and paper, and not jammed.

- ◆ Connected to the computer, print server, or network. If another computer or a print server is involved, check that it's powered on and functional.

Check the Program You're Printing From

If all is well with the printer, make sure you're not doing something wrong in the program from which you're trying to print. In particular, check that you're trying to print the right part of the document. For example, in a spreadsheet, make sure you haven't defined a print area that has the wrong contents. In a multipage document, check that you're trying to print the correct pages.

Running the Printing Troubleshooter

If the previous approach doesn't lead you to fix the problem, you can run Windows's Printing Troubleshooter and have it walk you through the steps of troubleshooting the problem:

1. Choose Start ➤ Help And Support. Windows displays a Windows Help and Support window.

2. Type **troubleshoot printer problems** in the Search box, and then press Enter. Windows displays a list of results.

3. Click the Troubleshoot Printer Problems link, and then follow its suggestions.

Configuring Your Print Server

Apart from the printer, which you saw how to configure earlier in this chapter, you can also configure the Windows print server—the software that controls the printers attached to your computer. In most cases, the default print server settings work fine, but you can improve your computer's performance and the printing experience of your print server's clients by setting the appropriate options. In particular, you may want to move the print server spool folder to a different location than its default location.

Opening the Print Server Properties Dialog Box

To set print server properties, open the Printers window, right-click in open space in the document area (where the printers are listed, right-click open space rather than one of the printers), choose Run as Administrator ➤ Server Properties from the context menu, and then authenticate yourself to User Account Control. (You can also simply choose Server Properties if you want to view the properties without having permission to set all of them.)

Windows displays the Print Server Properties dialog box, which contains four pages: Forms, Ports, Drivers, and Advanced.

Creating Custom Forms on the Forms Page

The Forms page of the Print Server Properties dialog box (see Figure 12.18) lets you create a new form. Take the following steps:

1. In the Forms On list box, select the existing form on which you want to base the new form.

2. Select the Create a New Form check box.

3. Type the name for the form in the Form Name text box.

4. Use the fields in the Form Description group box to specify the dimensions of the form, its margins, and the measurement units to use (Metric or English).

5. Click the Save Form button. Windows saves the form and adds it to the Forms On list box.

FIGURE 12.18
You can create custom forms on the Forms page of the Print Server Properties dialog box.

To delete a form you've added, select it in the Forms On list box, and then click the Delete button. Windows doesn't allow you to delete the built-in forms.

Configuring Ports on the Ports Page

On the Ports page of the Print Server Properties dialog box (see Figure 12.19), you can add new ports, configure existing ports, and delete ports you don't need anymore. The port configuration options available depend on the type of port involved—printer port, serial port, COM port, print server port, and so on. See the section "Setting Ports Page Options," earlier in this chapter, for a discussion of the different port types and the options you can set.

FIGURE 12.19
The Ports page of the Print Server Properties dialog box lets you add, delete, and configure printer ports.

Working with Printer Drivers

The Drivers page of the Print Server Properties dialog box (see Figure 12.20) lets you add new drivers, check the properties of existing drivers, replace existing drivers, or delete existing drivers. Normally, if you've set up one or more printers for printing on your computer, and they're printing correctly, you shouldn't need to make changes here. But you may need to make changes if:

◆ You share printers on the network with other computers that use different processor types or operating systems—for example, Itanium processors or 64-bit versions of Windows.

◆ You've removed a printer from your computer. Windows leaves the driver on your computer in case you need it again. If you don't, you can remove it using the Drivers page.

FIGURE 12.20

The Drivers page of the Print Server Properties dialog box lets you add or remove drivers and driver packages.

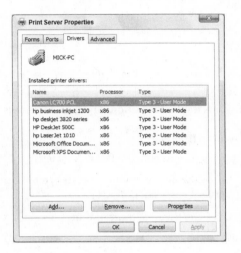

ADDING A DRIVER FOR ANOTHER PROCESSOR TYPE OR OPERATING SYSTEM

To add a driver, follow these steps:

1. On the Drivers page of the Print Server Properties dialog box, click the Add button. Windows launches the Add Printer Driver Wizard, which displays its Welcome screen.

2. Click the Next button. The wizard displays the Printer and Operating System Selection screen (see Figure 12.21).

3. Select the check box for each processor type or operating system used by a computer on your network that will print using a printer on this computer.

4. Click the Next button. The wizard displays the Printer Driver Selection screen. This screen has the same controls and works in the same way as the Install the Printer Driver screen of the Add Printer Wizard, shown in Figure 12.8 earlier in this chapter.

5. Select the printer's manufacturer in the Manufacturer list, and then select the model in the Printers list. You can also click the Have Disk button to supply a driver that you have on a disk.

FIGURE 12.21
On the Processors and Operating System Selection screen of the Add Printer Driver Wizard, select the check box for each processor type or operating system your network includes.

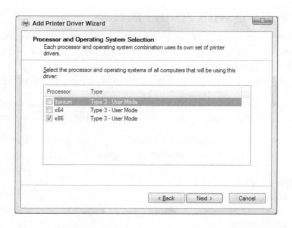

6. Click the Next button. The wizard displays the Completing the Add Printer Driver Wizard screen.

7. Click the Finish button. The wizard installs the driver and closes itself.

REMOVING A DRIVER

To remove a driver, take the following steps:

1. Select the driver in the Installed Printer Drivers list box on the Drivers page of the Print Server Properties dialog box.

2. Click the Remove button. Windows displays the Remove Driver and Package dialog box, shown here.

3. Select the Remove Driver Only option button if you want to remove only the driver. If you want to remove the driver and its package, select the Remove Driver and Driver Package option button.

4. Click the OK button. Windows displays a confirmation dialog box, as shown here.

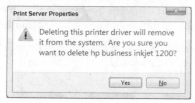

5. Click the Yes button. If you're removing the driver package as well as the driver, Windows displays the Remove Driver Package dialog box, shown here.

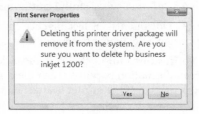

6. Click the Delete button. Windows removes the item or items.

7. Click the OK button. Windows closes the Remove Driver Package dialog box.

Choosing Advanced Print Server Options

The Advanced page of the Print Server Properties dialog box (see Figure 12.22) contains the following settings:

Spool Folder text box   The spool folder is a folder on your hard drive in which Windows stores the spool files for print jobs as they're being printed. Windows spools the data so that it can return control more quickly to the program that sent the print job. Spool files can be large, particularly for graphical documents, so you may want to move the spool folder to a drive that has plenty of space. The default location for the spool folder is on the partition that contains the Windows system files, but Windows will perform better if you move the spool folder to a different partition.

Log Spooler Error Events   Select this check box to make Windows write printer error events to the System log. This behavior is usually helpful.

Log Spooler Warning Events   Select this check box to make Windows write printer warning events to the System log. This behavior too is usually helpful.

FIGURE 12.22
The Advanced page of the Print Server Properties dialog box lets you control spooling and notifications.

Log Spooler Information Events   Select this check box to make Windows write printer information events to the System log. You probably don't need printer information (such as details on each document that was printed successfully) cluttering the System log.

Beep on Errors of Remote Documents   Select this check box to make the print server beep when an error occurs when printing a document from another computer.

Show Informational Notifications for Local Printers   Select this check box to make Windows display notification-area information pop-ups when the computer is printing to a local printer or a stand-alone network printer. If the printer is attached to the computer, these notifications usually don't help the user.

Show Informational Notifications for Network Printers   Select this check box to make Windows display notification-area information pop-ups when the computer is printing to a printer attached to another computer. This behavior is usually useful.

Printing Offline

If you're working offline, or if you want to queue up a number of print jobs and let them all run at once, put the printer offline. To do so, right-click the printer in the Printers window, and then choose Use Printer Offline from the context menu. You can then print to the printer as if your computer were connected to it, but instead of sending the data to the printer, Windows holds it in the print queue and saves it to disk.

When you've reconnected to the printer (or when you want to print, if you didn't disconnect), right-click the printer in the Printers window, and then choose Use Printer Online. Windows starts sending the print jobs to the printer. The printer must be a local printer—you can't print offline to a network printer.

Creating Multiple Entries for the Same Printer

If you want to use the same printer regularly in different ways, you can create two or more entries for it in the Printers window, and then set different properties for each entry. For example, you might set one printer entry to have a higher priority than the other, and then use that printer entry yourself while assigning the lower-priority printer entry to other users.

To create a new entry for the printer, install it again using the technique described earlier in this chapter. When you install the printer again like this, the Add Printer Wizard displays the Which Version of the Driver Do You Want to Use? screen, which offers you a Use the Driver That Is Currently Installed option button and a Replace the Current Driver option button. Given that the driver is the same, leave the Use the Driver That Is Currently Installed option button selected, and then click the Next button.

On the Type a Printer Name page, assign the printer a name that reflects the role you plan for it. For example, if you create a new entry for a printer so that you can use it to print to a file, include that information in the printer's name (and perhaps add it to the printer's Location and Comment fields as well).

After installing the printer, set properties for it to play the role you intend.

Printing to a File

Sometimes you may want to print a document to a file that you can send to someone else for printing or that you can use in another program. For example, if you need to have a document printed on a high-resolution device in your local print shop, you can print the document to a file, put the file on a portable medium, and take it along to the print shop. That way, the print shop doesn't need to have a copy of the program that created the document, the way it needs one if you copy the document onto a removable disk or recordable CD and take that along to the print shop instead.

You can print to a file in any of three ways:

Select the Print to File check box in the Print dialog box   When you print from a program, you can select the Print to File check box in the Print dialog box to print a particular job to a file rather than to a printer.

Configure a printer to always print to a file   By configuring a printer always to print to a file, you can turn every job you send to that printer into a print file.

Print to XML Paper Specification   By printing to Windows' XPS format, you can create a file that will look the same on any computer with an XPS viewer. (All versions of Windows Vista include an XPS viewer.)

ANOTHER MEANS OF PRINTING TO A FILE: PORTABLE DOCUMENT FORMAT (PDF)

If you often need to print to a file, or if you need to make read-only versions of documents and retain their layout, another option is to buy Adobe Acrobat. Acrobat produces documents in Portable Document Format (PDF), which you can view on most computer operating systems using the free Acrobat Reader, which is available from the Adobe website (http://www.adobe.com). Acrobat is more expensive than printing to a file, but in many cases it produces better results with service bureaus than simply printing to a file.

If you have Microsoft Office 2007, you can download from Microsoft's web site (http://www.microsoft.com) a component that allows the Office 2007 programs to create PDF files.

Printing to a File from the Print Dialog Box

To print to a file from the Print dialog box, follow these steps:

1. Issue a regular Print command as usual. (For example, choose File ➢ Print or press Ctrl+P.) Windows displays the Print dialog box.

2. Select the Print to File check box.

3. Choose any other appropriate printing options as usual for the program.

4. Click the OK button or the Print button, depending on the program. Windows displays the Print to File dialog box, as shown here.

5. Type the filename for the print file. If you want to specify the folder in which the print file is saved, enter the path to the folder before the filename. Otherwise, Windows saves the print file in the program's current folder.

6. Click the OK button. Windows closes the Print to File dialog box and the Print dialog box and prints the document to the file. Windows gives the file the .prn extension.

Setting a Printer to Always Print to a File

You can also set up a printer so that it prints to a file every time and doesn't let the user print to a physical printer. This capability is useful when you always need to create print files on a particular printer and don't want to risk actually printing a document by forgetting to select the Print to File check box in the Print dialog box, or if the printer in question is never available from your computer.

To make a printer always print to a file, select the FILE port in the Print to the Following Ports list box on the Ports page of the Properties dialog box for the printer. Windows clears any other port selected for the printer (unless you've selected the Enable Printer Pooling check box). When you click the OK button and Windows closes the Properties dialog box, Windows displays a disk on the printer icon to indicate that the printer is set up for printing to a file.

 Real World Scenario

SETTING "PRINT TO FILE" AS YOUR DEFAULT PRINTER

If you spend a lot of time on the road or in your local coffee shop, out of reach of any printer, you may want to set "Print to File" as your default printer. If you do, give the virtual printer an easy-to-remember name so that you don't have to guess whether you're printing to a real printer or not.

Printing to an XPS File

To print to an XPS file, follow these steps:

1. Issue a regular Print command as usual. (For example, choose File ➤ Print or press Ctrl+P.) Windows displays the Print dialog box.

2. In the list box or drop-down list for selecting the printer, choose the Microsoft XPS Document Writer item.

3. Choose any other appropriate printing options as usual for the program.

4. Click the OK button or the Print button, depending on the program. Windows displays the Save As dialog box.

5. Choose the folder in which to save the XPS file, and assign it a filename.

6. Click the Save button. Windows creates the XPS file.

Working with Fonts

Windows comes with a number of fonts that you can use to enhance your Windows display and your documents. You can add extra fonts as you need them, either by installing software that includes fonts (such as Corel WordPerfect Office or Microsoft Office) or by installing fonts directly.

A *font* is the name given to a typeface. A *typeface* is a set of characters. Normally, the characters in a typeface have similar characteristics, so that they look as though they belong together, but this isn't an absolute requirement.

Understanding Outline Fonts and Raster Fonts

Windows supports two categories of fonts:

Outline fonts   *Outline fonts* are the newest types of fonts. Windows renders outline fonts by using line and curve commands, which means that it can scale them to any size without distorting them and can rotate them. Windows supports three different types of outline fonts: TrueType fonts (which Windows has used for many years), OpenType fonts (a more recent extension of TrueType), and Type 1 fonts (which are created by Adobe Systems for use with PostScript printers and devices). TrueType fonts use the .ttf extension, OpenType fonts use the .otf extension, and Type 1 fonts use the .pfm extensions.

Raster fonts   *Raster fonts* are another older technology that Windows includes for backward compatibility. In a raster font, each character consists of a bitmap image that's displayed on the screen or printed on paper. Windows includes seven raster fonts: Courier, Modern, MS Sans Serif, MS Serif, Roman, Script, and Small Fonts. Like vector fonts, raster fonts use the .fon extension.

Some of the TrueType fonts are organized into TrueType collections, which use the .ttc extension.

Displaying the Fonts Window

To work with fonts, display the Fonts window by taking the following steps:

1. Choose Start ➢ Control Panel. Windows displays a Control Panel window.

2. Click the Appearance and Personalization link. Windows displays an Appearance and Personalization window.

3. Click the Fonts link. Windows displays the Fonts window.

Rather than having an alphabetical list of fonts, you may want to group the fonts into their different types by using the Font Type column header as shown in Figure 12.23.

Viewing and Printing a Font

To see what a font looks like, double-click its entry in the Fonts window. Windows displays the font in Font Viewer, which shows information on the font type, its file size, and copyright information, together with various sizes of the canonical sentence involving the quick brown fox and the lazy dog and the full set of numbers.

FIGURE 12.23
You can use the Font Type column header to sort the fonts into different types.

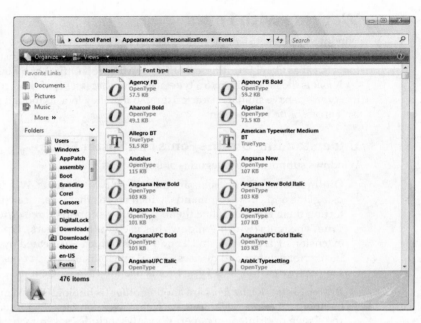

To print the information displayed, click the Print button. Windows displays the Print dialog box. Choose the printer and any options, then click the Print button. Windows closes the Print dialog box and prints the information.

To close Font Viewer, click the Close button (the × button).

Installing a Font

To install a font, take the following steps from the Fonts window:

1. Right-click blank space in the document area in the Fonts window, and then choose Install New Font from the context menu. Windows displays the Add Fonts dialog box (shown in Figure 12.24 with a font selected for installation).

FIGURE 12.24
Use the Add Fonts dialog box to add further fonts to your computer.

2. Use the Drives drop-down list and the Folders list box to navigate to the drive and folder that contain the font you want to install. (If necessary, click the Network button and use the Map Network Drive dialog box to map a network drive.)

3. In the List of Fonts list box, select the font or fonts you want to install. You can click the Select All button to select all the fonts in the List of Fonts list box.

4. Make sure that the Copy Fonts to Fonts Folder check box at the bottom of the Add Fonts dialog box is selected. This option causes Windows to copy the fonts you're installing to the Fonts folder, where you can manage them centrally. This is usually the best way to install fonts, especially when you're installing them from a removable medium (such as a CD). But if the fonts you're installing are already located on your hard drive, and you don't want to make copies of them in the Fonts folder, you can clear this check box. Windows then creates a pointer to the folder that contains the font.

5. Click the Install button, and then authenticate yourself to User Account Control. Windows installs the font or fonts.

6. Click the Close button. Windows closes the Add Fonts dialog box, returning you to the Fonts window.

GETTING MORE FONTS

Windows includes more than 300 fonts in a wide variety of styles, so you may not need to add any more fonts unless your documents have specific design needs.

If you do need more fonts, you can buy commercial font packages from most major software outlets and from many smaller vendors. But first, go to Microsoft's website (http://www.microsoft.com) and see if Microsoft is offering any fonts for free download. Then check out the free fonts that are available from many sites online: You may find a wide enough selection that you don't need to buy any fonts.

Deleting a Font

To delete a font, right-click it in the Fonts window, choose Delete from the context menu, and then authenticate yourself to User Account Control. (Alternatively, select the font and press the Delete key.) Windows displays the Delete File dialog box to confirm the deletion. Click the Yes button. Windows closes the dialog box and deletes the font.

 Real World Scenario

UNLOADING FONTS INSTEAD OF DELETING THEM

If you load your Fonts folder with thousands of fonts, Windows runs more slowly. Loading a huge number of fonts increases the amount of memory Windows needs and generally slows down the speed with which it can handle other tasks.

So it's a good idea not to load too many fonts at a time. But you don't have to delete fonts that you temporarily don't want to load. Instead, you can move them to another folder and store them there until you need them again. At that point, move the fonts back to the Fonts folder, and you can use them again in your programs.

If you work with many fonts, consider grouping them into a number of different folders so that you can quickly load the set of fonts you need for a particular type of document.

If you work with a huge number of fonts, consider getting a font-management solution such as Extensis Suitcase (`http://www.extensis.com`).

The Bottom Line

Understand printing terminology and how printing works in Windows   A printer is the hardware device that prints documents. The printer driver is the software used to control the printer. A print job is an item sent to a printer for printing. To print, you typically issue a Print command from a program. The program tells Windows that it needs to print the document. The printer driver receives the information the program is sending and spools it to the printer, saving the information to disk and passing it along to the printer as fast as the printer can handle.

Install a printer on your computer   Installing a USB printer should be as simple as connecting it to AC power and to your computer. Windows detects the printer automatically and installs the driver for it. If no driver is available, you may need to visit Windows Update or provide a driver on disk. To install a parallel printer, run the Add Printer Wizard manually by clicking the Add a Printer button in the Printers window, and specify the printer make and model.

Configure a printer's behavior to suit your needs   To make a printer your default printer, right-click it in the Printers window, and then choose Set as Default Printer from the context menu. To configure other settings for a printer, right-click its entry in the Printers window, choose Properties from the context menu, and then work in the Properties dialog box. The General page of the Properties dialog box has some of the most important options: You can change the printer's name, add a location (so that users know where it is), and add a comment explaining which printer this is and which print jobs it is for. The Advanced page of the Properties dialog box lets you limit the printer's availability—for example, to prevent users from printing during the night or at other inconvenient times.

Print documents and manage print jobs   The normal way to print a document is to open the document in the program that created the document, and then issue a Print command. You can also print in Explorer by dragging a document to the printer or a shortcut to the printer. To manage your print jobs, double-click the printer in the Printers window, or double-click an icon for the printer in the notification area, and then work in the window for the print queue.

Learn advanced printing techniques and print to a file   If your computer isn't always connected to your printer, you can put the printer offline by right-clicking it in the Printers window and choosing Use Printer Offline. You can then send print jobs to the printer while offline and have them print when you reconnect to the printer. To print to a file, either select the Print to File check box in the Print dialog box, or set up a printer entry to always print to file. Another option is to print to an XML Paper Specification file, which you can distribute to other Windows Vista users.

View, install, and delete fonts   To work with fonts, choose Start ➢ Control Panel, click the Appearance and Personalization link, and then click the Fonts link. The Fonts window displays the list of fonts installed on your computer. To install a font, right-click blank space in the document area in the Fonts window, choose Install New Font, and then use the Add Fonts dialog box to add the font. To remove a font, click it, and then press Delete. Instead of deleting a font, you can simply move it to another folder, so that you can restore it if you need it again.

Chapter 13

Managing Hardware, Drivers, and Power

◆ Find out what hardware you can use with Windows

◆ Install, connect, and disconnect hot-pluggable devices

◆ Install devices that are not hot pluggable

◆ Update, roll back, disable, and uninstall drivers

◆ Configure power management to improve battery life or reduce consumption

This chapter discusses how to install hardware on your computer and how to install, update, and roll back device drivers—the software that makes hardware function. It covers concerns for particular types of hardware and also shows how to configure power management on your computer.

Windows greatly simplifies the software end of the process of adding hardware. If the hardware is hot pluggable, Windows tries to locate and load the correct driver automatically. If Windows can't find a driver, you can use the Found New Hardware Wizard to provide the driver. If Windows can't find the hardware, you can use the Add Hardware Wizard to show Windows what the hardware is.

Other chapters discuss specific types of hardware. Chapter 12 discusses how to install, configure, and manage printers. Chapter 23 discusses how to install, configure, and use scanners and digital cameras. Chapter 25 discusses how to install, configure, and use games controllers.

Finding Out What Hardware You Can Use with Windows

To use computer hardware with Windows, you need the right *driver*—a piece of software that enables a hardware device and Windows to communicate with each other. Windows supports a wide range of hardware right out of the box and includes compatibility-tested drivers for many products. Windows can automatically download drivers for other devices, such as drivers that have been released since Windows itself was released.

By using the Windows Update feature to keep your copy of Windows up to date, and by downloading new drivers from hardware manufacturers' websites as necessary, you can also add the latest hardware to Windows. The devices you're more likely to have problems with are legacy devices more than a few years old, particularly those from smaller companies or from companies that have gone out of business.

To check whether a hardware item is compatible with Windows, follow these steps:

1. Choose Start ➤ Help and Support. Windows opens a Help and Support window.

2. Click the Troubleshooting link. Help and Support displays the Troubleshooting in Windows screen.

3. In the Hardware and Drivers section, click the Windows Vista Upgrade Adviser link. Help and Support opens a browser window to the Windows Vista Upgrade Adviser page on the Microsoft website, where you can check whether your hardware is compatible with Windows Vista.

Using Hot-Pluggable Devices

Hardware devices that use USB, FireWire, and PC Card (PCMCIA) connections are usually *hot pluggable*—you can plug in and unplug the device while Windows is running without any adverse effects. Windows automatically loads and unloads drivers for hot-pluggable devices as needed.

To install a hot-pluggable device for the first time, you must either be an Administrator or (if you're a Standard user or a Guest user) provide an Administrator password.

Once Windows has successfully installed the driver for the device, any user can plug the device in and use it.

Installing a Hot-Pluggable Device

When you plug in a hot-pluggable device for the first time, Windows displays a pop-up from the notification area to let you know that it has noticed the device, as shown here.

Windows then automatically looks for a driver to let Windows and the device communicate with each other. It first checks in its driver cache, which contains a wide variety of preinstalled drivers. If it doesn't find a driver there, and if your computer is connected to the Internet, it checks the Windows Update site for a driver for the device; if it finds a driver, it downloads it and installs it. If Windows is able to find a suitable driver in either the driver cache or Windows Update, it installs the driver, displaying a pop-up identifying the device as it does so, as in this example.

When the driver is installed and working, Windows displays a pop-up telling you that the hardware is ready to use, as shown here.

If Windows can't find a driver for the device, it starts the Found New Hardware Wizard, so that you can supply the driver for the device manually. See the section "Providing a Driver with the Found New Hardware Wizard," later in this chapter, for a walkthrough.

Removing a Hot-Pluggable Device

How you remove a hot-pluggable device depends on the type of device it is. Check to see whether Windows is displaying the Safely Remove Hardware icon (a gray card with a green circle and white check mark with a green arrow above it) in the notification area, as shown here (in black and white, second from the left).

If the Safely Remove Hardware icon appears, click it and see if the resulting context menu (see the example) displays an item for the device you're about to remove. If so, click that item.

PC Card devices always use the Safely Remove Hardware feature. Devices such as FireWire drives and USB memory-card readers typically have entries on the Safely Remove Hardware menu because Windows mounts them as drives, while items such as webcams and USB modems typically don't have entries. But check for an entry before removing a device.

If there *is* an item for the device on the Safely Remove Hardware menu, it'll read `Safely remove` *device*, where *device* is the name by which Windows knows the device (for example, `Safely remove USB Mass Storage Device - Drive(E:)`). Click this item and wait until Windows displays a pop-up telling you that it's safe to remove the device.

Looking at the previous illustration, you can see a problem that you'll often encounter: If you have two or more USB mass storage devices attached, the only way to tell them apart is by drive letter. To get around this problem, follow these steps:

1. Either double-click the Safely Remove Hardware icon in the notification area or right-click it and then choose Safely Remove Hardware from the context menu. Windows displays the Safely Remove Hardware dialog box, as shown here.

2. Select the Display Device Components check box to make the dialog box display the details of each device, as shown here.

3. From the description, identify the device you want to remove, click it in the Hardware Devices list box, and then click the Stop button to stop it. Windows displays the Stop a Hardware Device dialog box, as shown here.

4. Verify that you've selected the right device, and then click the OK button. Windows displays the Safe to Remove Hardware dialog box, as shown here.

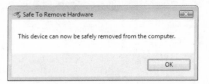

5. Click the OK button. Windows closes the Safe to Remove Hardware dialog box. You can then remove the device.

6. Click the Close button. Windows closes the Safely Remove Hardware dialog box.

If there's no entry for the device on the Safely Remove Hardware menu, or if the Safely Remove Hardware icon isn't displayed in the notification area (make sure that it's really not there and that it's not just temporarily hidden), you don't need to use the Safely Remove Hardware feature to remove the device. Simply unplug it. Windows notices that you've removed the device and unloads its driver.

Plugging a Hot-Pluggable Device in Again

When you plug a hot-pluggable device in again, Windows notices it and loads the driver without displaying any pop-up. At least, that's how it should work. In practice, Windows appears to have forgotten some hot-pluggable devices and decides to install them again.

Installing Devices that Are Not Hot Pluggable

Before installing a device that isn't hot pluggable, you must turn your computer off—and in most cases, disconnect the power cable and remove the battery (if the computer has one). For example, to install a PCI card, you'll need to open the computer's case, insert the card in a PCI slot and screw in the retaining screw, connect any cables needed, and then close the computer's case again.

When you restart your computer after installing the device, Windows normally detects the device during startup. If Windows can find a driver for the device, it loads the driver automatically and configures the device. If Windows can't find a driver, it launches the Found New Hardware Wizard.

Providing a Driver with the Found New Hardware Wizard

If Windows can't find a driver for a new device (hot pluggable or not), the Found New Hardware Wizard displays its Windows Needs to Install Driver Software screen (see Figure 13.1). This screen offers three choices:

Locate and Install Driver Software   Normally, you'll want to click this button to install the driver. You'll need to authenticate yourself to User Account Control to install the driver.

Ask Me Again Later   Click this button to defer setting up the device until later. For example, if you realize you don't have the driver disc with you, you might click this button. Next time you log on, the Found New Hardware Wizard appears again.

Don't Show This Message Again for This Device   Click this button if you don't want to install the driver for the device and you don't want the Found New Hardware Wizard to prompt you again—for example, because no Windows Vista–compatible driver is available yet. When you're ready to install the driver, you can do so as discussed in the next section.

FIGURE 13.1
The Windows Needs to Install Driver Software screen of the Found New Hardware Wizard sometimes names the device that needs the driver. If the wizard can't identify the type of hardware, the device appears as "Unknown Device."

When you click the Locate and Install Driver Software button, the wizard disappears, leaving only a notification-area pop-up telling you that it is installing software. When the wizard finds that it has no driver for the device, it displays the Windows Couldn't Find Driver Software for Your Device screen (see Figure 13.2). This screen offers you two choices:

Check for a Solution Click this button if you want Windows to consult Microsoft's online database for the latest information about the device in case there's extra information that will help you install the device. Normally, the wizard simply displays the Windows Was Unable to Install Your Unknown Device screen, which suggests that you visit the website of the device's manufacturer to see if a driver is available there. You can click the Close button to close the wizard, or click the Back button (in the upper-left corner of the window) to return to the Windows Couldn't Find Driver Software for Your Device screen, where you can click the Browse My Computer for Driver Software button.

Browse My Computer for Driver Software Click this button if you want to supply the driver from a CD or DVD, a floppy disk, or your hard disk or another connected disk. The wizard displays the Browse for Driver Software on Your Computer screen (see Figure 13.3).

Click the Browse button, use the resulting Browse for Folder dialog box to select the folder that contains the driver, and then click the OK button. The wizard enters the path in the Search for Driver Software in this Location text box. You can also type the path in this text box, but normally it's easier to browse to the folder.

Select the Include Subfolders check box if you want the wizard to search the folder's subfolders as well for the driver. (Searching the subfolders as well is usually a good idea.) Then click the Next button. The wizard searches for a suitable driver and, if it finds one, installs the device. If not, the wizard displays the Windows Was Unable to Install Your Unknown Device screen (see Figure 13.4). Click the Close button to close the wizard. Follow the instructions in the next section to install the device.

FIGURE 13.2
The Windows Couldn't Find Driver Software for Your Device screen lets you choose between checking online for a solution and browsing your computer for driver software.

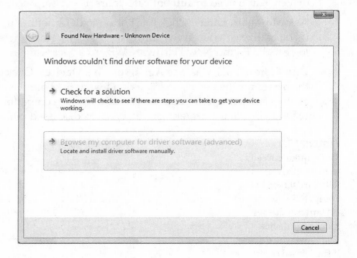

If the wizard doesn't find a suitable driver, or if a file is missing, it displays the Windows Encountered a Problem Installing the Driver Software for Your Device screen (see Figure 13.5). Click the Back button if you want to return to the Browse for Driver Software on Your Computer screen and try a different folder, or click the Close button if you want to close the wizard.

FIGURE 13.3
On the Browse for Driver Software on Your Computer screen, select the drive or folder that contains the software.

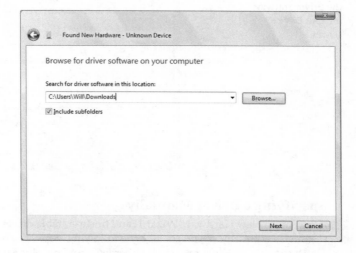

FIGURE 13.4
The wizard displays the Windows Was Unable to Install Your Unknown Device screen if it can't find a suitable driver.

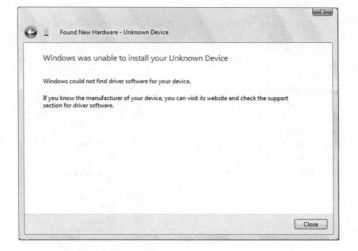

FIGURE 13.5
You may also run
into the Windows
Encountered a
Problem Installing
the Driver Software
for Your Device
screen.

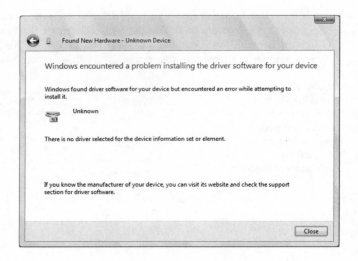

Specifying a Driver Manually

If the Found New Hardware Wizard can't find a suitable driver for a device, you may need to install the device manually. To do so, take the following steps. To show you examples of what you may see, the figures and illustrations show screens from installing various hardware devices rather than a single hardware device.

1. Press Windows Key+Break. Windows displays a System window.

2. In the Tasks panel on the left, click the Device Manager link, and then authenticate yourself to User Account Control. Windows displays a Device Manager window (see Figure 13.6).

FIGURE 13.6
You'll normally find
a device that doesn't
have a driver in
the Other Devices
category in Device
Manager.

3. Find the device that needs the driver. Device Manager shows an exclamation point next to each device that's not working. (For more detail on Device Manager, see the section "Opening Device Manager," later in this chapter.) If Windows doesn't know what the device is, look for an Unknown Device item in the Other Devices list. If it's not there, look in the appropriate category. For example, for a network card, look in the Network Adapters category.

4. Double-click the device's item. Device Manager displays the Properties dialog box for the device. The General page (see Figure 13.7) tells you that no driver is installed for the device.

5. Click the Driver tab. Device Manager displays the Driver page (see Figure 13.8).

FIGURE 13.7
The General page of the Properties dialog box for a device tells you what Windows knows about the device—in this case, not much beyond the fact that it is connected via USB.

FIGURE 13.8
Use the Update Driver button on the Driver page of the Properties dialog box for a device to specify a driver for the device.

6. Click the Update Driver button. Device Manager launches the Update Driver Software wizard, which displays its How Do You Want to Search for Driver Software? screen (see Figure 13.9).

7. Click the Browse My Computer for Driver Software button. The wizard displays the Browse for Driver Software on Your Computer screen (see Figure 13.10).

FIGURE 13.9
When specifying a driver manually, click the Browse My Computer for Driver Software button on the How Do You Want to Search for Driver Software? screen.

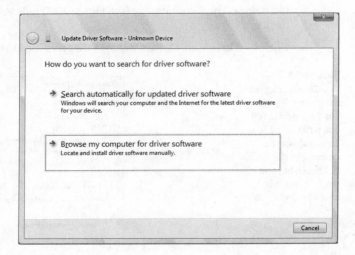

FIGURE 13.10
The Browse for Driver Software on Your Computer screen lets you choose between searching for drivers in a particular folder or choosing exactly the right drivers for the device.

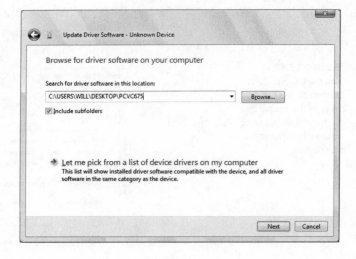

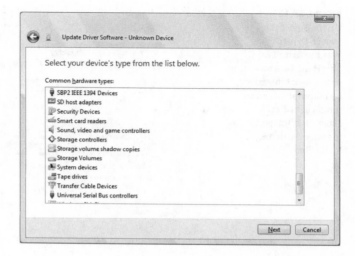

8. Click the Let Me Pick from a List of Device Drivers on My Computer button. Windows displays the Select Your Device's Type from the List Below screen (see Figure 13.11).

9. In the Common Hardware Types list box, select the type of device you're installing—for example, select Bluetooth Radios for a Bluetooth device, Display Adapters for a graphics card, or Monitors for an extra monitor.

   ◆ Some of the categories are cryptic—for example, Multifunction Adapters or Portable Devices.

   ◆ If you can't find a suitable category, select the Show All Devices item.

10. Click the Next button. The wizard displays the Select the Device Driver You Want to Install for This Hardware screen (see Figure 13.12). If you selected the Show All Devices item on the previous screen, it may take Windows a minute or two to assemble the list of drivers.

SEARCHING FOR DRIVER SOFTWARE FROM THE BROWSE FOR DRIVER SOFTWARE ON YOUR COMPUTER SCREEN

If you've downloaded a driver that wasn't available when you first tried to install a device, use the Browse button on the Browse for Driver Software on Your Computer screen of the Update Driver Software Wizard to select the folder that contains the driver. Then click the Next button to make the wizard search that folder for the driver. You don't need to go through the process of picking the driver from a list.

FIGURE 13.12
On the Select the Device Driver You Want to Install for This Hardware screen, either select the driver by manufacturer and model or click the Have Disk button to identify the driver by its file.

11. If Windows has a driver for the device, you can select it by clicking the manufacturer in the Manufacturer list box and the device in the Model list box. But usually the Found New Hardware Wizard will have identified the driver if Windows has it already, so you'll be visiting this page of the wizard only if you need to install a driver that Windows *doesn't* have. Click the Have Disk button. Windows displays the Install from Disk dialog box, shown here.

12. If you have the driver on a floppy disk or a CD or DVD, insert it in the appropriate drive and select the drive in the Copy Manufacturer's Files From drop-down list. If you have the driver on a local drive or network drive, click the Browse button, use the resulting Locate File dialog box (a common Open dialog box) to locate the driver file, and then click the Open button to enter its name and path in the Copy Manufacturer's Files From text box.

13. Click the OK button. The wizard displays the Select the Device Driver You Want to Install for This Hardware screen (see Figure 13.13) with the name of the hardware model or models identified by the driver.

FIGURE 13.13
When you specify
the driver to use, the
wizard displays this
Select the Device
Driver You Want
to Install for This
Hardware screen.
This screen tells
you whether or not
the driver is digitally
signed.

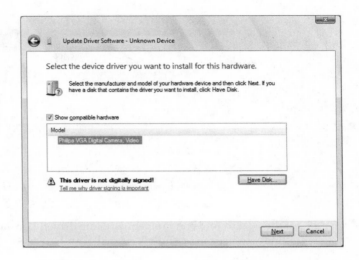

14. Select the proper driver if there are two or more models, and then click the Next button.

15. If Windows doesn't think the driver is correct for the device, it displays the Update Driver Warning dialog box (shown next), warning you that the hardware may not work and that your computer might become unstable or stop working. Click the Yes button if you're sure you want to install this driver. Otherwise, click the No button, and then select another driver.

16. If the driver doesn't have a valid digital signature, or if Windows can detect another obvious problem with it, the wizard displays a Windows Security dialog box such as the one shown next (which has been expanded to show its details). Click the Install This Driver Software Anyway button only if you're sure that the source of the driver is trustworthy. Otherwise, click the Don't Install This Driver Software button, and then look for a signed driver (for example, on the manufacturer's website).

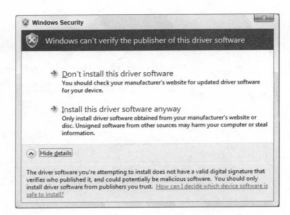

17. If the wizard finds no problem with the driver, it installs the driver and displays the Windows Has Successfully Updated Your Driver Software screen (see Figure 13.14).

18. Click the Close button. The wizard closes, returning you to the Properties dialog box for the device.

 Real World Scenario

YOU MAY SOMETIMES NEED TO INSTALL UNSIGNED DRIVERS

Ideally, every driver you install will be signed by its publisher so that you can be sure of its provenance. In practice, however, you may need to install unsigned drivers to get older hardware working with Windows Vista, especially when the device's manufacturer has gone out of business or been taken over by another company.

If a driver installation makes your computer unstable, use System Restore (see Chapter 16) to restore Windows to its state before you installed the driver.

WHAT HAPPENS IF YOU CHOOSE THE WRONG FILE

If the wizard can't find hardware information in the location you specified, it displays the Select Device message box telling you that the location you specified doesn't contain information about your hardware. The wizard then displays the Install from Disk dialog box again so that you can specify a different location for the file.

If you chose the wrong file, you can now choose the right one. But if the file doesn't work, you're probably stuck. You can click the Cancel button to close the Install from Disk dialog box and return to the Select the Device Driver You Want to Install for This Hardware page so that you can select a built-in driver, but that's about it. Click the Cancel button to cancel the wizard.

FIGURE 13.14
If all goes well, the Update Driver Software Wizard displays this screen after installing the driver.

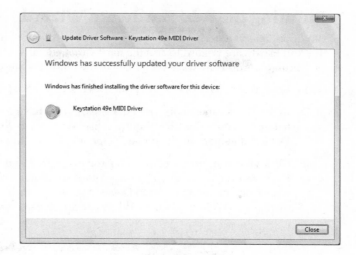

19. Click the Close button. Windows closes the Properties dialog box, returning you to Device Manager.

20. Choose File ➤ Exit or click the Close button (the × button). Windows closes Device Manager.

If there's a problem with the driver file you supply, the wizard may display the Windows Encountered a Problem Installing the Driver Software for Your Device screen (see Figure 13.15). From here, you can click the Back button to return to the Select Your Device's Type from the List Below screen of the wizard or click the Close button to close the wizard and give up on installing the device for now.

FIGURE 13.15
If the Update Driver Software Wizard displays the Windows Encountered a Problem Installing the Driver Software for Your Device screen, you will need to find a different driver for the device.

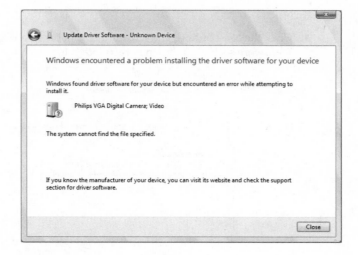

Running the Add Hardware Wizard

Windows detects most hardware you install, but if Windows doesn't detect a device, you can run the Add Hardware Wizard to add the hardware manually.

To run the Add Hardware Wizard, take the following steps:

1. Press Windows Key+Break. Windows displays a System window.

2. In the Tasks panel on the left, click the Device Manager link, and then authenticate yourself to User Account Control. Windows displays a Device Manager window. (For more detail on Device Manager, see the section "Opening Device Manager," later in this chapter.)

3. Click your computer's name at the top of the tree, and then choose Action ➤ Add Legacy Hardware. (You can also right-click your computer's name and choose Add Legacy Hardware from the context menu.) Device Manager launches the Add Hardware Wizard, which displays its Welcome to the Add Hardware Wizard screen, as shown here.

4. Click the Next button. The wizard displays the The Wizard Can Help You Install Other Hardware screen, as shown here, offering to search for the hardware.

5. Select the Install the Hardware that I Manually Select from a List option button.

6. Click the Next button. The wizard displays the From the List Below, Select the Type of Hardware You Are Installing page, as shown here.

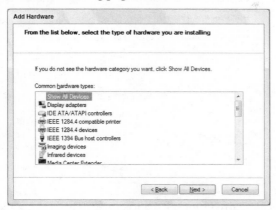

7. In the Common Hardware Types list box, select the type of hardware you're installing. If the device doesn't fit any of the descriptions, select the Show All Devices item.

8. Click the Next button:

◆ If you chose the Show All Devices item, the wizard displays the Select the Device Driver You Want to Install for this Hardware page, as shown here.

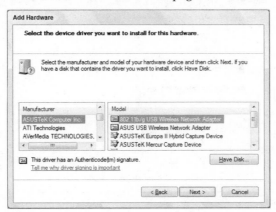

◆ If you chose a specific type of hardware, the wizard displays a list of that type of device. The following illustration shows a list of infrared devices.

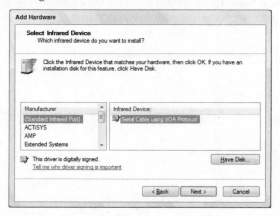

9. If Windows has a driver for the device, select it by clicking the manufacturer in the Manufacturer list box and the device in the Model list box. If you have a new driver, click the Have Disk button and use the resulting Install from Disk dialog box to specify the location of the driver.

10. Click the Next button. The wizard displays the The Wizard Is Ready to Install Your Hardware page, listing the hardware that's lined up for installation, as shown here.

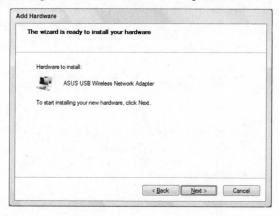

11. Click the Next button. The wizard installs the hardware and displays the Completing the Add Hardware Wizard page.

12. Click the Finish button. The Add Hardware Wizard closes itself. The hardware should be ready for use.

Working with Hardware Drivers

Without a functional driver, Windows can't use any piece of hardware. And using the wrong driver or a badly written driver can make Windows unstable or even make it crash.

Hardware manufacturers frequently release new versions of drivers for their hardware to improve performance, to banish bugs, or both. If you want to keep your hardware running to the best of its capacity, check the manufacturers' sites and the Windows Update site for updated drivers. In theory, Windows Update should be able to supply you with the latest drivers for most of your hardware. In practice, you can probably get the latest drivers more quickly by haunting the hardware manufacturers' websites and newsgroups.

To view, change, or uninstall the driver for a device, display the Driver page of the Properties dialog box for the device. The easiest way to display the Properties dialog box for the device is to go through Device Manager, which you will have met earlier in this chapter if you've been following along.

Opening Device Manager

To display the Device Manager window, take the following steps:

1. Press Windows Key+Break. Windows displays a System window.

2. In the Tasks panel on the left, click the Device Manager link, and then authenticate yourself to User Account Control. Windows displays a Device Manager window (see Figure 13.16).

Device Manager presents a categorized tree of the devices on the computer in its default view. Any device that isn't working or has a problem is marked with an exclamation mark icon, like the RAID Controller and the Unknown Device that appear in the Other Devices category in the figure. When all is well with a category of device, Device Manager presents the category collapsed. In the figure, the Display Adapters category and the Other Devices category are expanded to show their contents.

FIGURE 13.16
Use Device Manager to access hardware devices you want to configure.

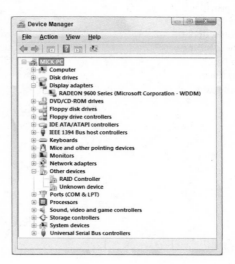

You can change the view by displaying the View menu and choosing Devices by Type (the default view), Devices by Connection, Resources by Type, or Resources by Connection from the menu. You can display hidden devices by choosing View ➤ Show Hidden Devices.

If you leave Device Manager open while you plug in a hot-pluggable device, you may need to refresh the listing in Device Manager to make it list the device. To do so, click the computer's entry at the top of the tree, and then choose Action ➤ Scan for Hardware Changes.

To check or set properties for a device, double-click its entry in Device Manager (or right-click the entry and choose Properties from the context menu). Windows displays the Properties dialog box for the device.

Checking the Details of a Driver

The Driver page of the Properties dialog box for a device shows some details of the driver: the provider of the driver (the company that supplied the driver to your computer), the date, the version, and the *digital signer*—the owner of the digital certificate applied to the driver. Figure 13.17 shows an example of the Driver page of the Properties dialog box for the driver for a RADEON 9600 graphics card.

To display further information, click the Driver Details button. Windows displays the Driver File Details dialog box, which displays further information: the filenames and paths of the driver files, the provider (the company that originally provided the driver), the file version, the copyright information, and the digital signer (again). Figure 13.18 shows an example of the Driver File Details dialog box.

FIGURE 13.17

The Driver page of the Properties dialog box shows essential information about the driver and provides buttons for accessing further details, updating the driver, rolling back an update, disabling the device, or uninstalling the driver.

FIGURE 13.18
The Driver File Details dialog box contains further information, including the filenames and paths of the driver files.

Updating a Driver

To update a driver, click the Update Driver Software Wizard on the Driver page of the Properties dialog box for the device. If you have a specific driver to install, follow the process explained in the section "Specifying a Driver Manually," earlier in this chapter. If you're just checking for a new driver on Windows Update, click the Search Automatically for Updated Driver Software button.

Rolling Back a Driver

If a new driver you've installed doesn't work, or doesn't improve things, revert to the previous driver by using the driver rollback feature. To use the rollback feature, click the Roll Back Driver button on the Driver page of the Properties dialog box for the device.

Disabling a Device

If you want to stop using a device temporarily, you can disable it. For example, you might want to disable a device that you think is making Windows unstable.

To disable a device, right-click it in Device Manager, and then choose Disable from the context menu. Windows displays a confirmation message box, such as that shown here. Click the Yes button. Windows closes the message box and disables the device.

Uninstalling a Device

If you want to stop using a device permanently and remove it from your computer, uninstall it first. To do so, follow these steps:

1. In Device Manager, right-click the device, and then choose Uninstall from the context menu. (Alternatively, display the Properties dialog box for the device, and then click the Uninstall button on the Driver page.) Windows displays the Confirm Device Uninstall dialog box, as shown here.

2. If you want to remove the device's driver as well as the device, select the Delete the Driver Software for This Device check box. Normally, it's best to leave the driver on your computer in case you install the device again, but if you're sure you won't reinstall it, you may want to reclaim the small amount of disk space the driver occupies.

3. Click the OK button. Windows closes the dialog box and uninstalls the device.

Adding Specific Hardware Items

The following sections discuss considerations for adding particular hardware items that need configuration beyond the driver. Many hardware items do not.

The easiest place to start configuring most hardware items is Device Manager.

Setting the DVD Region for a DVD Drive

The Properties dialog box for a DVD drive contains a DVD Region page (see Figure 13.19) that controls the DVD encoding region set for the DVD player. To change the region, select the country you want in the list box and click the OK button.

EXPERT KNOWLEDGE: DVD ENCODING REGIONS

In case you've managed to avoid the question of DVD encoding regions: As far as DVDs are concerned, the world is divided into eight regions or *locales*. Region 1 is the United States, Canada, and U.S. Territories. Region 2 is Europe, Japan, South Africa, and the Middle East. Region 3 is Southeast Asia, East Asia, and Hong Kong. Region 4 is Australia, New Zealand, the Pacific Islands, South America, Central America, Mexico, and the Caribbean. Region 5 is Eastern Europe, Mongolia, North Korea, the Indian subcontinent, and Africa, except South Africa. Region 6 is China. Region 7 is "reserved" (for off-world use, perhaps). And Region 8 is for international vessels such as airplanes and cruise ships.

DVD players are encoded to play only DVDs for their region. Almost all DVDs are encoded for the region in which they're intended to be sold. (There are also *all-region* DVDs that'll play in any region.) So to play a DVD, you need a player with a matching region code.

Most consumer-electronics DVD players are coded for one region only. Some players can play discs for two, more, or all regions. Other players can be *chipped* (modified, either by adding hardware, modifying the built-in hardware physically, or by entering an engineer's code to reprogram the device) to play DVDs with different regional encoding or even to play any regional encoding. Chipping is legal in most countries (though some manufacturers pretend to disagree) but typically costs a proportion of the cost of a cheap DVD player.

PC DVD drives are a little more flexible than most consumer-electronics DVD players. With most drives, you can switch region a certain number of times on a DVD drive before it goes into a locked state in which you can no longer change the region. The DVD Region page of the Properties dialog box for the DVD drive displays the number of times you can change the region again. Use them sparingly.

Why do DVDs have regional encoding anyway? In theory, it's to let the movie studios control the release of the movie in different countries. For example, U.S.-made movies are often released in the United States several months before they're released in Europe, and DVDs and videos of the movie are often released in the United States while the movie is still running in Europe. Regional encoding prevents most of the Europeans from viewing the movie on DVD until it's released with Region 2 encoding.

In practice, regional encoding also enables the distributors to charge different prices for DVDs in different countries without being undercut by imported DVDs from the least expensive regions. For example, at this writing, DVDs in Region 2 are substantially more expensive than those in Region 1, and the European Union has been investigating whether this constitutes price-fixing.

FIGURE 13.19
The DVD Region page of the Properties dialog box for a DVD drive displays the current encoding region for a DVD drive.

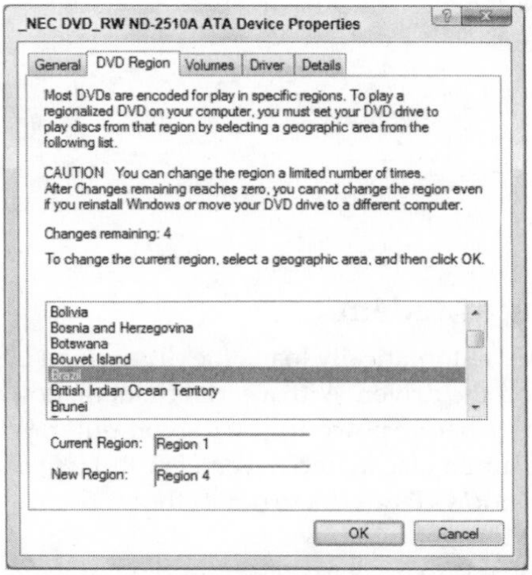

Adding a Removable Drive

The first time you plug in a removable drive or local drive, Windows displays an AutoPlay dialog box offering you choices for what to do with it. Figure 13.20 shows an example. The choices Windows offers depends on the content on the drive—for example:

Import Pictures   This item appears if the drive contains pictures—for example, digital photos.

View Pictures   This item also appears if the drive contains pictures. You may have a choice of using Windows (in other words, Explorer) or Windows Media Center.

Wireless Network Setup Wizard   This item appears if you've put the setup files for a wireless network on a USB drive. See Chapter 27 for details.

Open Folder to View Files   This item appears if the drive contains document files such as Word documents or Excel workbooks.

Speed Up My System   This item appears if the drive is of a type that Windows can use for ReadyBoost (see Chapter 15).

Select the action you want to take. If you want Windows to take this action for every device you add that contains this type of file, select the Always Do This For check box (this check box names the type of content involved—for example, Always Do This for Software and Games, or Always Do This for Pictures). Then click the OK button. Windows closes the AutoPlay dialog box and takes the action you specified.

FIGURE 13.20
The AutoPlay dialog box lets you specify which action you want Windows to take when you add a local disk or removable disk.

Adding a Modem

Windows automatically loads the driver for a USB modem, a PCI modem, or a PC Card modem if it can find the driver. With a serial modem, however, things are more hit and miss: If you connect the modem before powering on the computer, Windows may notice the modem and load the driver for it (assuming it can find the driver). But if you connect a serial modem while the computer is running, Windows tends not to notice the modem, even if you run the Add Hardware Wizard from the Device Manager window.

To force Windows to detect a serial modem, follow these steps:

1. Choose Start ➤ Control Panel. Windows opens a Control Panel window.

FIGURE 13.21

You may need to use the Phone and Modem Options dialog box to make Windows notice a serial modem.

2. In Control Panel Home view, click the Hardware and Sound link. Windows displays a Hardware and Sound window.

3. Click the Phone and Modem Options link. Windows displays the Phone and Modem Options dialog box.

4. Click the Modems tab. Windows displays the Modems page (see Figure 13.21).

5. Click the Add button, and then authenticate yourself to User Account Control. Windows launches the Add Hardware Wizard, which displays the Install New Modem screen, as shown here.

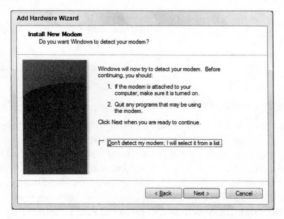

6. Make sure your modem is powered on and that no other program is using it. (If Windows doesn't know the modem is there, no program should be able to use it.)

7. Clear the Don't Detect My Modem; I Will Select It from a List check box.

8. Click the Next button. Windows attempts to detect the modem. You'll see a notification-area pop-up message saying that Windows is installing the modem.

9. The wizard should display a screen saying that the modem installation is finished. If it does, click the Close button to close the wizard. Sometimes, however, the wizard fails to notice the modem even though Windows is installing the driver software and then displaying a notification-area pop-up saying that the modem has been installed. If this happens, cancel the wizard, and then verify that the modem appears on the Modems page of the Phone and Modem Options dialog box.

SPECIFYING YOUR LOCATION

The first time you try to use a modem, Windows displays the Location Information dialog box (shown in Figure 13.22) demanding your location information unless you've given it already.

Specify the details: your country and region; your area code or city code; any carrier code you need to enter; any number you dial to access an outside line; and whether the phone system uses tone dialing (the norm for most modern exchanges) or pulse dialing. Then click the OK button. Windows closes the Location Information dialog box.

FIGURE 13.22
Sooner or later, Windows prompts you for information about your location. You need provide it only once.

SPECIFYING PHONE AND MODEM OPTIONS

After you close the Location Information dialog box, Windows displays the Phone and Modem Options dialog box with the Dialing Rules page foremost. Figure 13.23 shows this page of the dialog box.

Windows provides you with a default location named My Location with the area code you specified in the Location Information dialog box. Rename this location to something descriptive (for example, *Home* or the name of the city or town). Click the Edit button and enter the new name in the Location Name text box on the General page of the Edit Location dialog box that Windows displays. Then click the OK button. Windows closes the Edit Location dialog box. Click the OK button, and Windows closes the Phone and Modem Options dialog box.

For a laptop or other computer you take traveling, you'll probably want to create other locations as well. Chapter 14 discusses how to do this.

FIGURE 13.23
Edit your locations
on the Dialing Rules
page of the Phone
and Modem Options
dialog box.

Adding a Video Card

When you install a new video card, Windows may detect it on boot-up and display the Found New Hardware Wizard so that you can install the correct driver for it. Other times, you may have to change the video driver manually by using the Update Driver Software Wizard.

After installing the driver for the new video card, you usually need to restart Windows. When you log back on, Windows displays the Display Properties dialog box so that you can test and apply the screen resolution and color quality you want. See Chapter 3 for a discussion of how to choose a suitable screen resolution and color depth.

Adding a Monitor

Adding a monitor tends to be simplicity itself, involving only a couple of cables. But Windows often identifies a monitor simply as Plug and Play Monitor and assigns it a generic driver. This driver works well enough for undemanding programs, but to get the best performance, use the Update Driver Software Wizard to install the latest driver for your specific type of monitor.

If you're seeing corrupted images on your monitor, or if the mouse pointer doesn't respond properly to conventional stimuli, or if DirectX isn't working, you may need to change the graphics hardware acceleration on your computer. Only some graphics drivers allow you to change the hardware acceleration.

To change the hardware acceleration, take the following steps:

1. Right-click open space on the Desktop and choose Personalize from the context menu. Windows displays the Personalization window.

2. Click the Display Settings link. Windows displays the Display Settings dialog box.

3. Click the Advanced Settings button. Windows displays the Monitor and Graphics Card Properties dialog box. This dialog box's title bar shows the name of the monitor and the graphics card.

4. Click the Troubleshoot tab. Windows displays the Troubleshoot page.

5. If the Change Settings button is available (in other words, if it's not grayed out), click the Change Settings button, and then authenticate yourself to User Account Control. Windows displays the Display Adapter Troubleshooter dialog box, as shown here.

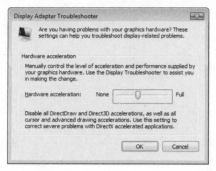

6. Move the Hardware Acceleration slider one notch at a time from Full (or wherever you find it) toward None until the problems disappear. At each setting, click the Apply button, and check your computer to see what effect the change has had.

7. When the screen seems to be behaving as it should, click the OK button. Windows closes the Monitor and Graphics Card Properties dialog box, returning you to the Display Settings dialog box.

8. Click the OK button. Windows closes the Display Settings dialog box.

Setting Up and Using Multiple Monitors

Windows Vista lets you attach multiple monitors (up to 10) to your computer to increase the amount of Desktop space available to you. This feature can make both work and play much easier—but it can also lead you to loading your desk with more monitors than it can comfortably provide a footing for.

This discussion of using multiple monitors concerns only desktop computers to which you can add one or more extra graphics cards. But Windows also includes a feature called DualView that lets you use multiple monitors with portable computers and graphics cards with multiple outputs. Chapter 14 discusses this feature.

If your graphics card supports two monitors, you should have no problem setting them up. Some graphics cards support two DVI monitors, while others can drive one DVI monitor and one VGA monitor. If in doubt about your graphics card's capabilities, consult its documentation or the manufacturer's website.

To use multiple monitors on separate graphics cards, make sure that your graphics cards work together (some graphics cards don't) and that your computer's motherboard supports multiple monitors (some motherboards don't).

The monitors, by contrast, don't need to know about each other, as each gets its own input just as if it were the only monitor attached to the computer. So any monitor should work. You can mix CRTs and LCDs provided that each graphics card you use can handle the monitor to which it's connected.

To set up multiple monitors, first get everything working to your satisfaction with one graphics card and one monitor (or two, if the graphics card supports two). Then power down your computer and insert the new graphics card. (You *can* install multiple graphics cards and monitors at a time, but unless you're very lucky and everything works, you'll be looking at some doubly confusing trouble-shooting.) Connect the second monitor, then power on everything. Don't be surprised if the boot-up display appears on the second monitor rather than your primary one. After you log on to Windows, it should discover the new hardware, which will trigger a Found New Hardware notification-area pop-up followed by the Found New Hardware Wizard. If Windows affects not to have noticed the new hardware, run the Add Hardware Wizard manually to add the graphics card and monitor.

Next, open the Display Settings dialog box: right-click the desktop, choose Personalize, and then click the Display Settings link in the Personalization window. (Figure 13.24 shows an example of the Display Settings dialog box.) For each monitor you want to use, select the monitor and then select the Extend the Desktop onto This Monitor check box. Once you've done that, let Windows know where the monitors are positioned in relation to each other by dragging the monitor icons into their relative positions. If you get confused as to which monitor is which, click the Identify Monitors button to have Windows flash up the number of each monitor on the monitor.

Your primary monitor is the monitor on which Windows displays the Welcome screen. You can change the primary monitor by clicking the icon for the monitor you want to make primary and selecting the This Is My Main Monitor check box. Because only the primary monitor can perform full DirectX acceleration and run DirectX programs full screen, it's almost always best to make your primary monitor the one that's connected to your fastest graphics card.

Set the screen resolution, color depth, and refresh rate for each monitor as usual (see Chapter 3 for details).

Once you close the Display Settings dialog box, you should have a substantially enlarged Desktop. By default, the Taskbar appears on your primary monitor, but you can drag it to any of the other monitors as you see fit. (If the Taskbar is unlocked, right-click it and choose Lock the Taskbar from the context menu to unlock the Taskbar so that you can move it.)

Maximizing a window maximizes it for the monitor it's currently (or mostly) on. You can extend a "normal" window across two or more monitors by dragging its window border to the appropriate size. Doing so can occasionally be useful when you need to see a lot of information at the same time.

CHECK THE HARDWARE COMPATIBILITY LIST BEFORE TRYING TO INSTALL MULTIPLE MONITORS

Setting up multiple monitors can be a tricky and frustrating business. With some combinations of motherboards and graphics cards, you need to install the graphics cards in the right sequence in order to get them to work. Others work fine immediately. Others never work.

Before you try to implement multiple monitors, check the Hardware Compatibility List (HCL) at the Microsoft website, http://www.microsoft.com, for details of the graphics cards that are known to work in multiple-monitor configurations with Windows.

FIGURE 13.24
Configuring two
monitors in a
multiple-monitor
setup

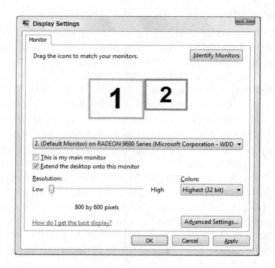

Configuring Power Management

If you have a laptop computer and use it on the road, power management tends to be an important part of your computing life. You've probably developed strategies to maximize your battery life while traveling, such as dimming the screen or slowing down the processor when you can accept poorer performance in the interests of longevity. (Chapter 14 discusses the features that Windows offers for portable computers.)

If you have a desktop computer, power management tends to be less of a concern, because leaving your computer running usually isn't a problem. But to keep your computer healthy, to keep your (or your employer's) electrical bill to a minimum, and perhaps to contribute to keeping the polar icecaps in place, it's a good idea to configure power management on your computer.

Windows offers a variety of power-management settings that let you closely manage your computer's power consumption. The following sections discuss these options.

To configure power management, open the Power Options Properties window as follows:

1. Choose Start ➤ Control Panel. Windows displays a Control Panel window.

2. Click the Hardware and Sound link. Windows displays the Hardware and Sound window.

3. Click the Power Options link. Windows displays the Power Options window (see Figure 13.25).

The Power Options window contains different options depending on how your computer is configured. For example, the window for laptop computers includes options such as Choose What Closing the Lid Does and Adjust the Display Brightness, which don't appear for desktop computers. The following sections show samples of power options from different computers rather than from a single computer.

FIGURE 13.25
The Power Options window lets you select a power plan and provides links for accessing other power options.

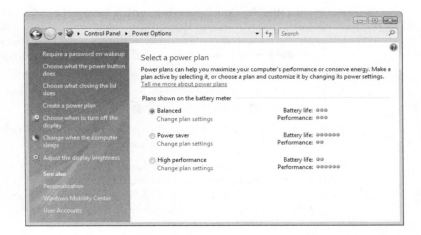

Choosing a Power Scheme

First, choose a power scheme and adjust it as necessary:

1. Open the Power Options window as discussed in the previous section.

2. In the Select a Power Plan area, select the option button for the power scheme you want to use: Balanced, Power Saver, or High Performance. Each of these schemes has preset settings for controlling whether and when the computer turns off the display, puts the computer to sleep, and adjusts the brightness of the display (on a laptop computer).

3. To see what the settings for the plan are, or to change them, click the Change Plan Settings link under the option button for the power plan you've chosen. Windows displays the Edit Plan Settings window (see Figure 13.26).

FIGURE 13.26
Use the Edit Plan Settings window to examine or configure the details of a power plan. This is the window for a laptop computer and includes settings for when the computer is running on battery and when it's plugged in. The window for a desktop computer has a single column of options and doesn't include the Adjust Display Brightness slider.

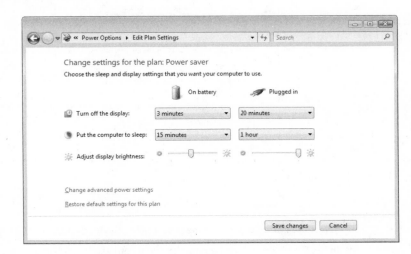

4. In the Turn Off the Display drop-down list, set the delay (in minutes or hours, or Never) before Windows should turn off the display or monitor. For a laptop computer, you'll typically want to set a short delay while it's running on battery (because the display typically uses more power than any other laptop component) and a longer delay while it's plugged in.

5. In the Put the Computer to Sleep drop-down list, specify how long Windows should wait before putting the computer to sleep.

6. For a laptop, drag the Adjust Display Brightness sliders to specify how bright the display should be while running on battery and while plugged in.

7. If you want to choose advanced power settings, click the Change Advanced Power Settings link, and then work as described in the section "Choosing Advanced Power Options," later in this chapter. Otherwise, save the changes to the power scheme by clicking the Save Changes button. Windows closes the Edit Plan Settings window, returning you to the Power Options window.

🌐 Real World Scenario

CREATING YOUR OWN POWER PLAN

Windows' three built-in power plans (Balanced, Power Saver, and High Performance) give plenty of flexibility for most people, especially if you customize these power plans to suit your needs. But you may want to create your own power plans to give yourself even more options.

To create a plan of your own, follow these steps:

1. In the Power Options window, click the Create a Power Plan link. Windows displays the Create a Power Plan window, as shown here.

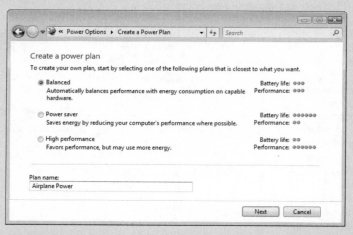

2. Select the option button for the power plan on which you want to base your custom plan.

3. In the Plan Name text box, type the name you want to give your plan.

4. Click the Next button. Windows displays the Change Settings for the Plan window, as shown here.

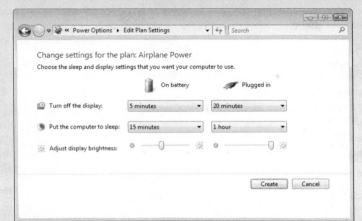

5. Choose settings for turning off the display, putting the computer to sleep, and (if appropriate), adjusting display brightness. For a laptop computer (as in this example), choose settings for both running on battery power and running when plugged in.

6. Click the Create button. Windows creates the power plan and adds it to the Select a Power Plan list in the Power Options window. You can then use the power plan by selecting its option button.

To delete a custom power plan, click its Change Plan Settings link in the Power Options window. In the Edit Plan Settings window, click the Delete This Plan link, and then click the OK button in the Power Options dialog box that Windows displays for confirmation (as shown here).

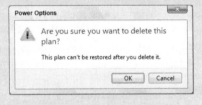

Choosing Power-Button, Lid, and Password-on-Wakeup Settings

Windows also lets you configure what happens when you press your computer's power button (or buttons), whether Windows requires the user to enter a password after waking the computer up from sleep, and what happens when you close the lid of a laptop. To choose these settings, follow these steps:

1. In the left pane of the Power Options window, click either the Require a Password on Wakeup link or the Choose What the Power Button Does link. Windows displays the System Settings window (see Figure 13.27).

   ◆ If your computer has two or more power buttons, the second link is called Choose What the Power Buttons Do.

   ◆ On a laptop, you can click the Choose What Closing the Lid Does link as well.

FIGURE 13.27

The System Settings window lets you configure actions for your computer's power buttons, choose what happens when you close the lid on a laptop, and specify whether to require a password when a user wakes the computer from sleep.

2. Use the When I Press the Power Button drop-down list or lists to specify what the computer should do when you press the power button: Do Nothing, Sleep, Hibernate, or Shut Down.

3. If the System Settings window contains a When I Press the Sleep Button drop-down list, use it to specify what the computer should do when you press the sleep button: Do Nothing, Sleep, or Hibernate.

4. For a laptop, use the When I Close the Lid drop-down lists to specify what the computer should do when you close the lid: Do Nothing, Sleep, Hibernate, or Shut Down.

5. If you want to change the settings in the Password Protection on Wakeup area, click the Change Settings That Are Currently Unavailable link, and then authenticate yourself to User Account Control. Windows makes the option buttons available. Select the Require a Password option button or the Don't Require a Password option button as appropriate.

6. Click the Save Changes button. Windows returns you to the Power Options window.

Choosing Advanced Power Options

The settings you've seen so far let you configure the most important power options, but Windows also lets you set advanced options. To do so, follow these steps:

1. In the Power Options window, click the Change Plan Settings link for the power plan you want to affect. Windows displays the Edit Plan Settings window.

2. Click the Change Advanced Power Settings link. Windows displays the Power Options dialog box (see Figure 13.28).

FIGURE 13.28
The Power Options
dialog box lets you
set advanced power
options such as the
performance mode
for wireless network
adapters or the battery-
alarm thresholds for
laptop computers.

3. Choose settings (see the description in the following sections). If a setting you want to change is unavailable, click the Change Settings That Are Currently Unavailable link, and then authenticate yourself to User Account Control.

4. If you want to choose settings for another power plan, select it in the drop-down list near the top of the dialog box, and then repeat step 3.

5. When you've finished choosing settings, click the OK button. Windows closes the Power Options dialog box and returns you to the Edit Plan Settings window.

If you need to reset the settings in the power plan to their defaults, click the Restore Plan Defaults button.

The following sections discuss the advanced power options that you can set. Which of these options is available depends on your computer's configuration and capabilities.

ADDITIONAL SETTINGS

This category contains the Require a Password on Wakeup setting. You need to click the Change Settings That Are Currently Unavailable link and authenticate yourself to User Account Control before you can change this setting. Normally, you'd set this setting in the System Settings window.

HARD DISK

This category contains the Turn Off Hard Disk After setting. The hard disk is one of the most power-hungry components of a computer, so turning off the hard disk saves a worthwhile amount of energy. After the hard disk has spun down, it will take a few seconds to spin back up when you start using the computer again.

WIRELESS ADAPTER SETTINGS

This category contains the Power Saving Mode setting for your computer's wireless adapter. You can choose Maximum Performance, Low Power Saving, Medium Power Saving, or Maximum Power Saving.

Many laptop computers allow you to switch off the wireless adapter altogether via either a hardware switch or a custom keyboard combination.

SLEEP

This category contains three settings:

Sleep After Specify the number of minutes to wait before putting the computer to sleep. Normally, you'd set this setting by using the Put the Computer to Sleep drop-down list in the Edit Plan Settings window.

Allow Hybrid Sleep Choose On or Off to control whether Windows uses *hybrid sleep*, a mode that saves power while enabling you to resume your work almost immediately.

Hibernate After Specify the number of minutes of inactivity that Windows should allow before it puts the computer into hibernation. Choose Never if you want to prevent hibernation.

POWER BUTTONS AND LID

This category contains the following settings:

Lid Close Action For a laptop, choose the action that Windows should take when you close the lid: Do Nothing, Sleep, Hibernate, or Shut Down. Normally, you'd set this setting in the System Settings window.

Power Button Action Choose the action that Windows should take when you press the power button: Do Nothing, Sleep, Hibernate, or Shut Down. Normally, you'd set this setting in the System Settings window.

Sleep Button Action Choose the action that Windows should take when you press the Sleep button: Do Nothing, Sleep, or Hibernate. Normally, you'd set this setting in the System Settings window.

Start Menu Power Button Choose the action that Windows should take when you click the Power button on the Start menu: Do Nothing, Sleep, or Hibernate.

PCI EXPRESS

This category contains the Link State Power Management setting, which lets you choose the Active State Power Management policy to use: Off, Moderate Power Savings, or Maximum Power Savings.

SEARCH AND INDEXING

This category contains the Power Savings Mode setting, which lets you choose which power plan to use for search and indexing: Power Saver, Balanced, or High Performance.

DISPLAY

This category contains the following options:

Turn Display Off After Specify how many minutes of inactivity Windows should allow before it turns off the display. Normally, you'll choose this setting in the Edit Plan Settings window.

Adaptive Display   Choose On or Off to specify whether Windows should increase the Turn Display Off After setting automatically if you keep turning it back on when it goes off. This setting is often helpful for getting the right display-off delay on laptops.

Display Brightness   For a laptop, choose the brightness to use when running on battery and when plugged in. Normally, you'll choose this setting in the Edit Plan Settings window.

MULTIMEDIA SETTINGS

This category contains the When Sharing Media setting, which lets you specify what Windows should do if your computer is sharing media (for example, songs) with other computers. If your computer goes to sleep, the other computers will no longer be able to access the media. Choose Allow the Computer to Sleep, Prevent Idling to Sleep, or Allow the Computer to Enter Away Mode, as needed. *Away mode* is a kind of somnolence in which the computer appears to be asleep but can still take actions such as recording TV shows or sharing media with other computers.

BATTERY

This category contains settings for managing low and critical battery levels, alarms, and actions. Chapter 14 discusses these settings in more detail as batteries are mostly used in portable computers.

The Bottom Line

Find out what hardware you can use with Windows   Windows works with a wide variety of hardware provided that you can find a suitable driver for each device. You can use the Windows Vista Upgrade Adviser page on the Microsoft website to find out whether a particular device is compatible with Windows Vista.

Install, connect, and disconnect hot-pluggable devices   Hot-pluggable devices are ones that you can plug in or unplug while Windows is running. Hot-pluggable devices use USB, FireWire, and PC Card connections. Windows automatically loads and unloads drivers for hot-pluggable devices as needed. You must be an Administrator or provide an Administrator password to install a hot-pluggable device. After that, any user can plug in or unplug a hot-pluggable device.

Install devices that are not hot pluggable   To install a device that isn't hot pluggable, turn off your computer and disconnect the power. Open the case, install and secure the device, and then close the case again. When you restart your computer after installing the device, Windows normally detects the device during startup. If Windows can find a driver for the device, it loads the driver automatically and configures the device. If Windows can't find a driver, it launches the Found New Hardware Wizard, which lets you tell Windows where to find the driver. If Windows doesn't detect the device, you can run the Add Hardware Wizard to install the device manually.

Update, roll back, disable, and uninstall drivers   To work with drivers, press Windows Key+Break, click the Device Manager link in the System window, and then authenticate yourself to User Account Control. Right-click the device whose driver you want to change, and then choose Properties from the context menu. Use the buttons on the Driver page of the device's Properties dialog box to update, roll back, disable, or uninstall a driver.

Configure power management to improve battery life or reduce consumption To improve battery life on a laptop computer or to reduce power consumption on a desktop, you can configure power options such as turning off the display or putting the computer to sleep after a specified period of inactivity. To work with these options, choose Start ➤ Control Panel, click the Hardware and Sound link, and then click the Power Options link. In the Power Options window, choose a power plan, and then click the Change Plan Settings link to customize its settings. Use the links in the left column of the Power Options window to access the main power configuration options.

Chapter 14

Using Windows Vista Home on a Portable Computer

◆ Access key mobile settings with Windows Mobility Center

◆ Use Windows' power-management features for portable computers

◆ Configure Tablet PC and Pen and Input settings

◆ Choose presentation settings to prevent interruptions during presentations

◆ Connect an external monitor to your laptop

◆ Use different locations in dial-up networking

◆ Transfer files between a desktop computer and a portable computer

◆ Synchronize files between two computers with Briefcase

This chapter discusses how to use the Windows Vista features that are mostly oriented to portable computers rather than desktop computers. You'll start by learning how to use Windows Mobility Center to access mobile-computing features, configure power-management settings for portable computers, and choose settings for Tablet PCs. After that, you'll find out how to choose settings for giving presentations on your laptop, how to connect an external monitor, how to create different locations to simplify dial-up networking in different places, and how to transfer and synchronize files between two computers.

Accessing Mobile Settings with Windows Mobility Center

Windows Mobility Center (see Figure 14.1) gives you quick access to a range of settings:

Display Brightness   Click the icon to display the Edit Plan Settings window for your current power plan. Drag the slider to increase or decrease the brightness of the display.

Volume   Click the icon to open the Sound dialog box. Select the Mute check box to mute the volume completely. Otherwise, drag the slider to set the volume.

Battery Status   Click the icon to open the Power Options window. Use the status readout to see how much battery power remains. Use the drop-down list to switch from one of your current power plans to another.

Wireless Network   Click the icon to launch the Connect to a Network Wizard, which you can use to connect to a network or to view your connection status. Use the status readout to see details of your current wireless network connection. Click the Turn Wireless Off button when you need to turn your wireless network adapter off. Click the resulting Turn Wireless On button to turn it back on.

External Display   Click the icon to display the Display Settings dialog box. Use the status readout to check whether Windows has detected an external display. If you've connected an external display, and Windows hasn't recognized it, click the Connect Display button to make Windows scan for the display.

Sync Center   Click the icon or the Sync Settings button to open a Sync Center window, in which you can create and manage synchronization partnerships.

Presentation Settings   Click the icon to display the Presentation Settings dialog box (see the section "Choosing Presentation Settings," later in this chapter). Click the Turn On button to turn on presentation mode; click the resulting Turn Off button to turn it off again.

The easiest way to open Windows Mobility Center is to click the Power icon in the notification area and then click the Windows Mobility Center link in the pop-up window. You can also choose Start ➢ Control Panel, and then click the Adjust Commonly Used Mobility Settings link in the Control Panel window.

To close Windows Mobility Center, click the Close button (the × button).

FIGURE 14.1
Use Windows Mobility Center to get an overview of your current mobility settings and to access options quickly.

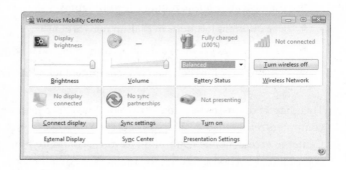

Using the Power-Management Features for Portable Computers

To get the best balance of performance and battery life from your portable, you'll probably need to configure its power settings carefully. In addition to the power-management features discussed in the previous chapter, Windows provides several power-management features for portable computers.

Using the Power Icon in the Notification Area

To work with power-management features on a portable computer, you use the Power icon in the notification area. Windows automatically displays this icon for a computer configured with a battery, so the icon should be there unless you've chosen to hide it. The icon shows a battery on its own when the computer is running on battery power. It shows a battery with a power lead when the computer is plugged in and receiving power.

ADDING THE POWER ICON TO THE NOTIFICATION AREA

If the Power icon doesn't appear in the notification area, you can add it as follows:

1. Right-click the Start button, and then choose Properties from the context menu. Windows displays the Taskbar and Start Menu Properties dialog box.

2. On the Notification Area page, select the Power check box.

3. Click the OK button. Windows closes the dialog box and adds the icon to the notification area.

To see how much battery power you have left and whether the battery is charging, hover the mouse pointer over the Power icon to display a pop-up window, as shown here.

To switch quickly from one power scheme to another, click the Power icon, and the select the appropriate option button in the pop-up window, as shown here.

To open the Power Options window, click the Power icon in the notification area, and then choose More Power Options from the pop-up window. If you choose not to display the Power icon, choose Start ➤ Control Panel, click the Hardware and Sound link, and then click the Power Options link.

Choosing Power Settings for Running on Batteries

As you saw in the previous chapter, the Edit Plan Settings dialog box for a portable computer lets you choose different settings for when the computer is running on batteries and when it is plugged in.

When you need to maximize battery life, set short delays for turning off the display and putting the computer to sleep. For example, if you work steadily at your computer, you might choose a delay of 2 minutes or 3 minutes for turning off the display and 5 minutes or 10 minutes for putting the computer to sleep. If you use your computer to work on documents that require pauses for thought, you may need to set a longer delay on turning off the display—having the screen black out when you're constructing a formula or a sentence can be very distracting.

Setting Battery Alarms, Notifications, and Actions

Sooner or (preferably) later, your battery will run out. To choose what Windows does when this happens, follow these steps:

1. In the Power Options window, click the Change Plan Settings link for the power plan you want to affect. Windows displays the Edit Plan Settings window for the plan.

2. Click the Change Advanced Power Settings link. Windows displays the Power Options dialog box.

3. Expand the Battery category so that you can see its settings (see Figure 14.2).

4. Expand the Critical Battery Action item, and then choose the action you want Windows to take when the battery reaches the critical level. (You'll define this level in a minute.) Your choices for when the computer is running on battery are Sleep, Hibernate, or Shut Down. When the computer is plugged in, you can also choose Do Nothing. Hibernate is usually the best choice, as it protects your data better than Sleep does. Shutting down the computer also protects your data, but it means that you'll need to perform a full startup when you plug in the computer rather than simply awaken it from hibernation.

5. Expand the Low Battery Level item, and then specify the percentage of battery power that Windows should treat as the low level. The default setting is 10 percent, which works well for many people.

6. Expand the Critical Battery Level item, and then specify the percentage of battery power that Windows should treat as the critical level—the point after which it's not safe to keep the computer running. The default setting is 5 percent, which should give enough battery life to ensure a successful hibernation or shutdown.

7. Expand the Low Battery Notification item, and then choose On or Off to control whether Windows warns you when the battery reaches its low level. Most people find the warning helpful, but you may prefer to work straight through to the critical level.

FIGURE 14.2

The settings in the Battery category of the Power Options dialog box lets you control what happens when your computer's battery runs out of power.

8. Expand the Low Battery Action item, and then choose the action you want Windows to take when the battery reaches the low level. Your choices are Do Nothing, Sleep, Hibernate, or Shut Down. Do Nothing is normally the most useful setting.

9. Click the OK button. Windows closes the Power Options dialog box and returns you to the Edit Plan Settings window.

10. Click the Save Changes button. Windows closes the Edit Plan Settings window and returns you to the Power Options window.

TROUBLESHOOTING: RECOVERING A HUNG LAPTOP

If your laptop gets so thoroughly hung that it no longer responds to the power button, even when you hold the power button down for four or five seconds, you may need to disconnect the laptop from the AC wall socket and remove the battery in order to reset it. But before you do, make sure that you're not missing a hardware reset button on the laptop. Many laptops have these, but to prevent you from pressing them accidentally, they're usually located in a really awkward position. For example, on some computers, you need to poke the end of a paper clip or a similar thin, blunt instrument through a small hole in the bottom of the machine to press the reset button. If in doubt, consult the manual for your laptop before poking it in a sensitive area.

Configuring Tablet PC and Pen and Input Settings

If you have a Tablet PC (one that accepts input via a stylus on its screen as well as via a keyboard and mouse), you can use the Tablet PC settings to control how the Tablet features work and the Pen and Input settings to configure how Windows reads pen input.

Configuring Tablet PC Settings

To configure Tablet PC settings, take the following steps:

1. Choose Start ➢ Control Panel. Windows displays a Control Panel window.

2. In Control Panel Home view, click the Hardware and Sound link. Windows displays the Hardware and Sound window.

3. Click the Tablet PC Settings link. Windows displays the Tablet PC Settings dialog box.

4. Choose Settings on the General page (see Figure 14.3).

    Handedness   In this group box, select the Right-Handed option button if you're right-handed and the Left-Handed option button if you're left-handed. This setting controls where Windows displays the menus, so that they're not covered by the hand you're using.

    Calibration   Select the orientation in the Orientation drop-down list: Primary Landscape, Primary Portrait, Secondary Landscape, or Secondary Portrait. You can then click the Calibrate button and use the resulting wizard to calibrate the digitizer.

FIGURE 14.3
On the General page of the Tablet PC Settings dialog box, tell Windows which hand you're using for the stylus, specify your display orientation, and calibrate the digitizer if you need to.

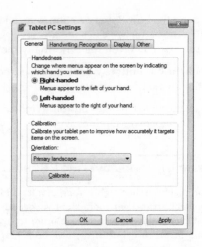

5. Choose settings on the Handwriting Recognition page (see Figure 14.4):

Use the Personal Recognizer   Select this check box to make Windows use personal handwriting recognition to improve its recognition of your handwriting. This feature is usually helpful.

Automatic Learning   In this group box, select the Use Automatic Learning option button if you want the recognizer to store the words you use so that it can recognize them more easily in future. You get better results by using this feature at the expense of a minor security concern (someone might be able to raid the recognizer and learn what you've been writing). Select the Don't Use Automatic Learning, and Delete Any Previously Collected Data option button if you want to guard against this concern.

FIGURE 14.4
On the Handwriting Recognition page of the Tablet PC Settings dialog box, choose whether to allow the recognizer to learn your writing and store the results.

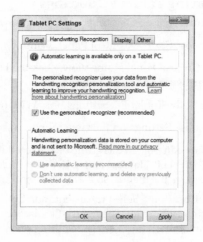

FIGURE 14.5

On the Display page of the Tablet PC Settings dialog box, select your screen orientation and set the order in which to cycle through orientations.

6. Choose settings on the Display page (see Figure 14.5):

Orientation In this drop-down list, select the screen orientation you want to use: Primary Landscape, Secondary Portrait, Secondary Landscape, or Primary Portrait. The Preview area shows an icon representing the orientation.

Sequence To change the sequence in which Windows cycles through the orientations when you press a tablet button, click the Change button. Windows displays the Orientation Sequence Settings dialog box, as shown next. Use the four numbered drop-down lists to specify the sequence, and then click the OK button.

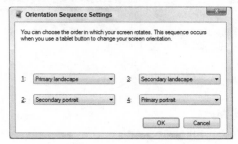

7. On the Other page, click the Go to Pen and Input Devices link if you want to open the Pen and Input Devices dialog box. Otherwise, click the OK button. Windows closes the Tablet PC Settings dialog box and applies your changes.

Configuring Pen and Input Devices Settings

To configure Pen and Input Devices settings, first open the Pen and Input Devices dialog box. If you opened it in the last step of the previous section, you're all set. Otherwise, take the following steps:

1. Choose Start ➢ Control Panel. Windows displays a Control Panel window.

2. In Control Panel Home view, click the Hardware and Sound link. Windows displays the Hardware and Sound window.

3. Click the Pen and Input Devices link. Windows displays the Pen and Input Devices dialog box.

CONFIGURING PEN OPTIONS

The Pen Options page of the Pen and Input Devices dialog box (see Figure 14.6) lets you change how Windows interprets actions you take with the pen and what effect clicking the pen buttons has.

Windows doesn't let you customize the effect of a single tap, which it always reads as a single click. But you can change the definition of a double-tap (which represents a double-click) and a press-and-hold gesture (which represents a right-click), and you can set up a gesture for starting the Tablet PC Input Panel.

FIGURE 14.6

You can change the pen actions for double-clicking and right-clicking on the Pen Options page of the Pen and Input Devices dialog box.

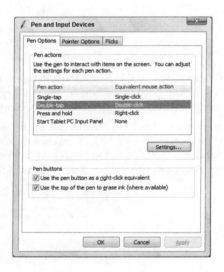

Customizing a Double-Tap

To customize a double-tap, follow these steps:

1. Click the Double-Tap item in the list box, and then click the Settings button. Windows displays the Double-Tap Settings dialog box (see Figure 14.7).

2. Drag the Speed slider left or right to decrease or increase the speed required to generate a double-tap.

3. Drag the Spatial Tolerance slider left or right to decrease or increase the distance Windows allows the pointer to move between taps in a double-tap. (If the pointer moves too far, Windows doesn't register the double-tap.)

4. In the Test Settings area, double-tap the graphic to make sure that you've chosen suitable settings. Windows changes the graphic when it registers a double-tap.

5. Click the OK button. Windows closes the Double-Tap Settings dialog box.

FIGURE 14.7

Use the Double-Tap Settings dialog box to change the speed and spatial tolerance of a double-tap gesture.

Customizing a Press-and-Hold Gesture

To customize a press-and-hold gesture, follow these steps:

1. Click the Press and Hold item in the list box, and then click the Settings button. Windows displays the Press and Hold Settings dialog box (see Figure 14.8).

2. Select the Enable Press and Hold for Right-Clicking check box if you want to be able to right-click by pressing and holding down the stylus.

3. Drag the Speed slider left or right to decrease or increase the speed with which Windows registers a press-and-hold gesture when you press the pen tip down and hold it there.

4. Drag the Duration slider left or right to decrease or increase the length of time that Windows allows you to perform a right-click action.

FIGURE 14.8

Use the Press and Hold Settings dialog box to change the speed and duration of a press-and-hold gesture.

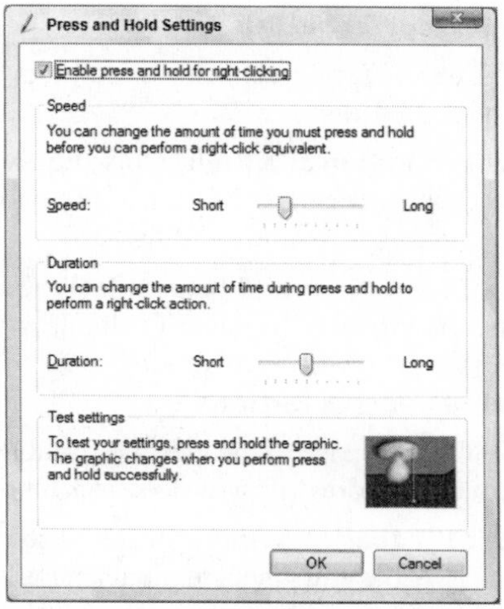

5. In the Test Settings area, press and hold the graphic to make sure that you've chosen suitable settings. Windows changes the graphic when it registers the press-and-hold gesture.

6. Click the OK button. Windows closes the Press and Hold Settings dialog box.

Defining a Gesture for Starting the Input Panel

To define a gesture for starting the Tablet PC Input Panel, follow these steps:

1. Click the Start Tablet PC Input Panel item in the list box, and then click the Settings button. Windows displays the Start Input Panel Gesture Settings dialog box, as shown here.

2. Select the Enable Start Input Panel Gesture check box if you want to be able to use a gesture to start the Input Panel.

3. Drag the Gesture Setting slider left or right to decrease the size of gesture you need to perform to start the Input Panel.

4. Hold your pen a short distance from the screen, and then move it quickly from side to side. If Windows doesn't recognize the gesture, adjust the Gesture Setting slider.

5. Click the OK button. Windows closes the Start Input Panel Gesture Settings dialog box.

Choosing Settings for the Pen Buttons

In the Pen Buttons group box, choose settings for the buttons on the pen you're using with your Tablet PC:

Use the Pen Button as a Right-Click Equivalent   Select this check box if you want to right-click by clicking the pen's button. Many people find clicking the pen's button much easier than performing the press-and-hold gesture.

Use the Top of the Pen to Erase Ink (Where Available)   Select this check box if you want to use the top of the pen (if it has a suitable top) to erase ink.

CONFIGURING POINTER OPTIONS

The Pointer Options page of the Pen and Input Devices dialog box (see Figure 14.9) lets you choose whether to have Windows provide feedback for pen taps and clicks and whether to display pen cursors:

Dynamic Feedback   In this group box, select the check box for each action on which you want Windows to give you visual feedback: Single-Tap, Double-Tap, Press the Pen Button, and Press the Pen Button and Tap. The circular symbols next to the check boxes show the feedback icons.

FIGURE 14.9
On the Pointer
Options page of the
Pen and Input Devices
dialog box, choose
whether to get visual
feedback and pen
cursors for pen
actions.

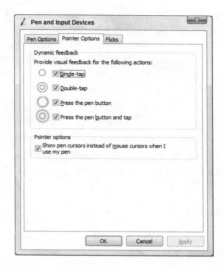

FIGURE 14.9
On the Pointer
Options page of the
Pen and Input Devices
dialog box, choose
whether to get visual
feedback and pen
cursors for pen
actions.

Pointer Options   Select the Show Pen Cursors instead of Mouse Cursors When I Use My Pen check box if you want Windows to show pen cursors when you're using your pen. This option is usually helpful.

CONFIGURING FLICKS OPTIONS

The Flicks page of the Pen and Input Devices dialog box (see Figure 14.10) lets you specify whether to use *flicks*, pen gestures for navigation and editing, and configure the sensitivity for recognizing flicks:

Use Flicks to Perform Common Actions Quickly and Easily   Select this check box to use flicks. If you don't want to use flicks, clear this check box to stop Windows from attempting to identify flicks in your pen movements.

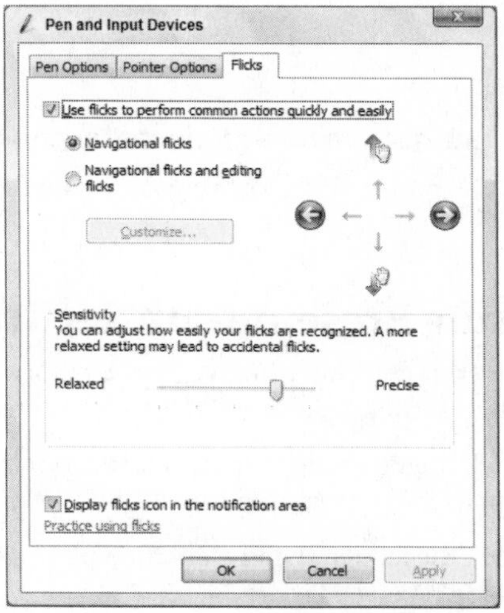

FIGURE 14.10
On the Flicks page
of the Pen and Input
Devices dialog box,
choose whether to
use flicks—and if
so, which ones.

Navigational Flicks/Navigational Flicks and Editing Flicks   Select the option button for the type of flicks you want to perform. If you select the Navigational Flicks option button, you can use flicks only for Back (flick left), Forward (flick right), Drag Up (flick up), and Drag Down (flick down) actions. If you select the Navigational Flicks and Editing Flicks option button, you can click the Customize button and use the Customize Flicks dialog box (see Figure 14.11) to customize the action for each flick.

Sensitivity   Drag the slider along the Relaxed–Precise spectrum to adjust how easily Windows recognizes your flicks. A setting toward the Precise end is usually best, as it prevents Windows from recognizing flicks that are in fact unintentional movements.

Display Flicks Icon in the Notification Area   Select this check box if you want Windows to display a Flicks icon in the notification area that you can use to access the Flicks options.

FIGURE 14.11
The Customize Flicks dialog box lets you change the action associated with one of the flick actions. You can also add a custom flick action by selecting the "(add)" item in a drop-down list.

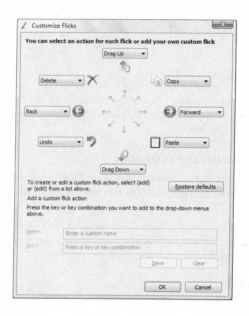

CLOSING THE PEN AND INPUT DEVICES DIALOG BOX

Click the OK button. Windows closes the Pen and Input Devices dialog box and applies your choices.

Choosing Presentation Settings

If you use your computer to give presentations, you can benefit by configuring Windows Vista's presentation settings. To do so, follow these steps:

1. Click the Power icon in the notification area, and then click the Windows Mobility Center link in the pop-up window. Windows displays the Windows Mobility Center window.

2. Click the icon in the Presentation Settings box. Windows displays the Presentation Settings dialog box (see Figure 14.12).

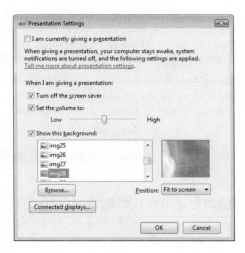

FIGURE 14.12
Choose settings for
Presentation mode in
the Presentation Set-
tings dialog box.

3. Clear the I Am Currently Giving a Presentation check box unless you're just about to give a presentation.

4. Select the Turn Off the Screen Saver check box if you want Windows to prevent the screen saver from starting during a presentation. Suppressing the screen saver is usually a good idea.

5. If you want Windows to automatically use a predetermined volume, select the Set the Volume To check box, and then drag the slider to a suitable position along the Low–High axis. This feature is designed to help you avoid starting a presentation with unsuitable volume settings left applied from your previous task.

6. If you want to use a particular background image, select the Show This Background check box, and then select the image. You can either choose one of Windows' images from the list box or click the Browse button and use the Browse dialog box to locate an image anywhere on your computer. Once you've chosen the image, look at the preview, and choose a different setting in the Position drop-down list if necessary. The options are Center, Tile, and Fit to Screen, just as for a desktop background image.

7. If you use the same external monitor for presentations, connect it to your computer, and then click the Connected Displays button. Windows displays the Current Displays dialog box, as shown here. Select the I Always Give a Presentation When I Use This Display Configuration check box, and then click the OK button. Windows closes the Current Displays dialog box, returning you to the Presentation Settings dialog box.

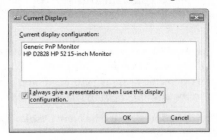

8. Click the OK button. Windows closes the Presentation Settings dialog box, returning you to the Windows Mobility Center window. When you're ready to start presenting, click the Turn On button in the Presentation Settings area. Windows puts your presentation settings into effect and displays the Presentation Settings Are On icon in the notification area.

To turn off Presentation mode, click the Presentation Settings Are On icon, and then choose Stop Presentation from the menu, as shown here. Alternatively, click the Turn Off button in the Presentation Settings area in Windows Mobility Center.

Connecting an External Monitor

To give yourself more space for your work than your laptop's screen can provide, you can connect an external monitor. Windows lets you display information on an external monitor in three ways:

Extend your desktop   Extending lets you use both your laptop's screen and the external monitor, displaying a different part of your desktop on each.

Mirror your desktop   Mirroring lets you display the same information on the external monitor as on your laptop's screen. Mirroring is mostly useful for presentations.

Use only the external monitor   Using only the external monitor lets you treat your laptop like a desktop. When you do this, you'll probably want to attach an external keyboard and mouse to your laptop.

To connect an external monitor to your laptop, follow these steps:

1. Connect the monitor to a power source and to your laptop's graphics port, and then switch the monitor on.

2. Windows normally detects the external monitor and displays the New Display Detected dialog box (see Figure 14.13). If Windows doesn't detect the monitor, open Windows Mobility Center and click the Connect Display button to make Windows scan for the monitor.

3. In the Extend Your Desktop area, select the Right option button or the Left option button to tell Windows whether you've placed the external monitor to the right of your laptop's screen or to the left. This setting applies only if you're extending the desktop.

4. Below the two screens, select the Duplicate My Desktop on All Displays option button if you want to mirror your desktop on the displays. Select the Show Different Parts of My Desktop on Each Display if you want to extend your desktop (as is most likely). Select the Show My Desktop on the External Display Only option button if you want to use only the external display.

5. If you're extending your desktop and have placed the external monitor above or below your laptop's screen, or if you need to change the resolution or refresh rate, click the Display Settings link. Windows opens the Display Settings dialog box, in which you can adjust the displays as discussed in the section "Setting Up and Using Multiple Monitors" in Chapter 13.

6. Click the OK button. Windows closes the New Display Detected dialog box, and you can start using the external display.

FIGURE 14.13
The New Display Detected dialog box lets you quickly set up a new display, choosing between extending your desktop and mirroring it.

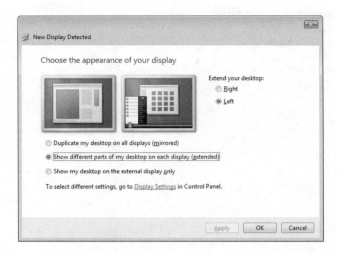

Using Dial-up Networking from Multiple Locations

If you travel with your portable computer, you'll probably want to create multiple locations for dial-up networking. Display the Phone and Modem Options dialog box by taking the following steps:

1. Choose Start ➤ Control Panel. Windows displays a Control Panel window.

2. In Control Panel Home view, click the Hardware and Sound link. Windows displays the Hardware and Sound window.

3. Click the Phone and Modem Options link. Windows displays the Phone and Modem Options dialog box.

Creating a New Location

To create a new location, take the following steps:

1. Click the New button on the Dialing Rules page of the Phone and Modem Options dialog box. Windows displays the New Location dialog box with the General page foremost (see Figure 14.14).

2. Type the name for the location in the Location Name text box.

3. In the Country/Region drop-down list, specify the country or region in which you'll use this location.

4. Type the area code for the location in the Area Code text box.

5. In the Dialing Rules group box, specify access numbers for outside lines and carrier codes for long-distance calls and international calls as appropriate.

6. If you need to disable call waiting, select the To Disable Call Waiting, Dial check box and enter the appropriate code in the text box, either by typing or by selecting one of the standard codes from the drop-down list.

FIGURE 14.14
Create the new
location on the
General page of
the New Location
dialog box.

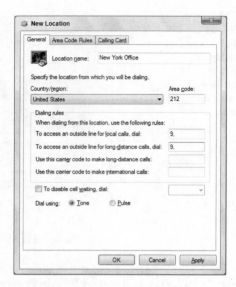

7. If the location uses pulse dialing, select the Pulse option button. (The Tone option button is selected by default.)

8. If necessary, create area code rules for dialing from the new location:

◆ Click the Area Code Rules tab. Windows displays the Area Code Rules page.

◆ Click the New button. Windows displays the New Area Code Rule dialog box (see Figure 14.15).

◆ Type the area code in the Area Code text box.

FIGURE 14.15
If necessary, use the
New Area Code Rule
dialog box to create
area code rules.

◆ In the Prefixes group box, select the Include All the Prefixes within This Area Code option button or the Include Only the Prefixes in the List Below option button as appropriate. If you choose the latter, click the Add button and use the resulting Add Prefix dialog box to specify the prefixes (separated by spaces or commas).

◆ In the Rules group box, select the Dial check box if these numbers require an extra number; if so, type it in the text box. Select the Include the Area Code check box if necessary.

◆ Click the OK button. Windows closes the New Area Code Rule dialog box and enters the rule in the Area Code Rules group box on the Area Code Rules page.

9. If you need to use a credit card or other payment card to pay for the call from the location, specify it by following the steps below.

◆ Click the Calling Card tab. Windows displays the Calling Card page of the New Location dialog box (see Figure 14.16).

◆ To use one of the card types listed in the Card Types list box, select its option button and enter the details in the Account Number text box and the Personal ID Number (PIN) text box.

◆ To add a calling card, click the New button. Windows displays the New Calling Card dialog box. Enter the details of the calling card on the four tabs of this dialog box, then click the OK button. Windows adds the new calling card to the list in the Card Types list box on the Calling Card page of the New Location dialog box.

10. Click the OK button. Windows closes the New Location dialog box and adds the new location to the Phone and Modem Options dialog box.

FIGURE 14.16

Use the Calling Card tab of the New Location dialog box to specify how to pay by card for calls.

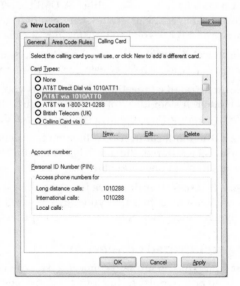

Editing a Location

To edit a location, select it in the Locations list box on the Dialing Rules page of the Phone and Modem Options dialog box, and then click the Edit button. Windows displays the Edit Location dialog box, which is a renamed version of the New Location dialog box. Make the necessary changes, and then click the OK button. Windows closes the Edit Location dialog box and applies your changes to the location.

Using a Location

To use a location, select it in the Phone and Modem Options dialog box and click the OK button. Windows closes the Phone and Modem Options dialog box and uses the location you chose for calls you dial.

Transferring Files between a Desktop Computer and a Portable

If you have both a desktop computer and a portable computer, chances are that you'll want to transfer files between them. You can use various methods of file transfer:

Use an Ethernet network or wireless network   If you've connected your computers to an Ethernet network or a wireless network, you can easily transfer files across the network.

Burn a CD or DVD   This method is good for moving large amounts of files, but it tends to be awkward for frequent file sharing.

Use a USB flash drive   A USB flash drive provides an easy way of moving up to several gigabytes of data from one computer to another.

Use a USB Easy Transfer cable   A USB Easy Transfer cable (as discussed in Appendix B) allows you to create a network between two computers using the USB ports. As long as the ports are USB 2.0, you can transfer files at a useful speed.

Use a FireWire cable   If both the computers involved have FireWire ports, you can connect them directly to each other using a six-pin-to-six-pin FireWire cable. See Chapter 27 for details.

Use an infrared connection   Infrared lets you connect two computers that are very close to each other. It's not ideal for file transfer, but if it's your easiest option, you'll probably find it effective enough. See the next section for details.

Use a Bluetooth connection   Bluetooth lets you create low-speed connections among networks. Like infrared, Bluetooth isn't ideal for file transfer, but it can be good enough. See the next section but one for details.

Use a Briefcase   A Briefcase is a special type of folder that lets you keep its contents synchronized with copies that you make on another computer. See the section "Using Briefcase to Synchronize Files between Two Computers," later in this chapter.

Using an Infrared Connection

If your laptop has an infrared connector, you can use it to transfer data between computers. Infrared used to be a popular technology for data transfer between portable computers, and most laptops used to have infrared ports built in. These days, infrared has largely been superseded by other data-transfer technologies (such as USB Easy Transfer, wireless networking, Ethernet, FireWire, or even Bluetooth). But infrared still works well enough, giving data transfer speeds of up to 4Mbps, and you may find it convenient.

WINDOWS VISTA DOESN'T SUPPORT PARALLEL CONNECTIONS OR SERIAL CONNECTIONS

Windows XP and most other earlier versions of Windows enabled you to connect one computer to another via a cable between the parallel ports or the serial ports. The parallel port is the large, 25-pin port used by old-style printers, while the serial port is a smaller, 9-pin port used for serial modems and other legacy devices. Windows could manage data transfer speeds of around 400Kbps with a regular parallel cable and 4Mbps with a special-purpose parallel cable. Serial cable connections could manage only 115Kbps, but this was enough for occasional file transfer in a pinch—for example, when you needed to move files from your old computer to your new computer.

Windows Vista supports neither parallel connections nor serial connections, either because the technology is outmoded (many new computers have neither serial ports nor parallel ports) or because the Incoming Connections feature required for cable connections represents a potential security threat. Instead, you need to use other data-transfer technologies—for example, USB Easy Transfer or Bluetooth.

CONFIGURING YOUR INFRARED HARDWARE

To configure your infrared hardware, follow these steps:

1. Choose Start ➢ Control Panel. Windows displays a Control Panel window.

2. In Control Panel Home view, click the Hardware and Sound link. Windows displays the Hardware and Sound window.

3. Click the Infrared link. Windows displays the Infrared dialog box (see Figure 14.17).

4. Choose settings on the Infrared page:

   Display an Icon on the Taskbar Indicating Infrared Activity   Select this check box to make the notification area display an infrared icon when there's another infrared-enabled device within range. This icon is usually helpful.

   Play a Sound When an Infrared Device Is Nearby   Select this check box if you want Windows to play a sound when it detects an infrared-enabled device within range. Depending on the situation, you may not need the aural alert as well as the visual alert.

FIGURE 14.17
Configure infrared
transfer options
on the Infrared
page of the Infrared
dialog box.

Allow Others to Send Files to My Computer Using Infrared Communications   Select this check box if you want to be able to receive files via infrared.

Notify Me When I Receive Files   Select this check box if you want Windows to display a pop-up telling you when you've received files via infrared.

Send Received Files Here   In this text box, enter the folder in which you want Windows to store files you receive via infrared transfer. Windows suggests your Desktop by default, which is handy for temporary storage of items you don't want to lose but not a good place for storing many files. Type the folder path or click the Browse button, use the Browse for Folder dialog box to select the folder, and then click the OK button.

5. If you have an infrared digital camera, choose settings on the Image Transfer page (see Figure 14.18):

Allow Digital Cameras to Use Infrared to Transfer Images Directly to My Computer   Select this check box if you want to transfer images via infrared. Infrared transfer is much slower than using a USB connection or a media card reader, but you may find it convenient.

Save Received Images Here   In this text box, enter the folder in which you want Windows to store images you receive via infrared transfer. Windows suggests your `Pictures` folder by default, which is normally a good choice. To change the folder, type the folder path or click the Browse button, use the Browse for Folder dialog box to select the folder, and then click the OK button.

Open Folder after Receiving Pictures   Select this check box if you want Windows to open an Explorer window automatically showing you the pictures you've received via infrared. This option is usually helpful, as it lets you make sure that the images were transferred successfully.

6. Click the OK button. Windows closes the Infrared dialog box and applies your choices.

Your computer's now set up to connect via infrared. If necessary, set up infrared on the other computer that you'll be using for the connection.

FIGURE 14.18
You can also transfer images from a digital camera to your computer via infrared.

CONNECTING VIA INFRARED

You're now ready to connect via infrared. To do so, bring the computers within range of each other, and make sure the infrared ports are pointing at each other. (If you're not sure where the infrared port is on a computer, consult its documentation.)

When the computers establish communication, Windows displays a pop-up message, as shown here, telling you that the other computer is within range (if you selected the Display an Icon on the Taskbar Indicating Infrared Activity check box). If you selected the Play a Sound when an Infrared Device Is Nearby check box, Windows also plays a sound.

Click the pop-up message to display the Infrared dialog box (see Figure 14.19), which you use for sending files.

Windows also displays a Send Files to Another Computer icon on the desktop, as shown here. You can drop files on this icon to send them to the other computer.

FIGURE 14.19
The Infrared dialog box lets you easily select files and send them to the other computer.

SENDING AND RECEIVING FILES

To send a file to the other computer, navigate to the file in the Infrared dialog box, select it, and then click the Send button. Windows displays the Sending Files dialog box, as shown here, while it prompts the recipient to accept the file and (if they do) transfers the file.

When the other computer sends one or more files to you, Windows displays the Infrared dialog box (as shown here) to ask if you want to receive the file or files. Click the Yes button or the Yes to All button, as appropriate, if you want the file or files. Otherwise, click the Cancel button to decline the offer.

While you're receiving one or more files, Windows displays the Receiving Files dialog box, as shown here. You can select the Close This Dialog Box When the Transfer Is Complete check box if you want Windows to close the dialog box automatically at the end of the transfer.

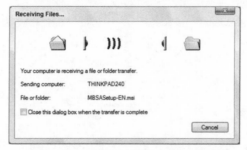

When the transfer is complete, Windows changes the Receiving Files dialog box to tell you that the files were successfully received, as shown here. Click the Close button to close the dialog box.

If you selected the Close This Dialog Box When the Transfer Is Complete check box, Windows simply closes the dialog box without displaying this message.

Closing an Infrared Connection

You can close the Infrared dialog box by clicking its Close button, but there's no way of directly closing an infrared connection. To stop the connection, simply bring your computer out of range of the other computer. Windows closes the connection automatically and removes the icons from the notification area and the Desktop.

Troubleshooting: Infrared Connections

To establish a connection via infrared, keep the limitations of infrared firmly in mind and position the computers accordingly:

Make sure the infrared ports are enabled Many laptops ship with the infrared ports disabled (partly to conserve battery power, partly as a security measure), so you have to turn them on before you can use them. In some cases, you must change a BIOS setting or use a manufacturer-supplied configuration utility to enable an infrared port, but you can usually enable it via Device Manager. Take the following steps:

1. Press Windows Key+Break. Windows displays a System window.

2. In the left panel, click the Device Manager link, and then authenticate yourself to User Account Control. Windows displays a Device Manager window.

3. Expand the Infrared Devices item in the tree. If the infrared device is disabled, it appears with an arrow pointing downward, as shown here.

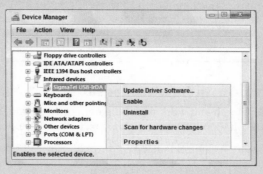

4. Right-click the infrared device, and then choose Enable from the context menu. Windows enables the device, refreshes the display in Device Manager, and removes the arrow.

5. Choose File ➢ Exit. Windows closes Device Manager.

6. Click the Close button (the × button). Windows closes the System window.

Distance   Keep the distance between the computers as short as possible. In theory, infrared works over distances of up to 3 feet. In practice, you'll find it much more reliable over distances of an inch to a foot.

Horizontal alignment   Keep the angle of alignment between the infrared ports as close to 90 degrees as possible. An infrared port throws out a 15–30-degree arc of infrared light, but the signal is strongest in the middle of the arc.

Vertical alignment   Position the two infrared ports on the same level as each other. infrared ports don't spread the beam out much vertically, so if the ports are at different levels, you may not be able to establish a satisfactory connection.

Clear path   Make sure the path between the infrared ports is clear. Even a sheet of paper can block infrared transmission quite effectively.

Avoid direct sunlight   Direct sunlight can interfere with an infrared signal because sunlight contains infrared rays. (Besides, your laptop won't thank you for being placed in direct sunlight.)

Reading this list may make you think that the infrared ports should be just about touching each other for maximum effect—and that's not far off. Get the ports as close to each other as is practical, and you'll experience fewer problems.

Using Bluetooth

Bluetooth is a handy technology for transferring modest amounts of data via wireless links over short distances (typically up to about 30 feet). Many recent computers have Bluetooth built in, but if yours doesn't, you can easily add it by connecting a Bluetooth adapter via USB. Bluetooth lets you synchronize data between your PC and devices such as handheld computers and mobile phones or transfer data from one computer to another.

WHY "BLUETOOTH"?

The name Bluetooth comes from the nickname of a 10th-century Danish king, Harald Bluetooth, who managed to unite Denmark and Norway mostly via diplomacy rather than warfare. The technology allows communication between disparate devices—which is a stretch, but the name is easy to remember.

OPENING THE BLUETOOTH DEVICES DIALOG BOX

To configure Bluetooth and work with Bluetooth devices, you use the Bluetooth Devices dialog box. To open the Bluetooth Devices dialog box, follow these steps:

1. Choose Start ➢ Control Panel. Windows displays a Control Panel window.

2. In Control Panel Home view, click the Hardware and Sound link. Windows displays the Hardware and Sound window.

3. Click the Bluetooth Devices link. Windows displays the Bluetooth Devices dialog box (see Figure 14.20). The Devices page will be blank unless you've already added a Bluetooth device.

FIGURE 14.20

The Bluetooth Devices dialog box contains four pages of options for configuring and using Bluetooth devices.

CONFIGURING BLUETOOTH ON YOUR COMPUTER

To make sure Bluetooth is set up suitably on your computer for adding a Bluetooth device or creating a Bluetooth network, take the following steps:

1. In the Bluetooth Devices dialog box, click the Options tab. Windows displays the Options page (see Figure 14.21).

2. In the Discovery group box, select the Allow Bluetooth Devices to Find This Computer check box. Selecting this check box makes your computer discoverable so that Bluetooth devices can find it.

 Real World Scenario

TURN ON DISCOVERY ONLY WHEN ADDING A DEVICE

You need turn on discovery (by selecting the Allow Bluetooth Devices to Find This Computer check box on the Options tab of the Bluetooth Devices dialog box) only when you're adding a new Bluetooth device. Once you've added the device, your computer doesn't need to be discoverable for the device to establish a connection, so you can turn discovery off to protect your computer from unwanted Bluetooth attention and attempts at connection.

FIGURE 14.21
Select the Allow Bluetooth Devices to Find This Computer check box on the Options page of the Bluetooth Devices dialog box to make your computer discoverable.

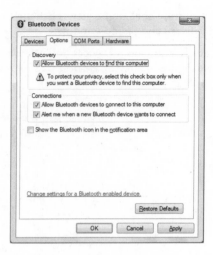

3. In the Connections group box, select the Allow Bluetooth Devices to Connect to This Computer check box and the Alert Me When a New Bluetooth Device Wants to Connect check box. Normally, you'll want to keep both these check boxes selected if you use Bluetooth devices.

4. Select the Show the Bluetooth Icon in the Notification Area check box if you want to have a Bluetooth icon appear in the notification area to give you access to the most useful Bluetooth commands, as shown here. This menu is the easiest way to access Bluetooth commands, so you'll probably want to display it.

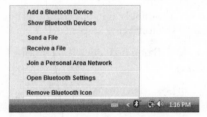

Leave the Bluetooth Devices dialog box open, as you'll need it in the next sections.

SETTING UP A BLUETOOTH DEVICE

This section shows you how to set up a Bluetooth device for use with your computer. The next section shows you how to use Bluetooth to create a network between two computers so that you can transfer files.

1. In the Bluetooth Devices dialog box, click the Add button on the Devices page. Windows launches the Add Bluetooth Device Wizard, which displays its Welcome screen, as shown here.

2. Make sure the device is operational. The Welcome screen mentions the steps you need to take, such as turning on the device and making it discoverable.

3. Select the My Device Is Set Up and Ready to Be Found check box, and then click the Next button. The wizard displays the Select the Bluetooth Device That You Want to Add screen, searches for Bluetooth devices, and lists them. The next illustration shows an example. If the device you want doesn't appear, make sure it's discoverable and powered on, and then click the Search Again button.

4. Select the item for the device you're adding, and then click the Next button. The wizard displays the Do You Need a Passkey to Add Your Device? screen, as shown here.

5. Select the option button for the passkey option you want to use:

Choose a Passkey for Me   Select this option button if the device doesn't have a preset passkey and you want Windows to create a pseudo-random passkey for you.

Use the Passkey Found in the Documentation   Select this option button if the device has a preset passkey that you must use to connect to it. Type the passkey in the text box.

Let Me Choose My Own Passkey   Select this option button if the device doesn't have a preset passkey and you want to create an easy-to-memorize passkey. Type the passkey in the text box.

Don't Use a Passkey   Select this option button if the device doesn't have a preset passkey and you don't want to use one. By not using a passkey, you run the risk of unauthorized users being able to access the device.

6. Click the Next button. The wizard displays the Windows Is Exchanging Passkeys screen, as shown here, showing instructions about what you need to do with the passkey on the other device.

7. If necessary, enter the passkey on the other device.

8. Once the connection is established, the wizard displays the Completing the Add Bluetooth Device Wizard screen. Click the Finish button to close the wizard.

Once you've connected a Bluetooth device, it appears on the Devices page in the Bluetooth Devices dialog box. Figure 14.22 shows an example.

FIGURE 14.22

The Devices page of the Bluetooth Devices dialog box divides your Bluetooth devices into different categories.

SET UP A BLUETOOTH NETWORK BETWEEN TWO COMPUTERS

To set up a Bluetooth connection between computers so that you can transfer files, you first add each computer as a Bluetooth device. Then you create a network between the two of the computers.

Set Up a Bluetooth Connection between Two Computers

To set up a Bluetooth connection between computers, take the following steps. The *target computer* is the computer to which you're connecting, and the *home computer* is the computer that's starting the connection.

1. On the target computer, open the Bluetooth Devices dialog box, and then click the Options tab.

2. Select the Allow Bluetooth Devices to Find This Computer check box.

3. On the home computer, open the Bluetooth Devices dialog box. Windows displays the Devices page when you open the dialog box.

4. Click the Add button. Windows launches the Add Bluetooth Device Wizard.

5. Select the My Device Is Set Up and Ready to Be Found check box, and then click the Next button. The wizard displays the Select the Bluetooth Device That You Want to Add screen, searches for Bluetooth devices, and lists them.

6. Select the item for the computer you want to connect to, and then click the Next button. The wizard displays the Do You Need a Passkey to Add Your Device? screen.

7. Select either the Choose a Passkey for Me option button or the Let Me Choose My Own Passkey option button. If you select the latter, type your passkey in the text box.

8. Click the Next button. The wizard displays the Windows Is Exchanging Passkeys screen.

9. When the home computer tries to connect to the target computer, Windows displays a notification-area pop-up message on the target computer, as shown here.

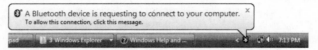

10. On the target computer, click the pop-up message. The Add Bluetooth Device Wizard displays the Enter the Passkey for the Bluetooth Device screen, as shown here. Type the password, and then click the Next button.

11. Once the connection is established, the wizard displays the Completing the Add Bluetooth Device Wizard screen on both the home computer and the target computer.

12. On the home computer, click the Finish button to close the wizard.

13. On the target computer, select the Turn Discovery Off check box on the Completing the Add Bluetooth Device Wizard screen if you want to stop the computer's being discoverable now that you've established the connection. Click the Finish button to close the wizard.

Create a Network across the Bluetooth Connection

Once you've added the target computer as a Bluetooth device, connect to it as follows:

1. On the home computer, click the Bluetooth Devices icon in the notification area, and then choose Join a Personal Area Network from the menu. Windows displays the Bluetooth Personal Area Network Devices dialog box (see Figure 14.23).

FIGURE 14.23

The Bluetooth Personal Area Network Devices dialog box lets you create a network connection to another computer via Bluetooth.

2. In the Bluetooth Devices list box, select the target computer, and then click the Connect button. Windows tries to create a connection, as shown here for a successful connection.

3. Choose Start ➤ Network. Windows opens a Network window. If there's an Information Bar across the top of the Network window saying "Network discovery and file sharing are turned off. Network computers and devices are not visible. Click to change," click the bar, choose Turn On Network Discovery and File Sharing, and then authenticate yourself to User Account Control. Windows displays the Network Discovery and File Sharing dialog box shown next, asking if you want to turn on network discovery and file sharing for all public networks. Click the No, Make the Network That I Am Connected to a Private Network button. The network computers then appear.

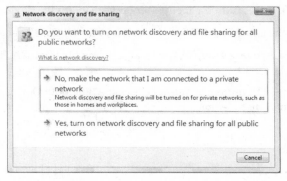

4. To see the folders that a computer is sharing, double-click the computer. You can then copy files from the shared folders. If the folders are shared with permission for you to change their contents, you can also copy files to the folders.

Disconnect the Bluetooth Network Connection

When you've finished transferring files across the Bluetooth network, disconnect the connection. Take the following steps:

1. On either the home computer or the target computer, click the Bluetooth Devices icon in the notification area, and then choose Join a Personal Area Network from the menu. Windows displays the Bluetooth Personal Area Network Devices dialog box.

2. In the Bluetooth Devices list box, select the connection you want to disconnect, and then click the Disconnect button. Windows displays the Warning dialog box shown here.

3. Click the Yes button. Windows disconnects the connection and closes the Bluetooth Personal Area Network Devices dialog box.

TRANSFER FILES WITH THE BLUETOOTH FILE TRANSFER WIZARD

Establishing a network connection between the two computers tends to be the most convenient way of transferring a large number of files. But if you need to transfer only a single file at a time, you can use the Bluetooth File Transfer Wizard instead. You must run the wizard on both the home computer and the target computer, which is clumsy if you're transferring files between two of your own computers. But if you need to transfer a file to someone else's computer, the wizard works well.

To transfer files using the Bluetooth File Transfer Wizard, follow these steps:

1. If the home computer hasn't previously connected to the target computer, make the target computer discoverable. Follow these steps:

   ◆ Click the Bluetooth Devices icon in the notification area, and then choose Show Bluetooth Devices from the menu. Windows displays the Bluetooth Devices dialog box.

   ◆ Click the Options tab. Windows displays the Options page.

   ◆ In the Discovery group box, select the Allow Bluetooth Devices to Find This Computer check box.

   ◆ Click the OK button. Windows closes the Bluetooth Devices dialog box and makes the computer discoverable.

2. On the home computer (the one sending the file), click the Bluetooth Devices icon in the notification area, and then choose Send a File. Windows launches the Bluetooth File Transfer Wizard, which displays the Select Where You Want to Send the File screen, as shown here.

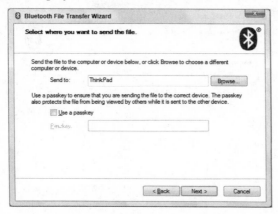

3. If the name of the target computer appears in the Send To text box, you're all set. (The name will appear there only if this was the last computer to which you connected via Bluetooth.) Otherwise, click the Browse button, select the computer in the Select Bluetooth Device dialog box (shown next), and then click the OK button. Windows enters the name in the Send To text box.

4. If you want to use a passkey for the connection, select the Use a Passkey check box, and then type the passkey in the Passkey text box. Using a passkey is good security practice, but if you're transferring a single file to someone else in an area that doesn't seem to be beset by eavesdroppers, you may prefer not to bother.

5. Click the Next button. Windows displays the Select the File You Want to Send page (shown here with a file chosen). Click the Browse button, select the file in the Browse dialog box, and then click the Open button.

6. On the target computer, click the Bluetooth Devices icon in the notification area, and then choose Receive a File. Windows launches the Bluetooth File Transfer Wizard, which displays the Windows Is Waiting to Receive the File screen, as shown here.

7. On the home computer, click the Next button. The wizard attempts to start the file transfer.

8. What happens next depends on whether you required a passkey.

◆ If you didn't require a passkey, the file transfer starts.

◆ If you did require a passkey, the target computer launches the Add Bluetooth Device Wizard, which displays the Enter the Passkey for the Bluetooth Device screen, as shown here.

◆ Type the passkey, and then click the Next button. The wizard then displays the Completing the Add Bluetooth Device Wizard screen.

◆ Select the Turn Discovery Off check box to turn off discovery and protect your computer from unauthorized access, and then click the Finish button. The Add Bluetooth Device Wizard closes, returning you to the Bluetooth File Transfer Wizard. (Having two wizards active at once is confusing, but the process does work.)

9. On the target computer, the wizard displays the Save the Received File screen, as shown here.

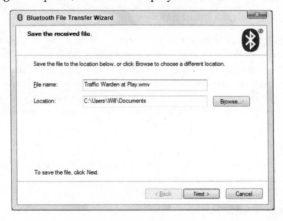

10. Change the filename and location as needed, and then click the Next button. The wizard completes the file transfer, saving the file under the name and path you just specified, and then displays the Completing the Bluetooth File Transfer Wizard screen on each computer.

11. On each computer, click the Finish button. The wizard closes.

Using Briefcase to Synchronize Files between Two Computers

The Windows Briefcase is a utility for creating Briefcases, a special type of folder that lets you keep its contents synchronized with copies that you make on another computer. Windows calls this special folder a "Briefcase." The classic scenario for using Briefcase—and the scenario from which Briefcase takes its name—is that you need to take files with you on a trip. You copy them from your desktop computer (or server) to the Briefcase on your laptop so that you can work on the files when you don't have access to the desktop computer or server. When you return home (or to the office), you synchronize the files contained in the Briefcase so that your desktop computer or the server contains the latest versions.

That's the classic scenario, and it can work pretty well. But if the original file on the desktop computer or the server has changed as well as the copy on your laptop having changed, overwriting either file with the other file is going to lose some changes. When this happens, Briefcase asks you what you want to do. Choosing the newer version of the file won't necessarily help—and even when standardizing on the newer version of the file is your solution, it can be complicated by the file on the laptop having been changed in a different time zone than the original file. When you run into a situation like this, you'll probably need to review both files and incorporate changes from both manually.

 Real World Scenario

YOU MAY NOT NEED TO USE BRIEFCASE

If you use both a desktop and a laptop, you may want to use Briefcase to keep files synchronized between the two—but here's an alternative worth considering. Instead of keeping the files on the desktop computer, and then synchronizing them with the laptop when you plan to use the laptop, keep the files on the laptop computer and share them with the desktop computer from there. This way, when you hit the road with the laptop, you'll know that you have the full set of files with you, and they'll all be up to date.

Using Briefcase

This section describes how to use Briefcase. It assumes that you've read the preceding sections about how Briefcase works and the perils of synchronization.

Creating a New Briefcase

You can create a Briefcase on the Desktop or in any folder—for example, on a removable disk or USB flash drive that you'll then transfer to the other computer. If you can connect the two computers so that you can transfer files or folders between them, the best place to create the Briefcase is on the hard drive of the laptop computer.

To do so, right-click the Desktop or open space in the folder and choose New ➤ Briefcase from the context menu. Windows creates a new briefcase and names it New Briefcase (or New Briefcase (2) if there's already a new Briefcase in the folder).

Renaming the New Briefcase

You can leave the new Briefcase with the name `New Briefcase` if you want, but usually it's a much better idea to assign it a descriptive name immediately. Rename the Briefcase by using standard Windows techniques. For example, select the Briefcase, press the F2 key to display an edit box around the name, type the new name, and then press the Enter key.

You can then double-click a Briefcase to open it in an Explorer window that includes Briefcase commands. The first time you open a Briefcase, Windows displays an introductory dialog box, as shown here. Click the Close button.

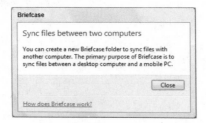

Adding Files to the Briefcase

To add files to the Briefcase, copy them there by using any form of the Copy command. For example, you can use the Copy to Folder dialog box or drag-and-drop to copy files to the Briefcase. When you copy an item to the Briefcase, Windows displays an Updating Briefcase dialog box rather than a Copying dialog box, so you know where you're copying them.

Working with Files in the Briefcase

Once you've got the files in the Briefcase, and the Briefcase on your laptop, you're ready to work with the files. Open them as you would any other files, edit them, save them, and close them.

You can also create new files in the Briefcase. A new file is called an *orphan*, because it doesn't have a parent file and isn't copied to the desktop computer or server during an update, so you'll need to copy it manually to wherever you want it to belong.

You can delete a file from the Briefcase as you would any other file. The file disappears into the Recycle Bin as usual, from where you can restore it if necessary. When you update the files, the original of that file will be deleted.

Viewing the Status of Briefcase Files

To view the status of files in the Briefcase, open the Briefcase in an Explorer window in Details view and examine the Status column, which lists the status—Up-to-Date, Needs Updating, or Orphan—of each file. (Details is the default view in which Briefcases open.) Figure 14.24 shows a small Briefcase open in an Explorer window.

For more specifics on the update status of a file or folder, right-click it and choose Properties to display its Properties dialog box, then click the Update Status tab to display the Update Status page (see Figure 14.25). This page includes a Find Original button that you can click to open an Explorer window showing the folder that contains the original of the file or folder.

FIGURE 14.24
You can view the status of Briefcase files by opening the Briefcase in an Explorer window.

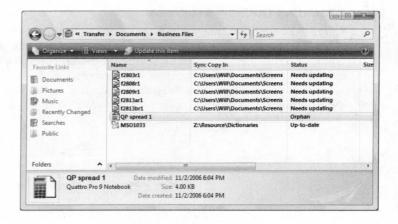

FIGURE 14.25
Use the Update Status page of the Properties dialog box for a file in a Briefcase to see its exact status.

Splitting a Briefcase File from Its Original

Sooner or later, you'll probably work on a file stored in Briefcase and create a file that you don't want to synchronize with the original of the file on the desktop computer or server. When this happens, you can *split* the file stored in Briefcase from its counterpart by selecting it in a Briefcase window, pressing Alt to display the menu bar, and then choosing Briefcase ➤ Split from Original. You can also issue this command by clicking the Split from Original button on the Update Status page of the Properties dialog box for the file.

Updating the Files in the Briefcase

When you bring the laptop back home, you need to update the files in the Briefcase so that the originals of the files contain any edits you made while on the road. Connect the laptop to the desktop computer or server, or put the disk containing the Briefcase in the desktop computer. Then issue an Update command in either of the two following ways:

◆ Right-click the icon for the Briefcase and choose Update All from the context menu.

◆ Open the Briefcase in an Explorer window and then click the Update All Items button on the toolbar.

To update just some of the items in the Briefcase, open an Explorer window to display the contents of the Briefcase, select the item or items you want to update, and click the Update This Item button or the Update the Selected Items button on the toolbar. (You can also right-click the item or selection and choose Update from the context menu.)

Briefcase checks the status of each file that you've requested (directly or indirectly) to update and displays the Update dialog box (see Figure 14.26) for you to confirm the actions to be taken.

To change an action, right-click the file and choose the appropriate option from the context menu. For a file that's marked to be deleted, the options are Delete, Create, and Don't Delete. For a file that's marked to be replaced, the options are → Replace (replace the original with the updated copy), ← Replace (replace the updated copy with the original), and Skip. You can also choose Details to display the Resolve Conflict dialog box (see Figure 14.27), which lets you decide which version of a file to keep.

When you've finished reviewing the updates and changing them if necessary, click the Update button. Briefcase makes the specified updates and closes the Update dialog box.

FIGURE 14.26

Check the status and update action for each file in the Briefcase before clicking the Update button.

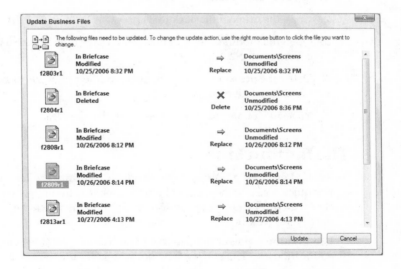

FIGURE 14.27

Use the Resolve Conflict dialog box to decide which version of a file to keep—or to determine that the files are apparently identical.

Troubleshooting Orphaned Files

The main problem that occurs with Briefcase (aside from when both the original file and the copy have been changed, and you have to decide between their competing claims to your affections or integrate the changes manually) is when one of the original files gets renamed or moved while its counterpart is being edited on the road. When this happens, Windows will tell you either that the file has been deleted or that "Filename Is an Orphan. It Was Not Updated."

If this happens, take the following steps:

1. Rename the modified copy of the file.

2. Copy the original file back to its previous location in Briefcase.

3. Open the modified copy of the file and save it under the name of the original file you just copied in step 2.

4. Delete the orphan file (the renamed modified copy whose contents you've just saved under the original filename).

5. Issue an Update command to synchronize the files.

The Bottom Line

Access key mobile settings with Windows Mobility Center Windows Mobility Center gives you quick access to the main settings for mobile computing. To open Windows Mobility Center, click the Power icon in the notification area and then click the Windows Mobility Center link in the pop-up window.

Use Windows' power-management features for portable computers The Power icon in the notification area lets you see whether your computer is running on battery power or on AC power, gives you a quick readout of battery status, and lets you quickly access Windows Mobility Center and the Power Options window. In the Power Options window, click the Change Plan Settings link for the power plan you want to configure, and then click the Change Advanced Power Settings link to display the Power Options dialog box. Use the settings in the Battery category to set battery alarms, notifications, and actions, such as making the computer hibernate when it reaches the critical battery level you set.

Configure Tablet PC and Pen and Input settings If your portable computer is a Tablet PC, use the Tablet PC Settings dialog box to configure screen orientation and handwriting recognition. Use the Pen and Input Settings dialog box to control how Windows interprets pen taps, gestures, and flicks.

Choose presentation settings to prevent interruptions during presentations Windows' presentation settings let you ensure that your screen saver doesn't start during a presentation, that the volume is correct, and that Windows knows which monitor to use. The easiest way to access the presentation settings is via Windows Mobility Center.

Connect an external monitor to your laptop When you connect an external monitor to your laptop, Windows displays the New Display Detected dialog box to let you specify whether to extend your Desktop onto the external monitor, mirror your laptop's screen on the external monitor, or use the external monitor instead of your laptop's screen. To choose further settings for an extended Desktop or an external monitor, such as placing it above the laptop's screen rather than to the left or right, open the Display Settings dialog box.

Use different locations in dial-up networking If you use dial-up networking with your portable computer in different places, create a dial-up location for each place containing the appropriate area code and dialing information so that you don't have to adjust dial-up connections manually. To create a new location, open the Phone and Modem Options dialog box, and then click the New button on the Dialing Rules page.

Transfer files between a desktop computer and a portable computer The easiest way to transfer files between a desktop computer and a portable computer is to use a home network— for example, a wired network or a wireless network. You can also use FireWire, infrared, USB Easy Transfer, or Bluetooth connections to transfer files. Alternatively, you can burn a CD or DVD, or use a USB flash drive to move files from one computer to another.

Synchronize files between two computers with Briefcase A Briefcase is a special type of folder that lets you keep its contents synchronized with copies that you make on another computer. You can create a Briefcase on the Desktop or in any Explorer window by right-clicking and choosing New ➤ Briefcase from the context menu. Double-click the Briefcase to open it, and you can then copy files and folders to it. When you need to update the files in the Briefcase, open it, and then click the Update All Items button on the toolbar.

Chapter 15

Troubleshooting and Optimizing Windows Vista

- ◆ Deal with program hangs
- ◆ Use Event Viewer to identify problems
- ◆ Keep Windows updated by using Windows Update
- ◆ Optimize your computer's performance
- ◆ Set suitable startup and recovery options
- ◆ Use Problem Reports and Solutions

Microsoft has made Windows Vista as reliable as possible—but things still sometimes go wrong: a program hangs, you start getting bizarre error messages about some strangely named component not having done something it should, or Windows starts to slow down, behave oddly, or become unstable.

This chapter discusses how to use the tools that Windows provides for dealing with such problems. It also discusses some steps you may want to take to optimize Windows in the hope of keeping it running smoothly and as swiftly as your hardware permits. And it shows you how to set up a dual-boot arrangement so that you can use both Windows and another operating system on your computer.

Dealing with Program Hangs

When a program hangs, the problem is usually obvious. The program stops responding to direct stimuli (keystrokes and mouse commands issued in its window) and indirect stimuli (for example, commands issued via the Taskbar or via another program). If you move another program window in front of the hung program's window and then move it away, the hung program's window fails to redraw correctly, leaving either parts of the window that you've moved or a blank, undrawn area on the screen.

Ending a Program

Sometimes Windows notices when a program has hung and displays the End Program dialog box automatically so that you can choose whether to end the program. Other times, you'll need to use Task Manager to tell Windows to end the program. To do so, take the following steps:

1. If you have Task Manager running already, switch to it. If not, press Ctrl+Alt+Delete, and then click the Start Task Manager button. Windows displays Task Manager with the Applications page foremost.

 **Real World Scenario**

A DIALOG BOX GETS STUCK BEHIND OTHER WINDOWS

If the End Program dialog box claims that "The system cannot end this program because it is waiting for a response from you," as in the next illustration, click the Cancel button, and see if the program has come back to life. Press Alt+Tab to attempt to access any application-modal dialog box that may be stuck behind the program that doesn't seem to be responding.

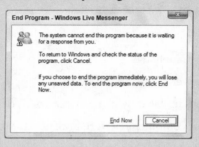

2. Select the task you want to end.

3. Click the End Task button. If Windows can end the task easily, it does so. Otherwise, Windows displays the End Program dialog box, of which Figure 15.1 shows an example.

4. Click the End Now button. Windows ends the program. You lose any unsaved data in the program.

FIGURE 15.1
If Windows can't close the program easily, it displays the End Program dialog box to let you end it forcibly.

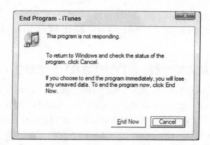

5. After shutting down the program and recovering the memory it was using, Windows may display a message box such as that shown next, inviting you to tell Microsoft about the problem. If you pass on this information to Microsoft, you can be sure that they're aware of the problem you've experienced; if enough people report the same problem, chances are that Microsoft will respond sometime in the future with a fix that Windows Update can download

for you. But understand that this error reporting isn't a personal service—Microsoft won't be contacting you directly with apologies for the problem you've suffered and a quick fix for it.

6. To view the details of the problem, click the View Details button. Windows enlarges the dialog box, as shown here.

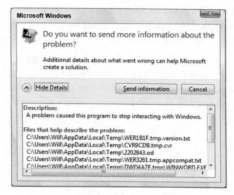

7. Click the Send Information button or the Cancel button as appropriate.

You can turn off or adjust this error reporting if you want. See the section "Using Problem Reports and Solutions," later in this chapter.

PREVENTING TASK MANAGER FROM STAYING ON TOP OF OTHER WINDOWS

By default, Task Manager appears with its Always on Top attribute on, so that it always appears as the topmost window on the Desktop, no matter which program window is active. Always having Task Manager on top makes it easy to keep track of Task Manager, but it means that Task Manager often blocks dialog boxes or error messages in the programs you're using, particularly at low screen resolutions such as 800 × 600.

If you find Task Manager useful and often keep it open to see what's happening with your programs, choose Options ➤ Always on Top to remove the check mark from the Always on Top menu item and make the Task Manager window behave like a normal program window. (To turn Always on Top back on, repeat the command.)

Ending a Process or a Process Tree

Instead of ending a program, you can end a process. A *process* is the executing environment in which program components called *threads* operate. Many programs run as a single process much of the time, but others involve multiple processes.

Ending a process may make your computer unstable, so it's a last resort rather than a routine action.

FINDING OUT WHICH PROCESS TO END

Process names can be hard to interpret—and you don't want to end the wrong process. Use any of these ways to find out which process represents a program:

Task Manager   Right-click a program on the Applications page in Task Manager and then choose Go to Process from the context menu. Windows selects the corresponding process on the Processes page. This command is useful when your computer is running properly, but you can't use it if the program you want has disappeared from the Applications page without closing its process.

Open the Properties dialog box for the process   Right-click the process on the Process page, and then choose Properties from the context menu. Windows displays the Properties dialog box for the process, as shown here. Look at the Description line to find out what the file is. If the description is unhelpful, look at the Location line, which tells you the folder that contains the file.

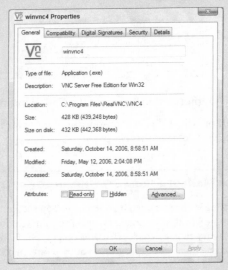

Search on the Web   Search for the process by name on the Web using a search engine such as Google (http://www.google.com). For many searches, the first or second hit is often to the LIUtilities website (http://www.liutilities.com), which provides details on processes and software for managing Windows.

To end a process, select it on the Processes page and then click the End Process button. Windows displays the Task Manager dialog box shown here, warning you that ending the process may make your system unstable or lose your data. If you're prepared to risk such consequences, click the End Process button. Windows terminates the process.

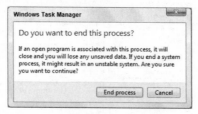

To end all the processes associated with a process, right-click the process, and then choose End Process Tree from the context menu. Windows displays the Task Manager Warning dialog box shown next with a variation of its message about the possible undesirable results of stopping processes. Click the End Process Tree button if you want to continue. Windows stops the processes.

Using Event Viewer to Identify Problems

If your computer seems to be behaving strangely, you can use Event Viewer to try to pinpoint the source of the problem.

To open Event Viewer, take the following steps:

1. Choose Start ➤ Control Panel. Windows displays Control Panel.

2. Click the System and Maintenance link. Windows displays the System and Maintenance window.

3. Click the Performance Information and Tools link. Windows displays the Performance Information and Tools window. You'll use the tools in this window later in this chapter.

4. In the left panel, click the Advanced Tools link. Windows displays the Advanced Tools window.

5. Click the View Performance Details in Event Log link, and then authenticate yourself to User Account Control.

6. Click the Administrative Tools link. Windows displays the Administrative Tools screen.

7. Double-click the Event Viewer shortcut. Windows starts Event Viewer (shown in Figure 15.2).

FIGURE 15.2

Use Event Viewer to identify problems and to learn what's happening behind the scenes in your computer.

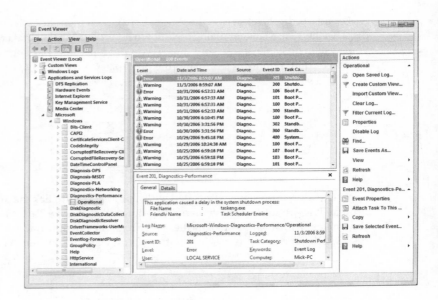

Event Viewer contains a mass of information, much of which is complex—so if you find it confusing, you're not alone.

Understanding the Event Viewer Window

The Event Viewer window consists of four main areas:

Console Tree The pane on the left of the Event Viewer window is the console tree. At the top of the tree is Event Viewer (Local), indicating that you're using Event Viewer to look at events on the local computer rather than events on a remote computer. The tree contains major categories such as Custom Views, Windows Logs, Applications and Services Logs, and Subscriptions. You can click the triangle to the left of an item to expand or collapse its contents.

Events List In the upper-middle part of the window, the Events list shows recent events that fall into the view you're currently using. For example, Windows opens Event Viewer showing the Operational log in the Diagnostics-Performance category of Windows logs, as in the figure.

Preview Pane Below the Events list, in the lower-middle part of the window, the Preview pane shows the information about the event selected in the Events list. You can toggle the Preview pane on and off by choosing View ➢ Preview Pane. Usually, having the Preview pane displayed is useful.

Actions Pane The pane on the right contains actions you can take on the current log and on the current event (if the Preview pane is displayed).

Understanding Logs

Event Viewer contains two types of event logs:

Windows Logs The Windows logs are the Application log, the Security log, the Setup log, the System log, and the Forwarded Events log. When you're getting started with Event Viewer, you'll probably want to start with these logs.

Application and Services Logs The Application and Services logs include logs for DFS Replication, Hardware Events, Internet Explorer, Key Management Service, Media Center, Microsoft Office Diagnostics, and Microsoft Office Sessions. The Console tree also contains a Microsoft folder that contains logs for individual Windows components.

THE SYSTEM LOG

The System Log contains information about Windows processes. The System Log uses the following three types of events:

Error events A notification that an error has occurred. Errors can be anything from mildly serious (for example, "The device U.S. Robotics 56K FAX EXT disappeared from the system without first being prepared for removal") to truly serious (for example, "Machine Check Event reported is a fatal TLB error").

Warning events A notification that something has gone wrong, but not disastrously so. For example, you might see a warning that "The browser was unable to retrieve a list of servers from the browser master on the network." This isn't bad—it just means that the browser (a service that finds out which resources are available on the network) has to find another browser master (a computer that's coordinating information on available resources).

Information events Events worth noting in the System Log but that are not considered errors and do not merit warnings. For example, when you start Windows, it starts the event log service and logs this as an Information event. Other examples include Windows' starting to use a network adapter that it has detected is connected to the network, or that the browser has forced an election on the network because a master browser was stopped.

Windows stores the System Log in the `System.evtx` file in the `%SystemRoot%\System32\Winevt\Logs` folder.

THE APPLICATION LOG

The Application Log contains information about programs running on the computer. Like the System Log, the Application Log supports three types of events: Error events, Warning events, and Information events. Program developers specify the events that their programs raise and which event type each event has.

Windows stores the Application Log in the `Appevent.evtx` file in the `%SystemRoot%\System32\Winevt\Logs` folder.

THE SECURITY LOG

The Security Log contains information on security-related events. In Windows Vista Home, these events are limited to Account Logon actions, Logon/Logoff actions, Policy Change actions (initiated by the System object), and System Events (such as the loading of authentication packages). Windows Home audits these events automatically. (In the Business and Ultimate versions of Windows Vista, you can enable auditing on files and folders, which lets you track which users take which actions on those files and in those folders.)

Windows stores the Security Log in the `Security.evtx` file in the `%SystemRoot%\System32\Winevt\Logs` folder.

THE SETUP LOG

The Setup Log contains information about applications you've installed. You may find that this log is empty.

Windows stores the Setup Log in the `Setup.evtx` file in the `%SystemRoot%\System32\Winevt\Logs` folder.

THE FORWARDEDEVENTS LOG

The ForwardedEvents Log contains information about events that Windows has collected from other computers you're monitoring using this computer. Normally, you won't need to use this capability on a home or home-office network, as you should be able to run Event Viewer on each of your computers easily enough. This capability is mostly used by network administrators who need to be able to monitor computers remotely. To monitor a computer remotely and receive forwarded events, you create a *subscription* to the computer. The subscription appears in the Subscriptions category in the console tree.

Unless you create a subscription, the ForwardedEvents Log will be empty. Windows stores the ForwardedEvents Log in the `ForwardedEvents.evtx` file in the `%SystemRoot%\System32\Winevt\Logs` folder.

THE APPLICATIONS AND SERVICES LOGS

The Applications and Services Logs contain events related to a single Windows component or a single application rather than systemwide events. These logs enable you to examine closely what a particular component or application has been doing.

The Applications and Services Logs come in four different types:

Admin Logs   Admin Logs contain events that indicate a problem. Windows assigns each event a code that you can look up for instructions on how to fix the problem.

Operational Logs   Operational Logs contain events that indicate an occurrence rather than a problem. For example, when you download a file successfully, the Background Intelligent Transfer Service (BITS) records four events: BITS creates a new job, starts to transfer the file, stops transferring the file, and closes the job as being complete.

Analytic Logs   Analytic Logs contain events that describe how programs and components are operating. Windows generates large numbers of these events.

Debug Logs   Debug Logs contain events related to debugging (troubleshooting) programs and are of interest to programmers rather than end users.

Admin Logs and Operational Logs are the ones you'll normally work with. Because most people won't need to use the Analytic Logs and Debug Logs, Event Viewer hides these logs. To display these logs, choose View ➢ Show Analytic and Debug Logs. Issue the command again to hide the logs once more.

Understanding Views

Windows collects data on so many events that it can be hard to find the events you need to examine. For example, say your computer is behaving erratically. Should you look in the Application Log in case there's a problem with a program, in the Security Log in case the problem is a security issue, or in the System Log because it might be a system problem?

To help you find events, Event Viewer lets you view events from different event logs at the same time. You can also filter events to create custom views, which you can then save for reuse in the future.

Viewing an Event Log

To view one of the Windows event logs, select it in the console tree. Event Viewer displays the events in the log in the Events list. Figure 15.3 shows an example of viewing the System Log.

To view the details of an event, click it so that you can see its contents (or some of them) in the Preview pane. To see the details more easily, open the Event Properties dialog box (see Figure 15.4) by taking one of these actions:

♦ Double-click the event.

♦ Right-click the event and choose Event Properties from the context menu.

♦ Click the event, and then click Event Properties in the Actions pane.

The General page in the Event Properties dialog box shows the date, time, type, user (if applicable), computer, source, category, and ID number of the event. The Details page lets you view an XML representation of the event (which is useful if you need to copy the event's details into a database using Extensible Markup Language, as administrators may do) or a "Friendly View" that provides the same information in an easy-to-read table. Click the Copy button to copy the details of the event to the Clipboard.

FIGURE 15.3
Viewing the System log in Event Viewer

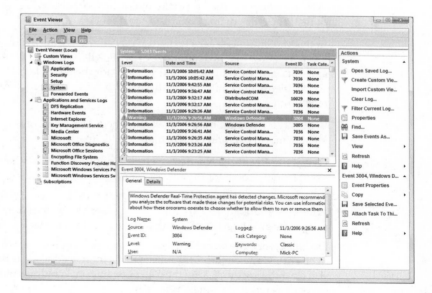

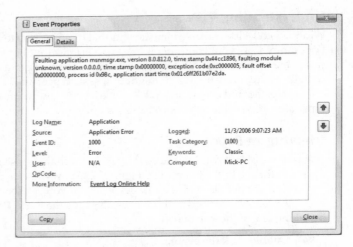

FIGURE 15.4
Use the Event
Properties dialog
box to view the prop-
erties for an event.

To view other events, you can leave the Event Properties dialog box open and click the Previous
Event button (the up-arrow button) and the Next Event button (the down-arrow button) to display
the details for the previous event or next event.

Managing the Event Logs

Event logs grow in size, particularly when many events occur that need logging. Windows offers
features to keep the size of your event logs under control.

To manage the event logs, take the following steps:

1. Right-click the event log you want to manage and choose Properties from the context menu.
   Windows displays the Properties dialog box for the log. Figure 15.5 shows the General page
   of the Properties dialog box for the System Log.

2. In the Maximum Log Size text box, you can specify the maximum size to which the file can
   grow. Windows sets a default size of 20,480KB (20MB) for the Application, System, Security,
   and ForwardedEvents logs, and 1,028KB for the Setup log. These sizes are large enough to
   collect plenty of events for identifying problems; you probably won't need to increase the
   maximum sizes.

3. In the When Maximum Log Size Is Reached area, select one of the option buttons to specify
   what Windows should do when the log file reaches its maximum size:

   Overwrite Events as Needed   Select this option button to have Windows delete the oldest
   event to make room for the newest event, thus keeping the log file around its maximum size.

   Archive the Log When Full, Do Not Overwrite Events   Select this option button to make
   Windows automatically archive the log when it becomes full. This is a good option if you
   need to be able to go back a long way in your logs to track persistent problems.

   Do Not Overwrite Events   Select this option button if you want to prevent Windows from
   overwriting any events. This means that you'll need to clear the event log manually. Until
   you clear the log by clicking the Clear Log button, Windows writes no more events to the log
   once it has reached its maximum size.

FIGURE 15.5

Use the General page of the Properties dialog box for an event log to specify a maximum size for the log file and which events to overwrite.

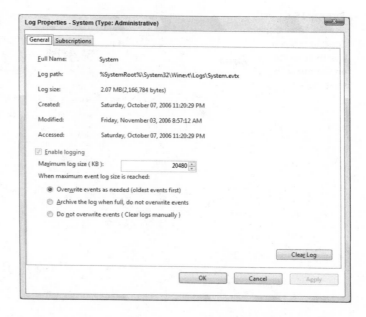

4. If you need to clear the log, click the Clear Log button. Event Viewer displays the dialog box shown next. Click the Save and Clear button if you want to save the log before clearing it; specify the filename in the Save As dialog box, and then click the Save button. Otherwise, click the Clear button to clear the log without saving its contents.

5. Click the OK button. Windows applies your changes and closes the Properties dialog box for the event log.

FILTERING THE EVENT LOG

To find the events in which you're interested, you can filter an event log. Take the following steps:

1. In the console tree, click the event log you want to filter.

2. Choose Action ➤ Filter Current Log. Windows displays the Filter Current Log dialog box (see Figure 15.6).

3. In the Logged drop-down list, choose the time frame for the events you want: Any Time, Last Hour, Last 12 Hours, Last 24 Hours, Last 7 Days, Last 30 Days, or a Custom Range you specify.

4. In the Event Level area, select the check box for each type of event you want to see: Critical, Error, Warning, Information, or Verbose.

FIGURE 15.6
Use the Filter Current
Log dialog box to
specify filtering
on the currently
selected log.

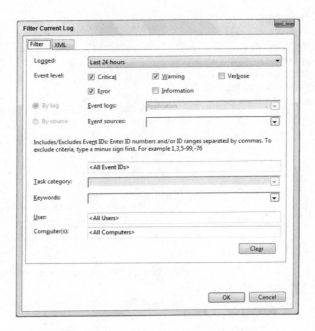

5. In the Includes/Excludes Event IDs text box, you can type particular event ID numbers or ranges of numbers that you want to find. This is expert usage; for normal usage, leave the <All Event IDs> item selected.

6. If you want to specify particular keywords for the filtering, click the drop-down list button, and then select the check box for each keyword you want to include. Here's an example of the options:

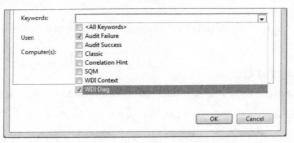

7. In the User text box, you can type a particular username if you want to see only events related to that user. Otherwise, leave the <All Users> item selected.

8. In the Computer(s) text box, you can type a particular computer name if you're monitoring remote computers and you want to see only the events related to a particular computer. Otherwise, leave the <All Computers> items selected.

9. Click the OK button. Windows closes the Filter Current Log dialog box and filters the contents of the current log to show only matching entries.

To remove the filtering, choose Action ➢ Clear Filter.

CLEARING THE EVENT LOG

To clear a log, right-click it in Event Viewer and choose Clear Log from the context menu. Event Viewer displays an Event Viewer dialog box asking if you want to save the log before clearing it. Click the Save and Clear button if you want to save the log before clearing it; specify the filename in the Save As dialog box, and then click the Save button. Otherwise, click the Clear button to clear the log without saving its contents.

Keeping Windows Updated with Windows Update

Windows Update is a feature that helps you keep Windows up to date by automatically checking for Windows updates, service packs, and fixes for security holes, and either installing them automatically or notifying the first available Administrator that they're available for installation. This section discusses how to use Windows Update in its default configuration and how to configure it to suit your needs.

Configuring What Windows Update Does

You can choose whether to run Windows Update automatically (on a schedule that Windows chooses) or manually at your convenience. Which setting you choose depends on your needs and what you want Windows Update to do for your computer.

CHOOSING WINDOWS UPDATE SETTINGS WHILE COMPLETING INSTALLATION

Your first chance to make this choice comes during the last stages of setting up Windows. After you've set up your Administrator user account, the Help Protect Windows Automatically screen appears and lets you choose which updates to install:

Use Recommended Settings If you choose this setting, Windows automatically installs important updates and recommended updates. Windows automatically checks online for solutions to problems your computer encounters. For example, if a particular program crashes, Windows checks online to see whether there's a fix. This behavior is usually useful, but there are a couple of problems you'll learn about in a minute.

Install Important Updates Only If you choose this setting, Windows automatically installs only the updates that are designated important—security updates and other critical updates.

Ask Me Later If you choose this setting, Windows doesn't use automatic updates, but it prompts you again periodically to decide whether to use automatic updates.

CHOOSING WINDOWS UPDATE SETTINGS SUBSEQUENTLY

The Help Protect Windows Automatically screen pressures you to choose automatic updates—which is arguably a good idea, because installing the latest patches and keeping Windows as fully protected as possibly is usually helpful. But installing these patches automatically has a couple of problems, as discussed in the "Why *Wouldn't* You Use Automatic Updates?" sidebar.

 **Real World Scenario**

WHY *WOULDN'T* YOU USE AUTOMATIC UPDATES?

In an ideal world, your computer would always be running the latest version of Windows, including all the latest patches to keep your computer protected against the most recent attacks and exploits developed by malefactors. Windows would check online every day for new patches and install them automatically for you.

In the real world, Windows Update automatically does this for you. But there are a couple of problems in practice:

Automatic Updates May Lose Your Work   If you allow Windows to apply automatic updates, Windows downloads the updates during the night (unless you change the time), installs them, and then reboots your computer if necessary to make the updates take effect. This behavior makes sense, but if you leave any program open with unsaved work in it, Windows automatically closes the program without saving your changes. The result is that you lose any work that you had not saved in the program. The remedy to this problem is obvious: When you leave your computer for the night, save all documents, and preferably close all programs as well. But many people find it more convenient to be able to leave their computer with unsaved work at any time of the day or night.

Automatic Updates May Remove Features from Windows   When you agree to automatic updates, you agree to let Microsoft update the software on your computer automatically without your being able to read about changes to the software's functionality or to the licensing agreements. If Microsoft deems certain features to be dangerous or otherwise undesirable, it can remove them without your consent. This concern might seem abstract, but in practice it's not. Even if the changes that Microsoft makes via automatic updates are designed to benefit you, they may have undesirable consequences in practice.

To change your settings for Windows Update, take the following steps:

1. Choose Start ➢ All Programs ➢ Windows Update. Windows displays the Windows Update window, as shown here.

FIGURE 15.7
Use the Change Settings window to specify whether Windows can install updates automatically or only with your approval.

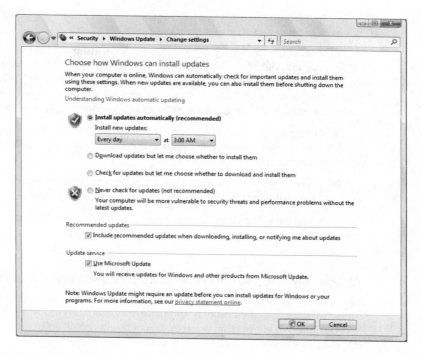

2. In the left panel, click the Change Settings link. Windows displays the Change Settings window (see Figure 15.7).

3. Select the appropriate option button for downloading and installing updates:

Install Updates Automatically   This option button is the best choice for convenience and security. Use the two drop-down lists to specify which day to use for updates (Every Day, Every Sunday, Every Monday, Every Tuesday, Every Wednesday, Every Thursday, Every Friday, or Every Saturday) and the time of day at which to search (the default setting is 3:00 AM). Choose the Every Day option if your computer has a permanent Internet connection and you're prepared to have Windows restart your computer without giving you the chance to save any unsaved work. Set the time drop-down list to a time when your computer will be powered on (rather than off) and you won't be interrupted by its use of your Internet connection.

Download Updates for Me But Let Me Choose Whether to Install Them   This option button lets you control when Windows installs any updates that it has automatically downloaded. Select this option button if you want to be able to control when the updates are installed. The disadvantage to this setting is that your computer remains unpatched and unprotected longer than if Windows had installed the updates automatically.

Check for Updates But Let Me Choose Whether to Download and Install Them   This option button lets you choose when to download any available updates (and, after you download them, when to install them). Select this option button if it's important that you control the use of your Internet connection's bandwidth rather than letting Automatic Updates hog it at inconvenient times.

Never Check for Updates   This option button lets you turn off Automatic Updates. Turning off Automatic Updates isn't usually a good idea, because it can leave your computer open to attack. But you may choose to turn off Automatic Updates and run Windows Update manually from the Start menu (choose Start ➤ All Programs ➤ Windows Update) at times when it's convenient for you to search for, download, and install updates.

4. If you want to include recommended updates as well as important updates, select the Include Recommended Updates When Downloading, Installing, or Notifying Me about Updates check box.

5. If you want to use the Microsoft Update service to receive updates for Windows and other Microsoft software, select the Use Microsoft Update check box.

6. Click the OK button, and then authenticate yourself to User Account Control. Windows closes the Change Settings window, applies your choices, and returns you to the Security window.

What Happens When Windows Update Runs Automatically

If you choose to have Windows Update download updates automatically, Windows checks for updates at the specified time. If updates are available, Windows starts downloading them as long as your Internet connection is either idle or being consistently lightly used over a period of time— for example, if your e-mail program is checking for mail every few minutes and finding nothing, but no other activity is taking place. If you've left Windows Update set to run at 3 AM (its default hour), chances are that your computer won't be doing much.

WHAT DOES WINDOWS UPDATE DO IF YOUR COMPUTER IS SLEEPING?

If your computer is sleeping and plugged in, Windows wakes it and downloads and installs the updates. If your computer is sleeping and on battery power, Windows doesn't wake it.

When Windows Update is downloading updates, it displays an icon in the notification area. You can make Windows display the status of the download (what percentage is complete) by hovering the mouse pointer over the icon. You can pause the download manually by clicking the icon and choosing Pause from the resulting menu, and resume a paused download by clicking the icon and choosing Resume from the menu.

If you choose to let Windows Update install updates automatically, Windows installs the updates as soon as it has finished downloading them. Windows then restarts your computer automatically. When you next log on, Windows displays a notification-area pop-up message telling you that it installed updates automatically.

If you choose the Download Updates, But Let Me Choose Whether to Install Them option button, Windows displays the New Updates Are Available icon in the notification area, as shown here.

Click the New Updates Are Available icon. Windows displays the Windows Update: Install Updates for Your Computer window, as shown here.

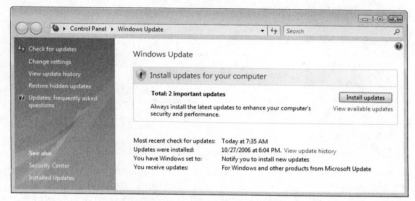

If you simply want to install all available updates, click the Install Updates button, and then authenticate yourself to User Account Control. Windows installs the updates.

If you want to see which updates are available so that you can decide whether to install them, click the View Available Updates link. Windows displays a list of updates, as shown here, with the check boxes selected automatically. Clear the check box for each update you don't want to install, click the Install button, and then authenticate yourself to User Account Control.

Downloading and Installing Updates Manually

If you choose to have Windows Update notify you when new updates are available, Windows Update checks periodically for new updates. When it finds some, it displays a New Updates Are Available icon in the notification area with a pop-up message telling you that new updates are available. When you click the icon or the message, Windows displays the Windows Update: Download and Install Updates for Your Computer window, as shown here.

If you simply want to install all available updates, click the Install Updates button, and then authenticate yourself to User Account Control. Windows installs the updates.

If you want to see which updates are available so that you can decide whether to install them, click the View Available Updates link. Windows displays a list of updates, as shown in the previous section, with the check boxes selected automatically. Clear the check box for each update you don't want to install, click the Install button, and then authenticate yourself to User Account Control.

Restarting Your Computer

After installing the updates, restart your computer if Windows tells you that you need to.

Viewing Installed Updates

To see which updates Windows has installed, click the View Update History link in the left panel in the Windows Update window. Windows displays the View Update History window (see Figure 15.8).

From here, you can click the Installed Updates link to display the Installed Updates window, which lets you remove some updates from your computer. However, Microsoft doesn't let you remove most updates from your computer, as they're considered essential to keeping Windows running securely.

Restoring Hidden Updates

If you decide to install updates manually, and you choose not to install some updates, you can change your mind and install them after all. To do so, take the following steps:

1. In the left panel in the Windows Update window, click the Restore Hidden Updates link. Windows displays the Restore Hidden Updates window.

FIGURE 15.8
The View Update
History window
lets you see which
updates Windows
has installed.

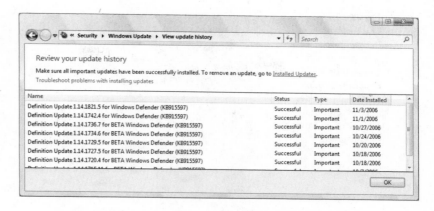

2. In the list box, select the check box for each update that you want to restore.

3. Click the Restore button, and then authenticate yourself to User Account Control. Windows restores the updates, and then prompts you to install them.

Optimizing Your Computer's Performance

This section discusses steps you can take to assess and optimize the performance of your computer and of Windows. These steps range from getting more RAM (if you need it) to setting suitable performance options for your computer or specifying the size and location of the paging file. You should also defragment your disk or disks as discussed in the section "Defragmenting Your Disks" in Chapter 10.

Checking Your Computer's Windows Experience Index Score

The best place to start optimizing performance is by checking your computer's Windows Experience Index in the Performance Information and Tools window. The Windows Experience Index is a measure of how well Windows thinks your computer is equipped to run Windows.

To view your computer's Windows Experience Index, take the following steps:

1. Choose Start ➤ Control Panel. Windows displays a Control Panel window.

2. Click the System and Maintenance link. Windows displays the System and Maintenance window.

3. Click the Performance Information and Tools link. Windows displays the Performance Information and Tools window (see Figure 15.9).

UNDERSTANDING THE WINDOWS EXPERIENCE INDEX SCORE

Windows Experience Index rates each of your computer's main components—the processor, memory, graphics capability, gaming graphics capability, and primary hard disk—on a scale of 1 to 5. Windows Experience Index gives the computer a *base score*, or overall score, that is the same as the lowest individual component score. For example, in the figure, the Gaming Graphics score is lowest at 4.0, so the computer receives a base score of 4.0.

Table 15.1 gives brief details of the kind of performance you can expect for a particular base score.

FIGURE 15.9
The Performance Information and Tools window gives your computer's Windows Experience Index score and provides links to tools that you can use to improve performance.

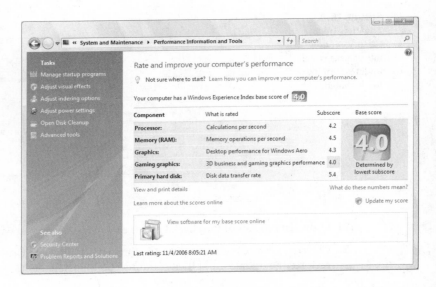

TABLE 15.1: Windows Experience Index Base Scores and Their Meanings

BASE SCORE	WINDOWS AERO UI	COMPUTER CAN	COMPUTER CAN'T
1 or 2	No	Run productivity applications	Run Windows Aero Play videos or TV
3	Yes	Run Windows Aero Play videos	Play HDTV
4 or 5	Yes	Run Windows Aero, all programs, and play videos and HDTV	—

UPDATING THE WINDOWS EXPERIENCE INDEX SCORE

If you've changed your computer's configuration (for example, by adding memory or installing a better graphics card), update your Windows Experience Index score to see what difference the change made. Set aside a few minutes when your computer's not busy with other tasks, and then click the Update My Score link in the Performance Information and Tools window. Windows displays the Windows Experience Index dialog box, as shown here, as it runs the test. Windows then updates the scores.

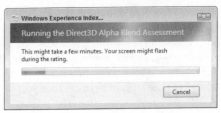

RAM: Does Your Computer Have Enough?

If your computer's performance seems disappointing, make sure that your computer has plenty of RAM to run Windows itself plus all the programs that may be running in the background. A total of 512MB is usually enough for running a single user session at reasonable speed, and 1GB is usually enough for several user sessions running conventional programs. If you want multiple users to be able to open large programs or large files at the same time, get 2GB or more.

RAM is normally the most affordable way of improving performance on your computer significantly. The exception is if your computer has a limited number of memory slots, all of which are full. In this case, you will need to discard some or all of your existing memory when you upgrade, which makes the upgrade more expensive.

To find out how much RAM your computer has, press Windows Key+Break, and then look at the Memory (RAM) readout in the System window. If the readout shows a figure other than one of the standard numbers (512MB, 768MB, 1,024MB, 1,280MB, 1,536MB, 1,792MB, or 2,048MB), the amount of RAM is the next higher figure. For example, if the readout shows 502MB, your computer has 512MB, and 10MB is being used for other purposes (typically video).

Using ReadyBoost to Supplement Your RAM

Increasing RAM is the best way to increase performance quickly, but Windows also allows you to improve performance by using a USB flash drive or certain other forms of memory (such as a MemoryStick device) as extra memory. This feature is called ReadyBoost and lets Windows cache (store) key files on the flash drive, from which it can access them much more quickly than if it caches them on the hard disk.

HOW READYBOOST WORKS

You can use only one device for ReadyBoost at a time. On that device, you can use anywhere from 256MB to 4GB. Windows lets you choose how much of a device's flash memory to assign to ReadyBoost.

Microsoft recommends having a 1:1 ratio of flash memory to system memory for modest performance and a 2.5:1 ratio for the best performance. For example, if your computer has 512MB RAM, you should assign 1,280MB of flash memory to get the best performance. Table 15.2 shows the figures for common memory configurations.

TABLE 15.2:   ReadyBoost RAM:Flash Memory Ratios

RAM (MB)	FLASH MEMORY	
	MODEST PERFORMANCE	BEST PERFORMANCE
512	512	1,280
768	768	1,920
1,024	1,024	2,560
1,280	1,280	3,200
1,536	1,536	3,840
1,792	1,793	4,480

TABLE 15.2: ReadyBoost RAM:Flash Memory Ratios *(CONTINUED)*

	FLASH MEMORY	
RAM (MB)	MODEST PERFORMANCE	BEST PERFORMANCE
2,048	2,048	5,120
3,072	3,072	7,680

 Real World Scenario

GETTING A FLASH DRIVE SUITABLE FOR READYBOOST

ReadyBoost is used mostly for small files and requires fast-performing memory. For ReadyBoost to work, the memory must be able to manage throughput of 2.5MB/s for 4KB random reads and 1.75MB/s for 512KB random writes across its full range of memory.

Many drives can meet these requirements—but many others can't. What's confusing is that the figures you'll see on devices measure sequential performance rather than random performance. For example, even if a device can manage 12MB/s sequential read, it may not be able to manage 2.5MB/s random reads.

One particular trap is that some flash drives that are marketed as having high speeds achieve those speeds by having a small amount of very fast memory that acts as a gateway to the rest of the memory. Such drives can turn in very fast sequential performance, but if the main memory isn't fast enough to meet ReadyBoost's random read and write requirements, you can't use the drive for ReadyBoost.

At this writing, there's no ReadyBoost-capable logo to indicate that a device is suitable for use. However, by the time you read this, there may be, so it's worth doing a little research before buying. If there's still no logo program, search online to find out which brands of flash drives have been found to work with ReadyBoost.

SETTING UP READYBOOST ON A DRIVE

To configure ReadyBoost on a drive, follow these steps:

1. Connect the drive to your computer via USB. Windows displays the AutoPlay dialog box containing options for the drive. Here's an example:

2. Click the Speed Up My System button. Windows displays the ReadyBoost page of the Properties dialog box for the drive (see Figure 15.10). If the drive is already connected to your computer, choose Start ➤ My Computer, right-click the drive, and then choose Properties from the context menu. In the Properties dialog box, click the ReadyBoost tab.

3. Select the Use This Device option button.

4. Drag the Space to Reserve for System Speed slider, or adjust the value in the text box, to specify how much of the drive to use.

5. Click the OK button. Windows closes the Properties dialog box and starts using the device as extra memory.

FIGURE 15.10

The ReadyBoost page of the Properties dialog box for a USB flash drive lets you specify how much of the drive to devote to speeding up your computer with ReadyBoost.

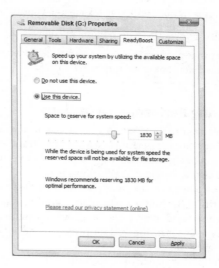

FORCE WINDOWS TO USE READYBOOST ON A DRIVE THAT IT DEEMS TOO SLOW

If Windows claims "this device doesn't have the required performance characteristics for use in speeding up your system," click the Test Again button to make sure. Sometimes Windows reads marginal devices as viable the second time around.

If Windows still finds the device too slow, you can force Windows to use the device for ReadyBoost by editing the Registry. If the device really is to slow, you may not benefit from forcing Windows to use ReadyBoost on it, but you can try the device and see if it improves performance.

To force Windows to use the device, take the following steps:

1. Close the Properties dialog box.

2. Unplug the device from the USB port.

3. Press Windows Key+R. Windows displays the Run dialog box.

4. Type **regedit** and press Enter or click the OK button. Windows launches Registry Editor.

5. Expand the HKEY_LOCAL_MACHINE hive and navigate to the Microsoft\WindowsNT\ CurrentVersion\EMDMgmt key.

6. Select the USBSTOR key for the device (look at the end of the long ID number to see a text string that's related to your device). Registry Editor displays the value entries for the device.

7. Double-click the DeviceStatus value entry, use the Edit DWORD (32-Bit) Value dialog box to set its value to 2 with the Hexadecimal option button selected, and then click the OK button.

8. Double-click the ReadSpeedKBs value entry, use the Edit DWORD (32-Bit) Value dialog box to set its value to 1,000 with the Hexadecimal option button selected, and then click the OK button.

9. Double-click the WriteSpeedKBs value entry, use the Edit DWORD (32-Bit) Value dialog box to set its value to 1,000 with the Hexadecimal option button selected, and then click the OK button.

10. Plug the device back in. Windows displays the AutoPlay dialog box.

11. Click the Speed Up My System button, and then use the controls on the ReadyBoost page of the Properties dialog box to set up ReadyBoost.

Choosing Performance Options

Next, make sure that Windows is configured to give the best performance possible for your needs.

Getting the best performance out of Windows on a computer that isn't screamingly fast is partly a question of choosing the right balance between visual sophistication and speed: the more graphics and visual effects that Windows is using, the slower their display will be, and the heavier the demands placed on the processor as well as the graphics subsystem. The more visual effects you can sacrifice, the better performance you'll get.

You also need to give the foreground program as much of a boost as possible, so make sure that memory usage is optimized for programs rather than system cache, and set an appropriate size for your paging file.

To set performance options, follow these steps:

1. Press Windows Key+Break. Windows displays the System window.

2. In the left panel, click the Advanced System Settings link. Windows displays the Advanced page of the System Properties dialog box (see Figure 15.11).

3. Click the Settings button in the Performance group box. Windows displays the Performance Options dialog box.

4. On the Visual Effects page of the Performance Options dialog box (see Figure 15.12), select one of the option buttons:

   ◆ Select the Let Windows Choose What's Best for My Computer option button to have Windows apply the mixture of settings it deems most appropriate to your computer's speed and your graphics card's capabilities.

   ◆ Select the Adjust for Best Appearance option button to turn on all the effects.

   ◆ Select the Adjust for Best Performance option button to turn off all the effects.

◆ Select the Custom option button if you want to apply a custom set of effects. Then select the check boxes for the effects you want to use. Most of the effects are self-explanatory—for example, the Animate Windows When Minimizing and Maximizing check box controls whether Windows animates windows when minimizing, maximizing, and restoring them. The fewer visual effects you use, the better the performance you'll enjoy, but the plainer and less subtle the Windows interface will seem.

5. Click the Advanced tab. Windows displays the Advanced page of the Performance Options dialog box (see Figure 15.13).

FIGURE 15.11

The Advanced page of the System Properties dialog box is the starting place for setting performance options.

FIGURE 15.12

To improve performance, turn off unnecessary visual effects on the Visual Effects page of the Performance Options dialog box.

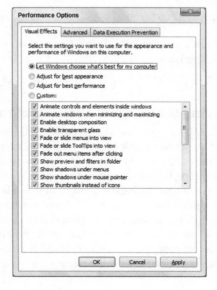

FIGURE 15.13
On the Advanced
page of the Perfor-
mance Options
dialog box, make
sure that processor
scheduling and
memory usage
are optimized for
applications.

6. In the Processor Scheduling group box, make sure that the Programs option button is selected. The Programs option button causes Windows to give priority to the foreground program—the active program—giving you faster response time in it. (Select the Background Services option button only if you're using this computer as a sort of server and are not running programs on it or if you want a background task, such as Backup Utility, to get more attention so that it'll run faster.) For the Programs option, Windows allocates short, variable-length *quanta* (time slices) to programs, whereas for the Background Services option, Windows allocates longer, fixed-length quanta.

7. If necessary, change the size of the paging file by following the instructions in the next section.

8. Click the OK button. Windows applies your changes and closes the Performance Options dialog box.

9. Click the OK button. Windows closes the System Properties dialog box.

Specifying the Size and Location of the Paging File

The *paging file* is space reserved on the hard disk for Windows to use as virtual memory. *Virtual memory* involves storing memory information on the hard disk so that more information can be loaded into memory (both real and virtual) at the same time. Windows juggles virtual memory automatically, swapping information between the RAM and the paging file, so its use should be imperceptible to you. (You'll hear the hard drive working, but then, the hard drive works so much when Windows is running that you'll hear it even when no virtual memory swapping is taking place.)

Being able to load more information into memory at a time is good, but because the hard drive is much slower to access than RAM, storing memory information in virtual memory makes your computer run more slowly than it would if it were to store all memory information in RAM. Windows allows you to turn off the paging file to force the OS to use RAM all the time. But given the demands that Windows can make on memory, Microsoft doesn't recommend it—even if you have a huge amount of RAM (say, 2GB or more).

Windows automatically creates the paging file on the drive that Windows itself is installed on, not because this is the best place to have it—it isn't—but because it'd be antisocial to put it anywhere else. (If you're familiar with Linux, you'll know that it requires a separate partition for its swap file, which is roughly analogous to the paging file in Windows.) You may well want to move the paging file to a different partition to improve performance by separating the disk read and write requests for the system folder from those for the paging file.

You might also want to move your paging file to a faster drive than the drive it's currently on. For example, if you have a small but very fast drive in your computer as well as a slower but much larger drive, you might want to move the paging file to the faster drive to improve performance. (This would work for a large and fast drive as well—but you'd probably have installed Windows on that drive in the first place, so the paging file would already be there.) Similarly, you may be able to improve performance by moving the paging file to an otherwise unused drive if you have one.

Before you move the paging file, though, there's a gotcha you need to know about. For Windows to be able to create a memory dump file for debugging STOP errors, you need to have a paging file on the boot partition. (See the section "Setting Startup and Recovery Options" later in this chapter for a discussion of memory dumps.) So in most cases it's best to split the paging file between the boot partition and one or more other partitions. When you do this, Windows uses an internal algorithm to determine which paging file to use, allowing it to use the paging file on the less frequently accessed partition (or partitions) in preference to that on the boot partition (which will be heavily accessed).

The paging file takes up anything from about 750MB to several gigabytes. By default, the paging file is initially set to 1.5 times the amount of RAM in the computer: a 768MB paging file for a computer with 512MB of RAM, 1,533MB for 1GB of RAM, and so on. So if you have a small drive or partition, you may want to move the paging file off it when you start running low on disk space. You can also split the paging file between different partitions if you're running low on space on all the partitions or if you want to optimize performance. (More on this in a moment.)

The paging file is called PAGEFILE.SYS. It's a hidden and protected operating system file, so if you feel the urge to look at its entry in an Explorer window, you'll need to select the Show Hidden Files and Folders option button and clear the Hide Protected Operating System Files check box on the View page of the Folder Options dialog box to see it. (To display the Folder Options dialog box, choose Organize ➢ Folder and Search Options in an Explorer window.)

Windows won't let you delete the paging file directly. You *can* delete the paging file by booting another operating system and attacking it from there, but there's little point in doing so—you can manage the paging file easily enough by following the procedure described next.

WHAT'S THE HUGE FILE CALLED *HIBERFIL.SYS*?

If you look for the paging file, you may also see the hibernation file, HIBERFIL.SYS. (Your computer will have a hibernation file only if your computer supports hibernation.)

By default, the hibernation file is stored on the same drive as the paging file, and is approximately the same size as the amount of RAM your computer contains. For example, if the computer has 1GB of RAM, the hibernation file will be about 1GB as well. That's because Windows writes the contents of RAM to the hibernation file before entering hibernation—RAM doesn't store information when it's powered down.

EXPERT KNOWLEDGE: USE A FIXED-SIZE PAGING FILE ON EACH PHYSICAL DRIVE

As you can see in the following list, Windows lets you specify the size and location of your paging file. You can choose to place a paging file of just about any size on each fixed drive. (You can also place paging files on writable removable volumes, but this is seldom a good idea.) Or you can choose not to use a paging file at all.

For optimum performance, create one paging file on each physical hard drive in your computer, and make each paging file a fixed size by choosing the Custom Size option button and entering the same value in the Initial Size text box and the Maximum Size text box. Using a fixed-size paging file means not only that Windows doesn't need to waste time resizing the paging file on the fly but also, more importantly, that the paging file can be written to disk in one contiguous area of the hard disk in question rather than fragmented over various parts of the disk. If the paging file isn't fragmented, access to virtual memory will be faster. Also—less of a bonus but important when things go wrong—memory dumps are less likely to contain errors if the paging file isn't fragmented than if it is.

Instead of creating a fixed-size paging file, you can create one on its own partition and allow Windows to manage its size. Having no other files on the partition will prevent fragmentation from occurring.

To ensure that there's plenty of space in your fixed-size paging files, make their total size (on all drives together) equal to twice the amount of RAM in your computer.

When creating your paging files, make sure that you're clear about which volume resides in which partition of which physical drive so that you can avoid putting two or more paging files in different partitions on the same physical drive. (Doing so will rob you of the performance benefits of spreading out your paging files.) Also, don't put your paging files on removable hard drives. Instead, use a USB flash drive or a similar device for ReadyBoost.

To specify the size and location of the paging file, follow these steps:

1. Click the Change button in the Virtual Memory group box on the Advanced page of the Performance Options dialog box. Windows displays the Virtual Memory dialog box (see Figure 15.14).

FIGURE 15.14

The Virtual Memory dialog box lets you specify the size of the paging file and the drive on which to locate it.

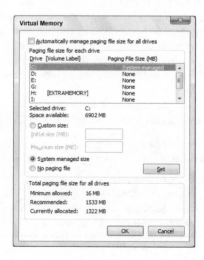

2. If you want to manage the paging file, clear the Automatically Manage Page File Size for All Drives check box. While this check box is selected, the other controls in the Virtual Memory dialog box are disabled.

3. In the Drive list box, select the drive (or one of the drives) that contains the paging file.

4. In the Paging File Size for Selected Drive list box, specify the size of the file:

   ◆ If you want Windows to manage the paging file's size, select the System Managed Size option button.

   ◆ If you want to manage the paging file's size yourself, select the Custom Size option button. Enter appropriate values in the Initial Size text box and the Maximum Size text box, based on the Recommended readout and the Currently Allocated readout in the Total Paging File Size for All Drives group box. Click the Set button.

   ◆ To remove the paging file from this drive, select the No Paging File option button. Click the Set button.

5. Specify paging file sizes for the other drives as appropriate by repeating steps 3 and 4.

6. Click the OK button. Windows closes the Virtual Memory dialog box and returns you to the Advanced page of the Performance Options dialog box.

7. Click the OK button. Windows closes the Performance Options dialog box and returns you to the Advanced page of the System Properties dialog box.

You'll need to restart Windows before your changes to the paging file take effect.

 Real World Scenario

USING NO PAGING FILE IS USUALLY NOT A GOOD IDEA

If you want, you can use the No Paging File option on each drive that currently contains a paging file to remove that paging file, leaving you with no paging file at all. Unless you have a huge amount of RAM— 2GB or more, depending on how many user sessions you typically have running at once and on how many programs and files each typically uses—this isn't usually a good idea.

In theory, turning off the paging file should speed up Windows (again, given plenty of RAM) because Windows won't waste time writing memory data to disk and retrieving it from there. But in practice, turning off the paging file doesn't seem to deliver much of a performance boost, and it increases the likelihood of Windows's running out of memory and crashing.

FOR SECURITY, CLEAR THE PAGING FILE AT SHUTDOWN

Because your paging file can contain sensitive information, you may want to clear its contents when Windows shuts down. To do so, see "Clearing the Paging File at Shutdown" in Chapter 11.

Controlling Data Execution Prevention

Data Execution Prevention (DEP) is a security feature against rogue code in malware or documents. DEP cordons off some particular memory areas (identified by their addresses) as "protected" or "nonexecutable" (NX for short), which means that programs cannot be executed (run) from them.

For DEP to work fully, your computer's processor must support NX. All new Intel and AMD processors support NX, as do many recent processors. If your computer has an older processor that doesn't support NX, DEP won't be available, and the controls on the Data Execution Prevention tab of the Performance Options dialog box will be disabled. Software DEP will still work.

If your computer's processor supports NX, Windows turns on DEP automatically for all programs, and you should leave it on for all programs unless it prevents you from running a vital program. The programs you've installed on your computer don't run from nonexecutable memory areas, so they run normally unless something goes wrong. But when a virus, worm, or other malware tries to execute, it does so from a nonexecutable memory area, which allows Windows to identify the problem and close the program.

When DEP closes a program, it displays the Data Execution Prevention Alert dialog box to warn you that it has done so. If this is a program you need to be able to run, click the Change Settings button and configure an exception for the program. To create an exception, you must be an Administrator user rather than a Standard user (or the Guest user).

To configure DEP, click the Data Execution Prevention tab of the Performance Options dialog box to display the Data Execution Prevention page (see Figure 15.15). Here you can select the Turn On DEP for Essential Windows Programs and Services Only option button or the Turn On DEP for All Programs and Services Except Those I Select option button. If you select the latter, use the Add and Remove buttons to control the list of DEP exceptions.

Click the OK button to close the Performance Options dialog box when you've made your selection. You'll need to restart Windows to make the changes take effect.

FIGURE 15.15

Data Execution Prevention prevents programs such as viruses from executing in protected memory areas on your PC.

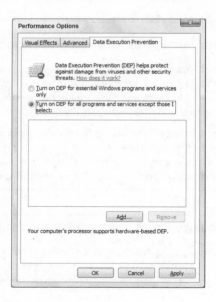

SETTING ENVIRONMENT VARIABLES

From the Advanced page of the System Properties dialog box, you can click the Environment Variables button to display the Environment Variables dialog box (shown here).

Environment variables have largely been superseded by Registry values, so you probably won't need to do much in this dialog box. You *can* use the New, the Edit, and the Delete buttons to create, edit, and delete user variables and system variables, but you shouldn't need to do so. And you *can* find out some information about Windows and your system from the System Variables list box—but most of this information is more easily found elsewhere. For example, you'll find processor information in the System Info applet, which you can access from the Help and Support Center window.

Click the OK button to close the Environment Variables dialog box.

Setting Startup and Recovery Options

Windows includes several startup options that you should know about if you're running a dual-boot setup. (If you're not, just ignore these options: They don't apply to you at the moment.) You can also specify what Windows should do when it encounters a system failure—an error bad enough to crash the system.

To set startup and recovery options, follow these steps:

1. Click the Settings button in the Startup and Recovery group box on the Advanced page of the System Properties dialog box. Windows displays the Startup and Recovery dialog box (see Figure 15.16).

2. If you have a dual- or multiple-boot system, choose options in the System Startup group box:

   ◆ In the Default Operating System drop-down list, select the operating system that you want to boot by default.

FIGURE 15.16
Use the System
Startup options
in the Startup and
Recovery dialog box
to specify the default
operating system
to boot and for how
long Windows should
display the boot list
of operating systems.
Use the System Fail-
ure options to specify
what Windows should
do if it suffers a system
failure.

◆ If you want Windows to display the boot list of operating systems for a number of seconds before booting one, so that you can boot an operating system other than the default one, select the Time to Display List of Operating Systems check box and enter a suitable value in the text box. You can enter any value from 0 seconds to 999 seconds. The default value is 30 seconds, but most people find a shorter value more useful—long enough to give you time to select the operating system (or just tap a key) without needing fast reflexes, but short enough to pass quickly if you just want to boot the default operating system.

3. Whether you're using a single-boot system or a multiple-boot system, leave the Time to Display Recovery Options When Needed check box selected, and enter a suitable number of seconds in its text box. When Windows is rebooting after a failed boot, it displays the Recovery Options menu so that you can restart it in Safe mode if you want.

4. Choose options in the System Failure group box:

Write an Event to the System Log check box Select this check box if you want Windows to write an event to the System Log. (The section "The System Log," earlier in this chapter, shows you how to view and interpret the System Log.)

Automatically Restart check box Select this check box if you want Windows to automatically reboot if there's a system failure. (Windows reboots after writing that event to the System Log and sending an administrative alert, if you left those check boxes selected.)

Write Debugging Information group box In the drop-down list, select the type of debugging information that you want Windows to write in the event of a crash. Your choices are None, Small Memory Dump, Kernel Memory Dump, and Complete Memory Dump. The None choice turns off the writing of debugging information. A Small Memory Dump creates a file with a name built of the prefix MINI, the date in MMDDYY format, a hyphen, the number of the dump, and the DMP extension. For example, the first dump on Christmas Day 2007 is named MINI122507-01.DMP. The dump file is stored in the directory specified in the

Small Dump Directory text box and contains the smallest possible amount of memory information to be useful for debugging. With each crash, Windows creates a new file. To create a Small Memory Dump, Windows needs a paging file of at least 2MB on the boot volume of your computer. A Kernel Memory Dump dumps only the kernel memory into a file called MEMORY.DMP by default and needs between 50 and 800MB of space for the paging file on the boot volume (not on another volume). A Complete Memory Dump, as its name suggests, dumps all the information contained in system memory when the crash occurred. Again, this goes into a file named MEMORY.DMP by default. To create a complete memory dump, you need to have a paging file on the boot volume (again, not on another volume) of at least the size of your computer's RAM plus 1MB (for example, a paging file of at least 1,025MB if your computer has 1GB RAM). Choose the location and name for the dump file in the text box in the Write Debugging Information group box, and select the Overwrite Any Existing File check box if appropriate. (This check box isn't available for Small Memory Dump, because this option creates a sequence of files automatically.)

5. Click the OK button. Windows closes the Startup and Recovery dialog box.

 Real World Scenario

THE SYSTEM FAILURE OPTIONS DON'T ALWAYS WORK

The recovery options in the System Failure group box aren't a panacea. Any crash serious enough to be called a system failure will almost invariably result in the loss of any unsaved data sitting around in the programs affected.

Windows Vista suffers occasional lockups, particularly with misbehaving hardware drivers. If your system hangs (freezes), you'll probably need to reboot it manually, because the auto-reboot functionality will be frozen as well. After rebooting, you'll find that no event was written to the System Log and no administrative alert was sent, because Windows was just as blindsided by the hang as you were.

TESTING A CRASH OR MEMORY DUMP

To check how the memory dump works, or to experience a crash in action, try using the CrashOnCtrlScroll Registry key as discussed in the "For Testing Only: Crashing Your Computer on Cue" sidebar in Chapter 11. On some computers, this produces a dump followed by a reboot. On other computers, it produces a custom Blue Screen of Death and nothing beyond it.

Using Problem Reports and Solutions

Windows' Problem Reports and Solutions feature lets you find solutions for problems your computer is having.

To get started with Problem Reports and Solutions, open the Problem Reports and Solutions window by following these steps:

1. Choose Start ➤ Control Panel. Windows displays a Control Panel window.

2. Click the System and Maintenance link. Windows displays a System and Maintenance window.

3. Click the Problem Reports and Solutions link. Windows displays the Problem Reports and Solutions window (see Figure 15.17).

If the Solutions to Install area shows any solutions to install, choose whether to install them.

FIGURE 15.17
The Problem Reports and Solutions window lets you see which problems Windows has identified on your computer and check for solutions to them.

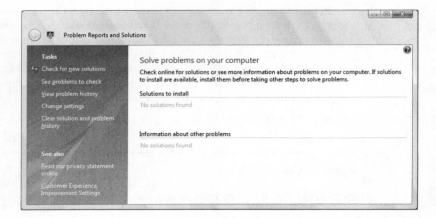

Checking for New Solutions

To check for new solutions to problems, click the Check for New Solutions link in the left panel in the Problem Reports and Solutions window. Windows displays the Problem Reports and Solutions: Checking for Solutions dialog box, as shown here, while it reports problems and checks for solutions. You can click the Show Details link to see the name of the problem that Windows is currently reporting.

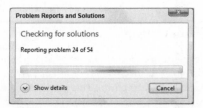

When Windows has finished reporting problems, it may display the Problem Reports and Solutions dialog box shown in Figure 15.18 requesting your permission to send more information to try to solve some of the problems. Click the View Problem Details button to display the details, as shown in the figure, so that you can see what information Windows will send. Click the Send Information button if you want to proceed.

FIGURE 15.18
Windows may need to send further information to Microsoft in order to find solutions to the problems.

Seeing Problems with Your Computer

To see which problems Windows has identified on your computer, click the See Problems to Check link. Windows displays the Problem Reports and Solutions: Check for Solutions to These Problems window (see Figure 15.19). Select the check box for each problem you want to check online, and then click the Check for Solutions button.

Viewing Your Problem History

To view the record of problems that Windows has identified on your computer, click the View Problem History link in the left panel in the Problem Reports and Solutions window. Windows displays the Problem Reports and Solutions: Problems Windows Has Identified window (see Figure 15.20).

FIGURE 15.19
In the Problem Reports and Solutions: Check for Solutions to These Problems window, select the check box for each problem you want to evaluate, and then click the Check for Solutions button.

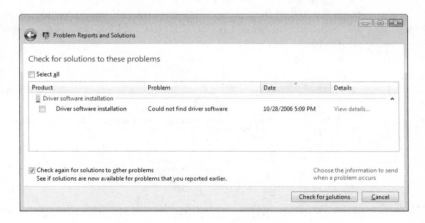

FIGURE 15.20
Use the Problem
Reports and Solutions:
Problems Windows
Has Identified
window to get an
overview of the
problems your
computer has had.

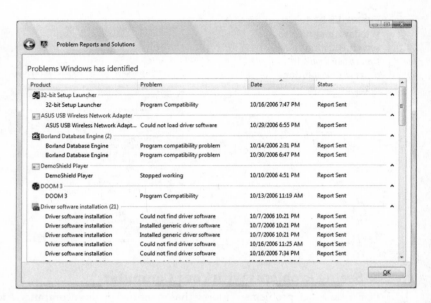

You can sort the problems by any column—for example, by the Product column or by the Date column—or group by a column. To take an action on a problem, right-click it, and then choose Check for a Solution, Delete, View Solution (if available), or View Problem Details from the context menu.

When you've finished working in the Problem Reports and Solutions: Problems Windows Has Identified window, click the OK button. Windows returns you to the Problem Reports and Solutions window.

Change Your Settings for Problem Reports and Solutions

To change the settings for Problem Reports and Solutions, click the Change Settings link in the left panel of the Problem Reports and Solutions window. Windows displays the Problem Reports and Solutions: Choose How to Check for Solutions to Computer Problems window, as shown here.

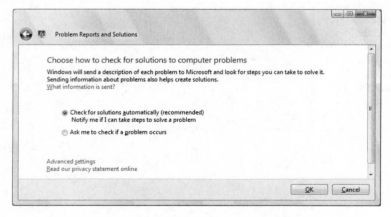

FIGURE 15.21

The Problem Reports and Solutions: Advanced Settings for Problem Reporting window lets you turn problem reporting off for all your programs or block it for particular programs.

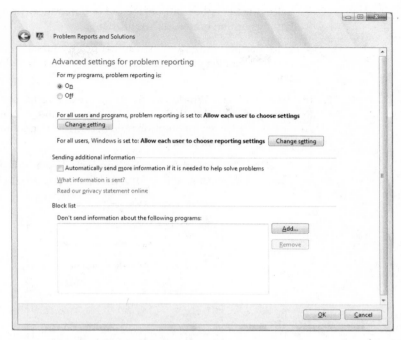

Select the Check for Solutions Automatically option button if you want Windows to check automatically whenever a problem occurs. If you have a permanent Internet connection, this option is usually handy. Otherwise, select the Ask Me to Check if a Problem Occurs option button. Windows then prompts to decide whether to check for a solution each time a problem occurs.

To reach the advanced settings for Problem Reports and Solutions, click the Advanced Settings link. Windows displays the Problem Reports and Solutions: Advanced Settings for Problem Reporting window (see Figure 15.21). Choose settings as follows:

1. In the For My Programs, Problem Reporting Is area, select the On option button if you want to report problems for programs you run. Otherwise, select the Off option button.

2. In the For All Users and Programs, Problem Reporting Is Set To area, examine the setting: On, Off, or Allow Each User to Choose Settings. To change this setting, follow these steps:

   ◆ Click the Change Setting button. Windows displays the Problem Reports and Solutions: For All Users, Turn Windows Problem Reporting dialog box, as shown here.

◆ Select the On option button, the Off option button, or the Allow Each User to Choose Settings option button, as appropriate.

◆ Click the OK button, and then authenticate yourself to User Account Control. Windows closes the dialog box and returns you to the Advanced Settings for Problem Reporting window.

3. In the For All Users, Windows Is Set To area, examine the setting: Allow Each User to Choose Reporting Settings, Ask Each Time a Problem Occurs, Automatically Check for Solutions, or Automatically Check for Solutions and Send Additional Information, if Needed. To change the setting, follow these steps:

◆ Click the Change Setting button. Windows displays the Problem Reports and Solutions: Choose a Reporting Setting for All Users dialog box, as shown here.

◆ Choose the appropriate option button.

◆ Click the OK button, and then authenticate yourself to User Account Control. Windows closes the dialog box and returns you to the Advanced Settings for Problem Reporting window.

4. If you want Windows to automatically send any extra information needed to resolve the problem, select the Automatically Send More Information if It Is Needed to Help Solve Problems check box.

5. If you want to exclude a particular program from error reporting, click the Add button, use the resulting Problem Reports and Solutions dialog box to select the program's executable file, and then click the Open button. Windows adds the program to the Don't Send Information about the Following Programs list box. You can remove a program from this list box by clicking the program's name and then clicking the Remove button.

6. Click the OK button. Windows closes the Problem Reports and Solutions: Advanced Settings for Problem Reporting window and returns you to the Problem Reports and Solutions: Choose How to Check for Solutions to Computer Problems window.

7. Click the OK button. Windows returns you to the Problem Reports and Solutions window.

Clearing Your Solution and Problem History

If you need a fresh start with Windows' problems and solutions, click the Clear Solution and Problem History link in the left pane of the Problem Reports and Solutions window. Windows displays the Problem Reports and Solutions: Windows Uses Problem Reports to Check for Solutions dialog box, as shown here.

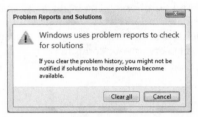

If you're sure you want to clear all the problems and solutions, click the Clear All button.

The Bottom Line

Deal with program hangs If a program stops responding, Windows may automatically display the End Program dialog box to allow you to end the program. If not, press Ctrl+Alt+Delete, and then click the Start Task Manager button. Select the program on the Applications page of Task Manager, and then click the End Task button. If ending the task doesn't close the program, you may need to end the program's process or process tree from the Processes page in Task Manager.

Use Event Viewer to identify problems Event Viewer lets you examine various categories of system events to find out what has happened or what has gone wrong. To open Event Viewer, choose Start ➤ Control Panel, click the System and Maintenance link, click the Performance Information and Tools link, click the Advanced Tools link, and then click the View Performance Details in Event Log link.

Keep Windows updated using Windows Update The Windows Update feature helps you keep Windows up-to-date by automatically checking for Windows updates. Windows Update can install updates automatically, or you can review available updates and then install them manually if you choose to. The disadvantage to installing updates manually is that some require Windows to restart, which loses you any unsaved work if you are not at your computer to save it.

Optimize your computer's performance Windows provides various tools for improving your computer's performance. Normally, you'll want to start by opening the Performance Information and Tools window (choose Start ➤ Control Panel, click the System and Maintenance link, and then click the Performance Information and Tools link) and checking your computer's Windows Experience Index score. If the score is inadequate for your needs, you can improve performance by adding RAM, using a USB flash drive as ReadyBoost memory, enlarging the paging file or move it to a different drive, or reducing the visual complexity of Windows.

Set suitable startup and recovery options If you've set up Windows as a dual-boot system with another operating system, you can choose the default operating system and the length of time for which Windows displays the boot list of operating systems. You can also configure what happens when Windows encounters a system failure—for example, you might dump the kernel memory and reboot the computer.

Use Problem Reports and Solutions The Problem Reports and Solutions feature lets you examine the problems that Windows has found with your computer. You can force Windows to check for solutions, view your problem history, and choose problem-reporting settings either for just yourself or for all users of your computer.

Chapter 16

Backup and Disaster Recovery

- ◆ Back up the data you value, and restore it when necessary
- ◆ Understand Windows File Protection
- ◆ Use System Restore to protect your computer and recover from problems
- ◆ Deal with problems booting your computer

Backup is one of the more tedious and least enjoyable parts of maintaining a computer—but even those who truly detest backup find it preferable to losing all their data.

This chapter shows you how to use the Backup program to protect your data and restore it when needed. It explains Windows File Protection, a mechanism for restoring essential system files that get deleted. It shows you how to use System Restore to create snapshots of your system to which you can restore it if things go wrong. And it explains how to deal with problems booting your computer.

Backing Up Your Data—and Restoring It

This section discusses how to use Windows's Backup program and wizards to back up your data for protection against problems and restore it when problems arise. It starts by talking about *why* you must back up your data, and the equipment and media you'll need to do so, before discussing the actual procedures for using the Backup program, which goes by the name Backup Status and Configuration.

To run Backup Status and Configuration, choose Start ➤ All Programs ➤ Accessories ➤ System Tools ➤ Backup Status and Configuration.

Why You Must Back Up Your Data

If you've used most any computer for any length of time, you likely don't need to be told why you *must* back up your data: because if you don't, you may lose it irretrievably. Windows Vista is arguably more stable than any other version of Windows yet released, but Windows Vista itself can still crash, as can any program running on it. If Windows or a program crashes, you will lose unsaved data.

Even if all your software is stable, your data is at risk from several other threats, of which the following are the most frequent repeat offenders:

Hardware problems   If your hard drive develops bad sectors or gets corrupted, you can lose anything from a file to all your files. Or your computer may get physically damaged: Laptops can get dropped, spilled on, or baked (or frozen) when left in cars. Desktop computers usually avoid such trials of gravity, precipitation, and thermodynamics but are threatened by the attention of children, pets, and worse.

Electrical problems Even if you use an uninterruptible power supply (UPS) to protect against power outages, severe electrical storms or disruptions can still damage your computer.

Viruses, worms, and other malware Even if you always use antivirus software and firewalls to protect your computer from as many threats as possible, you may run into a virus, worm, or other type of malware that damages your data.

User error You or another user may overwrite or delete files, deliberately or by accident.

Theft and vandalism Whether at work, at home, on the road, or in the air, your computer could be stolen. Even if you use a third-party encryption solution to secure your data against prying eyes, you'll still need a backup so that *you* can get at it.

The only reason for *not* backing up your data is if you're prepared to lose everything on your computer at a moment's notice. For example, say you keep a computer set aside for playing games or for testing buggy software, and you never put any valuable data on it. You might then be prepared to reinstall Windows and all applications from scratch at any point.

 Real World Scenario

BACKUP IS EVEN MORE VITAL FOR BUSINESS

If you're using Windows in your home business, backing up your files is even more vital for a couple of reasons:

1. You may be obliged to keep records of your business for a certain number of years.

2. However humble they may seem to you—a customer database in Address Book, spreadsheets in Works or Excel workbooks containing income and expenses, pending orders in Access, proposals in Word or WordPad—those files are probably even more vital to your business than you imagine. A survey conducted by McGladrey and Pullen, LLP, a firm of UK accountants, found that any company that's unable to get at its data for 10 days will *never* recover fully, and 43 percent of them will go out of business sooner or later.

What to Back Up

There's a temptation to back up *everything* on your computer, so that, if needed, you could restore it to the state it was in before the problem occurred with your computer or your data. But there's not much sense in doing this, because some of the files on your computer are essentially useless and others are easily replaceable. For example, there's no sense in backing up your paging file or your hibernation file, because they don't contain any data that you can actually use. And if you still have your Windows installation DVD (or installation source files), you can reinstall your operating system files easily. Generally speaking, you'll want to back up your data files—the information you've created—and your configuration files, but not the system files and program files that you can easily reinstall from CD or DVD.

Backup Status and Configuration *does* let you back up just about all the data on your computer, but you won't want to do this frequently, because it takes a long time and requires capacious backup media. In most cases, you'll do better to craft a strategy of regular complete backups with frequent incremental backups that will provide near-total cover of the files you've sweated over. That means backing up your data files and configuration files.

Backup Status and Configuration makes this process fairly easy, but you can help make it even easier by arranging your folders suitably for backup. In particular, keep your documents in a separate folder structure than your program files, as Windows encourages you to do (and as most Windows guidelines–compliant programs also suggest).

When to Back Up Your Data

Back up your data regularly and frequently enough that you never expose yourself to the chance of losing more data than you can recreate comfortably and easily. If you use your computer mostly for e-mail and entertainment, you might be comfortable backing it up only once a week or once every couple of weeks. If you use your computer for business, you might want to back it up every day, or even every few hours.

Instead of performing ultra-frequent backups, you may prefer to manually copy your current working documents to a removable medium (such as a USB key drive or a CD recorder running packet-writing software) every few hours. Doing so can be quicker and easier than running backup software.

UNDERSTANDING DIFFERENT TYPES OF BACKUPS

Windows files have an *archive bit* that can be set on or off to indicate the backup status of the file. When the archive bit is on, the file needs backing up; when the bit is off, the file doesn't need backing up. Most backup operations set the archive bit to the Off position once they've backed up the file. The next time a program changes a file, it sets the archive bit to the On position again, so the backup program knows that the file needs to be backed up once more.

The normal form of backup is to simply copy all the files and folders to the backup medium. Doing so takes a lot of time and space—and when you've copied all the files and folders once, you don't need to back them up again until they change. You can then perform partial backups such as these types:

Differential backup   A differential backup backs up all the files that have been changed since the last full backup. Differential backups *don't* clear the archive bit and thus grow in size. Say you perform a full backup on a Friday, then a differential backup on each other weekday. Monday's differential backup contains files that have changed on Saturday, Sunday, and Monday; Tuesday's contains changes from Saturday through Tuesday; and so on. To restore a computer using a full backup and a differential backup, you need only the latest differential backup and the full backup.

Incremental backup   An incremental backup backs up all the files that have been changed since the last full backup or incremental backup. An incremental backup clears the archive bit for the files it backs up, so that they don't need backing up until they change again. Incremental backups after the first have the advantage of being smaller than differential backups (again, after the first), but they have the corresponding disadvantage that you need to reapply each incremental backup in turn on top of the last full backup to fully restore the file set. If your backup media are capacious enough to store differential backups, differential is a better option than incremental.

Daily backup   A daily backup backs up only the files modified on the day you run the backup. To get full coverage with daily backups, you need to run them every day: Skip a day, and you might miss backing up an important file. But if you're conscientious about backing up daily, and you know the date on which you last changed the file you're looking for, you should be able to find it easily.

In Windows Vista Home, Backup Status and Configuration automatically manages your backups for you, freeing you from having to decide which type of backup to perform. Backup Status and Configuration isn't infallible, but it usually works pretty well.

Choosing Backup Media

Ideally, you want to back up your data to a medium that's capacious enough to hold it all but portable enough to keep in a safe place. The medium would also be inexpensive enough for you to be able to create backups as frequently as needed—perhaps every day.

At this writing, these are the best media for backing up a computer running Windows Vista Home:

◆ Recordable DVDs let you store 4.7GB on a single-sided disc or 9.4GB on a double-sided disc. Recordable CDs are too low in capacity to be practical for any but the most modest backups.

◆ A network drive can provide plenty of space, good space, and extreme simplicity for a backup, but ideally you need to have offsite backup as well. (If your network is extensive enough that your network drive *is* effectively offsite, you're on to a winner here.)

◆ A second (or subsequent) hard disk offers the capacity and speed for a complete backup. External USB 2.0 or FireWire hard drives offer portability as well. If you can afford a pair of external hard drives, they make a very effective backup mechanism. (And if you're an iPod enthusiast who keeps upgrading to Apple's latest offerings, you might find yourself with several surplus older-model iPods that will make great portable backup drives.)

◆ Online backup offers easy access from any computer that can connect to the Internet—but compared to other backup media, it's slow and expensive. If you have enough money and a fast enough Internet connection, you can back up *all* your data online. But for most people, online is an option only for small amounts of data. Backup Status and Configuration can't back data up directly to online storage, but you can copy backup files to such storage manually.

RESTRICTIONS ON BACKUP MEDIA AND DRIVES

Windows can't save backups to tape drives or to flash drives. Nor can you back up data to the same disk that contains it or to the system disk or the startup disk (also called the *boot* disk).

For technical reasons, Windows can back up only files stored on NTFS drives, not on FAT32 drives.

Configuring Backup and Running Your First Backup

To configure backups and run your first backup, take the following steps:

1. Choose Start ➢ All Programs ➢ Accessories ➢ System Tools ➢ Backup Status and Configuration. The first time you run Backup Status and Configuration, it displays the Automatic File Backup Is Not Set Up screen (see Figure 16.1).

⊕ Real World Scenario

KEEP KEY FILES ONLINE IN CASE OF DISASTER

With backup, you don't need to put all of your virtual eggs in one basket. Whatever form of backup you choose for most of your files, consider backing up key files in a safe location online. This can be particularly valuable if you travel for work and need immediate access to backups of your data if a crisis strikes—for example, if your laptop stops working when a flight attendant pours your coffee on it.

---

2. Click the Set Up Automatic File Backup button, and then authenticate yourself to User Account Control. Windows launches the Back Up Files Wizard, which scans for backup devices and then displays the Where Do You Want to Save Your Backup? screen (see Figure 16.2).

3. Choose between using a local disk and a network folder:

   ◆ If you want to use a hard disk, CD, or DVD, select the On a Hard Disk, CD, or DVD option button, and then choose the drive in the drop-down list.

   ◆ If you want to use a network folder, select the On a Network option button. Click the Browse button. Windows displays the Browse for Folder dialog box. Select the folder, and then click the OK button.

4. Click the Next button. The wizard displays the Which Disks Do You Want to Include in the Backup? screen (see Figure 16.3).

5. Select the check box for each disk you want to include. If you clear one or more check boxes, the wizard displays the warning symbol at the bottom of the screen to make sure that you know you are not backing up all of the disks on your computer.

FIGURE 16.1
The Automatic File Backup Is Not Set Up window appears the first time you run Backup Status and Configuration.

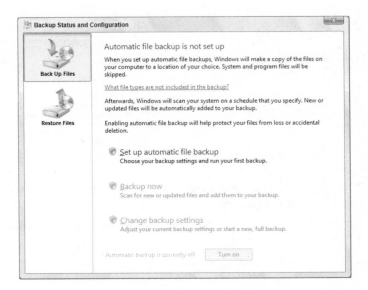

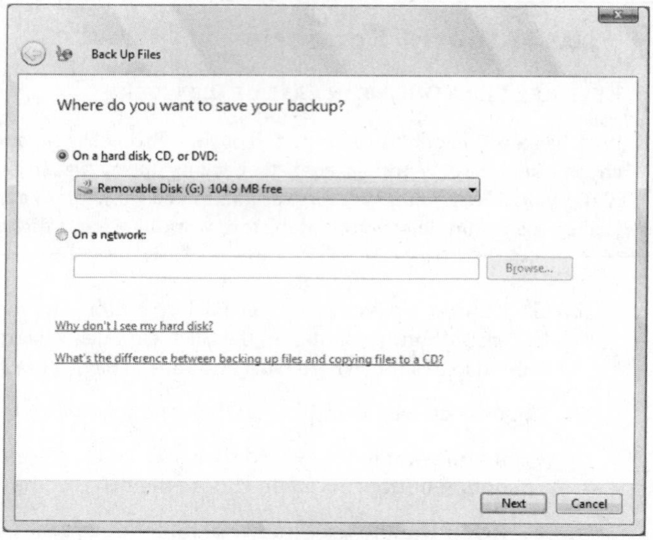

FIGURE 16.2
On the Where Do
You Want to Save
Your Backup? screen,
select the hard disk,
CD, DVD, removable
disk, or network drive
on which to save the
backup.

FIGURE 16.3
On the Which
Disks Do You Want
to Include in the
Backup screen, select
the check box for
each disk you want
to include.

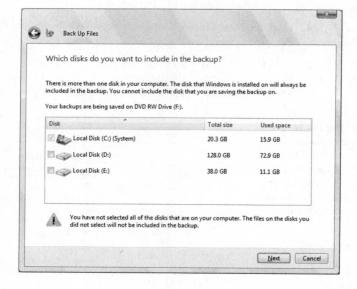

6. Click the Next button. The wizard displays the Which File Types Do You Want to Back Up? screen (see Figure 16.4).

7. Select the check box for each file type you want to back up.

8. Click the Next button. The wizard displays the How Often Do You Want to Create a Backup? screen (see Figure 16.5).

Be Careful When Backing Up Compressed Files

The Compressed Files category on the Which File Types Do You Want to Back Up? screen includes several file types that can be very large. To keep down the size of your backups and the time they take to run, you may prefer not to include these file types in the backups.

ZIP Files Zip is a widely used format for compressing and archiving data. You may want to back up zip files instead of the individual uncompressed files that you put in the zip files.

CAB Files CAB (Cabinet) files are used for storing and distributing data. Windows doesn't provide a tool for creating Cabinet files, so you're not likely to create them yourself. Most of the Cabinet files on your computer will probably come from Microsoft or other companies. You may not need to back up these files.

ISO Files ISO files are image files for CDs or DVDs. If you've downloaded an ISO file, you will normally do better to burn it to CD or DVD rather than back it up with your other files.

WIM Files WIM (Windows Imaging) files are disk-image files containing operating systems. Despite compressing their contents as far as possible, WIM files tend to be very large. For this reason, you may prefer not to back up WIM files. On the other hand, you will almost certainly not create WIM files yourself, so your computer may not contain any.

VHD Files VHD (Virtual Hard Disk) files are used by Microsoft's Virtual PC program, which allows you to run other operating systems on top of Windows. VHD files tend to be several gigabytes each, so you may prefer not to include them in regular backups. However, unless you use Virtual PC or a compatible program, your PC will probably not contain any VHD files.

FIGURE 16.4

On the Which File Types Do You Want to Back Up? screen, select the file types you want. Move the mouse pointer over a category of files to see a description in the Category Details box.

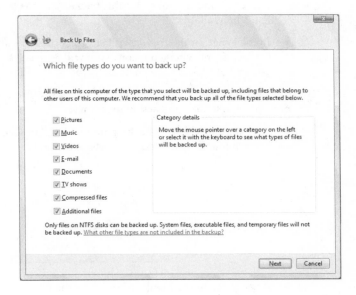

FIGURE 16.5
On the How Often
Do You Want to
Create a Backup?
screen, choose the
frequency and timing
of your backups.

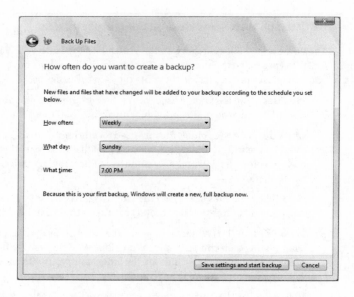

9. Choose the schedule for your backups as follows. No matter which choice you make here, Backup will perform a full backup right away.

   ◆ In the How Often drop-down list, select Daily, Weekly, or Monthly.

   ◆ In the What Day drop-down list, select the day of the week (for a Weekly backup) or the date of the month (for a Monthly backup). For a Daily backup, the What Day drop-down list is unavailable.

   ◆ In the What Time drop-down list, select the hour at which to start the backup running. Choose a time when your computer will be powered on but you won't be using it. (While you can work during a backup, the backup will run faster if you don't.)

10. Click the Save Settings and Start Backup button. The wizard scans your backup media and prompts you to take any action necessary:

   ◆ For example, if you're backing up to a DVD or CD, the wizard displays the Label and Insert a Blank Disk dialog box, as shown here.

   ◆ When you insert a blank CD or DVD, the wizard displays the Are You Sure You Want to Format This Disk? dialog box, as shown here. Select the Don't Ask Again for This

Backup check box if you want to suppress such questions for the rest of this backup (usually a good idea), and then click the Format button.

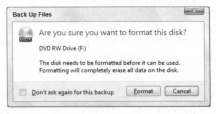

11. Once the wizard knows that your backup media is viable, it scans the files to back up, and then backs them up. If your backup needs further CDs or DVDs, the wizard will prompt you to insert them.

12. When the backup is complete, Backup Status and Configuration displays its main screen (see Figure 16.6), which shows details of your last backup. Click the Close button (the × button) to close the Backup Status and Configuration window.

FIGURE 16.6
When you complete your first backup, Backup Status and Configuration makes the Back Up Now button and the Change Backup Settings button available.

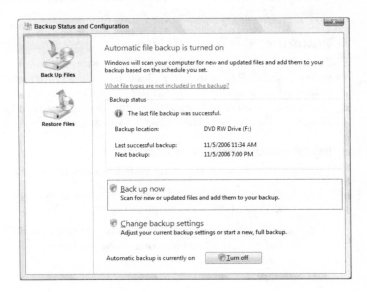

Running an Unscheduled Backup

You can run an unscheduled backup at any point by clicking the Back Up Now button in the Backup Status and Configuration window and authenticating yourself to User Account Control.

Backup displays a pop-up message over the notification area to tell you that the backup is running, as shown here. You can click this message to display the progress window.

When the backup is complete, Backup displays a pop-up message over the notification area to let you know, as shown here.

Changing Your Backup Settings

To change your backup settings, click the Change Backup Settings button in the Backup Status and Configuration window, and then authenticate yourself to User Account Control. The Backup Wizard runs you through the process described in the section "Configuring Backup and Running Your First Backup," earlier in this chapter. When you've specified the kind of backup you want, you can click the Save Settings and Exit button on the How Often Do You Want to Create a Backup? screen if you want to exit Backup. If you want to create a new full backup now, select the Create a New, Full Backup Now in Addition to Saving Settings check box, and then click the Save Settings and Start Backup button.

Turning Off Automatic Backup

To turn off automatic backup, click the Turn Off button in the Backup Status and Configuration window, and then authenticate yourself to User Account Control. When you want to turn automatic backup on again, click the Turn On button, and again authenticate yourself to User Account Control.

Restoring Files from Backup

Backup Status and Configuration lets you restore either some files from backup or all the files on your computer. Restoring some files is useful if you (or someone else) have deleted files by accident. Restoring all files is useful after a disaster such as a hard drive failure.

For either kind of restoration, open the Backup Status and Configuration window by choosing Start ➤ All Programs ➤ Accessories ➤ System Tools ➤ Backup Status and Configuration.

RESTORING SOME FILES FROM BACKUP

To restore files from backup, take the following steps:

1. In the Backup Status and Configuration window, click the Restore Files button. The Restore Files Wizard starts and displays the What Do You Want to Restore? screen (see Figure 16.7).

2. Select the Files from the Latest Backup option button if the files you want are in your most recent backup. If the files are in an earlier backup, select the Files from an Older Backup option button.

FIGURE 16.7
For a partial backup, the What Do You Want to Restore? screen lets you choose between restoring files from the last backup and files from an older backup.

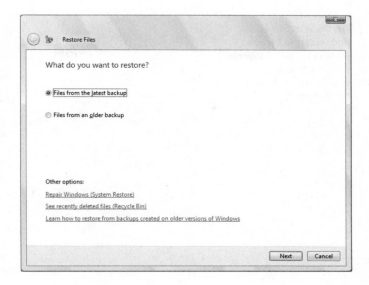

3. Click the Next button. Windows displays the Select the Files and Folders to Restore screen (shown in Figure 16.8 with some folders added to the restoration list). If you selected the Files from an Older Backup option button, the wizard displays the Select the Date to Restore From screen, which lists available backups. Select the backup you want, and then click the Next button. Windows then displays the Select the Files and Folders to Restore screen.

4. Build your list of files and folders to restore by using the Add Files button, the Add Folders button, and the Search button:

   ◆ To add one or more single files, click the Add Files button, use the Add Files to Restore dialog box (which is a renamed Open dialog box) to select the files, and then click the Add button.

   ◆ To add one or more folders, click the Add Folders button, use the Add Folders to Restore dialog box (which is another renamed Open dialog box) to select the folders, and then click the Add button.

   ◆ To search for files or folders, click the Search button. Windows displays the Search for Files to Restore dialog box (see Figure 16.9). Type the search term in the Search For text box, and then click the Search button. In the results list box, select the check boxes for the files you want, and then click the Add button. If the Search for Files to Restore dialog box is still open when you've finished searching, click the Close button.

   ◆ To remove one or more items you've added, select the item or items, and then click the Remove button. To remove all items, click the Remove All button.

5. Click the Next button. The wizard displays the Where Do You Want to Save the Restored Files? screen (see Figure 16.10).

FIGURE 16.8
Use the Select the Files and Folders to Restore screen to line up the files and folders you want to restore from the backup.

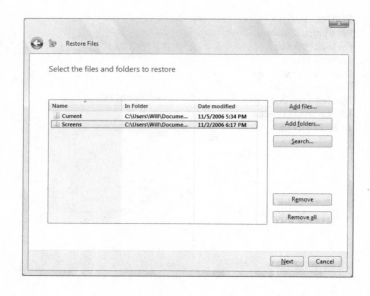

FIGURE 16.9
If you're not sure which folder contains the files you want to restore, use the Search for Files to Restore dialog box to find them.

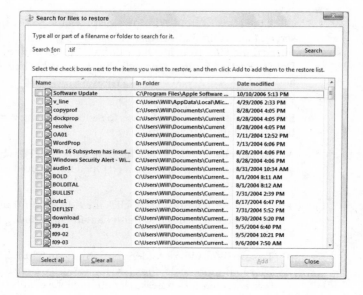

FIGURE 16.10

The Where Do You Want to Save the Restored Files? screen lets you choose whether to use the same locations (overwriting the existing files if necessary) or another folder.

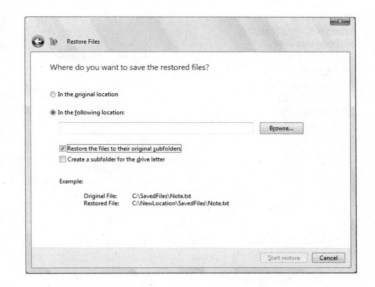

6. Choose where to place the files you're restoring:

   In the Original Location   Select this option button if you want to restore the files to their original folders, overwriting any versions that remain in those folders. This option is good if you've deleted or damaged the files.

   In the Following Location   Select this option button if you want to put the files in a different folder than where the originals are (or were). Click the Browse button, use the Browse for Folder dialog box to select the folder, and then click the OK button. Select the Restore the Files to Their Original Subfolders check box if you want the wizard to create the original subfolder structure *in the new folder you specify*. Select the Create a Subfolder for the Drive Letter check box if you want to include the drive letter in the subfolder structure within the new folder.

7. Click the Start Restore button. The wizard displays the Restore Progress screen as it restores the files and folders.

8. If you're restoring files and folders to their original locations, and if the restoration will overwrite existing files and folders with the same names, the wizard displays the Copy File dialog box (see Figure 16.11) to let you decide whether to copy and replace files, cancel the copy, or rename the canceled files. Select the Do This for All Conflicts check box if you want your decision to apply to all the file and folder conflicts in the restoration.

9. When the backup is complete, the wizard displays the Successfully Restored Files screen.

10. Click the Finish button. The wizard closes, returning you to the Backup Status and Configuration window.

FIGURE 16.11
When restoring files and folders to the original locations, you may need to decide whether to overwrite existing files and folders.

RESTORING ALL FILES FROM BACKUP

When you need to restore all files from backup (for example, when recovering from a disaster with a hard disk), take the following steps:

1. In the Backup Status and Configuration window, click the Advanced Restore button, and then authenticate yourself to User Account Control. The Restore Files (Advanced) Wizard starts and displays the What Do You Want to Restore? screen (see Figure 16.12).

FIGURE 16.12
For a full restoration, the What Do You Want to Restore? screen lets you choose between restoring files from the last backup, files from an older backup made on this computer, and files from a backup made on another computer.

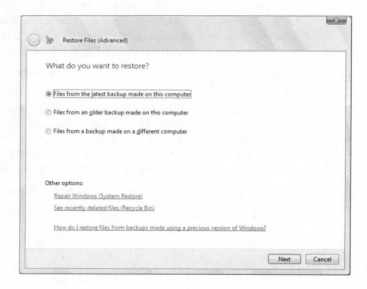

2. Select the appropriate option button:

Files from the Latest Backup Made on this Computer   Select this option button to restore the computer from the latest backup. This is what you're most likely to want. When you click the Next button, the wizard displays the Select the Files and Folders to Restore screen.

Files from an Older Backup Made on this Computer   Select this option button if you've found that the latest backup suffered a problem (for example, it was infected with the same malware that caused a problem with your computer's hard disk) and you need to go back to a previous backup.

Files from a Backup Made on a Different Computer   Select this option button if you're trying to restore your data on a new computer because the computer on which you made the backup has failed.

3. Click the Next button, and specify the backup you want to use:

◆ If you're using the latest backup, the wizard already knows which backup to use. Go to the next step.

◆ If you're using an older backup from this computer, the wizard displays the Select the Date to Restore From screen, which lists available backups by date. Select the date of the backup you want to use.

◆ If you're using a backup made on a different computer, the wizard displays the Where Is the Backup That You Want to Restore? screen (see Figure 16.13). For a backup on a hard disk or optical disk, select the Hard Disk, CD, or DVD option button, insert the optical disk, and then choose the drive from the drop-down list. For a backup in a network folder, select the Shared Folder on the Network option button, click the Browse button, use the Browse for Folder dialog box to select the folder, and then click the OK button. Click the Next button. The wizard displays the Select the Date to Restore From screen, which lists available backups by date. Select the date of the backup you want to use.

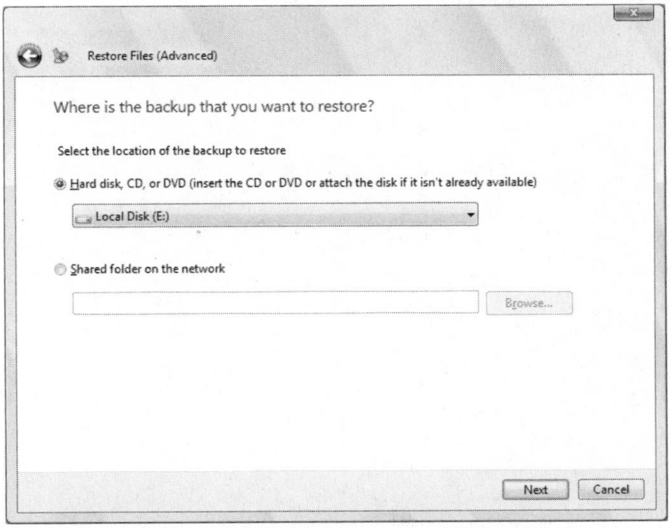

FIGURE 16.13
The Where Is the Backup That You Want to Restore? screen lets you specify the location of a backup that you've created on another computer—for example, the computer whose data you're trying to recover to a new computer.

4. Click the Next button. The wizard displays the Select the Files and Folders to Restore screen (see Figure 16.14).

5. If you want to restore all the files in the backup, select the Restore Everything in This Backup check box. The wizard removes the controls for adding files. Otherwise, build your list of files and folders to restore by using the Add Files button, the Add Folders button, and the Search button:

◆ To add one or more single files, click the Add Files button, use the Add Files to Restore dialog box (which is a renamed Open dialog box) to select the files, and then click the Add button.

◆ To add one or more folders, click the Add Folders button, use the Add Folders to Restore dialog box (which is another renamed Open dialog box) to select the folders, and then click the Add button.

◆ To search for files or folders, click the Search button. Windows displays the Search for Files to Restore dialog box (see Figure 16.15). Type the search term in the Search For text box, and then click the Search button. In the results list box, select the check boxes for the files you want, and then click the Add button. If the Search for Files to Restore dialog box is still open when you've finished searching, click the Close button.

◆ To remove one or more items you've added, select the item or items, and then click the Remove button. To remove all items, click the Remove All button.

FIGURE 16.14
The Select the Files and Folders to Restore screen lets you choose between restoring the entire backup and restoring just the files and folders you list.

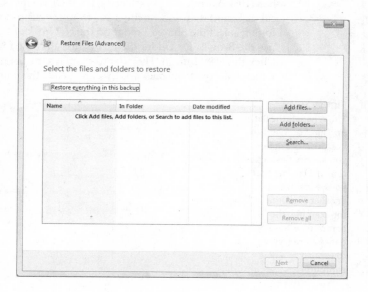

FIGURE 16.15

Use the Search for Files to Restore dialog box to find files with a particular name.

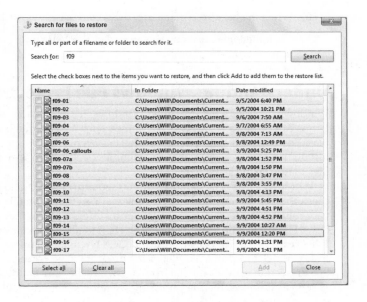

6. Click the Next button. The wizard displays the Where Do You Want to Save the Restored Files? screen.

7. Choose where to place the files you're restoring:

   In the Original Location Select this option button if you want to restore the files to their original folders, overwriting any versions that remain in those folders. This option is good if you've deleted or damaged the files.

   In the Following Location Select this option button if you want to put the files in a different folder than where the originals are (or were). Click the Browse button, use the Browse for Folder dialog box to select the folder, and then click the OK button. Select the Restore the Files to Their Original Subfolders check box if you want the wizard to create the original subfolder structure *in the new folder you specify*. Select the Create a Subfolder for the Drive Letter check box if you want to include the drive letter in the subfolder structure within the new folder.

8. Click the Start Restore button. The wizard displays the Restore Progress screen as it restores the files and folders, and then displays the Successfully Restored Files screen.

9. If you're restoring files and folders to their original locations, and if the restoration will overwrite existing files and folders with the same names, the wizard displays the Copy File dialog box to let you decide whether to copy and replace files, cancel the copy, or rename the canceled files. Select the Do This for All Conflicts check box if you want your decision to apply to all the file and folder conflicts in the restoration.

10. When the backup is complete, the wizard displays the Successfully Restored Files screen.

11. Click the Finish button. The wizard closes, returning you to the Backup Status and Configuration window.

Understanding Windows File Protection

Windows includes a feature called Windows File Protection that limits the damage you or programs can cause to Windows system files, such as dynamic-link libraries (DLLs) and executable files. You probably won't decide to delete system files, but poorly written programs, wayward installation routines, or malware sometimes overwrite system files with unauthorized versions of files that have the same name.

Windows File Protection uses digital signatures and catalog files produced by code signing to check that the files are authorized versions. You may remember from Chapter 13 that Windows is very reluctant to let you install a driver that doesn't have the appropriate digital signature. Windows File Protection extends this protection to all key system files, including all SYS, DLL, EXE, TTF (TrueType font), FON (font), and OCX (ActiveX component) files.

If you delete a protected file, or if a program overwrites or replaces a protected file, Windows File Protection restores the file from its own cache or from the distribution media for the software as soon as it notices the file is missing. Windows then displays an alert message box to an administrator notifying them that the file has been replaced.

There are no interface settings for Windows File Protection: It's on all the time.

Checking Files with System File Checker

If you suspect that there may be a problem with your files, you can run the System File Checker tool to scan your protected system files and verify their versions. If System File Checker finds a protected file has been damaged or overwritten, it replaces it with the correct file from its cache. You may need to provide your Windows DVD if System File Checker needs files that aren't held in the cache.

To run System File Checker, follow these steps:

1. Choose Start ➤ All Programs ➤ Accessories. Windows displays the Accessories folder on the Start menu.

2. Right-click the Command Prompt, choose Run As Administrator from the context menu, and then authenticate yourself to User Account Control. (If you're logged in as a Standard user or the Guest user, you'll need to provide an Administrator password.) Windows displays an Administrator: Command Prompt window.

3. Type the **sfc** command with the appropriate options using the following syntax

   ```
   sfc [/scannow] [/verifyonly] [/scanfile=<file>] [/verifyfile=<file>] [/
   offwindir=<offline Windows directory>] [/offbootdir=<offline boot directory>]
   ```

These are the parameters:

Parameter	Makes System File Checker
/scannow	Scan all protected system files immediately and repair any problem files.
/verifyonly	Scan all protected system files but not repair any problem files.

Parameter	Makes System File Checker
/scanfile	Scan the file specified and repair it if there's a problem.
/verifyfile	Scan the specified file but not repair any problem in it.
/offwindir	Use the specified offline Windows directory.
/offbootdir	Use the specified offline boot directory.

Checking System Files and Drivers with File Signature Verification

Windows includes a tool called File Signature Verification for checking that critical files on your computer include the appropriate digital signatures. You can run File Signature Verification by choosing Start ➢ Run, typing **sigverif** in the Open text box, and clicking the OK button.

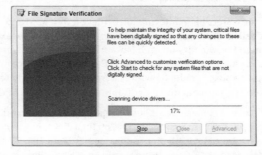

You can click the Advanced File Signature Verification Settings dialog box, which lets you specify exactly what to search for, where to search, and how and where to log the results.

When File Signature Verification has finished running, it displays a message box such as the one shown here to let you know what it found.

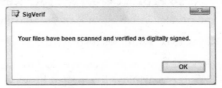

Using the System Restore Feature

Windows's System Restore feature provides a way of recovering from the consequences of installing the wrong hardware driver (or a buggy driver) or a dysfunctional piece of software.

How System Restore Works

System Restore uses a system of *restore points* that include information about the state of the computer's software configuration when the restore point was created. Windows creates some restore points automatically (one after the first boot, then one every 24 hours) and before you install an unsigned driver or a program that uses the Windows Installer or the InstallShield installer. To supplement these automatic restore points, you can create restore points manually whenever you want to. For example, you might choose to create a restore point manually before you install a new driver or program so that you can be sure a suitable restore point exists and you can identify it easily.

If your computer starts misbehaving, you can return your computer to one of the restore points before whatever change precipitated the trouble. You run System Restore and specify the restore point you want to return to. Windows then restores the computer's software configuration using the information stored in the restore point.

System Restore is very impressive technology, but it can't fix every problem. It affects only your system files (as opposed to your data files or backup files), so rolling back the computer to an earlier state doesn't delete any data files you've created or downloaded in the meantime. Likewise, returning to a restore point doesn't reinstate any data files that you've deleted since that point in time.

SYSTEM RESTORE: THE SMALL PRINT

System Restore stores the restore point information in files on your hard disk. The more restore points Windows creates automatically and you create manually, the more space they take up. Windows automatically reserves space for System Restore files on each hard drive volume that's protected with System Restore. Windows takes 300MB to start with, and can increase the amount of space up to 15 percent of the space on the disk. Windows fills this space gradually with restore point information as it creates restore points, so you don't lose all the reserved space at once—it disappears only as System Restore actually uses it.

Windows Vista doesn't let you change the amount of space System Restore takes up on a hard disk (as Windows XP did). However, you can turn System Restore off for a disk that you don't want to protect with System Restore. Windows then deletes all the restore points from that disk, freeing up the space they occupied. Normally, you need use System Restore only on the drive that contains your Windows files and your program files.

Choosing Which Disks to Protect with System Restore

To choose which disks you protect with System Restore, take the following steps:

1. Press Windows Key+Break. Windows displays the System window.

2. In the left panel, click the System Protection link, and then authenticate yourself to User Account Control. Windows displays the System Protection page of the System Properties dialog box (see Figure 16.16).

3. In the Available Disks list box, select the check box for each disk you want to protect. Clear the other check boxes.

   ◆ Your system disk appears with a Windows icon before it and the word (System) after it. Normally, you'll want to make sure the check box for this disk is selected. If you clear this check box, Windows displays the System Protection dialog box shown next to make sure you understand that turning off System Restore will delete all existing restore points. Click the Cancel button unless you're determined to turn System Restore off.

   ◆ When a check box is already selected, the Most Recent Restore Point column lists the most recent restore point created for that disk.

4. If you want to create a restore point now, click the Create button. Windows displays the System Protection: Create a Restore Point dialog box, as shown here. Type a descriptive name for the restore point (you don't need to include the date and time, as Windows adds them automatically), and then click the Create button. Windows creates the restore point, and then displays a System Protection dialog box to tell you that it has done so. Click the OK button.

5. Click the OK button. Windows closes the System Properties dialog box.

FIGURE 16.16

The System Protection page of the System Properties dialog box lets you choose which drives to protect with System Restore. You can also create a restore point immediately.

Restoring Your System to a Restore Point

To restore your computer to a restore point, take the following steps:

1. Close all programs that you're running.

2. Choose Start ➢ All Programs ➢ Accessories ➢ System Tools ➢ System Restore, and then authenticate yourself to User Account Control. Windows launches System Restore, which displays the Restore System Files and Settings screen.

3. Click the Next button. System Restore displays the Choose a Restore Point screen (see Figure 16.17).

4. Select the appropriate restore point, and then click the Next button. System Restore displays the Confirm Your Restore Point screen (see Figure 16.18).

FIGURE 16.17

On the Choose a Restore Point screen, select the restore point to which you want to return your computer.

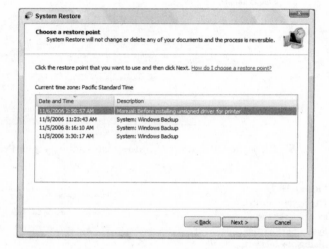

FIGURE 16.18

Before restoring your computer, System Restore asks you to confirm your choice of restore point.

5. Make sure you've chosen the right restore point, and then click the Finish button. System Restore displays a final confirmation message box, as shown here.

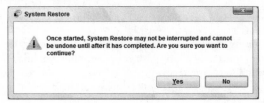

6. Click the Yes button. System Restore displays a status dialog box as it prepares to restore your computer. System Restore then shuts down your computer, restores the files, and restarts Windows. After you log on, you see a System Restore dialog box telling you whether the restoration completed successfully, as shown here. Click the OK button.

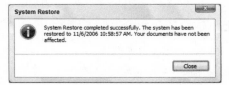

7. Check your system to make sure it's running correctly.

8. If the restoration didn't produce the effect you wanted, run System Restore again. You can choose a restore point further in the past or undo your last restoration (choose the Undo: Restore Operation restore point on the Choose a Restore Point screen).

Deal with Boot Problems

This section shows you how to deal with boot problems by using Last Known Good Configuration, Startup Repair, Safe Mode, and System Configuration Utility.

Restoring the Last Known Good Configuration

System Restore can work wonders—provided that your system can boot Windows. But if your system can't boot Windows, you need to take other measures. Your first step should be to try restoring the Last Known Good Configuration, as discussed in "Restoring the Registry to Its Last Known Good Configuration" in Chapter 11. Failing that, try using Startup Repair, as described in the next section.

Using Startup Repair to Fix Boot Problems or Run System Restore

If using the Last Known Good Configuration does you no good, or if you want to go nuclear without taking conventional recovery steps, try Startup Repair. Startup Repair is the modern equivalent of booting from a boot floppy to fix problems in your Windows configuration, but it also lets you launch System Restore, run Windows Memory Diagnostic Tool, and open a Command Prompt window so that you can issue other commands to repair Windows.

Real World Scenario

RUNNING SYSTEM RESTORE FROM SAFE MODE OR FROM SYSTEM RECOVERY OPTIONS

The normal way of running System Restore is from a normal Windows session, as described in this section. But if things have gone badly wrong with your computer, you may need to run System Restore in Safe Mode from the Windows Error Recovery screen (shown next) or the Advanced Boot Options screen. To enter Safe Mode, select the Safe Mode option on one of these screens, and then press Enter.

```
                        Windows Error Recovery

Windows did not shut down successfully. If this was due to the system not
responding, or if the system was shut down to protect data, you might be
able to recover by choosing one of the Safe Mode configurations from the
menu below:
(Use the arrow keys to highlight your choice.)

    Safe Mode
    Safe Mode with Networking
    Safe Mode with Command Prompt

    Start Windows Normally


Description: Start Windows with only the core drivers and services.




 ENTER=Choose
```

Once you're working in Safe Mode, the only difference from the procedure described here is that your mouse may not be working. If so, you'll need to navigate to System Restore, and through its screens, by using the keyboard.

If your computer has suffered a problem that won't let it boot to Safe Mode, run Startup Repair as discussed in the next section, and then launch System Restore from inside Startup Repair

To launch Startup Repair, take the following steps:

1. Boot from your Windows DVD as if you were installing Windows from scratch. Wait while Setup loads all the files required for setup.

2. On the first Install Windows screen, choose your language and (if necessary) the keyboard you're using, and then click the Next button. The second Install Windows screen appears.

3. Click the Repair Your Computer link. Windows displays the first System Recovery Options dialog box, which lists each installation of Windows Vista on your computer (see Figure 16.19).

4. Click the Next button. Windows displays the second System Recovery Options dialog box (see Figure 16.20).

FIGURE 16.19
In the first System Recovery Options dialog box, select the installation of Windows that you want to recover. Normally, you'll have only one installation of Windows Vista. If any installation is missing, click the Load Drivers button.

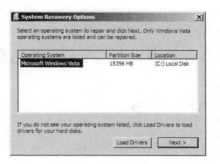

FIGURE 16.20
The second System Recovery Options dialog box gives you access to the full range of recovery tools.

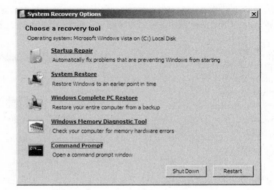

The following sections discuss the Startup Repair, System Restore, Windows Memory Diagnostic Tool, and Command Prompt recovery tools. The Windows Complete PC Restore recovery tool isn't available on Home versions of Windows Vista Home—it's available only on the Business and Ultimate versions.

IF YOU DON'T HAVE A WINDOWS INSTALLATION DVD

If you bought your computer with Windows preinstalled, you may not have a Windows installation DVD. Instead, press F8 during bootup to display the Advanced Boot Options screen, and see if your computer's manufacturer has included a Startup Repair option there for running Startup Repair from a Windows image file on a hidden partition. If a Startup Repair option appears, select it to run Startup Repair.

Some computer manufacturers don't offer this option. If yours doesn't, consult your computer's documentation for any custom boot screen of options that the computer includes. For example, some computers include a manufacturer-specific key that you can press during bootup to display a screen of system options.

If your computer doesn't offer this means of recovery either, you may need to borrow a Windows DVD from a friend in order to be able to use Startup Repair. (Don't *install* Windows from that DVD—just use the DVD to launch Startup Repair, and then repair your installation of Windows.)

USING THE STARTUP REPAIR TOOL

The Startup Repair tool attempts to fix any problems that are preventing Windows from booting—for example, damage to the computer's boot sector or boot files. Click the Startup Repair link in the second System Recovery Options dialog box to launch the Startup Repair tool, and then allow it to work. Figure 16.21 shows an example of Startup Repair in operation.

Startup Repair is often effective, but it's not always able to get Windows working again. If Startup Repair displays a dialog box such as that shown in Figure 16.22, you'll need to either tackle the problem yourself (for example, by using Command Prompt) or reinstall Windows. Click the Send Information about This Problem button to send information to Microsoft (if Windows is able to establish an Internet connection).

USING SYSTEM RESTORE FROM STARTUP REPAIR

If you're not able to run System Restore when you're logged in normally or from Safe Mode, you should be able to run it from Startup Repair. Click the System Restore link in the second System Recovery Options dialog box, and then follow through the process of choosing the restore point.

FIGURE 16.21
The Startup Repair tool tries to fix problems that are stopping Windows from booting successfully.

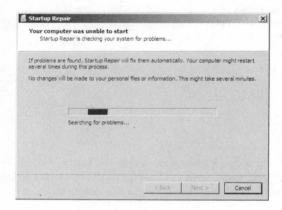

FIGURE 16.22
Startup Repair is unable to repair some kinds of damage.

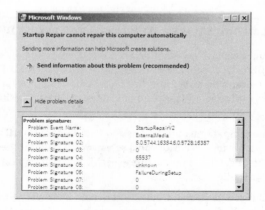

USING WINDOWS MEMORY DIAGNOSTIC TOOL

To check your computer's memory for hardware errors, click the Windows Memory Diagnostic Tool link in the second System Recovery Options window. Windows displays the Windows Memory Diagnostic Tool dialog box, as shown here.

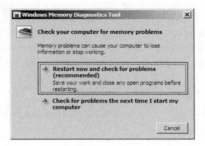

Click the Restart Now and Check for Problems button if you want to test straight away. Otherwise, click the Check for Problems the Next Time I Start My Computer option button if you want to try some other options in Startup Repair before restarting. When Windows runs the memory tests, you'll see a screen like Figure 16.23.

FIGURE 16.23

You can use Windows Memory Diagnostic Tool to check for errors in your computer's memory.

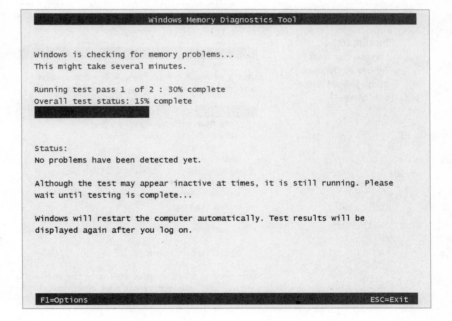

USING COMMAND PROMPT FROM STARTUP REPAIR

To issue other commands than the System Recovery Options dialog box allows, click the Command Prompt link. Windows opens a Command Prompt window, in which you can issue many of the same commands that you can use in Command Prompt when Windows is running. For example, you can create, rename, and delete directories, and copy or move files.

The command you're perhaps most likely to need is the DISKPART command, which displays a screen that you can use to create and delete disk partitions. DISKPART is a powerful tool that can wreck your computer's operating system much more effectively than most malware if you use it incorrectly—so if you do use it, make sure you know what you're doing.

Exiting Startup Repair

To exit Startup Repair and restart your computer, click the Restart button in the second System Recovery Options dialog box.

Booting into Safe Mode

If Windows starts to boot but then won't run successfully, try booting into Safe Mode so that you can troubleshoot the problem. To boot into Safe Mode, restart Windows (or start it if it's not currently running). When the computer is restarting, press the F8 key so that Windows displays the Windows Advanced Options menu (see Figure 16.24). (If your computer has a multiboot configuration, press the F8 key from the Windows Boot Manager screen.) Then select the Safe Mode option (or another, more appropriate, option) from the menu and press the Enter key to boot with it.

FIGURE 16.24
Use the Windows
Advanced Options
menu to boot into
Safe Mode.

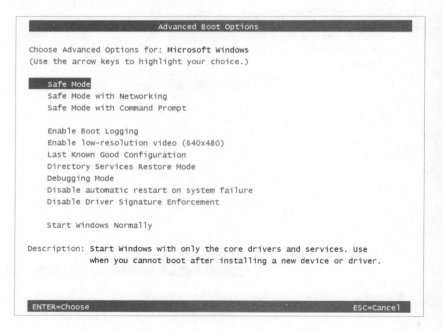

The Windows Advanced Options menu offers the options listed in Table 16.1.

TABLE 16.1: Options on the Windows Advanced Options Menu

OPTION	EXPLANATION
Safe Mode	Starts Windows with as few services and drivers as is possible, and uses the VGA.SYS alternative VGA video driver (at 640×480 resolution, and in 16-color mode) to force video compatibility. Use Safe Mode for troubleshooting drivers and services, including video driver problems.
Safe Mode with Networking	Starts Windows in Safe Mode but adds the network drivers and services. Use this option for troubleshooting drivers and services when you need to connect to a network (for example, to get replacement files) or for troubleshooting networking.
Safe Mode with Command Prompt	Starts Windows in Safe Mode but with a command prompt instead of the Explorer shell. Use this option for troubleshooting using command-line tools or when your mouse seems to be causing the problem. To shut down Windows, press Ctrl+Alt+Delete and use the Shut Down command. Alternatively, issue the explorer command and choose the Yes button in the Desktop dialog box that Windows displays, then use the Start button to shut down Windows as usual.
Enable Boot Logging	Turns on logging of the boot process for any Safe Mode option except Last Known Good Configuration. Windows logs the boot information in the NTBTLOG.TXT file in the %systemroot% folder.
Enable Low-Resolution Video (640 × 480)	Starts Windows using VGA (640 × 480) resolution but with the current video driver rather than the backup video driver (VGA.SYS). Use this option for troubleshooting display resolutions when the driver itself isn't the problem—for example, if the refresh rate or display size is set higher than the monitor can handle.
Last Known Good Configuration	Starts Windows using the Last Known Good Configuration. See the section "Restoring the Registry to Its Last Known Good Configuration" in Chapter 11 for a discussion of this option.
Directory Services Restore Mode	Applies only to Windows-based domain controllers, not to computers running Home versions of Windows Vista.
Debugging Mode	Enables debugging mode using the COM2 serial port. To use this option, use the COM2 serial port to connect this computer to another computer that's running a debugging program. Expert stuff.
Disable Automatic Restart on System Failure	Turns off Windows' normal behavior of restarting the computer after a system failure. Restarting the computer is usually helpful, but it may prevent you from seeing error messages that will enable you to look up and troubleshoot the problem.

TABLE 16.1:   Options on the Windows Advanced Options Menu *(CONTINUED)*

OPTION	EXPLANATION
Disable Driver Signature Enforcement	Turns off Windows' feature that prevents you from loading device drivers that have improper digital signatures. Disabling driver signature enforcement removes one layer of protection against malware, but you may occasionally need to do this to get your computer working again.
Start Windows Normally	Starts the computer normally. Use this option when Windows automatically displays the Windows Advanced Options menu after rebooting following an incomplete start caused by problems that you've eliminated (for example, power problems) or when you've displayed the Windows Advanced Options menu by mistake. (You can also press Esc to return to the previous screen.)

Using System Configuration Utility to Disable Startup Items or to Clean Boot

System Configuration Utility is a graphical tool for troubleshooting your system configuration (as opposed to a tool for *configuring* your system) by disabling startup programs and services that you suspect of causing problems at bootup.

RUNNING SYSTEM CONFIGURATION UTILITY

To run System Configuration Utility, follow these steps:

1. Press Windows Key+R. Windows displays the Run dialog box.

2. Type **msconfig** in the text box, press Enter or click the OK button, and then authenticate yourself to User Account Control. The System Configuration Utility window then appears.

Once System Configuration Utility is running, you can work with the options on its five pages. Most of the action takes place on the General page (shown foremost in Figure 16.25), which provides overarching options that turn on or off the sets of options presented on the other four pages.

OPENING SYSTEM CONFIGURATION UTILITY TO A PARTICULAR PAGE

To display a particular page of System Configuration Utility, you can use the *−n* switch when launching it from the Run dialog box, where *n* is a number between 1 and 5 representing the page you want to display. The pages are numbered from left to right:

msconfig -1   General page (displayed by default)

msconfig -2   Boot page

msconfig -3   Services page

msconfig -4   Startup page

msconfig -5   Tools page

FIGURE 16.25
System Configuration
Utility is a trouble-
shooting tool that
lets you turn off boot
elements—drivers,
services, initializa-
tion files—in order to
pin down problems.

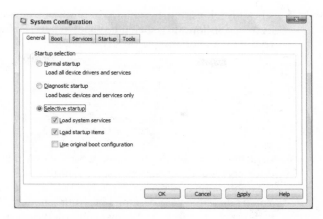

The General page offers three main option buttons:

Normal Startup—Load All Device Drivers and Services   This option button, which is selected by default, causes Windows to load all drivers and services. Leave this setting alone if the computer is operating normally. (But if it is, you probably won't be using System Configuration Utility.)

Diagnostic Startup—Load Basic Devices and Services Only   Select this option button when you want to strip down the device drivers that Windows loads and the services that Windows starts to a bare minimum. The services that Windows disables when you select this option prevent you from using some of the tools in Control Panel. This option is primarily useful for determining whether you have a problem with a basic driver or service or whether the problem lies later on in the boot process.

Selective Startup   Selecting this option button lets you selectively turn off items by using the check boxes below the Selective Startup option button. These check boxes relate to the sets of controls presented on the other four pages of System Configuration Utility and are discussed in the following sections.

How to Proceed with System Configuration Utility

The basic methodology for troubleshooting boot problems using System Configuration Utility is to perform a clean boot to eliminate all possible causes of the problem, and then gradually load drivers, start services, and launch startup programs until the problem reoccurs and you can isolate it. Take the following steps:

1. Close any other programs and run System Configuration Utility.

2. On the General page, select the Selective Startup option button.

3. Clear the Load System Services check box and the Load Startup Items check box. If your version of Windows comes from your computer manufacturer rather than from a retail box, there may be other check boxes (for custom features); if so, clear those check boxes too.

4. Make sure the Use Original Boot Configuration check box is selected.

5. Click the OK button. System Configuration Utility applies your changes and displays the System Configuration dialog box shown here, telling you that you may need to restart the computer and offering to do so for you.

6. Click the Restart button. System Configuration Utility causes Windows to reboot. When Windows comes back up and you log on, Windows will probably display a pop-up message over the notification area saying that it has blocked some startup programs (see Figure 16.26). You'll notice that your desktop looks different from normal, as Windows has turned off most of its graphical effects, and items such as audio services and networking may not be working.

7. Click the Blocked Startup Programs in the notification area, and then choose Run Blocked Program ➤ System Configuration Utility from the menu. (Windows Defender blocks System Configuration Utility from running.) Authenticate yourself to User Account Control. You then see the System Configuration Utility dialog box shown here. Because graphical effects are turned off, this dialog box has square corners and appears in shades of gray.

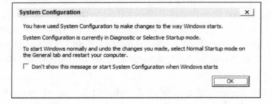

8. If appropriate, select the Don't Show This Message or Start System Configuration When Windows Starts check box. (Usually, having this dialog box displayed and System Configuration Utility launched automatically is a helpful reminder.)

9. Click the OK button. Windows launches System Configuration Utility (unless you told it not to).

10. Try running a few programs. If Windows seems to be working all right, select the Load System Services check box on the General page of System Configuration Utility, click the OK button, and click the Restart button in the System Configuration dialog box that appears.

FIGURE 16.26
System Configuration Utility suppresses not only some startup programs but also many of Windows' graphical effects.

If Windows *isn't* running properly, work with the items on the Startup page of System Configuration Utility to identify the service that's causing the trouble. Disable that service to prevent it from running. See the section "Controlling the Loading of System Services," later in this chapter, for details.

11. When Windows restarts, click the Blocked Startup Programs in the notification area, and then choose Run Blocked Program ➤ System Configuration Utility from the menu. Then see if Windows seems to be running stably. If it is, select the Load Startup Items check box, click the OK button, and then let System Configuration Utility restart the computer again.

If Windows *isn't* running properly, work with the controls on the Startup page of System Configuration Utility to identify the program that seems to be causing the instability. Prevent that program from running. See the section "Controlling Which Programs Are Started at Startup," later in this chapter, for details.

If the problem seems to be with your boot configuration file rather than with the drivers, services, or startup programs, use the controls on the Boot page of System Configuration Utility to adjust your boot configuration. See the section "Using a Modified Boot Configuration," later in this chapter, for details.

Once you've identified the problem and removed it, select the Normal Startup—Load All Device Drivers and Services check option button on the General page of System Configuration Utility and click the OK button. Let System Configuration Utility reboot your computer, and verify that it's running normally after it comes back up.

CONTROLLING THE LOADING OF SYSTEM SERVICES

The Services page of System Configuration Utility (see Figure 16.27) lets you disable individual services from running. The list shows the service name, the manufacturer of the service, and its status (Running or Stopped). You can sort the entries by any column by clicking the column heading. Select the Hide All Microsoft Services check box to hide the entries for all Microsoft services and make it easier to spot third-party services that might be causing problems.

You can turn off all services by clicking the Disable All button on the Services page or by clearing the Load System Services check box on the General page.

FIGURE 16.27

On the Services page of System Configuration Utility, you can disable individual services that you suspect of causing problems.

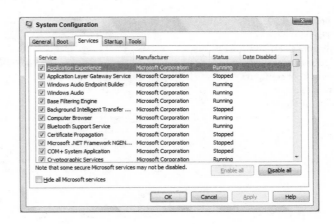

CONTROLLING WHICH PROGRAMS ARE STARTED AT STARTUP

To control which programs Windows starts at startup, use the check boxes on the Startup page of System Configuration Utility (see Figure 16.28). To disable all startup programs, click the Disable All button on the Startup page or clear the Load Startup Items check box on the General page.

USING A MODIFIED BOOT CONFIGURATION

You can modify your computer's boot configuration by using the controls on the Boot page of System Configuration Utility (see Figure 16.29).

To adjust the boot configuration, select the operating system entry you want to affect in the list box and click the appropriate control:

Set As Default Click this button to set the selected item as the default operating system to load.

Delete Click this button to delete the selected item. You can't delete the default OS.

Timeout text box Change the value in this text box to change the time for which the boot menu is displayed.

FIGURE 16.28
On the Startup page of System Configuration Utility, you can prevent individual programs from starting up automatically.

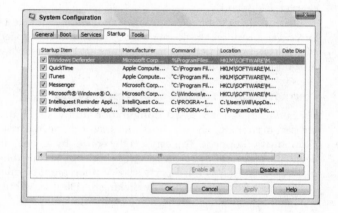

FIGURE 16.29
The Boot page of System Configuration Utility lets you adjust your boot configuration to overcome boot problems.

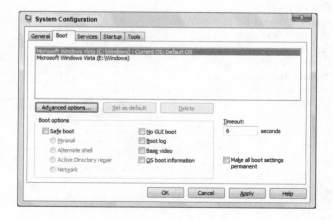

Boot Options group box   Select the check boxes for the options you want to use (see Table 16.2 for the meaning of the options). If you select the Safe Boot check box, select the appropriate option button as well.

Make All Boot Settings Permanent   Select this check box to apply your boot settings permanently.

In extreme situations, you may need to limit the memory that Windows uses or prevent Windows from dynamically assigning resources to PCI devices. To do so, click the Advanced Options button and choose options in the BOOT Advanced Options dialog box (see Figure 16.30). Again, the options add switches to the selected entry in the boot menu, and Table 16.2 shows their meaning.

FIGURE 16.30
The BOOT Advanced
Options dialog
box lets you tell
Windows how many
processors and how
much memory to
use, and configure
other advanced
boot options for
troubleshooting.

TABLE 16.2:   Boot Options Switches

SWITCH	EXPLANATION
Safe Boot: Minimal	Boots Safe Mode (with the minimal set of drivers and services).
Safe Boot: Alternate Shell	Boots Safe Mode with a command prompt instead of the Explorer shell.
Safe Boot: Active Directory Repair	Boots Safe Mode for restoring Active Directory from a backup. This setting is not applicable to Home versions of Windows Vista.
Safe Boot: Network	Boots Safe Mode with network support.
No GUI Boot	Disables the VGA video driver used to display graphics during the boot process.
Boot Log	Makes Windows create a log of the boot process in a file named NTBTLOG.TXT in the *%systemroot%* folder. View the log to see which drivers load successfully and which don't.

TABLE 16.2: Boot Options Switches *(CONTINUED)*

SWITCH	EXPLANATION
Base Video	Makes Windows use the standard VGA display driver when moving to graphical mode.
OS Boot Information	Forces Windows to display driver names while they're being loaded and, after that, information on the file-system check. This switch is useful for determining at what point the boot process is failing.
Number of Processors	Limits Windows to using the specified number of processors or processor cores.
Maximum Memory	Limits Windows to using the specified number of megabytes of memory.
PCI Lock	Prevents Windows from dynamically assigning input/output addresses and interrupt requests (IRQs) to PCI devices, leaving the devices as configured by the BIOS.
Detect HAL	Makes Windows detect the correct hardware abstraction layer (HAL) being used to translate Windows commands into commands the computer's hardware can understand.
Debug	Enables kernel-mode debugging. If you select this check box, you can choose settings for debugging in the Global Debug Settings group box. The Debug Port check box and drop-down list let you specify which port to use: COM1, COM2, COM3, COM4, 1394 (FireWire), or USB. For a COM port, select the Baud Rate check box and specify the baud rate to use. For an IEEE1394 (FireWire) port, select the Channel check box and specify the channel to use. For a USB port, enter the target name in the USB Target Name text box.

The Use Original Boot Configuration check box on the General page of System Configuration Utility lets you switch between your original boot configuration and the modified version you've created by using the controls on the Boot page. As soon as you make changes on the Boot page, System Configuration Utility automatically clears the Use Original Boot Configuration check box, so you'll need to select this check box if you've changed your mind about the modifications you've made.

USING THE TOOLS PAGE TO LAUNCH TOOLS

The Tools page of System Configuration Utility (see Figure 16.31) lets you launch widely useful tools for configuring and troubleshooting Windows. In the list box, select the tool you want to launch, and then click the Launch button.

FIGURE 16.31

Use the Tools page of System Configuration Utility to launch tools to help you configure and troubleshoot Windows.

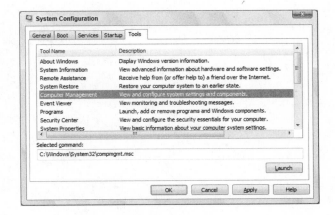

The Bottom Line

Back up the data you value, and restore it when necessary   If you have any valuable data, you must back it up so that you can restore it in case disaster strikes your computer. You don't need to back up your program files or other files that you can quickly restore from software CDs, but rather the data that you yourself have created. Launch Backup Status and Configuration by choosing Start ➤ All Programs ➤ Accessories ➤ System Tools ➤ Backup Status and Configuration, click the Set Up Automatic File Backup button, and then follow through the process for setting up automatic backups and performing a complete backup immediately.

Understand Windows File Protection   Windows File Protection helps prevent you from disabling your computer by deleting files you shouldn't delete—or by having malware overwrite such files for you. Windows File Protection automatically replaces deleted system files. You can also run System File Checker to detect and replace damaged system files, and you can use File Signature Verification to check that critical files include the appropriate digital signatures.

Use System Restore to protect your computer and recover from problems   System Restore automatically creates restore points, snapshots of your computer's configuration, to which you can restore Windows if your computer's configuration becomes unstable. You can specify which drives to protect with System Restore, and create restore points manually, by working on the System Protection page of the System Properties dialog box. To restore your computer to a restore point, choose Start ➤ All Programs ➤ Accessories ➤ System Tools ➤ System Restore, and then follow through the wizard. You can also run System Restore from the Windows Advanced Options menu or from Startup Repair if it won't run from a normal Windows session.

Deal with problems booting your computer   If your computer won't boot, first try selecting the Last Known Good Configuration item on the Windows Advanced Options menu. If that doesn't work, launch Startup Repair from your Windows DVD or from a manufacturer-specific configuration menu, and then run the Startup Repair item. If the first part of bootup works, but the latter part doesn't, you may need to boot into Safe Mode and use the troubleshooting options available. You may also need to run System Configuration Utility, which lets you turn off individual components during the boot process so that you can identify which component is causing instability.

Part 3

Using Windows Vista's Communication Tools

Chapter 17

E-mail with Windows Mail

◆ Collect the information you need to get started with Windows Mail

◆ Choose options for Windows Mail

◆ Suppress junk e-mail messages

◆ Read, send, and reply to e-mail

◆ Manage your e-mail messages

◆ Filter your e-mail to make it more manageable

◆ Add, remove, and configure mail accounts

◆ Customize the Inbox

◆ Back up your e-mail

This chapter discusses how to use the e-mail features of Windows Mail, the powerful e-mail and newsreader program built into Windows. (The next chapter discusses how to use the newsreader features.)

Before you can do anything with Windows Mail, you need to configure it to work with your ISP, so that's the first order of business. After that, the chapter shows you how to create and send e-mail messages, read e-mail messages, and send and receive attachments. Along the way, you'll learn how to filter your e-mail, how to block e-mail from certain people, and how to implement e-mail security.

Getting Started

To work through this chapter, you'll need to have an Internet connection (either broadband or via a modem) and an account with an ISP or e-mail provider. Also, gather the following information: your logon name and password, your e-mail address, your incoming mail server and its type (POP or IMAP), your outgoing mail server, and whether to use Secure Password Authentication (SPA).

For the next chapter, you'll also need to know the name for your ISP's news server, whether you have to log on to it, and (if you do log on) whether you must use Secure Password Authentication. So if you're asking your ISP for information, include those questions.

Starting Windows Mail

As long as Windows knows that Mail is your default mail program, the easiest way to start Windows Mail is to choose Start ➤ E-mail.

WINDOWS MAIL NO LONGER SUPPORTS HOTMAIL ACCOUNTS

Most versions of Outlook Express, the predecessor of Windows Mail, were able to access both free and paid-for Hotmail accounts, which made Outlook Express a popular way of checking Hotmail. Sadly, Microsoft has gradually restricted this access, first preventing Outlook Express from accessing free accounts (while still allowing access to paid accounts) and now preventing Windows Mail from accessing Hotmail at all.

To access Hotmail from an e-mail program rather than a web browser, use Outlook rather than Windows Mail.

 Real World Scenario

CHANGING YOUR DEFAULT E-MAIL PROGRAM

Windows Mail is included with Windows (at this writing)—but it's far from the only game in town. Other popular e-mail programs include Eudora (from Qualcomm Inc., http://www.eudora.com), Netscape Mail (from Netscape Communications; http://www.netscape.com), Mozilla Thunderbird (from Mozilla, http://www.mozilla.org), and Microsoft's heavier-duty e-mail program, Outlook (which comes in various versions of Microsoft Office, but which you can also buy as a separate program).

If you've installed another e-mail program, you may need to instruct Windows which one to use as the default e-mail program. To do so, right-click the Start button and choose Properties from the context menu to display the Taskbar and Start Menu Properties dialog box, and then click the Customize button. In the E-mail Link drop-down list in the Customize Start Menu dialog box, select the program, then click the OK buttons to close first the Customize Start Menu dialog box and then the Taskbar and Start Menu Properties dialog box.

Alternatively, create a shortcut to Windows Mail on your Quick Launch toolbar, on your Desktop, or in another handy location. If you want to run Windows Mail automatically each time you start Windows—not a bad idea, given how vital e-mail is these days—put a shortcut to Windows Mail in your Startup group (see the section "Making Programs Run at Startup" in Chapter 4).

Setting Up E-mail with Windows Mail

The first time you start Windows Mail, you'll need to set it up to work with your Internet connection and ISP. Follow these steps:

1. Choose Start ➤ E-mail. Windows launches Windows Mail, which notices that you don't have an account set up and so displays the Your Name screen to help you to set one up.

2. In the Display Name text box, enter your name the way you want it to appear in outgoing messages. (For example, you might choose to use your full name with middle initial, or you might prefer to use your diminutive and your last name. Or you might choose an alias.)

3. Click the Next button. The wizard displays the Internet E-mail Address screen.

4. Type your e-mail address in the E-mail Address text box.

5. Click the Next button. The wizard displays the Set Up E-mail Servers screen (shown in Figure 17.1):

   ◆ In the Incoming E-Mail Server Type drop-down list, choose POP3 or IMAP, as appropriate for your ISP. (If you're curious about these acronyms and their implications, see the next sidebar.)

   ◆ In the Incoming Mail (POP3 or IMAP) Server text box, enter the name of your ISP's incoming mail server.

   ◆ In the Outgoing E-Mail Server (SMTP) text box, enter the name of your ISP's outgoing mail server.

   ◆ If the outgoing mail server requires authentication to send messages, select the Outgoing Server Requires Authentication check box.

6. Click the Next button. The wizard displays the Internet Mail Logon page (shown in Figure 17.2).

7. Enter your account name in the E-mail Username text box and your password in the Password text box.

8. Select the Remember Password check box if you think it's wise. Using this option saves you time typing your password when you retrieve your mail, but it means that anyone who can access your user account on the computer can check your mail, too.

9. Click the Next button. The wizard displays its Congratulations page, telling you that you've successfully entered all the information needed to set up your e-mail account.

10. If you don't want Windows Mail to download folders from an IMAP or HTTP e-mail account, select the Do Not Download My E-mail and Folders at This Time check box.

11. Click the Finish button. The wizard closes itself and downloads the e-mail and folders unless you told it not to.

FIGURE 17.1
On the Set Up E-mail Servers page of the Internet Connection Wizard, specify the e-mail servers you'll use.

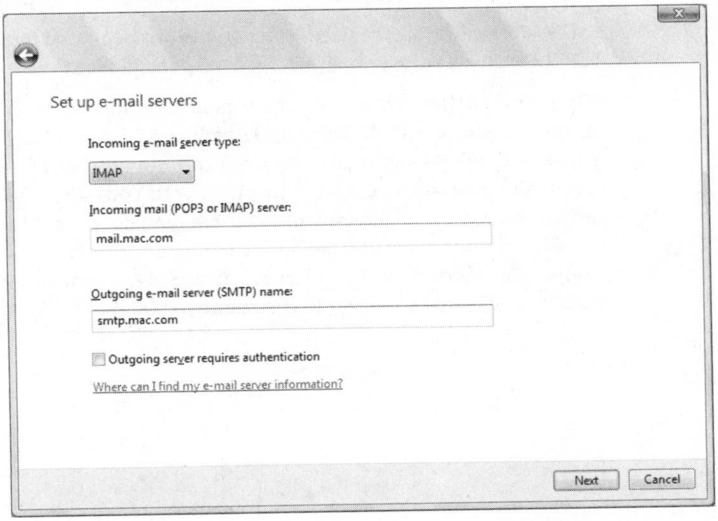

FIGURE 17.2
On the Internet Mail
Logon page of the
Internet Connection
Wizard dialog box,
specify your account
name and password.

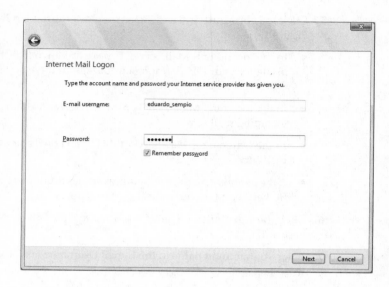

EXPERT KNOWLEDGE: POP3, IMAP, HTTP, AND SMTP

E-mail settings are full of acronyms: POP3, IMAP, HTTP, SMTP, and others. What do they mean, and how much should you worry about them?

To answer the second question first, you shouldn't worry about them too much beyond giving Windows Mail the correct information. Usually you won't have a choice of server types—your ISP will support either POP3 or IMAP for incoming mail and will use SMTP for outgoing mail.

Here's what these terms mean:

HTTP   Hypertext Transfer Protocol, the protocol on which much of the Web is based.

SMTP   Simple Mail Transfer Protocol, the protocol used for sending e-mail. SMTP is part of the TCP/IP protocol suite (which is largely responsible for the running of the Internet).

POP3   Post Office Protocol, the common or garden variety Internet mail-server protocol for storing and passing on mail. POP3 works well and is very widely used, but it doesn't have advanced features that IMAP has. POP3's major limitation is that when you check your mail, you have to download all the messages waiting for you. You can leave copies of all your messages on the server, but each time you download them, you download everything waiting for you. Some e-mail programs are bright enough to download only the messages that they haven't downloaded before. (Tech moment: POP3 actually uses SMTP to move the messages from the one server to another and from the server to the client.)

IMAP   Internet Mail Access Protocol, a newer protocol than POP3 and one that has more features. IMAP offers strong authentication and supports Kerberos security, but from the average user's point of view, IMAP's big advantage is that it's smart enough to allow you to manage your mail on the server. You can download just the headers of the messages so that you can decide which you want to download, delete messages off the server without reading them, and shuttle them between different folders on the server. These capabilities make IMAP especially useful for checking mail from multiple computers—for example, when traveling.

For e-mail users, IMAP offers many advantages over POP3. (The only disadvantage is that you may have to do more configuration with IMAP than with POP3, depending on how smart your mail client is.) Unfortunately, many ISPs aren't enthusiastic about implementing IMAP because doing so would probably result in a huge amount more mail lying around on their servers than is currently on them (which is already more than enough). Given that spam still seems to be increasing, and that legitimate (non-spam) advertising e-mail messages seem to be getting not only more frequent but also larger, *and* that more people are using e-mail and sending more messages and attachments, you can understand their concern.

The Windows Mail Screen

Once you've configured Windows Mail, and thereafter when you start it, it displays your local Inbox (see Figure 17.3).

If you chose not to have Windows Mail store your password, you'll need to log on when you launch Windows Mail. Figure 17.4 shows an example of the Logon dialog box you'll see.

If you change your mind about having Windows Mail store your username and password, select the Remember My Credentials button in the Windows Security: Logon dialog box before clicking the OK button.

FIGURE 17.3
The Inbox in the Local Folders structure

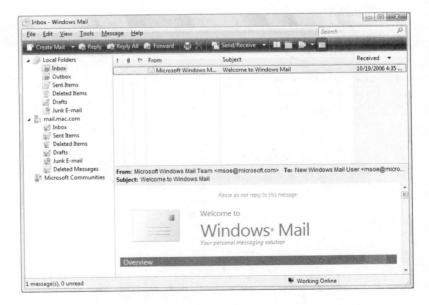

FIGURE 17.4

If you didn't save your password, you'll need to enter it in the Windows Security: Logon dialog box in order to log on to the mail servers.

Choosing Options for Windows Mail

At this point, you *could* start sending e-mail straight away, but it's a good idea to configure Windows Mail first. This section discusses the configuration options that Windows Mail offers.

Because of its complexity, Windows Mail has a host of options, many of which it's a good idea to know about. Because there are so many options, you may prefer to skim this section rather than read it in detail, and then return to it when you find there's an aspect of Windows Mail's behavior you want to change.

To configure Windows Mail, choose Tools ➤ Options. Windows Mail displays the Options dialog box. Then choose settings as appropriate.

General Page Options

The General page of the Options dialog box (see Figure 17.5) contains three sets of options.

FIGURE 17.5

The General page of the Options dialog box lets you choose how frequently to check for new mail and whether to play a sound when new messages arrive.

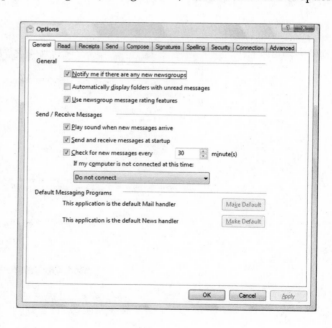

GENERAL AREA

The General area of the General page contains three options:

Notify Me if There Are Any New Newsgroups   Select this check box if you want Windows Mail to notify you of new newsgroups on the news server you're using. This option is a double-edged sword: It may be good to learn about new newsgroups that might interest you, but new newsgroups are created so often that leaving this option selected means that Windows Mail will offer you new newsgroups every time you fire up the newsreader. You may prefer to check for new newsgroups manually every now and then.

Automatically Display Folders with Unread Messages   Select this check box you want Windows Mail to automatically display e-mail folders and newsgroup folders that contain messages you haven't read. Most people find this option helpful. If you don't, clear this check box.

Use Newsgroup Message Rating Feature   Select this check box if you want to be able to use Windows Mail's feedback features for rating messages in newsgroups.

SEND/RECEIVE MESSAGES AREA

The Send/Receive Messages area of the General page contains four options:

Play Sound When New Messages Arrive   Select this check box to have Windows Mail automatically play a sound when it receives a new message. Clear this check box if you prefer to be uninterrupted; the Windows Mail status bar will still indicate any new messages that come in.

Send and Receive Messages at Startup   Select this check box if you want Windows Mail to send any pending mail and receive any incoming mail when you start it. Clear this check box if you want to choose when to send and receive mail.

Check for New Messages Every *NN* Minutes   Select this check box if you want Windows Mail to check for messages at regular intervals. Specify the interval in the text box (the default is 30 minutes). Clear this check box if you prefer to check for messages manually.

If My Computer Is Not Connected at This Time   If you leave the Check for New Messages check box selected, use this drop-down list to specify what you want Windows Mail to do if your computer isn't connected to the Internet when Windows Mail needs to send and receive mail. Choose Do Not Connect if you don't want Windows Mail to dial a connection. Choose Connect Only When Not Working Offline when your computer is disconnected from its Internet connection (for example, if it's a laptop and you're on the move). Choose Connect Even When Working Offline for dial-up Internet connections.

DEFAULT MESSAGING PROGRAMS AREA

The Default Messaging Programs area of the General page notes whether Windows Mail is your default mail handler and news handler. In Figure 17.5, Windows Mail is both; but if it's not, you can click the Make Default button to make it the default.

Read Page Options

The Read page of the Options dialog box (see Figure 17.6) contains three areas: Reading Messages, News, and Fonts.

FIGURE 17.6
The Read page of
the Options dialog
box lets you choose
whether Windows
Mail should automati-
cally download a mes-
sage you start viewing
in the Preview pane.

READING MESSAGES AREA

The Reading Messages area of the Read page contains the following options:

Mark Message Read after Displaying for *NN* Seconds   Select this check box if you want Windows Mail to mark a message as having been read when you've displayed it for the specified number of seconds in the Preview pane. Adjust the number of seconds if you want to be able to browse
quickly through messages in the Preview pane without Windows Mail marking them as read.
Clear this check box if you prefer to mark messages as read manually.

Automatically Expand Grouped Messages   Select this check box if you want Windows Mail
to automatically expand threads of messages in newsgroups. Clear this check box to have Windows Mail display just the original message.

Automatically Download Message When Viewing in the Preview Pane   Select this check
box if you want Windows Mail to download the body of a message when you select its header
in the message list. Most people find this option useful—but be warned that you'll also get any
attachments the message has, which can slow things down greatly if you have a dial-up Internet
connection. If you clear this check box, you can press the spacebar to display the body for the
header you've selected.

Show ToolTips in the Message List for Clipped Items   Select this check box to have Windows
Mail display a tooltip over a message header when the header is too long to fit in its column. To
display the tooltip, hover the mouse pointer over the header.

Highlight Watched Messages   In this drop-down list, select the color you want to use for
watched conversations. (More on this later in the chapter.)

NEWS AREA

The News area of the Read page contains two options:

Get *NN* Headers at a Time   These controls let you choose between downloading the specified number of headers from the newsgroup (if there are that many; otherwise you get however many there are) and downloading all the messages. If you frequent very busy newsgroups, select this check box, and reduce the number in the text box if necessary.

Mark All Messages As Read When Exiting a Newsgroup   Select this check box if you want Windows Mail to mark all messages in a newsgroup as read when you exit the newsgroup. Clear this check box to have Windows Mail mark the messages as read only when you've read them (this is normal behavior). This check box is useful if you tend to browse newsgroups that have a high volume of traffic with many posts that you don't want to read or manually mark as read but that you want to treat as read the next time you open the newsgroup.

FONTS AREA

This area contains two buttons:

◆ The Fonts button displays the Fonts dialog box, in which you can choose font settings for reading messages. For example, you might increase the font size or choose a different font.

◆ The International Settings button displays the International Read Settings dialog box, in which you can specify whether to use default encoding for all incoming messages. You shouldn't need to do this unless you find yourself coming up against apparently garbled messages that use different language encoding.

Receipts Page Options

The Receipts page of the Options dialog box (see Figure 17.7) contains three areas: Requesting Read Receipts, Returning Read Receipts, and Secure Receipts.

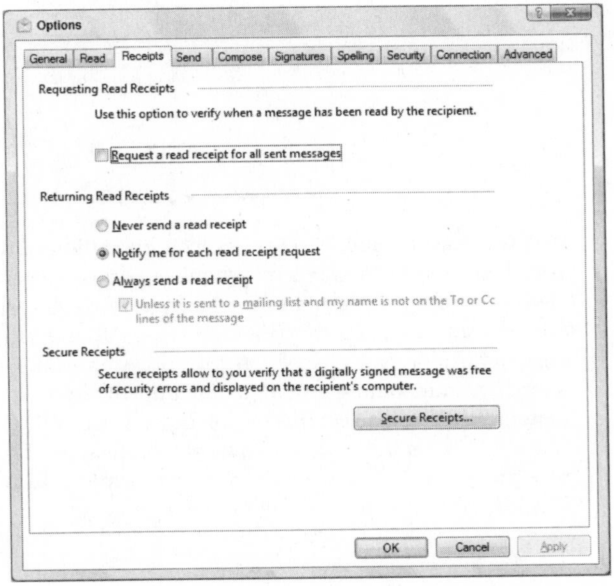

FIGURE 17.7
On the Receipts page of the Options dialog box, choose whether to request read receipts and whether to send read receipts that others request.

REQUESTING READ RECEIPTS AREA

The Requesting Read Receipts area of the Receipts page contains only one option, but it's an important one: the Request a Read Receipt for All Sent Messages check box.

Select this check box if you want to try to get a notification of when the recipient opens ("reads") the message. Whether you receive a receipt depends on whether the recipient has chosen to send receipts and on whether the ISP's mail server supports requesting receipts. Receipts often don't work, so don't rely on them.

If you want to request receipts only on certain messages you send, leave this check box cleared and choose Tools ➢ Request Read Receipt from the New Message window when composing a message for which you want a receipt. Similarly, if you want to request receipts on all but a few messages you send, select this check box and choose Tools ➢ Request Read Receipt from the New Message window to turn off the request on any given message.

A read receipt appears as a regular message in your Inbox, with the subject *Read:* and the original subject (for example, *Read: Dinner at 8?* for a message with the subject "Dinner at 8?") and details of when the message was sent and when it was read.

RETURNING READ RECEIPTS AREA

The Returning Read Receipts area of the Receipts page contains three option buttons and a check box for specifying how Windows Mail deals with requests you receive for read receipts.

Never Send a Read Receipt   Select this option button to make sure that Windows Mail never sends read receipts. This setting helps you avoid others tracking your e-mail reading habits, but it also prevents you from sending an e-mail receipt on those (usually rare) occasions when it might be helpful. (Windows Mail simply suppresses the requests without mentioning them to you.)

Notify Me for Each Read Receipt Request   Select this option button if you want Windows Mail to warn you about each request for a read receipt, as shown here. You can then decide whether to send the read receipt or not. Most people find this the best setting, because you find out whenever someone requests a receipt but you can decide whether to send it.

Always Send a Read Receipt   Select this option button if you want Windows Mail to go ahead and send a read receipt whenever anyone asks for one. This setting isn't a good idea for anyone who accepts e-mail from strangers, as the read receipts can confirm to spammers that your e-mail address is live (in other words, that it's in use). However, if you use the Safe Senders Only option (see the section "Suppressing Junk E-mail Messages," later in this chapter) to restrict your incoming e-mail to only approved senders, sending a read receipt on request isn't dangerous. If you select this option button, select the Unless It Is Sent to a Mailing List and My Name Is Not on the To or Cc Lines of the Message check box to prevent you from sending read receipts to mailing lists. Sending these receipts will annoy everyone on the group if they're not filtered out by software or by humans.

🌐 **Real World Scenario**

As Well As Read Receipts, Web Bugs Can Track Your Reading E-Mail

Read receipts aren't the only way that someone can track that you've read a message. Instead (or in tandem), a sender can include in an HTML-formatted message a hyperlink to a graphic or other content on a website. When Windows Mail goes to retrieve that graphic or content in order to display it to you, the sender of the message will know that you've read the message. (If you display the message multiple times, causing multiple downloads of the data, they'll know that too.)

These items are called "Web bugs," and the Security page of the Options dialog box (discussed in the section "Security Page Options," later in this chapter) gives you a way to deal with them.

Secure Receipts Area

The Secure Receipts area of the Receipts page contains only the Secure Receipts button. If you want to receive secure receipts for digitally signed messages you send, or send secure read receipts in response to digitally signed messages you receive, click the Secure Receipts button. Windows Mail displays the Secure Receipt Options dialog box (see Figure 17.8), which contains similar options to the Returning Read Receipts area, except for secure receipts. Choose the options you want and click the OK button.

FIGURE 17.8
For secure receipts, click the Secure Receipts button and work in the Secure Receipt Options dialog box.

Sending Secure Receipts Is Safe—But You May Still Not Want to Send Them

When you receive a digitally signed message, you can be sure that the sender is who they claim to be— at least, in as far as you can trust the certification authority that issues their digital certificate. So sending secure receipts is safe enough.

Even so, it's usually best to select the Ask Me if I Would Like to Send a Secure Receipt option button rather than the Always Send a Secure Receipt option button, so that you remain in control of which receipts Windows Mail sends.

Send Page Options

The Send page of the Options dialog box (see Figure 17.9) contains three areas, as discussed in the following sections.

FIGURE 17.9
The Send page of the Options dialog box

SENDING AREA

The Sending area of the Send page contains the following options:

Save Copy of Sent Messages in the "Sent Items" Folder   Select this check box to have Windows Mail save a copy of each message you send in the Sent Items folder. Clear this check box if you don't want to keep copies of messages you send.

Send Messages Immediately   Select this check box if you want Windows Mail to send messages immediately rather than put them in your Outbox until you issue a Send and Receive command or the next scheduled mail check occurs. Usually, you'll want to select this check box if you have an always-on Internet connection; if you have a dial-up connection that you don't keep connected as much as possible, clear this check box unless you want to launch the connection whenever you finish a message.

Automatically Put People I Reply to in My Contacts List   Select this check box if you want Windows Mail to create Contacts list entries for any person whose message you reply to who doesn't already have an entry. This option can be a labor saver, but it can also pack your Contacts list with useless entries consisting of just an e-mail address. If you prefer to add contacts manually (for example, if you send replies to people you don't want to keep as contacts), clear this check box.

Automatically Complete E-mail Addresses When Composing   Select this check box if you want Windows Mail to attempt to help you out by suggesting e-mail addresses from your Address Book to match addresses you type in the To, Cc, and Bcc fields in message windows. This option can be helpful, but it doesn't suit everyone—if you have contacts with similar names, this feature makes it easier to pick the wrong person or wrong e-mail address by accident. If you find this feature problematic, turn it off so that you can type the addresses in peace.

Include Message in Reply   Select this check box to include the message in the reply. Clear this check box to create blank replies.

Reply to Messages Using the Format in which They Were Sent   Select this check box to have Windows Mail create replies in the same format—plain text or HTML—as the message. This option is intended to help prevent you from sending HTML messages to people who prefer text, and vice versa, and is usually a good idea. Clear this check box to send all messages in the format you specify in the Mail Sending Format area.

 Real World Scenario

FAILINGS OF THE AUTOMATICALLY-ADD-CONTACTS FEATURE

The Automatically Put People I Reply To in My Contacts List option can be useful, but it has a couple of problems:

◆ First, if you make the mistake of replying to spam (either to buy or to request your removal from the spammer's list), this option will add the spammer's address to Address Book too.

◆ Second, if someone who already has a contact entry in your Address Book writes to you using an e-mail address other than their usual one, you'll get a duplicate entry for them that you'll later need to weed out of your Contacts list to keep it current and accurate. Having multiple contact items for the same person can be confusing and a waste of time.

SHOULD YOU USE PLAIN TEXT OR HTML? AND WHAT ABOUT STATIONERY?

In the early days of the Internet, all e-mail was plain text, because that was all that e-mail programs were designed to send. Plain-text messages were as plain as the term suggests, but they were small, and they traveled quickly through Internet servers and the wires. Then HTML mail was developed.

The advantages of HTML formatting (also called rich-text formatting) are clear: You can add to your messages not only formatting (such as colors, bulleted lists, and paragraph styles) but also hyperlinks, graphics, and background colors. By using HTML formatting, you can create messages that pack far greater punch than plain-text messages. From the recipient's point of view, the mail can look more or less like a web page—full of color, light, and impact.

Provided, of course, that the recipient can receive HTML mail. If they can receive only plain-text e-mail, they'll receive a plain-text version of your message plus a text version containing all the HTML codes. If the message contained pictures, they'll come through as attachments, and the recipient will need to view them separately. The resulting message will look pretty sorry, and all your effort in formatting it will be wasted. So it's not a great idea to send HTML mail to someone who can receive only plain-text messages.

These days, most e-mail programs can receive HTML mail and display it accurately, but some cannot. For security reasons, some computer users prefer to reject HTML mail. If you receive HTML mail from someone, you can be sure that their e-mail client can handle HTML, so you're safe sending them an HTML reply. And if you know the recipient is using Windows Mail, you can feel free to send HTML mail. But if you know that someone is using plain-text e-mail, don't send them HTML mail if you can avoid it. Simple enough—but if you're used to sending HTML mail, it's easy to forget that some people won't be able to read it, especially when you're sending messages to multiple recipients.

So for much of the time, you're probably safe in sending HTML mail. But think before you add gratuitous formatting to your messages. Just because you can add, say, a picture or a background color to your messages doesn't mean that you should. Use these features only if they will enhance the recipient's reading or understanding of your message. This is doubly true for colorful stationery, which tends to be more appropriate to personal settings than business settings. For example, if you wrote to your bank, you'd probably use regular paper (or letterhead) rather than a colorful greeting card. Likewise, if you send your bank e-mail, use no stationery or simple stationery rather than inappropriately colorful stationery.

Last, remember that HTML messages are larger than plain-text messages, particularly if you stuff them with finery. Anyone who has a slow Internet connection probably won't welcome an HTML message bloated with stationery and pictures where a humbler text-only message would have sufficed.

MAIL SENDING FORMAT AREA

In this area, select the HTML option button or the Plain Text option button to specify which format to use for mail you send. This setting is overridden by the Reply to Messages Using the Format in which They Were Sent option if you selected its check box.

If you want to adjust the settings for the format you choose, click the HTML Settings button or the Plain Text Settings button. The HTML Settings dialog box (shown on the left in Figure 17.10) contains the following settings:

Encode Text Using   Normally, you should choose Quoted Printable (the default setting) in this drop-down list. The other choices are None and Base 64.

Allow 8-Bit Characters in Headers   Select this check box if you want Windows Mail to display foreign character sets, double-byte character sets, and extended ASCII characters in the header without encoding. If you don't know what these character sets are, clear this check box, and Windows Mail encodes these characters in the header.

Send Pictures with Messages   Select this check box if you want Windows Mail to send pictures or background images included in the message with the message. Clear this check box if you don't want to send pictures (Windows Mail includes a reference to the picture instead) or if the recipients will already have access to the pictures—for example, if the recipients are on the same network as you.

Indent Message on Reply   Select this check box if you want Windows Mail to indent the text of a message to which you're replying. Usually, indenting the original message is a good idea, because it enables the recipient to distinguish it from your reply. If you clear this check box, Windows Mail left aligns the original message.

Automatically Wrap Text at *NN* Characters, When Sending text box   This option is available only if you choose the None setting in the Encode Text Using drop-down list. Set the number of characters at which to wrap the lines of text in outgoing messages. This is so that they don't wrap when displayed in text-only e-mail clients or when indented in replies. As a standard line length for text-only e-mail clients is 80 characters, the default setting of 76 characters allows for an indent of three or four characters on a reply before wrapping occurs. To allow two indentations without wrapping, choose a setting of 72 characters.

The Plain Text Settings dialog box (shown on the bottom in Figure 17.10) lets you choose between sending messages in MIME format and Uuencode format. (See the next sidebar for a quick explanation of MIME and Uuencode.) If you choose MIME, you can specify text encoding and whether to allow 8-bit characters in headers, just as you could in the HTML Settings dialog box. For either MIME or Uuencode, you can specify the number of characters for text wrapping. The Plain Text Settings dialog box offers a different indentation option:

Indent the Original Text with ">" When Replying or Forwarding check box   Select this check box if you want to indent original text in replies and forwarded messages and preface the indentation with an angle bracket (>) character. Clear this check box if you want original text to appear flush left.

News Sending Format Area

The News Sending Format area of the Send page essentially duplicates the Mail Sending Format area, except that its controls apply to news rather than mail. Select the HTML option button or the Plain Text option button as appropriate, and use the HTML Settings button or the Plain Text Settings button to set options for that format.

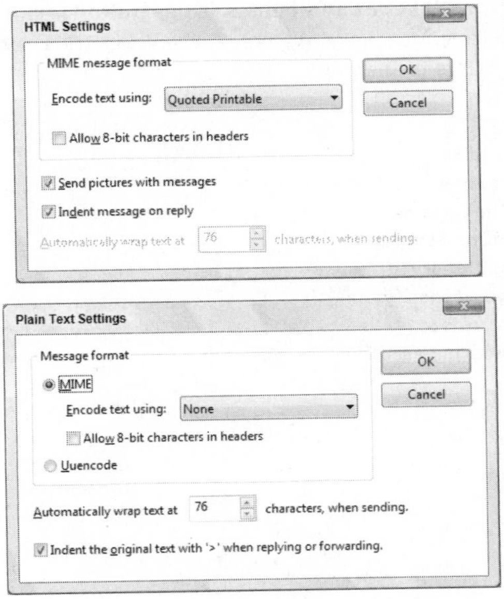

Figure 17.10

Use the HTML Settings dialog box (top) or the Plain Text Settings dialog box (bottom) to specify formatting for your messages.

EXPERT KNOWLEDGE: MIME AND UUENCODE

MIME is the acronym for Multipurpose Internet Mail Extension, an Internet specification for sending multimedia and multipart messages. MIME is widely used, and you should use it unless you have a good reason not to. S/MIME is the abbreviation for Secure MIME, a MIME extension that adds RSA security to MIME. (RSA is an encryption algorithm named after the initials of its creators: Rivest, Shamir, and Adleman.) S/MIME is a good choice for secure e-mail.

Uuencoding is a method of converting a binary file (for example, a graphic or an audio file) into a text file so that it can be sent in a text-only message. Uuencode is the utility for uuencoding, and there's a corresponding utility called Uudecode for decoding the resulting text (usually after transfer) back to the binary file. Uuencode and Uudecode essentially enabled the transfer of binary files via e-mail and newsgroups, but they've largely been superseded by MIME. You'll still find uuencoded files in some newsgroups and on systems that need to maintain backward compatibility with old standards.

Compose Page Options

The Compose page of the Options dialog box (see Figure 17.11) contains three sets of options for composing mail and news.

COMPOSE FONT AREA

The Compose Font area contains four controls:

Mail text box and Font Settings button This text box displays the font and font size currently selected for mail. Click the Font Settings button to display the Font dialog box, in which you can change the font, font size, style, and effects (for example, underline, strikeout, and color).

News text box and Font Settings button This text box displays the font and font size currently selected for news. Again, you can click the Font Settings button to display the Font dialog box to change the settings.

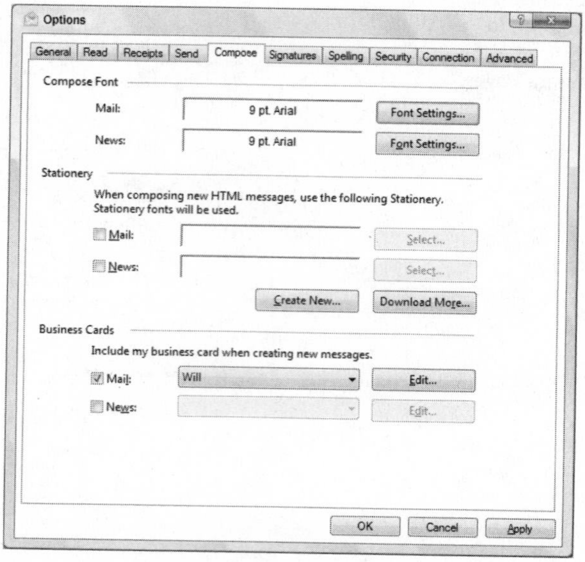

FIGURE 17.11
Use the controls on the Compose page of the Options dialog box to set fonts, choose stationery (if needed), and specify business cards to include with messages.

STATIONERY AREA

The Stationery area contains controls for specifying the stationery to use for HTML messages for mail and news. To use stationery, select the Mail check box or the News check box, and then click the Select button. Windows Mail displays the Select Stationery dialog box. Select the stationery item to use, and click the OK button.

Click the Create New button to start the Stationery Setup Wizard, which walks you through the process of creating custom stationery by choosing a background, font settings, and margins.

Click the Download More button to open a browser window showing the Windows Mail area on the Microsoft website, which offers more stationery files.

BUSINESS CARDS AREA

The Business Cards area contains controls for specifying a business card to include as a vCard with mail and news messages you send. To include a business card, select the Mail check box or the News check box as appropriate, and then choose the business card from the drop-down list, which contains the contacts in your Contacts list. To edit the business card, click the Edit button. Windows Mail displays the Properties dialog box with the details for the contact.

Signatures Page Options

The Signatures page of the Options dialog box (shown in Figure 17.12 with a signature added) contains three sets of options for creating signatures and adding them to your messages. A *signature* is text that usually gives your name (or assumed name), e-mail address or other immediately relevant contact information, and sometimes an epigram or quote. Use a signature only if it will benefit recipients of your messages.

These options are best explained through the process of creating and using signatures.

FIGURE 17.12
The Signatures page lets you create signatures to add to your outgoing messages.

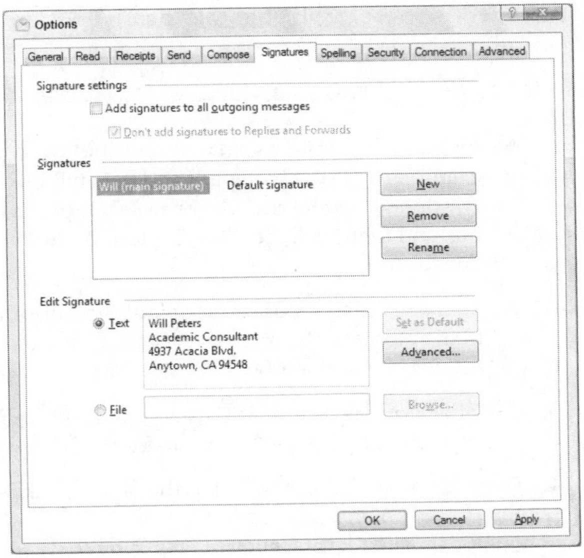

KEEP YOUR SIGNATURES SHORT—AND DON'T INCLUDE PICTURES

Signatures are best kept short. Try not to be one of those people who become so delighted by the possibilities of signatures that they include far too much text.

You can also put a picture in a signature by creating an HTML file that gives the path and filename of the picture, but this also is seldom a good idea.

To create signatures and add them to your messages, follow these steps:

1. Click the New button. Windows Mail adds to the Signatures list box a signature named Signature #1 (or the next available number), selects it, and positions the insertion point in the Edit Signature text box.

2. Type the text for the signature.

   ♦ If you have multiple accounts and want to use the signature for only one of them, click the Advanced button. Windows Mail displays the Advanced Signature Settings dialog box, shown next. Select the check box for the account, and click the OK button. Windows Mail closes the Advanced Signature Settings dialog box and applies the signature to that account.

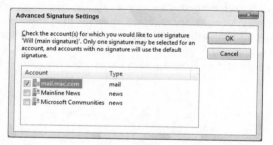

   ♦ Instead of creating a signature in Windows Mail, you can create one in a text file (for example, by using Notepad) and then tell Windows Mail to use it. To use a file, select the File option button, click the Browse button, use the resulting Open dialog box to select the file, and then click the Open button. Windows Mail enters the path and filename in the File text box.

   ♦ To make the signature your default signature, click the Set As Default button. (Windows Mail automatically makes the first signature you create the default, so you need take this action only with subsequent signatures.)

3. Click the Rename button. Windows displays an edit box around the signature's name in the Signatures list box. Type the name for the signature, and then press the Enter key.

4. To delete a signature, select it in the Signatures list box, and then click the Remove button.

5. Select the Add Signatures to All Outgoing Messages check box if you want to do just that.

◆ If you select this check box, select or clear the Don't Add Signatures to Replies and Forwards check box. Windows Mail selects this check box by default to prevent you unintentionally adding signatures to replies and forwarded messages (which probably won't need signatures).

◆ If you choose not to add signatures to all your outgoing messages, you can apply a signature to an individual message from the New Message window by choosing Insert ➢ Signature.

Spelling Page Options

The Spelling page of the Options dialog box (shown in Figure 17.13) lets you choose how to check spelling in the messages you send.

FIGURE 17.13
Configure spell-checking options for your outgoing messages on the Spelling page of the Options dialog box.

SETTINGS AREA

The Settings area of the Spelling page contains only one option:

Always Check Spelling Before Sending check box   Select this check box if you want Windows Mail to check the spelling automatically when you send a message. Many people find this setting helpful for avoiding potentially embarrassing spelling mistakes. If this isn't a concern, or if you prefer to check spelling manually when you want, clear this check box.

WHEN CHECKING SPELLING, ALWAYS IGNORE AREA

The When Checking Spelling, Always Ignore area of the Spelling page contains the following options:

Words in UPPERCASE   Select this check box to make the spelling checker ignore any words that are all uppercase.

Words with Numbers   Select this check box to make the spelling checker ignore any words that contain numbers.

The Original Text in a Reply or Forward   Select this check box if you want the spelling checker to ignore the text of any message that you forward or reply to. In most cases, there's little point in correcting other people's spelling.

Internet Addresses check box   Select this check box if you want the spelling checker to ignore any URLs or other Internet addresses in a message. You'll seldom want to spell-check these items.

LANGUAGE AREA

The Language area of the Spelling page contains only one option:

Language   In this drop-down list, verify that the correct language for checking spelling is selected.

Security Page Options

The Security page of the Options dialog box (see Figure 17.14) contains options for securing Windows Mail. These options work closely with those you set for Internet Explorer (discussed in Chapter 2).

VIRUS PROTECTION AREA

The Virus Protection area of the Security page contains the following options:

Select the Internet Explorer Security Zone to Use   Select the Internet Zone option button or the Restricted Sites Zone option button. Usually, the Restricted Sites Zone option button is a better choice, but you may lose some functionality when you select it.

Warn Me When Other Applications Try to Send Mail As Me   Select this check box if you want Windows Mail to warn you when other programs try to send mail under your identity. This setting offers some protection against viruses that send mail in your name, but it may also object to some legitimate operations. For example, sending Remote Assistance requests via e-mail may trigger this warning.

Do Not Allow Attachments to Be Saved or Opened That Could Potentially Be a Virus check box   Select this check box if you want Windows Mail to refuse documents of file types that might contain viruses. This setting offers you some protection against viruses, but it may cause Windows Mail to discard some harmless documents because their file type is suspect. In many cases, you'll be better off using good, up-to-date antivirus software than using this setting. See the sidebar "Protecting Yourself against Malicious Attachments," later in this chapter, for advice on how to handle attachments.

FIGURE 17.14
Choose security settings on the Security page of the Options dialog box.

DOWNLOAD IMAGES AREA

The Download Images area contains only one setting, but it's a crucial one: the Block Images and Other External Content in HTML E-mail check box. This check box, which is selected by default, prevents Web bugs (such as transparent, one-pixel-square graphics) from executing in Windows Mail. Web bugs can be used to track when and how often you open a message, so you'll probably want to keep this check box selected to prevent Web bugs from operating.

When this feature blocks images or other content, Windows Mail displays a bar like the one shown here to let you know. Click the bar if you want to download the pictures and display them. This manual loading is a small price to pay for the privacy this setting provides.

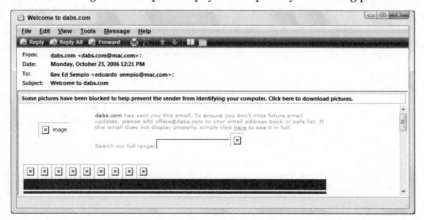

SECURE MAIL AREA

The Secure Mail area of the Security page contains options for specifying how to handle secure mail—messages that are either encrypted to protect their contents or signed with a digital certificate to verify the sender.

Before you can send an encrypted message, you must add the recipient's certificate to your Contacts list. Likewise, anyone who wants to send you an encrypted message must have your public key.

Digital IDs   Click this button to display the Certificates dialog box (discussed in the section "Using Digital Certificates" in Chapter 2).

Get Digital ID   Click this button to open a browser window containing information from the Microsoft website on where to obtain a digital certificate.

Encrypt Contents and Attachments for All Outgoing Messages   Select this check box if you want to try to encrypt all the messages and attachments you send. You need to have the recipient's certificate in your Contacts list in order to send an encrypted message or attachment. If you select this option and send messages or attachments to people whose digital certificates you don't have, Windows Mail warns you of the problem and offers you the choice of sending the item without encryption or canceling sending it.

Digitally Sign All Outgoing Messages   Select this check box if you want to digitally sign all the messages you send.

To choose advanced security settings, click the Advanced button. Windows Mail displays the Advanced Security Settings dialog box (see Figure 17.15), which offers the following options:

Warn on Encrypting Messages with Less than This Strength drop-down list   Select the minimum acceptable level of encryption for messages: 40 bits, 56 bits, 64 bits, 128 bits, or 168 bits. (See the next sidebar for an explanation of the bit-ness of encryption—but basically, the higher the number, the more secure.) Windows Mail then warns you if you're about to send a message with a lower level of encryption.

Always Encrypt to Myself When Sending Encrypted Mail   Select this check box if you want Windows Mail to encrypt with your digital certificate the copy of the message that it puts in your Sent Mail folder. (If you don't encrypt this copy, you won't be able to read it.)

FIGURE 17.15
The Advanced Security Settings dialog box lets you choose settings for encryption and digital signing.

Include My Digital ID When Sending Signed Messages Select this check box to send your digital certificate with a digitally signed message so that the recipient can use the public key to read it. (If the recipient already has your public key, you don't need to send the digital certificate again.)

Encode Message Before Signing (Opaque Signing) Select this check box if you want to encode your digitally signed messages in order to keep the signature secure. If you use this option, the recipient's e-mail program must support S/MIME. Otherwise, they won't be able to read the message.

Add Senders' Certificates to My Windows Contacts Select this check box to have Windows Mail automatically add certificates from messages you receive to your Contacts list. This option is usually a good way to build your collection of certificates so that you can gradually send secure messages to more people (assuming you want to do so).

Check for Revoked Digital IDs list Select the Only When Online option button or the Never option button to specify when to check that digital IDs you receive are current and haven't been revoked.

Click the OK button. Windows Mail closes the Advanced Security Settings dialog box and returns you to the Options dialog box.

 Real World Scenario

SHOULD YOU USE ENCRYPTION? AND IF SO, HOW MUCH?

Internet e-mail is inherently insecure, because it passes through a shared medium (the Internet). The standard analogy used to illustrate the insecurity of Internet e-mail is that of a postcard sent through the mail: At any point, anyone who can get hold of it can read its contents. Conversely, anyone looking for that particular postcard would have a hard time finding it among all the other mail being sent unless they were able to intercept it close to its source or its destination.

So the standard advice goes that you shouldn't write anything in an unencrypted e-mail that you wouldn't mind the whole world reading, because anyone who reads the e-mail could publish it worldwide almost instantly by posting it on a website or to a newsgroup. (The recipient could also do this, but presumably you trust them enough to read the content of the message.)

There's much truth in this, but most people send unencrypted e-mail all day long without suffering any adverse consequences. However, if you want to make sure that nobody who intercepts a message can read it, you need to secure the message by using encryption.

As you saw a page or so ago, Windows Mail offers various strengths of encryption: 40 bit, 56 bit, 64 bit, 128 bit, and 168 bit. Which should you use?

Very generally speaking, the more bits, the more secure the encryption, and the more processing power it takes to encode and decode. The weakest encryption strengths, 40 bit and 56 bit, used to be the strongest encryption the U.S. government allowed software firms to export. (Unlike with beer, export-strength encryption is weaker than the normal article.) The next strength, 64-bit encryption, is marginally stronger than 40-bit and 56-bit, but probably not enough so to be worth using if you're concerned about security. While 128-bit encryption is considered strong encryption, if you want as much protection as possible, you should go straight to the 168-bit level.

Connection Page Options

The Connection page of the Options dialog box (see Figure 17.16) contains only three options:

Ask Before Switching Dial-up Connections Select this check box if you want Windows Mail to check with you before switching from a connection that isn't working to another connection. If you have only one dial-up connection, you don't need to worry about this setting.

Hang Up After Sending and Receiving Select this check box if you want Windows Mail to hang up your dial-up connection once it has finished sending and receiving mail when you issue a Send and Receive command. This setting is most useful with pay-as-you-go Internet connections.

Change button Click this button to display the Connections page of the Internet Properties dialog box (discussed in the section "Preventing Internet Explorer from Connecting Automatically" in Chapter 2).

FIGURE 17.16
The Connection page of the Options dialog box lets you tell Windows Mail how to deal with dial-up connections.

Advanced Page Options

The Advanced page of the Options dialog box (see Figure 17.17) lets you configure an assortment of settings.

CONTACT ATTACHMENT CONVERSION

Choose what you want Windows Mail to do with attachments.

◆ Select the Always Convert Contacts Attachments to vCard option button if you want to create vCards that you can use not only with Windows Vista but also with earlier versions of Windows.

◆ Select the Ask Me Every Time option button if you want Windows Mail to prompt you to decide each time you receive a vCard.

◆ Select the Leave Contact Attachments in Contact Format if you want Windows Mail to leave the attachments in the Contact format. This format is compatible with Windows Vista but not with earlier versions of Windows.

IMAP

Select the Use the "Deleted Items" Folder with IMAP Accounts check box if you want Windows Mail to move items you delete to your Deleted Items folder. This behavior is usually helpful. If you clear this check box, Windows Mail leaves deleted items in your message list until you delete them from the IMAP server. (This is the way IMAP is supposed to work, but many people find it odd to delete an item but have it remain in place.)

FIGURE 17.17
Choose settings for contacts, IMAP, message threads, and replies on the Advanced page of the Options dialog box.

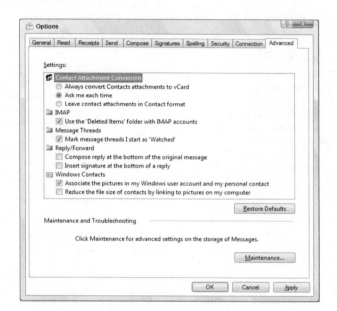

MESSAGE THREADS

Select the Mark Message Threads I Start as "Watched" check box if you want Windows Mail to set a watch on message threads that you initiate. This setting is usually helpful.

REPLY/FORWARD

Select the Compose Reply at the Bottom of the Original Message check box if you want Windows Mail to position the insertion point at the bottom of a message that you're forwarding or to which you're replying. If you clear this check box, Windows Mail places the insertion point at the beginning of the message, where the recipient's eye will find it first.

Select the Insert Signature at the Bottom of a Reply check box if you want Windows Mail to add a signature to each reply. If you clear this check box, Windows Mail adds a signature only to each new message.

WINDOWS CONTACTS

Select the Associate the Pictures in My Windows User Account and My Personal Contact check box if you want Windows to apply the pictures you choose for your Windows user account to your own contact item as well. If you've applied a photo of yourself to your user account, you may want to select this check box. If you're using one of Windows' standard pictures, leaving this check box clear is probably a better idea.

Select the Reduce the File Size of Contacts by Linking to Pictures on My Computer check box if you want to keep down the size of contact files by linking pictures rather than including pictures in the contacts themselves.

Maintenance Options

To choose maintenance options for Windows Mail, click the Maintenance button on the Advanced page of the Options dialog box. Windows displays the Maintenance dialog box (see Figure 17.18), which contains options for keeping Windows Mail running smoothly without silting up your hard disk.

FIGURE 17.18
The Maintenance dialog box lets you choose when to get rid of deleted items, how often to compact the Windows Mail database, and where to store your messages.

These are the options in the Maintenance dialog box:

Empty Messages from the "Deleted Items" Folder on Exit   Select this check box to have Windows Mail empty all the deleted messages in your Deleted Items folder when you exit Windows Mail. By default, Windows Mail keeps the deleted messages until you empty the Deleted Items folder manually. Getting rid of the deleted items is better security, but it prevents you from recovering items you've deleted by accident in an earlier session.

Purge Deleted Messages When Leaving IMAP Folders   Select this check box to have Windows Mail dispose of all messages you've marked as deleted when you close an IMAP folder. If your server is POP3 rather than IMAP, you don't need to worry about this option.

Purge Newsgroup Messages in the Background   Select this check box if you want Windows Mail to dispose of newsgroup messages automatically rather than you disposing of them manually. Use the next two check boxes to control which messages Windows Mail purges.

Delete Read Message Bodies in Newsgroups   Select this check box if you want Windows Mail to delete all the message bodies of messages you've read when you quit Windows Mail. This option saves a lot of space, but it means that you'll need to download a message again if you want to reread it.

Delete News Messages *NN* Days After Being Downloaded   Select this check box and specify the number of days in the text box if you want Windows Mail to automatically delete messages after a set time. Clear this check box if you want to keep old messages for reference.

Compact the Database on Shutdown Every *NN* Runs   Select this check box if you want Windows Mail to automatically compact its database of messages when you close Windows Mail after running it the specified number of times. The default number is 100, but if you use Windows Mail heavily and leave it running throughout each Windows session, reduce the number so as not to leave too long an interval between compactions.

Clean Up Now   Click this button to display the Local File Clean Up dialog box, which provides actions for compacting and deleting messages. The section "Cleaning Up Messages" later in this chapter discusses these actions.

Store Folder   Click this button to display the Store Location dialog box, which you can use for changing the folder in which your message store is located. The section "Moving Your Message Store" later in this chapter discusses this process.

Troubleshooting area   If you're having problems communicating with a mail or news server, you can select the Mail check box, the News check box, or the IMAP check box, to make Windows Mail log the commands used for that server. The log file may help cast light on the problem. The log files have the extension LOG and are named after the account they log. For example, the HTTP mail log is called HTTPMail.log, and the news log for the account news.pacbell.com would be called news.pacbell.com.log. You'll find these files in the message store folder. (To find out where the message store folder is, click the Store Folder button.)

Suppressing Junk E-mail Messages

Junk e-mail, or *spam*, is a sad fact of life for most people online. Windows Mail provides a strong suite of features to help you minimize the menace.

To find these options, choose Tools ➤ Junk E-mail Options. Windows Mail displays the Junk E-mail Options dialog box. The following sections discuss the options contained on the five pages of this dialog box.

Setting Junk E-mail Options

The Options page of the Junk E-mail Options dialog box (see Figure 17.19) lets you set the level of protection you want from junk e-mail:

No Automatic Filtering. Mail from Blocked Senders Is Still Moved to the Junk E-mail Folder   Select this option button only if you want to be sure that any message that might be legitimate (no matter how remote the possibility) ends up in your Inbox rather than in the Junk E-mail folder. If you receive a message from a sender whom you've blocked by name (see the section "Creating a Blocked Senders List," later in this chapter), Windows Mail puts it in the Junk E-mail folder.

Low: Move the Most Obvious Junk E-mail to the Junk E-mail Folder   Select this option button to have Windows Mail filter out the most obvious junk mail and place it in your Junk E-mail folder. On this setting, your Inbox will still receive junk e-mail messages that Windows Mail can't definitively condemn as junk. This setting is usually a good choice for normal mail use.

High: Most Junk E-mail Is Caught, but Some Regular Mail May Be Caught As Well   Select this option button if you find that the Low setting is letting too much junk e-mail through to your Inbox. This setting makes Windows Mail take a more aggressive line, condemning any ambiguous messages as junk. Check your Junk E-mail folder frequently for non-junk messages that Windows Mail has wrongly identified as junk.

Safe List Only: Only Mail from People or Domains on Your Safe Senders List Will Be Delivered to Your Inbox   Select this option button when you want to ensure no junk e-mail arrives in your Inbox. Windows Mail accepts only messages from senders you've designated safe (see the next section) and puts all other messages in the Junk E-mail folder.

Permanently Delete Suspected Junk E-mail instead of Moving It to the Junk E-mail Folder   Select this check box if you want Windows Mail to delete suspected junk e-mail without consulting you. Even if you use the Low option button for filtering, deleting junk e-mail without review is seldom a good idea. Before using this setting, review your Junk E-mail folder for a while and make sure that the filtering level you've set is picking up only junk messages.

Creating a Safe Senders List

Windows Mail comes with filters for determining what's junk mail and what's not, but you can help it considerably by creating a Safe Senders list of people and domains whom you trust never to send junk and a Blocked Senders list of people and domains whose messages you always consider junk.

FIGURE 17.19
On the Options page of the Junk E-mail Options dialog box, set the level of filtering you want to use.

To create the Safe Senders list, work on the Safe Senders page of the Junk E-mail Options dialog box (see Figure 17.20). Take the following steps:

1. Click the Add button. Windows Mail displays the Add Address or Domain dialog box, as shown here.

2. In the text box, type either a full e-mail address (for example, `julia@example.com`) or just the domain (for example, `example.com`). Use a full e-mail address whenever possible, as most domains have many users. (For example, adding `hotmail.com` or `yahoo.com` to the Safe Senders list would be a mistake.) Click the OK button. Windows Mail closes the Add Address or Domain dialog box and adds the address or domain to the list box.

3. If you need to change an existing entry in the list, click it, click the Edit button, and then work in the Edit Address or Domain dialog box, which works just like the Add Address or Domain dialog box. If you need to remove an entry from the list, select it, and then click the Remove button.

FIGURE 17.20
Create a Safe Senders list to make sure messages you want to receive never go into the Junk E-mail folder.

4. If you want Windows Mail to treat your contacts as if they were on the Safe Senders list (without your needing to add them explicitly), select the Also Trust E-mail from My Windows Contacts check box.

5. Select the Automatically Add People I E-mail to the Safe Senders List check box if you want Windows Mail to add such people to the Safe Senders list. Whether this is a good idea depends on whom you send messages to.

Creating a Blocked Senders List

The Blocked Senders list is the counterpart to the Safe Senders list—a list of people and domains whose messages you always want to treat as junk. Use the Add button, Edit button, and Remove button on the Blocked Senders page of the Junk E-mail Options dialog box (see Figure 17.21) to put together your list of addresses and domains.

FIGURE 17.21
Build a Blocked Senders list of e-mail addresses and domains whose messages are always junk.

Blocking Messages by Top-Level Domain or Language Encoding

The International page of the Junk E-mail Options dialog box (see Figure 17.22) lets you implement two more forms of blocking:

By Top-Level Domain If you find you receive only spam from certain top-level domains, you can block that entire domain. For example, you might choose to block the Nigeria domain or the Nauru domain.

Language Encoding If your Inbox suffers from spam written in a particular character set (for example, Arabic or Korean) in which you don't receive worthwhile messages, you can block that language encoding.

The International page of the Junk E-mail Options dialog box lets you block messages by top-level domain or language encoding.

To block by top-level domain, follow these steps:

1. Click the Blocked Top-Level Domain List button. Windows Mail displays the Blocked Top-Level Domain List, as shown here.

2. Select the check box for each domain you want to block. If you want to block all domains except a few, click the Select All button, and then clear the check box for each domain you want to allow. Normally, however, you'll want to block only specific domains that seem to give you only spam.

3. Click the OK button. Windows Mail closes the Blocked Top-Level Domain List dialog box, returning you to the International page of the Junk E-mail Options dialog box.

To block by language encoding, follow these steps:

1. Click the Blocked Encoding List button. Windows Mail displays the Blocked Encodings List dialog box, as shown here.

2. Select the check box for each language encoding you want to block. Should you want to block all encodings except a few, click the Select All button, and then clear the check box for each encoding you want to allow (you'll probably want to allow Western European and US_ASCII). Most likely, you'll need to block only particular encodings that are proving troublesome.

3. Click the OK button. Windows Mail closes the Blocked Encodings List dialog box, returning you to the International page of the Junk E-mail Options dialog box.

Configuring Phishing Settings

Phishing is the practice of sending a fake e-mail message to try to learn personal information or financial information (such as credit card or bank details) or perpetrate some other kind of financial scam. For example:

◆ A message may claim there is a problem with your PayPal account and state that it has been frozen. To use it again, you should click a link in the message, which takes you to a site that appears to be the PayPal logon page—but is in fact a facsimile site designed to grab your logon name and password.

◆ A message may claim to be from your bank, saying that there's a problem with your account. To sort out the problem, you should click a link in the message. What your browser shows is your bank's real web page, but the logon area actually has a superimposed section into which you unwittingly enter your details—and share them with the fraudsters.

◆ A message claims your e-mail address has won an international online lottery. Just call this number to find out how to get your prize—and spend 10 minutes in voicemail hell at super-premium international rates before finding out that it's bogus.

The Phishing page of the Junk E-mail Options dialog box (see Figure 17.23) contains two options to help you avoid getting stung by phishing messages:

Protect My Inbox from Messages with Potential Phishing Links   Select this check box to make Windows Mail watch for messages that may contain phishing links. Windows Mail warns you that the links may be dangerous.

Move Phishing E-mail to the Junk Mail Folder   Select this check box if you want Windows Mail to move suspected phishing messages directly to the Junk Mail folder rather than placing them in your Inbox. This check box is available only when the previous check box is selected. Normally, it's best to clear this check box and deal with suspected phishing messages in the Inbox, in case they're actually genuine.

FIGURE 17.23

Normally, you'll want to turn on the Protect My Inbox from Messages with Potential Phishing Links feature on the Phishing page of the Junk E-mail Options dialog box.

Receiving a Suspect Message

When Windows Mail downloads a message that it suspects of being junk or phishing, it displays the message box shown here to alert you to the message.

If you don't want Windows Mail to display this dialog box again, select the Please Do Not Show Me This Dialog Again check box. Click the Open Junk E-mail Folder button if you want to examine the message immediately, or click the Close button if you want to simply close the dialog box. You can also click the Junk E-mail Options button to open the Junk E-mail Options dialog box.

Reading and Sending E-mail

This section shows you how to read e-mail messages; how to send messages; how to reply to messages, and how to forward messages; and how to work with vCards (virtual business cards) and attachments.

Reading E-mail Messages

To read incoming e-mail, go to the Folder List on the left of the Windows Mail window and click the Inbox for the mail account you want to read. Windows Mail displays your Inbox, which lists the messages and displays icons to indicate information about the message headers. Figure 17.24 shows the Inbox in the Local Folders structure. As you can see in the figure, there's another Inbox in the Main Account folder structure.

◆ The Attachment icon means that the message has one or more files attached to it. (You'll learn how to work with attachments later in this chapter.)

◆ The Unread Message icon indicates that a message has not been read.

◆ The Read Message icon indicates that a message has been read. You can mark a message as unread or read by right-clicking its header and choosing Mark As Unread or Mark As Read, as appropriate, from the context menu.

FIGURE 17.24
The Inbox

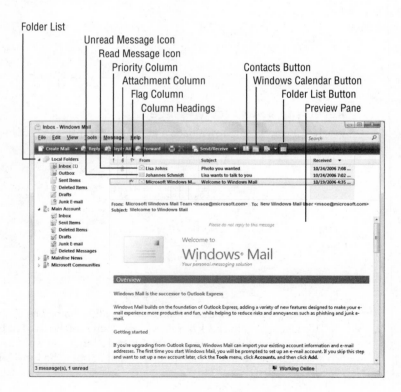

♦ A flag is a mark you can set on a message to indicate that you need to deal with it. To set or remove a flag, click in the Flag column beside the message's header.

♦ If a message is marked as high priority, it displays a red exclamation point in the Priority column.

To read a message in the Preview pane, click it in the message headers listing. Windows Mail displays it in the Preview pane.

To read a message in a separate window, double-click its message header listing. Windows Mail displays the message in a separate window, as shown in Figure 17.25.

To sort your messages by one of the column headings, click the heading once for an ascending sort (alphabetical order) or twice for a descending sort (reverse-alphabetical order).

To view a subset of your messages, choose View ➢ Current View ➢ Hide Read Messages or View ➢ Current View ➢ Hide Read or Ignored Messages. To restore the view to all messages, choose View ➢ Current View ➢ Show All Messages.

If you have multiple messages from the same conversation (on the same topic, with the same subject), choose View ➢ Current View ➢ Group Messages by Conversation to group the messages. Issue the command again to ungroup the messages.

To ignore a conversation that's going on, select one of the messages and choose Message ➢ Ignore Conversation.

Sending E-mail

You can generate e-mail in Windows Mail by creating new messages, replying to messages you've received, or forwarding either messages you've received or messages you've created and sent before.

FIGURE 17.25
Instead of reading a message in the Preview pane, you can display it in a separate window if you prefer.

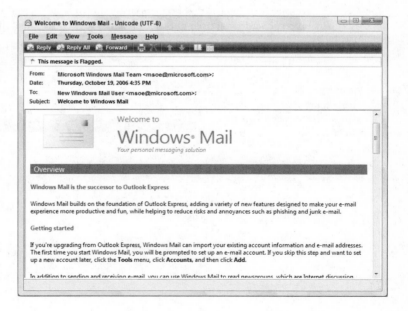

TROUBLESHOOTING: "SERVER NOT FOUND" ERROR

A "Server not found" error from Windows Mail may mean that your Internet connection isn't working when Windows Mail expects it to be. If you want Windows Mail to dial the connection automatically when necessary, select the Dial Whenever a Network Connection Is Not Present check box on the Connection page of the Options dialog box.

COMPOSING A NEW MESSAGE

To create a new message, take the following steps:

1. Click the Create Mail button on the toolbar. Windows Mail opens a message window containing a new message. Figure 17.26 shows an example.

   ◆ To create a message using Windows Mail's stationery, click the Create Mail button's drop-down list button and choose the type of stationery from the drop-down menu. If you've set Windows Mail to use a type of stationery as the default, choose No Stationery from the drop-down menu when you need to create a blank message.

   ◆ To create a message to a contact, click the Contacts button. Windows Mail opens an Explorer window showing your Contacts folder. Click the contact, and then click the E-mail button on the toolbar.

2. If you have multiple e-mail accounts, choose the account from which you want to send the account by using the drop-down list at the right end of the From text box.

3. Enter the e-mail address of the recipient or recipients in the To text box and the names of cc: recipients in the Cc: text box. Separate multiple addresses with semicolons. You can either type each address in or choose it from Address Book as follows:

   ◆ Click the To: button. Windows Mail displays the Select Recipients dialog box (shown in Figure 17.27).

FIGURE 17.26
Create your message in the New Message window.

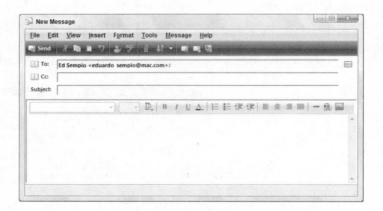

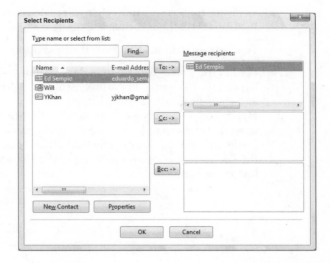

FIGURE 17.27
Use the Select Recipients dialog box to specify the recipients for the message.

◆ In the Type Name or Select from List list box, select the name and click the To: button, the Cc: button, or the Bcc: button to add the selected name to the appropriate box of message recipients.

◆ Add further names to the To:, Cc:, and Bcc: lists as applicable, and then click the OK button. Windows Mail closes the Select Recipients dialog box and adds the recipients to the appropriate boxes in the New Message window.

4. Click in the Subject text box and enter the Subject line for the message. The more descriptive, informative, and concise the Subject line is, the more useful it will be to the recipients of the message—and the more likely they will be to read the message.

5. In the message box, enter the text of the message:

◆ You can enter and edit the text using the standard Windows commands (such as cut-and-paste, and drag-and-drop) and format the text (if you're sending a formatted message) by using the buttons on the Formatting toolbar, shown in Figure 17.28.

FIGURE 17.28
Use the Formatting toolbar to format your messages if necessary.

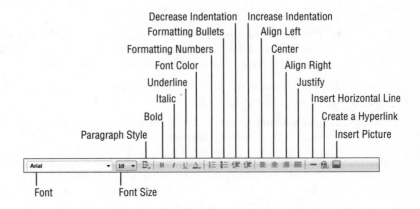

◆ To switch the message from plain text to rich text (HTML) or vice versa, choose Format ➢ Rich Text (HTML) or Format ➢ Plain Text.

◆ To insert a horizontal line, click the Insert Horizontal Line button on the toolbar.

◆ If you type a recognizable hyperlink, Windows Mail automatically converts it to a hyperlink. To insert a hyperlink manually, select the text to include in the hyperlink and click the Create a Hyperlink button on the toolbar. Windows Mail displays the Hyperlink dialog box (shown next). Choose the type of hyperlink from the Type drop-down list (for example, http for a regular connection, https for a secure connection, mailto for an e-mail link), enter the URL or address in the URL text box, and then click the OK button. Windows Mail closes the Hyperlink dialog box and inserts the hyperlink in the message.

◆ To insert a picture, click the Insert a Picture button. Windows Mail displays the Picture dialog box, which is a standard Windows Open dialog box given a new name. Select the picture, and then click the Open button. Windows Mail closes the Picture dialog box and inserts the picture in the message at the insertion point. If you want to control how the picture appears, right-click the picture and choose Properties from the context menu. Windows Mail displays the Picture dialog box, shown next. In the Alternate Text text box, enter text to be displayed in case the recipient cannot view the picture. Choose alignment and border thickness options in the Layout group box and horizontal and vertical spacing options in the Spacing group box, and then click the OK button. Windows Mail closes the Picture dialog box and applies the changes to the picture in the message.

6. If you want to override for this message your default setting for requesting read receipts, choose Tools ➢ Request Read Receipt. If you've turned on digital signing and want to request a secure receipt, choose Tools ➢ Request Secure Receipt.

7. If you want to override for this message your default setting for encrypting messages, choose Tools ➢ Encrypt.

8. If you want to override for this message your default setting for digitally signing messages, choose Tools ➢ Digitally Sign.

9. You're now ready to send the message. Read through the message quickly to make sure it conveys what you want it to and that you haven't written anything rash or ambiguous. Spell-check the message if necessary by clicking the Spelling button or choosing Tools ➢ Spelling. Then click the Send button or choose File ➢ Send to send the message on its way.

If you try to send an encrypted message without having a digital certificate with which to encrypt it for yourself, Windows Mail displays the Security Warning dialog box shown next. Choose the Yes button to send the message unencrypted, or choose the No button to cancel sending the message so that you can change the encryption setting or find your digital certificate.

If you try to send an encrypted message to someone whose digital certificate you don't have, Windows Mail displays the Windows Mail dialog box shown next. Click the Don't Encrypt button to send the message without encryption. Click the Cancel button to cancel sending the message.

Real World Scenario

CREATING MORE COMPLEX HTML MESSAGES

As you've seen in this section, Windows Mail offers some basic formatting options for HTML messages. But if you want to create a complex layout for a message, you'll do better to use a custom web-design program (for example, FrontPage) to create it as a web page. Then paste the contents of the page into the message in Windows Mail. Before sending the message to others, send a copy to yourself to make sure everything works.

Replying to an E-mail Message

To reply to a message from the Inbox, click the Reply button on the toolbar, or right-click the message header and choose Reply to Sender from the context menu. Alternatively, press Ctrl+R.

To reply to a message from a message window, click the Reply button on the toolbar in the message window.

If you weren't the only recipient of a message, you can use the Reply to All feature to reply quickly to all the recipients of that message (and to cc: everyone on the Cc: list, if the message has one). From the Inbox, click the Reply All button on the toolbar, or right-click and choose Reply to All from the context menu. Alternatively, press Ctrl+Shift+R. From a message window, click the Reply All button on the message window's toolbar.

Windows Mail opens a message window for the reply. Compose your reply, add any extra recipients, and send the message as usual.

When you reply to a message, Windows Mail adds RE: to the Subject line so that the recipient can easily see that the message is a reply.

Adding a vCard to Your Outgoing Messages

You can include a *vCard*—a virtual business card—with your outgoing messages either automatically or manually. Usually it's better to include vCards manually when necessary so that you don't barrage your friends and colleagues with useless vCards. vCards are small, but they travel as attachments to messages, so they can make attachments folders silt up.

To send a vCard with every message, select the Mail check box in the Business Cards area of the Compose page of the Options dialog box (Tools ➤ Options), then choose the appropriate contact entry from the context menu.

To send a vCard manually, specify the vCard as described in the previous paragraph, but then clear the Mail check box in the Business Cards area. You can then choose Insert ➤ My Business Card from a message window to add the vCard to a message.

EXPERT KNOWLEDGE: RESIZING PICTURES YOU SEND VIA E-MAIL

Large graphics files can be slow to transmit. Windows lets you resize (or, more accurately, down-resolve) a graphics file to produce a smaller file size that will transmit more quickly.

To use this feature, take the following steps:

1. Open an Explorer window to the folder containing the file. For example, you might choose Start ➤ Pictures.

2. Select the file, and then click the E-mail button on the toolbar. (Alternatively, right-click the file and choose Send To ➤ Mail Recipient from the context menu.) Windows displays the Attach Files dialog box, as shown here.

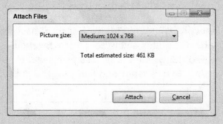

3. In the Picture Size drop-down list, select the Smaller item, the Small item, the Medium item, or the Large item, as appropriate. (Each size lists the resolution used.) To send the pictures at full size, choose the Original Size item.

4. Click the Attach button. Windows creates a new version of the file or files using the specified resolution, starts a new message, and attaches the file or files.

5. Address the message, finish it, and then send it as usual.

Adding vCards You Receive to the Address Book

When you receive a vCard as an attachment, you can quickly add it to the Address Book by taking the following steps:

1. Click the icon for the vCard in the message window and choose Open from the pop-up menu. Alternatively, select the message in your Inbox and click the icon for the vCard in the Preview pane header. Windows Mail displays the Mail Attachment dialog box, as shown here.

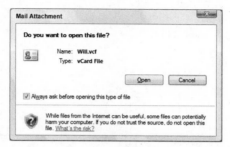

2. Click the Open button. Windows Mail displays the Properties dialog box for the vCard.

3. Click the Add to Address Book button to make the contact information editable, and then edit it as usual.

Forwarding a Message

You can easily forward a message to someone else. To forward a message from the Inbox, click the Forward button on the toolbar or right-click the message header and choose Forward from the context menu. Alternatively, press Ctrl+F.

To forward a message from a message window, click the Forward button on the toolbar in the message window.

Windows Mail opens a message window for the forwarded message. Choose recipients, enter your contribution to the message, and then send it as usual.

When you forward a message, Windows Mail adds Fw: to the Subject line so that the recipient can easily see that the message was forwarded. You can delete this addition if you want, just as you can give the message a different Subject line.

Sending and Receiving Attachments

In addition to sending and receiving e-mail messages, you can send and receive files as attachments to messages. Attachments are a great way of sharing files and getting information from point A to point B.

SENDING ATTACHMENTS

To send a file as an attachment, start a message as usual (or reply to a message, or forward a message), and then click the Attach button on the toolbar. Windows Mail displays the Open dialog box. Select the file or files to attach, and click the Open button. Windows Mail closes the Open dialog box and displays the Attach box on the message (shown in Figure 17.29) with details of the attachment. You can then complete and send the message as usual.

FIGURE 17.29

When you've attached one or more files to a message, the message displays the Attach box.

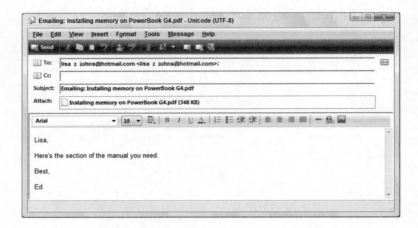

 Real World Scenario

YOU MAY NEED TO SPLIT UP LARGE FILES FOR E-MAIL TRANSFER

If the attachment you're sending is much larger than 1MB, it may be rejected by a mail server on the way. If this happens (or to prevent this from happening), select the Break Apart Messages Larger than *NN* KB check box on the Advanced page of the Properties dialog box for the mail account and specify a value of 1MB (1,024KB) or smaller in the text box. Windows Mail then breaks up the message into parts, and the recipient can recombine the parts, by using either an e-mail program with recombining capability (for example, Windows Mail or Outlook) or a separate recombining utility. See the "Configuring an Individual Account" section later in the chapter for details.

RECEIVING ATTACHMENTS

When someone sends you a file with an attachment, the message header in your Inbox displays an Attachment icon, as you saw earlier in this chapter. If you open the message in a message window, it displays an Attach box.

To save an attachment, take the following steps:

1. Make sure the attachment is safe. See the next sidebar for details.

2. Select the message header.

3. Choose File ➤ Save Attachments. Windows Mail displays the Save Attachments dialog box (see Figure 17.30).

4. For each attachment, specify a destination location in the Save To text box (use the Browse button and the resulting Browse for Folder dialog box if necessary), then click the Save button.

5. Check the detached file with virus-checking software before you open it.

FIGURE 17.30
Use the Save Attachments dialog box to save the attachments from an e-mail message to a folder of your choosing.

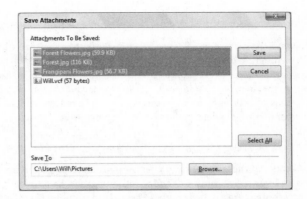

If you receive an attachment that has been broken into multiple parts, select all the messages in the Inbox, right-click one of them, and select the Combine and Decode command.

EXPERT KNOWLEDGE: PROTECTING YOURSELF AGAINST MALICIOUS ATTACHMENTS

Attachments are one of the easiest ways for a malicious hacker to attack your computer, so have your wits about you each time you open an attachment. This sidebar discusses the ways in which attachments can pose a threat to your computer and the best way to protect yourself.

AN EXECUTABLE FILE OR SCRIPT FILE CAN DO DAMAGE

The most straightforward threat is an attachment containing an undisguised executable file or script file that you can be persuaded to run. By the beginning of the twenty-first century, most computer users know that it's a really bad idea to execute an executable file or script file that they receive as an e-mail attachment—even if it comes from someone they know, trust, or even love—so most malefactors have taken to disguising the executables or scripts they send.

AN APPARENTLY HARMLESS FILE MAY BE A DISGUISED EXECUTABLE OR SCRIPT

Even if you've chosen to display file extensions (as discussed in Chapter 9), the true extension of the file can be hidden behind a part of the filename masquerading as the extension.

For example, if Windows is hiding extensions (as it does by default), and someone sent you the executable file NewXtinapic.jpg.exe, it would appear to be named NewXtinapic.jpg. Since JPG is a graphics file format, you might think it safe to open the file—but opening it directly would cause the executable file to run. (Trying to open the file from a graphics program would cause an error, as the graphics program wouldn't be able to open the executable file.)

Even if you'd cleared the Hide Extensions for Known File Types check box on the View page of the Folder Options dialog box (from Explorer) so that Windows displays most extensions, a file with one of the super-hidden extensions (.url, .jse, .js, .shs, .lnk, .shb, .job, .vbe, .vbs, .scf, or .wsf) would still appear to be a different type of file. For example, New Shakira Hit.mp3.js would appear to be named New Shakira Hit.mp3.

A DOCUMENT FILE MAY CONTAIN VBA OR OTHER EXECUTABLE CODE

Even if the file is of the file type its extension suggests, it can still be dangerous. For example, a file created by a program that acts as a Visual Basic for Applications (VBA) host—such as a Word or WordPerfect document, an Excel workbook, a PowerPoint presentation, or an AutoCAD drawing—can contain executable code in macros or user forms that can attack your computer. VBA and other scripting languages can take extensive actions on a computer—anything from formatting a disk to installing a back-door administration program or silently e-mailing your most private files to persons unknown.

ALWAYS VIRUS CHECK ALL ATTACHMENTS YOU RECEIVE

Because of these dangers, it's best *never* to open *any* attachment *from anyone* without virus checking it first. Even if you know the sender and you've checked their e-mail address to make sure the message and attachment are really from that person, bear in mind that their computer could be infected with a virus that's using the e-mail client automatically to spread itself. Alternatively, your apparent correspondent's e-mail account could have been hijacked, either at the computer or at the server, and used to distribute malware. Or the person could have sent you, intentionally and in good faith, a document that they didn't know had been infected with a virus.

The best way to virus check all documents is to use antivirus software that monitors all the comings and goings on your PC, including the e-mail you receive (and send). Such antivirus software may slow down an older PC enough to be annoying, but it's still far better than having to disinfect a computer that's caught a virus. Restoring data from backup takes time and effort. And having to re-create data files you've lost because of an attack that struck when you didn't have a backup takes longest of all. So it's well worth investing in an antivirus program that automatically checks all incoming e-mail and attachments—and running it all the time.

TURN OFF THE PREVIEW PANE IN WINDOWS MAIL

For extra security, you may want to avoid using the Preview pane in Windows Mail, because the act of displaying the message in the Preview pane can run a script that can trigger some kinds of virus. (To stop using the Preview pane, choose View ➤ Layout. Windows Mail displays the Window Layout Properties dialog box. Clear the Show Preview Pane check box in the Preview Pane area, and then click the OK button.) However, because the Preview pane helps you process your e-mail quickly, and because most viruses travel as attachments, most people choose to continue using the Preview pane. Some antivirus programs can also guard against this type of script.

USE THE "DO NOT ALLOW ATTACHMENTS TO BE SAVED " OPTION

As discussed in the section "Security Page Options," earlier in this chapter, the Security page of the Options dialog box for Windows Mail includes a check box called Do Not Allow Attachments to Be Saved or Opened That Could Potentially Be a Virus. If you select this check box, Windows Mail won't let you save or open attachments whose file types *could* contain a virus or code. These file types include executable files and scripts, of course, but also include documents that could contain VBA code or code in another scripting language.

The problem with this option is that when you use it, Windows Mail typically ends up "protecting" you from a large number of harmless files that you want to work with, such as Word documents that contain customized toolbars. So if you use this option, you'll need to toggle it on and off frequently: Keep it on until Windows Mail notifies you that it has suppressed an attachment because it might be dangerous; turn it off so that you can set your antivirus program on the file and decide if it's a friend or a foe; and then turn it back on again so that Windows Mail is protecting you once more.

Because of all this maneuvering, many people find that antivirus software, run constantly and updated whenever possible, provides a more satisfactory solution to the problem of dangerous attachments. This is especially true because malefactors can produce new types of viruses that inhabit supposedly harmless files. For example, JPEG images used to be safe, but now they can be loaded with code that can be run automatically by an extractor program that has been surreptitiously installed on your computer. (If the extractor program hasn't been installed on your computer, the code in the doctored JPEG images does nothing.)

Managing Your E-mail Messages

To keep your Inbox in order, you'll need to manage your messages carefully, by deleting messages, moving them to folders, and being able to locate messages for reference. You may also have to move your message store, and you should certainly back it up to safeguard against data loss.

Deleting a Message

To delete a message from the Inbox, select it and click the Delete button (the × button) on the toolbar or press the Delete key. Doing so moves the message to the Deleted Items folder.

To delete everything in the Deleted Items folder, right-click the folder, choose Empty "Deleted Items" Folder from the context menu, and then click the Yes button in the confirmation message box that appears.

Cleaning Up Messages

If you send and receive many messages, and subscribe to many newsgroups, the messages and posts can take up a lot of space on your hard disk. To reduce the amount of space taken up, or the amount of information stored, follow these steps:

1. Choose Tools ➤ Options. Windows Mail displays the Options dialog box.

2. Click the Advanced tab. Windows Mail displays the Advanced page.

3. Click the Maintenance button. Windows Mail displays the Maintenance dialog box.

4. Click the Clean Up Now button. Windows Mail displays the Local File Clean Up dialog box (shown in Figure 17.31).

5. In the Folders For text box, make sure the right account is selected: Windows Mail for all your accounts, or a specific mail or news account by name. If it's not, click the Select button, select the account in the resulting Windows Mail dialog box, and click the OK button.

FIGURE 17.31
In the Local File
Clean Up dialog box,
select the action you
want to take to free
up more disk space.

6. Click the button for the action you want to take:

Remove Messages   Click this button to delete the bodies of downloaded messages but keep the headers. Because the bodies tend to be bulkier than the headers (especially for messages that have attachments), this action can recover a good amount of space.

Delete   Click this button to delete all the messages (both headers and bodies). This action reclaims even more space, but it doesn't leave much behind.

Reset   Click this button to delete all the messages (again, both headers and bodies) *and* reset the folder so that it will download the message headers again. This action is best saved for when an account has become corrupted.

7. Click the Close button. Windows Mail closes the Local File Clean Up dialog box and returns you to the Maintenance dialog box.

8. Click the Close button. Windows Mail closes the Maintenance dialog box and returns you to the Options dialog box.

9. Click the OK button. Windows Mail closes the Options dialog box.

Moving a Message to a Folder

You can move a message to a folder in several ways:

◆ From the Inbox, click the message header and drag it to the appropriate folder in the Folders pane.

◆ From the Inbox, right-click the message and choose Move to Folder from the context menu, or choose Edit ➤ Move to Folder. Windows Mail displays the Move dialog box. Select the folder and click the OK button.

◆ From a message window, choose File ➤ Move to Folder. Windows Mail displays the Move dialog box. Proceed as described in the previous paragraph.

You can also copy a message to a folder (instead of moving it) by using the Copy to Folder command instead of the Move to Folder command.

Moving Your Message Store

By default, Windows Mail puts your *message store* (the file that contains your messages) in a file named WindowsMail.MSMessageStore in a folder within your user account folder. This is normally a good place to store your messages, but you can move your Windows Mail message store to a different folder if need be—for example, if the current drive is getting full. The folder to which you move the message store must be empty.

To move the message store, follow these steps:

1. Choose Tools ➤ Options. Windows Mail displays the Options dialog box.

2. Click the Advanced tab. Windows Mail displays the Advanced page.

3. Click the Maintenance button. Windows Mail displays the Maintenance dialog box.

4. Click the Store Folder button. Windows Mail displays the Store Location dialog box, as shown here.

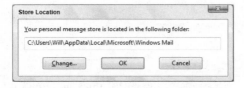

5. Click the Change button. Windows Mail displays the Browse for Folder dialog box.

6. Select the folder for the new location and click the OK button. Windows Mail moves the folder and returns you to the Store Location dialog box.

7. Click the OK button. Windows Mail displays a dialog box telling you that the store location will not be changed until you shut down Windows Mail.

8. Click the OK button. Windows Mail closes the Store Location dialog box and returns you to the Maintenance dialog box.

9. Click the Close button. Windows Mail closes the Maintenance dialog box and returns you to the Options dialog box.

10. Click the OK button. Windows Mail closes the Options dialog box.

11. If you want to move your message store immediately, exit Windows Mail immediately. You'll see an Explorer Copy window as Windows copies the files. Once the copy operation is complete, Windows Mail restarts.

Finding a Message

To find a particular message, take the following steps:

1. Click the Find button page, or choose Edit ➤ Find ➤ Message. Windows Mail displays the Find Message window (shown in Figure 17.32).

2. Enter such information as you can muster about the message in the From, To, Subject, and Message text boxes; specify dates in the Received Before and Received After boxes if possible; and select the Message Has Attachment(s) check box or the Message Is Flagged check box if applicable to narrow the field further.

FIGURE 17.32
Use the Find Message window to find a particular message by specifying information it contains.

3. Click the Find Now button. The Find Message window displays the messages it finds in a list box at the bottom of the window.

4. Double-click a message to open it.

Filtering Your E-mail

Business queries, love letters, spam, messages from your family, and solicitations for mass-mailing software and pornography—these days, you never know exactly what to expect in your Inbox, but most people can count on an increasing number of messages arriving.

To help you manage the mayhem, Windows Mail lets you try to block junk e-mail (as discussed earlier in this chapter) and create rules for filtering e-mail and news. By creating a rule that defines certain conditions, you can take action when a matching message arrives. That action can be anything from moving or copying the message to a particular folder, to forwarding the message automatically to people, to deleting it unread. For example, you could create a rule that deleted any message that contained the word *marketing*.

Creating Rules for Filtering E-mail

Your first priority in filtering should be to filter the e-mail you receive. By filtering e-mail, you can move messages to different folders or even delete them without your ever seeing them.

To create a rule for filtering e-mail, take the following steps:

1. Choose Tools ➢ Message Rules ➢ Mail. Windows Mail displays the New Mail Rule dialog box. Figure 17.33 shows the New Mail Rule dialog box with a rule underway.

2. In the Select the Conditions for Your Rule list box, select the condition or conditions under which you want the rule to operate. For example, you might choose the Where the From Line Contains People condition in order to take action on messages from a particular e-mail account. (You get to specify which people in a moment.) You might also choose the Where the Subject Line Contains Specific Words condition to filter the subject line for particular words.

3. In the Select the Actions for Your Rule list box, select the action that you want Windows Mail to take when the condition is met. For example, you might choose the Move It to the Specified Folder action to move the message to a particular folder. (Again, you get to specify which folder in a moment.)

FIGURE 17.33
Use the New Mail
Rule dialog box to
create rules for
filtering e-mail.

4. In the Rule Description list box, Windows Mail has built the general rule. Now click one of the underlined values to edit it.

◆ Continuing the example, you'd click the Contains People link. Windows Mail displays the Select People dialog box (shown next). Enter a name in the text box and click the Add button to add it to the list box. Or click the Address Book button to display the Rule Addresses dialog box, select the names, move them to the Rule Addresses list box, and click the OK button. Windows Mail closes the Rule Addresses dialog box and updates the Contains condition in the Rule Description list box to reflect the names you chose.

◆ You'd then click the And link in the Rule Description list box. (This link appears when you've created two or more criteria that can be complementary.) Windows Mail displays the And/Or dialog box (shown next). Select the Messages Match All of the Criteria option button if you want messages to meet each condition for the rule to kick in, or select the Messages Match Any One of the Criteria option button to have one condition suffice. (The example uses the Messages Match All of the Criteria option button.) Click the OK button. Windows Mail closes the And/Or dialog box and updates the Rule Description list box.

◆ You'd then click the Contains Specific Words link. Windows Mail displays the Type Specific Words dialog box (shown next with several words added). Type one word at a time into the text box, then click the Add button to add them. Click the OK button. Windows Mail closes the Type Specific Words dialog box and updates the Where the Subject Line Contains condition to contain the words.

◆ You'd then click the Specified link. Windows Mail displays the Move dialog box. Select the folder in the folder structure as usual (create a new folder if necessary), and then click the OK button. Windows Mail closes the Move dialog box and returns you to the New Mail Rule dialog box.

5. In the Name of the Rule text box, type a descriptive name for the rule.

6. Click the OK button. Windows Mail closes the New Mail Rule dialog box, creates the rule, and displays the Message Rules dialog box (shown in Figure 17.34).

7. Click the Apply Now button. Windows Mail displays the Apply Mail Rules Now dialog box (shown in Figure 17.35).

CREATING A RULE THAT APPLIES IF A MESSAGE *DOESN'T* CONTAIN THE SPECIFIED INFORMATION

You can also create a rule that applies if a message does *not* contain the specified information—for example, if a message does not come from a specified sender. To do so, click the Options button in the selection dialog box (the Select People dialog box, the Type Specific Words dialog box, or another selection dialog box). Windows Mail displays the Rule Condition Options dialog box, as shown here.

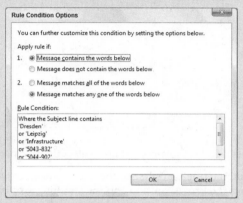

Choose options as appropriate to the rule you're creating. For example, here you might select the Message Does Not Contain the Words Below option button. When you've finished, click the OK button to return to the selection dialog box.

FIGURE 17.34

Manage your mail rules on the Mail Rules page of the Message Rules dialog box.

FIGURE 17.35
In the Apply Mail
Rules Now dialog box,
choose which rules to
apply to which folder.

8. In the Select Rules to Apply list box, select the rules you want to apply.

9. By default, the rule is applied to the folder you were working in when you created it. If necessary, use the Browse button and the resulting Apply to Folder dialog box to designate a different folder, and click the OK button. If the folder has subfolders to which you want to apply the rules, select the Include Subfolders check box.

10. Click the Apply Now button to apply the rules you chose. Windows Mail displays a message box telling you that it has applied the rules to the folder.

11. Click the OK button. Windows Mail closes the message box.

12. Click the Close button. Windows Mail closes the Apply Mail Rules Now dialog box and returns you to the Message Rules dialog box.

13. If you're using multiple mail rules, use the Move Up and Move Down buttons to arrange the rules in the best order.

14. Click the OK button. Windows Mail closes the Message Rules dialog box.

Next, if possible, send yourself a message that meets the condition—or wait until someone else sends you a message that does meet it. Make sure the filter catches the message. If not, adjust the filter until it works.

Blocking a Sender

Despite the junk e-mail filter, you may still receive spam—or you may decide that you no longer want to receive messages from someone whom you found acceptable before. When this happens, you can block either the sender or the sender's entire domain directly from the Inbox:

◆ To block a sender, choose Message ➤ Junk E-mail ➤ Add Sender to Blocked Sender's List.

◆ To block a sender's entire domain, choose Message ➤ Junk E-mail ➤ Add Sender's Domain to Blocker Senders List.

When you take either of these actions, Windows Mail displays the following dialog box to tell you that it has made the addition to your Blocked Senders list.

To unblock a sender that you've blocked, choose Tools ➤ Junk E-mail Options, and then work on the Blocked Senders page of the Junk E-mail Options dialog box.

 Real World Scenario

MINIMIZING SPAM

If you've used e-mail for more than a few days, you probably know what spam is—unsolicited commercial e-mail offering you a variety of supposedly can't-miss opportunities for medicines, pyramid and multilevel marketing schemes, mail-order spouses, pornography, or spam-them-yourself software.

Despite the Junk E-mail filter's efforts and those of any filters you create, and no matter how determinedly you block any sender or domain that offends you, spam will still get through to you. When it does, there's only one thing to do: Delete it.

It's never worth responding to spam (unless you want to buy whatever the spammer is selling). *Never* reply to spam that thoughtfully provides an address for removing yourself from the spammer's list, because sending mail to this address proves that your e-mail address is a live one: The spammer will put you on the list of live addresses that they share with other spammers, so you'll get more spam. And never respond to spam with flames, either—however much vitriol you muster, nobody will read the message, and again you prove that the address from which you sent it is live.

When posting to newsgroups, use a variation of your e-mail address that'll trip up robotic harvesting of e-mail addresses but will let sentient beings read your e-mail address easily. (More on this in the next chapter.)

Think twice before you make your e-mail address available in online directories (or indeed offline directories). Balance your privacy against the need of other people to find your e-mail address for positive reasons. Alternatively, get a secondary e-mail account (perhaps a free account), make that account's address available, and be prepared for a high noise-to-signal ratio on that account. By doing so, you can keep your primary e-mail account mainly on signal but still publicize an e-mail address at which people with whom you haven't shared your primary address can contact you.

If you're interested in actively fighting spam, check out the website of the Coalition Against Unsolicited Commercial Email (CAUCE; http://www.cauce.org).

Adding, Removing, and Configuring Mail Accounts

One e-mail account is enough for many people, but if you separate business from pleasure, you may need to use two or more accounts. You may also need to configure your accounts—for example, if you change your password or your ISP changes mail server.

Adding Another Mail Account

If you have multiple mail accounts, you can add them all to Windows Mail and manage them all together. To add another mail account to Windows Mail, take the following steps:

1. Choose Tools ➢ Accounts. Windows Mail displays the Internet Accounts dialog box with the Mail page foremost (shown in Figure 17.36).

2. Click the Add button. Windows Mail starts the Internet Connection Wizard, which displays the Select Account Type screen.

3. Select the E-mail Account item, and then click the Next button. The wizard displays the Your Name screen.

4. Enter the details for the account just as you did with your first account in "Setting Up E-mail with Windows Mail" at the beginning of this chapter.

Removing a Mail Account

To remove a mail account, select the account in the Internet Accounts dialog box and click the Remove button. Windows Mail displays a Remove Internet Account dialog box to confirm that you want to delete the account. Click the OK button.

FIGURE 17.36
Use the Internet Accounts dialog box to create new accounts and set properties for existing accounts.

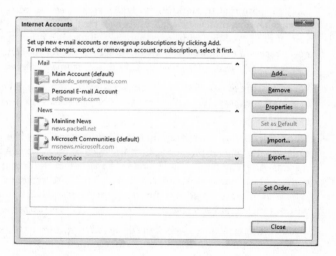

Configuring an Individual Account

You may have thought there were plenty of configuration options earlier in the chapter when you configured Windows Mail—but Windows Mail also lets you configure individual accounts. For example, you might need to change the server used for incoming or outgoing mail; you might want to change the name for the account so that it's easier to recognize when Windows Mail is checking it; or you might want to use a particular digital certificate for one account but not for others.

To change the properties of an account, choose Tools ➢ Accounts. Windows Mail displays the Internet Accounts dialog box. Select the account, and then click the Properties button. Windows Mail displays the Properties dialog box for the account.

The next sections discuss the options on the pages of the Properties dialog box. The number of pages in the Properties dialog box varies depending on the type of account: It has five pages for a POP3 account, and six pages for an IMAP account.

GENERAL PAGE PROPERTIES

The General page of the Properties dialog box (see Figure 17.37) for a mail account contains the following settings:

Mail Account area Enter the descriptive name for the mail account in the text box. This is the name that you see when Windows Mail is accessing the account or otherwise dealing with it. Windows Mail gives the account the mail server's name, but you can usually improve on this.

User Information area Enter or adjust your name, organization, e-mail address, and reply address in the four text boxes. The name and e-mail address will be filled in already with the information you entered while setting up the account. Specify the organization if you want to use one. Enter a reply address only if you want replies to your e-mail to be automatically sent to a different e-mail address than the address entered in the E-mail Address text box.

Select the Include This Account When Receiving Mail or Synchronizing check box if you want Windows Mail to check this account for new messages each time you check for new messages.

FIGURE 17.37
The General page of the Properties dialog box for a mail account

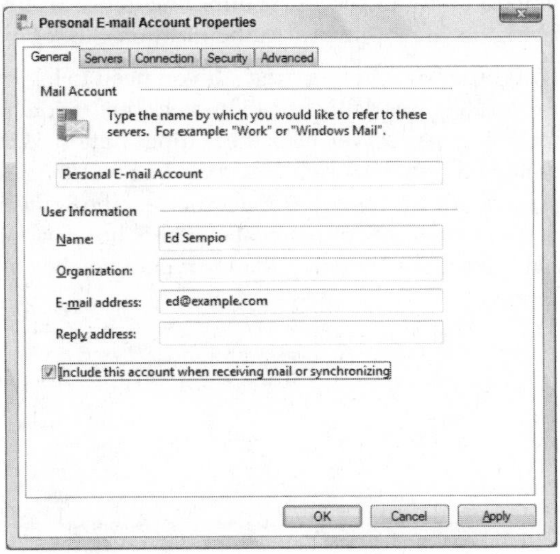

SERVERS PAGE PROPERTIES

The Servers page of the Properties dialog box (see Figure 17.38) for a mail account contains the following settings:

> **Server Information area**   Enter or adjust the information for the incoming mail server and the outgoing mail server. If you entered this information correctly when setting up the account, you should need to change it only if your ISP changes server type or server name.

FIGURE 17.38
The Servers page of the Properties dialog box for a mail account is where you can change your password or the server address.

> **Incoming Mail Server area**   Enter or adjust your account name and password. Select the Remember Password check box if you want Windows Mail to store your password; clear it if you don't. If this server requires you to use Secure Password Authentication, select the Log on Using Secure Password Authentication check box.

> **Outgoing Mail Server area**   If you need to log on to your outgoing mail server, select the My Server Requires Authentication check box. If you have to use different settings than those for your incoming mail server, click the Settings button. Windows Mail displays the Outgoing Mail Server dialog box (shown next). Select the Log on Using option button. Enter your account name and (if you wish) your password. Select or clear the Remember Password check box and the Log on Using Secure Password Authentication check box as appropriate. Then click the OK button. Windows Mail closes the Outgoing Mail Server dialog box and returns you to the Properties dialog box.

CONNECTION PAGE PROPERTIES

The Connection page of the Properties dialog box for a mail account lets you instruct Windows Mail to use a specific dial-up connection or LAN connection for connecting to the account.

To use a specific connection, select the Always Connect to This Account Using check box and select the connection in the drop-down list. Clicking the Settings button displays the Properties dialog box for the connection. Clicking the Add button starts the Set Up a New Connection Wizard so that you can create a new connection.

SECURITY PAGE PROPERTIES

The Security page of the Properties dialog box (see Figure 17.39) for a mail account contains the following settings:

Signing Certificate area   To specify a digital certificate to use for signing messages from this account, click the Select button. Windows Mail displays the Select Default Account Digital ID dialog box. Select the certificate and click the OK button. Windows Mail closes the Select Default Account Digital ID dialog box and enters the name of the certificate in the text box in the Signing Certificate area.

Encrypting Preferences area   To specify an encryption certificate and algorithm, click the Select button and use the resulting Select Default Account Digital ID dialog box to enter the name of the certificate in the text box. If necessary (and it shouldn't be), change the algorithm in the Algorithm drop-down list.

FIGURE 17.39
The Security page of the Properties dialog box for a mail account

ADVANCED PAGE PROPERTIES

The Advanced page of the Properties dialog box (see Figure 17.40) for a mail account contains a full house of advanced options.

Server Port Numbers area   If necessary, change the port number in the Outgoing Mail (SMTP) text box from the default setting (25) to another port specified by your ISP. Likewise, change the port number in the Incoming Mail (POP3) text box if your ISP uses a different port. Also if necessary, select the This Server Requires a Secure Connection (SSL) check box. Again, your ISP will let you know if you need to apply this setting.

Server Timeouts area   If Windows Mail is timing out when you feel it shouldn't be, drag the slider to increase the length of the server timeout interval.

Sending area   Select the Break Apart Messages Larger than *NN* KB check box and enter an appropriate value in the text box if you want Windows Mail to automatically divide large files you attach to a message into a number of smaller parts. This option is useful for making sure that large files don't get rejected by mail servers. Most mail servers these days allow at least 1MB files to pass, so you might enter 1,024KB as the limit.

Delivery area   This area of the dialog box is displayed only for POP3 servers. Select the Leave a Copy of Messages on Server check box if you want to leave a copy of messages on the server while downloading the full set of messages. This option is useful when you need to check your mail from a computer other than your usual one but later download the same messages to your usual computer, so as to have the full set of messages on your usual computer. Don't use this option on your usual computer, because the number of messages on the server will build up as you receive more mail, and Windows Mail will download all of them each time you check mail. To reduce this problem, if you leave a copy of messages on the server, you can select the Remove from Server after *NN* Days check box and use the text box to specify the number of days after which Windows Mail should instruct the server to delete the messages you've downloaded. You can also select the Remove from Server When Deleted from "Deleted Items" check box to make Windows Mail tell the server to delete the messages you've downloaded after you've deleted them *and* removed them from your Deleted Items folder (for example, by emptying the Deleted Items folder).

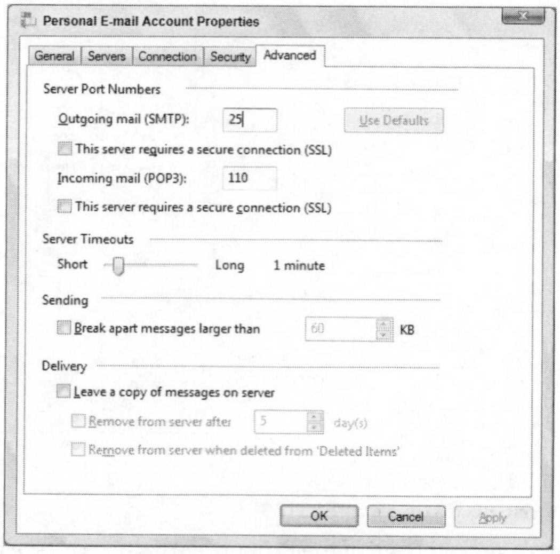

FIGURE 17.40

The Advanced page of the Properties dialog box for a mail account

IMAP PAGE PROPERTIES

The IMAP page of the Properties dialog box (shown in Figure 17.41) for a mail account appears only for accounts that use an IMAP server. It contains the following options:

Folders area In the Root Folder Path text box, enter the name of the root folder—the folder that contains all your folders. For a Unix server, this is usually the `Mail` folder in the folder named with your username. For example, if your username is `ppiper`, your root folder path would usually be `~ppiper/Mail`. (Don't add a forward slash (/) to the path, because this invalidates the name.) For a Cyrus IMAP server, the root folder is the Inbox.

Leave the Check for New Messages in All Folders check box selected if you want Windows Mail to check all folders (including hidden folders) for new messages.

Special Folders area If you want to store Windows Mail's Sent Items folder, Drafts folder, Deleted Items folder, and Junk E-mail folder on the IMAP server, select the Store Special Folders on IMAP Server check box and enter the appropriate paths in the text boxes.

When you've finished adjusting properties in the Properties dialog box, click the OK button. Windows Mail closes the Properties dialog box and returns you to the Internet Accounts dialog box. Click the Close button to return to Windows Mail.

FIGURE 17.41
The IMAP page of the Properties dialog box for an IMAP mail account

Customizing the Inbox and Backing Up Your Mail

This section shows you how to customize the columns displayed in your Inbox, how to configure the Inbox layout and the toolbar, and how to back up your e-mail items.

Customizing the Columns Displayed in the Inbox

By default, the Inbox displays six columns: Priority, Attachment, Flag, From, Subject, and Received. For most purposes, these are the most widely useful columns. Windows Mail offers five more columns—Mark for Offline, Sent, Size, To, and Watch/Ignore—that you can add if you want. You can also remove the default columns, specify widths for all the columns you display, and change the order in which they appear.

To customize the columns displayed in the Inbox, take the following steps:

1. Right-click a column heading and choose Columns from the context menu, or choose View ➢ Columns. Windows Mail displays the Columns dialog box (shown in Figure 17.42).

2. In the list box, clear the check box for any column that you don't want to appear. Select the check box for any column you want to add. For any column you display, you can specify a suitable width in the The Selected Column Should be *NN* Pixels Wide text box.

3. To rearrange the order of the columns, select a column and use the Move Up or Move Down button.

4. Click the OK button. Windows Mail closes the Columns dialog box and implements your changes to the Inbox.

FIGURE 17.42
Use the Columns dialog box to quickly change the configuration of your Inbox.

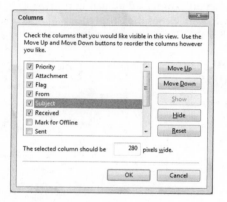

Customizing the Inbox Layout and the Toolbar

In addition to changing the columns displayed, you can customize the layout of your Inbox, displaying only the elements you want, arranging the Preview pane where you need it, and customizing the toolbar. Take the following steps:

1. Choose View ➢ Layout. Windows Mail displays the Layout page of the Window Layout Properties dialog box (shown in Figure 17.43).

2. In the Basic area, select the check boxes for the components you want to see, and clear the check boxes for the components you want to hide. Most of the items you've seen already, but there are a couple you haven't:

◆ The Folder bar is a vertical bar that you can display at the left side of the Inbox to provide navigation between the main Windows Mail folders (the Inbox, the Outbox, the Sent Items folder, the Deleted Items folder, and the Drafts folder). Normally, you won't need to use the Folder bar.

◆ The Views bar is a horizontal bar that appears below the toolbar and provides a drop-down list of different views: Show All Messages, Hide Read Messages, or Hide Read or Ignored Messages.

FIGURE 17.43
Use the Window Layout Properties dialog box to show only the parts of Windows Mail that you want to see.

3. In the Preview Pane area, choose options for the Preview pane:

   ◆ Clear the Show Preview Pane check box if you don't want to use the Preview pane.

   ◆ If you do use the Preview pane, choose the Below Messages option button or the Beside Messages option button to determine its placement.

   ◆ Select the Show Preview Pane Header check box if you want to have the Preview pane header displayed. (The Preview pane header is the gray strip at the top of the Preview pane that shows information about the current message.)

4. If you want to customize the toolbar, click the Customize Toolbar button. Windows Mail displays the Customize Toolbar dialog box, as shown here. Work as follows:

   ◆ To remove a button from the toolbar, select it in the Current Toolbar Buttons list box, and then click the Remove button.

   ◆ To add a button to the toolbar, select the item in the Current Toolbar Buttons list above which you want the item to be added. Then select the item in the Available Toolbar Buttons list box and click the Add button.

   ◆ To move a button up or down the toolbar, select it in the Current Toolbar Buttons list box, and then click the Move Up button or the Move Down button.

   ◆ To control how text appears for items, choose Selective Text on Left, Show Text Labels, or No Text Labels in the Text Options drop-down list.

   ◆ To control how icons appear, choose Small Icons or Large Icons in the Icon Options drop-down list.

   ◆ If you mess up the toolbar and need to reset it, click the Reset button.

   ◆ When you've finished choosing toolbar options, click the Close button. Windows Mail closes the Customize Toolbar dialog box and returns you to the Windows Layout Properties dialog box.

5. Click the OK button. Windows Mail closes the Window Layout Properties dialog box and applies your choices.

Backing Up and Restoring Your Windows Mail Folders

If you use Windows Mail extensively, and you use most of the features discussed in this chapter, you'll soon have not only a large quantity of data stored in Windows Mail but also a considerable amount of effort invested—writing and responding to messages, building your list of contacts, configuring your accounts and the Junk E-mail options, and constructing rules to highlight important mail and deflect as much unwanted mail as possible. It only makes sense to back up your Windows Mail folders and configuration so that you can restore your data and your configuration should disaster strike.

The easiest way to back up your Windows Mail data is to use Backup Utility as discussed in Chapter 16. If you store your Windows Mail data in the default location (within your user profile folders), you can back it up by backing up your profile, and restore it by restoring your profile. This data includes your folders, Internet accounts (mail, news, and directory services), mail rules, news rules, and blocked senders.

Alternatively, you can back up individual components by using the following commands:

♦ You can export and import individual mail, news, or directory service accounts by using the Export button and the Import button on the All page or the Category page (Mail, News, or Directory Service) of the Internet Accounts dialog box (Tools ➤ Accounts).

♦ You can back up the message store for an identity by backing up the `Windows Mail` folder in the appropriate folder. The easiest way of getting to the message store is to display the Store Location dialog box by clicking the Store Folder button in the Maintenance dialog box, copy the path to the folder, press Windows Key+R, paste the path into the Run dialog box, and click the OK button. Windows opens an Explorer window to the folder.

♦ Similarly, you can back up an individual mail folder within the message store. Open the message store as described in the previous paragraph and back up the appropriate DBX file.

♦ To restore a mail folder, choose File ➤ Import ➤ Messages, and then follow through the steps of the Windows Mail Import Wizard.

The Bottom Line

Collect the information you need to get started with Windows Mail To use Windows Mail, you need an Internet connection (either broadband or via a modem) and an account with an ISP or e-mail provider. Make sure you know your logon name and password, your e-mail address, your incoming mail server and its type (POP or IMAP), your outgoing mail server, and whether to use Secure Password Authentication (SPA). Choose Start ➢ E-mail, and then follow through the process of setting up your e-mail account.

Choose options for Windows Mail Windows Mail comes with default settings that work well for many people, but to get the most out of Windows Mail, you will probably need to customize some settings. Choose Tools ➢ Options, and then work on the many pages of the Options dialog box.

Suppress junk e-mail messages To help you reduce the amount of spam that arrives in your Inbox, Windows Mail provides features for blocking junk e-mail messages. Choose Tools ➢ Junk E-mail Options to open the Junk E-mail Options dialog box. You can then choose a preset level of junk e-mail detection, create a Safe Senders list and a Blocked Senders list, block messages by domain or by language encoding, and choose settings for identifying phishing messages.

Read, send, and reply to e-mail To read incoming e-mail, go to the Folder List on the left of the Windows Mail window and click the Inbox for the mail account you want to read. Windows Mail displays your Inbox, which lists the messages and displays icons to indicate information about the message headers. Click the message you want to read.

To create a new message, click the Create Mail button on the toolbar, and then work in the resulting message window. To reply to a message, click the Reply button on the toolbar. To forward a message, click the Forward button on the toolbar, and then address the message.

Manage your e-mail messages To delete a message from the Inbox, select it and click the Delete button (the × button) on the toolbar. Windows Mail moves the message to the Deleted Items folder. To empty the Deleted Items folder, right-click the folder, choose Empty "Deleted Items" Folder from the context menu, and then click the Yes button in the confirmation message box that appears.

To move a message from the Inbox to a folder, click the message header and drag it to the appropriate folder in the Folders pane.

To clean up messages, choose Tools ➢ Options, click the Advanced tab in the Options dialog box, and then click the Maintenance button. In the Maintenance dialog box, click the Clean Up Now button, select the account, and then choose which messages to remove.

Filter your e-mail to make it more manageable Apart from filtering out junk mail, you can create rules to apply filtering to your messages. Choose Tools ➢ Message Rules ➢ Mail, and then use the options in the New Mail Rule dialog box to define the rule.

Add, remove, and configure mail accounts To add another e-mail account to Windows Mail, choose Tools ➢ Accounts, click the Add button in the Internet Accounts dialog box, and then work through the Internet Connection Wizard. To remove a mail account, select the account in the Internet Accounts dialog box and click the Remove button. To change the properties of an account, click it in the Internet Accounts dialog box, click the Properties button, and then work in the Properties dialog box.

Customize the Inbox To customize the columns displayed in the Inbox, choose View ➤ Columns, and then use the controls in the Columns dialog box to specify which columns Windows Mail should display and the order in which you want them. To customize the layout of your Inbox, choose View ➤ Layout, and then work in the Window Layout Properties dialog box.

Back up your e-mail To back up your Windows Mail data, use Backup Utility (see Chapter 16). If you store your Windows Mail data in the default location, you can back it up by backing up your user profile.

Chapter 18

Reading News with Windows Mail

◆ Understanding the dangers of newsgroups

◆ Setting up Windows Mail to read newsgroups

◆ Reading newsgroup messages

◆ Posting to a newsgroup

◆ Creating rules for filtering news

◆ Working offline

News in this chapter refers to Internet discussion forums, called *newsgroups*, a very loose collection of discussion areas based on the Network News Transport Protocol (NNTP). A *newsgroup* consists of the messages (and sometimes attachments) that people post to the list. These messages, often referred to as *posts*, are available to anyone who chooses to take part in the group (or, in a moderated newsgroup, anyone the moderators allow to take part).

Internet newsgroups encompass most every topic under the sun, the moon, and the earth. In the olden days of the early 1990s, newsgroups were divided up into a relatively formalized informal structure based around a dozen or so hierarchies of newsgroups with names such as `alt` (alternative topics), `biz` (business topics), `comp` (computer topics), and assorted others, with many subgroups under each hierarchy. Nowadays, in concert with the near anarchy into which the Web has grown, newsgroups are often named capriciously, so the best way to find a newsgroup covering topics you're interested in is to search for keywords (or get a recommendation from a friend).

This chapter discusses how to use the newsreader features of Windows Mail to read messages posted to Internet newsgroups and to post messages yourself. It assumes that you've already read the previous chapter and are familiar with Windows Mail's mail features. In this chapter, you'll need to do a little more setup, configuring Windows Mail to access the right news server.

Understanding the Dangers of Newsgroups

Before you dive into Internet newsgroups, there are several things that you should keep in mind— even if you're fully up to speed on the dangers of the Internet and the Web in general.

First, Internet newsgroups are public. In most cases, anyone who can get online can post to them. If you dip into the right newsgroups (or maybe the *wrong* newsgroups), you'll sooner or later run into the full range of online humanity.

Some of these people post things that most people would much rather they didn't. Sooner or later (probably sooner), you're likely to run into such posts.

MEMBERS-ONLY NEWSGROUPS TEND TO HAVE HIGHER STANDARDS

In addition to public, free-for-all newsgroups, you may be invited to join members-only newsgroups. Such newsgroups usually expect a high standard of participation from their members.

Second, much of the information you find in newsgroups is incomplete, inaccurate, wrong, misinformation, disinformation, lies, or advertising. Evaluate any information carefully before deciding to trust it.

Third, newsgroups tend to get archived. (For an example of an archive, point your web browser at Google Groups, http://groups.google.com/, where you can search through millions of posts.) This archiving means that every throwaway post has a good chance of remaining available more or less forever—or at least long enough to severely embarrass the poster. Before you dash off an inflammatory post, remember that it may stick around to haunt you for years. Likewise, don't post any personal information that you don't want to share with the whole wired world.

Fourth, spammers use *bots* (robot programs) to harvest e-mail addresses from newsgroups, both for direct use and for selling to other people. (Perhaps you've already received spam offering you *2 million valid e-mail addresses for only $29.99*? Many of those e-mail addresses have been harvested from newsgroups.) This harvesting means that if you expose your real e-mail address, you're likely to get spam almost immediately from the current crop of spammers.

Many people who post to newsgroups change their e-mail addresses in a way that will defeat bots but enable humans to establish the real e-mail address with a minimal application of sentience. For example, if your e-mail address is peterpiper@pacbell.net, you might post with an address of peterpiper@removethis.pacbell.net and add a note saying "remove removethis from the address when replying." This type of custom addition to an address is enough to defeat most bots while remaining manageable for anyone with even minimal command of English. (Another option is to set up a free e-mail account that you're prepared to dump at any time if it starts receiving unwelcome attention.) Other people consider it unwise to include any form of their e-mail address in public newsgroups. Others yet are happy to expose their real addresses.

Fifth, many of the more specialized newsgroups tend to attract an expert audience that doesn't tolerate off-topic or ill-considered questions well. Before posting, be sure to read the Frequently Asked Questions list (the FAQ) for the newsgroup, and check through its archives to make sure that the topic of your posting (a) is on topic for the newsgroup, and (b) hasn't been answered several times already in the last three months.

Setting Up Windows Mail to Read Newsgroups

When you set up Windows Mail for e-mail, it automatically sets itself up with a news account for the Microsoft Communities newsgroups. This account gives you access to a wide range of Microsoft-related newsgroups.

For wider reading, you'll probably want to set Windows Mail up to read newsgroups provided by your ISP or another online service provider. To set up Windows Mail to read newsgroups, take the following steps:

1. Open Windows Mail as usual (for example, choose Start ➢ E-mail).

2. Choose Tools ➢ Accounts. Windows Mail displays the Internet Accounts dialog box.

3. Click the Add button. Windows Mail displays the Select Account Type screen (see Figure 18.1).

4. Select the Newsgroup Account item, and then click the Next button. Windows Mail displays the Your Name screen.

5. In the Display Name text box, type the name you want to use for your posts. Depending on whether you'll be posting personally or professionally, you may want to use a pseudonym or a variation of your name.

6. Click the Next button. Windows Mail displays the Internet News E-mail Address screen.

7. In the E-mail Address text box, type the e-mail address that you want to use for your posts. As discussed in the previous section, you may want to use a variation of your real e-mail address to throw off spammers.

8. Click the Next button. The wizard displays the Internet News Server Name screen (see Figure 18.2).

9. Type the name of your news server in the News (NNTP) Server text box. If you don't know the name, consult your ISP.

10. If you need to log on to the news server, select the My News Server Requires Me to Log On check box. (Many news servers don't require you to log on.)

11. Click the Next button. If you didn't select the check box in the previous step, the wizard displays its Congratulations page. Go to step 13.

12. If you did select the My News Server Requires Me to Log On check box, the wizard displays the Internet News Server Logon screen. Enter your account name and password. Select the Remember Password check box if you think the convenience of not having to enter the password outweighs the marginal risk of storing it. Then click the Next button. The wizard displays the Congratulations page.

FIGURE 18.1
On the Select Account Type screen, select the Newsgroup Account item.

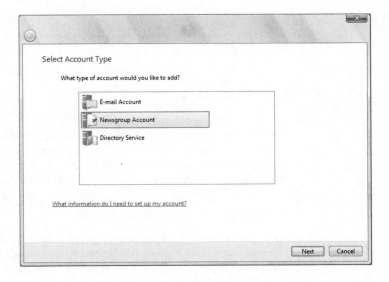

FIGURE 18.2
On the Internet News
Server Name screen,
enter the name of
the news server and
specify whether it
requires you to log on.

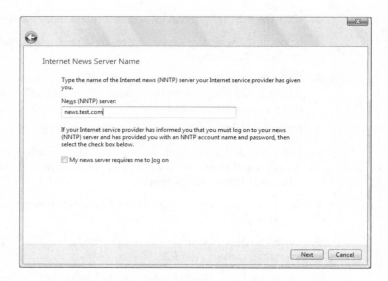

13. Click the Finish button. The wizard closes, returning you to the Internet Accounts dialog box.

14. Click the Close button. Windows Mail displays the Subscribe to Newsgroups dialog box, shown here:

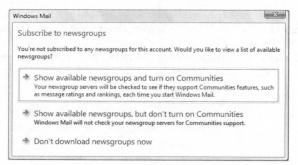

15. Click the appropriate button:

♦ If you want to use Windows Mail's Communities features (which include the ability to see message ratings and rankings) and download a list of newsgroups, click the Show Available Newsgroups and Turn on Communities button. At this writing, many newsgroups do not support Communities, and in others, the Communities features appear not to be fully implemented—but matters may have improved by the time you read this.

♦ If you just want to download a list of newsgroups, click the Show Available Newsgroups, but Don't Turn on Communities button.

♦ If you don't want to download the list of newsgroups now, click the Don't Download Newsgroups Now button. You'll need to download the list of newsgroups at some point, but if you're currently using a dial-up connection, you might prefer to leave the download until later.

16. If you chose to download the newsgroups, Windows Mail displays the Downloading News-groups dialog box while it downloads them. Skip ahead to the section "Downloading the List of Newsgroups."

Changing the Properties for a News Account

You can change the properties for a news account you've set up by working in its Properties dialog box. For example, you might want to change the name that Windows Mail displays for the news account to something more descriptive, or you might need to change your password or connection information.

To display the Properties dialog box for the account, take either of the following actions:

◆ Right-click the news account in the Folders pane and choose Properties from the context menu.

◆ Choose Tools ➢ Accounts. Windows Mail displays the Internet Accounts dialog box. In the News section, select the account, and then click the Properties button.

GENERAL PAGE PROPERTIES

The General page of the Properties dialog box (see Figure 18.3) for a news account contains the following options:

News Account area In the text box, enter the name that you want displayed for the news account. Changing the name doesn't affect the server.

User Information area Enter or adjust your name, organization, e-mail address, and reply address in the four text boxes. Select the Include This Account when Checking for New Messages check box if you want Windows Mail to check this account's newsgroups for new messages each time you check for new messages. (Doing so tends to slow down checking for mail.)

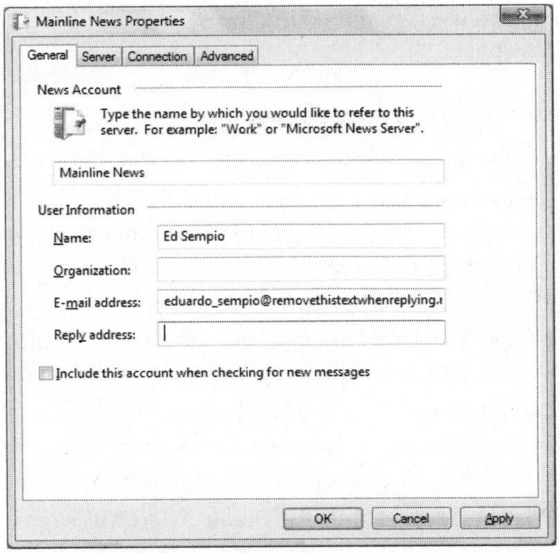

FIGURE 18.3
The General page of the Properties dialog box for a news account lets you rename the server and adjust the user information displayed.

SERVER PAGE PROPERTIES

The Server page of the Properties dialog box (see Figure 18.4) for a news account contains the connection information for the server that you entered during setup. Change this information if necessary to connect to the server. (For example, your ISP might start requiring you to log on or to use Secure Password Authentication.)

FIGURE 18.4

The Server page of the Properties dialog box for a news account lets you change the server or specify logon information.

CONNECTION PAGE PROPERTIES

The Connection page of the Properties dialog box for a news account lets you specify which connection to use for connecting to the account. In many cases, you won't need to change the settings on this page.

ADVANCED PAGE PROPERTIES

The Advanced page of the Properties dialog box (see Figure 18.5) contains the following options:

Server Port Number area If necessary, change the port number in the News (NNTP) text box from the default setting (119) to another port specified by your ISP. Also if necessary, select the This Server Requires a Secure Connection (SSL) check box. Again, your ISP will let you know if you need to apply this setting.

Server Timeouts area If Windows Mail is timing out when you feel it shouldn't be, drag the slider to increase the length of the server timeout interval.

Descriptions area Select the Use Newsgroup Descriptions check box if you want Windows Mail to download newsgroup descriptions. Doing so can be informative but slows down the downloading of the list of newsgroups.

Posting area Select the Break Apart Messages Larger than *NN* KB check box and enter an appropriate value in the text box if you want Windows Mail to automatically divide large files you post into a number of smaller parts. (This setting is primarily useful if you're posting large attachments, but it will also help protect the readers of the newsgroups if you start posting million-word theses on a regular basis.) Select the Ignore News Sending Format and Post Using check box and select the HTML option button or the Plain Text option button if you want Windows Mail to override the format in which you compose your messages.

When you've finished choosing options in the Properties dialog box, click the OK button. Windows Mail closes the Properties dialog box and applies your choices.

FIGURE 18.5
The Advanced page of the Properties dialog box for a news account provides options for server connections, downloading news-group descriptions, and posting messages.

Downloading the List of Newsgroups

As mentioned in the previous section, Windows Mail encourages you to download the list of news-groups from the news server you've just added. (This list contains the names and brief details of the newsgroups available to you—it doesn't include all the contents of the newsgroups.) If you prefer not to do so right away, you can download the list the first time you issue the Tools ➤ Newsgroups command.

Windows Mail displays the Downloading Newsgroups dialog box while downloading the list of newsgroups. The number of newsgroups available depends on the ISP. Some ISPs offer as many newsgroups as they can get (50,000 or more), whereas others provide only the newsgroups that they think their customers want (or should want).

When Windows Mail has finished downloading the list of newsgroups, it displays the list in the Newsgroup Subscriptions box. The next section covers how to subscribe to newsgroups.

READING A NEWSGROUP THAT YOUR ISP DOESN'T PROVIDE

If your ISP doesn't provide a newsgroup that you want to read, Google may be able to help. Choose Start ➤ Internet, browse to http://groups.google.com, and then use the links to browse to the newsgroup or search for it. You can subscribe to receive groups via e-mail.

Subscribing to Newsgroups

At this point, you're ready to start reading news. You can do this either by subscribing to newsgroups that interest you or simply by opening newsgroups that might interest you and browsing through them.

To subscribe to a newsgroup, follow these steps:

1. Click the Newsgroups button on the toolbar, or choose Tools ➤ Newsgroups, or press Ctrl+W. Windows Mail displays the Newsgroup Subscriptions dialog box (shown in Figure 18.6 with two groups subscribed).

2. In the list box, select a newsgroup that you want to subscribe to, and click the Subscribe button to subscribe:

   ◆ The Newsgroup Subscriptions dialog box has three pages: All, Subscribed, and New. Typically, you'll want to start on the All page, so that you can access all the newsgroups. Once you've subscribed to the newsgroups you're interested in, use the Subscribed page to access them quickly, and use the New page to check out new newsgroups from time to time.

   ◆ To filter the thousands of newsgroups down to a manageable number, enter search text in the Display Newsgroups Which Contain text box. For example, if you're interested in hardware for PC-compatible computer systems, you could enter `comp.sys.ibm.pc.hardware` to display the set of newsgroups that contain that string of text, as shown in the figure. (As mentioned earlier in this chapter, `comp` is one of the main hierarchies of newsgroups that persist to this day.)

   ◆ Select the Also Search Descriptions check box if you want to search the newsgroup descriptions for the terms in the Display Newsgroups Which Contain text box. (Many of the newsgroups lack descriptions, however, so this step may not get you far.)

FIGURE 18.6
Subscribe to newsgroups in the Newsgroup Subscriptions dialog box.

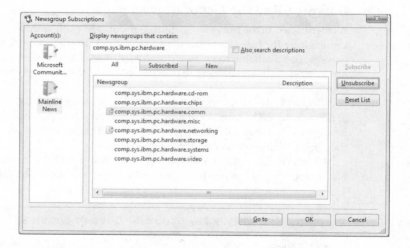

- Windows Mail places an icon to the left of newsgroups you're subscribed to, as you can see with the `comp.sys.ibm.pc.hardware.comm` and `comp.sys.ibm.pc.hardware.networking` newsgroups in the figure.

- To unsubscribe from a newsgroup you're subscribed to, select the newsgroup and click the Unsubscribe button.

- To download the latest newsgroups, click the Reset List button. You'll see the Downloading Newsgroups dialog box again.

3. When you've assembled your list of newsgroups, click the OK button. Windows Mail closes the Newsgroup Subscriptions dialog box and returns you to its main page, where the Folders pane lists the newsgroups you subscribed to under the news server.

To read a newsgroup without subscribing to it, select its name in the Newsgroup Subscriptions dialog box and click the Go To button. Windows Mail displays the newsgroup.

 Real World Scenario

WHEN YOU CAN'T FIND A NEWSGROUP YOU KNOW EXISTS

If a newsgroup you want to read isn't available even after you have reset your list of newsgroups, your ISP probably doesn't carry it. Try requesting the ISP to carry it—if it's a new newsgroup, it may not have appeared on their radar yet. If they won't carry it (for example, because other people might find its content offensive), you might need to read it on Google Groups (`http://groups.google.com`) or buy a subscription to a dedicated news server that carries it.

Reading Newsgroup Messages

To read the messages in a newsgroup you've subscribed to, double-click the newsgroup in the Folders pane to display it. Windows Mail downloads the first batch of headers for the newsgroup—up to 300, at the default setting, if there are that many—and displays them in the Header pane.

Click a message to display it in the Preview pane, as shown in Figure 18.7. Alternatively, double-click a message to display it in a separate window. If a message has an attachment, you can open it by using the same techniques as for e-mail messages with attachments.

"COMBINE AND DECODE" A LARGE FILE POSTED IN MULTIPLE PARTS

When a large file has been posted in multiple parts, you can reconstitute it by downloading the messages for each part, selecting the messages, right-clicking one of them, and choosing Combine and Decode from the context menu.

FIGURE 18.7
As with e-mail, you can read newsgroups in the Preview pane or in a separate window.

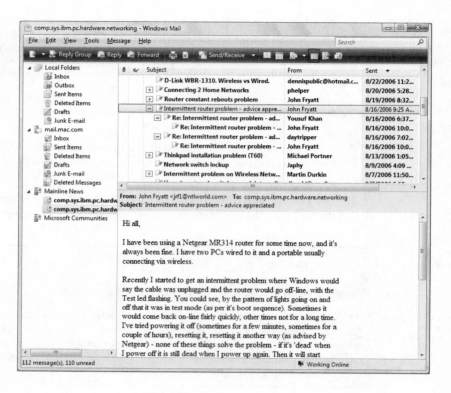

Where posters have replied to a message using the same Subject line, the messages are *threaded* (linked together in a sequence). You can expand a collapsed thread by clicking the plus (+) sign next to it, and collapse an expanded sign by clicking its minus (–) sign. Each generation of a threaded message is indented more than the previous generations, as shown here.

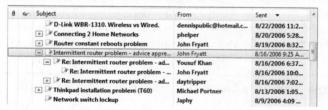

The status bar shows you the current status of your subscription to the newsgroup: how many messages there are in the newsgroup, how many you've read, and how many more you haven't downloaded yet.

To download message headers you haven't downloaded yet, click the Get Next Headers button (the rightmost button on the toolbar) or choose Tools ➤ Get Next 300 Headers. To display another newsgroup, double-click it in the Folders pane.

Posting to a Newsgroup

You can post to a newsgroup either by creating a new post or by replying to a post:

◆ Click the Write Message button on the toolbar to start a new post. Don't use stationery for a post to an Internet newsgroup, because chances are that many people won't be able to see it—they'll probably have to download it as an attached graphic, which improves nobody's temper. Windows Mail starts a new post to the newsgroup.

◆ To reply to the newsgroup, click the Reply Group button on the toolbar. Windows Mail creates a reply message to the group, quoting the text of the original post (shown in Figure 18.8). Reduce this text to the minimum needed for context, because surplus quoted text is a killer in highly trafficked newsgroups.

Once you've written your post, set it aside for 10 minutes. Then read it carefully to make sure its meaning is clear, that there's nothing offensive in it, and that you're not about to annoy people by writing in all capitals (doing so is considered to be shouting). Make changes as necessary, and spell-check it if appropriate. Then click the Send button to send the post.

You may also want to reply only to the author of the post (particularly if you don't want to broadcast your response to the post) or to forward the post to someone else:

◆ To reply only to the author of the post, click the Reply button on the toolbar. Windows Mail creates a regular reply for you, as if you were replying to an e-mail message.

◆ To forward a post, click the Forward button on the toolbar. Windows Mail creates a regular forwarded message.

FIGURE 18.8

Creating a reply to a newsgroup post

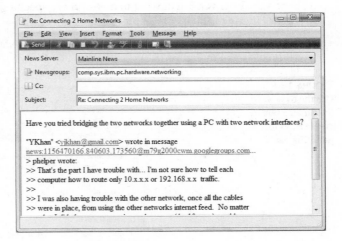

Posting an Attachment

To attach a file to a post, follow the same procedure as for an e-mail message:

1. Click the Attach File to Message button or choose Insert ➤ File Attachment. Windows Mail displays the Open dialog box.

2. Select the file.

3. Click the Open button. Windows Mail attaches it to the post.

If you're posting large attachments, make sure that you've selected the Break Apart Messages Larger than *NN* KB check box on the Advanced page of the Properties dialog box for the news account and entered an appropriate value in the text box. What's an appropriate file size will depend on the size of the files you're posting and the sensitivity (or lack of sensitivity) of the news server. For example, if you're posting your latest compositions in MP3 format, consider breaking the files down into segments of 100KB or so by using this option.

 Real World Scenario

AVOIDING COPYRIGHT ISSUES

Don't post any copyrighted material that you don't have specific permission to distribute. See the section "Understanding Copyright Issues" in Chapter 19 for a brief discussion of copyright.

Creating Rules for Filtering News

In Chapter 17, you learned how you can filter e-mail to take actions automatically on messages that match certain criteria. Windows Mail lets you filter news messages as well. For example, you might want to create a rule that captured every message with particular keywords in the header.

Here's the brief version of what to do (for more specifics, look at the section titled "Creating Rules for Filtering E-mail" in Chapter 17):

1. Choose Tools ➢ Message Rules ➢ News. Windows Mail displays the New News Rule dialog box (shown in Figure 18.9).

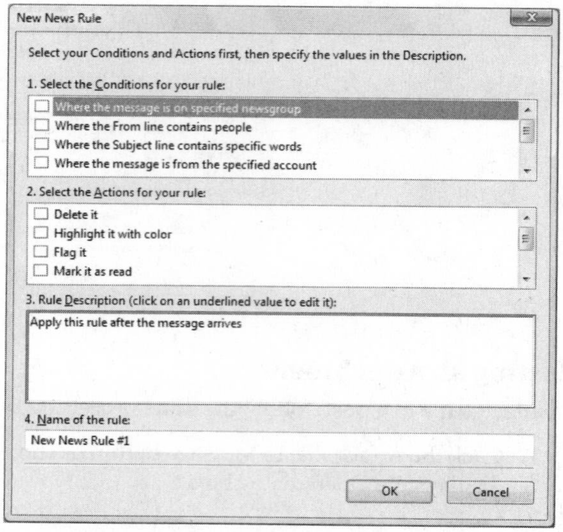

FIGURE 18.9
Use the New News Rule dialog box to create rules for handling news.

New News Rule
Select your Conditions and Actions first, then specify the values in the Description.
1. Select the Conditions for your rule:
☐ Where the message is on specified newsgroup
☐ Where the From line contains people
☐ Where the Subject line contains specific words
☐ Where the message is from the specified account
2. Select the Actions for your rule:
☐ Delete it
☐ Highlight it with color
☐ Flag it
☐ Mark it as read
3. Rule Description (click on an underlined value to edit it):
Apply this rule after the message arrives
4. Name of the rule:
New News Rule #1
OK   Cancel

2. In the Select the Conditions for Your Rule list box, select the conditions to apply to the messages.

3. In the Select the Actions for Your Rule list box, select the actions to take when the conditions are met.

4. In the Rule Description list box, click the links to edit them as appropriate.

5. In the Name of the Rule text box, type a descriptive and easily understood name for the rule.

6. Click the OK button. Windows Mail closes the New News Rule dialog box and displays the Message Rules dialog box.

7. Click the Apply Now button. Windows Mail displays the Apply News Rules Now dialog box.

8. Select the rule in the Select Rules to Apply list box.

9. Click the Browse button, and then use the resulting Apply to Folder dialog box to apply the rule to a different newsgroup if necessary.

10. Click the Apply Now button to apply the rule. Windows Mail displays a message box telling you when the rule has been applied.

11. Click the OK button. Windows Mail closes the message box.

12. Click the Close button. Windows Mail closes the Apply News Rules Now dialog box.

13. Click the OK button. Windows Mail closes the Message Rules dialog box.

Working Offline

If you don't have a permanent Internet connection, you can work offline with newsgroups. In short, you download the headers for the newsgroups, mark those you want to download, and then download them when you go back online.

To work offline, follow these steps:

1. When you're ready to go offline, choose File ➢ Work Offline. Windows Mail stops working online and switches to offline mode. The status bar displays *Working Offline*.

2. Browse the headers for the newsgroups you subscribe to. Mark any messages you want to download:

   ◆ To mark a message for downloading, right-click it and choose Download Message Later from the context menu. Windows Mail marks the message with an arrow to indicate that it will be downloaded.

   ◆ To mark a thread for downloading, right-click one of the messages in it and choose Download Conversation Later from the context menu. Windows Mail marks the messages with arrows.

3. When you're ready to go back online, choose File ➢ Work Online or double-click the *Working Online* indicator on the status bar.

4. With the newsgroup selected, choose Tools ➢ Synchronize Newsgroup. Windows Mail displays the Synchronize Newsgroup dialog box (shown in Figure 18.10).

FIGURE 18.10
In the Synchronize
Newsgroup dialog
box, specify which
items to download.

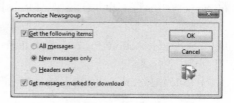

5. Make sure the Get Messages Marked for Download check box is selected. To download further headers, select the Get the Following Items check box and the Headers Only option button.

6. Click the OK button. Windows Mail downloads the items you specified.

7. Choose File ➤ Work Offline to go offline again to read the items.

The Bottom Line

Understanding the dangers of newsgroups   Newsgroups can offer a wide variety of interesting and useful information, but they can also contain inaccurate, offensive, or dangerous material. Evaluate all material critically rather that taking it at face value. Don't send inflammatory posts that you may later regret when they end up in a news archive. Consider disguising your e-mail address so that it cannot be harvested by spammers' bots, or use a disposable e-mail address for your posts.

Setting up Windows Mail to read newsgroups   To set up Windows Mail to read newsgroups, choose Tools ➤ Accounts, click the Add button, choose the Newsgroup Account item on the Select Account Type screen, and then follow the wizard. You'll need to supply a name (perhaps your own, perhaps a pseudonym), an e-mail address (perhaps disguised), and a news server name (accurate). You can change the name of a news account after creating it by working on the General page of its Properties dialog box. To subscribe to newsgroups, click the Newsgroups button on the toolbar, and then work on the three pages of the Newsgroup Subscriptions dialog box.

Reading newsgroup messages   Once you've subscribed to a newsgroup, double-click its listing under the news server in the Folders pane to open the newsgroup and display messages in it. Click a message to display it in the Preview pane.

Posting to a newsgroup   To create a new post to a newsgroup, click the Write Message button on the toolbar. To reply to a post in the newsgroup, click the Reply Group button. To reply only to the person who posted (without posting to the newsgroup), click the Reply button. Before sending your post, it's a good idea to take a short break and then reread it to make sure it says exactly what you want and isn't inflammatory.

Creating rules for filtering news   You can filter news messages by using much the same techniques as for e-mail messages. Choose Tools ➤ Message Rules ➤ News, and then work with the options in the New News Rule dialog box.

Working offline   If your Internet connection is dial-up or temporary, you can use Windows Mail's offline features to arrange which messages to download, and then download them all at once. Choose File ➤ Work Offline to go offline. Right-click a message and choose Download Message Later to mark a message for downloading, or right-click a message in a thread and choose Download Conversation Later. Choose File ➤ Work Online to go back online. Select the newsgroup, choose Tools ➤ Synchronize Newsgroup, specify which items to download, and then click the OK button to download them.

Chapter 19

Publishing Information to the Web

- ◆ Resolve content, copyright, and quality issues
- ◆ Create your own website
- ◆ Create a Space on Windows Live Spaces
- ◆ Write a blog
- ◆ Post materials to content-specific sites

The Web allows you to make your own material available to the whole wired world—provided that you have a place to put it. This chapter discusses four leading ways of publishing information on the Web from Windows Vista: creating your own website, creating a Space on Windows Live Spaces, writing a blog, or posting materials to content-specific sites.

Deciding What to Publish

First, decide what you will publish. Perhaps you've decided already—anything from your family photos to your political opinions, from your recipes to your music and videos.

But before you publish anything, there's one issue you *must* consider: copyright. And there's another issue you really ought to consider: quality control. This section discusses those issues.

Understanding Copyright Issues

Before you publish any material to the Web, make sure you can legally do so. This means either understanding the basics of copyright law or consulting a lawyer. You can guess which of these options costs more. Nonetheless, this chapter isn't to be construed as legal advice and is not a substitute for it. If you have any questions about copyright issues, seek the counsel of an attorney, preferably one who specializes in intellectual property rights.

Here is the absolute minimum you should know about copyright:

- ◆ If you created an original work yourself, you hold the copyright to it. For example, if you take an original digital photo, write an original story, or compose an original song, you hold the copyright to it. (If the work isn't original, you've probably infringed copyright. For example, taking a digital photo of someone else's work is not likely to create an original work.) You can post that work to the Web if you want. And you can try to defend your copyright against anyone who infringes it.

- ◆ As the copyright holder, you have five main rights to the work: the Reproduction Right (making copies of the work), the Distribution Right (distributing it), the Modification Right or Derivative Works Right (creating other works based on the work), the Public Performance Right (performing or transmitting the work), and the Public Display Right (displaying the work in a public place). You can exercise these rights yourself or grant them to other people. For example, the author of a book often grants to a publisher the Reproduction Right and the Distribution Right, so that the publisher can print copies of the book and distribute them.

◆ If someone else created the work, you probably need to get explicit permission to publish or distribute it. The fact that someone has posted a work on a website or a newsgroup doesn't make it public domain (discussed in the next paragraph), and you should be wary of airy claims by such posters that works are in the public domain.

◆ Some works are in the *public domain*, a notional area that contains all works that are not protected by copyright and which you can therefore publish and distribute freely. Some works are never protected by copyright, because they're not copyrightable due to their nature (for example, facts andURLs are not copyrightable), because they're not copyrighted (for example, U.S. government publications under the authorship of the federal government are not copyrighted), or because the creator of the work has chosen to put it in the public domain (such a work will usually contain a statement saying that it has been placed in the public domain). Other works go out of copyright because the copyright has expired or has been lost. If in doubt, do a copyright search at the Copyright Office (`http://www.copyright.gov`), or use a qualified copyright search firm.

Beware the Copyright Grabbers

Some website hosting services use their Terms and Conditions to claim copyright of any original material you post. Read the small print before you post anything on these services.

Those are the bare bones of what you need to know about copyright to avoid committing copyright violations left, right, and center. Here are some resources for understanding copyright:

◆ Brad Templeton's *10 Big Myths about Copyright Explained* site (`http://www.templetons.com/brad/copymyths.html`) debunks the biggest myths about copyright.

◆ The U.S. Copyright Office (`http://www.copyright.gov`) offers several resources on copyright, including the Copyright FAQ (`http://www.copyright.gov/help/faq/`) and a Copyright Basics section (`http://www.copyright.gov/circs/circ1.html`).

◆ The Copyright Clearance Center (`http://www.copyright.com`) provides a central location for getting permission to reproduce many copyrighted works. (For others, you may need to contact the creator of the work directly.)

Performing Quality Control

As you'll have noticed if you've spent more than a few hours surfing, the Web already suffers from a severe lack of quality control. If you plan to publish to the Web, try not to add to this problem.

Historically, the high cost of publishing a work has acted as a strong incentive for the publisher to ensure that the work is of a high enough quality that it will appeal to its intended audience. For example, if a publisher publishes a book that's so bad (or on so unappealing a topic) that nobody buys it, they lose money. If a record company issues an unlistenable CD, they're unlikely to achieve significant sales (and they may even have to pay the artist huge sums of money to make her go away). And if an artist paints wretched pictures, the chances of their finding a market are slim.

By contrast, the Web is more or less a free-for-all. The cost of publishing to the Web can be extremely low (or nothing): You need do little more than create files and post them on a website or blog, and anyone with an Internet connection and web browser can access them. If they don't like what they find at your site, they probably won't return, but the cost to you remains minimal.

But if you want people to look at what you post, make sure that its quality is at least acceptable:

◆ Don't post just anything (or *everything*) you have. Select the best items and post them. If they draw acclaim (or rapture), consider posting more.

◆ Spell-check any text you post. If your grammar is poor, get someone competent to check it for you. Involve an editor or proofreader if you're looking to be professional and persuasive. (For editors and proofreaders, the unedited and unproofed content on the Web can be painful to experience but at the same time gratifying in that it illustrates the need for their often unseen and unsung services.)

◆ Use graphics in moderation—and make sure they contribute to your site. Pointless or large graphics increase the time it takes web pages to load, which pleases nobody.

◆ Produce any audio material to a reasonable standard. Your band's live tapes might not make the cut unmixed; mixed, they might.

◆ Produce any video material to a higher standard. Today's broadband connections can handle modest amounts of video comfortably, but nobody wants to waste hours downloading huge video files only to find their content is worthless. Instead of posting video on your own site, you may prefer to use a video-sharing site such as YouTube (`http://www.youtube.com`).

Create Your Own Website

The most flexible option for publishing your material on the Web is to create your own website. You can control the structure, layout, and look of your site, so you should be able to create exactly the type of site you want—subject to the limitations of websites and the tools you use. The disadvantage to creating your own site is that doing so typically takes more effort that using the other options discussed later in this chapter.

Deciding Where to Host Your Site

If you decide to create your own site, you need to decide where to host it:

Space provided by your ISP   Many ISPs provide web space with your Internet service (along with one or more e-mail addresses). If your web-publishing plans are modest, this space may be more than adequate. When choosing an ISP, factor in how much web space they give you and how much traffic they allow your site before charging you for extra bandwidth.

Other Web hosts   If your ISP doesn't provide adequate space or bandwidth, you can use a web-hosting firm instead. Such firms specialize in hosting websites and registering domains. To find a suitable firm, consult friends who have their own websites, put **web hosting** into your favorite search engine, or consult a host-finding site such as FindMyHosting.com (`http://www.findmyhosting.com`) or Web Hosting Stuff (`http://www.webhostingstuff.com`). For a reliable website, it's usually best to pay a modest fee for web hosting. Bargain-basement web hosts may not be reliable or responsive, and most free web hosts support their business by posting ads on your site, which tends to detract from its appeal.

Creating Web Content

When you have your own website, you can use any program capable of producing HTML to create your web pages. Here are some examples:

Notepad Notepad (choose Start ➢ All Programs ➢ Accessories ➢ Notepad) can be a handy tool for creating web pages—provided that you know the HTML codes you need. The advantage of using a text editor such as Notepad is that you can create compact HTML that contains no unnecessary elements that more complex programs may insert automatically.

Microsoft Word If you have Microsoft Word, you can easily save Word documents as HTML files. Choose the "Web Page, Filtered" format in the Save As Type drop-down list in the Save As dialog box to create an HTML page from a document. (The Single File Web Page format and the Web Page format create HTML files that contain Word-related information, such as document properties and even VBA code, that are useless in your web pages.)

Web Page Editor For creating a complex website, you may prefer to use a web page editor such as Microsoft FrontPage or Adobe Dreamweaver. Such editors let you switch quickly between viewing the HTML code and the page that the code produces.

Getting Material to Your Website

The standard way of getting material onto your website is to create and assemble the material offline and then upload it to the website via FTP. If you're uploading a new version of a page, the upload overwrites the existing page. You can spend as long as you need to create and save the content, and because the files you're working with are stored on a local drive, you can access them at full speed.

USING WINDOWS VISTA'S FTP CAPABILITIES

Internet Explorer and Windows Explorer include basic FTP capabilities. To transfer files via Internet Explorer and Windows Explorer, take the following steps:

1. Choose Start ➢ Internet. Windows launches Internet Explorer.

2. In the Address bar, enter the FTP address, username, and password (if you choose) using the following format:

```
ftp://username[:password]@ftpserver/url
```

3. Click the Go button or press the Enter key. If you specified your password, Internet Explorer connects to the FTP server and displays the folder. If you chose not to specify your password, Internet Explorer displays the Login As dialog box, in which you can enter your password and choose whether to save it.

CREATE A FAVORITE FOR THE FTP SITE

Once you've connected to the FTP site, create a favorite for it so that you can access it quickly in the future.

The FTP site appears in the Internet Explorer window as a series of links:

◆ Click the Up to Higher Level Directory link to go up to the parent directory or folder (the folder that contains the folder you're currently viewing).

◆ Click the link for a folder to open that folder.

◆ Click the link for a file to download that file.

Downloading is easy from within the Internet Explorer window, but if you need to upload files to the FTP site, you must open a Windows Explorer window to it. To do so, choose Page ➢ Open FTP Site in Windows Explorer. Internet Explorer may display an Internet Explorer Security dialog box like the one shown here, warning you that "A website wants to open web content using this program on your computer."

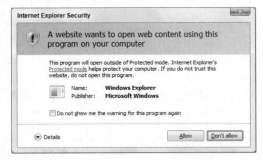

Verify that the program is Windows Explorer, and then click the Allow button. A Windows Explorer window opens showing the contents of the website. You can then transfer files by using standard Windows Explorer techniques:

◆ To upload a file, drag it to the FTP site's Windows Explorer window.

◆ To download a file, drag it from the FTP site's Windows Explorer window to another Windows Explorer window.

Using an FTP Client

Internet Explorer and Windows Explorer provide functional FTP, but if you need more powerful FTP capabilities, get a graphical FTP client such as WS_FTP Pro (http://www.ipswitch.com) or CuteFTP (http://www.globalscape.com). Such FTP clients streamline the process of uploading and downloading many files and folders.

Create a Space on Windows Live Spaces

Windows Live Spaces is Microsoft's free social-networking site. Windows Live Spaces was formerly known as MSN Spaces before Microsoft brought it into the fold of Live services.

A Space lets you create standard elements such as your profile, a blog, a photo book, and lists of items you like (for example, songs or movies). By filling in all the blanks, you can quickly create a personal web presence that gives visitors some idea of you, your interests, and your tastes. You can choose whether to make your Space public (so that anybody on the Internet can view it) or restrict it to a list of friends whom you choose. These features are attractive for social networking, but you may find them limiting if you want to create either a focused website or a blog that doesn't have distractions.

To create a Windows Live Space, you must have a Windows Live ID, which is the new name for what used to be Microsoft Passport. If you have a Hotmail account or an MSN account, you already have a Windows Live ID. If not, you can sign up for a Windows Live ID by pointing your web browser to `http://get.live.com/windowsvista/winlive/` or taking the following steps:

1. Choose Start ➢ Control Panel. Windows displays a Control Panel window.

2. Click the System and Maintenance link. Windows displays the System and Maintenance window.

3. Click the Welcome Center link. Windows displays the Welcome Center window.

4. In the Offers from Microsoft area, double-click the Go Online to Learn about Windows Live icon.

Write a Blog

Blog (or *web log*) sites such as Blogger.com (`http://www.blogger.com`) make it easy to create an ongoing journal in reverse chronological order, so that the most recent item appears at the top (where the reader sees it first). Blog sites tend to follow a mostly standard format but allow you to customize it by using different templates. Blogs are typically best suited for text-based information, but some sites host other kinds of blogs, such as video blogs.

Posting to a Blog

The procedure for posting to a blog varies from site to site. Most blog sites provide a web-based mechanism for creating blog posts through a web browser; you can either type the text directly into the boxes on the web page or copy it from an existing document and paste it in. Many sites also allow you to post from other devices, including mobile phones.

Blogging from Microsoft Word 2007

If you have Microsoft Word 2007, you can publish a document directly to a blog on certain blogging sites, including Windows Live Spaces and Blogger. To set Word up for blogging, take the following steps:

1. In Word, click the Office Button, and then click New. Word displays the New Document dialog box.

2. In the Templates box, click the Blank and Recent item, and then choose the New Blog Post item.

3. Click the Create button. Word creates a new blog document, displays the Blog Post tab of the Ribbon, and opens the Register a Blog Account dialog box.

4. Click the Register Now button. Word displays the New Blog Account dialog box, as shown here.

5. In the Blog drop-down list, select your blog provider, and then click the Next button. Word displays a dialog box with options for the blog provider you chose, as in the example shown here for Blogger.

6. Enter your username and password, select the Remember Password check box if you want Word to store the password for your convenience, and choose any other options that are available. Then click the OK button. Word sets up the account for blogging.

Once you've created your post in the Word document, you can publish it by choosing Office Button ➤ Publish ➤ Blog.

Post Materials to Content-Specific Sites

If you have only a particular type of content to post, consider a content-specific site. For example:

◆ If your only content is videos of your band performing, you might post them to YouTube (http://www.youtube.com) or a similar video site, where they may receive more views than on your own website.

◆ If you have only photos to post, you might use a photo-specific site such as Flickr (http://www.flickr.com).

The Bottom Line

Resolve content, copyright, and quality issues You can freely publish any material that you've created yourself and whose rights you haven't assigned to anyone else. You'll need permission to distribute anyone else's copyrighted content. While you can publish material of any quality at all to the Web, higher-quality content tends to draw more eyeballs and more return visits.

Create your own website   For full control over your web presence, create your own website, either on space provided by your ISP or on space you rent from a web-hosting company. You can create HTML files using any tool from Notepad upward, but you'll probably want to get a web page editor if you're creating a full-featured site.

Create a Space on Windows Live Spaces   Windows Live Spaces lets you quickly create a personal web presence within a canned format. You can make your Space available only to specified friends or to everyone online.

Write a blog   A blog lets you easily create an online journal, with the most recent post appearing at the top of the page. You typically create blog content by using a web page, but you may also be able to post from other devices or directly from Microsoft Word 2007.

Post materials to content-specific sites   Content-specific sites such as YouTube (videos) or Flickr (photos) let you post particular content types for others to browse. Such sites can provide greater visibility for your material than a personal website or a Space.

Chapter 20

Instant Messaging with Windows Live Messenger

◆ Get and install Windows Live Messenger

◆ Start Messenger for the first time

◆ Configure Messenger to suit your needs

◆ Add and remove contacts

◆ Chat with your contacts

◆ Block and unblock users

◆ Change your online status

◆ Transfer files to and from your contacts

This chapter shows you how to use Windows Live Messenger, the instant-messaging software designed to be used with Windows Vista. Windows Live Messenger (hereafter referred to simply as *Messenger*) provides solid instant-messaging capabilities: You can keep a list of online contacts, see at a glance which of them are online, and communicate instantly with them via text-based chat, voice, and even video (if you have the hardware). You can also transfer files to your buddies and receive files from them.

Instant messaging (IM) is a great way to keep in touch with people, because the conversation takes place in real time. If someone is online at the same time you are, you can communicate with them. Messenger notifies you when your contacts come online (and notifies your contacts when *you* go online), so you know who's available to chat. If the person with whom you want to communicate isn't online, you can send them an "offline instant message"—a message that they'll receive the next time they sign in.

To use Messenger, you must have a Windows Live ID, the latest version of what used to be called Microsoft .NET Passport. If you have a Hotmail account or MSN account, you already have a Windows Live ID. If not, you can sign up for one in minutes.

Getting and Installing Messenger

Messenger came built into Windows XP, and some other earlier versions of Windows, but it's not included in standard distributions of Windows Vista. However, your computer's manufacturer may have included Messenger—so have a look for Messenger on the Start menu before you download it.

To download and install Messenger, follow these steps:

1. Choose Start ➢ All Programs ➢ Windows Live Messenger Download. If that item doesn't appear on the All Programs menu, open Internet Explorer (for example, choose Start ➢ Internet) and go to http://get.live.com/messenger/overview.

2. Click the link to download Windows Live Messenger. In the File Download – Security Warning dialog box, click the Save button, and then choose the folder in which to save it.

3. When the download is complete, click the Run button in the Download Complete dialog box to start the installation.

4. If Internet Explorer displays a Security Warning dialog box, click the Run button to proceed.

5. Follow through the installation. The key decision comes with the Terms of Use and Privacy Statement screen, where you must decide to accept the terms of service and privacy statement in order to use Messenger. Read the terms carefully, and follow the URL to the Privacy Statement, to make sure that you know what you're agreeing to. For example, you must agree that:

    ◆ You will not use Messenger to send or receive any material protected by intellectual property laws unless you own the rights or have received consent to distribute the material.

    ◆ Microsoft may automatically update the version of Messenger you're using.

    ◆ Microsoft can change the terms of use and privacy statement without telling you. To find out the changes, you must check online. If you continue using Messenger after such a change, even if you don't know about it, you're deemed to have agreed to the change.

    ◆ Microsoft may monitor your communications and disclose your details to comply with the law, to respond to legal process, or for other reasons.

6. On the Choose Additional Features and Settings screen (see Figure 20.1), clear the check box for any feature you don't want to install. Your options include:

    ◆ **Windows Live Messenger Shortcuts**—Having a shortcut on your Desktop and the Quick Launch toolbar can be handy, but you can always launch Messenger from the Start menu, or set it to launch automatically when you log on to Windows.

    ◆ **Windows Live Sign-in Assistant**—The Assistant enables you to use two or more Windows Live IDs from the same Windows user account. You can save the password for each of the Windows Live IDs, so you can sign in easily using any of the IDs.

    ◆ **MSN Home**—Selecting this check box changes Internet Explorer's home page to MSN Home. If you have a preferred home page, clear this check box.

    ◆ **Windows Live Toolbar** If this check box appears, clear it, because the Windows Live Toolbar requires Windows XP rather than Windows Vista. (Windows Vista already includes most of the features available in Windows Live Toolbar.)

7. When the setup routine ends, click the Close button. Messenger then starts automatically.

FIGURE 20.1

On the Choose Additional Features and Settings screen of the Windows Live Messenger setup routine, clear the MSN Home check box unless you want to use MSN Home as your home page in Internet Explorer.

Starting Messenger for the First Time

The first time you start Messenger, you need to provide the details of your Windows Live ID and you will also choose options. Follow these steps:

1. To start Messenger, choose Start ➤ All Programs ➤ Windows Live Messenger. Alternatively, if a Messenger icon appears in the notification area, double-click it. Figure 20.2 shows the initial Messenger window.

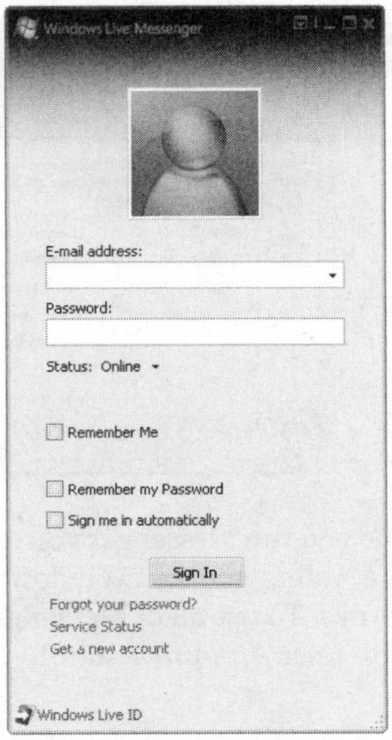

FIGURE 20.2

If you already have a Windows Live ID (for example, a Hotmail account), you're ready to sign in to Messenger. If not, click the Get a New Account link.

2. If you don't have a Windows Live ID yet, click the Get a New Account link toward the bottom of the window. Messenger causes Windows to open a browser window to the Windows Live web page on which you can sign up for a Windows Live ID. Follow the process, being sure to read the terms and conditions carefully.

3. Type your Windows Live ID in the E-mail Address text box, and then type your password in the Password text box.

4. If you want Messenger to remember your Windows Live ID, select the Remember Me check box. Messenger makes Windows store the details of your Windows Live ID, so that it is associated with your Windows user account. Storing the Windows Live ID lets you log on to Messenger more easily (or automatically) in future, but it has security implications that you may want to consider first. See the sidebar titled "Decide Whether to Associate Your Windows Live ID with Your Windows User Account."

5. If you want Messenger to save your password, select the Remember My Password check box. Saving your password enables you to log in effortlessly (or log in automatically), but it means that anyone who can access your computer while you're logged on and active can log on to Messenger as you. (Other people can't learn your password, but they don't need to: They need only tell Messenger to log on as you.)

6. If you want Messenger to sign you in automatically, select the Sign Me in Automatically check box. When you select this check box and log on to Windows, this setting helps ensure that you spend each Windows session signed in to Messenger. Be sure that this is what you want before you select the Sign Me in Automatically check box.

7. Click the Sign In button to sign in to Messenger.

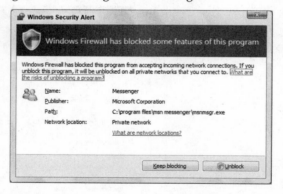

The first time you run Messenger you may see a Windows Security Alert dialog box, such as the one shown here, telling you that Windows Firewall has blocked some features of the program on all public networks. To use all of Messenger's features, click the Unblock button, and then authenticate yourself to User Account Control.

Once you've started Messenger, it displays an icon in your notification area. Click this icon to display a menu of actions you can take with Messenger, as shown here.

When Messenger appears on your screen, it may tell you that you don't have anyone in your contact list and suggest you click the Add a Contact button to start adding contacts. Figure 20.3 shows Messenger with a few contacts added. As you can see in the figure, Messenger also tells you the number of new messages you have in your Hotmail or MSN account (if you have any).

You're probably itching to add some contacts and get on with messaging. Before you do that, however, configure Messenger by choosing options as described in the next section.

FIGURE 20.3
Messenger with some
contacts added

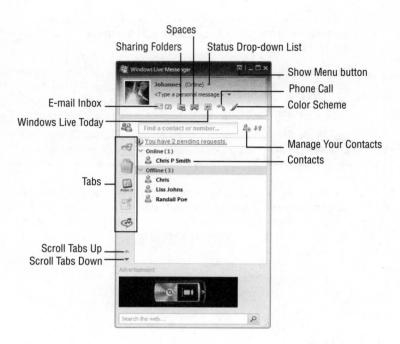

Configuring Messenger to Suit Your Needs

Messenger has many configuration options that let you change its behavior considerably. You don't need to set all of them at once, but it's a good idea to know about them before using Messenger. At the very least, you should edit your public profile so that you know what information other people can access about you.

Click the Status drop-down list (the drop-down button near the top of the window that shows your name), and then choose Personal Settings to display the Options dialog box. You can then configure your choice of the options described in the following sections.

Personal Page Options

The Personal page of the Options dialog box (see Figure 20.4) contains several important settings and some trivial ones.

My Display Name area   In the Type Your Name as You Want Others to See It text box, enter the name you want Messenger to display for you. You can display whatever name you like, barring some sensitive words and trademarked terms that Microsoft excludes. Most likely, you'll want to use your name, nickname, or a combination of the two that makes clear who you are. Don't use your e-mail address as your name, because making your e-mail address public in this way may bring it to the attention of spammers.

In the Type a Personal Message for Your Contacts to See text box, you can type a message that appears next to your name in contact listings when you're online. You might want to change this text every day to show what you're up to; if so, you can change it more easily by clicking in the <Type a Personal Message> area in the Messenger window and typing the message there. If you want just your name to appear, leave this text box blank. If you want Messenger to display the artist and song you're currently listening to in Windows Media Player, select the Show Song Information from Windows Media Player as a Personal Message check box.

My Display Picture area   If you want Messenger to display a picture for you, select the Show My Display Picture and Allow Others to See It check box. Your display picture is the one that appears next to your name in the main Messenger window. To change the picture, follow these steps:

1. Click the Change Picture button. Messenger displays the My Display Picture dialog box (see Figure 20.5).

2. If you want to use a canned picture, choose it in the list box. To add a picture of your own, click the Browse button, use the resulting Select a Display Picture dialog box to select the picture, and then click the Open button. Messenger crops the picture automatically and displays it in the Preview box. To use a picture or animated character from a commercial site, click one of the links below the list box. If you prefer not to display a picture, select the Don't Show a Picture check box.

3. Click the OK button. Messenger closes the My Display Picture dialog box and applies the picture you chose.

FIGURE 20.4
On the Personal page of the Options dialog box, set your display name and choose whether to display emoticons.

FIGURE 20.5
The My Display Picture dialog box lets you choose a canned picture to be your Messenger personality, use a picture of your own, or create an animated display character.

My Public Profile area Messenger works with Microsoft's Windows Live Spaces service, which provides structured online space for you to create an online presence, including a personal profile, photo albums, details of music you like, and similar information. If you're already a Windows Live Spaces user, you can click the Edit Profile button in the My Public Profile area to access your Space on MSN Spaces. If you're not a Windows Live Spaces user, clicking the Edit Profile button leads you to a signup screen for Windows Live Spaces.

My Status area Select the Show Me as "Away" when I'm Inactive for *NN* Minutes check box if you want Messenger to change your status to Away after the specified period of inactivity. (Adjust the number of minutes in the text box as necessary. The default setting is 5 minutes, which is too short for many busy people.) Clear this check box if you don't want Messenger to monitor you in this way. If you clear this check box, Messenger changes your status to Away when your screen saver kicks in. (If you're not using a screen saver, your status will remain Online until you change it.)

Select the Show Me as "Busy" and Block My Alerts When I'm Running a Full-Screen Program, Such As a Slide Presentation check box if you want Messenger to block alerts (and set your status to Busy when you're using a program full-screen. This setting is good for making sure that Messenger doesn't intrude on work (such as a presentation you're running) or games.

My Webcam area Select the Allow Others to See that I Have a Webcam check box if you want Messenger to include a webcam symbol next to your listing. This symbol helps your contacts see that you have a webcam connected and functional in case they want to make a video call to you.

General Page Options

The General page of the Options dialog box (see Figure 20.6) includes important items for controlling how Messenger runs and the items it shows.

Sign In area Select the Automatically Run Windows Live Messenger When I Log on to Windows check box if you want Messenger to run automatically at the start of each Windows session. If you prefer to run Messenger manually at your convenience, clear this check box.

Select the Open Windows Live Messenger Main Window When Windows Live Messenger Starts check box if you want the main Messenger window to appear when Messenger starts. Seeing the main window is usually a good idea, as it reminds you that Messenger is running. If you clear this check box, the Messenger icon appears in the notification area.

Select the Allow Automatic Sign in When Connected to the Internet check box if you want Messenger to sign you in automatically when you start Messenger and your computer is connected to the Internet.

Select the Show Windows Live Today after Signing in to Messenger check box if you want Messenger to open the Windows Live Today window, which shows you the mail you've received on Hotmail or MSN, the MSN Today home page, and the MSNBC home page.

Displaying My Contacts area Select the Show Display Pictures from Others check box if you want to see others' pictures in Messenger. Seeing the pictures can help you keep participants straight in busy conversations.

Quality Improvement area Select the Allow Microsoft to Collect Anonymous Information about How I Use Windows Live Messenger check box if you want to participate in Microsoft's Customer Experience Improvement Program.

Video Carousel area Select the Show Video Carousel in the Main Windows Messenger Live Window check box if you want Messenger to display miniature videos at the bottom of the main window. Clear this check box if you don't want to watch the videos or if bandwidth is limited.

Effects area Select the Show Shadows under Window Frames check box if you want Messenger to display drop shadows under window frames. Clear this check box if you don't need this extra visual adornment. (Your computer's graphics card probably deserves a break.)

FIGURE 20.6
On the General page, choose whether to let Messenger automatically sign you in.

Messages Page Options

The Messages page of the Options dialog box (see Figure 20.7) lets you control how your instant messages appear and behave.

FIGURE 20.7
Among other refinements, the Messages page lets you suppress emoticons, nudges, and winks. You can also choose to keep a history of your Messenger conversations.

General Message Settings area   To change the font used in your IM windows, click the Change Font button, and then use the resulting Set My Message Font dialog box.

Select the Show Emoticons check box if you want to let standard emoticons ("smileys" and other expressive characters) appear in your message windows. Select the Show Custom Emoticons check box if you want to let custom (user-defined) emoticons appear as well.

Select the Show Timestamps on Messages check box if you want each message to show the time at which it was received. Timestamps can be helpful when you're tracking several slow-moving conversations. In faster-paced conversations, you will probably find you don't need the timestamps.

Select the Show "Contact Says:" before Every Message check box if you want the contact's name and the word "says" to appear before each message. Having your contacts' names appear is usually helpful in keeping straight who said what.

Select the Allow Me to Send and Receive Nudges check box if you want to be able to use Nudges. A nudge vibrates the conversation window to get the contact's attention. Clear this check box if you find nudges annoying.

Select the Play Winks Automatically When They Are Received check box if you want Messenger to play winks automatically. Winks are animations that can add zip to your conversations. They may also drive you crazy. If you clear this check box, you can play a wink manually by clicking its link in the conversation window.

Select the Play Voice Clips Automatically When They Are Received check box if you want Messenger to play voice clips when they arrive. Clear this check box if you prefer to play voice clips manually at your convenience.

Offline Instant Message Settings area Select the Show My Offline Messages Automatically When I Sign In option button if you want Messenger to automatically open your offline messages when you sign in. Select the Show a Link to My Offline Messages in the Main Window options button if you prefer to see only a link to your offline messages so that you can open them at a time that suits you.

Message History area Select the Automatically Keep a History of My Conversations check box if you want Messenger to automatically log your conversations. Saving conversations can be handy if you use Messenger for business or technical discussions and need to retain the details. Set the folder for Messenger to use in the Save My Conversations in this Folder text box.

Select the Show My Last Conversation in New Conversation Windows check box if you want Messenger to insert your last conversation with a particular contact in a new conversation you start with that contact. This setting helps you to pick up a conversation where you left off.

Handwriting area Select the Show the Handwrite Tab in Conversation Windows check box if you want Messenger to include the Handwrite tab (so that you can write using a tablet).

Alerts and Sounds Page Options

The options on the Alerts and Sounds page (see Figure 20.8) let you control whether Messenger alerts you to events and which sounds (if any) Messenger plays.

FIGURE 20.8
On the Alerts and Sounds page, make sure Messenger is set to alert you only to events you want to learn about.

Alerts area   Select the Display Alerts When Contacts Come Online check box if you want Messenger to pop up an alert above the notification area when one of your contacts comes online.

Select the Display Alerts When a Message Is Received check box if you want Messenger to pop up an alert when you receive an instant message.

Select the Display Alerts When E-Mail Is Received check box if you want Messenger to pop up an alert when you receive e-mail on your Hotmail or MSN account.

Select the Display Alerts When New Videos Are Available check box if you want Messenger to pop up an alert when new videos are available on MSN Videos.

Select the Display Alerts When a Sharing Folder Is Updated check box if you want Messenger to pop up an alert when one of your contacts adds a file to a sharing folder (a folder you're sharing with one or more contacts).

Sounds area   Messenger can play sounds to give you an aural cue for events such as incoming calls, nudges, a contact signing in, or an instant message or e-mail message arriving. To change which sound Messenger plays for an event, follow these steps:

1. Select the event in the Windows Live Messenger Events list box. The text box under the Windows Live Messenger Events list box shows the path and name of the current sound file. Click the Play button if you want to hear the sound.

2. To change the sound, click the Browse button, use the resulting Open dialog box to select the sound, and then click the Open button.

3. To prevent Messenger from playing a sound for an event, clear the event's check box in the Windows Live Messenger Events list box.

Sharing Folders Page Options

Messenger lets you share files with your contacts in two ways:

◆ By sending a single file at a time during a conversation.

◆ By using a *sharing folder*, a folder that's shared between you and the contact. Any files you put in the sharing folder are shared with the contact. Likewise, any files your contact puts in the folder are shared with you. A sharing folder simplifies the process of transferring files.

Use the options on the Sharing Folders page of the Options dialog box (see Figure 20.9) to control whether Messenger uses sharing folders:

1. If you want to use sharing folders, select the Use Sharing Folders Instead of Sending One File at a Time check box.

2. In the Manage Which Contacts Have a Sharing Folder Stored on This Computer area, specify which contacts get sharing folders by moving them from the All Contacts list to the Sharing Folders list. Select a contact in the All Contacts list, and then click the Add button to add the contact to the Sharing Folders list. To remove a contact from the Sharing Folders list, click the contact's entry, and then click the Remove button.

3. If you want Messenger to automatically create a sharing folder for a contact who doesn't already have one, select the Automatically Create Sharing Folders When I Send Files to My Contacts check box.

FIGURE 20.9

The Sharing Folders page of the Options dialog box lets you control which contacts get sharing folders on your computer and whether Messenger creates sharing folders automatically.

File Transfer Page Options

The File Transfer page (see Figure 20.10) offers the following options:

File Transfer Options area   In the Save Received Files in This Folder text box, specify the folder in which you want Messenger to place the files your contacts send to you. The default folder is the My Received Files folder in your Documents folder. (Messenger creates this folder automatically the first time you receive a file.) To change the folder, click the Browse button, use the Browse for Folder dialog box to select the folder, and then click the OK button.

To scan the files for malware, select the Scan Files for Viruses Using check box. You can then choose between using your existing antivirus program (assuming you have one, as you should) or Windows Live Safety Scanner, which at this writing is the only scanner that can check shared folders. To use your antivirus program, click the Browse button, use the resulting dialog box to select the program, and then click the Open button. To use the Windows Live Safety Scanner, click the Install button, and then follow through the process for downloading and installing Windows Live Safety Scanner.

If you want Messenger to refuse any file types that are dangerous, such as script files, select the Automatically Reject File Transfers for Known Unsafe File Types check box. You may find that this setting also prevents you from receiving some file types that you actually want, such as program files.

Automatic Background Sharing area   Select the Automatically Share Backgrounds and Accept Shared Backgrounds check box if you want Messenger to share the background images you use in conversation windows with the other participants. Similarly, Messenger accepts the backgrounds that your contacts have chosen to share.

FIGURE 20.10
On the File Transfer page of the Options dialog box, choose where to save files you receive and how to scan them for viruses.

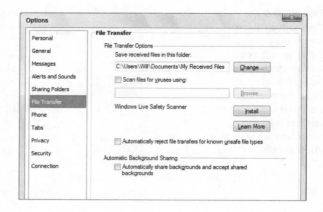

Phone Page Options

The Phone page of the Options dialog box (see Figure 20.11) lets you specify your country or region code and your home, work, and mobile phone numbers. You can also click the Mobile Settings button to access the MSN site for setting up a mobile phone account so that you can receive messages sent by your Messenger contacts on your mobile phone, or click the Settings button to access the MSN Direct site for setting up a Smart Watch.

Tabs Page Options

The Tabs page of the Options dialog box (see Figure 20.12) lets you choose the order in which tabs appear. You can restore the default order by clicking the Restore Defaults button.

FIGURE 20.11
On the Phone page of the Options dialog box, specify your country or region code and enter the phone numbers you want Messenger to know.

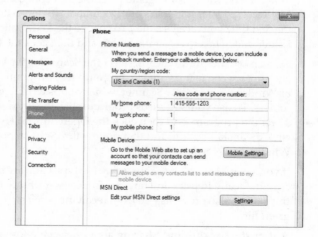

Use the controls on the
Tabs page to change
the order in which
tabs appear. To get rid
of the tabs, select the
Hide Tabs check box.

Privacy Page Options

The Privacy page of the Options dialog box (see Figure 20.13) is where you maintain your Allow List (people who can see your online status and can send you messages) and your Block List (people who can do neither).

To move a contact from one list to another, select them in the appropriate list box and click the Allow button or the Block button. By default, Messenger prevents all other users except your contacts from contacting you and viewing your status until you explicitly allow them. If you want to make yourself publicly available, click the All Others item in the Block List box, and then click the Allow button.

FIGURE 20.13
On the Privacy page of
the Options dialog
box, maintain your
Allow List and your
Block List to control
who may and may not
contact you.

To see which users have added you to their contact lists, click the View button. Messenger displays the Who Has You in Their Contact List? dialog box, which contains a list of names. You can right-click a name and choose Add to Contacts from the context menu to add the person to your list of contacts.

Select the Alert Me When Other People Add Me to Their Contact List check box if you want Messenger to notify you when another user adds you to their contact list. This check box is available only if you move the All Others item from the Block List box to the Allow List box. Otherwise, Messenger selects this check box and makes it unavailable.

Security Page Options

The Security page of the Options dialog box (see Figure 20.14) contains the following options:

Security area   Select the Always Ask Me for My Password When Checking Hotmail or Opening Other Microsoft Passport Enabled Web Pages check box if you want to enter your Passport password manually each time it's required by a website. Entering the password manually improves your security, but you may find yourself needing to enter the password too often for speedy or comfortable browsing.

If you're using a public computer, or you're sharing a Windows user account with other people, select the This Is a Shared Computer so Don't Store My Address Book, Display Picture, or Personal Message on It check box. If you share your computer with other people (for example, your family) but have your own user account, you don't need to select this check box for security.

Select the Allow Me to Connect Directly to My Contacts When Sending Messages check box if you want Messenger to send messages directly to your contacts' computers rather than routing them through the Windows Live Messenger service. Connecting directly may give faster performance but poses a slight security concern.

Select the Allow Voice Clips to Be Sent, Received, and Temporarily Stored on My Computer check box if you want to use voice clips. Clear this check box if you don't want to use voice clips to conserve bandwidth or for security reasons.

Select the Allow Links in the Conversation Window check box if you want to allow Messenger to display clickable hyperlinks in conversation windows. The danger of hyperlinks is that someone might direct you to a site that's offensive or that contains malware.

Select the Allow Windows Live Messenger to Start a Conversation from a Link in a Web Browser check box if you want to be able to start a Messenger conversation by clicking a link in your web browser. The security concern here is that you might start a conversation with someone other than who you intended to reach.

Contact Storage area   Select the Encrypt Contact List Data so That It Is Not Accessible Outside of Windows Live Messenger check box if you want to keep your contact list data encrypted. This is a good idea for security.

Connection Page Options

The Connection page of the Options dialog box (see Figure 20.15) shows you what kind of Internet connection you're using—for example, a wired network connection that uses port-restricted Network Address Translation (NAT), such as a DSL router.

If Messenger isn't connecting to the server, you can click the Start button to launch the Connection Troubleshooter.

If you need to specify proxy server settings for connecting to the Internet, click the Advanced Settings button, and then work in the Settings dialog box. Normally, you'll set these settings for Internet Explorer rather than for Messenger.

FIGURE 20.14
The Security page of the Options dialog box lets you prevent Messenger from signing you into Microsoft Passport–enabled sites automatically.

FIGURE 20.15
The Connection tab of the Options dialog box lets you check your connection method and troubleshoot problems with it.

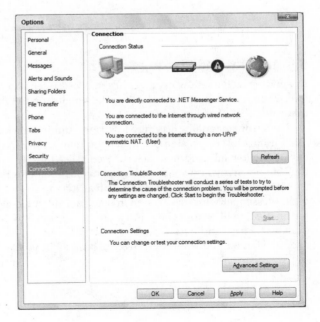

Setting Up Audio and Video

If you have speakers (or headphones) and a microphone, you can use them to make voice calls via Messenger. If you have a webcam or another live video camera, you can make video calls as well. To set up Messenger for making voice and video calls, follow these steps:

1. Make sure your sound and video hardware is plugged in and working.

2. Click the Show Menu button, and then choose Tools ➢ Audio and Video Setup to start the Audio and Video Setup Wizard.

3. Follow the steps of the wizard, selecting your speakers and setting the playback volume, selecting the microphone and setting the recording volume (see Figure 20.16), and then selecting your webcam.

FIGURE 20.16
The Audio and Video Setup Wizard walks you through setting up your speakers, microphone, and webcam.

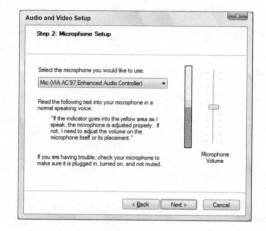

Signing Out and Signing Back In

Depending on the settings you've chosen, Messenger may automatically sign you in when you start it or when it launches automatically after you log on to Windows. If you chose not to sign in automatically, click the Sign In button.

To sign out manually, leaving Messenger running, click the Show Menu button, and then choose File ➢ Sign Out. If you sign out while you're in a conversation, Messenger displays a dialog box explaining that all windows will be closed. Click the OK button to continue signing out, or click the Cancel button if you want to end the conversation before signing out.

Normally, you'll want to sign back in as the same user. To do so, click the Sign In button in the main Messenger window. To sign in using a different Windows Live ID, click the drop-down button on the E-mail Address box, and then choose Sign in with a Different E-mail Address to clear the existing address and password (if it is saved). You can then type the new address and password, choose whether you want Messenger to remember you, and then click the Sign In button.

Adding and Removing a Contact

You can add a contact to your list of contacts by using their instant messaging name, by adding them when they contact you, or by reciprocating when they add you as a contact.

Adding a Contact by Instant Messaging Address

If you know a contact's instant messaging address, you can add them to your contact list as follows:

1. Click the Add a Contact button in the Messenger window, or click the Show Menu button and then choose Contacts ➤ Add a Contact. Messenger displays the Windows Live Contacts – Add a Contact dialog box with the General category displayed (see Figure 20.17).

2. In the Instant Messaging Address text box, type your contact's IM address.

3. To personalize the invitation that Messenger sends to your contact, select the Type a Personal Invitation check box, and then type the message in the text box that appears. For example, you might make sure the contact can identify you clearly from your IM identity.

4. If you want to add mobile phone information, select the country or region in the drop-down list, and then enter the number in the text boxes.

5. If you want to use a nickname for the contact, type it in the Nickname text box.

6. In the Group drop-down list, select the contact group to which you want to add the contact—for example, Friends or Family.

FIGURE 20.17
Use the Add a Contact dialog box to add a contact by their instant messaging address.

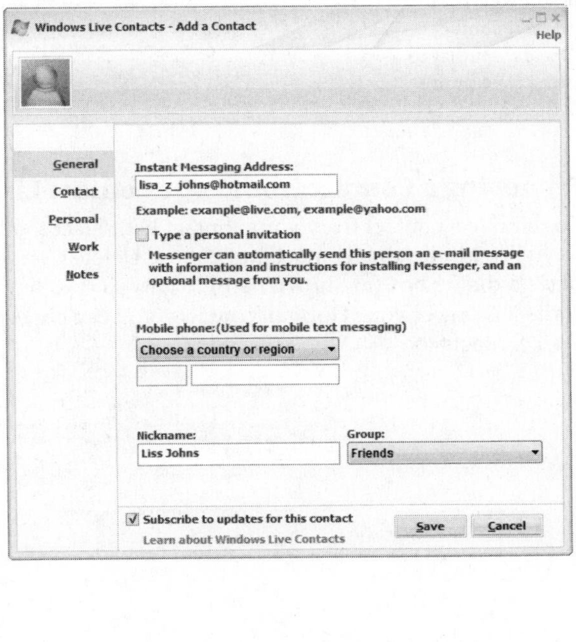

7. Select the Subscribe to Updates for this Contact check box if you want Messenger to automatically pick up new information about this contact from their Windows Live ID.

8. Add more information about the contact if you want by using the fields in the other categories. For example, click the Contact category in the left pane, and then enter details such as the contact's first, middle, and last names, or their phone numbers.

9. Click the Save button. Messenger sends a request to the contact asking them to be one of your contacts.

Adding a Contact when People Add You to Their Contact List

You can also add a contact quickly by adding a person who adds you to their contact list (unless you've configured Messenger not to notify you when this happens).

When someone adds you to their contact list, Messenger displays the Windows Live Messenger dialog box shown in Figure 20.18 asking whether you want to allow this person or block them. Select the Allow this Person to See when You Are Online and Contact You option button or the Block This Person from Seeing When You Are Online and Contacting You option button as appropriate. If you want to add the person to your contact list, leave the Add This Person to My Contact List check box selected. If not, clear it. Then click the OK button. Messenger closes the dialog box and takes the actions you specified.

FIGURE 20.18

Messenger displays this Windows Live Messenger dialog box when someone adds you to their contact list. Decide whether to allow the contact or block them.

Removing a Contact from Your Contact List

To remove a contact from your contact list, select their entry and press the Delete key. Alternatively, right-click the contact and choose Delete Contact from the context menu. Messenger displays a dialog box (as shown here) to let you decide whether to block the contact as well. If the contact is one of your Hotmail contacts, you can choose whether to remove them from your Hotmail contacts too.

Chatting

To chat with a Messenger user, double-click the user's entry in the Online list, or right-click the user's entry in the Online list and choose Send an Instant Message from the context menu.

Messenger opens a conversation window for chatting with the user. Figure 20.19 shows an example. Type a message into the text box and press the Enter key (or click the Send button) to send it.

The other user receives a screen pop, as shown here, telling them that you've sent them a message and a minimized conversation window. The user can display the conversation window by clicking the screen pop (if they're quick enough to catch it before it disappears) or by clicking the conversation window's button on the Taskbar.

Figure 20.20 shows a chat getting started in a conversation window. Note the readout at the bottom that tells you that your contact is typing a message. This alert helps you avoid sending overlapping messages and having the conversations spiral off into multiple threads.

Adding More People to a Conversation

To add another person to your current conversation, click the Invite Someone to This Conversation button, or click the Show Menu button and then choose Actions ➤ Invite a Contact to This Conversation. Messenger displays the Select Contacts dialog box showing your contacts who are online. Select the person, and then click the OK button.

Including Emoticons in Your Messages

To include *emoticons* (also called *smileys* or *glyphs*) in your messages, click the Emoticons button and click the appropriate button on the grid.

FIGURE 20.19
Starting a conversation in Messenger

FIGURE 20.20
Chatting in a conversation window. The readout at the bottom warns the user that the other participant is typing a message.

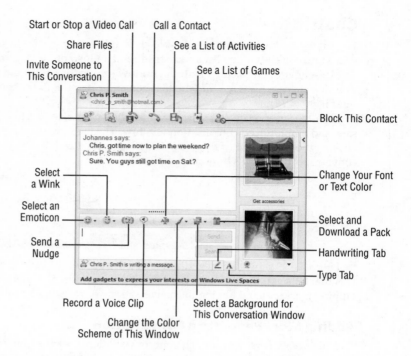

If you use emoticons frequently, you may prefer to type them so that you don't need to remove your hands from the keyboard. To see the keystrokes for an emoticon, hover the mouse pointer over the emoticon and read the tooltip that appears.

FIGURE 20.21
The My Emoticons dialog box contains a Pinned Emoticons list that can contain up to 40 emoticons that are pinned in place on the grid that appears in the conversation window. If the Pinned Emoticons list is full, you must unpin an emoticon from it before you can pin another to it.

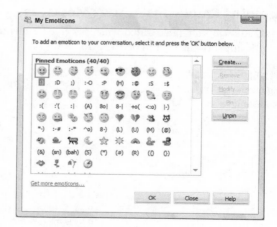

To see more emoticons, click the More link on the Emoticons grid. Messenger displays the My Emoticons dialog box (see Figure 20.21), which allows you to change the emoticons that appear on the grid. You can also create custom emoticons from your own graphics files by clicking the Create button and working in the Add a Custom Emoticon dialog box.

You can buy more emoticons from the Kiwee site by clicking the Get More Emoticons link in the My Emoticons dialog box.

When you send a sequence that contains the text sequence for an emoticon, Messenger converts the text sequence and displays the emoticon on both your screen and that of the person (or people) you're chatting with.

If you turn off the display of emoticons on the Messages page of the Options dialog box, you see the characters that represent the emoticon instead.

Setting Font, Style, and Color for Text You Send

If you want to be distinctive, you can change the font, style, and color for text you send to others and that you see on your screen. For the text you see in the Messenger windows, you can change the size as well. (You can't change the size of the text others see, and they can't change the size you see.)

To set the font, style, color, and size, click the Change Your Font or Text Color button. Messenger displays the Change My Message Font dialog box. Choose settings you like, and then click the OK button to apply them.

Adding Voice to a Conversation

If both participants have functioning audio hardware, you can add voice to a Messenger conversation between two people. (You can't use voice in a conversation that has three or more people.)

To add voice to your current conversation, click the Call a Contact button in the conversation window, and then click Call Computer on the drop-down menu. Messenger displays a Speakers volume control and a Microphone Mute check box and notifies the person you're chatting with that you want to have a voice conversation. They get to accept this or decline it. If they accept, Messenger establishes the connection.

To hang up the voice portion of the call, click the Hang Up link or press Alt+Q.

Adding Video to a Conversation

If one or both participants have video hardware installed, you can add video to a Messenger conversation between two people. (As with voice, you can't use video in a conversation that has three or more people.)

To add video to a conversation, click the Start or Stop a Video Call button. Messenger invites your contact to take part in the video conversation. If they accept, Messenger displays the video picture and extra controls (see Figure 20.22).

To change the size of the incoming video, click the upper Options button, choose Size from the menu, and then choose the size you want from the submenu.

To stop transmitting or receiving video, click the Start or Stop a Video Call button.

FIGURE 20.22
A video call starts with the video in a window, but you can display the video full screen if you choose.

Start or Stop My Contact's Webcam   Full Screen   Mute Your Speakers

Start or Stop My Webcam   Options Button

Mute Your Microphone

Blocking and Unblocking Contacts

To block somebody from chatting with you, take one of the following actions:

◆ In a conversation window with the contact you want to block, click the Block This Contact button.

◆ In a conversation window with multiple people, click the Block button and choose the contact from the pop-up menu.

◆ From the main Messenger window, right-click the contact and choose Block Contact from the context menu.

When you block a user from a conversation window, Messenger displays a dialog box telling you that the blocked user will not be able to contact you or see your online status. When you unblock a user, Messenger displays a similar dialog box telling you that the other user *will* be able to do these things. In either case, you get an OK button to proceed with the blocking or unblocking, a Cancel button to cancel it, and a Don't Show Me This Message Again check box that you can select to suppress this message in the future.

To unblock a user, take one of the following actions:

◆ In a conversation window, click the Unblock button.

◆ In a conversation window with multiple participants, click the Block or Unblock button, and then select the blocked contact from the submenu.

◆ In the Windows Live Messenger window, right-click the blocked contact and choose Unblock Contact from the context menu.

Changing Your Status

To let people know what you're up to, you can change the status that Messenger displays for you. To do so, click your name in the main Messenger window and then choose Online, Busy, Be Right Back, Away, On the Phone, Out to Lunch, or Appear Offline from the pop-up menu. You can also set your status by clicking the Show Menu button, choosing File ➢ My Status, and then selecting the status from the submenu.

When you change your status to Appear Offline, Messenger displays a dialog box warning you that all windows will be closed. Click the OK button if this is okay, or click the Cancel button to cancel the status change.

Transferring Files

Messenger lets you transfer a single file at a time during a conversation, but it also provides the sharing folders feature for effortlessly sharing multiple files.

Sending a File

To send a file to someone via Messenger, take the following steps:

1. You can send a file either from the main Messenger window or from a conversation window:

   ◆ In the main Messenger window, right-click the contact and choose Send Other ➢ Send a Single File from the context menu. Messenger displays the Send a File To dialog box, which is a renamed version of the standard Open dialog box.

   ◆ In a conversation window, click the Share Files button, and then choose Send a Single File from the drop-down menu.

2. Navigate to the file, select it, and click the Open button. Messenger contacts the user, asking them if they want to accept or decline the file. You can cancel the transfer by pressing Alt+Q or clicking the Cancel link.

3. If the user accepts the file, Messenger displays a progress readout in the conversation window. When the file transfer is complete, Messenger tells you so.

If the user doesn't accept the transfer, or if it fails, Messenger tells you that the user declined the file or the file could not be sent.

Sending Files via Sharing Folders

Instead of sending a single file, you can use Messenger's sharing folders feature to share files. A sharing folder is a folder shared with a particular contact.

To share files via sharing folders, follow these steps:

1. Set up a sharing folder for the contact. The easiest way to do this is to right-click the contact in the main Messenger window, and then choose Create a Sharing Folder from the shortcut menu. You can also create sharing folders on the Sharing Folders page of the Options dialog box.

2. Open the sharing folder either from the main Messenger window or from a conversation window:

   ◆ In the main Messenger window, right-click the contact, and then choose Open Your Sharing Folder from the shortcut menu.

   ◆ In a conversation window, click the Share Files button, and then choose Open Your Sharing Folder from the drop-down menu.

3. The first time you open a sharing folder, Messenger displays a message box urging you not to share unauthorized materials. You can select the Don't Show Me This Again check box to suppress these messages in the future. The sharing folder then appears (see Figure 20.23).

4. Add files to the sharing folder. Either drag files to it from a Windows Explorer window, or click the Add Files button, use the resulting Send a File To dialog box to select the files, and then click the Open button.

5. When your contact is online, Messenger automatically synchronizes the files in the sharing folder, and then informs your contact via a pop-up message or (if they're in a conversation with you) via a link in the conversation window.

FIGURE 20.23
A sharing folder lets you share files automatically with a contact.

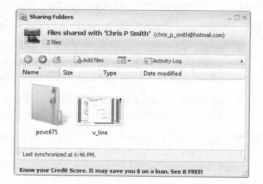

Receiving a File

Receiving a file via Messenger is even easier than sending one. Here's what happens:

1. If you're using pop-ups, Messenger displays a pop-up telling you that someone is trying to send you a file. (Messenger identifies the user and the file by name.)

2. Click the pop-up to display the conversation window. (If you're already in a conversation with this user, you'll go directly to this step.)

3. To accept the file and put it in your Received Files folder, click the Accept link (or press Alt+C). To put the file in another folder, click the Save As link (or press Alt+S), use the Save Incoming File As dialog box to specify the folder, and then click the Save button. To decline the file, click the Decline link (or press Alt+D).

4. If you choose to accept the file, Messenger displays a Windows Messenger dialog box warning you that files may contain harmful viruses or scripts and advising you to make sure that the file you're receiving is from a trustworthy source. Click the OK button to dismiss this dialog box. You can select the Don't Show Me This Message Again check box before dismissing the dialog box, if you're fully aware of malware tricks and you carefully check every file you receive before running it.

5. Messenger transfers the file and then displays a link that you can click to open the file.

To access your received files folder, click the Show Menu button, and then choose File ➤ Open Received Files.

Receiving Files via Sharing Folders

When a contact sends you files via a sharing folder, Messenger displays a pop-up message or a link in a conversation window with that contact. Click the pop-up message or the link to open the sharing folder and see the files. You can then copy or move the files to other folders as needed.

The Bottom Line

Get and install Windows Live Messenger Download the latest version of Windows Live Messenger by choosing Start ➤ All Programs ➤ Windows Live Messenger Download or opening Internet Explorer and then going to http://get.live.com/messenger/overview. Run the file to install it. You must accept the Terms of Use and Privacy Statement, which are worth reading carefully.

Start Messenger for the first time Choose Start ➤ All Programs ➤ Windows Live Messenger to start Messenger. Thereafter, you can launch Messenger from its icon in the notification area.

Configure Messenger to suit your needs Messenger has a wide variety of settings that you should explore to get the most use out of Messenger with the greatest security and convenience. To open the Options dialog box, click your name when signed in, and then choose Personal Settings from the menu.

Add and remove contacts If you know a contact's IM address, add the contact by clicking the Add a Contact button in the Messenger window and then working in the Add a Contact dialog box. You can also add a contact when someone adds you to their contact list.

Chat with your contacts To chat with a contact, double-click the contact's name in the main Messenger window. Type a message in the conversation window that Messenger opens, and then click the Send button or press Enter. If the contact accepts the invitation to the conversation, the chat begins. You can add voice to a conversation by clicking the Call a Contact button in the conversation window and then clicking Call Computer. To add video to a conversation, click the Start or Stop a Video Call button.

Block and unblock contacts   To prevent a contact from chatting with you, click the Block This Contact button in a conversation window, or right-click the contact in the main Messenger window and choose Block Contact. To allow the contact to chat with you again, unblock the contact.

Change your online status   To change your online status, click your name in the main Messenger window and then choose Online, Busy, Be Right Back, Away, On the Phone, Out to Lunch, or Appear Offline.

Transfer files to and from your contacts   To send a file to a contact in a conversation, click the Share Files button, and then choose Send a Single File. Select the file, and then click the Open button. Your contact then has the option to accept or decline the file. To send multiple files, set up a sharing folder for the contact by right-clicking the contact in the main Messenger window, and then choosing Create a Sharing Folder. You can then place files in that folder, and Messenger automatically shares them with your contact when the contact is online.

Chapter 21

Giving and Getting Remote Assistance

◆ Understand what Remote Assistance is and what security considerations are involved

◆ Turn on Remote Assistance and set limits for how it can be used

◆ Send a remote access invitation via e-mail

◆ Send a Remote Assistance invitation via Windows Live Messenger

◆ Receive help via Remote Assistance

◆ Provide Remote Assistance to someone else

Remote Assistance is a powerful Windows feature that lets you permit a designated helper to connect to your computer, see what's going on, and help you out of trouble. The helper—a friend, an administrator, or a Microsoft support professional; whomever you choose—can control the computer directly if you give them permission, or you can simply chat with them and apply yourself such of their advice as you deem fit. Or you can use Remote Assistance to help another person who requests your assistance.

Remote Assistance works with Windows Vista, Windows XP, and Windows Server 2003, but not with earlier versions of Windows, such as Windows 98 and Windows Me.

Understanding the Basics of Remote Assistance

Remote Assistance lets a user who needs help share the display of their screen and, if they wish, control of their computer, with another user across a network or Internet connection. For ease of reference, the user requesting assistance is termed the *novice*, though they may be an experienced user. The user providing assistance is termed the *expert*; again, the usual connotations needn't apply.

To use Remote Assistance, both the novice's computer and the expert's computer must be running Windows Vista, Windows XP, or Windows Server 2003. The novice sends an invitation via e-mail or via Windows Live Messenger, or saves it as a file (for example, to a network location designated for Remote Assistance request files, or on a floppy or CD that they then put in the snail mail). When the expert responds, the novice decides whether to accept their help.

Each of the three methods of requesting Remote Assistance has its advantages and disadvantages. An e-mail invitation lets the novice include details of the problem with which they need help—but the novice doesn't know when the expert will check their e-mail, or if the novice will be online when the expert tries to respond. A Messenger invitation will be received immediately, but you can only send the invitation when the expert is online. A file invitation is harder to transfer to the expert and may not receive a response in a short enough time frame to be helpful.

On the other end of the wire, you can provide help via Remote Assistance. You can either wait for someone to send you an invitation by any of the three methods discussed here, or you can offer Remote Assistance unsolicited.

HOW REMOTE ASSISTANCE DIFFERS FROM REMOTE DESKTOP CONNECTION

Like Remote Desktop Connection (discussed in Chapter 30), Remote Assistance uses Windows's Terminal Services feature to achieve its effects. Terminal Services (also discussed in Chapter 30) is a technology that passes keystrokes, mouse movements and clicks, and video display information across a network or Internet connection, allowing remote control of a computer running Windows Vista Business or Ultimate.

Although the two have some similarities, Remote Assistance is substantially different from Remote Desktop Connection. Remote Desktop Connection is designed to let you remotely control a computer on which you have a user account. While you're remotely controlling the computer, the monitor attached to the computer displays the Welcome screen (or the Log On to Windows screen, depending on how it's configured), so nobody physically at the computer can see what you're doing or take actions on the computer until you disconnect. By contrast, you can't connect to a computer using Remote Assistance unless there's somebody (the novice) at the computer who can respond to the request for the Remote Assistance session. Both the novice and the expert see the screen of the novice's computer. And the novice has control of their computer until and unless they specifically decide to grant the expert control of it.

Security Considerations for Remote Assistance

Like all remote-control technologies, Remote Assistance has serious security implications that you need to consider before using it.

If you give another person remote control of your computer, they can take actions almost as freely as if they were seated in front of the computer. You can watch these actions, and you can take back control of the computer at any time, but you may already be too late: It takes less than a second to delete a key file, and only a little longer to plant a virus or other form of malware.

Even if you *don't* give the expert control, and simply chat, keep your wits about you when deciding which of their suggestions to implement. Malicious or ill-informed suggestions can do plenty of damage if you apply them without thinking. Never take any actions that could compromise your security or destroy your data. Above all, treat any incoming files with the greatest of suspicion and virus-check them using an up-to-date antivirus program before using them.

One particular problem is that you can't tell that the person at the other computer is who they claim to be. For this reason alone, always protect the Remote Assistance invitations that you send via e-mail or save to a file with a strong password known only to the person from whom you're requesting help. That way, if someone else is at their computer or is impersonating them, they won't be able to respond to the Remote Assistance invitation you send.

Provided that you choose your helper wisely and don't take any rash actions, Remote Assistance is pretty secure. Windows encrypts the Remote Assistance connection, so it's not likely that anybody will be able to hack into it.

Turning On Remote Assistance

Remote Assistance must be turned on before you can use it. To turn on Remote Assistance on your computer, take the following steps:

1. Press Windows Key+Break. Windows opens the System window of Control Panel.

2. Click the Remote Settings link, and then authenticate yourself to User Account Control. Windows displays the Remote page of the System Properties dialog box (see Figure 21.1).

3. Select the Remote Assistance Invitations Can Be Sent from This Computer check box. Selecting this check box lets you (and other users of this computer) send Remote Assistance invitations via e-mail, asking other people for help.

4. If you simply want to turn on Remote Assistance, click the OK button, and Windows closes the System Properties dialog box. But what you probably should do is set the limits for Remote Assistance, as described in the next section. Leave the System Properties dialog box open and read on.

FIGURE 21.1

The Remote page of the System Properties dialog box lets you turn Remote Assistance on and off. You can also choose whether to allow users to receive Remote Assistance from instant messaging contacts.

Setting Limits for Remote Assistance

For security, you may prefer to prevent your helper from ever controlling your computer remotely. You can also change the length of time for which Remote Assistance invitations last before they expire, and decide whether to accept Remote Assistance connections only from computers running Windows Vista and later versions of Windows rather than versions earlier than Windows Vista.

To set limits for Remote Assistance, take the following steps:

1. Click the Advanced button in the Remote Assistance group box on the Remote page of the System Properties dialog box. Windows displays the Remote Assistance Settings dialog box (shown in Figure 21.2).

FIGURE 21.2
The Remote Assistance Settings dialog box lets you prevent your helper from controlling your computer, change the life span of Remote Assistance invitations, and limit connections to computers running Windows Vista and later versions of Windows.

2. In the Remote Control group box, clear the Allow This Computer to Be Controlled Remotely check box if you don't want your helpers to be able to control the computer. Even when this check box is selected, you need to approve each request for control of the PC manually, so leaving it selected is not a great security threat.

3. In the Invitations group box, use the two drop-down lists to specify an expiration limit for Remote Assistance invitations that your computer sends out. Depending on how soon you expect your helpers to be able to respond, you might set anything from 30 minutes to a couple of days.

4. If you want to prevent computers running Windows XP and other pre-Vista versions of Windows that support Remote Assistance from connecting to your computer, select the Create Invitations That Can Only Be Used from Computers Running Windows Vista or Later check box. The Windows Vista version of Remote Assistance is marginally more secure than earlier versions, but unless you're certain that your helper is using Windows Vista, it's best to clear this check box.

5. Click the OK button. Windows closes the Remote Assistance Settings dialog box, returning you to the System Properties dialog box.

6. Click the OK button. Windows closes the System Properties dialog box.

You're now ready to start sending out invitations for Remote Assistance.

Sending a Remote Assistance Invitation via E-mail

E-mail is an easy way to get a Remote Assistance invitation to your helper. E-mail isn't as quick as sending an invitation via an instant-messaging program (as discussed in the next section), but it has the advantage that you don't need to be sure your helper is online before you can send the invitation.

You can send a Remote Assistance invitation either via a standard e-mail program (such as Microsoft Outlook or Windows Mail) or via a web-based e-mail program (such as Hotmail or Gmail). Some e-mail programs aren't able to send Remote Assistance invitations automatically; in this case, you can create a Remote Assistance invitation file and attach it manually to an e-mail message.

Sending a Remote Assistance Invitation via a Standard E-mail Program

To send a Remote Assistance invitation as an e-mail message via your existing e-mail account, follow these steps:

1. Choose Start ➤ All Programs ➤ Maintenance ➤ Windows Remote Assistance. Windows opens a Windows Remote Assistance window (see Figure 21.3), asking whether you want to ask for help or offer help.

2. Click the Invite Someone You Trust to Help You button. Windows displays the next screen (see Figure 21.4).

3. Click the Use E-mail to Send an Invitation button. Windows displays the Choose a Password for Connecting to Your Computer screen (see Figure 21.5).

4. Type your chosen password in each of the text boxes, and then click the Next button. Remote Assistance displays the Starting Your E-mail screen, and then creates a new e-mail message in your default e-mail program. Remote Assistance attaches to the message a small file named RATicket.MsRcIncident, which contains details of the Remote Assistance connection. Figure 21.6 shows an example of this message in Windows Mail, the e-mail program that comes with Windows Vista.

   If Help and Support Center can't find your e-mail program, it displays the Your E-mail Invitation Was Not Sent screen (see Figure 21.7). If you haven't yet set up your e-mail program, set it up now, and then try running Remote Assistance again. More likely, Remote Assistance doesn't work with your e-mail program because your e-mail program doesn't support the Messaging Application Programming Interface (MAPI) standard, a layer of code that enables programs to send messages automatically. In this case, you can save the Remote Assistance invitation as a file, and then attach it manually to an e-mail message. Click the Next button. Windows displays the Save the Invitation as a File screen, discussed in the next section.

FIGURE 21.3
Tell Windows that you want to ask for Remote Assistance rather than offer it to someone else.

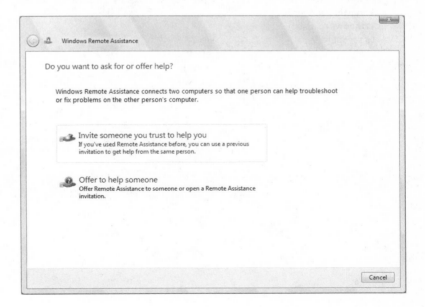

FIGURE 21.4
The How Do You Want to Invite Someone to Help You? screen of Windows Remote Assistance lets you decide between using e-mail to send the invitation and saving the invitation as a file that you can attach to a web-based e-mail message (for example, on Hotmail or Gmail).

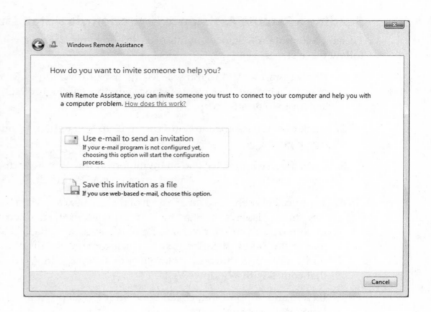

FIGURE 21.5
On the Choose a Password for Connecting to Your Computer screen, type a password of six characters or more. If you use a shorter password, Windows refuses to accept it.

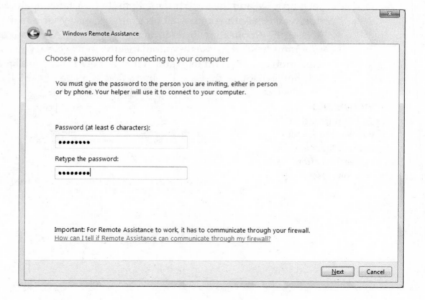

FIGURE 21.6
Remote Access starts
an e-mail message for
you with canned text
explaining how the
recipient can access
your computer.

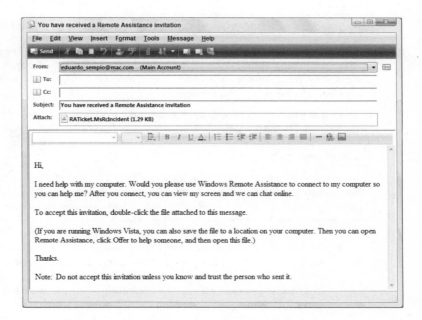

FIGURE 21.7
If you see this screen,
you'll need to save the
Remote Assistance
invitation as a file and
attach it to an e-mail
message manually.
You can use this tech-
nique when you need
to send the invitation
via a web-based e-mail
program such as Hot-
mail or Gmail.

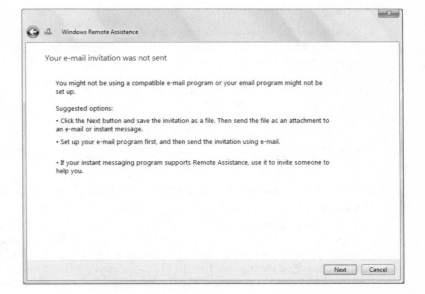

PASSWORDS IN REMOTE ASSISTANCE ARE AWKWARD, BUT YOU MUST MAKE THEM STRONG

The password is both Remote Assistance's strength and its weakness. The password is your main means of ensuring that only the person you intend can actually connect to your computer, so it's essential to use a password strong enough to protect yourself against malefactors. The problem is that you need to communicate the password to your helper.

Given that you're sending the Remote Assistance invitation via e-mail, you may be tempted to include the password in the invitation message itself. Don't do this, as it removes all the security that the password adds. It's much better to tell the expert the password on the phone, in person (if possible), or via instant messaging.

Make the password a strong one: at least six characters long, not a name or a real word in any language, and including at least one symbol and at least one number. Use a new password for each Remote Assistance invitation rather than establishing a standard password with your helper and then reusing it.

---

5. Address the message and edit its text as needed. The canned text includes a "Personal message:" section at the end for you to add text that will help the recipient identify you (if your name is widely used) and persuade them to come to your help. You may get better results from adding personal text at the beginning of the message so that the canned text seems less awkward. Consider also editing the Subject line from its default text ("You have received a Remote Access invitation"), which may look like spam to some recipients.

6. Click the Send button (or whichever button your e-mail program uses) to send the message.

After you've sent the message, you see the Windows Remote Assistance window with the "Waiting for incoming connection" message, as shown here. Minimize the window while you're waiting to hear back from your helper.

Sending a Remote Assistance Invitation via a Web-Based E-mail Program

If you want to use a web-based e-mail program to send the Remote Assistance invitation, you must save the invitation to a file and then attach it to an e-mail message manually. On the How Do You Want to Invite Someone to Help You? screen, click the Save This Invitation as a File button. Windows displays the Save the Invitation as a File screen (see Figure 21.8), which suggests saving the invitation as the file `Invitation.msrcincident` on your Desktop. You can choose a different location if you want, but the Desktop is as good a location as any, because you should delete the invitation file once you've sent it. The Type a Password text box and the Confirm the Password text box contain the password you typed already. You can change the password if you want, but normally you shouldn't need to.

Click the Finish button. You'll see the Windows Remote Assistance window with the "Waiting for incoming connection" message. Minimize this window, go to your e-mail program, and create a message to your helper. Attach the `Invitation.msrcincident` file to the message, send the message, and then delete the invitation file from your desktop.

When your helper contacts you, work as described in the section "Receiving Remote Assistance," later in this chapter.

FIGURE 21.8
On the Save the Invitation as a File screen, save the invitation to a folder in which you can easily find it when you need to attach it to an e-mail message.

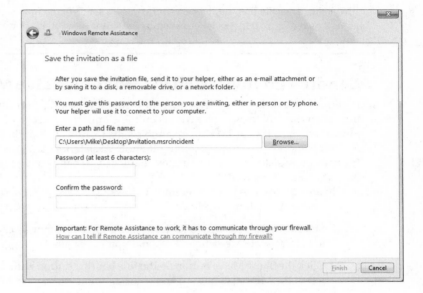

CHANGE YOUR DEFAULT PROGRAM FOR E-MAIL

When you try to send a Remote Assistance invitation via e-mail, you may find that Windows tries to use the wrong e-mail program. If this happens, it's because Windows is set to use a different e-mail program as a default program than the program you're using.

To change the default program for e-mail, choose Start ➢ Default Programs. In the Default Programs window, click the Set Your Default Programs item to display the Set Your Default Programs window. In the Programs list box on the left, click your mail program, and then click the Set as Default button. Click the OK button to close the Set Your Default Programs window.

OTHER WAYS OF TRANSFERRING A REMOTE ASSISTANCE INVITATION FILE

Once you've saved a Remote Assistance invitation file as described in "Sending a Remote Assistance Invitation via a Web-Based E-mail Program," you don't have to send it via e-mail. You can also transfer it via a physical medium or via a network if you prefer.

If the expert is within walking distance, you can put the invitation file on a floppy disk, recordable CD, or USB drive and take it to them. Or you could copy the invitation file to a network drive, and then phone the expert to tell them where it is and what the password is.

You might also need to send the invitation via physical mail. A Remote Assistance invitation file is tiny, so it fits easily on a floppy disk. But if you're sending the medium through the mail, consider using a recordable CD instead, because the mail-scanning systems instituted since 9/11 may damage floppies.

Sending an Invitation via Windows Live Messenger

If you use Windows Live Messenger for instant messaging, you can send a Remote Assistance invitation directly to a contact who is online. Similarly, you can offer Remote Assistance to one of your contacts if your IM conversation seems to indicate that they're struggling. If you've configured Windows to accept incoming Remote Assistance offers (as discussed in "Setting Limits for Remote Assistance," earlier in this chapter), you can receive Remote Assistance offers from your IM contacts as well.

Chapter 20 explains how to set up Windows Live Messenger and use it for instant messaging. To send an invitation via Windows Live Messenger, follow these steps:

1. Start Messenger as usual. If Messenger is already running, click its icon in the notification area to activate Messenger. Log on if you're not already logged on.

2. Click the Show Menu button on the title bar (the button with a drop-down arrow, just to the left of the Minimize button) and choose Actions ➢ Request Remote Assistance. Messenger opens a Windows Live Contacts window for you to select the contact. Click the contact's name, and then click the OK button.

REQUEST REMOTE ASSISTANCE FROM AN EXISTING CONVERSATION

You can also request Remote Assistance from a conversation you're having with a contact. Click the See a List of Activities button and choose Request Remote Assistance from the My Activities list, or click the Show Menu button and choose Actions ➢ Request Remote Assistance.

1. Messenger opens an Instant Message window on the specified user's computer and displays a note saying that you've invited the user to start Remote Assistance. To cancel the invitation, click the Cancel link in the Instant Message window, or press Alt+Q.

2. If the expert accepts the invitation, Windows prompts you to create a password for the connection, as shown here.

3. Type the password in the Type a Password text box, type it again in the Confirm the Password text box, and then click the OK button.

4. You now need to communicate your password to the expert. The obvious way to communicate it is by typing it into Messenger, but this is totally insecure. It's much better to communicate the password by voice, even if doing so is much harder than using text. You might also send the password via e-mail. (There's a risk that the password might be intercepted, but in this case it's separate from the invitation, which you've transferred via Messenger.)

5. Wait for your helper to connect, and then proceed as described in "Receiving Remote Assistance," later in this chapter.

Receiving Remote Assistance

This section explains allowing the expert to connect to your computer, receiving assistance via chat or remote control, and disconnecting the expert when you no longer need their help.

Allowing the Expert to Connect to Your Computer

When the expert responds to an invitation, Windows displays a message box such as the one shown here, asking if you want the expert (it gives the name) to connect and warning you that the expert will be able to see whatever is on your desktop. Close any programs you don't want the expert to see, and then click the Yes button.

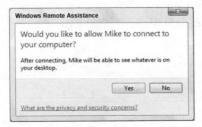

DETAILS ABOUT REMOTE ASSISTANCE

If you don't take any action for a few minutes when the expert tries to connect to your computer, Windows times out the connection.

Remote Assistance automatically configures its settings based on the speed of the connection established with the expert, so that it sends only an appropriate amount of information. But if the connection between you and the expert is slow (for example, a modem connection), it will take 30 seconds to a minute for the expert to see changes that appear on your screen in milliseconds—so you need to be patient. (Exactly how long it takes depends on the nature of the changes and the screen resolution you're using as well as on the speed of the connection.)

If you're using the Vista Aero user interface, and the expert's computer will not be able to display it correctly, Windows displays a notification-area pop-up message telling you that the color scheme has been changed to Windows Vista Basic because "a running program isn't compatible with certain visual elements of Windows." If you want to see more detail, you can click the pop-up message to display the dialog box shown here. Select the Don't Show Me This Again check box if you want to dispense with this warning in future, and then click the OK button. Your screen then uses the simpler Vista Basic user interface until you close Remote Assistance.

Receiving Assistance

Once the Remote Assistance session is established, Remote Assistance displays on the novice's screen the Remote Assistance window shown in Figure 21.9, which provides basic information about what's happening and control buttons.

CHATTING WITH THE EXPERT

You can chat with the expert via text. Click the Chat button to display a chat pane and ongoing status messages, type the message in the text box, and then press Enter or click the Send button. Figure 21.10 shows an example of chat.

FIGURE 21.9
During a Remote Assistance session, this Remote Assistance window provides a status information and control buttons.

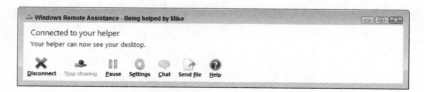

FIGURE 21.10
Use chat to tell the
expert which problem
you need them to
solve.

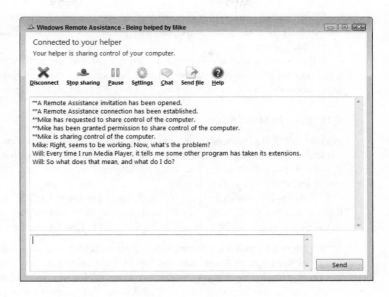

GIVING THE EXPERT CONTROL OF YOUR COMPUTER

If the expert requests control of your computer, Windows displays the Remote Assistance dialog box shown next.

Select the Allow *Helper* to Respond to User Account Control Prompts check box if you want your helper to be able to click through User Account Control windows. Granting this authority makes providing the help much easier for your helper, but it also enables them to make critical changes to your computer—so you should not select this check box unless you completely trust your helper.

Click the Yes button if you want to give your helper control of your computer. Otherwise, click the No button. You can regain control by pressing the Esc key, by pressing Alt+T, or by clicking the Stop Sharing button.

If the expert leaves the Remote Assistance connection untouched for around an hour when they have control of your computer, Remote Assistance times out the connection and closes it. You'll need to establish a new connection if you need further assistance.

CHANGING REMOTE ASSISTANCE SETTINGS

As you saw a moment ago, Remote Assistance lets you press Esc to stop the expert from sharing control of your computer. Using Esc this way allows you a quick escape, but it prevents both you and the expert from using Esc to cancel dialog boxes or other features. It even prevents you from using Esc in any key combination.

If you find this restriction awkward, you may want to disable this meaning of Esc. You can do this by clicking the Settings button and clearing the Use ESC Key to Stop Sharing Control check box in the Settings dialog box shown in Figure 21.11. This dialog box also contains three other settings:

◆ **Save a Log of This Session** Select this check box if you want to save a log (a written record) of the Remote Assistance session so that you can review it afterward if necessary. You'll find this log in the Remote Assistance Logs folder in your `Documents` folder. Remote Assistance names the logs with the date and time. For example, the log file `20070212140806.xml` was created on February 12, 2007, at 2:08.06 PM. You can double-click one of these files to open it in Internet Explorer.

◆ **Bandwidth Usage** Drag the slider up and down the Low–High axis to tell Remote Assistance how much bandwidth optimization to use:

No Bandwidth Optimization When the slider is at the High setting, Windows applies no bandwidth optimization, which gives the expert the most accurate picture of the novice's desktop. Use this setting when the expert and novice are connecting over a network connection or a fast Internet connection.

Don't Allow Full Window Drag When the slider is one notch down from the More setting, Windows doesn't display the contents of windows when you drag them. Instead, you see only the window frame.

Turn Off Background When the slider is in its middle position, Windows also turns off the desktop background. Use this setting for medium-speed Internet connections (for example, slow DSL or ISDN connections).

Use 8-Bit Color When the slider is at the Low setting, Windows reduces the color depth to 8 bits (256 colors). This setting degrades the display considerably but makes the display information much faster to transfer. Use this setting for dial-up or other slow connections.

◆ **Allow Helper to See Credential Requests** Click this button and then authenticate yourself to User Account Control to let your helper respond to User Account Control dialog boxes. To prevent the helper from responding to User Account Control dialog boxes again, click the Don't Allow Helper to See Credential Requests button that replaces the Allow Helper to See Credential Requests button.

Click the OK button when you've chosen the settings you want.

FIGURE 21.11
Drag the Bandwidth
Usage slider to specify
which visual effects
Windows should turn
off to reduce band-
width and make the
display faster for
the expert.

DISCONNECTING THE EXPERT

To disconnect the expert, click the Disconnect button. Remote Assistance checks to make sure you want to do this, as shown next. Click the Yes button. Windows closes the connection and restores your Desktop to its full complement of colors (if you or Windows chose to optimize performance for the expert).

When the expert disconnects, Windows displays a Remote Assistance dialog box telling you so. Click the OK button to close this dialog box, and then close the Windows Remote Assistance window.

CANCELING WAITING FOR REMOTE ASSISTANCE

If you fix the problem yourself, or decide to stop waiting for the expert to respond to your invitation, click the Cancel button. Windows displays the Are You Sure You Want to Stop Waiting? dialog box, shown here. Click the Yes button. Once you've done so, the expert will no longer be able to connect to your computer.

REUSING A REMOTE ASSISTANCE INVITATION

Once you've created and used a Remote Assistance invitation, you can use it again from the How Do You Want to Invite Someone to Help You? screen (see Figure 21.12).

For security, you should always create a new password when reusing a Remote Assistance invitation, even though this means you'll need to communicate the new password to the expert.

FIGURE 21.12

You can reuse a Remote Assistance invitation, but it's best to assign a different password and filename when you do so.

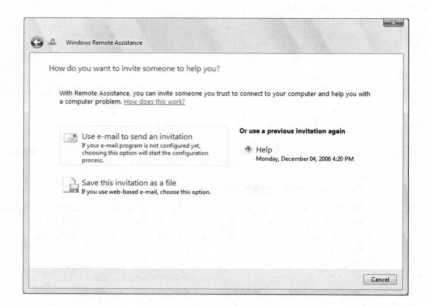

Providing Remote Assistance

You can provide Remote Assistance either by responding to a Remote Assistance invitation that a novice has sent or given to you or by offering assistance.

Responding to a Remote Assistance Invitation

When someone sends you a Remote Assistance invitation, you can accept it as follows:

◆ **E-mail** You receive an e-mail message with the Subject line "You have received a Remote Assistance invitation" (or another subject if the sender has changed the canned text). The message comes with explanatory text augmenting whatever message text the requester entered, and an attached file with the name RATicket.MsRcIncident. Open the file by double-clicking it. Alternatively, in Windows Mail, click the Attachment icon, select the file from the drop-down menu, select the Open It button in the Mail Attachment dialog box, and click the OK button.

◆ **Messenger** You see a Conversation window telling you that the person "is inviting you to start using Remote Assistance." Click the Accept link (or press Alt+T) to accept the invitation or click the Decline link (or press Alt+D) to decline it.

◆ **File** Double-click the invitation file to open it.

Windows prompts you for the password for the connection, as shown here. Type the password and press Enter or click the OK button.

Windows displays a Remote Assistance window and shows the Attempting to Connect message as it prompts the novice to accept the connection. If the novice accepts it, the Remote Assistance session starts.

TROUBLESHOOTING: WHEN REMOTE ASSISTANCE CAN'T CONNECT THROUGH A FIREWALL

If Remote Assistance can't connect through your firewall or Internet connection–sharing device, make sure that TCP port 3389 is open. You shouldn't need to open this port manually on Windows Firewall, because Windows Firewall opens it automatically when Remote Assistance comes knocking. But you may need to open it (or have a network administrator open it for you) on other firewalls or Internet connection–sharing devices.

If you're not able to establish a Remote Assistance connection from an invitation sent via e-mail (or via a file drop), try establishing a connection via Messenger instead. The advantage of this method is that because Messenger already has a connection between the novice's computer and the expert's computer, Remote Assistance is better positioned to deal with firewall problems. If the expert's computer doesn't receive a Remote Assistance connection attempt from the novice's computer within five seconds of the expert's acceptance of the Messenger invitation, the expert's computer sends what's called a *forward connect* to the location specified in the invitation. Usually, this backup attempt at communication is enough to solve communications problems caused by firewalls and Internet connection–sharing devices.

TROUBLESHOOTING: "REMOTE ASSISTANCE CANNOT MAKE THE CONNECTION" ERROR

The error message "Remote Assistance cannot make the connection" (see the dialog box shown below), which occurs when the expert opens the invitation and tries to establish a connection with the novice, can mean any of the following:

◆ The novice's Internet connection is down.

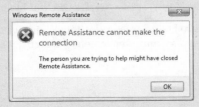

◆ The novice's IP address has changed, and Remote Assistance has no way of identifying the computer's new IP address. (If both computers are on the same network, Remote Assistance can look up the computer from the name information contained in the Remote Assistance invitation, but it can't do this across the Internet.) If the expert can communicate with the novice via e-mail or chat, the expert can learn the novice's new IP address, open the rcBuddy.MsRcIncident file in a text editor such as Notepad, and enter the new IP address to make the connection work. But in most cases it's easier to have the novice resend the invitation from Help and Support Center. If the expert can communicate with the novice via Messenger, the novice can issue a new invitation in Messenger.

◆ The novice has closed the Remote Assistance window, which makes the Remote Assistance invitation expire.

◆ A firewall other than Windows Firewall is blocking the connection.

Offering Remote Assistance

If you think someone needs your help, you can offer it to them. The easiest way to offer Remote Assistance is via Messenger, but you can also offer Remote Assistance by starting a connection directly to the person's computer.

OFFERING REMOTE ASSISTANCE VIA MESSENGER

You can offer Remote Assistance via Messenger in either of these ways:

◆ In an existing conversation, click the Show Menu button and choose Actions ➤ Offer Remote Assistance.

◆ In the main Messenger window, click the Show Menu button and choose Actions ➤ Offer Remote Assistance. In the Select a Contact window, select the contact to whom you want to offer Remote Assistance, and then click the OK button. Messenger opens a conversation window with your contact and offers them Remote Assistance.

If your contact clicks the Accept link, Windows prompts them to create a password for the connection. Windows then prompts you for the password. If you enter the correct password, the Remote Assistance session starts, and the novice has the choice of accepting the incoming connection.

OFFERING REMOTE ASSISTANCE VIA AN IP ADDRESS OR AN INVITATION

You can also offer Remote Assistance directly if you know the novice's computer's name or IP address or you have an existing Remote Assistance invitation from the novice. Follow these steps:

1. Choose Start ➤ All Programs ➤ Maintenance ➤ Windows Remote Assistance. Windows displays the Do You Want to Ask for or Offer Help? window.

2. Click the Offer to Help Someone button. Windows displays the Choose a Way to Connect to the Other Person's Computer screen (see Figure 21.13).

FIGURE 21.13
The Choose a Way to Connect to the Other Person's Computer screen lets you connect via the computer name or IP address or via an existing invitation.

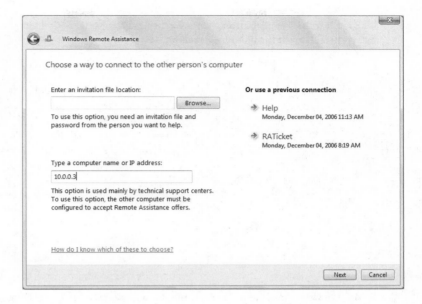

3. Choose how to connect:

   ◆ In the Type a Computer Name or IP Address text box, type the computer's name or the IP address. (If you don't know the IP address, see the sidebar "Finding Out a Computer's IP Address" for instructions on how to find it out.) Click the Finish button.

   ◆ If you have an invitation file, click the Browse button, use the Open dialog box to navigate to and select the file, and then click the Open button. Click the Finish button.

   ◆ If you want to reuse a previous connection, click it in the Or Use Previous Connection list.

4. If Windows can connect to the novice's computer, it prompts the novice to accept the connection. If you have started the Remote Assistance session by using the computer's name or IP address, Windows prompts the novice to create a password for the connection, and then prompts you to enter the password.

FINDING OUT A COMPUTER'S IP ADDRESS

To find out a computer's IP address, follow these steps:

1. Right-click the Network icon in the notification area and choose Network and Sharing Center from the shortcut menu. Windows opens a Network and Sharing Center window.

2. In the area that gives details on your network, click the View Status link. Windows displays a Status dialog box for the connection.

3. Click the Details button. Windows displays the Network Connection Details dialog box, as shown here. Look at the IP Address readout.

4. Click the Close button to close the Network Connection Details dialog box, click the Close button to close the Status dialog box, and then click the Close button (the × button) to close the Network Center window.

Providing Remote Assistance

If Windows is able to contact the novice's computer, and if the novice accepts the Remote Assistance connection, Windows displays the Remote Assistance window (shown in Figure 21.14). As you can see, this features a chat pane, a view pane that shows the novice's Desktop, and assorted command buttons. If the novice's Desktop uses multiple monitors, the Remote Assistance window displays all of them in one window.

CHATTING WITH THE NOVICE

To chat with the novice via text, click the Chat button to display the chat pane if it's not currently displayed. Type a message in the text box and press the Enter key or click the Send button to send it.

To hide the chat pane so that you can see more of the remote screen, click the Chat button again.

FITTING THE REMOTE DISPLAY TO YOUR SCREEN

You can scale the remote display to shrink it down to fit in the area available on your screen by clicking the Fit to Screen button, and restore it to its actual size by clicking the Fit to Screen button again (see Figure 21.15). (You can't make the remote display larger than its actual size, no matter how much screen real estate you have.) Depending on the resolution you and the novice have set, scaling the display may make the fonts illegible, but viewing the whole screen at once may make it easier for you to see what's happening on the computer than being able to see only a partial screen and having to scroll to see its outer reaches.

FIGURE 21.14

Once connected to the novice's computer, you see the entire screen, including the novice's Remote Assistance controls.

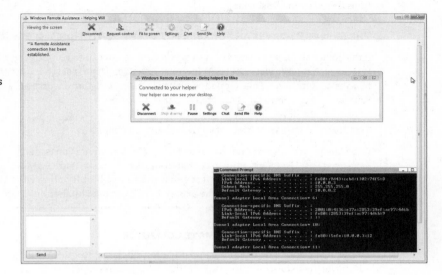

FIGURE 21.15

When you're supplying the assistance in a Remote Assistance session, you can view the screen and chat with the novice. Fitting the desktop to your screen is often helpful, even though it makes icons small and text hard to read.

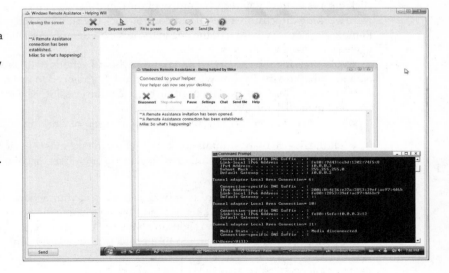

TROUBLESHOOTING: SOLVING PROBLEMS RESPONDING TO REMOTE ASSISTANCE INVITATIONS ISSUED FROM MESSENGER

This sidebar discusses how to deal with the two most common problems with Remote Assistance invitations issued from Messenger.

THE EXPERT RECEIVES AN "UNABLE TO ACCEPT INVITATION" MESSAGE

If the novice sends a Remote Assistance invitation to an expert running a version of Windows other than Windows Vista, Windows XP, or Windows Server 2003, that person is likely to see the message "Unable to accept invitation." This happens because Remote Assistance works only with these three versions of Windows, not with earlier versions.

THE NOVICE DOESN'T RESPOND TO THE EXPERT'S REPLY

If the novice doesn't respond to the expert's reply to an invitation issued via Messenger, the novice may have used Fast User Switching to switch to another account. Because Messenger keeps running in a disconnected session, the expert will see that the novice is still online with Messenger, but because the novice won't be able to see that the expert is trying to take up their invitation, they won't respond.

SHARING CONTROL OF THE REMOTE COMPUTER

To request control of the remote computer, click the Request Control button. Windows displays a Remote Assistance dialog box on the remote screen asking the novice if they want to give you control. (You'll see this Remote Assistance dialog box in the Remote Assistance window.) If they click the Yes button, you receive control of the computer and can take any action with it as if you were working directly on it. To release control, click the Stop Sharing button (either the one in your Remote Assistance window or the one in the novice's Remote Assistance window that you're controlling) or press the Esc key.

Avoid pressing the Esc key when taking keyboard actions on the remote computer. Even combinations that use the Esc key will release control. If you need to use Esc, click the Settings button on the novice's Remote Assistance button bar, clear the Use ESC Key to Stop Sharing Control check box, and then click the OK button.

When you have control of the remote computer, you're working in the novice's security context:

♦ If the novice is an Administrator user, you can take most any action on the computer. If the novice has granted you authority to click through User Account Control dialog boxes, you can act freely.

♦ If the novice is a Standard user, you're limited in your actions. If the novice is the Guest, you're even more limited. If you're just trying to show the novice how to do something they ought to be able to do, you shouldn't have any problem working within a Standard or Guest account, but if you're trying to fix a problem, the security context may give you grief.

TRANSFERRING FILES TO AND FROM THE REMOTE COMPUTER

To transfer a file to the remote computer, click the Send File button. Windows displays an Open dialog box. Navigate to the file, and then click the Open button to send it. The novice then gets to decide whether to keep the file and in which folder to save it. (If you have control of the computer, you can make these decisions.)

To transfer a file from the remote computer to your computer, have the novice click the Send File button in their Remote Assistance window. Alternatively, if you have control of the computer, you can do this yourself.

DISCONNECTING FROM THE REMOTE COMPUTER

To disconnect from the remote computer, click the Disconnect button. Then close the Remote Assistance window manually. Unless you expect you'll need to reconnect to the remote computer to help the novice further during the time remaining before the Remote Assistance invitation expires, delete the invitation file before you forget.

If the novice disconnects the connection, Windows adds the message "The Remote Assistance connection has ended" to the session log.

TROUBLESHOOTING: AVOIDING LOSS OF CONTROL OF THE REMOTE COMPUTER

When you, the expert, have taken control of the remote computer, you may need to take steps to avoid losing control of it:

◆ You lose control of the remote computer if its screen resolution changes. You then need to request control again. The most likely cause of the screen resolution changing when you have control is your changing it manually, so this is an action to avoid. The screen resolution may also change if the screen saver on the remote computer starts while you're working. If you're planning an extended session on a remote computer without the novice present at it (for example, if you're using a slow connection), check the screen saver early on and increase its delay if necessary.

◆ You lose control if the remote computer goes into standby or hibernation. Again, if you're planning an extended Remote Assistance session, you might start by checking the standby and hibernation settings on the remote computer. If the remote computer is a portable, find out whether it's running on battery power and, if so, how much power is left. Standby and hibernation times are usually shorter when a portable is running on battery power, so ask the novice to plug in the portable computer if possible.

◆ You lose control if another user logs on to the remote computer. If the novice is present at the computer, this shouldn't happen. If the novice is going to step away for a while, and there's a danger that someone else might try to use the computer, consider asking the novice to put a warning sign on the computer.

You also lose control if the novice stops control, disconnects you, or closes the Remote Assistance session. But there's not much you can do to prevent the novice from taking these actions beyond asking them not to.

The Bottom Line

Understand what Remote Assistance is and what security considerations are involved

Remote Assistance lets you request assistance across a network or Internet connection from someone you trust, termed the "expert." You can let the expert only view your screen and chat with you, or you can allow the expert to take control of your computer and even click through User Account Control dialog boxes. Letting the expert take control of your computer poses a considerable security risk, because you must trust both the expert's good intentions and technical skill. Even if you don't give the expert control, you should evaluate each help suggestion carefully before implementing it.

Turn on Remote Assistance and set limits for how it can be used   To turn on Remote Assistance, press Windows Key+Break, and then click the Remote Settings link in the System window of Control Panel. Click the Continue button in the User Account Control window. On the Remote page of the System Properties dialog box, select the Remote Assistance Invitations Can Be Sent from this Computer check box. To prevent the computer from being controlled remotely, click the Advanced button, and then clear the Allow this Computer to Be Controlled Remotely check box.

Send a remote access invitation via e-mail   Choose Start ➤ All Programs ➤ Maintenance ➤ Windows Remote Assistance, click the Invite Someone You Trust to Help You button, and then click the Use E-mail to Send an Invitation button. Type a password for the connection, and then click the Next button. Windows starts an e-mail message with canned text and a Remote Assistance invitation attached. Address the message and send it. If you use a web-based e-mail program, select the Save This Invitation as a File button on the How Do You Want to Invite Someone to Help You? screen, name the file, and then attach it to an e-mail message manually.

Send a Remote Assistance invitation via Windows Live Messenger   To send a Remote Assistance invitation via Windows Live Messenger, click the Show Menu button and choose Actions ➤ Request Remote Assistance. Pick the contact in the resulting window and click the OK button. Alternatively, start a conversation with the contact, click the Show Menu button in the conversation window, and then choose Actions ➤ Request Remote Assistance.

Receive help via Remote Assistance   When the expert tries to connect to your computer, accept the connection. You can then chat with the expert and follow the expert's suggestions, or allow the expert to take control of your computer. Click the Stop Sharing button to regain control of your computer from the expert. Click the Disconnect button to end the Remote Assistance session.

Provide Remote Assistance to someone else   To respond to a Remote Assistance invitation, open the e-mail attachment or file, or click the Accept link in a Messenger conversation. Enter the password when prompted. Windows opens a Remote Assistance window showing the novice's screen. Use chat to tell the novice what to do, or click the Request Control button to request control of the novice's computer so that you can fix the problem. Use the Send File button if you need to transfer a file from your computer to the novice's computer or vice versa. When you've finished, click the Disconnect button to break the connection.

Part 4

Audio, Video, and Games

In this section:

Chapter 22

Windows Media Player and Windows Media Center

- ◆ Enjoy audio, video, and more with Windows Media Player
- ◆ Watch and record TV with Windows Media Center
- ◆ Control input and output with the Volume icon and Sounds
- ◆ Record audio with Sound Recorder

This chapter shows you how to use Windows Media Player and Windows Media Center. Windows Media Player is the powerful multimedia player included with all versions of Windows Vista; it not only provides features for enjoying audio, video, and DVDs, but also supports copying compact discs (CDs) to your hard disk in compressed formats and burning custom audio CDs.

Windows Media Center is a program for recording and watching TV, and playing and burning CDs and DVDs. Windows Media Center comes with Windows Vista Home Premium (and with Windows Vista Ultimate) but not with Windows Vista Home Basic. Much of Windows Media Center's functionality is simple to use, so this chapter covers it only briefly.

This chapter also shows you how to use the Volume icon to control input and output and how to record audio using the Sound Recorder applet.

Using Windows Media Player

This section shows you how to use Windows Media Player for enjoying audio and video. Microsoft has made Windows Media Player as easy to use as possible—but it also has many configuration options that you should know about so that you can make the best use of the program.

Getting Started with Windows Media Player

Start Windows Media Player by choosing Start ➢ All Programs ➢ Windows Media Player.

CHOOSING INITIAL SETTINGS

The first time you run Windows Media Player, the program displays its Welcome screen (see Figure 22.1), which offers you the choice between Express Settings and Custom Settings.

FIGURE 22.1
The Welcome
screen lets you
choose between
Express Settings
and Custom Settings
for Windows Media
Player.

The easiest choice is to select the Express Settings option button and then click the Finish button. You can change these settings later. But if you want to control what Windows Media Player does from the start, follow these steps:

1. Click the Custom Settings, and then click the Next button. Windows displays the Select Privacy Options screen (see Figure 22.2), which lets you choose the options you want:

   Display Media Information from the Internet This check box controls whether Windows Media Player automatically downloads information from the Internet for the CDs and DVDs you insert in your optical drives. For example, when you load an audio CD, Windows Media Player downloads the artist, CD, and track data so that you can create compressed files easily with the correct names. Usually, this is helpful, but it can potentially reveal which CDs and DVDs you're playing.

FIGURE 22.2
The Select Privacy
Options screen lets
you choose whether
to download media
information automat-
ically and whether
to participate in
Microsoft's Customer
Experience Improve-
ment Program.

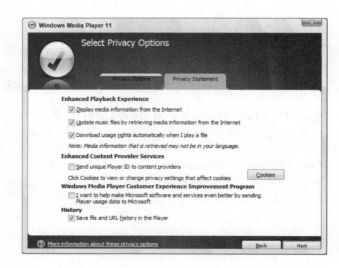

Update Music Files by Retrieving Media Information from the Internet This check box controls whether Windows Media Player updates your music files by retrieving missing tag information from the Internet. This feature too is largely positive except that it could reveal which music files you have.

Download Usage Rights Automatically When I Play a File This check box controls whether Windows Media Player automatically acquires licenses for content that's protected by digital rights management (DRM) technologies. This is usually a good idea, but you may prefer to be prompted each time a license is needed.

Send Unique Player ID to Content Providers This check box controls whether Windows Media Player passes an identifier to streaming media servers to enable the servers to monitor the connection and adjust the stream to improve playback quality. You may need to select this check box to get high-quality streaming audio.

Cookies Windows Media Player uses Internet Explorer's cookies (discussed in the section "Handling Cookies" in Chapter 2). Click the Cookies button to access the controls for configuring cookie handling.

I Want to Help Make Microsoft Software and Services Even Better by Sending Player Usage Data to Microsoft Select this check box if you want Windows Media Player to send Microsoft data on your playing habits automatically. Windows Media Player sends the information anonymously, but many people still feel uncomfortable being monitored.

Save File and URL History in the Player Select this check box if you want Windows Media Player to save information about the files and streams you've played. Clear this check box if you'd prefer not to keep this data.

2. Click the Next button. Windows Media Player displays the Customize the Installation Options screen.

3. Choose whether to create shortcuts on the Desktop and Quick Launch toolbar:

   ◆ Select the Add a Shortcut to the Desktop check box if you want to have a Windows Media Player shortcut on your Desktop. You probably don't need to create a shortcut here.

   ◆ Select the Add a Shortcut to the Quick Launch Bar check box if you want to have a Windows Media Player shortcut on your Quick Launch toolbar. This shortcut is more useful than the Desktop shortcut.

4. Click the Next button. Windows Media Player displays the Select the Default Music and Video Player screen.

5. If you want to use Windows Media Player as your default music and video player, select the Make Windows Media Player the Default Music and Video Player option button. Otherwise, select the Choose the File Types that Windows Media Player Will Play option button.

6. Click the Next button. If you decided to make Windows Media Player the default player, Windows Media Player displays the Choose an Online Store screen; go to the next step. If you decided to choose the file types, Windows displays the Set Program Associations window for Windows Media Player (see Figure 22.3). This window shows the file extensions that Windows Media Player can play and the program to which they are currently

assigned. Select the check box for any file extension currently assigned to another program that you want to transfer to Windows Media Player, and then click the Save button. Windows Media Player displays the Choose an Online Store screen.

7. Choose the appropriate option button, and then finish the installation:

◆ Select the URGE option button if you want to use the URGE music service for buying and downloading songs, click the Install button, and follow through the process for downloading and installing URGE. If the Microsoft Windows Media Configuration Utility – Security Warning dialog box appears, click the Run button, and then authenticate yourself to User Account Control. Depending on your Internet Explorer cookie settings, you may also be prompted to let urge.com place cookies on your computer. Select the Apply My Decision to All Cookies from This Website check box, and then click the Allow button.

◆ Otherwise, select the Don't Set Up a Store Now option button, and then click the Finish button. (The Install button swaps places with the Finish button depending on which option button you choose.)

Once you've completed the installation, the Windows Media Player window appears (see Figure 22.4), showing the songs on your computer. Even if you haven't added any songs yourself, your computer will normally have the sample songs that come with Windows Vista.

FIGURE 22.3
Use the Set Program Associations window to transfer to Windows Media Player any file extensions that are currently assigned to other programs (such as QuickTime Player in this example).

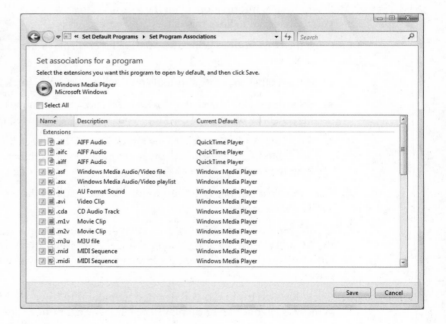

UNDERSTANDING PLAY MODES

Windows Media Player offers four play modes: Full mode, Compact mode, Skin mode, and Mini mode.

Full Mode   Windows Media Player appears in a normal window that you can resize or maximize as needed. Full mode is good for watching video (or DVDs) and for navigating your media library, but it takes up too much screen space when you're just listening to music.

FIGURE 22.4
Windows Media Player in its Full mode, occupying a normal window

Compact Mode   Click the Switch to Compact Mode button in the lower-right corner of the Full mode window, and Windows Media Player appears in Compact mode, as shown here. The title bar shows the artist, composer, album, and song title in sequence. You can click the Return to Full Mode button in the lower-right corner of the window to return to Full mode.

Skin Mode   Skin mode applies a custom *skin*, or graphical look, to Windows Media Player, as shown here.

♦ To choose a skin, right-click the command bar at the top of the Windows Media Player window (just below the title bar), and then choose View ➤ Skin Chooser from the menus. Choose one of the skins in the left panel to display it in the right; when you find one you want, click the Apply Skin button. To download more skins, click the More Skins button, and then use the resulting browser window to download skins.

♦ To switch to Skin mode, press Ctrl+2 or right-click the command bar and choose View ➤ Skin Mode from the menus.

♦ To switch back to Full mode, press Ctrl+1 or click the Switch to Full Mode button. (The location of this button depends on the skin.)

Mini Mode   Mini mode (shown next) reduces Windows Media Player to a toolbar containing control buttons.

♦ To switch to Mini mode, minimize Windows Media Player, and then accept Windows Media Player's invitation to display Windows Media Player as a toolbar. After that, Windows Media Player will run as a toolbar when you minimize it.

♦ To stop Windows Media Player appearing as a toolbar, right-click the notification area, and then choose Toolbars ➤ Windows Media Player to remove the check mark from the Windows Media Player item on the menu.

♦ You can display the current track information by hovering the mouse pointer over the toolbar, or by clicking the button with the up- and down-arrows.

♦ To switch back to Full mode, click the Restore button at the lower-right corner of the toolbar.

EXPERT KNOWLEDGE: DIGITAL RIGHTS MANAGEMENT, LICENSES, AND COPY-PROTECTION TECHNOLOGIES

Being able to store audio and video in digital format on a PC, play them back easily, and even transfer them via the Internet or removable media is great for consumers of audio and video content. But it can be way less than great for creators of audio and video content: These computer capabilities pose a severe threat to their livelihoods by compromising their copyrighted works and robbing them of sales.

COMPUTERS HAVE MADE DIGITAL PIRACY EFFORTLESS, FAST, AND CHEAP

In the past, audio and video works have largely been distributed on physical media, such as CDs, audio-cassettes, LPs, videocassettes, and DVDs. The tangible nature and physical presence of such media generally make it clear when a theft has occurred: Physical media can't walk out of stores by themselves. Making unauthorized copies of a work distributed on a physical medium such as a videotape involves cost (for the media for the copies and for any duplicating equipment needed), time (typically real-time copying), and effort. Distributing those copies involves further cost, time, and effort. And the illegality of such pirated works is widely understood: Most consumers are aware that it's illegal to distribute (let alone sell) copies of copyrighted works. Besides, copies of works on analog media (such as videotape or audiotape) are lower fidelity than the originals, so the inauthenticity of late-generation copies is clear.

By contrast, any work stored in a digital medium accessible by a PC can be copied in seconds at almost zero cost, and the copies are perfect every time. These perfect copies can be distributed via the Internet, again at negligible cost. And they can be distributed in quantities and over distances unthinkable for physical media. For example, if someone buys a CD in Sioux Falls, makes MP3 files of its tracks, and makes them available on a file-sharing service, anyone with Internet connectivity anywhere in the world—from Vladivostok to Tierra del Fuego, from Juneau to Java—can download them and then distribute them further.

PROTECTING THE RIGHTS OF CONTENT CREATORS

At this writing, several technologies exist to protect the rights of content creators (and their authorized distributors) while allowing consumers to use the content. For example, most DVDs use an encryption system called Content Scrambling System (CSS), which requires an encryption key in order to be decoded. CSS keys were licensed and tightly controlled by the DVD-Copy Control Association (DVD-CCA)—tightly controlled, that is, until Norwegian hackers in the LiVid (Linux Video) group created a utility called DeCSS by reverse-engineering some unencrypted code they discovered in a sloppily constructed software DVD player. Now that DeCSS is widely available, CSS-encrypted content can be deciphered by anyone who has the code.

Perhaps the most promising of the technologies designed to protect content is the digital license. A *digital license* is encrypted information that links a particular copy of a downloaded work to a particular computer or individual. For example, in the current model of digital licenses for audio, if you download a track that uses a digital license, you buy or are otherwise granted a license to play the track on the computer on which you downloaded it. If you transfer the track to another computer, it won't play, because the computer lacks the necessary license information.

So far, so good. But in order to be viable enough to become widely accepted, digital licenses need to be not only easy and intuitive to use but also compatible with both generally used technology and with the prevailing laws. For example, the First Sale Doctrine laid out in the Copyright Act allows consumers to sell or give a copy they've legitimately acquired of a copyrighted work to another person. Any copyright-protection technology that prevents consumers from doing this effectively (for example, because any subsequent recipient would not be able to view or listen to the work because it was locked by encryption and a nontransferable license to the first purchaser's computer) would be open to heavy-duty legal challenges.

Leaving aside such details for the moment, digital licenses are now being used to secure some copyrighted content. Windows Media Player adopts a two-pronged approach to digital licenses for audio content, supporting digital licenses for both tracks you buy and download and tracks you copy from CD. Windows Media Player automatically issues a license for each track you copy from a CD (unless you set it to copy tracks without licensing them).

At this writing, Windows Media Player lets you choose whether to use digital licenses or to be free, easy, and possibly illegal. As long as you use those tracks on the PC with which you created them, there's no problem with using licenses. But if you want to be able to play the tracks from another computer, you face a problem, because the license ties the associated digital media file to the PC for which the license is issued: You'll need to acquire a new license or transfer a license from the original computer. Similarly, you may not be able to download a copy of a licensed track to a portable player without performing some licensing gymnastics.

Simply *playing* a track from another computer should be fine, legally, because it's the same file that you created from the CD. So should be moving the track to another computer that belongs to you and using it on that computer. Only if you create an illegal copy of the track (or if you distribute it) should there be a problem. More on this later in the chapter; but you can see that the implementation of digital licenses tends to be problematic, partly because of the nature of digital licenses and partly because of the assumption of those who implemented the technology that anything unlicensed will tend to be licentious. There's no good reason for using digital licenses for the tracks you copy from CD unless you can't trust yourself (or other users of your computer) not to take illegal actions with them. In fact, this is how Microsoft pitches DRM: It'll prevent you from unwittingly doing anything illegal.

If you choose to use digital licenses for the tracks you copy from CD and the tracks you purchase and download (or download for free), you must back up your licenses in case you lose them and need to restore them. If your computer crashes, if you reinstall Windows, or if you install another operating system, you'll need to restore your licenses in order to be able to use the tracks.

License files are small, so you can store a good number of them on a floppy disk, CD, or USB key. If you're not good at keeping your removable media in order, or if you want to protect them against local or natural disasters, back them up to an Internet drive instead.

BEWARE OF NON-CD AUDIO DISCS

Since around 2001, some of the major record companies have been releasing audio discs that use copyright-protection technologies intended to prevent users from ripping and encoding their contents on computers and (by extension) sharing the resulting files with other people in authorized ways.

Typically, copy-protected discs include some form of deliberate corruption designed to confuse computer CD and DVD drives, which are more sensitive than audio-only CD drives because they need to be able to read data CDs as well as audio CDs. Some of the copy-protection mechanisms mess with the error-correction capabilities built into CD players, raising concerns that these discs will degenerate faster than genuine CDs because they're less resistant to scratches. Others work by surreptitiously using Windows' AutoPlay feature to install a custom CD driver the first time you load the CD. The driver then prevents you from ripping the CD. (Such copy-protection can be avoided by turning off AutoPlay for your optical drives or suppressing AutoPlay temporarily by pressing the Shift key while you load a CD, so it's not fully effective.)

These protected discs play fine on most audio CD players, though some cause problems on older CD players and specialized CD players, such as car CD players. But they won't play on many (perhaps most) computer CD drives. Other CD drives—particularly DVD drives and CD-RW drives—can play these discs (and rip and encode them) without problems. If you have such a drive, and you rip and encode a copy-protected audio disc, you will have committed a crime under Title I of the Digital Millennium Copyright Act (DMCA), which makes it illegal to "circumvent a technological measure that effectively controls access to a work protected under this title." If you do this "willfully and for purposes of commercial advantage or private financial gain" (which can include providing another person with a track you've ripped and encoded and receiving just about anything—even a single audio track—from them in return), you can be savaged with fines of up to a half-million dollars and a sentence of 5 years in jail.

Technically and legally, these copy-protected audio discs are *not* compact discs, because they don't conform to the Red Book compact disc specification. This means that, legally, such discs can't be sold as CDs and must not bear the CD logo that certifies that the disc is a CD. This distinction may sound like nit-picking, but it's not: Much of the success of the CD as a format over the past 20-odd years has been built on the fact that all CD players could play all CDs—without fail, and without unpleasant surprises.

Probably the worst of these non-CD audio discs so far were the ones that Sony-BMG issued in 2005 using the XCP copy-protection system. If the user clicked the Agree button in a pop-up window that appeared when they inserted the disc, the disc automatically installed software that included a *rootkit*, a tool used by malicious hackers to hide malware from users. After a firestorm of complaint, Sony-BMG recalled the discs, issued a patch intended to remove the rootkit, and agreed to settle several class-action lawsuits.

Setting Up Sharing

When Windows Media Player detects another computer running Windows Media Player on the same network, it prompts you to set up sharing by displaying a notification-area icon and a pop-up message, as shown here.

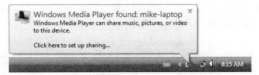

Click the pop-up message. Windows displays the Windows Media Player Library Sharing dialog box, as shown here.

If you want to go ahead and start sharing, click the Allow button, and then authenticate yourself to User Account Control. If you want to review your sharing settings (as you'll probably want to do at first), click the Sharing Settings button. Windows Media Player displays the Media Sharing dialog box (see Figure 22.5).

FIGURE 22.5
Use the Media Sharing dialog box to set up sharing of songs and videos via Windows Media Player.

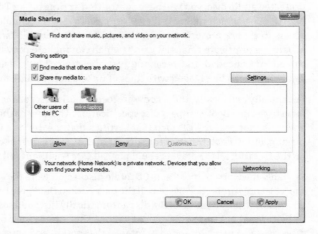

If you want to be able to play media files that other users and computers are sharing, select the Find Media That Others Are Sharing check box.

If you want to be able to share your media files with other users of this computer or with other computers, take the following steps:

1. Select the Share My Media To check box. Windows Media Player enables the Settings button and the list box showing users and computers.

2. Click the Settings button. Windows Media Player displays the Media Sharing – Default Settings dialog box (see Figure 22.6).

FIGURE 22.6
Use the Media Sharing – Default Settings dialog box to specify which media types and ratings to share by default with other devices and computers.

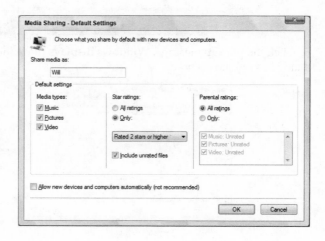

3. Specify which media and ratings to share:

Share Media As   In this text box, type the name you want to give your shared media. Windows suggests your username.

Media Types   In this area, select the Music check box, the Pictures check box, or the Video check box to indicate which items you want to share.

Star Ratings   In this area, select the All Ratings option button if you want to share all your media. If you want to share only media you've given a certain star rating, select the Only option button, and then select the rating in the drop-down list: Rated 1 Star or Higher, Rated 2 Stars or Higher, Rated 3 Stars or Higher, Rated 4 Stars or Higher, or Rated 5 Stars. Select the Include Unrated Files check box if you want to include files to which you haven't yet assigned a rating.

Parental Ratings   In this area, select the All Ratings option button if you want to share files no matter what rating they have, or select the Only option button, and then select the check boxes in the list box to specify which files to share.

4. If you want to apply these sharing settings to all computers and devices that join the network, select the Allow New Devices and Computers Automatically check box. Normally, you'll want to apply different ratings to different devices and computers to prevent any user from getting an earful or eyeful of unsuitable content.

5. Click the OK button. Windows Media Player closes the Media Sharing – Default Settings dialog box, returning you to the Media Sharing dialog box.

6. In the main list box, select the computer that you want to affect, or select the Other Users of this PC item if you want to affect the other users of your computer.

7. Click the Allow button if you want to let the computer or users share your media, or click the Deny button if you don't want to let them.

8. If you need to change your computer's Sharing and Discovery settings, click the Networking button, and then work in the resulting Network and Sharing Center window. For example, you might want to change your Media Sharing settings. Close the Network and Sharing Center window to return to the Media Sharing dialog box.

9. Click the OK button, and then authenticate yourself to User Account Control. Windows applies the sharing settings you chose, and the computers or users to whom you assigned the permission can access the shared parts of your media library.

Configuring Windows Media Player

Windows Media Player offers many configuration options on the 10 or 11 pages of its Options dialog box (the DVD page appears only if your computer has a DVD drive). The following sections discuss the most important options. To start configuring Windows Media Player, choose Tools ➤ Options. Windows Media Player displays the Options dialog box.

PLAYER PAGE OPTIONS

Almost all of the options on the Player page (see Figure 22.7) are worth knowing about.

FIGURE 22.7
The Player page of the Options dialog box for Windows Media Player.

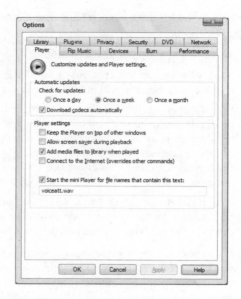

Automatic Updates Group Box

Choose how often Windows Media Player should check for updates. If you have an always-on Internet connection, select the Once a Day option button or the Once a Week option button; if not, the Once a Month option button is probably a better choice. Select the Leave the Download Codecs Automatically check box if you want Windows Media Player to download and install any new *codecs* (coder/decoder software) it needs to play back audio streams or files. Clear this check box if you prefer to have Windows Media Player prompt you before it installs new codecs.

You can check for updates manually at any point by choosing Help ➤ Check for Updates.

Player Settings Group Box

The Player Settings group box contains the following check boxes:

Keep the Player on Top of Other Windows   Select this check box if you want to keep Windows Media Player on top of all other running windows. This setting is useful if you use Compact mode or Skin mode.

Allow Screen Saver during Playback   Select this check box if you want the screen saver to be able to start while Windows Media Player is playing music. Whether this is a good idea depends on how you use your computer.

Add Music Files to Library When Played   Select this check box if you want to add to your music library any music file that you play that isn't already in the library. (For example, you might start a song playing by double-clicking it in an Explorer window.) If you select this check box, you can also select the Include Files from Removable Media and Network Shares check box (which is cleared by default) if you want to add music files from removable disks and network drives.

Connect to the Internet (Overrides Other Commands) Select this check box if you want Windows Media Player to be able to connect to the Internet even if you've told other programs to work offline.

Start the Mini Player for File Names That Contain This Text Select this check box if you want Windows Media Player to run in Mini mode when you receive a file that has a particular name. The default name, `voiceatt.wav`, is used for voicemail messages.

Enable Picture Support for Devices Select this check box (which is cleared by default) if you want Windows Media Player to synchronize JPG pictures with a portable device that supports them.

RIP MUSIC PAGE OPTIONS

The Rip Music page of the Options dialog box (see Figure 22.8) contains options that control the ripping (extracting and copying) of music from CDs to your hard drive. These options are largely set-and-forget, though you may want to use different music quality settings for different CDs that you copy. The options are described in the following sections.

FIGURE 22.8
The Rip Music page of the Options dialog box for Windows Media Player

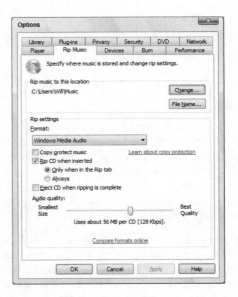

Rip Music to This Location

This group box contains a label that shows the folder in which Windows Media Player creates the compressed files containing music. The default location is your `Music` folder, in which Windows Media Player creates folders by artist and, within these, folders by album name. To change the location, click the Change button, use the resulting Browse for Folder dialog box to navigate to and select the location, and then click the OK button.

By default, Windows Media Player names the files by track number and track name (or *song title*, as Windows Media Player refers to it)—for example, `01 My Love.WMA`. To change the naming, click the File Name button and work in the resulting File Name Options dialog box (shown in Figure 22.9). Select the check boxes for the items you want to include in the filename (track number, song title, artist, album, and so on). Use the Move Up and Move Down buttons to shuffle the selected items into order. And use the Separator drop-down list to specify which separator character to use: none, a space, a dash, a dot, or an underline. Then click the OK button. Windows Media Player closes the File Name Options dialog box and applies your choices.

FIGURE 22.9

Use the File Name Options dialog box to tell Windows Media Player how to name the files you rip from CD.

Rip Settings

In the Format drop-down list, select the file format you want to use for the files: Windows Media Audio, Windows Media Audio Pro, Windows Media Audio (Variable Bit Rate), Windows Media Audio Lossless, MP3, or WAV. (See the next sidebar for details on how Windows Media and MP3 stack up to each other.)

OTHER MUSIC PROGRAMS YOU MIGHT WANT TO USE

You can get various high-quality MP3 rippers and encoders for free. Two of the leading programs are Apple Computer's iTunes, which you can download for free from the Apple website (http://www.apple.com) and Musicmatch Jukebox (http://www.musicmatch.com), which comes in a free Basic version and a paid Plus version. Both iTunes and Musicmatch Jukebox also play music (some rippers don't), but you may also want to get a dedicated MP3 player, such as Winamp (http://www.winamp.com), rather than using Windows Media Player all the time.

Select the Copy Protect Music check box if you want to use Windows Media Player's features for personal licensing of CD tracks you copy. See the sidebar, "Digital Rights Management, Licenses, and Copy-Protection Technologies," for a discussion of the advantage and disadvantages of using this feature. Clear this check box if you want more flexibility in what you can do with WMA files.

Select the Rip CD When Inserted check box if you want Windows Media Player to automatically start ripping each CD you insert. Select the Only When in the Rip Tab option button if you want to rip CDs only when you've displayed the Rip tab in Windows Media Player; if not, select the Always option button. Select the Eject CD When Ripping Is Complete check box if you want Windows Media Player to open the CD tray after it finishes ripping. Both settings are good for building your music library quickly, but automatic ejection is a bad idea for a laptop computer that you use out and about (as opposed to on your desk).

Use the Audio Quality slider to specify the quality at which to encode the files you copy. Windows Media Player offers different bit rates graded from Smallest Size to Best Quality for the Windows Media Audio, Windows Media Audio Pro, and Windows Media Audio (Variable Bit Rate) formats, while the Windows Media Audio Lossless format offers only one setting.

Higher bit rates take up more space but sound better. Experiment with this setting on a variety of music and find the bit rate that suits you best:

◆ If you want to create the best-sounding files possible, use Windows Media Lossless.

◆ If you want to use the files with a portable player that has limited memory, use the lowest bit rate that sounds good on the player.

 Real World Scenario

UNDERSTANDING THE WINDOWS MEDIA AUDIO FORMATS

In an ideal world, you'd rip all your CDs—no, scratch that: you wouldn't need to rip your CDs at all. But in the next-best scenario, you'd rip all your CDs to a single format that provided the ideal balance of audio quality (high) with file size (small).

Nobody has invented that world yet, and Microsoft has chosen to muddy the waters by providing four Windows Media Audio file formats. Which should you choose—or should you use the MP3 format instead? And what about the WAV format?

Here's what you need to know:

◆ WMA Lossless is considered "mathematically lossless"—technically, it doesn't lose any of the audio data. By comparison, the other three formats of WMA and MP3 use lossy compression, so they discard some audio data. The disadvantage to WMA Lossless is that the files are very large (around 25MB for a four-minute song), so they take up a lot of space on your computer and you can't fit many of them on a portable player. Many portable players don't play this format.

◆ WMA Lossless sounds great to most people, but some audiophiles claim that it doesn't sound quite as good as CD-quality audio, which uses a comprehensive range of samples across the whole area of audio frequencies audible to the human ear. If you can tell the difference, you should probably stick with the WAV format. WAV is uncompressed, so the audio should be as perfect as the audio source. One disadvantage of WAV is that the file format doesn't provide tags (containers) for information such as the artist, CD, and song. But Windows Media Player can finesse this for you, associating this information with the WAV file in its database. The other disadvantage of WAV is that the files are huge (around 36MB for a four-minute song). Many portable players don't play WAV files.

◆ Unless you've got amazing ears, very good hi-fi, or both, the advantages of compression outweigh the disadvantages. Compressed files are small enough to store in large numbers on computers, to carry in small numbers on portable players, and to transfer easily via removable media, networks, or the Internet.

◆ Windows Media Audio uses a standard bit rate—in other words, it saves the same amount of data for each passage of music. Windows Media Audio (Variable Bit Rate) uses a variable bit rate, saving more data for more complex passages of audio and less for simpler ones. A variable bit rate normally gives higher-quality audio at the same file size, or a smaller file size for similar quality. Windows Media Player may take longer to encode variable bit rate files, but if your computer is capable of running Windows Vista adequately, this shouldn't be a concern. Some older portable players don't support Windows Media Audio (Variable Bit Rate).

◆ Windows Media Audio Pro is a high-compression format that produces good audio quality at small file sizes. Windows Media Audio Pro is most suitable for portable players with low storage capacity, such as flash-memory players and mobile phones. Many portable players don't support Windows Media Audio Pro.

◆ MP3 and WMA use different encoding methods, but the results are roughly comparable in quality.

◆ MP3 is a more widely used file format than WMA, but WMA is catching up fast, especially as it has become the main audio format for online music stores such as Napster and Walmart.com. A wide variety of software MP3 players are available for every conceivable computing platform, and you can get hardware MP3 players in an impressive variety of shapes and sizes. Many software MP3 players and some hardware MP3 players can handle WMA files as well as MP3 files.

◆ All the Windows Media Audio formats are proprietary and support digital rights management. MP3 and WAV are not proprietary and do not support digital rights management.

Whether you choose MP3, WMA, or another format will probably boil down to what you want to do with digital audio, how high your standards are, and how much time, effort, and money you're prepared to invest.

If all you want to do is rip your CDs, encode them, and store the results on your hard disk so that you can play them back from your computer, Windows Media Player and one of the Windows Media Audio formats provide an effective solution. Choose a format bit rate that delivers satisfactory audio quality through your sound card and speakers, load the first CD, and start ripping. In this case, you might even choose to use the Copy Protect Music feature, because it ensures that you can't inadvertently break the law by using the files on another computer. (You can transfer them to another computer, but because it doesn't have the right license information, it won't be able to play them.)

If you want to use digital audio on a portable player, make sure that the player supports your chosen Windows Media Audio format before you buy it or (if you already have the player) before you rip all your CDs.

DEVICES PAGE OPTIONS

The Devices page of the Options dialog box (see Figure 22.10) lets you configure your optical drives, display, speakers, and any portable music players.

Setting Properties for a CD Drive or DVD Drive

To set properties for a CD drive or DVD drive, select it in the Devices list box and click the Properties button. Windows Media Player displays the Properties dialog box for the drive. Figure 22.11 shows an example of the Properties dialog box for a DVD drive.

In the Playback group box and the Rip group box, choose between the Digital option button and the Analog option button. (Depending on the drive, the Analog option button may not be available.)

FIGURE 22.10
The Devices page of the Options dialog box lists your CD drives, DVD drives, and portable devices.

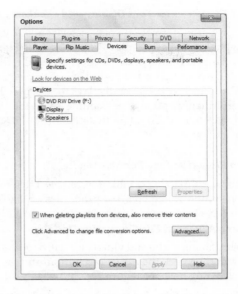

FIGURE 22.11
To choose analog or digital audio, display the Properties dialog box for the drive.

Digital audio extraction is preferable to analog audio extraction because it maintains a higher-fidelity signal. The main reason not to use digital audio extraction is if your CD drive does not support it or cannot deliver it successfully. If you choose digital audio extraction, you can select the Use Error Correction check box if you want Windows Media Player to use its error-correction features to try to remove errors that occur during ripping. Error correction uses a bit more processor power when copying; it slows down copying considerably; and its effect is often undetectable—but it's a good idea to use error correction for copying music, because any defects in the copied tracks tend to be much more annoying than spending a few extra minutes copying each CD.

Click the OK button. Windows Media Player closes the Properties dialog box for the optical drive.

Setting Properties for Your Display and Speakers

To set properties for your display, select it in the list box and click the Properties button. Windows Media Player opens a Display Properties dialog box. Use the controls in the dialog box to change the pixel aspect ratio so that the circle is round rather than distorted, and then click the OK button.

To set properties for your speakers, click their entry in the list box and click the Properties button. Windows Media Player displays the Speaker Properties dialog box. Choose sound playback and performance options (for example, select the Use 24-Bit Audio for Audio CDs check box if you use High Definition Compatible Digital CDs—HDCDs—or other extra-quality CDs), and then click the OK button.

Setting Properties for a Portable Device

To set properties for a portable device, select it in the list box, click the Properties button, and work in the resulting dialog box. The properties available depend on the type of device.

Choosing Advanced File Conversion Options

If synchronizing audio and video files with a portable device seems to be taking too long, or if quality is suffering, click the Advanced button, and then work with the options in the File Conversion Options dialog box (see Figure 22.12).

Allow Video Files to Convert in the Background   Select this check box if you want to let Windows Media Player convert video files when your computer isn't playing media and has had no keyboard or mouse input for 10 minutes. This setting is usually helpful, because it allows Windows Media Player to convert videos ready for synchronization.

Allow Audio Files to Convert in the Background   Select this check box if you want to let Windows Media Player convert audio files when your computer is idle. Audio conversion takes less time than video conversion, but if you're using a lower audio quality on your portable player (so that you can fit more content on it), you may want to use this feature.

Deinterlace Video Files When Converting   Select this check box only if your video files are interlaced and you need to play them on a device that uses a progressive-scan display (for example, a Portable Media Center). Most video files are deinterlaced, so you'll seldom need this option. (*Interlacing* is a method of scanning every odd-numbered line in a picture, followed by every even-numbered line, to give faster results, rather than scanning each line in sequence, as progressive scan does.)

Choose Quality over Speed When Converting Video   Select this check box if the quality of your converted videos is too low.

Store Files Temporarily to This Location   Select the folder you want to use for temporary storage of converted files (before they're synchronized), and specify the amount of space to make available. If your computer is out of disk space, you can reclaim any used space by clicking the Delete Files button—but Windows Media Player will need to create the files again for your next synchronization.

When you've finished choosing conversion options, click the OK button. Windows Media Player returns you to the Devices page of the Options dialog box.

FIGURE 22.12

The File Conversion
Options dialog box
lets you tell Windows
Media Player to
convert audio and
video files in the back-
ground to speed up
synchronization.

BURN PAGE OPTIONS

The Burn page (see Figure 22.13) of the Options dialog box lets you change the following settings:

General In the Burn Speed drop-down list, select the speed you want to use: Fastest, Fast,
Medium, or Slow. Use Fastest unless you find the discs have problems; in which case, lower the
speed. Select the Automatically Eject the Disc after Burning check box if you want Windows
Media Player to eject the disc. On a laptop computer, you may want to clear this check box in
case the drive is obstructed.

Audio CDs Select the Apply Volume Leveling across Tracks on the CD check box if you want
to apply volume leveling, also called *normalization*—making all the songs conform to a more or
less uniform volume. Volume leveling can help you avoid getting your ears blasted, but it can
also reduce the dramatic impact of songs.

FIGURE 22.13

The Burn page of the
Options dialog box
lets you set the burn
speed, apply normal-
ization, and convert
music to a lower
bit rate so that more
fits on a disc.

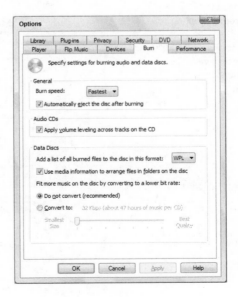

Data Discs   In the Add a List of All Burned Files to the Disc in this Format drop-down list, choose WPL (Windows Playlist) if you'll use the disc only on Windows. Choose M3U (an MP3 playlist format) if you'll use the disc on other operating systems as well. Select the Use Media Information to Arrange Files in Folders on the Disc check box if you want Windows Media Player to put the songs in a folder structure of artists and albums rather than all in a single folder. If you want to pack more music onto the disc by using a lower bit rate, select the Convert To option button, and then drag the slider to the quality you want. Otherwise, select the Do Not Convert option button to leave the songs at their existing bit rates.

PERFORMANCE PAGE OPTIONS

The Performance page (see Figure 22.14) of the Options dialog box offers these options:

Connection Speed   Select the Detect Connection Speed option button if you want Windows Media Player to detect your connection speed. This setting usually works well. If you find the results disappointing, try selecting the Choose Connection Speed option button and specifying the speed in the drop-down list.

Network Buffering   Select the Use Default Buffering option button to make Windows Media Player buffers the default number of seconds of audio before starting to play it. (The *buffer* is the quantity of audio that Windows Media Player downloads before starting to play an audio stream and holds in reserve so that it can even out any minor interruptions in the audio stream when it's playing.) If you hear interruptions in the audio with the default buffering, note the buffering time the next time you access streaming audio, then try selecting the Buffer For option button and specifying a larger number in the Seconds text box. The disadvantage to buffering more audio is that you have to wait longer for the audio to start playing, but if you're prepared to put up with a little delay, a larger buffer can help smooth out the playback.

FIGURE 22.14
You may need to specify a connection speed or adjust buffering on the Performance page of the Options dialog box.

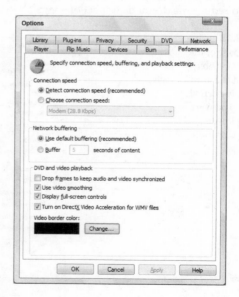

DVD and Video Playback   On a computer with poor video performance, you may need to select the Drop Frames to Keep Audio and Video Synchronized check box to prevent the audio and video by going out of sync because the video can't keep up. Windows Media Player then drops as many video frames as necessary, which gives a jerky effect—so use this setting only if you must.

Select the Use Video Smoothing check box if you want Windows Media Player to *interpolate* (add extra) frames for video files with low frame rates to create a smoother effect. This setting is usually helpful.

Select the Display Full-Screen Controls check box if you want Windows Media Player to display the full-screen controls on top of the video. Having the controls is usually helpful. Windows Media Player fades the controls away after a few seconds.

Select the Turn On DirectX Video Acceleration for WMV Files check box if you want Windows Media Player to use DirectX acceleration when playing files in the Windows Media Video format. This acceleration is usually helpful.

If you want to change the color of the video border, click the Change button, select the color in the Color dialog box, and then click the OK button.

Library Page Options

The Library page (see Figure 22.15) of the Options dialog box contains options for specifying how to create and maintain your media library.

Sharing

In this group box, click the Configure Sharing button to display the Media Sharing dialog box, which you can use to set up sharing. See "Set Up Sharing," earlier in this chapter, for details.

FIGURE 22.15

Use the Library page of the Options dialog box to specify how to add files to your media library.

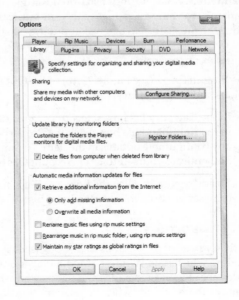

Update Library by Monitoring Folders

To specify which folders Windows Media Player monitors for new media files, click the Monitor Folders button and work in the Add to Library dialog box. Monitor as few folders as possible so that Windows Media Player doesn't waste processor cycles searching your entire neighborhood for new files. See the section "Adding Files to Your Media Library," later in this chapter.

Automatic Media Information Updates for Files

This group box contains the following settings:

Retrieve Additional Information from the Internet   Select this check box to have Windows Media Player download and apply missing tag information (such as album names or cover art) to your files; clear this check box if you want Windows Media Player to leave the tag information alone. If you select this check box, choose between the Only Add Missing Information option button (the default) or the Overwrite All Media Information option button, which lets Windows Media Player overwrite any existing tag information it considers wrong. Overwriting all can be annoying if you've customized tags.

Rename Music Files Using Rip Music Settings   Select this check box if you want Windows Media Player to rename music files using tag information and the format you specified in the File Name Options dialog box.

Rearrange Music in Rip Music Folder, Using Rip Music Settings   Select this check box if you want Windows Media Player to move files to different folders following the organization scheme you specified in the File Name Options dialog box. This option can be useful if you use only Windows Media Player to play your music files. If you want to manage your music files manually, clear this check box—otherwise, you may not find your music files where you left them.

Maintain My Star Ratings as Global Ratings in the Media Files   Select this check box if you want to save your star ratings with your music files. This behavior is usually helpful: If you then move the music files to a new computer, you still have your ratings.

PLUG-INS PAGE OPTIONS

On the Plug-ins page (see Figure 22.16) of the Options dialog box, you can choose options for visualizations and other features:

◆   In the Category list box, select the type of item you want to affect, and then select the item in the right-hand list box. Click the Properties button to display a Properties dialog box for any configurable options in the item. To remove the item, click the Remove button, and then authenticate yourself to User Account Control.

◆   To add a plug-in, click the Look for Plug-ins on the Web link, and then use the resulting browser window to download and install components.

PRIVACY PAGE OPTIONS

The Privacy page of the Options dialog box (see Figure 22.17) contains a complex set of options for controlling which data Windows Media Player downloads for you automatically, which data it provides about your media files and habits, and whether it saves your play history. You will have set some of these settings when you set up Windows Media Player.

FIGURE 22.16
Use the Plug-ins page to add, remove, and configure plug-in components for Windows Media Player.

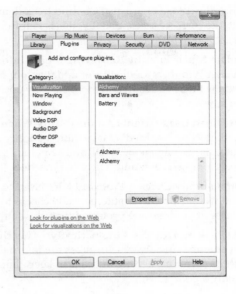

FIGURE 22.17
Choose privacy options on the Privacy page of the Options dialog box.

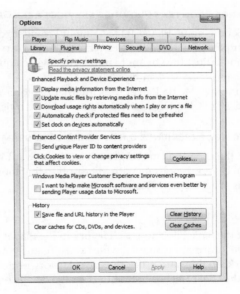

ENHANCED PLAYBACK AND DEVICE EXPERIENCE GROUP BOX

The Enhanced Playback and Device Experience group box contains the following options:

Display Media Information from the Internet   This check box controls whether Windows Media Player automatically downloads information from the Internet for the CDs and DVDs you insert in your optical drives. For example, when you load an audio CD, Windows Media

Player downloads the artist, CD, and track data so that you can create compressed files easily with the correct names. Usually, this is helpful, but it can potentially reveal which CDs and DVDs you're playing.

Update Music Files by Retrieving Media Info from the Internet This check box controls whether Windows Media Player updates your music files by retrieving missing tag information from the Internet. This feature too is largely positive except that it could reveal which music files you have.

Download Usage Rights Automatically When I Play or Sync a File This check box controls whether Windows Media Player automatically acquires licenses for content that's protected by digital rights management (DRM) technologies. This is usually a good idea, but you may prefer to be prompted each time a license is needed.

Automatically Check if Protected Files Need to Be Refreshed This check box controls whether Windows Media Player automatically checks to see whether your protected files need updated licenses. If you're using protected files, this setting is usually helpful.

Set Clock on Devices Automatically This check box controls whether Windows Media Player automatically synchronizes the internal clock on a device (such as a portable player) with its own time setting in order to keep time-limited digital licenses coordinated. This is usually a good idea.

ENHANCED CONTENT PROVIDER SERVICES AREA GROUP BOX

The Send Unique Player ID to Content Providers check box controls whether Windows Media Player passes an identifier to streaming media servers to enable the servers to monitor the connection and adjust the stream to improve playback quality. You may need to select this check box to get high-quality streaming audio.

Windows Media Player uses Internet Explorer's cookies (discussed in the section "Handling Cookies" in Chapter 2), which you can access quickly by clicking the Cookies button.

CUSTOMER EXPERIENCE IMPROVEMENT PROGRAM GROUP BOX

Select the check box in this group box if you want Windows Media Player to share your Windows Media Player usage data with Microsoft so that they can learn how real users use the program. The data is shared anonymously.

HISTORY AREA

Select the Save File and URL History in the Player check box if you want Windows Media Player to save information about the files and streams you've played. Clear this check box if you'd prefer not to keep this data. Click the Clear History button to clear your current file and URL history, or click the Clear Caches button to clear the details on the CDs and DVDs you've loaded recently.

SECURITY PAGE OPTIONS

The Security page of the Options dialog box (see Figure 22.18) contains the following options:

Run Script Commands When Present This check box controls whether Windows Media Player runs script commands embedded in digital media content. Scripts can be malicious, so it's best to keep this check box cleared.

Run Script Commands and Rich Media Streams When the Player Is in a Web Page This check box controls whether Windows Media Player runs scripts or streams when the player is embedded in a web page. Selecting this check box increases your security but may cost you functionality.

Play Enhanced Content That Uses Web Pages without Prompting Select this check box if you want to suppress prompting about enhanced content delivered via web pages. Normally, it's safer to have Windows Media Player prompt you before it starts displaying web pages.

Show Local Captions When Present Select this check box if you want Windows Media Player to display any available Synchronized Accessible Media Interchange (SAMI) captions during playback. (SAMI is closed captioning for Windows multimedia files.)

Zone Settings Windows Media Player shares Internet Explorer's security zones (discussed in the section "Choosing Security Options" in Chapter 2), which you can access quickly by clicking this button.

FIGURE 22.18
The Security page of the Options dialog box.

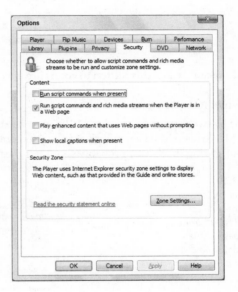

DVD PAGE OPTIONS

The DVD page (see Figure 22.19) appears if your computer has a DVD drive and decoder installed. This page offers these options:

DVD Playback Restrictions To implement parental control on DVDs played on the computer, click the Change button. Windows Media Player displays the Change Rating Restriction dialog box, as shown next. Select the maximum permitted rating in the Prevent Others from Playing DVDs That Are Rated Higher Than drop-down list, click the OK button, and then authenticate yourself to User Account Control.

Language Settings If you want to change your default languages for DVDs and videos, click the Defaults button. Windows Media Player displays the Default Language Settings dialog box, as shown next. Choose the languages in the Audio Language drop-down list, the Lyrics, Captions, and Subtitles drop-down list, and then DVD Menu drop-down list, and then click the OK button. The Title Default setting gives you the primary language with which the DVD was encoded.

Advanced Click this button to configure speaker settings.

NETWORK PAGE OPTIONS

On the Network page (see Figure 22.20), you can choose which protocols to use for receiving audio and video streams over a network. Unless you know your protocols well enough not to need advice on configuring them, you probably shouldn't mess with the default selections.

FIGURE 22.19
You can set DVD restrictions such as PG-13 and NC-17 from the DVD page of the Options dialog box.

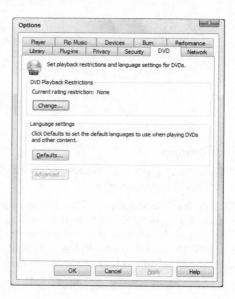

FIGURE 22.20
You shouldn't need to change the settings on the Network page of the Options dialog box.

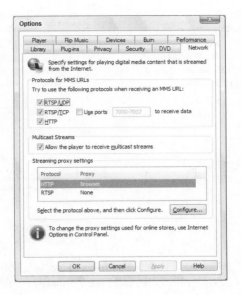

Adding Files to Your Media Library

You can add files to your media library by ripping your CDs to audio files (see the section "Ripping a CD," later in this chapter), by having Windows Media Player automatically monitor folders for new media files, or by using drag and drop.

ADDING FILES FROM AUTOMATICALLY MONITORED FOLDERS

To set up Windows Media Player to add media files automatically from certain folders, take the following steps:

1. Right-click the command bar (right-click just to the right of the Forward button) and choose File ≻ Add to Library from the menus. Windows Media Player displays the Add to Library dialog box (see Figure 22.21). If you see the smaller version of the dialog box, click the Advanced Options button to reveal the rest of it.

2. If you just want to monitor Windows' media folders (such as the Music folder in your user account), select the My Personal Folders option button. If you want to monitor media folders that other users of this computer and other computers on your network are sharing, select the My Folders and Those of Others That I Can Access option button. The list box shows the folders Windows Media Player is set to monitor and their folder type—for example, your Music folder is typically designated the Rip Folder.

3. To add another folder, click the Add button, select the folder in the Add Folder dialog box, and then click the OK button. To remove a folder, select it in the list box, and then click the Remove button.

FIGURE 22.21
The Add to Library dialog box lets you set up folders for Windows Media Player to monitor for new files.

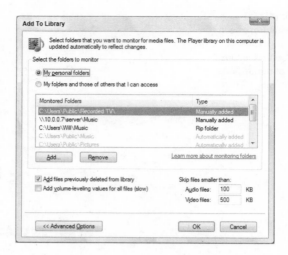

4. If you want Windows Media Player to restore any files that you've deleted from your music library, select the Add Files Previously Deleted from Library check box.

5. If you want to apply normalization to all files, select the Add Volume-Leveling Values for All Files check box. This process can take a long time if you're adding many files.

6. In the Skip Files Smaller Than area, use the Audio Files text box and the Video Files text box to specify the smallest size of files that you want to include (the default settings, 100KB for audio files and 500KB for video files, work well for many people). These minimum sizes help you avoid adding very short audio files (for example, system sounds) and video clips to your media library.

7. Click the OK button. Windows Media Player displays the Add to Library by Searching Computer dialog box, as shown next, while it searches for files and then adds them to your media library.

8. For best results, let Windows Media Player finish adding the files. If you need to start using Windows Media Player before that, you can click the Close button to close the dialog box. Windows Media Player continues adding the files in the background, but the process takes longer.

ADDING FILES VIA DRAG AND DROP

If you don't want to put all your audio or video files into the folders you've set Windows Media Player to monitor, you can add a file or folder to your media library by using drag and drop. Open a Windows Explorer window, position it so that you can see the Library item on the left of the Windows Media Player window, and then drag the file or folder from the Windows Explorer window to the Library item.

Playing Audio Files

To play a song from the music library, take the following steps:

1. Click the drop-down arrow on the Library button on the command bar, and then choose Music from the drop-down menu. Windows Media Player displays the Library page showing your music (see Figure 22.22).

2. Use the items in the left panel to navigate to the song you want. For example, click the Artist item in the Library category to display a list of artists, and then double-click the artist to display the songs by that artist.

3. Double-click the song, or click it and then click the Play button at the bottom of the Windows Media Player window.

FIGURE 22.22
The Library page in Windows Media Player lets you view your files in various ways.

Creating Playlists

To make a sequence of songs you want to play, create a playlist. Take the following steps:

1. Click the drop-down arrow on the Library button on the command bar, and then choose Music from the drop-down menu. Windows Media Player displays the Library page showing your music.

2. Press Ctrl+N or click the drop-down arrow on the Library button, and then choose Create Playlist. Windows Media Player displays a playlist pane at the right side of the window, gives it the name Untitled Playlist, and selects the name so that you can overwrite it.

CHOOSING VISUALIZATIONS

When it's playing audio, Windows Media Player shows *visualizations* (graphical displays) on the Now Playing page. To toggle a visualization to full screen, press Alt+Enter or click the View Full Screen button in the lower-right corner of the Windows Media Player window. Press the Esc key (or Alt+Enter again) to toggle off full screen. To change the visualization, click the Now Playing drop-down button, choose Visualizations from the menu, and then make a choice from one of the submenus.

3. Type a new name over the text, and then press the Enter button. Windows Media Player adds the playlist to the Playlists list in the left pane.

4. Drag songs to the playlist to add them.

5. To change the order of the songs in the playlist, drag them up or down.

6. Click the Save Playlist button. Windows Media Player saves the playlist.

You can also create Auto Playlists—playlists in which Windows Media Player picks the tracks for you according to the criteria you specify. To create an Auto Playlist, follow these steps:

1. Click the drop-down arrow on the Library button on the command bar, and then choose Create Auto Playlist from the drop-down menu. Windows Media Player displays the New Auto Playlist dialog box (see Figure 22.23).

2. Type the name for the playlist in the Auto Playlist Name text box.

3. Use the Controls in the main box to specify which songs to include in the playlist.

4. Click the OK button. Windows Media Player closes the New Auto Playlist dialog box and adds the playlist to the Playlists category.

To play a playlist, double-click it.

FIGURE 22.23
Use the New Auto Playlist to set up the parameters for an automatically selected playlist.

PLAYING A CD

When you insert a CD in an optical drive, Windows normally displays the AutoPlay dialog box (see Figure 22.24). You can click the Play Audio CD Using Windows Media Player button to start the CD playing in Windows Media Player. You can select Always Do This for Audio CDs check box if you want each CD you insert to start playing in Windows Media Player.

Once you've inserted a CD and dealt with AutoPlay (if it runs), you can play a CD in Windows Media Player by double-clicking its entry in the left pane.

If your computer is connected to the Internet, Windows Media Player attempts to retrieve the CD information when you insert the CD.

FIGURE 22.24
The AutoPlay dialog box lets you set up Windows Media Player to play or rip CDs automatically. If you prefer to be prompted each time, clear the Always Do This for Audio CDs check box before making your choice.

USING THE GRAPHIC EQUALIZER AND SOUND EFFECTS

Windows Media Player includes a graphic equalizer for improving the sound that emerges from your speakers or headphones. When a song is playing, click the Now Playing button to display the Now Playing screen, and then click the Now Playing drop-down button and choose Enhancements ➤ Graphic Equalizer. Figure 22.25 shows the graphic equalizer.

The graphic equalizer is straightforward to use:

◆ To turn the graphic equalizer on and off, click the Turn On link or Turn Off link.

◆ To apply a preset equalization, choose it from the Select Preset drop-down list.

◆ To apply custom equalization, drag each frequency-band slider to an appropriate position. The frequency bands start with the lowest frequencies at the left side and progress to the highest frequencies at the right side.

◆ To specify whether the frequency-band sliders move independently or together, click one of the three buttons on the control to the left of the frequency bands. Click the top button to make the sliders move independently. Click the middle button to make the sliders move together in a loose group. Click the bottom button to make the sliders move together in a tight group.

◆ To close the graphic equalizer, click its Close button (the × button).

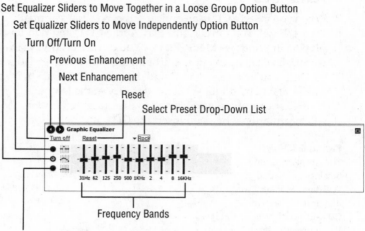

FIGURE 22.25
Use the graphic equalizer to improve the sound of audio.

To apply sound effects, click the Now Playing drop-down button and choose Enhancements ➤ SRS WOW Effects. Windows Media Player displays the SRS WOW Effects panel. From here, you can use the Turn On link and Turn Off link to turn the effects on and off, set bass boosting with the TruBass slider, set the WOW effect with the WOW Effect slider, or choose a different speaker setting.

Ripping a CD

Windows Media Player makes it easy to rip an audio CD to your hard drive and encode it to the compressed format you specified on the Rip Music page in the Options dialog box—for example, WMA.

EXPERT KNOWLEDGE: WHAT CAN YOU LEGALLY DO WITH DIGITAL AUDIO?

If you're going to enjoy digital audio, you need to know what you can and cannot do with it. Here's what you can legally do:

◆ Listen to streaming audio from a website or an Internet radio station, even if the site or person streaming the audio is doing so illegally.

◆ Record audio from a medium you own (for example, a CD) to a different medium (for example, a cassette) so that you can listen to it at a different time or in a different place.

◆ Download a digital file that contains copyrighted material from a website or FTP site *provided that the copyright holder has granted the distributor permission to distribute it.*

◆ Download a digital file from a computer via P2P technology *provided that the copyright holder has granted the distributor permission to distribute it.*

◆ Create digital-audio files (for example, WMA files or MP3 files) of tracks on CDs you own for your personal use.

◆ Distribute a digital-audio file to which you hold the copyright or for whose distribution the copyright holder has granted you permission.

♦ Download (or copy) legal digital-audio files in other supported formats to portable audio devices or PDAs.

♦ Broadcast licensed audio across the Internet.

Here are some of the key things that you cannot legally do with audio:

♦ Download a digital-audio file that contains copyrighted material if the copyright holder has not granted the distributor permission to distribute it.

♦ Distribute a digital-audio file that contains copyrighted material if the copyright holder has not granted you permission to distribute it.

♦ Lend a friend a CD so that they can create digital-audio files from it.

♦ Borrow a CD from a friend and create digital-audio files from it.

♦ Upload digital-audio files from a portable audio player that supports music uploading (which most portable players don't) to another computer. (In this scenario, you're using the portable player to copy the files from one computer to another.)

CD-quality audio files are huge, taking up about 9MB per minute. (This is why about 74 minutes of audio fits on a 650MB CD.) WMA and MP3 files can be encoded at various bit rates, either using a constant bit rate or a variable bit rate. A variable bit rate allocates the available space more intelligently to the content, with more complex audio passages taking more space than simpler passages, but a constant bit rate is compatible with more hardware and software players. The higher the bit rate, the more data is saved, and the higher the quality. WMA Lossless encoding saves the most data of all and delivers the highest quality. For putting music on portable devices, you'll probably want to use either WMA or WMA Variable Bitrate with either the Best Quality setting or the next setting down the scale. If the device has minimal memory, use the Windows Media Audio Pro format.

To copy a CD, follow these general steps:

1. Load the CD in your CD drive. If the AutoPlay dialog box appears (see Figure 22.24 earlier in this chapter), you can click the Rip Music from CD Using Windows Media Player button if you want to rip straight away, but it's usually a better idea to check the tag information before ripping so that you're sure it's correct.

2. In Windows Media Player, click the Rip tab. Windows Media Player displays the Rip page. Windows Media Player automatically retrieves the CD information and displays it.

3. If necessary, edit the information retrieved. You can edit any of the changeable fields (such as the track names, the artist's name, or the genre) by clicking the field twice (with a pause in between—*not* double-clicking) or clicking once and then pressing the F2 key. Windows Media Player displays an edit box around the field. Type the correction and press the Enter key.

4. Select the check boxes for the tracks you want to copy. Use the check box in the column header to change the status of all the individual check boxes at once.

5. Click the Rip button. Windows Media Player starts ripping and encoding the music, adding the tracks to the Media Library when they're finished. Figure 22.26 shows Windows Media Player ripping a CD.

If you notice a problem, click the Stop Rip button to stop ripping the tracks.

FIGURE 22.26
Windows Media Player makes it easy to rip the songs from a CD to your hard disk.

Playing a DVD

If your computer has a DVD drive (as almost all Vista-capable computers do), you can play a DVD by putting it in the drive. If the AutoPlay dialog box appears, as shown here, click the Play DVD Movie Using Windows Media Player button if you want to play the DVD with Windows Media Player. If you prefer use Windows Media Center instead, click the Play DVD Movie Using Windows Media Center. Either way, you can select the Always Do This for DVD Movies check box if you want to apply your choice to future DVDs you load.

If play doesn't start automatically, double-click the DVD's entry in the left panel in the Library window to start it playing. Windows Media Player uses the standard Play controls for DVDs and displays a list of the DVD chapters in the playlist area.

To make the most of your DVDs, you'll probably want to view them full screen. To do so, click the View Full Screen button in the lower-right corner of the Windows Media Player window or press Alt+Enter. Windows Media Player switches to full-screen view. You can display pop-up controls on screen by moving the mouse. These disappear after a few seconds when you stop moving the mouse.

EDITING MP3 AND WMA TAGS

WMA files and MP3 files include a *tag*, a virtual container with slots for several pieces of information, such as the artist's name, the track name, the album name, the genre, and so on. By using these tags, you can not only keep your music clearly identified but you can also sort the tracks by any of the pieces of information. For example, you could sort tracks by artist or by album.

The best way to tag your songs correctly is to check the tag information before importing a file—for example, before ripping a CD. But you'll often need to edit the tag on a file afterward. To do so, take the following steps:

1. Display the Library window and navigate to the song.

2. Right-click the song and choose Advanced Tag Editor from the shortcut menu. Windows Media Player displays the Advanced Tag Editor dialog box (shown here).

3. Enter the tag information on the various pages of the dialog box.

4. Click the OK button. Windows Media Player closes the Advanced Tag Editor dialog box and applies the tags to the audio file.

Playing Videos

Playing a video file could hardly be easier:

◆ To play a video file listed in your Media Library, double-click it.

◆ To play a video file that's not listed in your Media Library, right-click the command bar, choose File ➢ Open and use the resulting Open dialog box to select the video to open.

◆ To play a streaming video from a website, click its link.

Controlling Windows Media Player via Keyboard Shortcuts

Windows Media Player provides graphical controls for its functions, but you can also control the program using the keyboard using the commands shown in Table 22.1.

TABLE 22.1:   Keyboard Controls for Windows Media Player

TO DO THIS	PRESS
Zooming and Playing Videos	
Zoom the video to 50 percent	Alt+1
Zoom the video to 100 percent	Alt+2
Zoom the video to 200 percent	Alt+3
Toggle full screen display	Alt+Enter
Toggle captions and subtitles on and off	Ctrl+Shift+C
Fast-forward	Ctrl+Shift+F
Rewind video	Ctrl+Shift+B
Changing Modes and Views	
Switch to Full mode	Ctrl+1
Switch to Skin mode	Ctrl+2
Toggle "classic" menus in Full mode	Ctrl+M
Switch to or from full-screen mode	F11
Return from full-screen mode	Esc
Go back to the previous view	Alt+←
Go forward to the previous view (before you went back)	Alt+→
Switch to the first view after Recently Added	Ctrl+7
Switch to the second view after Recently Added	Ctrl+8
Switch to the third view after Recently Added	Ctrl+9

TABLE 22.1:   Keyboard Controls for Windows Media Player *(CONTINUED)*

To Do This	Press
Playing Songs and Items	
Start or pause play	Ctrl+P
Stop play	Ctrl+S
Toggle repeat	Ctrl+T
Go to the next item or chapter	Ctrl+F
Go to the previous item or chapter	Ctrl+B
Toggle shuffle on and off	Ctrl+H
Move the focus to the search box	Ctrl+E
Stop playing or close a file	Ctrl+W
Switch to fast play speed	Ctrl+Shift+G
Switch to normal play speed	Ctrl+Shift+N
Switch to slow play speed	Ctrl+Shift+S
Ctrl+Windows Key+0/1/2/3/4/5	Rate the playing item as 0/1/2/3/4/5 stars
Controlling the Volume	
Toggle muting on and off	F7
Decrease the volume	F8
Increase the volume	F9
Enlarge album art	F6
Reduce album art	Shift+F6
Maintaining Your Media Library	
Display the Add to Library dialog box	F3
Display the Open URL dialog box	Ctrl+U
Edit text for the selected item	F2
Change the view in the Details pane	F4

Burning Discs from Windows Media Player

Windows Media Player includes a feature for burning audio CDs directly from playlists. You can use MP3, WAV, and WMA files to create CDs. If you want to include tracks in other formats on CDs you burn, convert them to WAV format first.

To burn a CD from Windows Media Player, take the following steps:

1. Click the Burn drop-down button, and then choose Audio CD from the drop-down list. Windows Media Player displays the Burn pane on the right side of the window.

2. Drag songs or a playlist from your library to the Burn pane. Windows Media Player creates a list called Current Disc (see Figure 22.27). The readout at the top of the pane shows the CD's capacity and the amount of time left. If there are too many songs to fit on a single disc, Windows Media Player creates a second list (further down the Burn pane) called Next Disc.

3. If necessary, drag songs up or down the list in the Burn pane to get them into your preferred order.

4. Insert a blank CD in your CD drive.

5. Click the Start Burn button. Windows starts burning the disc, displaying its progress next to the track it's working on.

6. When Windows Media Player has closed the disc, it ejects the CD. Check the CD manually to make sure that it works (for example, put it back in the drive and try playing it). If it works, label it before you forget.

FIGURE 22.27
Use the Burn pane on the right side of the Windows Media Player window to put together your CD's contents.

Using Windows Media Center

If you have Windows Vista Home Premium rather than Windows Vista Home Basic, you can use Windows Media Center to play DVDs and videos, watch and record TV, listen to music, or view your pictures.

Windows Media Center is designed to be easy to use, so this section gives you the broad outlines rather than every detail, showing you the main actions you're likely to want to take but not every possible action.

Starting Windows Media Center

To start Windows Media Center, choose Start ≻ All Programs ≻ Windows Media Center. Windows Media Center displays its opening screen (see Figure 22.28). To reach the item you want, move up or down the vertical scrolling list of categories; the list wraps around, so you can reach any item by going either up or down, although one way will be longer than the other.

You can navigate Windows Media Center in any of these ways:

Remote Control   Press the ←, →, ↑, and ↓ buttons to navigate, and press the Select button to select the current item.

Mouse   Click the item you want, or move the mouse to display a caret that you can click. You can also simply hover the mouse pointer above a caret to keep moving in that direction.

Keyboard   Press the ←, →, ↑, and ↓ buttons to navigate, and press the Select button to select the current item.

FIGURE 22.28
The Windows Media Center opening screen. Windows Media Center is designed to be navigated using a remote control, so using a mouse can feel labored.

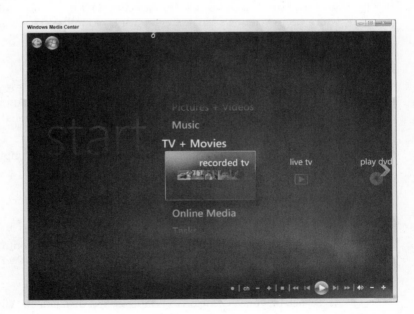

From any screen, you can click the Back button in the upper-left corner of Windows Media Center to return to the previous screen, or click the Home button (to the right of the Back button) to return to the Home screen.

Windows Media Center appears full screen by default. You can toggle between full-screen mode and windowed mode by pressing Alt+Enter.

Understanding the Windows Media Center Categories

These are the categories that Windows Media Center uses:

Pictures and Videos   Includes the Picture Library item (which lets you view your photos) and the Video Library item (which lets you view your videos).

Music   Includes the Music Library item (which lets you play your Windows Media Player songs), the Radio item (which lets you listen to radio via the Internet), and the Search item (which lets you search for music).

TV and Movies   Includes the Recorded TV item (which lets you watch shows you've recorded), the Live TV item, and the Play DVD item.

Online Media   Includes the Program Library item, which lets you play some of the games on your computer.

Tasks   Includes the Settings item (see the next section), the Shutdown item (for exiting Windows Media Center or locking or shutting down your computer), the Burn CD/DVD item, the Sync item (for synchronizing devices), and the Add Extender item (for adding an extender to send audio or video across your home network). Tasks also includes the Media Only mode item, which keeps Windows Media Center displayed full screen and hides its Minimize and Close buttons.

Setting Up Windows Media Center

Unless someone else has set up Windows Media Center on your computer, you'll probably want to start by setting up Windows Media Center. Many of the default settings work fine, but you'll have to configure Windows Media Center to work with your aerial or set-top box. To do so, take the following steps:

1. Connect your aerial or your set-top box to your PC's TV input. For example:

   ◆ Connect an aerial to an RF input.

   ◆ Connect a composite video input to an RCA connector.

   ◆ Connect an S-video input to an S-video connector.

2. If your Windows Media Center setup uses an infrared control cable, connect it to your PC and position the "eye" over the infrared receiver on your set-top box.

3. Switch on your set-top box (if you have one).

4. Switch on your PC, log on to Windows, and then launch Windows Media Center.

5. Navigate to the Tasks category, and then select the Settings item. Windows Media Center displays the Settings screen.

6. Select the TV item. Windows Media Center displays the TV screen.

7. Select the Set Up TV Signal item, and then follow through the TV Signal Wizard, which walks you through the process of choosing your region (for example, United States), downloading the latest TV setup options for that region, and configuring your TV signal. Usually the wizard does a good job of identifying your TV signal (see Figure 22.29), but if your setup confuses the wizard, select the No, Proceed to Manual TV Signal Setup option button, and then make the necessary choices manually.

The other settings that you should configure at this point are the Recorder settings, because recording TV creates large files. To configure the Recorder settings, take the following steps:

1. From the TV screen, select the Recorder item. Windows Media Center displays the Recorder screen.

2. Click the Recorder Storage item. Windows Media Center displays the Recorder Storage screen (see Figure 22.30).

3. In the Record on Drive box, choose the drive on which to record. The more space you have available, the more hours of TV you can record.

4. In the Maximum TV Limit box, specify the amount of space you want to devote to TV recording. Windows Media Center grabs most of the free space, so you may need to reduce the setting.

5. In the Recording Quality box, choose the recording quality you want to use: Best, Better, Good, or Fair. The higher the quality, the larger the files. Good quality is adequate for most purposes, but you'll need to check whether it suits your monitor (or TV) and your eyes.

6. Click the Save button. Windows Media Center saves your settings and returns you to the Recorder screen.

FIGURE 22.29
Windows Media Center gives you the option of reverting to manual setup if automated setup can't find the right signal.

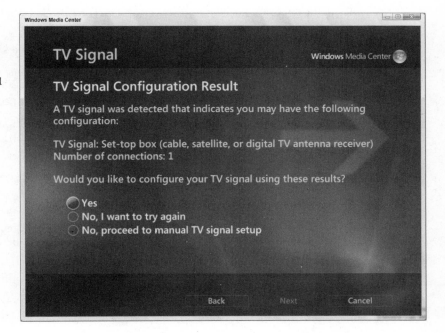

FIGURE 22.30
It's a good idea to check the Recorder Storage settings to make sure that Windows Media Center doesn't fill your entire hard drive with recordings.

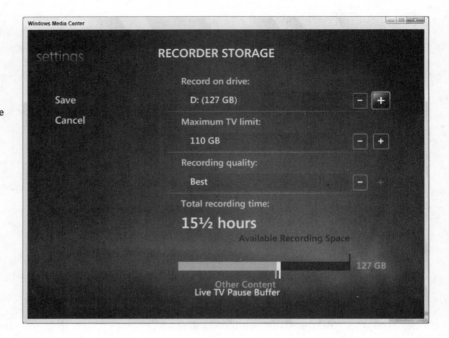

7. Select the Recording Defaults item. Windows Media Center displays the Recording Defaults screen (see Figure 22.31).

8. In the Keep box, choose Until Space Needed, For 1 Week, Until I Watch, or Until I Delete, as appropriate. (You can override these default settings for individual shows.)

9. In the Quality box, choose Best, Better, Good, or Fair, as needed.

10. In the Start When Possible box, choose the amount of extra time you want to record at the beginning of a program in case it's running early (or if you just love commercials): On Time (the riskiest setting), 1 Minute Before, 2 Minutes Before, 3 Minutes Before, or 4 Minutes Before.

11. In the Stop When Possible box, choose the amount of extra time you want to record at the end of a program in case it's running late: On Time (if you trust broadcasters), 1 Minute After, 2 Minutes After, 3 Minutes After, or 4 Minutes After.

12. In the Preferred Audio Language box, choose the language you want to use. Windows Media Center picks up your Windows language, so you may well not need to change this setting.

13. In the Series Only Recording Defaults: Keep Up To box, specify how many recordings of a series to keep: As Many as Possible, or one of the numbered items (for example, 3 Recordings).

14. Click the Save button. Windows Media Center saves your settings and returns you to the Recorder screen.

FIGURE 22.31
The Recording Defaults screen lets you specify how much time before and after a show's scheduled limits to record.

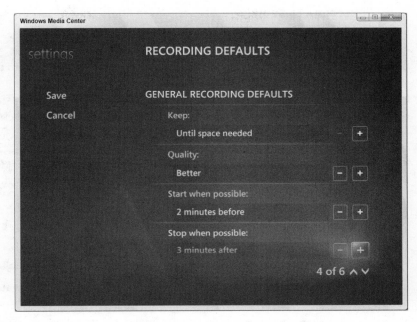

Now click the Back button to return to the TV screen. You may want to set up one of the other options:

Guide   Lets you change the order of channels, edit channels, add listings to channels, add missing channels, restore default channel settings, or set up TV guide listings.

Configure Your TV or Monitor   Starts a wizard that walks you through the process of setting up Windows Media Center on your monitor. If Windows Media Center looks fine already, you don't need to do this.

Audio   Lets you choose different audio settings. You may be happy with the default setting, Stereo.

Subtitle   Lets you turn on the display of subtitles. You may not need them.

You may prefer to return to this screen after experimenting with Windows Media Center and realizing that one of the default settings doesn't suit you.

Watching and Recording TV

Windows Media Center makes watching and recording TV pretty much as easy as doing so with a "real" TV.

WATCH LIVE TV

To watch live TV, select the TV + Movies item, and then select Live TV. Windows Media Center displays the current feed from your aerial or set-top box. Use the controls displayed on the window to change channel, adjust the volume, or start recording the current show.

RECORD A TV SHOW

You can record a TV show in any of these ways:

Live While watching live TV, click the Record button. Windows Media Center starts recording from that moment, not from the beginning of the show (or from the point at which you started watching).

From the Guide On the Home screen, select the TV + Movies item, and then select the Guide item. Move to the show you want to record, right-click, and then select Record.

By Time and Channel On the Home screen, select the TV + Movies item, and then select the Recorded TV item. Select the Add Recording item, and then use the controls on the Manual Record screen (see Figure 22.32) to specify the channel, date, and time. In the Frequency box, choose whether to record once, every day, or each week on a particular day (for example, Every Tuesday).

WATCH A RECORDED SHOW

To watch a show you've recorded, follow these steps:

1. On the Home screen, select the TV + Movies item, and then select the Recorded TV item.

2. On the Recorded TV screen, select the show you want to watch. You can select the Date Recorded item to sort the shows by date, or the Title item to sort them by title.

If you want to override your default Keep Until setting for a particular show, click the Keep Until item to display the Keep Until screen. You can then choose Do Not Change, Keep Until Space Needed, Keep Until (*Date*), Keep Until I Watch, or Keep Until I Delete.

FIGURE 22.32
The Manual Record screen lets you set up recording for a single program or a series.

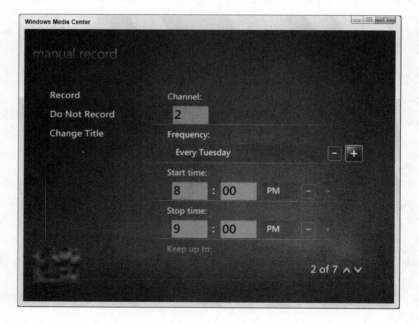

Watching a DVD

To watch a DVD, insert it in your DVD drive. If Windows displays the AutoPlay dialog box, click the Play DVD Movie Using Windows Media Center button. (Select the Always Do This for DVD Movies first if you want to use Windows Media Center for every DVD you insert.) Windows opens the DVD in Windows Media Center, and you can control it using the controls on screen.

If Windows doesn't display the AutoPlay dialog box, select TV + Movies in Windows Media Center, and then select Play DVD.

Listening to Music

To listen to music, follow these steps:

1. On the Home screen, select the Music category, and then select the Music Library item. Windows Media Center displays the Music Library screen.

2. Click one of the buttons to browse by albums, artists, genres, songs, playlists, composers, years, or album artists.

3. Select the item you want to play. Windows Media Center displays the Song Details screen.

4. Click the Play Song button to start it playing, or click the Add to Queue button to add it to the play queue.

Setting Output Volume and Recording Volume

When your computer is playing audio, you can control the volume either by using the Volume icon in the notification area or by using the program's own volume control.

The Volume icon in the notification area is usually the easiest means of controlling the volume when you don't have a program running full screen. To adjust the volume, click the Volume icon, and then drag the slider in the Volume window (shown here) up or down as needed. Click the Mute button once to mute the audio completely; click again to remove the muting.

RESTORING THE VOLUME ICON TO THE NOTIFICATION AREA

Windows Vista normally displays the Volume icon in the notification area. If the Volume icon doesn't appear, follow these steps to restore it:

1. Right-click the Start button, and then choose Customize from the context menu. Windows displays the Taskbar and Start Menu Properties dialog box.

2. Click the Notification Area tab. Windows displays the Notification Area page.

3. In the System Icons group box, select the Volume check box.

4. Click the OK button. Windows closes the Taskbar and Start Menu Properties dialog box and displays the Volume icon.

Changing the Relative Loudness of Devices and Programs

Windows Vista lets you change the relative loudness of devices and programs, so you can (for example) prevent Windows' system sounds from intruding too far into your music or videos. To adjust the relative loudness, follow these steps:

1. Click the Volume icon in the notification area, and then click the Mixer link at the bottom of the volume window. Windows displays the Volume Mixer window, as shown here.

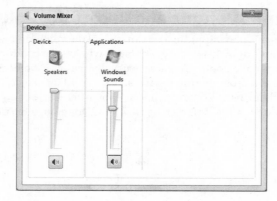

2. Drag the Device slider to set the volume you want for the main sound output.

3. Drag the Applications slider to set the volume you want for Windows sounds.

4. Click the Close button (the × button). Windows closes the Volume Mixer window.

Configuring Audio Playback

To configure audio playback, right-click the Volume icon in the notification area, and then choose Playback Devices from the context menu. Windows displays the Sound dialog box with the Playback page foremost.

What you'll find on the Playback page and what you can do with what you find, depends on your computer's audio configuration. If you have an analog audio output with speakers attached, you'll probably find only an item named Speakers. If you have a digital output device, it will appear as a Digital Output Device.

Either way, click the device you want to affect.

CONFIGURING AN ANALOG SPEAKER SYSTEM

If your computer has an analog speaker system, you should be able to configure it using the Speaker Setup Wizard. On the Playback page of the Sound dialog box, click the Speakers item, and then click the Configure button. The Speaker Setup Wizard launches and walks you through the process of choosing your speaker configuration, specifying your full-range speakers (see Figure 22.33) and making other available choices.

FIGURE 22.33

You can use the Speaker Setup Wizard to tell Windows what speaker arrangement you're using.

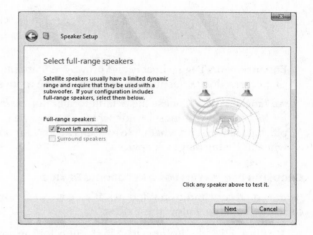

CHOOSING PROPERTIES FOR A PLAYBACK DEVICE

For any type of playback device, you can choose properties by clicking the device on the Playback page, clicking the Properties button, and then working in the Properties dialog box for the device. The number of pages in the Properties dialog box varies depending on the type of device. Figure 22.34 shows the Properties dialog box for analog speakers on the left and a digital output device on the right.

Here's what you can do on the pages:

General Page   Change the device's name or icon, view information about the audio controller and the jack on the device, and enable or disable the device.

Custom Page   Choose custom options for the device—for example, enable an S/PDIF port.

Supported Formats Page   Test which formats a digital receiver can decode—for example, DTS Audio, Dolby Digital, or Microsoft WMA Pro Audio. Test which sample rates your digital receiver supports (for example, 44.1kHz and 48.0kHz).

Levels Page   Set volume levels and balances for different outputs (see Figure 22.34 for an example). Mute a digital output device.

FIGURE 22.34
The Properties dialog box for an analog device (left) contains different pages to the Properties dialog box for a digital device (right).

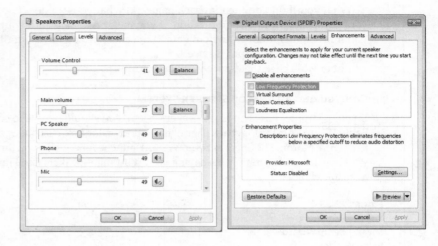

Enhancements Page   Enable and preview enhancements such as virtual surround sound or room correction (adjusting the audio to suit the room's characteristics).

Advanced Page   Choose the default format (for example, 16-bit, 44,100Hz audio). Choose Exclusive-mode settings: Decide whether to allow a program to take exclusive control of the playback device and whether to give an Exclusive-mode program priority over other programs when using the playback device.

CHOOSING PROPERTIES FOR A RECORDING DEVICE

Before you record audio on Windows, it's a good idea to make sure your recording device is set up correctly. To do so, follow these steps:

1. Right-click the Volume icon in the notification area, and then choose Recording Devices from the context menu. Windows displays the Recording page of the Sound dialog box (see Figure 22.35). (If you still have the Sound dialog box open, all you need do is click the Recording tab to display the Recording page.)

2. To configure a microphone, click it, and then click the Configure button. Windows displays the Speech Recognition Options window. Click the Set Up Microphone link, and then work through the Microphone Setup Wizard.

3. To check or change properties for a recording device, select it on the Recording page, and then click the Properties button. Windows displays the device's Properties dialog box, which contains several pages of options for configuring the device. The pages typically include some or all of the following:

   General Page   Change the device's name or icon, view information about the audio controller and the jack on the device, and enable or disable the device.

   Custom Page   Choose custom options for the device—for example, apply a 20-decibel boost to a microphone to get a more powerful signal.

   Levels Page   Set the input level for a microphone.

Advanced Page Choose the default format (for example, 16-bit, 44,100Hz audio). Choose Exclusive-mode settings: Decide whether to allow a program to take exclusive control of the recording device and whether to give an Exclusive-mode program priority over other programs when using the recording device.

4. To set a device as the default, click in the list box, and then click the Set Default button.

5. Click the OK button. Windows closes the Sound dialog box.

FIGURE 22.35
Use the Recording page of the Sound dialog box to configure recording devices and specify a default device.

Recording Audio Files with Sound Recorder

If you need to record audio from a real-time source (for example, your voice), use Sound Recorder. Sound Recorder is a simple program, but it's good enough for basic recording.

Sound Recorder records audio at a bit rate of 96Kbps, which is high enough to produce decent quality but not audiophile quality. Sound Recorder records in WMA format on Windows Vista Home Premium, but it records in WAV format on Windows Vista Home Basic. The advantage of WMA format is that it uses compression, so your files don't take up much room. By contrast, WAV format is uncompressed and takes up about 15 times as much space as WMA.

To start Sound Recorder, choose Start ➢ All Programs ➢ Accessories ➢ Sound Recorder. Windows launches Sound Recorder, as shown here.

To record a sound file with Sound Recorder, take the following steps:

1. Use Record Control to select the input you want to use. Choose appropriate volume and balance settings.

2. If you currently have a file open in Sound Recorder, choose File ➢ Open. Sound Recorder closes the current file, prompting you to save it if it contains unsaved changes, and displays the Open dialog box. Open the extended blank file that you created.

3. Get the input ready. For example, bring your microphone close to your mouth or throat, or feed in a signal through the Line In jack.

4. Click the Start Recording button.

5. Start the input.

6. Click the Stop Recording button to stop recording. Sound Recorder displays the Save As dialog box.

7. Choose the folder, type a filename, and then click the Save button. Sound Recorder closes the file and opens a new file so that you can record more audio if you want.

To close Sound Recorder, click the Close button (the × button).

The Bottom Line

Enjoy audio, video, and more with Windows Media Player   Windows Media Player is a powerful multimedia player that lets you enjoy audio, video, and DVDs. Windows Media Player includes many configuration options, some of which are important to understand. You can add audio files to your media library by copying them from your CDs or by dragging them from a Windows Explorer window. You can play audio files or video files by double-clicking them on the Library page. To play a DVD, either click the Play DVD Movie Using Windows Media Player button in the AutoPlay dialog box that Windows displays, or double-click the DVD's entry on the Library page.

Watch and record TV with Windows Media Center   Windows Media Center lets you watch and record TV and enjoy DVDs, videos, music, and more. You'll need to configure Windows Media Center to recognize your TV signal, and it's a good idea to make sure the settings for recording TV won't fill your hard drive with files. After that, Windows Media Center is mostly plain sailing, whether you navigate it with a remote control, a mouse, or the keyboard.

Control input and output with the Volume icon and Sounds   The easiest way to manage audio volume is with the Volume icon in the notification area. Right-click the Volume icon to display a menu of commands for accessing the Playback page and Recording page of the Sounds dialog box, which let you configure audio playback and recording devices.

Record audio with Sound Recorder   Sound Recorder is a basic utility for recording audio via a microphone. On Windows Vista Home Premium, Sound Recorder records in the compressed Windows Media Audio format, but on Windows Vista Home Basic it records in the uncompressed WAV format.

Chapter 23

Working with Pictures and Videos

- ◆ Work with pictures in Explorer
- ◆ Install a scanner or a digital camera
- ◆ View and manage pictures and videos with Windows Photo Gallery
- ◆ Import video from a camcorder
- ◆ Create your own movies with Windows Movie Maker
- ◆ Create DVDs with Windows DVD Maker

Windows provides strong features for working with pictures and videos—everything from easily viewing and rotating a picture to making a video of your own. The chapter starts by discussing the tools that Windows provides for manipulating pictures via Explorer. It then discusses how to install scanners and digital cameras, how to scan documents, and how to retrieve images from a digital camera. After that, it covers how to capture still pictures from a video camera and how to copy your pictures to the Web. It shows you how to get started with Windows Movie Maker, Windows's built-in tool for capturing, editing, and exporting digital video, and how to create DVDs with Windows DVD Maker.

Working with Pictures in Windows Explorer

Windows includes two folders designed specifically for working with pictures:

Pictures   The Pictures folder is a folder in your user account for you to keep your pictures. This folder is normally private, but you can choose to share pictures in it with other users. Windows programs for working with pictures, such as Paint and Windows Photo Gallery, use the Pictures folder as the default folder for opening and saving pictures.

Public Pictures   The Public Pictures folder is a subfolder of the Public folder that's shared with all other users of your computer. Depending on the sharing settings that you or an administrator have chosen, the Public Pictures folder may be shared with other users of your network as well.

Both the Pictures folder and the Public Pictures folder use the Pictures and Videos folder template, which adds to the toolbar several special buttons for previewing the selected picture, running a slide show, printing pictures, and more. You can apply the Pictures and Videos folder template to other folders to add these features to them.

Opening Your *Pictures* Folder

To open your `Pictures` folder, choose Start ➤ Pictures. Windows opens a Windows Explorer window showing the contents of your `Pictures` folder. Figure 23.1 shows an example.

The easiest way to open your computer's `Public Pictures` folder is to open your `Pictures` folder (as just described), click the Public link in the Favorite Links list, and then double-click the `Public Pictures` folder in the document area.

FIGURE 23.1

The toolbar in the Pictures folder contains buttons for performing special actions with pictures. Some buttons appear only when you've selected one or more pictures, as in this example.

Previewing a Picture

To preview a picture, either double-click it, or click it and then click the Preview button. Windows opens the picture in your default picture-viewing program. Unless you've changed Windows' standard settings, that program is Windows Photo Gallery, which you'll learn about later in this chapter.

Viewing a Slide Show of Pictures

To view a slide show of pictures, follow these steps:

1. Select the pictures you want to include in the slide show. If you want to include all the pictures in the folder, you don't need to select any.

2. Click the Slide Show button on the toolbar. Windows starts a slide show, displaying the first picture full screen and momentarily showing a bar of controls for the show (see Figure 23.2).

FIGURE 23.2
Use the control bar to
control the slide show.
Windows hides the
control bar after a few
seconds, but you can
pop it up by moving
the mouse pointer.

3. Windows automatically displays the next picture after a few seconds, but you can also use
   the controls to run the slide show as needed:

   ◆ Click the Next button to move to the next picture. You can also press →, ↓, or Page Down.

   ◆ Click the Previous button to go back to the previous picture. You can also press ←, ↑, or
   Page Up.

   ◆ Click the Pause button to pause the slide show, and click the resulting Play button to
   restart it. You can also press the spacebar for both play and pause.

   ◆ To change the theme of the slide show, click the Themes button, and then make a choice
   from the pop-up menu (shown here). The different themes are better experienced than
   described, so play with the various choices, and find which one suits your pictures best.

◆ To change the speed of the slide show, shuffle it, switch looping on or off, or mute the sound, click the Settings button, and then choose options from the pop-up menu (shown here).

4. To stop the slide show, click the Exit button on the toolbar, or press the Esc key.

Printing a Picture

To print one or more pictures, follow these steps:

1. Select the picture or pictures you want to print.

2. Click the Print button on the toolbar. Windows launches the Print Pictures Wizard, which displays the How Do You Want to Print Your Pictures? window, as shown here.

3. In the Printer drop-down list, select the printer you want to use. If you change the printer, Windows makes any necessary changes to the settings in the Paper Size drop-down list, the Quality drop-down list, and the Paper Type drop-down list.

4. In the Paper Size drop-down list, choose the size of paper you want to use.

5. In the Quality drop-down list, verify that Windows has chosen the correct print quality. If you want to print at draft quality, select that quality in the drop-down list.

6. In the Paper Type drop-down list, select the type of paper you want to use. For example, you might choose to print pictures on photographic paper rather than plain paper.

7. In the list on the right side of the window, choose the type of picture you want to print: Full Page Photo (normally the default choice), a standard size (such as two 4″ × 6″ pictures or four 3.5″ × 5″ pictures), or a contact sheet (containing a large number of tiny pictures).

8. In the Copies of Each Picture box, choose whether to print one copy of each picture (the default setting) or more.

9. If you want Windows to adjust the picture's dimensions to fit the available area on the paper, select the Fit Picture to Frame check box. To leave the picture's dimensions unchanged, clear this check box.

10. If you want to turn off Windows' automatic sharpening of pictures that you print (which is intended to make them look better but doesn't suit all pictures), click the Options link. Windows displays the Print Settings dialog box, as shown here. Clear the Sharpen for Printing check box, and then click the OK button. The Print Settings dialog box also contains the Only Show Options That Are Compatible with My Printer check box, which you can clear to make sure that Windows offers you all available settings. Normally, you're better off staying with the settings that are compatible with your printer.

11. Click the Print button. The wizard prints the pictures to the printer and then closes.

Sending Pictures via E-mail

To send pictures via e-mail, follow these steps:

1. Select the picture or pictures.

2. Click the E-mail button on the toolbar. Windows displays the Attach Files dialog box, as shown here.

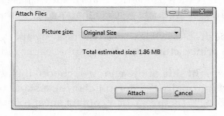

3. In the Picture Size drop-down list, select the size you want:

Smaller: 640 × 480   This size is good for sharing pictures with someone who has a slow Internet connection, but the pictures are suitable only for viewing on screen at a small size, not for printing.

Small: 800 × 600   This size provides moderate quality for viewing on screen with a relatively small file size or for use in web pages.

Medium: 1024 × 768   This size produces pictures that can be used as desktop backgrounds on a monitor running at standard XGA (1024 × 768) resolution (for example, a typical 15-inch monitor).

Large: 1280 × 1024   This size produces pictures suitable for use as desktop backgrounds on a monitor running at the 1280 × 1024 resolution (for example, a typical 17-inch monitor) or for printing at modest sizes (for example, at 5″ × 7″). The file size is relatively large, so the pictures transfer slowly over a dial-up Internet connection.

Original Size   This option sends the pictures at their original size. Use this option if you want to send the pictures at their full quality.

4. Click the Attach button. Windows changes the file size (unless you chose Original Size) and starts a message in your default e-mail program (for example, Windows Mail).

5. Address the message and send it as usual.

Installing a Scanner or Digital Camera

To install a scanner or digital camera, connect it to your computer. If Windows notices the scanner or camera, it displays a notification-area pop-up, and then attempts to locate the software for the device. If Windows doesn't have drivers for the scanner or camera, install them manually from the manufacturer's installation media or website.

If Windows doesn't automatically detect your scanner or camera, use the Scanner and Camera Installation Wizard to identify it. Start the wizard by taking the following steps:

1. Choose Start ➢ Control Panel. Windows displays Control Panel.

2. Click the Hardware and Sound link. Windows displays the Hardware and Sound window.

3. Click the Scanners and Cameras link. Windows displays the Scanners and Cameras dialog box, as shown here.

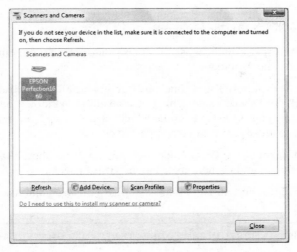

4. If the scanner or camera doesn't appear, click the Add Device button, and then authenticate yourself to User Account Control. Windows starts the Scanner and Camera Installation Wizard, which displays the Welcome to the Scanner and Camera Installation Wizard page.

To install your scanner or camera, follow the wizard. This example goes through the steps involved in installing a camera:

1. Click the Next button. The Scanner and Camera Installation Wizard displays the Which Scanner or Camera Do You Want to Install? page (shown in Figure 23.3).

FIGURE 23.3

On the Which Scanner or Camera Do You Want to Install? page of the Scanner and Camera Installation Wizard, select the driver or provide one of your own.

2. Use the Manufacturer list and the Model list to specify your camera, or use the Have Disk button and its resulting dialog boxes to give Windows a new driver.

3. Click the Next button. The Scanner and Camera Installation Wizard displays the Connect Your Device to Your Computer page.

4. Connect the device, and choose the appropriate port in the Available Ports list. Alternatively, leave the Automatic Port Detection item selected.

5. Click the Next button. The Scanner and Camera Installation Wizard displays the What Is the Name of Your Device? page, which lets you adjust Windows' name for the device or enter a new name. This is the name under which the device appears in the Scanners and Cameras window, so make sure it's descriptive and clear.

6. Click the Next button. The Scanner and Camera Installation Wizard displays the Completing the Scanner and Camera Installation Wizard page.

7. Click the Finish button. The wizard completes the installation, and then closes itself.

AVOID USING SERIAL PORTS WHEN CONNECTING OLDER DIGITAL CAMERAS

Most modern digital cameras connect via USB; some also offer the option of using FireWire. Older digital cameras offer the choice between a serial port and USB.

If faced with the choice between serial and USB, choose USB every time, even if it's the slow USB 1.*x* rather than the fast USB 2.0. Even USB 1.*x* transfers pictures many times faster than a serial connection.

Using Windows Photo Gallery

Windows Photo Gallery is a program for managing and viewing pictures and videos. Windows Photo Gallery consists of a viewer component that shows you a single picture or video at a watchable size with a small set of controls, and a management component for organizing and tagging your pictures and videos.

Opening Windows Photo Gallery

To open Windows Photo Gallery, choose Start ➢ All Programs ➢ Windows Photo Gallery. Figure 23.4 shows Windows Photo Gallery with the Pictures category selected, showing the sample pictures that Windows installs automatically on your computer.

The left list provides different ways of accessing your pictures and videos:

◆ Click the Pictures item in the All Pictures and Videos category to see all the pictures in the gallery.

◆ Click the Recently Imported category to see pictures you've imported recently.

◆ Click one of the items in the Tags category to see pictures tagged with that word.

◆ Use the Date Taken categories to navigate to pictures by the year, month, and date they were taken.

FIGURE 23.4
Windows Photo
Gallery is a program
for viewing and
manipulating digital
pictures and videos.

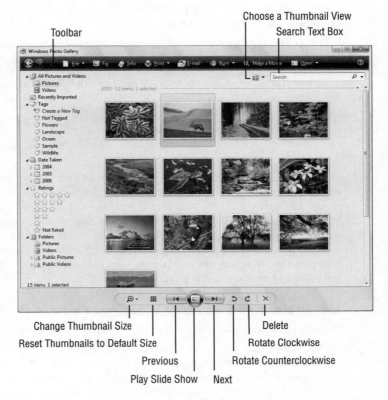

Toolbar

Choose a Thumbnail View

Search Text Box

Change Thumbnail Size

Reset Thumbnails to Default Size

Previous

Play Slide Show   Next

Delete

Rotate Clockwise

Rotate Counterclockwise

◆ The Ratings category allows you to see only pictures that have a certain star rating (or no rating).

◆ The Folders category lets you navigate quickly among the folders that contain pictures and videos.

To search for pictures by filename or tag information, type a search term in the Search text box. As you type, Windows narrows down the items displayed to those that meet your criteria. To clear a search, click the × button in the Search text box.

Once you've navigated to the pictures you want, select a picture in the main area to manipulate it.

Using Different Views and Sizes

Windows Photo Gallery starts you off viewing the pictures or videos as thumbnails, a size that lets you get an overview of a couple dozen pictures or videos at once.

To change the size of the pictures or videos, click the Change Thumbnail Size button and drag the slider up (to increase the size) or down (to decrease the size). You can also press Ctrl++ (Ctrl and the plus key) to increase the size or Ctrl+− (Ctrl and the hyphen key) to decrease the size.

To reset the pictures or videos to their standard size, click the Reset Thumbnails to Default Size button or press Ctrl+0.

To change the view, click the Choose a Thumbnail View button, and then choose Thumbnails, Thumbnails with Text, or Tiles from the menu:

Thumbnails   Displays each picture or video without any text.

Thumbnails with Text   Displays each picture or video with the date and time it was taken.

Tiles   Displays each picture or video with brief details alongside it, as shown here.

The Choose a Thumbnail View button also lets you group and sort the pictures or videos in much the same way you can group and sort files in Explorer windows. For example, you might choose Group By ➢ Rating to group the pictures or videos by rating, or choose Sort By ➢ Date Modified to sort the pictures or videos by the date on which you'd last modified them. For both sorting and grouping, you can choose between Ascending order and Descending order.

The Choose a Thumbnail View button also contains commands for displaying and hiding a table of contents pane, which appears between the navigation pane and the document area, and refreshing the list of pictures and videos.

Manipulating a Picture or Video from within the Gallery

You can perform some basic manipulations from within the gallery.

Rotate a Picture   To rotate a picture by 90 degrees, select the picture, and then click the Rotate Counterclockwise button or the Rotate Clockwise button. You can right-click the picture and choose Rotate Counterclockwise or Rotate Clockwise from the context menu, or press Ctrl+, (Ctrl and the comma key) to rotate counterclockwise or Ctrl+. (Ctrl and the period key) to rotate clockwise.

Tag a Picture or Video   To tag a picture or video, click it, and then click the Info button on the toolbar. Windows Photo Gallery displays the Info pane with the picture or video's details on the right side of the window (see Figure 23.5). Click the Add Tags link (or press Ctrl+T) to display a text box for adding tags. Type the tag, and then press Enter to add it. You can then add further tags as needed, or move to another picture or video and add tags to it. When you've finished working in the Info pane, click its Close button (the × button).

Rate a Picture or Video   To rate a picture or video, click it, and then click the Info button on the toolbar. Windows Photo Gallery displays the Info pane. Click the number of stars you want to assign, counting from the left—for example, click the fourth star to assign a four-star rating. To remove a rating, right-click the picture or video, and then choose Clear Rating from the context menu.

Set a Picture as Your Desktop Background   To set a picture as your desktop background, right-click it, and then choose Set as Desktop Background from the context menu. (This move works in any Explorer window—it's not specific to picture folders.)

Viewing a Picture or Video

To view a picture or video, double-click it in the gallery. Windows Photo Gallery switches to the viewer mode and displays the picture or video at a larger size (see Figure 23.6). If you chose a video, Windows Photo Gallery starts it playing automatically.

FIGURE 23.5
Use the Info pane to add tags to a picture or to change its rating.

FIGURE 23.6
Viewing a picture in Windows Photo Gallery.

Change Display Size

Actual Size

Previous

Play Slide Show

Next

Rotate Counterclockwise

Rotate Clockwise

Delete

The viewer window is easy to use:

- To zoom in or out on a picture, click the Change Display Size button, and then drag the slider up or down. To reset the picture to its actual size, click the Actual Size button or press Ctrl+Alt+0.

- Click the Next button to display the next picture or video, or click the Previous button to display the previous picture or video.

- Click the Play Slide Show button (or press the F11 key) to start playing a slide show from the current picture or video.

- To rotate the picture by 90 degrees, click the Rotate Counterclockwise button or the Rotate Clockwise button.

- To move the picture to the Recycle Bin, click the Delete button (or press the Delete button on your keyboard), and then click the Yes button in the Delete File dialog box that Windows displays (as shown here).

- To tag or rate the picture or video, click the Info button, and then work in the Info panel, as discussed earlier, to tag or rate the picture or video.

Click the Back to Gallery button on the toolbar when you want to return from the viewer to the gallery.

Importing Pictures from a Scanner

To import pictures from a scanner, follow these steps:

1. In Windows Photo Gallery, choose File ➤ Import from Camera or Scanner. Windows displays the Import Pictures and Videos dialog box.

2. In the Scanners and Cameras list, select the scanner, and then click the Import button. Windows displays the New Scan dialog box (shown in Figure 23.7 with settings chosen).

3. In the Profile drop-down list, select the scanning profile you want to use. For a picture, you'll most likely want the Photo profile; for a document, use the Document profile. You can also create a custom profile by choosing Add Profile in the drop-down list, and then working in the Add New Profile dialog box.

4. Unless your scanner has two or more scanning decks (for example, one for paper documents and another for slides), you won't be able to change the setting in the Source drop-down list. In the figure, the only choice is Flatbed.

5. In the Color Format drop-down list, choose Color for a color document. If you want to produce a grayscale scan from a color picture, choose Grayscale. If you're scanning a document, choose Black and White.

FIGURE 23.7
Use the Preview button in the New Scan dialog box to make sure the picture is straight in the scanner and to set the scan area.

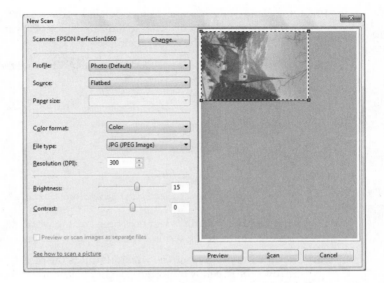

6. In the File Type drop-down list, select the file format to use for the images. Your choices are BMP, JPG, PNG, or TIF:

◆ BMP (bitmap image) uses no compression, so it produces large files. But this format can be read by a wide variety of old software, so it may be useful for backward compatibility. Because a bitmap retains the full amount of information about the image, it's a good format for archiving images to recordable CDs so that you can work with them later.

◆ JPG (JPEG image; Joint Pictures Experts Group) is the default format. JPG uses lossy compression, so you lose image quality when you use this format, but the results are good for general use. JPG files have a relatively small file size, which is good for saving and transferring the images.

◆ PNG (PNG image; Portable Network Graphics) is a lossless compression format designed for handling computer-generated images on the Web. PNG is generally considered less suitable than JPG for scanned images or photographs.

◆ TIF (TIFF image; Tagged Image File Format) uses lossless compression, so it produces medium-large files. TIFFs are widely used, but not as widely as BMPs. (Not all TIFFs are compressed, but the ones that the Scanner and Camera Wizard produces are compressed.)

7. In the Resolution (DPI) text box, specify the resolution you want to use. The highest resolution you can use is the highest resolution your scanner supports.

8. If you want to adjust the brightness or contrast of the picture, drag the Brightness slider or the Contrast slider.

9. Click the Preview button. The Wizard scans the picture and displays a preview on the right side of the New Scan dialog box.

10. If the picture you're scanning is less than a full page, or if you want to save only part of the picture, drag the dotted border to indicate which part you want. You can drag either one of the edges or one of the corner handles.

11. Click the Scan button. The wizard scans the picture, and then displays the Importing Pictures and Videos dialog box, as shown here.

12. In the Tag These Pictures text box, type any tag words you want to assign to the picture. If you enter multiple tag terms, separate them with semicolons.

13. Click the Import button. The wizard imports the picture, and then displays a pop-up message over the Recently Imported category in Windows Photo Gallery to indicate that you can find the picture there.

Importing Pictures from a Digital Camera

If your digital camera connects directly to your computer via USB or another technology that enables Windows to recognize the camera, the camera appears in the Scanners and Cameras list in the Import Pictures and Videos dialog box. You can then import pictures directly into Windows Photo Gallery by choosing File ➤ Import from Camera or Scanner, selecting the camera, clicking the Import button, and then following through the resulting wizard.

These days, however, most cameras come with removable storage media, such as CompactFlash cards, SD or XD cards, or Memory Stick cards. With such storage media, you'll normally import pictures by putting the media card into a media reader built into or connected to your computer. Take the following steps:

1. Remove the media card from the camera, and insert it in the media card reader. When Windows notices the card, it displays an AutoPlay dialog box such as the one shown here.

2. If you always want to take the same action with pictures, select the Always Do This for Pictures check box. If you want to keep the flexibility to handle pictures in different ways, leave this check box cleared.

3. Click the Import Pictures Using Windows link. Windows displays the Importing Pictures and Videos dialog box, as shown here.

4. If you want to configure the way Windows names the pictures and the folder in which it places them, click the Options link. Windows displays the Import Settings dialog box (see Figure 23.8). If you've already configured settings, go to step 11.

5. In the Settings For drop-down list, make sure Cameras is selected. (You can also use the Import Settings dialog box to choose settings for importing pictures from scanners and from optical discs.)

6. In the Import To drop-down list, specify the folder inside which you want to put the folders containing the pictures you import. The default folder is your Pictures folder, which works well if you want to keep the pictures to yourself. If you want to share your pictures with others, putting them in the Public Pictures folder may be a better choice.

FIGURE 23.8
In the Import Settings dialog box, choose settings for naming and storing picture files you import from a camera.

7. In the Folder Name drop-down list, select the naming convention you want for the folders Windows creates for you within the folder you chose in the previous step. Your choices are Date Imported + Tag, Date Taken + Tag, Date Taken Range + Tag, Tag + Date Imported, Tag + Date Taken, Tag + Date Taken Range, or plain Tag.

8. In the File Name drop-down list, choose how to name the files: Tag (using the tag you specify), Original File Name, or Original File Name (Preserve Folders). The Preserve Folders option carries over the subfolder structure created on the camera to your computer. Normally, the Original File Name option is the most useful, as it gives you files that follow a numbering sequence. You can then rename the files manually as needed.

9. In the Other Options area, choose other options:

Prompt for a Tag on Import Select this check box if you want Windows to prompt you for a tag with the Importing Pictures and Videos dialog box.

Always Erase from Camera After Importing Select this check box if you want Windows to erase the picture files automatically from the camera or memory card after importing them. Usually, it's better to make sure that the files have imported successfully, and then erase them from the camera using the camera's own commands.

Rotate Pictures on Import Select this check box if you want Windows to rotate pictures that are marked as having been taken in different orientations. Only some cameras store this information in picture metadata, so even if you select this check box, you may still need to rotate pictures manually.

Open Windows Photo Gallery After Import Select this check box if you want Windows to open Windows Photo Gallery automatically after importing your pictures so that you can view the pictures. This option is usually helpful if you use Windows Photo Gallery to manage your pictures.

10. Click the OK button. Windows closes the Import Settings dialog box and displays a message box warning you that it needs to restart Import Pictures and Video to make these changes take effect. Click the OK button. Windows restarts Import Pictures and Videos, and displays the Importing Pictures and Videos dialog box again.

11. If you want to use a tag, type it in the Tag These Pictures text box.

12. Click the Import button. Windows imports the pictures, as shown here, and then displays Windows Photo Gallery (unless you cleared the Open Windows Photo Gallery After Import check box).

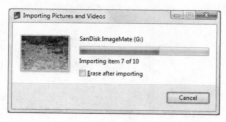

13. To view your new pictures, click the Recently Imported category on the left of the Windows Photo Gallery window.

🌐 Real World Scenario

DOES NAMING BY TAG HELP YOU?

Whether naming by tag makes sense depends on what you take pictures of, how you import your pictures in batches, and how general your tags are. For example, if you're happy to tag all the pictures you're importing simply with "vacation" or "Christmas 2006," naming by tag is reasonable. If you want to tag each picture separately, naming folders by tags won't be helpful.

The Folder Name drop-down list suggests that you can't avoid naming by tags, as "tag" appears in each choice. But if you choose one of the naming options that includes a date, and then don't enter a tag in the Importing Pictures and Videos dialog box, you can have Windows name the folder only using the date.

Fixing a Picture

Windows Photo Gallery includes tools for making basic fixes to pictures, such as adjusting the exposure and color, cropping the picture, and removing red eye. To fix a picture, follow these steps:

1. In the gallery window, click the picture, and then click the Fix button on the toolbar. Windows Photo Gallery switches to viewer mode and displays the picture and the Fix panel. Alternatively, open the picture in the viewer, and then click the Fix button on the toolbar in the viewer to display the Fix panel, as shown here.

2. If you want to improve the exposure and color, you may want to try using the Auto Adjust feature first to see what good it does. Click the Auto Adjust button, and Windows Photo Gallery tries to improve the exposure and color. If you like the results, keep them (or improve them further); if not, click the Undo button to undo the automatic adjustment.

3. To adjust the exposure manually, click the Adjust Exposure button. Windows Photo Gallery displays the Brightness slider and Contrast slider, as shown here. Drag a slider to the right to increase the brightness or contrast, or to the left to decrease it.

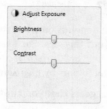

4. To adjust the color balance manually, click the Adjust Color button. Windows Photo Gallery displays the Color Temperature slide, the Tint slider, and the Saturation slider, as shown here. Drag these sliders to produce colors that please you.

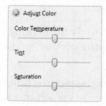

5. To crop the picture, click the Crop Picture button. Windows Photo Gallery displays the Crop Picture controls, as shown here.

   ◆ In the Proportion drop-down list, choose Original if you want to keep the same proportions as the original picture; choose Custom if you want to be able to crop unconstrained by proportions; or choose one of the preset sizes (for example, 16 × 9) or Square.

   ◆ If you want to rotate the cropping frame (for example, from landscape orientation to portrait orientation), click the Rotate Frame button.

   ◆ Drag a handle on the frame to resize the frame.

   ◆ To move the frame, click in it and drag.

   ◆ When you've selected the part of the picture you want, click the Crop button.

6. To remove red eye, zoom using the Change Display Size slider so that you can see the eyes in close-up. Click the Fix Red Eye button, and then drag a rectangle around the eye containing the redness.

7. When you've finished fixing the picture, click the Back to Gallery button. Windows Photo Gallery saves the changes you made to the picture.

Change the Date or Time Stamp on a Picture

One of the great things about digital cameras is that they automatically record the date and time you take a picture in the picture's metadata. But one of the wretched things about digital cameras is that you can easily forget to set the date—or the date may revert to the beginning of the millennium because the camera's battery ran out. Either way, it's all too easy to end up with pictures that have the wrong date on them—or the wrong time.

Windows Photo Gallery lets you change the date and time on pictures. To do so, follow these steps:

1. In the gallery, select the pictures whose date you want to change. For example, you might want to change the date on all the pictures you recently imported.

2. Click the Info button to display the Info pane.

3. Click the Date readout to display a drop-down box around the date.

4. Either type the new date, or click the drop-down arrow, and choose the date from the panel.

5. To change the time, click the Time readout, and then use the controls to adjust the time.

If you need to change only the time stamp (without changing the date), follow these steps:

1. In the gallery, select the pictures whose time stamp you want to change.

2. Right-click anywhere in the selection, and then choose Change Time Taken from the context menu. Windows Photo Gallery displays the Change Time Taken dialog box, as shown here.

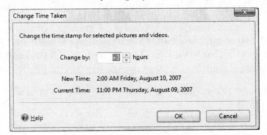

3. Use the spin buttons in the Change By box to specify the number of hours by which to change the time. The New Time readout shows the effect of the change.

4. Click the OK button. Windows Photo Gallery closes the Change Time Taken dialog box and changes the time stamp on the pictures.

Capturing Still Pictures from a Video Camera

To capture still pictures from a video camera, connect it to your computer and take the following steps:

1. Choose Start ➢ All Programs ➢ Accessories ➢ Paint. Windows launches Paint.

2. Choose File ➢ From Scanner or Camera. If you have multiple devices, Paint displays the Select Device dialog box. If you have only one device configured, Paint doesn't need to ask you which device to use.

3. Select the device and click the OK button. Paint displays the Capture Pictures from Video dialog box with a feed running from the camera into the left pane.

4. Click the Capture button to capture the current frame. Paint displays a thumbnail of the resulting picture in the right pane.

5. Capture further frames if you want.

6. Choose the thumbnail of the picture you want in the right pane, then click the Get Picture button. Paint closes the Capture Pictures from Video dialog box and displays the captured frame as a new picture in Paint, where you can work with it and save it as usual.

Importing Video from a Camcorder

Windows includes an Import Video tool that lets you import video from a DV camcorder either into Windows Photo Gallery or into Windows Movie Maker (discussed next). You may find it handy to put your video clips into Windows Photo Gallery and then choose which of them to put into a Windows Movie Maker project rather than importing all the clips directly into Windows Movie Maker and then performing quality control there.

Connecting Your DV Camcorder to Your Computer

There are two main ways to connect a DV camcorder to a Windows computer:

FireWire connection   Most DV camcorders use a FireWire or IEEE 1394 connection. If your computer doesn't have a FireWire port, you can add one via a PCI card (for a desktop) or a PC Card (for a laptop).

USB 2.0 connection   Some DV camcorders support streaming video over USB 2.0, which allows you to import video via a USB 2.0 connection. To find out whether your DV camcorder supports USB video streaming, either consult the manual or follow these steps:

1. Connect your DV camcorder to your computer via USB.

2. Press Windows Key+Break. Windows displays the System window.

3. In the left panel, click the Device Manager link, and then authenticate yourself to User Account Control. Windows displays Device Manager.

4. Check to see whether the camera appears as a USB Video Device. If so, it supports streaming; if not, it doesn't.

5. Click the Close button (the × button) to close the Device Manager window and the System window.

To import video from a DV camcorder, take the following steps:

1. Connect your DV camcorder to your computer. Plug in the camcorder's power supply to ensure that you don't run out of battery power.

2. Turn on the camera in VCR mode or playback mode. Windows recognizes the camera and displays the AutoPlay dialog box, as shown here.

3. If you always want to import video when you connect your DV camcorder, select the Always Do This for This Device check box. (You might also want to play back video from the computer to the DV camcorder—in which case, leave this check box cleared.)

4. Click the Import Video link. Windows launches the Import Video Wizard, which displays the Enter a Name for the Videotape You Will Import screen (see Figure 23.9).

5. In the Name text box, type a descriptive name for the video you're importing. The wizard suggests "Videotape," but you should be able to improve on this.

6. In the Import To drop-down list, select the destination folder for the video. The wizard suggests your Videos folder, which works well for private projects. For shared projects, you may want to choose the Public Videos folder instead.

7. In the Format drop-down list, select the file format you want to use:

Audio Video Interleaved (Single File) This choice creates a single file in the AVI format containing all the video from the tape (or that part you choose to transfer). This choice is good if you're capturing a single scene in its entirety or you want to create a video file that you can distribute to others without any editing. AVI is a widely viewable format, but it creates large files (taking up to 13GB per hour of video), so it can quickly fill up even a large hard disk.

Windows Media Video (Single File) This choice creates a single file in the Windows Media Video format containing all the video from the tape (or that part you choose to transfer). WMV is a compressed video format and takes up around 2GB per hour, making it a better choice than AVI if you need to store a lot of video. This choice is useful if you want to distribute the full video in Windows Media Video format without editing the video content (for example, you might adjust the audio). You can edit the video using Windows Movie Maker, but if you plan to edit it extensively, use the Windows Media Video (One File per Scene) format instead.

FIGURE 23.9
On this screen of the Import Video Wizard, name your material, choose the destination folder, and select the file format.

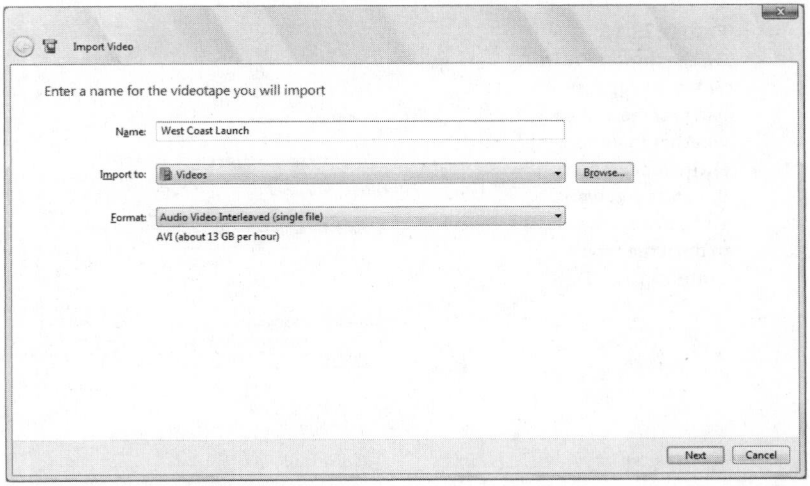

Windows Media Video (One File per Scene)   This choice creates a separate file in the Windows Media Video format for each scene that the wizard detects in the video. The wizard uses breaks in the timecode to determine when one scene ends and another begins. This method isn't infallible, but it usually works pretty well, and you can use Windows Movie Maker to split up clips, or join clips together, if necessary.

8. Click the Next button. The wizard displays the Import Entire Videotape or Just Parts? screen (see Figure 23.10).

9. Select the appropriate option button:

Import the Entire Videotape to My Computer   Use this option when you want to import all the video rather than segments—for example, if you've recorded a performance or a sports match.

Import the Entire Videotape and Then Burn It to DVD   Use this option if you want to get the tape's contents onto DVD without any quality control. This isn't normally a good idea, but you may disagree. Type the title for the DVD in the DVD Menu Title text box.

Only Import Parts of the Videotape to My Computer   Use this option if you want to record only parts of the tape—for example, because the tape contains various types of contents or contains some contents that you've already imported.

10. Click the Next button. What happens next depends on your choice:

◆ If you chose the Import the Entire Videotape to My Computer option button, the wizard displays the Importing Video screen (see Figure 23.11), records the video, and saves it to a file. The wizard then closes and displays Windows Photo Gallery so that you can view the video.

◆ If you chose the Import the Entire Videotape and Then Burn It to DVD option button, Windows DVD Maker prompts you to insert a disc. Once you've done so, the wizard displays the Importing Video screen (shown above), records the video, and then burns it to DVD using Windows DVD Maker. The wizard then closes.

FIGURE 23.10
On the Import Entire Videotape or Just Parts? screen, choose whether to import the entire tape or just the parts you want. You can also choose to burn the tape's contents to DVD.

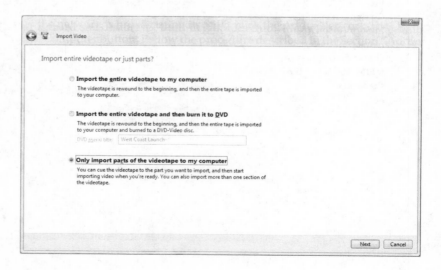

◆ If you chose the Only Import Parts of the Videotape to My Computer option button, the wizard displays the Cue the Videotape and then Start Importing Video screen (see Figure 23.12). Use the controls to move to the right position in the tape, and then click the Start Video Import button. Click the resulting Stop Video Import button when you want to stop recording. You can then repeat the process to record another clip. If you want to record a specific length of time, select the Stop Importing After check box, and specify the number of minutes. When you've finished recording, click the Finish button. The wizard closes and displays Windows Photo Gallery so that you can view the video clips.

FIGURE 23.11

If you choose to import the entire videotape, the wizard rewinds the tape to the beginning and then imports it.

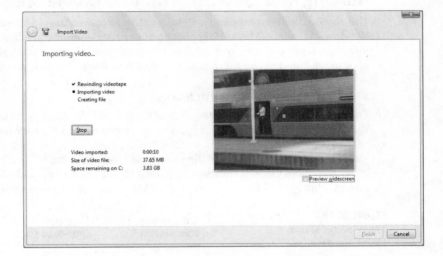

FIGURE 23.12

On the Cue the Video-tape and Then Start Importing Video screen, use the Digital Video Camera Controls buttons to move to where you want to start record-ing, and then click the Start Video Import button.

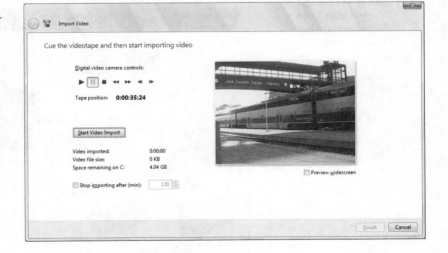

IMPORTING VIDEO FROM A VIDEOTAPE

If your video is on a videotape rather than on a camcorder tape, you should still be able to record it using the Import Video Wizard. You need one of the following:

◆ A DV camcorder that allows you to pass an analog signal through it, digitizing it on the way.

◆ An analog video capture device on your computer. (Many TV tuner cards can do this.)

Making Movies with Windows Movie Maker

This section discusses how to use Windows Movie Maker, the video-editing program included with Windows. Windows Movie Maker lets you import video clips and edit them, break a movie file down into clips to make it more manageable, add narration or a soundtrack to a movie, add video files to your movies, and save your movies in convenient formats so that you can share them with others.

Starting Windows Movie Maker

To start Windows Movie Maker, choose Start ➢ All Programs ➢ Windows Movie Maker. Pin Windows Movie Maker to your Start menu if you'll need to work with it frequently.

You can also launch Windows Movie Maker from Windows Photo Gallery. Select a picture or a video either in the gallery or in the viewer, and then click the Make a Movie button on the toolbar. Windows Photo Gallery launches Windows Movie Maker and adds the picture or clip to a new project. Figure 23.13 shows the Windows Movie Maker interface with some video clips imported.

FIGURE 23.13
The Windows Movie Maker interface includes a Tasks pane that you can toggle on and off by clicking the Show or Hide Tasks button or choosing View ➢ Tasks.

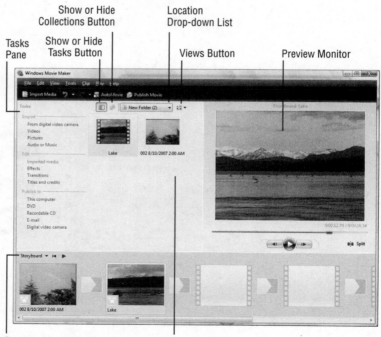

Capturing Video from a DV Camcorder

If you need to capture video from a DV camcorder for a movie, choose File ➤ Import from Digital Video Camera or click the From Digital Video Camera link in the Import section of the Tasks pane. Windows Movie Maker launches the Import Video Wizard and selects the Windows Media Video (One File per Scene) item in the Format drop-down list on the Enter a Name for the Videotape You Will Import screen. Follow through the wizard, as described earlier in this chapter.

Importing an Audio, Video, or Picture File

Windows Movie Maker also lets you import existing audio, video, and picture files for use in your movies. To import a file, click the Videos link, the Pictures link, or the Audio or Music link in the Import section of the Tasks pane. Windows Movie Maker displays the Import Media Items dialog box showing the contents of your Videos folder, your Pictures folder, or your Music folder as appropriate. Select the file, and then click the Import button to import it.

Saving the Project

To save your movie project, take the following steps:

1. Choose File ➤ Save Project. Windows Movie Maker displays the Save Project As dialog box.

2. By default, Windows Movie Maker saves files in your Videos folder. If necessary, navigate to a different folder (for example, the Public Videos folder).

3. Type the name for the project file in the File Name text box.

4. Click the Save button. Windows Movie Maker closes the Save Project As dialog box and saves the project in the Windows Movie Maker Project (MSWMM) format.

Editing a Movie

To edit a movie, use the links in the Edit area of the Tasks pane to switch among the collections of clips you've captured or imported, the video effects you can apply, the video transitions you can place between clips, and Windows Movie Maker's features for adding titles or credits. These links work like option buttons—only one link can be clicked at a time, and clicking one link deselects all the other links. You can also click the Show or Hide Collections button to display the Collections pane in place of the Tasks pane, and then use the Collections pane (shown here) to navigate among effects, transitions, and imported media.

Normally, you'll want to start by working with clips. Click the Imported Media link in the Edit section of the Tasks pane if it's not currently selected. You can then use the Location drop-down list in the toolbar to switch among your collections.

If you need to work extensively with collections, click the Show or Hide Collections button on the toolbar to display the Collections pane (shown here) instead of the Tasks pane. Click the Tasks button on the toolbar when you want to restore the Tasks pane.

VIEWING A CLIP

To view a clip, select it in the list of clips. (Windows Movie Maker displays this list in Thumbnail view by default, but you can click the Views button and then choose Thumbnails, or choose View ➢ Details from the menu bar, to use Details view instead.) Windows Movie Maker displays the first frame of the clip in the preview pane.

You can then move through the clip by using the controls below the preview pane. Figure 23.14 shows these controls with labels.

RENAMING A CLIP

To rename a clip, use one of the standard Windows renaming techniques in the list box: Click the clip's name twice with a pause in between; click the clip's name, and then press the F2 key; or right-click the clip, and then choose Rename from the context menu. Windows displays an edit box around the name. Type the new name for the clip, and then press the Enter key or click elsewhere.

FIGURE 23.14
Use these controls to manipulate a clip.

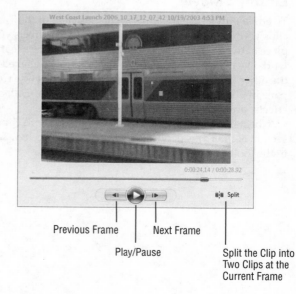

SPLITTING A CLIP

To split a clip, navigate to the frame at which you want to split it. Then click the Split Clip button. Windows Movie Maker splits the clip into two. It saves the first part under its previous name and saves the second part under a new name formed by appending (1) (or the next available number) to the clip's original name. For example, if you split a clip named `Party Scene`, Windows Movie Maker names the second part `Party Scene (1)`.

COMBINING TWO OR MORE CLIPS

To combine two or more clips, select them in the Contents pane, right-click somewhere in the selection, and then choose Combine from the context menu. Windows Movie Maker combines the clips under the name of the first clip.

COPYING AND MOVING CLIPS

You can move clips by using drag-and-drop and copy them by using Ctrl+drag-and-drop. You can copy and move clips either within a collection or from one collection to another.

Arranging the Clips on the Storyboard

Once you've got a clip trimmed or combined so that it shows what you want it to, drag it into place on the storyboard, the filmstrip-like control at the bottom of the window. Figure 23.15 shows several clips placed on the storyboard.

To display the preview on the Preview Monitor of a clip on the storyboard, click the clip. To play a clip, right-click it and choose Play Storyboard from the context menu. To play the whole sequence of clips on the storyboard, click the Rewind Storyboard button and then the Play Storyboard button.

To remove a clip from the storyboard, select it, and then press the Delete key.

FIGURE 23.15
Place the clips on the storyboard in the order you want them to appear in the movie.

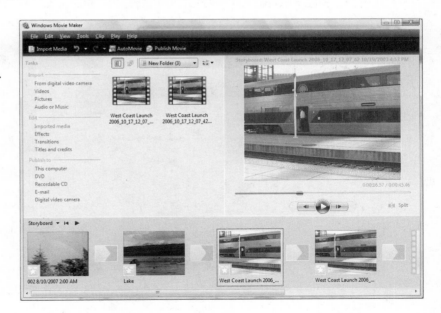

TRIMMING A CLIP ON THE TIMELINE

Once you've put a clip on the storyboard, you can trim it so that only part of it is shown in the movie. To do so, follow these steps:

1. Choose View ➤ Timeline, or click the drop-down button above the left end of the storyboard and choose Timeline from the menu. Windows Movie Maker displays the timeline in place of the filmstrip (see Figure 23.16).

2. Select the clip on the timeline so that it appears on the Preview Monitor.

3. Using the controls on the Preview Monitor, move to the first frame that you want to include in the movie.

4. Choose Clip ➤ Trim Beginning.

5. Again using the controls on the Preview Monitor, move to the last frame that you want to include in the movie.

6. Choose Clip ➤ Trim End.

7. Play the clip to check that the result is to your liking. If not, set the trim points again. You can also trim a clip by dragging the inward-pointing black arrow at the start or end.

To remove trimming from a clip, select it, and then choose Clip ➤ Clear Trim Points.

FADING ONE CLIP INTO ANOTHER

By default, Windows Movie Maker cuts from one clip to the next, as you might expect. To create a fade from one clip to another, take the following steps:

1. If the storyboard is displayed, choose View ➤ Timeline (or press Ctrl+T) to display the timeline.

FIGURE 23.16
Use the timeline to implement fading from one clip to another.

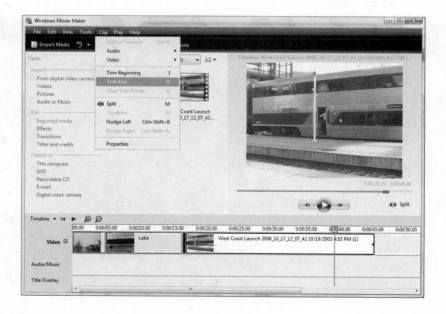

2. If necessary, click the Zoom In or Zoom Out buttons to adjust your view of the timeline so that the timeline displays an appropriate length of time for editing the clips.

3. Drag the later clip left so that it overlaps the clip with which you want to fade it. The amount of overlap sets the length of the fade.

RECORDING NARRATION

To record narration for your movie, take the following steps:

1. If the storyboard is displayed, choose View ➢ Timeline (or press Ctrl+T) to display the timeline.

2. Choose Tools ➢ Narrate Timeline. Windows Movie Maker displays the Narrate Timeline pane (shown in Figure 23.17 with all its controls displayed).

3. The first time you use the Narrate Timeline pane in a session, click the Show Options link, and verify the selection in the Audio Device drop-down list. Change it if necessary.

4. To mute the sound, select the Mute Speakers check box.

5. Speak into your microphone at a sample volume, and drag the Input Level slider to set a suitable recording level.

6. Click the Start Narration button and start the narration as Windows Movie Maker plays the clip.

7. When you've finished the narration, click the Stop Narration button. Windows Movie Maker displays the Save Windows Media File dialog box.

8. Specify the filename and folder for the file, and then click the Save button. Windows Movie Maker closes the dialog box and saves the narration track. It then adds a box for the narration track in the audio track under the pictures in the timeline.

9. Click the Close button to close the Narrate Timeline pane.

FIGURE 23.17
Use the Narrate Timeline pane to add narration to a movie.

Setting Audio Levels

To set the balance of audio levels between the video track and the audio track, choose Tools ➤ Audio Levels. Windows Movie Maker displays the Audio Levels dialog box (shown here). Drag the slider to a suitable position, and click the Close button (the × button) to close the Audio Levels dialog box.

Adding Transitions between Clips

To add an effect to a clip, click the Effects link in the Edit section of the Tasks pane, or choose Effects in the Location drop-down list. Windows Movie Maker displays the Effects list. Drag the effect you want to the storyboard and drop it on the clip you want to affect.

Adding Transitions, Titles, and Credits

To add transitions to your movie, click the Transitions link in the Edit section in the Tasks pane, or choose Transitions in the Location drop-down list. Windows Movie Maker displays the Transitions list. Drag the transition you want to the storyboard and drop it in the transition space between the two clips you want to affect.

To add titles or credits to your movie, click the Titles and Credits link in the Edit section in the Tasks pane. Windows Movie Maker displays the Where Do You Want to Add a Title? pane. Click the appropriate link (for example, click the Title at the Beginning link) and use the resulting pane to add the text in the place you specified. Use the links in the More Options section to change the title animation or to choose a different font and color for the text. When you've added the title or credit, Windows Movie Maker automatically closes the pane.

Saving the Movie

To save the movie you've created, click the appropriate link—This Computer, DVD, Recordable CD, E-mail, or Digital Video Camera—in the Publish To list in the Tasks pane. Windows Movie Maker launches the Publish Movie Wizard. Follow through the steps of saving the movie.

Creating DVDs with Windows DVD Maker

Windows DVD Maker is a basic program for creating DVDs containing pictures or videos. You can use Windows DVD Maker to create DVDs from scratch or to burn videos you create in Windows Movie Maker.

You can't use Windows DVD Maker to burn DVDs containing data files or bootable DVDs (such as those you use to install Windows). For creating data files, use Explorer's burning functionality. For bootable DVDs and other specialized DVD formats, use third-party DVD-burning software such as Easy DVD Creator.

Launching Windows DVD Maker

To launch Windows DVD Maker, choose Start ➤ All Programs ➤ Windows DVD Maker. Figure 23.18 shows the Windows DVD Maker interface with a project underway.

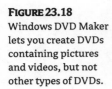

FIGURE 23.18
Windows DVD Maker lets you create DVDs containing pictures and videos, but not other types of DVDs.

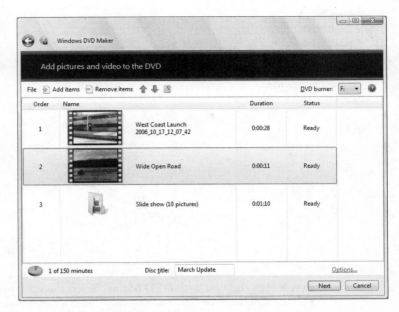

You can also launch Windows DVD Maker indirectly:

◆ In Windows Movie Maker, when you choose to burn your movie to a DVD, Windows Movie Maker announces that it will save your project, close it, and open Windows DVD Maker.

◆ In Windows Photo Gallery, when you choose to burn a DVD, the program launches Windows DVD Maker automatically.

Choosing Options for Windows DVD Maker

Before you create your first project in Windows DVD Maker, make sure its options are set suitably. Once you've set them, you may not need to change them for subsequent projects, unless you need to create different types of DVDs.

To choose options for Windows DVD Maker, follow these steps:

1. Click the Options link in the lower-right corner of the window. Windows DVD Maker displays the DVD Options dialog box (see Figure 23.19).

2. In the Choose DVD Playback Settings group box, decide what type of playback to use:

   Start with DVD Menu Select this option button to make a DVD that begins with a menu that lets the user control playback, as on most commercial DVDs. This is the "normal" type of DVD playback.

FIGURE 23.19
In the DVD Options
dialog box, choose the
video format, the DVD
aspect ratio, and how
you want to organize
playback on the DVD.

Play Video and End with DVD Menu   Select this option button to make a DVD that starts playing automatically and ends by displaying a menu that lets the user control playback. This functionality is sometimes useful, but it tends to surprise users accustomed to DVDs that start with a menu.

Play Video in a Continuous Loop   Select this option button to make a DVD that starts playing and loops back to the beginning when it reaches the end. This type of DVD is useful for situations such as a kiosk at a trade show.

3. In the DVD Aspect Ratio group box, select the option button for the aspect ratio you want your DVD to have: 4:3 (standard TV format) or 16:9 (widescreen).

4. In the Video Format group box, select the NTSC option button if you want to use the NTSC format (which is used in North America). Select the PAL option button if you want to use the PAL format (which is used in Europe and some other locations). NTSC is the abbreviation for National Television System Committee, a U.S. standardization organization established in 1940, which defined the NTSC encoding system. PAL is the acronym for Phase-Alternating Line, a different TV-encoding system.

5. In the DVD Burner Speed drop-down list, select the speed you want to use: Fastest, Medium, or Slow. Fastest is usually the best choice unless you find that DVDs don't burn correctly using it.

6. In the Temporary File Location text box, you can specify the folder in which you want Windows DVD Maker to store temporary files while preparing to burn the DVD. Leave the `<Default>` location selected (it's shown between the angle brackets like that) unless one of the following criteria applies:

◆ Your computer's main hard disk has less than 5GB of free space, and you need to use another disk (for example, an external disk).

◆ Your computer has two or more internal hard disks, one of which is faster than the other, and you want to move the temporary file location to the faster disk.

7. Click the OK button. Windows DVD Maker closes the DVD Options dialog box.

Starting Your Project

When you launch Windows DVD Maker, it displays the Add Pictures and Video to the DVD screen. Take these two preparatory steps to start your project:

1. Make sure that Windows DVD Maker has selected the correct drive in the DVD Burner drop-down list. The setting should be correct unless you have two or more DVD burners.

2. In the Disc Title text box, type the name for your DVD.

Adding Pictures and Videos to the DVD

If you launched Windows DVD Maker from Windows Movie Maker or Windows Photo Gallery, you will already have added content to the DVD. If you launched Windows DVD Maker manually, or if you want to add further content or rearrange the existing content, follow these steps:

1. Add items to the DVD in either of these ways:

    ◆ Click the Add Items button. Windows displays the Add Items to DVD dialog box, which is a standard Open dialog box given a different name. Select the file or files you want to add, and then click the Add button.

    ◆ Drag picture or video files from an Explorer window or from Windows Photo Gallery.

2. Arrange the items into the order you want. Either drag an item up or down the list to reposition it, or select it, and then click the Move Up button or the Move Down button.

3. If you need to remove an item from the list, select it, and then click the Remove Items button or press the Delete key.

4. Watch the readout in the lower-right corner to see how much of the DVD's available time the current content takes up.

Setting Up the Menus for Your DVD

When you've finished adding pictures and videos to the DV, click the Next button. Windows DVD Maker displays the Ready to Burn Disc screen (see Figure 23.20).

At this point, you can go ahead and click the Burn button to burn the disc with the content you've arranged already and the menu style that Windows DVD Maker has chosen to apply. But what you'll normally want to do is set up custom menus for your DVD and preview them to make sure they're what you want. To do so, follow these steps:

1. Click the Menu Text button. Windows DVD Maker displays the Change the DVD Menu Text screen (see Figure 23.21).

2. In the Font drop-down list, select the font you want to use for the menu text. Use the three buttons below the Font drop-down list to change the font color (the A button), toggle boldface on or off, or toggle italic on or off.

3. In the Disc Title text box, change the name for the disc if necessary. Windows DVD Maker suggests the name you entered on the first screen.

4. In the Play Button text box, change the text for the Play button if necessary.

5. In the Scenes Button text box, change the text for the Scenes button if necessary. This is the button that the user can click to see a listing of the DVD's contents.

FIGURE 23.20
The Ready to Burn Disc screen in Windows DVD Maker lets you start burning the disc immediately, but you can also preview the disc and customize the menu system.

FIGURE 23.21
The Change the DVD Menu Text screen lets you change the name of the disc and the navigation buttons. You can also add notes to the DVD.

6. In the Notes Button text box, change the text for the Notes button if necessary, and then type the text for the notes in the Notes text box.

7. Check the preview to see the effect of the changes you've made, and then click the Change Text button. Windows DVD Maker applies the changes and returns you to the Ready to Burn Disc screen.

FIGURE 23.22
The Customize the Disc Menu Style screen lets you set up a foreground video, a background video, and audio for the menu.

8. To customize the menu structure, click the Customize Menu button. Windows DVD Maker displays the Customize the Disc Menu Style screen (see Figure 23.22).

9. If you want to change the font used for the menus, use the Font drop-down list and the three buttons below it.

10. To play a video in the foreground of the menus, click the Browse button alongside the Foreground Video text box, select the video in the Add Foreground Video dialog box, and then click the Add button. The upper preview box shows the effect of your choice.

11. To play a video in the background of the menus, click the Browse button alongside the Background Video text box, select the video in the Add Background video dialog box, and then click the Add button. Again, the upper preview box shows the effect of your choice. Background video can not only make DVDs unnecessarily complex but also make your computer work harder during playback, so don't feel you have to add a background video just because you can.

12. To play audio while the menus are displayed, click the Browse button alongside the Menu Audio text box, select the audio in the Add Audio to the Menu dialog box, and then click the Add button.

13. To change the type of buttons used for the scenes, click the Scenes Button Styles button, and then choose the style from the drop-down list. The lower preview box shows the effect of your choice.

14. If you want to save your choices as a style that you can reapply to other projects, click the Save as New Style button, type a name in the Save as New Style dialog box, and then click the OK button. Windows DVD Maker adds a Custom Styles category to the Menu Styles drop-down button on the Ready to Burn Disc screen and adds your new style to this category.

15. Click the Change Style button. Windows DVD Maker applies the changes and returns you to the Ready to Burn Disc screen.

16. To set up a slide show, click the Slide Show button. Windows DVD Maker displays the Change Your Slide Show Settings screen (see Figure 23.23).

17. Use the controls in the Music for Slide Show area to set up the music for the slide show:

    ◆ To add a song, click the Add Music button, select the song in the Add Music to Slide Show dialog box, and then click the Add button.

    ◆ To move a song up or down the order, select it, and then click the Move Up button or the Move Down button.

    ◆ To remove a song, click it, and then click the Remove button.

18. If you want to extend the slide show automatically so that it uses as much time as the music you've chosen, select the Change Slide Show Length to Match Music Length check box. When you do this, Windows DVD Maker disables the Picture Length drop-down list. Otherwise, use the Picture Length drop-down list to select the number of seconds for which you want to display each picture.

19. Choose the transition from picture to picture in the Transition drop-down list.

20. If you want Windows DVD Maker to use pan and zoom effects for the slideshow, select the Use Pan and Zoom Effects for Pictures check box. Pan and zoom can look good, but it can rapidly become clichéd.

21. Click the Change Slide Show button. Windows DVD Maker applies your changes and returns you to the Ready to Burn Disc screen.

FIGURE 23.23
The Change Your Slide Show Settings screen lets you add music to a slide show.

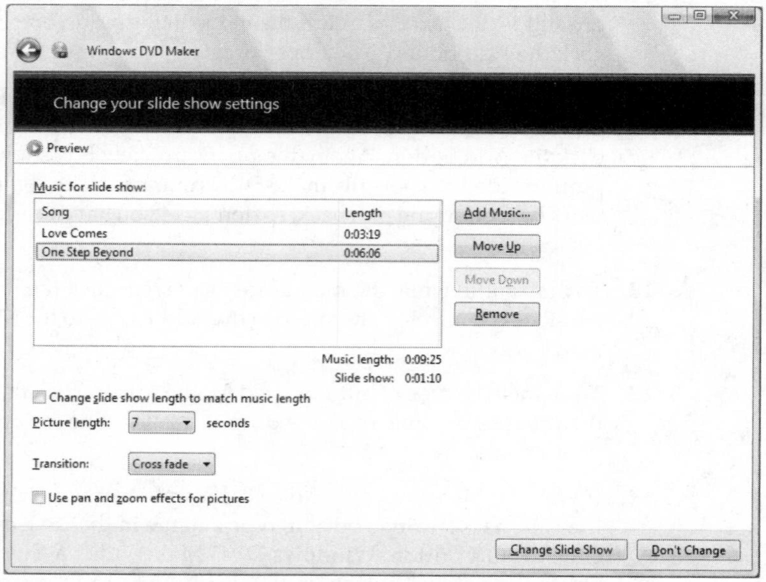

Previewing and Burning the DVD

By this point, you should be ready to preview the DVD. Click the Preview button, and use the resulting Preview Your Disc window (see Figure 23.24) to preview the disc. Go back and make any changes you find are necessary.

FIGURE 23.24

The Preview Your Disc window provides DVD player–style controls so that you can check the navigation on the DVD before burning it.

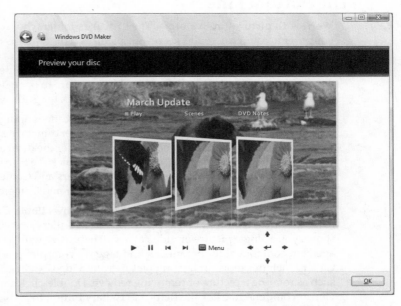

When you're satisfied with your DVD, click the Burn button. Windows DVD Maker displays the Burning dialog box (shown here) as it burns the DVD.

When it has finished burning the DVD, Windows DVD Maker ejects the DVD and offers you the chance to make another copy of the disc, as shown here. If you want to create another DVD, click the Make Another Copy of This Disc button. Otherwise, click the Close button.

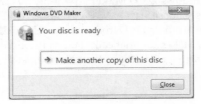

If you want to save the DVD project so that you can work with it again, choose File ≻ Save, and then use the Save Project dialog box to save the file. Then choose File ≻ Exit. Windows DVD Maker closes. If you didn't save the project, Windows DVD Maker asks whether you want to do so.

The Bottom Line

Work with pictures in Explorer   The Pictures folder (choose Start ≻ Pictures) is a folder in your user account for you to keep your pictures. This folder is normally private, but you can choose to share pictures in it with other users. The Public Pictures folder is a subfolder of the Public folder that's shared with all other users of your computer and may be shared with other users of your network as well. Double-click a picture to open it in Windows Photo Gallery. To start a slide show, select the pictures, and then click the Slide Show button on the toolbar.

Install a scanner or a digital camera   To install a scanner or digital camera, connect it to your computer. Normally, Windows notices the scanner or camera, displays a notification-area pop-up message, and then attempts to locate the software for the device. If Windows doesn't notice the scanner or camera, choose Start ≻ Control Panel, click the Hardware and Sound link, and then click the Scanners and Cameras link. In the Scanners and Cameras dialog box, click the Add Device button, and then work through the Scanner and Camera Installation Wizard.

View and manage pictures and videos with Windows Photo Gallery   Windows Photo Gallery (choose Start ≻ All Programs ≻ Windows Photo Gallery) consists of a viewer component that shows you a single picture or video at a watchable size with a small set of controls, and a management component for organizing and tagging your pictures and videos. Windows Photo Gallery includes tools for tagging pictures and videos and performing basic manipulations, such as rotating a picture or removing red eye. Double-click a picture or video to open it in the viewer component. Click the Return to Gallery button to go back to the gallery component.

Import video from a camcorder   To import video, connect your DV camcorder via FireWire or USB 2.0 (if it supports USB streaming). In the AutoPlay dialog box, click the Import Video link, and then work your way through the steps in the Import Video Wizard. You can choose between importing the entire videotape and importing only the segments that you choose.

Create your own movies with Windows Movie Maker   Windows Movie Maker enables you to create movies from video clips, pictures, music, and narration. Choose Start ≻ All Programs ≻ Windows Movie Maker to launch Windows Movie Maker. Use the links in the Import section of the Tasks pane to import materials; use the links in the Edit section and the commands on the Tools menu to arrange the materials on the storyboard, add effects and transitions, and record narration; and use the links in the Publish To section to export the movie to a file, a DVD or CD, e-mail, or a DV camera.

Create DVDs with Windows DVD Maker   Windows DVD Maker lets you create DVDs containing pictures and videos. Choose Start ≻ All Programs ≻ Windows DVD Maker to launch Windows DVD Maker, or choose to burn a DVD from Windows Movie Maker or Windows Photo Gallery to launch Windows DVD Maker automatically. Follow through the wizard-style interface to add content to the project and arrange it in the order you want, set up menus, and then burn the project to a DVD.

Chapter 24

Burning CDs and DVDs

- ◆ Understand the essentials of recording CDs and DVDs
- ◆ Configure your burner drive with suitable settings
- ◆ Burn files to disc using the Live File System format
- ◆ Burn files to disc using the Mastered format
- ◆ Burn discs from other programs

Provided that you have an optical drive capable of burning discs, Windows Vista lets you burn both CDs and DVDs. Recordable and rewritable discs are an inexpensive and easy method of backing up important data or simply transferring files from one computer to another.

This chapter explains the essentials of recording CDs and DVDs, shows you how to configure your burner drive, and then walks you through the process of burning files to disc using the two formats that Windows offers, Live File System and Mastered.

Understanding the Essentials of Burning Discs

Before you start burning discs, it's a good idea to have a rough idea of the capacity of CDs and DVDs, understand the difference between recordable and rewritable discs, and know which of Windows' two burning formats to use and when.

CD and DVD Capacity

CDs are handy for transferring or backing up relatively small amounts of data:

- ◆ Regular CD-R discs hold 650MB, the same amount as a standard audio CD. (A disc with 650MB holds 74 minutes of uncompressed audio.)
- ◆ Extended-capacity CD-R discs hold 700MB, a small increase that's worth having if you don't have to pay extra for it. A disc with 700MB holds 80 minutes of uncompressed audio.
- ◆ You can also find higher-capacity CDs that go up to 870MB, or 99 minutes of music.

DVDs are great for backing up large files (such as video files) or collections of smaller files (for example, your collection of MP3 files):

- ◆ Single-sided DVDs can hold up to 4.37GB, depending on the formatting used.
- ◆ Double-sided DVDs can hold up to 8.74GB, again depending on the formatting used.

Recordable Discs and Rewritable Discs

CDs and DVDs on which you can record data come in two basic types:

CD-R and DVD-R discs   CD-R discs and DVD-R discs, usually referred to as *recordable discs*, are discs that you can record data to only once. Once you finish recording data, you can't change the information on the disc.

CD-RW and DVD-RW discs   CD-RW and DVD-RW discs, usually referred to as *rewritable discs*, are discs on which you can record data multiple times. You can record data to the disc in multiple recording sessions until it is full. You can then erase all the data from the disc (a process that some recording programs call *formatting*) and use it again. Rewritable discs specify a theoretical safe maximum number of times that you can reuse them, but if you value your data, you'd be wise not to push them that far. Rewritable discs are a little more expensive than recordable discs, but if you need to be able to rewrite the discs, the extra expense is worthwhile.

Windows uses the term *writable disc* to refer to recordable and rewritable discs interchangeably.

Choosing which File System to Use

Windows lets you burn CDs and DVDs using the Live File System format or the Mastered format.

Live File System Format   This file system is "live" in that you can copy files to the disc at any point after you've loaded the disc in your optical drive and formatted the disc with the Live File System. The advantage of the Live File System format is that you can copy files to it in as many operations as you need. The disadvantage is that some older drives, operating systems, and devices cannot read discs burned using the Live File System format.

Mastered Format   With this file system, you arrange the files that you want to burn to the disc, and then burn them all at once in a single operation. The advantage of the Mastered format is that it's more compatible with older drives, operating systems, and other devices than the Live File System format is. For example, if you need to create a disc that you can use with a Mac, use Mastered format rather than Live File System format.

Configuring Your Burner Drive

Before you try to burn a disc, it's a good idea to check the settings that Windows has chosen for your recorder drive. You may want to adjust the configuration or change the drive used for holding temporary files when burning a disc on the Desktop.

To configure a recordable disc drive, follow these steps:

1. Choose Start ➤ My Computer. Windows displays a Computer window.

2. Right-click the recordable disc drive, and then choose Properties from the context menu. Windows displays the Properties dialog box for the drive.

3. Click the Recording tab. Windows displays the Recording page (shown in Figure 24.1).

4. Choose settings that meet your needs:

   Select a Drive that Windows Can Use as the Default Recorder for Your System   In this drop-down list, select the drive you want to use for recording. Windows lets you use only one drive at a time for recording. If your computer has only one recordable drive, you should find that Windows has already selected it. If you have two or more recordable drives, you may need to change Windows' choice here.

Choose a Drive that Has Sufficient Free Space to Burn a Disc   In this drop-down list, select the hard disk drive on which Windows should store an *image* of the disc (temporary files containing the data to be written to the disc) when creating the disc. If your computer has a DVD drive that you'll use to burn DVDs, you will need to have enough space to contain a complete DVD, plus a little overhead. For example, if you'll be burning 4.7GB DVDs, make sure that the drive you choose has at least 5GB free. For performance's sake, this disk drive must be a local disk rather than a network disk. You must authenticate yourself to User Account Control when you change disks.

Automatically Eject the Disc after a Mastered Burn   Select this check box to make Windows eject the disc when it has finished writing to it in a mastered burn. This feature is normally useful, because the ejection can be a visual signal that the disc is done, but you may want to disable ejection when burning discs on a laptop that you're using in a tight space.

5. To make sure that Windows automatically closes the current burning session when you eject the disc, click the Global Settings button, and then authenticate yourself to User Account Control. Windows displays the Global Settings dialog box, as shown here.

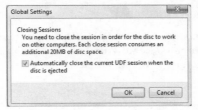

FIGURE 24.1
Check the configuration of your recordable disc drive on the Recording page of its Properties dialog box.

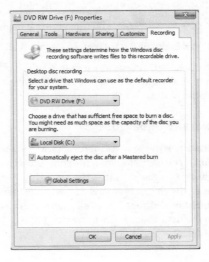

6. Select the Automatically Close the Current UDF Session When the Disc Is Ejected check box. (UDF is the Universal Disk Format, a file system used for optical discs.) By closing the burning session, you make the disc usable by other computers when you eject it. The only downside to closing the burning session is that each time you close the session, you waste 20MB of space on the disc. You'd clear this check box only if you needed to be able to eject a disc you'd been burning, then reinsert the disc and continue your previous burning session.

7. Click the OK button. Windows closes the Properties dialog box and applies your choices.

 Real World Scenario

CHOOSING A BURNER

Because of its value for backup and file transfer, a burner is almost indispensable nowadays. Most new PCs (both desktops and laptops) include an optical drive that can burn both CDs and DVDs. But some lower-spec PCs include a drive that can play DVDs but burn only CDs, not DVDs.

This sidebar tells you what you need to know if you're looking to upgrade your computer's DVD burner or add a new DVD burner.

TECHNICAL TERMS: WORM AND WARM

If someone's trying to confuse you about writable media, they may use the terms WORM and WARM. Discs that can be recorded to only once are *Write Once, Read Multiple* (or *WORM*) media, while rewritable discs are *Write and Read Multiple* (or *WARM*) media.

SPEED

CD recording speeds and DVD recording speeds are both measured in Xs—1X is the lowest speed, 2X is twice as fast, and so on. But the Xs are different for CDs and DVDs:

CD 1X is 150KB per second (the nominal read rate of the first CD drives).

DVD 1X is 1,350KB per second, or around 9X in CD speeds.

At this writing, DVD speeds go up to 16X, which is the equivalent of 144X in CD speeds. At 16X, a DVD drive can typically burn a complete DVD in around 5 or 6 minutes, including the time required to start and finish the writing. A 10X drive takes 7 or 8 minutes, and an 8X drive around 9 minutes.

BUFFERING AND UNDERRUNS

The faster a drive tries to write (or rewrite) a disc, the more susceptible it is to buffer underrun problems. A *buffer underrun* happens when the computer's hard drive subsystem can't deliver data to the burner quickly enough for the writing to run smoothly. The data stream from the computer is likely to be irregular because the computer tends to system tasks and user input at the same time as burning a disc, so burners include a buffer to store a certain amount of data to let the recorder smooth out any inconsistencies in the data stream. The bigger the buffer, the bigger the disruptions in the data stream that the recorder can smooth out.

But if the computer is working hard at other tasks, even a big buffer may not be enough to prevent a buffer underrun, which wrecks the disc being recorded. Drives with buffer underrun protection let the disc-burning laser pause when a buffer underrun is about to occur and then pick up from the point it left off. Buffer underrun protection can save you plenty of time and wasted discs, so it's worth looking for if you're planning to buy a new burner.

INTERNAL OR EXTERNAL?

Generally speaking, an internal drive will cost you less than an external drive, but you'll need to have a drive bay free in your computer for an internal drive, and you'll have to do a little work with cables (or have someone else do it for you). An external drive will usually cost more, will occupy space on your desk, and will need its own power supply. In addition, most external drives are much noisier than internal drives because they contain their own fans. But if you need to add a burner to a notebook, or if you want to be able to move the drive from computer to computer without undue effort, or if you're looking for an easy connection, you'll need an external drive.

CONNECTION TYPE

Internal drives use an EIDE connection (EIDE is short for Enhanced IDE, and IDE is short for Integrated Drive Electronics). External drives can connect through either USB or FireWire. For a Windows PC, a USB 2.0 connection is normally best, but if your PC has FireWire built in, FireWire is a good alternative. Avoid USB 1.x connections, which can burn CDs slowly (at up to 4X CD speeds) but are too slow for burning DVDs.

Burning Files to Disc Using the Live File System Format

If you want to be able to add files to a DVD or CD gradually as needed, use the Live File System format. Follow these steps:

1. Insert a blank disc in your computer's burner. Depending on the AutoPlay settings you've chosen for the drive, Windows may display an AutoPlay dialog box like the one shown here. If so, select the Always Do This for Blank DVDs check box or Always Do This for Blank CDs check box if you want to set the default; and, in any case, click the Burn Files to Disc Using Windows button.

2. Windows displays the Burn a Disc dialog box, as shown here.

3. In the Disc Title text box, type the name for the disc. Windows suggests a short form of the current date, which is useful for backups, but other data deserves a more descriptive name.

4. If you want to go ahead using the standard burning settings, which produce a disc that's readable on Windows Vista, Windows XP, and Windows Server 2003, but may not be readable on earlier versions of Windows or other operating systems (such as Mac OS X), go to the next step. If you want to adjust the format used, follow these steps:

◆ Click the Show Formatting Options link. Windows displays the hidden part of the dialog box, as shown here.

◆ Click the Change Version link. Windows displays the Select a UDF Version dialog box, as shown here.

◆ In the UDF Version drop-down list, choose the UDF version you want: 1.50 is compatible with Windows 2000 and later versions of Windows; 2.00 is compatible with Windows Vista, Windows XP, and Windows Server 2003; 2.01 is the default setting (compatible with Windows Vista, Windows XP, and Windows Server 2003); and 2.50 is compatible with Windows Vista only.

◆ Click the OK button. Windows closes the Select a UDF Version dialog box.

5. Click the Next button. Windows formats the disc, and then displays an Explorer window showing the disc's contents (nothing), as shown here.

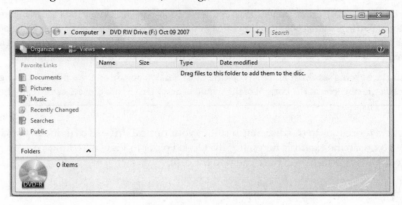

6. To add files to the disc, drag them from another Explorer window; or use standard Copy and Paste commands; or right-click a file or folder, choose Send To, and then select the burner drive from the Send To submenu. Windows copies the files to the disc, keeping you updated about its progress as usual, as in this example, and warns you if there's not enough space on the disc.

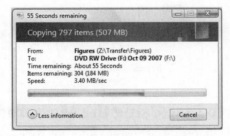

7. Add further files as needed. You can leave the disc in your optical drive as long as you don't need the drive for another disc. (This is the whole point of the Live File System format.)

8. When you want to remove the disc, eject it as usual by taking one of these actions:

   ◆ Choose Start ➤ Computer, right-click the optical drive's entry, and then choose Eject from the context menu.

   ◆ Press the Eject button on your optical drive or a dedicated eject key on your laptop computer or your keyboard.

9. Windows displays a notification area pop-up message as it closes the session, and then ejects the disc.

CLOSING THE BURNING SESSION MANUALLY

If you cleared the Automatically Close the Current UDF Session When the Disc Is Ejected check box in the Global Settings dialog box, Windows doesn't close the burning session when you eject the disc. This means that you can reinsert the disc in the drive and resume the burning session—but it also means that you must close the session manually before you can use the disc on another computer.

To close the burning session manually, click the Close Session button on the toolbar. For variety, you can also right-click the disc icon at the bottom of the window, and then choose Close Session from the context menu.

To add more files to the disc, reinsert it in your optical drive. If Windows displays an AutoPlay dialog box, as in the example here, click the Open Folder to View Files link. You can then drag further files to the disc's window to burn them to the disc.

Burning Files to Disc Using the Mastered Format

If you choose to burn your discs all at once to ensure the widest possible compatibility with older drives, operating systems, and devices, follow these steps to burn files to disc:

1. Insert a blank disc in your computer's burner. Depending on the AutoPlay settings you've chosen for the drive, Windows may display an AutoPlay dialog box like the one shown here. If so, select the Always Do This for Blank DVDs check box or Always Do This for Blank CDs check box if you want to set the default; and in any case, click the Burn Files to Disc Using Windows button.

2. Windows displays the Burn a Disc dialog box, as shown here.

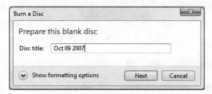

3. In the Disc Title text box, either accept Windows' suggestion (a short form of the current date) or type a more descriptive name.

4. Select the Mastered option button.

5. Click the Next button. Windows displays an Explorer window showing the disc's contents (nothing).

6. To add files to the disc, drag them from another Explorer window; or use standard Copy and Paste commands; or right-click a file or folder, choose Send To, and then select the burner drive from the Send To submenu.

◆ Windows copies the files to the storage area for the disc, not actually to the disc itself.

◆ If the disc doesn't contain enough space for the files you copy, Window warns you, as in the next illustration.

◆ After copying the files, Windows displays a pop-up message above the notification area to remind you that you have files waiting to be burned to disc, as shown here.

7. When you've added to the disc all the files you want it to contain, click the pop-up message to display the burner drive's Explorer window, or simply navigate to the burner drive's window manually. The window shows the list of Files Ready to Be Written to the

Disc with faded icons and a downward-pointing arrow to indicate that they're temporary file destined to be burned to CD and then deleted, as shown here.

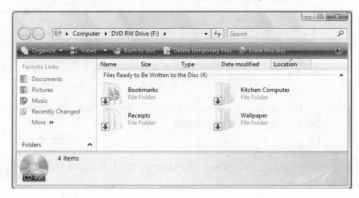

8. Click the Burn to Disc button on the toolbar. Windows launches the Burn to Disc Wizard, which displays the Prepare This Disc screen, as shown here.

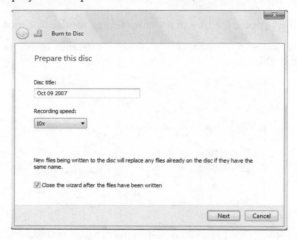

9. In the Disc Title text box, type the name for the disc.

10. In the Recording Speed drop-down list, you can select the recording speed to use for the disc. Normally, Windows chooses the fastest possible speed that the burner and the disc support, so you shouldn't need to change it. However, if a burn fails, you may want to choose a lower speed when retrying the burn.

11. Select the Close the Wizard After the Files Have Been Written check box if you want the wizard to close after completing the burn. Clear this check box if you want to be able to burn another disc containing the same files without having to restart the wizard.

12. Click the Next button. If you're using a recordable disc rather than a rewritable disc, the wizard displays the dialog box shown next to make sure you understand you can write to the disc only once. Click the Yes button.

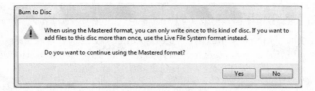

13. The wizard begins burning the disc and displays its progress, as shown here.

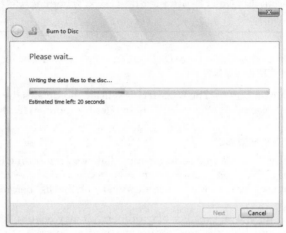

14. When the wizard has finished burning the disc, it ejects the disc. If you selected the Close the Wizard After the Files Have Been Written check box, the wizard closes; if you cleared this check box, it displays the You Have Successfully Written Your Files to the Disc screen, as shown here. If you want to create another disc with the same contents, you can then select the Yes, Burn These Files to Another Disc check box and click the Next button (the Finish button changes to Next when you select the check box). Otherwise, click the Finish button to close the Wizard.

> **GIVE WINDOWS ENOUGH TIME TO COPY ALL THE FILES TO THE STORAGE AREA**
>
> When you tell Windows to copy files to the storage area, the copy operation may take several minutes. Allow the copy operation to complete before you click the Burn to Disc button, or else the files won't all be present and correct, and problems will result with the burn.
>
> Windows doesn't lock the storage area even when you start the Burning Wizard, but after you start the wizard, you can't add any more files to the storage area for inclusion on the CD. You *can* paste more files to the storage area, but they won't be written to the CD you're burning, and they'll be deleted when the CD-burning operation ends.

15. If you want to create another CD containing the same files, select the Yes, Write These Files to Another CD check box.

16. Click the Finish button. The wizard closes itself and deletes the files from the storage area unless you selected the Yes, Write These Files to Another CD check box.

Testing Your New Disc

When you've finished creating a disc, test it immediately by reinserting it in your computer's optical drive. If Windows displays an AutoPlay window, choose to view the files. In the resulting Explorer window, open some of the files. Make sure all is well with the disc before archiving it or sending it to its destination.

If the disc you create won't read or play properly, it may have suffered recording errors. Try burning the disc again, but, this time, reduce the burning speed.

When Things Go Wrong Writing the Disc

If something goes wrong burning the disc, the wizard displays a screen telling you that there was a problem and offering you options for fixing or working around the problem. The following illustration shows an example of what you can do when the wizard has run into an error while burning the disc.

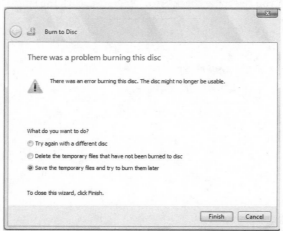

TROUBLESHOOTING: AVOIDING AVOIDABLE PROBLEMS WHILE BURNING

Even with today's powerful computers, burning a disc can be a demanding task that requires plenty of processor cycles and a steady stream of data. You can help your computer by not disturbing its concentration while it's burning. In particular:

◆ Don't run processor-intensive programs or operations. That means no terrain mapping and no video rendering, of course, not to mention the more demanding games. But you should also watch for other programs that tend to hog processor cycles. A perennial culprit is Visual Basic for Applications (VBA) macros in programs such as those in Microsoft Office, which tend to take every available processor cycle. Many macros execute quickly, but you should avoid running those that take longer while you're burning.

◆ Don't try to suspend your computer or put it into hibernation while burning a disc. Under most circumstances, this is likely only to happen if the computer is running on batteries or an uninterruptible power supply (UPS) and the battery state or UPS state triggers suspension or hibernation. Avoid burning a disc on battery power if possible (you'll know if it's not) and be prepared to lose a disc you're burning if a power outage knocks you back to UPS power.

◆ Don't let your screen saver kick in while you're burning a disc. The screen saver might do the burn no harm, but it won't do it any good. Either don't use a screen saver (better by far) or configure your screen saver to start after a period of inactivity long enough to cover even a burn that's been slowed down to a crawl by media problems.

Clearing the Storage Area for a Mastered Burn

If you've set up a disc for burning to Mastered format, and you end up deciding not to create the disc after all, clear the storage area by deleting the files in it so that they're not left hanging around.

To clear the storage area, click the Delete Temporary Files button on the toolbar. Windows displays the Confirm Delete dialog box, as shown here. Click the Yes button to delete the files. Windows deletes the files and removes the Files Ready to Be Written to the CD heading from the Explorer window.

Erasing All Files from a Rewritable CD

You can erase all the files from a rewritable disc so that all its space is free again. To do so, take the following steps:

1. Choose Start ➢ Computer. Windows opens a Computer window.

2. Double-click the burner drive. Windows displays the disc's current contents.

3. Click the Erase this Disc button on the toolbar. Windows launches the Burn to Disc Wizard, which displays the Ready to Erase Disc screen, as shown here.

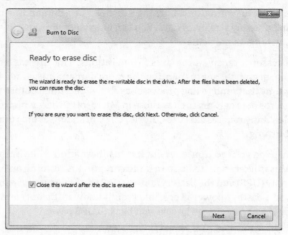

4. Select the Close This Wizard After the Disc Is Erased check box if you want the wizard to close itself after erasing the disc.

5. Click the Next button. The wizard erases the files on the disc, keeping you informed of its progress. When it has finished, it closes (if you selected the check box) or displays the Erase Completed Successfully screen (as shown here). Click the Finish button to close the wizard.

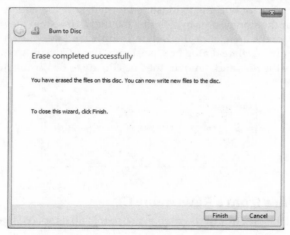

Burning Discs from Other Programs

Apart from burning discs directly from Explorer, Windows lets you burn discs from Windows Media Player and Windows DVD Maker. See Chapter 22 for coverage of Windows Media Player's burning capabilities and Chapter 23 for coverage of burning from Windows DVD Maker.

You can also start the process of burning a disc from Windows Movie Maker. When you do, Windows Movie Maker starts Windows DVD Maker and passes the disc-burning project over to it.

The Bottom Line

Understand the essentials of recording CDs and DVDs CDs are useful for recording modest amounts of data—up to 700MB or a little more. Single-sided DVDs can hold up to 4.37GB, and double-sided DVDs can hold up to 8.74GB. You can record a recordable disc once and a rewritable disc multiple times. The Live File System format lets you record multiple separate sessions to a disc that is compatible only with recent version of Windows, while the Mastered format lets you record a single session to a disc but have it be compatible with most computers, operating systems, and devices.

Configure your burner drive with suitable settings Before burning discs, configure your burner drive to make sure that Windows has identified the correct burner, and make sure that the hard disk selected for containing the image has more than enough space even for a full DVD.

Burn files to disc using the Live File System format The Live File System format is Windows' default format for burning discs, so you can accept the default settings when you load a blank disc. Drag files from an Explorer window to the disc's window to burn them to the disc. Windows automatically closes the burning session when you eject the disc.

Burn files to disc using the Mastered format To burn a disc using the Mastered format, choose the Mastered option button in the Burn a Disc dialog box. When you drag files to the disc's window, Windows queues them for burning to the disc. Click the Burn to Disc button on the toolbar in the Explorer window to start burning the disc.

Burn discs from other programs Windows Media Player and Windows DVD Maker include built-in features for burning discs. See the chapters covering those programs for details on burning with them.

Chapter 25

Playing Games on Windows Vista

- ◆ Enjoy Windows Vista's bundled games
- ◆ Configure games (or get rid of them)
- ◆ Choose hardware for serious gaming
- ◆ Add and configure game controllers
- ◆ Get the best performance from games

All work and no play makes Jack a dull computer, so Windows Vista comes not only complete with enough games to entertain you for a while but also capable of running a wide variety of other games, from the simple, but absorbing, to the graphically intense and complex.

This chapter starts by discussing briefly the nine games that come with Windows, which range from old favorites (such as Solitaire and FreeCell) to classic games such as chess (a welcome addition) and mahjong. The chapter then goes on to discuss the hardware you'll need for "serious" games, how to install and configure game controllers, and how to get the best performance from your computer when running games.

Playing the Bundled Games

Windows includes enough games to keep you entertained the next time you get stuck waiting for a connection in an airport—even if you're thoroughly sick of Solitaire, that old standby.

Opening the Games Folder

To reach the games, choose Start ➢ Games. Windows displays a window showing the contents of the Games folder (see Figure 25.1).

At first, the Games folder contains only those games that come built into Windows (plus any games that your computer's manufacturer installed). However, Windows adds games you install to the Games folder, making the Games folder the central place for managing games.

FIGURE 25.1
Windows' built-in
games include
Chess Titans, a
3D chess game.

Understanding the Ratings for Games

To help you avoid playing any unsuitable games or trying to run games that your computer isn't capable of running, Windows shows ratings for its built-in games and for any rated games you install. When you select a game in the Games folder, the right panel displays the following information:

Game Recommended Rating   The performance level that Microsoft recommends for you to be able to play the game satisfactorily. For example, 2.0. This score is on the Windows Experience Index scale discussed in the section "Checking Your Computer's Windows Experience Index Score" in Chapter 15.

Game Required Rating   The performance level that the game requires for your computer to play it at all. For example, 1.0 means that any Vista-capable computer can run the game (although the player's experience may be poor).

Current System's Rating   This is the Windows rating for your computer. You can click the Performance Information and Tools link to display the Performance Information and Tools window (also discussed in Chapter 15).

Rating System and Rating   The symbol at the bottom of the right panel shows the current rating system for games—for example, the ESRB icon shown in the figure represents the Entertainment Software Rating Board—and the rating given to the game (for example, Everyone).

The panel at the bottom of the Games window shows you details about the game: its name, the publisher (with a link to the website), the developer (also with a link), the product version, and the genre (for example, Family Entertainment or Adult).

Launching a Game

To launch a game, double-click its icon in the Games window, or click the icon, and then click the Play button on the toolbar.

Windows's Built-in Games

Windows includes nine single-player games, with revamped versions of long-time games such as Minesweeper, Solitaire, and FreeCell augmented by new additions, such as Chess Titans and Purble Place.

CHESS TITANS

Chess Titans is a 3D chess game that lets you play against either your computer or a human opponent. You can play in either a "top-down" orientation, as if you were looking straight down at the board from above, or from the angle at which a player might see the board (see Figure 25.2). You can change the angle of the board temporarily by right-dragging on the board.

To get started with Chess Titans, choose Game ➢ Options, and then choose options in the Options dialog box (shown next):

◆ The most important option is the Difficulty slider, which controls how hard the computer makes the game.

◆ Most of the other options are self-explanatory—for example, select the Always Save Game on Exit check box if you want the program to save the game automatically when you close the program.

FIGURE 25.2
Chess Titans highlights the allowed moves when you click the piece you want to move. Click the square for the move you want.

◆ The Graphics Quality slider controls the five check boxes below it. The farther you drag the slider to the right, the more check boxes become selected.

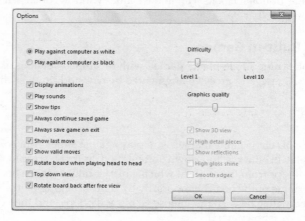

FREECELL

FreeCell (see Figure 25.3) is a solitaire variation that involves building descending columns of cards of opposite colors until you can transfer each suit in ascending order onto the four home cells.

To enable you to do so, there are four free cells (from which the game gets its name), each of which can hold one card at a time. All million FreeCell games are theoretically winnable, though some are much harder than others. The Game ➤ Hint command (which is new in this version of FreeCell) can point you in the right direction for your next move if you haven't run out of options.

FIGURE 25.3
Windows Vista's version of FreeCell includes a Game ➤ Change Appearance command that lets you customize or randomize the deck of cards and the background.

You can start a new random game by choosing Game ➤ New Game (or pressing the F2 key) or a new game of a specified number by choosing Game ➤ Select Game (or pressing the F3 key), entering the game number in the resulting Game Number dialog box, and clicking the OK button.

HEARTS

Hearts is a computerized implementation of the classic four-person card game. In this implementation, the computer plays the other three players. The Hearts Options dialog box (Game ➤ Options, or press the F5 key) lets you turn off animation (for the movement of the cards), sounds, and tips; choose whether to always continue your last saved game; and whether to save your game automatically when you close the program. You can also change the names of your cybernetic opponents from West, North, and East if you wish.

INKBALL

Inkball is a new game in Windows Vista. The game board consists of a rectangle with a variable arrangement of blocks (see Figure 25.4), one or more holes of different colors, and one or more balls of different colors (the balls use the same colors as the holes). You use a pen to try to prevent a ball from going into a hole of the opposite color. You can place dots and lines off which the balls bounce; when a ball hits a dot or line, the ball clears it off the board.

MAHJONG TITANS

Mahjong Titans (see Figure 25.5) is a solitaire game in which you try to clear the board by removing matching pairs of free tiles from the board. The Options (choose Game ➤ Options) let you turn off animations, sound, and tips, and choose whether to save games on exit and continue saved games.

FIGURE 25.4

To get started with Inkball, choose a difficulty from the Difficulty menu, and then choose Game ➤ New Game or press the F2 key.

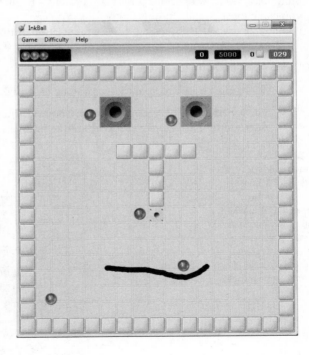

FIGURE 25.5
In Mahjong Titans, you remove pairs of free tiles—ones that you can take from the board without upsetting any of the other tiles around them. Press the H key to get a hint.

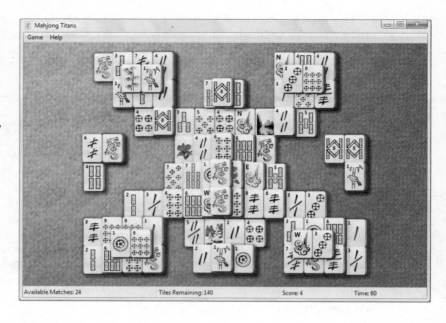

MINESWEEPER

Minesweeper (see Figure 25.6) is a classic Windows logic game in which you attempt to clear a minefield. Minesweeper has three sizes of field—Beginner, Intermediate, and Advanced—that you can choose in the Options dialog box. You can also create custom minefields up to 30 rows wide by 24 rows high by using the Custom option button.

These are the basics of Minesweeper:

◆ Click a square to clear it.

◆ Right-click a square to mark it as a mine (one click) or a possible mine (another click).

◆ Click both left and right buttons on a square whose mines you've marked to clear the surrounding area as far as any unmarked mines.

FIGURE 25.6
Windows Vista's version of Minesweeper features improved animations. You can even choose to sweep flowers rather than mines (choose Game ➢ Change Appearance).

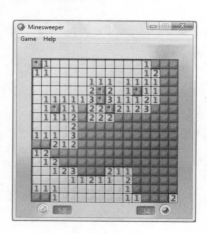

PURBLE PLACE

Purble Place, a new addition to Windows Vista, offers three educational games for teaching colors, shapes, and pattern recognition. For example, the Comfy Cakes game (see Figure 25.7) involves selecting a shape, choosing a color, and then picking a decoration.

SOLITAIRE

The classic solitaire card game, Solitaire (see Figure 25.8) should need little introduction, even though the Windows Vista version offers enhanced graphics.

The Options dialog box (choose Game ➢ Options) lets you choose the following:

- Whether to draw one card or three.

- Whether to use standard scoring, Vegas scoring (with or without cumulative scoring), or no scoring.

- Whether to time the game.

- Whether to display animations, play sounds, and show tips.

- Whether to save the game automatically when you exit, and whether to continue a saved game when you restart.

SPIDER SOLITAIRE

Spider Solitaire is a challenging solitaire game. The Options dialog box (choose Game ➢ Options) lets you choose among Beginner, Intermediate, and Advanced levels of difficulty; choose whether to display animations, play sounds, and show tips; and decide whether to save the game automatically when you exit, and whether to continue a saved game when you restart.

If you're new to Spider Solitaire, press the H key or choose Game ➢ Hint to see an available move.

FIGURE 25.7
The Purble Place games can help keep young minds busy.

FIGURE 25.8
Solitaire has had
a makeover for
Windows Vista, but
it's still a reliable
source of entertain-
ment. Choose Game ➤
Hint or press the H key
to get a hint on the
next card to move.

Configuring Games

The Games folder includes options for configuring games. You can choose a games rating system, hide games so that they don't appear in your Games folder, or reinstate games that you've hidden. Working outside the Games folder, you can remove some or all games from your computer so that standard users can't access them.

Choosing a Games Rating System

Windows comes set to use the Entertainment Software Rating Board (ESRB) ratings for games. If you prefer to use another rating service, follow these steps:

1. In the Games folder, click the Parental Controls button on the toolbar, and then authenticate yourself to User Account Control. Windows displays the Parental Controls window.

2. In the left panel, click the Select a Games Ratings System link. Windows displays the Game Rating Systems window.

3. Select the option button for the games rating system you want, and then click the OK button. Windows closes the Game Rating Systems window and returns you to the Parental Controls window.

Hiding Games from View—and Reinstating Them

If you don't want to play a game, you can hide it so that it doesn't appear in the Games folder, letting you see your other games more easily. To hide a game, right-click it in the Games folder, and then choose Hide This Game from the context menu. Any user can hide and reinstate games for his or her own account. The changes you make don't carry through to any other user's account.

To restore the games you've hidden, follow these steps:

1. In the Games window, click the Options button on the toolbar. Windows displays the Set Up Games Folder Options dialog box, shown here.

2. Click the Unhide Games button. Windows restores all hidden games to the list in the Games folder.

3. Click the OK button. Windows closes the Set Up Games Folder Options dialog box.

CHOOSING OTHER SETTINGS IN THE SET UP GAMES FOLDER OPTIONS DIALOG BOX

In the Set Up Games Folder Options dialog box, you can also do the following apart from unhiding games:

◆ Clear the Download Information about Installed Games check box to prevent Windows from downloading additional information about the games you've installed on your computer. (For example, you might see Windows downloading information about games as a privacy issue.)

◆ Clear the List Most Recently Played Games check box if you don't want Windows to track your games usage.

◆ Click the Clear History button to clear your game-playing history.

Removing Games from Your Computer

If you want to prevent yourself or a standard user from playing games on your computer, you can remove Windows' built-in games. To do so, follow these steps:

1. Choose Start ➢ Control Panel. Windows displays a Control Panel window.

2. In Control Panel Home view, click the Programs link. Windows displays the Programs window.

3. Under the Programs and Features heading, click the Turn Windows Features On or Off link. Windows displays the Windows Features window, as shown here.

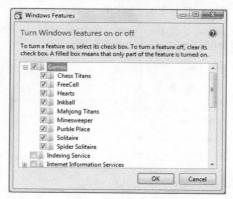

4. To remove all the games, clear the Games check box. To remove some games, click the plus (+) sign to expand the Games category, and then clear the check box for each game you want to remove.

5. Click the OK button, and then wait while Windows "configures the features" (as it describes the process). Windows then closes the Windows Features window.

Installing a Game

You can install a game in the same way as any other program:

1. Insert the game's CD or DVD in your computer's optical drive. Windows displays the AutoPlay dialog box for the disc, as in the example shown here:

2. Click the Run Autorun.exe link or a similar link to start the installation program running.

3. On the installation screen, click the Install button or link, authenticate yourself to User Account Control, and then follow through the remaining steps in the setup routine.

ADDING OLDER GAMES TO THE GAMES FOLDER

If you install an older game that's not fully aware of newer versions of Windows, you may find that it doesn't appear in the Games folder. If this happens, you can add it to the Games folder by dragging the executable file for the application from the folder in which the setup routine installed it.

Choosing Hardware for Serious Gaming

Any computer that can run Windows Vista at a decent pace should be able to run most games well enough for you to see what they're like. If your computer can handle the Aero Glass user interface, its graphics hardware should be good enough to produce an acceptable video display for light-duty gaming. But to get the most out of more demanding games, you need heavier-duty hardware than Windows Vista itself needs.

Sound Card and Speakers or Headphones

Basic sound systems such as those you find in run-of-the-mill bargain PCs are fine for standard audio tasks such as Windows system sounds and listening to Internet radio, and may be good enough for a little light CD, WMA, or MP3 audio if your ears aren't too picky. But to enjoy the sonic excesses of serious gaming, you need a sound system built for it.

For most people, that means getting a sound card that delivers 3D audio and environmental audio, and a subwoofer system with surround sound or home-theater capabilities (for example, a Dolby 5.1 setup—five satellites and a subwoofer—or 7.1 setup). Subwoofer systems are more expensive than subless systems, but because the subwoofer does the heavy lifting, it tends to be the most important part of a speaker upgrade.

When buying speakers, choose ones designed for the use or uses you'll give them: Some speakers are designed for classical music, some for rock, and some for rockets and explosions. Speakers that overlap the latter two categories may be your best bet, unless you have no interest in music.

Headphones come in enough styles—circumaural (over the ear), supra-aural (on the ear), and assorted buds (in the ear)—designs, and sizes that they're almost entirely a personal choice. While cheap headphones are almost guaranteed to sound bad, you don't need to spend a huge amount to get acceptable sound quality and comfort.

Generally speaking, sound quality and comfort are what you should look for in headphones. Style and looks should be secondary considerations (if you consider them at all).

Video Card

Games are one area where an investment in a high-powered video card with plenty of video memory can pay dividends. At this writing, entry-level Vista-capable video cards have 128MB of video memory, serious video cards have 256MB of video memory, and gaming-enthusiast video cards have 512MB. (Video cards with 1GB of video memory are available, but the prices are high and the uses highly specialized.) The latest and greatest graphics cards use PCI Express rather than AGP.

Before splashing out on the most expensive video card around, look at a round-up of video cards and their capabilities at a games website such as GameSpot (http://www.gamespot.com). Unless you have a high-resolution monitor and are determined to run games at the highest resolution possible, you probably don't need the latest video card, let alone a pair of them.

Joystick, Game Pad, Steering Wheel, or Other Human Interface Device

Keyboards and mice are great for regular input to Windows computers, but to enjoy most games to the max, you'll probably want to add a game controller such as a joystick, game pad, or steering wheel with rudder pedals. These devices are commonly referred to as *game controllers* or *human interface devices*.

Which type of device you choose depends of course on the types of games that you want to play. *Force-feedback devices* (such as joysticks) provide better tactile sensation for some games (for example, flying simulations). As you'd expect, they cost more than regular devices.

Adding and Configuring Game Controllers

This section discusses how to add and configure game controllers, such as those discussed in the previous section.

Adding a Game Controller

Most modern game controllers connect via USB. When you plug in the controller, Windows detects it automatically and launches the Found New Hardware Wizard to install a driver. If Windows has an appropriate driver for the controller, the wizard loads it automatically; if not, it prompts you to supply a driver. Do so.

Opening the Game Controllers Dialog Box

To configure game controllers, you use the Game Controllers dialog box. To open this dialog box, take the following steps:

1. Choose Start ➤ Control Panel. Windows displays a Control Panel window.

2. In Control Panel Home view, click the Hardware and Sound heading. Windows displays the Hardware and Sound window.

3. Click the Game Controllers heading. Windows displays the Game Controllers dialog box, as shown here.

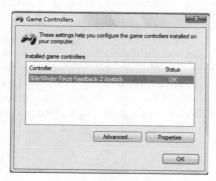

Choosing the Game Controller to Use for Older Programs

If you play games extensively, you may need to install multiple game controllers on the same PC—for example, a joystick and a gaming pad. To tell Windows which game controller to use for legacy games, take the following steps:

1. Click the Advanced button in the Game Controllers dialog box. Windows displays the Advanced Settings dialog box, as shown here.

2. In the Preferred Device drop-down list, select the game controller you want to use.

3. Click the OK button. Windows closes the Advanced Settings dialog box and applies your choice.

Testing and Calibrating a Game Controller

To test and calibrate a game controller, take the following steps:

1. Select the game controller in the Installed Game Controllers list box in the Game Controllers dialog box.

2. Click the Properties button. Windows displays the Properties dialog box for the game controller with the Test page foremost. Figure 25.9 shows the Test page of the Properties dialog box for a SideWinder Force Feedback 2 Joystick.

3. Use the controls on the Test page to make sure that your game controller is working as it should. For example, in the Properties dialog box shown, you can check the range of movement on the axes and make sure that the buttons and the point-of-view hat control are working correctly.

FIGURE 25.9
The Test page of the Properties dialog box for a game controller lets you test and calibrate the controller.

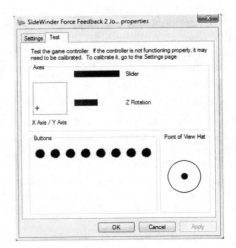

4. If you decide you need to calibrate your controller, click the Settings tab. Windows displays the Settings page (see Figure 25.10).

5. Click the Calibrate button. Windows starts the Device Calibration Wizard.

6. Follow the prompts as the Device Calibration Wizard walks you through calibrating your game controller. When the wizard finishes, it returns you to the Properties dialog box for the controller.

7. Click the OK button. Windows closes the Properties dialog box, applies the settings you chose, and returns you to the Game Controllers dialog box.

FIGURE 25.10
The Settings page (right) includes the Calibrate button for starting the Device Calibration Wizard.

Getting the Best Performance on Games

To get the best performance on games, follow the recommendations in this list.

Get plenty of RAM   You've heard this before many times in this book, but many computers don't have enough RAM to run demanding programs effectively without frequent swapping to disk. You can run Windows Vista with 512MB of RAM, but many games are happiest with another 512MB or 1GB dedicated to them. Physical RAM is preferable, but you will also get a performance boost by using flash memory in a ReadyBoost configuration.

Prefer PCI Express to AGP   If you have the choice between a PCI Express graphics card and an AGP graphics card, choose the PCI Express graphics card.

If using AGP, assign a big AGP aperture size   AGP video cards can offload some video-processing tasks onto system RAM so that they can devote their video memory to dealing with the most exciting and demanding video-processing tasks. To get the most benefit from this, assign a big AGP *aperture size*, the amount of RAM that your computer makes available to your graphics card for processing video information. Restart your computer and display the BIOS screen. (On many computers, you can do this by pressing the Delete key or the F2 key during boot-up.) Find the setting called AGP Aperture Size (or something similar, depending on your

BIOS), and increase it to a value that's around half the amount of system RAM you have. (You'll be limited to the settings that the BIOS provides, but choose a setting around this amount.) Save the values and exit the BIOS screen. AGP will then be able to take as much RAM as it needs for video-processing tasks.

Assign plenty of swap-file space   Give Windows plenty of space for the paging file so that it can write to disk as much information as it needs. (See the section "Specifying the Size and Location of the Paging File" in Chapter 15 for details.)

Get the latest stable drivers   Get the latest stable versions of drivers for your hardware. If your hardware is from big-name or enthusiastic manufacturers, you'll probably be able to download new drivers via Windows Update. But for the latest drivers the moment they're released, visit the hardware manufacturers' websites directly. Resist any temptation to test beta drivers, because they can destabilize your computer. Though System Restore (discussed in Chapter 16) can work wonders, you probably won't want to use it any more frequently than you have to.

Keep your disks defragmented   Keep your disks defragmented, as discussed in Chapter 10. This speeds up the retrieval of game data from the hard drive and optimizes the performance of virtual memory.

Choose appropriate display settings   Choose a screen resolution, color depth, and refresh rate appropriate to the game you're playing. For example, for action games, you may want to reduce the resolution, color depth, and refresh rate to increase the frame rate of the game and produce a smoother flow of play. For a nonaction game that uses high-quality graphics, you'll probably want a higher resolution, color depth, and refresh rate. (If your hardware is supremely rugged, handsome, and windswept, you may be able to manage an impressive frame rate with high resolution and true color.)

Disable high-end graphics features you can't afford   If your computer is struggling to run a game fast enough for you, you may be able to turn off some of the flashier features to buy yourself more speed. For example, some games let you turn off high-quality textures and shadows. You might also be able to lower the sound quality used.

Stop unnecessary software   Before running a game, exit as many open programs as possible to free up memory. Check your startup group for background services that may be running when you don't need them to. If you're using a screen saver, disable it so that it won't try to kick in while you're playing a game.

The Bottom Line

Enjoy Windows Vista's bundled games   Choose Start ➤ Games to open a window showing the Games folder. Windows includes nine games that range from revamped versions of old stalwarts (such as Solitaire and FreeCell) to a new chess game and the Purble Place educational games.

Configure games (or get rid of them)   Windows comes set to use the Entertainment Software Rating Board ratings for games, but you can choose another rating system by clicking the Parental Controls button on the toolbar, and then clicking the Select a Games Ratings System link. You can hide a game by right-clicking it and then choosing Hide this Game from the context menu; and you can reinstate games by clicking the Options button on the toolbar, and then working in the Set Up Games Folder Options dialog box. To install a game, run its setup routine.

Choose hardware for serious gaming   If you're serious about games, you'll probably want a sound card and speakers (or headphones) to match. Many different video cards are available for desktop PCs, but you will probably not need to buy the highest level of video card unless you need seriously high resolutions for games. However, you will almost certainly need a joystick or game pad to supplement your mouse and keyboard for playing games.

Add and configure game controllers   To configure games controllers, choose Start ➢ Control Panel, click the Hardware and Sound heading, and then click the Game Controllers heading. Use the options in the Game Controllers dialog box to configure your game controllers.

Get the best performance from games   To improve performance from games, make sure your computer has plenty of RAM. A PCI Express graphics card is a better bet than an AGP card; but if you're stuck with AGP, assign plenty of memory to it. Either way, make sure your swap file is large enough to allow Windows to run smoothly. Defragment your hard disks, choose display settings suitable for the game rather than for boasting, disable high-end graphics features that cause disappointing performance for games, and exit any programs that you don't need to have running while you play the games.

Part 5

Networking Windows Vista Home Edition

In this part:

Chapter 26

Understanding Windows Networking

- ◆ Understand the benefits of networking your home or home office

- ◆ Know what network architectures and protocols are

- ◆ Plan a network that's right for your needs

- ◆ Choose hardware for a wired network

- ◆ Choose hardware for a wireless network

This chapter discusses what a network is, why you might want to implement one in your home or home office, and what hardware you'll need to get in order to implement a network. Along the way, it tells you what you need to know about network architectures, network topologies, and network equipment.

Windows includes all the software you need to create a fully functional network. Depending on what kinds of computers you have, you may not even need to buy any extra hardware, as most modern computers include a wired network port, a wireless network adapter, or both. If you do need to buy hardware, it shouldn't be too expensive, and setting up the network should be easy.

If your computer is already connected to a network, you can skip this chapter and the next and go directly to Chapter 28 (which discusses how to share resources, such as printers) or Chapter 29 (which explains how to secure your network).

Why Network Your Home or Home Office?

A *network* is simply computers connected to each other so that they can share resources or exchange information. A network can consist of as few as two computers or as many computers as are connected to the Internet. In a home or a home office, you'll probably have anything from a couple of computers to a half-dozen computers networked together.

By networking your computers, you can share files and resources, so that you can perform the following actions and more:

- ◆ Transfer files from one computer to another. (For one-time use, such as when you're upgrading from an old computer to a new one, you might choose to use a direct connection via a USB, FireWire, infrared, or Bluetooth port instead of establishing a connection via network cards.)

- ◆ Share files. For example, if several users need to collaborate on a project from different computers, you can give them all access to a networked drive to use as a central location.

- Back up files easily from each of the networked computers. By centralizing backup to one computer or standard media, you can protect your files against loss and corruption.

- Share Internet connections, thus making better use of broadband connections (such as DSL, cable, and satellite connections) or simply reducing hardware and telephone costs.

- Share printers, CD and DVD recorder drives, scanners, and other hardware.

- Play multiplayer games with either other users of your network or people on the Internet (or both).

Network Architectures

There are two basic network architectures: *client/server networks* and *peer-to-peer networks*. The following sections discuss the key points of each. Both are worth considering for your home or home-office network. At this writing peer-to-peer networks are far more popular for such small networks, but client/server networks deserve more consideration than they get.

Client/Server Networks

Client/server networks are the type of networks used by most companies that have more than a dozen or so users. In a *client/server network* (also sometimes called a *server-based network*), there are two different types of computers: *server computers* that provide services, such as file storage and printing, and *client computers* that use those services. The point of using servers is to centralize files, coordinate the sharing of resources, and improve security while decreasing the number of points of failure. In most client/server networks, the client computers are managed by software running on the servers, but looser arrangements, in which the client computers enjoy some autonomy while tasting the benefits that servers can deliver, are possible too.

A client/server network can have just one server, but most corporate networks of any size have multiple servers of different types, each type having a specialized purpose. *File servers* provide networked storage for the users' files. *Print servers* manage printers, queuing the print jobs that the users send and coordinating the printers. *Applications servers* run programs so that users' desktop PCs can be 98-pound weaklings or the modern equivalent of dumb terminals. *Internet-access servers* such as proxy servers handle users' Internet requests, routing demands for URLs outward and the corresponding data inward. (Most proxy servers are set to check incoming and outgoing information for sins such as sports sites and sex sites on the way.) *E-mail servers* handle e-mail and groupware. *Fax servers* coordinate the sending and receiving of faxes.

The servers make it easier to manage, back up, and troubleshoot the network. Instead of having files scattered all around the building (or the campus, or offices spread right across North America) on the hard drives of individual users' computers, the administrators can have files saved on network drives that they can easily back up (and restore if necessary) from a central location. Instead of having an inexpensive and flaky printer crowding each user's cubicle, the administrators can funnel printing through centralized printers the size of refrigerators, making troubleshooting and management easy. Instead of installing programs locally (on the users' hard drives), they can install them on the applications server, where they can maintain and upgrade them with minimal effort. Security and permissions are handled centrally through the servers, so an administrator can easily prevent users from taking actions they shouldn't.

Needless to say, there's a downside to this centralization as well. If everyone in the office has been well behaved and stored all their files on the file server (as they're usually told to do), nobody will be able to do any work on those files if the file server crashes. If the Internet-access server takes an extended coffee break, all users' contact with the Internet and the Web is cut off. And if one of the cubicle-sized printers decides to eat paper rather than churn it out at 40 sheets a minute, even the network administrators won't be able to print out their resumes.

That said, when client/server networks work well, they work *very* well. With proper planning, client/server networks can *scale* (grow) to have thousands of workstations on them, whereas (even with good planning) peer-to-peer networks seldom work well with more than a couple dozen workstations.

Figure 26.1 shows part of a client/server network, omitting most of the clients so that the figure fits on the page.

Normally, the server or servers in a client/server network run a server operating system such as Windows Server 2003, Mac OS X Server, Linux, or Unix. But this isn't an absolute requirement. If you want, you can set up a small client/server network in which the server runs Windows Vista, Windows XP, or even an earlier version of Windows. More on this in a moment.

FIGURE 26.1

In a client/server network, servers centralize tasks such as file storage, faxing, e-mail, and Internet access.

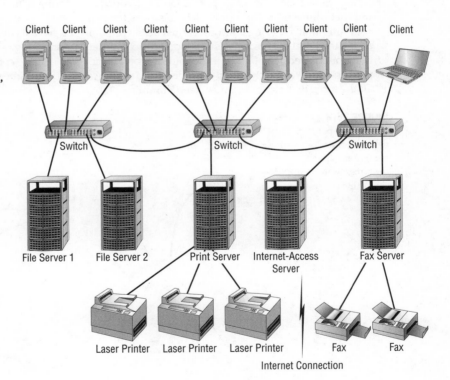

Peer-to-Peer Networks

In a *peer-to-peer network*, the computers are all equals—*peers*—from the administration and security points of view. Instead of connecting to one or more servers, the peer computers connect to each other. Instead of getting services from servers, the peer computers get services from each other and provide each other with services. Instead of being managed centrally by administrators, each peer computer is managed by its user, making security and backup more difficult without deliberate coordination by the users.

Typically, each computer on a peer-to-peer network is both a client and a server: It's a client when it accesses a resource on another computer, and it's a server when it supplies a resource to another computer. (Sometimes, a computer in a peer network acts only as a client, accessing resources on other computers but, itself, not sharing any resources with its peers.) For example, when you share a folder with other users, your computer is acting as a server. And when you access the printer connected to another computer, your computer is acting as a client. But most of the time, you don't need to worry about whether your computer is acting as a client or as a server, because it all happens seamlessly behind the scenes. You set up the sharing, and after that, the resources are available, and you can use them. It's as simple as that.

Figure 26.2 shows a simple peer-to-peer network that's sharing folders, two printers, and a dial-up Internet connection. This figure also illustrates the main weakness of peer-to-peer networks: Each computer that's sharing a resource must be powered on and have its operating system functioning all the time that the resource is needed. If the computer that's sharing folders is switched off (or has hung or crashed), the files in those folders won't be accessible. If the computer that's sharing the printers is powered off, nobody will be able to print. And for the Internet connection to be accessible all the time, that computer must keep humming along.

FIGURE 26.2

In a peer-to-peer network, the computers share resources with each other.

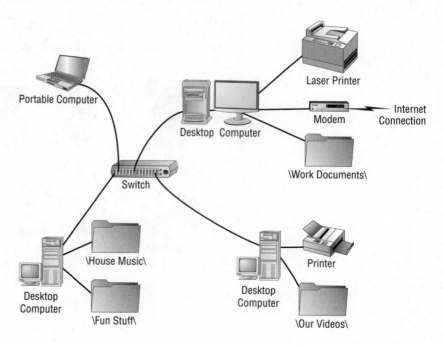

Peer-to-peer networks have another disadvantage worth mentioning here—a disadvantage that you can't see in the figure. Sharing a resource occupies some of the computer's processing power and memory, making it less responsive for its regular duties, such as running programs for the person using it.

If you compare Figure 26.2 with Figure 26.1, you can see that the line between a client/server network and a peer-to-peer network can be fine. If one of the computers were sharing all the resources, it'd be a server, and the network would be a client/server network rather than a peer-to-peer network.

EXTRA INFORMATION: NETWORK TOPOLOGIES

One factor that you probably won't need to worry about when putting together a home network is its *topology*—the way in which the components of the network are related to each other in terms of layout. But when troubleshooting problems with the network, you may find helpful to understand the topology.

Each network has a physical topology and a logical topology:

Physical Topology   The way in which the connections among the devices in the network are arranged.

Logical Topology   The way in which the data travels along the wires of the network or across the wireless connections.

STAR TOPOLOGY

The *star topology* is the most used topology for networks nowadays, because it's easy to implement and fault tolerant. In a star topology, all the computers connect to a central switch or hub (or several switches or hubs connected to each other). Both the client/server network shown in Figure 26.1 and the peer-to-peer network shown in Figure 26.2 use star topologies. Wireless networks also use a star topology, with the wireless access point at the center.

A star topology uses more cable than a bus topology (discussed in the next section), because each computer is wired to the switch or hub. Extra cable costs more money, of course, but for a small network, the difference in cabling cost between a star topology and a bus topology isn't usually a significant amount. And because each computer is connected to the switch or hub, a cable failure affects only one computer.

The switch, hub, or wireless access point in a star topology does represent a single point of failure. But because these devices are typically reliable, and because you can keep a spare device relatively cheaply, this isn't usually a problem.

BUS TOPOLOGY

In a *bus topology*, all the computers and devices are attached to a single run of cable. As you can see in the next illustration, which illustrates a bus topology, the bus is a simple network design, and one that's economical on cable. The terminators at each end of the bus tell the signal that it's reached the end of the cable and that it should stop rather than bouncing back along the cable.

The main drawback to a bus topology is that any break in the cable takes down the entire network. Bus topologies are seldom used for Ethernet and Fast Ethernet nowadays, but they're used in other networking technologies, such as some phone-line networks.

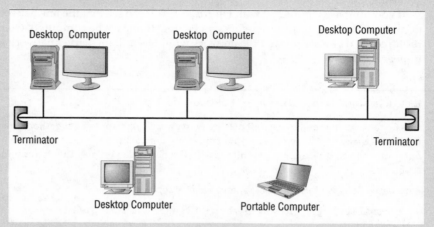

OTHER TOPOLOGIES: RING AND MESH

There are two other physical topologies, ring and mesh, but these are seldom used nowadays:

◆ In a *ring topology*, the computers are laid out in a topological ring, with each connected to its two neighbors. Ring topologies aren't fault tolerant, and because each computer on the network needs two cables, they tend to be more expensive than star or bus topologies.

◆ *Mesh topologies* are fault tolerant and are used where uptime is vital. In a true mesh, each computer is directly connected to each other computer, giving a network diagram that looks like a mesh or a cat's cradle. A true mesh involves a huge number of connections and is rarely implemented for more than a handful of computers. More frequently, a partial mesh topology is implemented, with the most critical computers having multiple connections to each other so that they can maintain connectivity even if they lose a connection or two.

LOGICAL TOPOLOGIES

There are three widely used logical topologies:

◆ In a *logical bus topology*, the signal travels to all the computers on the network, but only the computer identified by the address picks the packets of data off the wires. Ethernet uses a logical bus topology.

◆ In a *logical ring topology*, the signal travels around the network from one attached computer to the next. Each computer checks to see if the signal is intended for it; if it isn't, the computer passes the signal along to the next computer. When the signal reaches the computer identified by the address, that computer picks the packets off the wire, and they travel no farther. A token ring network is an example of a logical ring topology.

◆ In a *logical mesh topology*, the signal can take any of a number of paths from its source to its destination. The Internet is an example of a logical mesh topology.

Network Protocols

A *network protocol* is a set of rules that lay out how data is transmitted between computers (or other devices) on a network. For two devices to communicate effectively, they must use the same protocol.

TCP/IP

For local networking and most Internet connections, Windows uses the Transmission Control Protocol/Internet Protocol, which is known as *TCP/IP* for short. TCP/IP is the suite of protocols on which the Internet is based. Windows supports two different versions of TCP/IP:

◆ Internet Protocol Version 6 (TCP/IPv6) is the latest version of TCP/IP. TCP/IPv6 offers far more IP addresses than TCP/IPv4—enough for every person on the planet to have various different IP addresses for computers and gadgets—and will become the standard protocol for most networks. At this writing, relatively few computers support TCP/IPv6, as most of them still run TCP/IPv4.

◆ Internet Protocol Version 4 (TCP/IPv4) is the standard version of TCP/IP that has been used for several years now both for the Internet and for private networks. TCP/IPv4 still works well but has run short of IP addresses because it was designed at a time when the number of devices connected to the Internet seemed likely to remain small.

Windows Vista comes set to use both TCP/IPv6 and TCP/IPv4. When Windows Vista establishes a network connection, it tries using TCP/IPv6 first. If TCP/IPv6 doesn't work, Windows falls back to TCP/IPv4.

OTHER NETWORKING PROTOCOLS WINDOWS NO LONGER SUPPORTS

Earlier versions of Windows included support for other networking protocols that Windows Vista doesn't support. These protocols include:

NetBEUI NetBIOS Enhanced User Interface (NetBEUI, pronounced "net-booey") is a local area network protocol that many previous versions of Windows supported.

AppleTalk AppleTalk is a networking protocol used by Macs. However, because Mac OS X uses TCP/IP, lack of AppleTalk shouldn't be a problem.

IPX/SPX IPX/SPX (Internetwork Packet Exchange/Sequenced Packet Exchange) is a set of protocols developed by Novell, Inc. and used in Novell's NetWare network operating system. Home networks seldom require IPX/SPX, although some unusual consumer-level devices require it.

Special-Purpose Network Protocols

Windows uses various other network protocols for particular purposes that include the following:

Dial-Up Network Connections Windows uses Point-to-Point Protocol (PPP) for dial-up connections such as Internet connections via modems or ISDN.

Broadband Internet Connections Windows uses Point-to-Point Protocol over Ethernet (PPPoE) for broadband Internet connections such as cable connections and DSL connections.

Virtual Private Network Connections   Windows uses Point-to-Point Tunneling Protocol (PPTP) and Layer 2 Tunneling Protocol (L2TP) for virtual private network (VPN) connections. (Chapter 30 discusses how to create and use VPN connections.)

Automatic Network Configuration and Device Discovery   Windows uses Universal Plug and Play (UPnP) to enable networked devices to communicate their presence to each other and configure themselves to work with each other. For example, if you enable Internet Connection Sharing (ICS) on an Internet connection, it uses UPnP to advertise its presence to other computers so that they can connect to the Internet through the shared connection.

In most cases, Windows handles the protocols shown in the above list seamlessly, so you don't need to worry about them. For example, if you set up a dial-up networking connection by using the Set Up a Connection or Network feature, Windows configures the connection to use PPP by default; if you set up a broadband connection, Windows will automatically use PPPoE. If you enable ICS, Windows automatically uses UPnP. However, you may sometimes need to configure a protocol manually.

EXPERT KNOWLEDGE: IP ADDRESSES AND HOW THEY WORK

You don't need to know this information in order to implement a Windows network, but understanding what Internet Protocol (IP) addresses are and how they work can be a great help when troubleshooting network problems.

TCP/IP uses an IP address to identify each computer or device on a network:

◆   An IPv4 address is written in decimal numbers and takes the form $x.x.x.x$, where each x is a number between 0 and 255—for example, 216.43.28.244.

◆   An IPv6 address is written in hexadecimal notation (base 16: using the numbers 0–9, and the letters A–F). An IPv6 address consists of eight groups of hexadecimal characters separated by colons. Written out in full, an IPv6 address might look like this: 3dce:ffff:0000:2f3b:02ba:00ff:fe28:9c5a. You can also compact many IPv6 addresses by suppressing any leading zeroes in a section. For example, the compact form of the previous address is 3dce:ffff:0:2f3b:2ba:ff:fe28:9c5a. Usually, it's easiest to write IPv6 addresses out in full, because they're easier to read that way. There's also another convention for compacting IPv6 addresses: if part of the address contains only zeroes, you can omit that part, and indicate its omission by putting a double colon in the appropriate place. For example, the previous address can be written as 3dce:ffff::2f3b:2ba:ff:fe28:9c5a, with the double colon indicating that the 0000 section is missing.

In IPv4, IP addresses are either public or private. *Public IP addresses* are centrally assigned by the Internet's registration authorities, which keep detailed records of which organization or individual has which IP address. *Private IP addresses* are IP addresses that you can assign yourself for internal use within your network. Private IP addresses are *nonroutable*, which means that packets sent to private IP addresses can't be passed across routers and so can't escape from your network to the Internet.

IPv4 has three private address ranges. The range 10.0.0.0 to 10.255.255.255 is used for large organizations. The range 172.16.0.0 to 172.31.255.255 is used for medium-sized organizations. The range 192.168.0.0 to 192.168.255.255 is used for small networks and home networks. Windows' Internet Connection Sharing (ICS) uses the last-mentioned range for home and small-office networks.

A computer can get an IP address in three ways:

DHCP   Dynamic Host Configuration Protocol (DHCP) is a protocol for assigning IP addresses automatically to computers and networked devices on demand and reclaims them when they're no longer being used. In a Windows domain–based network, the DHCP service runs on a server (for example, Windows 2003 Server) to allocate the addresses. Many devices designed for sharing Internet access in the home or small office, such as residential gateways, implement a basic DHCP service as well. ICS includes a DHCP allocator, which is a stripped-down DHCP server.

IPv6 has a *stateless autoconfiguration* mechanism that allows it to automatically configure its own IP address using one or more network prefixes that it gets from an IPv6 router on its network.

Set a Fixed Address Manually   You can set a fixed address manually. In most cases, using DHCP is more efficient than allocating fixed IP addresses manually, because DHCP prevents a computer that's switched off (or disconnected) from keeping an IP address when another computer might need it. But in some cases it's useful to keep a fixed IP address for a given computer so that you always know which address it's using. Besides, if you're using only half a dozen or so computers and other devices on your network, you won't run short of IP addresses.

Self-Allocation   For when you haven't set a fixed IP address manually and no DHCP server is reachable, Windows can allocate itself an IP address automatically, a feature called Automatic Private IP Addressing (the acronym is APIPA), in case you're not using DHCP (or fixed IP addresses) or your DHCP allocator isn't available. If Windows doesn't get a response to its request for an IP address, it automatically chooses an IP address in the range 169.254.0.1 to 169.254.0.254 and checks to see if any other computer already on the network is already using this address. If the IP address is free, Windows Home assigns itself that address; if not, it chooses another, checks that, and so on. Windows keeps checking the network for a DHCP server and, if it finds one, applies for an IP address, to which it then switches.

Planning Your Network

This section discusses how to go about planning your network. You need to make the following decisions:

◆   Should the network be client/server or peer-to-peer?

◆   Should the network be wired, wireless, or a mixture of the two?

◆   If the network will be wired, which wired networking technology will you use?

◆   Where will you keep your files?

◆   Which resources will you share on the network?

Client/Server or Peer-to-Peer?

Most home networks and many home-office networks are peer-to-peer networks, but you should evaluate creating a client/server network instead of a peer-to-peer network.

Even if your network needs are relatively modest, it's worth considering having a server, especially if you have a spare computer, or a pensioned-off old laptop or desktop, that you'd like to get a bit more use out of. A server doesn't have to have a fast processor or a ton of RAM. Nor does it need to be running Windows Vista. If you've gotten a new computer because your old computer couldn't handle Windows Vista, you might be able to continue using that old computer with a less demanding operating system on it—for example, Windows XP or Linux (if you can handle Linux). The server doesn't have to manage the computers on the network—it just has to provide resources and services to authenticated users.

PROVIDING SERVICES VIA DEDICATED DEVICES

Instead of centralizing resources on a server that you keep running all the time, so that you don't have individual computers sharing resources, you can add to the network dedicated devices for sharing resources. For example, you could add a DSL router to share your Internet connection, or a print server to share one or more of your printers.

You can also get stand-alone, dedicated file servers designed for home-office or small-office use, although these tend to be far more expensive than a humble PC providing equivalent capabilities. Each of these is an independent device that connects to your network hub. Once it's connected, the device can be accessed by any computer that's running.

Wired, Wireless, or Both?

After you decide between a client/server network and a peer-to-peer network, your second decision should be whether you want a wired network, a wireless network, or a combination of the two.

Both wired and wireless networks offer advantages and disadvantages. Wired networks have three main advantages over wireless networks: speed, cost, and reliability. Wireless networks offer two main advantages over wired networks: flexibility and lack of cables. The following sections examine these advantages.

One point on which wired networks and wireless networks are nearly tied is simplicity. In theory, a wireless network should be easier to implement than a wired network, because less hardware is involved—for example, there are no cables. But it doesn't always work out that way in practice, as anyone will attest who has spent time struggling to configure a wireless access point to talk to the wireless network adapter located right next to it.

Wired networks are relatively simple to configure. You add a network card to each computer, attach a cable to the network card and the switch or hub, and you're in business.

Another point on which wired networks often score over wireless networks is security: Because the range of a wireless access device often extends beyond the physical boundaries of the location it's covering, someone can tap into the network from outside the location. But as you'll see in the section "Securing Your Wireless Network" in Chapter 29, if you take some basic measures to secure it, a wireless network can be secure enough for most conventional use.

ADVANTAGES OF WIRED NETWORKS OVER WIRELESS NETWORKS

This section discusses the advantages of wired networks over wireless networks: speed, cost, and reliability.

🌐 Real World Scenario

INCREASING THE RANGE OF WIRELESS NETWORKS WITH ANTENNAE

If the reason you choose a wireless network is to be able to move your computer freely about your house, office, or area, you may find you need to extend the range of the network beyond what the equipment can manage. Although many products promise ranges of 1,000 feet or more, real-world ranges tend to be much shorter, and often shorter than you need to cover even a modest area.

To increase the range of a wireless network, keep these points in mind:

◆ When buying equipment, look for an access point and a wireless network adapter that have a connector for an external antenna. Such a connector gives you the flexibility to attach any compatible antenna.

◆ The built-in antennae on many wireless network adapters are hard to orient for maximum effect. On a PC Card–style network adapter, much of the coverage is actually directed up and down rather than outward, where you would probably want it. (You might get better wireless range by standing your laptop on edge, but your work, play, or neck would suffer.)

◆ Omnidirectional antennae provide the widest coverage. (The coverage is actually pancake shaped and in the horizontal plane rather than spherical, because moles don't need boosted signals and airplanes tend not to appreciate them.)

◆ Yagi antennae provide extended range in a general direction.

◆ Parabolic grid antennae provide the greatest range in a more specific direction. Wireless enthusiasts can get ranges of 20 miles or more with boosted Wi-Fi, given a suitably open landscape.

Speed

Wired networks offer higher speed than wireless networks. Gigabit Ethernet is usually the best choice for a wired network and provides speeds of up to 1Gbps. You may need only Fast Ethernet, the next level down from Gigabit Ethernet, which provides 100Mbps and is included as the wired port in many wireless access points.

Wireless networks offer speeds up to a claimed 300Mbps, depending on the products used, but most real-world speeds are in the 11Mbps–54Mbps range. All wireless adapters drop down to lower speeds if unable to connect at their top speeds. The more distance and the more walls, floors, or other obstacles you put between your wireless adapter and the nearest access point, the lower the transmission speed is.

Most of the highest speeds are based on the 802.11n protocol for wireless networks. At this writing, the protocol is still at the draft stage, but manufacturers have released many devices based on different interpretations of the standard. Many of these devices do not interoperate well with devices from other manufacturers. The latest widely supported standard is the 802.11g Wi-Fi standard, which offers theoretical transfer rates of 54Mbps, as does the less widely used 801.11a standard. The most widely used standard, 802.11b Wi-Fi, has a maximum transfer speed of 11Mbps.

Cost

Wired network adapters cost less than wireless network adapters. You can get a bargain-basement wired network adapter for $10, though you'll usually be better advised to spend more like $20 to $50. Then you'll need a switch (costing around $5 to $10 per port) or a hub (costing a little less but providing much less functionality).

Most wireless network adapters cost between $30 and $100. You can create a peer-to-peer network with two or more adapters, but to improve performance, you may want to get a wireless access point instead. Most hardware wireless access points cost between $70 and $250, depending on which extra features they have—a switch or hub for connecting your wired computers, a print server for sharing your printer, or even a feature for playing music from a computer to your home stereo.

Reliability

Wired networks tend to be more reliable than wireless networks. Unless there's a problem with one of the network cards, the cables, or the switch (or hub), a wired network should deliver its full performance all the time.

By contrast, throughput on a wireless network can be affected not only by the distance and obvious obstacles such as walls and floors but also by its immediate surroundings. For example, if you put a stack of books next to your laptop's wireless network adapter, you may reduce its range. If you're using your laptop on your lap, your body may block part of the signal.

ADVANTAGES OF WIRELESS NETWORKS OVER WIRED NETWORKS

This section discusses the advantages of wireless networks over wired networks: flexibility and the lack of cables.

Flexibility

Because the computers in a wireless network aren't constrained by cables, a wireless network offers greater flexibility than a wired network. You can move the computers from room to room without trailing cables. Even if you're not interested in roaming with your laptop, being able to move it about freely can be a boon.

For desktop computers, the mobility offered by a wireless network connection is less of a draw, although it can come in useful for shared computers. For example, if you put a desktop computer on a wheeled workstation, you can move it easily from room to room (or from schoolroom to schoolroom).

You can also get multifunction wireless devices that act as a network access point, a print server, and an Internet sharing device. If you can find one of these devices that suits your needs and is within your budget, you should be able to connect your key devices with a minimal number of wires.

Lack of Cables

Wireless networks are great for locations where, for whatever reason, you don't want to (or cannot) install cables. For example, in a temporary office location, you can set up a wireless network without having unsightly cables strung like trip wires from room to room. Likewise, if you're renting an apartment whose landlord wouldn't appreciate your drilling holes from room to room (or floor to floor) or stapling cables or raceways along the baseboards, a wireless network will probably seem more attractive than a wired network.

Voice over IP Phones

Depending on the type of wireless network you implement, you may be able to add Voice over IP (VoIP) phones to it, so that you could make phone calls via your Internet connection from a cordless phone that connects to your wireless network. You can also add VoIP to a wired network, but you'll be tethered to your PC for calls, which most people find less appealing.

COMBINING WIRED AND WIRELESS IN YOUR NETWORK

You can get the best of both worlds by combining wired and wireless in your network. For example, you may want to implement a wired network with a wireless access point that allows your laptops to connect via wireless network interface cards from wherever in the building they happen to be. The wired portion of your network will be fast, and the wireless portion of your network will be flexible. The cost will be considerably more than that of a wired-only network, but it should be less than that of a wireless-only network.

If you decide to combine wired and wireless networks, create the wired network as described in "Installing a Wired Network" in Chapter 27, and then add wireless to it as described in "Setting Up a Wireless Network" (also in Chapter 27).

Where Will You Keep Your Files?

Your next decision is where to keep the files on the network. It's vital to make this decision when implementing the network, because it can save you a great deal of time and effort later on.

In a peer-to-peer network, each user typically saves the files they create (or download) on the hard drive of their computer. To share files, they either use the Public folder on their computer, designate another folder on their computer for sharing, or use a folder someone else is sharing on another computer.

There's nothing to stop you from keeping your files scattered about on the hard drives (or even removable drives) of all the computers attached to the network. But the files will be difficult to back up effectively from their various locations, and unless each user of the network has a good memory, it'll become hard to remember which file is stored in which folder on which computer. Windows Vista's search capabilities can help you find the files you need, but it's much better to organize the files into a more-or-less formal structure so that you don't need to search.

To keep your shared files in order, designate a minimum number of shared locations. This is one of the strongest arguments for creating a client/server network rather than a peer-to-peer network. By concentrating all your shared files on the server, you'll be able to back them up easily. All the users of the network should be able to find the shared files without wasting time and effort. And because the server will be running all the time, you'll avoid the problem that arises when a user wants to access a file in a shared folder whose host computer is currently powered down or whose operating system has crashed or hung.

HOW MUCH SPACE DO YOU NEED FOR YOUR FILES?

If you decide to keep all your shared files in a central location, estimate how much space you'll need for the files. It's always difficult to know how much space you need until you find out that you have far too little, but you need to start by making an educated guess at the amount of space required so that you can provide it to start with.

How much space you need will vary wildly depending on the types of files you want to share. If you're networking your home office, you'll probably want to share documents, spreadsheets, presentations, address books, and so on. If you're networking your computers to make their entertainment resources available to each computer in the household, you may need much more space. For example, if you're planning to implement a network so that you can play your vast collection of music files from any connected computer, you'll need many gigabytes of storage space. If you want to share video files, you'll probably need hundreds of gigabytes. You might even want to look into creating a redundant array of inexpensive disks (RAID) on a network file server for maximum space and speed.

Which Resources Will You Share?

Next, make a list of the resources that you want to share via the network—your files and folders, your Internet connection, your printers, and other devices.

Once you've set up Discovery and Sharing (as discussed in the section "Setting Up Discovery and Sharing" in Chapter 9), Windows lets you share files and folders, an Internet connection, and printers from one computer to another. For example, if Computer A is sharing a printer, Computers B and C can print to it via the network. If Computer B is sharing its Internet connection, Computers A and C can use the Internet connection to access the Internet. With custom software, you can also share other resources. For example, you can network your TV or your DVD, or implement a video-communication or baby-monitoring program across the network.

You may also want to share other resources that you can't share directly like this. For example, you can't share a digital camera or scanner among computers unless you unplug the device and carry it from computer to computer. So the best way to share a digital camera or scanner is to set it up on a computer that any member of the household can use. If the server is in a central location, it may be the best computer for this role.

Choosing Network Hardware for a Wired Network

Once you've decided to implement a wired network, you have a further choice to make: Gigabit Ethernet or Fast Ethernet, FireWire, phone line (HomePNA), or power line (HomePlug). The following sections discuss how to choose hardware for each of these types of wired network.

Choosing Hardware for a Gigabit Ethernet or Fast Ethernet Network

For a Gigabit Ethernet or Fast Ethernet network, you need network interface cards, cables, and a switch or hub.

NETWORK INTERFACE CARDS

If you've decided to go with Gigabit Ethernet, your choices are simple:

Desktop Computer   Buy a PCI Gigabit Ethernet network card. If your computer doesn't have a PCI slot free, you can use a USB 2.0 Gigabit Ethernet network adapter, but the transmission speed will be limited to less than Gigabit Ethernet's maximum 1Gbps because USB 2.0's maximum speed is 480Mbps.

Laptop Computer   Buy a PC Card Gigabit Ethernet network adapter. Alternatively, you can use a USB 2.0 Gigabit Ethernet network adapter, but the transmission speed will be limited to USB 2.0's 480Mbps top speed.

For Fast Ethernet, your choices are similar, but you may also be able to get an ISA card instead of a PCI card for a desktop. PCI is more convenient, but if all your computer's PCI slots are full, ISA may be an easy solution. USB 2.0 is a reasonable choice for Fast Ethernet, because Fast Ethernet's maximum speed is far slower than USB 2.0's maximum speed.

BUY GIGABIT ETHERNET UNLESS YOU'VE A GOOD REASON NOT TO

At this writing, Gigabit Ethernet is the best choice if you're buying new network equipment. While Gigabit Ethernet equipment is still more expensive than Fast Ethernet equipment, its much higher performance makes the relatively small price premium worthwhile.

If you have Fast Ethernet equipment for most of your network, it's still worth getting Gigabit Ethernet equipment for any new items. Gigabit Ethernet equipment can drop down to Fast Ethernet speeds as needed, and you will most likely upgrade your network to Gigabit Ethernet at some point in the future.

Even if you have Fast Ethernet cards and switches, make sure any cables you buy are Gigabit Ethernet capable, because you can use them for higher data rates if you upgrade your network interface cards and switches. The cables should last for many years unless you allow dogs, rodents, or small children near them.

 Real World Scenario

SCRIMPING ON NETWORK HARDWARE SELDOM PAYS OFF

Network hardware is unglamorous compared to graphics cards, fast processors, and thundering subwoofer systems, but don't make the mistake of buying the cheapest hardware you can find for your network just because the network is boring. In particular, don't skimp on the switch (or hub) and the cables. You can shave a few bucks off the price, but you need your network to be reliable because it will be carrying your valuable data. False economies you make here can cost you far more in troubleshooting and downtime in the future.

Whichever types of network card you choose, make sure they're listed on the Windows Hardware Compatibility List (HCL) at the Microsoft Windows Hardware Quality Labs website, `http://www.microsoft.com/whdc/hcl/default.mspx`.

CABLE

When choosing cable, keep these points in mind:

◆ For Gigabit Ethernet or Fast Ethernet, use either Category 5E (Cat 5E for short) or Category 6 (Cat 6) unshielded twisted-pair (UTP) cable. For Fast Ethernet, you can also use Category 5 cable, but Cat 5E or Cat 6 is a better choice in case you upgrade to Gigabit Ethernet.

◆ If you need to run cable in suspended ceilings, inside walls, or between the floors of a building, get plenum cable. Plenum cable has a Teflon coating designed to resist catching fire and to give off nontoxic smoke if it does catch fire. (A *plenum* is an enclosed space that's full of matter.)

◆ For fast and easy connection, buy ready-made cables. Most networking suppliers stock cables anything from 18 inches to 100 feet in length and in a wide variety of colors. Colored cables can help you identify different cables more easily in a crowded environment, but if you want your cables to be inconspicuous, you'll probably want to settle for the color that best matches your décor.

♦ If you need a lot of cables, or if you prefer cables of exactly the right length rather than ready-made lengths, you can make your own cables easily enough. You'll need a reel of cable, some RJ-45 connectors, and a crimping tool with a die for crimping RJ-45 connectors. You'll probably also want to get a cable-stripper tool for stripping the outer plastic sheath off the cable neatly, but you can strip it with a knife if you have the steady hand and patience required. Buying a crimping tool, a reel of cable, and connectors can save you money over buying a large number of ready-made cables.

SWITCH OR HUB

In the star network topology used for Gigabit Ethernet and Fast Ethernet, the switch forms the central point of the network, with the network cables from all the computers and other network-aware devices plugging into its ports. For Fast Ethernet, you can also use a hub (which typically is cheaper than a switch), but a switch is a better choice (see the nearby sidebar for the reasons why).

EVEN FOR FAST ETHERNET, BUY A SWITCH INSTEAD OF A HUB

For Fast Ethernet, you can use a hub instead of a switch, but network performance will be poorer. When a computer sends data, the hub receives it on one port and broadcasts it on all the other connected ports so that the computer or device to which the data is addressed can receive it.

This arrangement is effective but inefficient, as a lot of data bounces around the network unnecessarily. Say you have eight computers, named A through H, connected to your hub. When A is sending data to B, it sends it to the hub, and the hub broadcasts the data to all the ports but the port the data is coming in on—in other words, the ports to which computers B through H are connected. B picks the data off the wire. The data to ports C through H is unnecessary and decreases the performance of the network.

A *switch* (sometimes called a *switching hub*) handles the data more intelligently. The switch builds a table of the hardware addresses of the computers and devices connected to its ports. Then, instead of taking the data passed to it on one port and sending it on all other connected ports, it examines the address on the data and passes the data along only to the appropriate port (and thus to the appropriate computer). By doing this, a switch provides more available bandwidth on the network and improves performance.

When buying a switch, keep the following points in mind:

♦ Buy a switch with enough ports for both your current needs and your future needs. If you have four computers in your home or office now, but might add either more computers or more network-aware devices in the near future, it makes little sense to buy a four-port switch. Instead, buy an eight-port or 12-port switch.

♦ Alternatively, make sure that your four-port switch includes an uplink port, so that you can attach another switch to it.

♦ For Gigabit Ethernet, make sure the switch is triple-speed (10-, 100-, and 1,000-capable) so that when you connect all the equipment to it, it lets each port communicate at the full speed of the device attached to it rather than knocking the whole network back to the speed of the slowest device. If you have both standard Ethernet (10BaseT) equipment and Fast Ethernet (100BaseT) equipment, make sure that your switch is dual speed.

♦ Buy an unmanaged switch rather than a managed switch. An *unmanaged switch* is one that looks after itself once you've connected it to your network. High-performance networks often use *managed switches*, on which the administrator can configure the performance of each port—for example, allowing a computer connected to one port large amounts of bandwidth and a high quality of service while making a computer connected to another port scratch along with minimal bandwidth and a miserable quality of service. Managed switches are far more expensive than unmanaged switches.

Choosing Hardware for a Phone-Line Network

Phone lines can be one of the easiest ways to network your home quickly, provided that you have wires and jacks where you need them. (If you don't, you *can* run extension leads—but these offer little advantage over network cable.)

Here's what you need to know about phone-line networks:

◆ Phone-line networks are limited in speed. The industry body, the Home Phoneline Networking Alliance (HomePNA; `http://www.homepna.org`), has so far set three standards:

HomePNA 1.0   Up to 1Mbps

HomePNA 2.0   Up to 10Mbps—the same speed as a regular Ethernet network

HomePNA 3.0   Up to 240Mbps—faster than Fast Ethernet

◆ The phone jacks you use for the network need to be on the same phone line.

◆ Most phone-line network adapters include a splitter, so that you can use the network and the phone at the same time.

◆ Most phone-line network adapters plug into a USB port, PC Card slot, or a PCI slot.

◆ Phone-line networks use a physical bus topology and a logical bus topology. This means that you don't need a hub. It also means that if you cut the phone line, the whole network stops working. Phone lines are terminated automatically, so you don't need to add termination devices to the ends of the bus.

This is about all you need to know. If the speed is adequate for your needs, and you have the jacks, you can buy a phone-line networking kit, plug in the adapters, and install the software, and you should be all set.

CREATING SMALL NETWORKS WITH FIREWIRE

You can also connect FireWire-enabled computers by using FireWire cables. (If a computer doesn't have a FireWire port, you can add one or more by using a PCI card or a PC Card, provided that you have a PCI slot or a PC Card slot free.) These cables are far more expensive than network cables but give good performance.

Because FireWire can transfer data very fast (up to 400Mbps for IEEE 1394a, and up to 800Mbps for IEEE 1394b), and because it's plug and play, it can be a great networking solution for a home or home office. The main problem with FireWire networking is that the maximum cable length is 15 feet (4.5 meters), so each of the computers on the FireWire network needs to be within 15 feet of another computer or of a FireWire hub. That 15 feet needs to be "as the cable flies"—around or over any obstacles that the cable can't go through, and preferably not strung like a thigh-high trip wire between desks.

You can also bridge a FireWire network with an Ethernet network. So if you have a cluster of computers in the den, you can network them to each other with FireWire, and then network one of them to an Ethernet network with a cable run to the distant reaches of your dwelling.

Choosing Hardware for a Power-Line Network

Power-line networking tends to make eyebrows rise, but a power-line network can be one of the easiest ways to network your home, simpler even than phone-line networks because most dwellings have many more electrical outlets than they do phone jacks. You shouldn't need to buy any cables for a power-line network beyond the cables for connecting the computer's USB port to the electrical socket.

Early power-line networks managed only 12Mbps or 14Mbps, making them competitive with regular Ethernet and workable for modest networks. Recent power-line networks, however, reach speeds of 200Mbps—twice as fast as Fast Ethernet and plenty fast enough for most residential use. Most power-line network adapters require a power conditioner to make sure that the computer receives no untoward signal from variations in the power supply that normal electrical equipment can shrug off.

Various manufacturers, including Belkin (http://www.belkin.com), Linksys (http://www.linksys.com), and NetGear (http://www.netgear.com), make power-line network equipment. Some power-line network adapters plug into an Ethernet connection on the computer, while others connect via USB. For information, visit the HomePlug Powerline Alliance web page (http://www.homeplug.org).

Power-line networks have a couple of limitations worth mentioning. One is that some power-line networks don't work well with bidirectional printer cables: You need to disable the features that let the printer give feedback to the computer, such as telling the computer that it's out of ink or that it's managed to jam again on your expensive letterhead.

A second limitation is that, because multiple apartments or even houses can be on the same ring main, power-line networking can inadvertently network you with your neighbors. So it's vital that you implement security on a power-line network to protect your data and your devices.

Choosing Hardware for a Wireless Network

Choosing hardware for a wireless network is both easier and harder than choosing hardware for a wired network. It's easier in that you need less equipment—you can skip the cables for a start—but harder in that you should evaluate that equipment even more carefully than you would wired networking equipment.

For a simple wireless network involving two computers, you need nothing more than a pair of wireless network interface cards. For desktop computers, USB 2.0 network adapters that attach via a cable are the best choice, as you can position the main part of the adapter and angle its antenna to get optimum reception. PCI card network interface cards and USB network adapters that protrude from the USB socket are more discreet but give you less flexibility in aiming the antenna. For portable computers, PC Card or CardBus network interface cards are usually the best choice—although a USB 2.0 network adapter that attaches via a cable can give you better reception, it will also rob you of some of the portability that you presumably want from your laptop.

For a more complex or more capable wireless network, get a wireless access point for the wireless network interface cards to connect to. The access point typically plugs into your Ethernet switch (or hub), forming a wireless bridge to the network and letting the wireless computers access the wired portions of the network. Some wireless access points include small switches or hubs (for example, with four ports). Look for at least Fast Ethernet speeds on such ports; Gigabit Ethernet speeds are preferable.

Usually it's best to get all your wireless equipment from the same manufacturer or from manufacturers known to be friendly to each other. At this writing, standards-based 802.11g devices and 802.11b devices operate mostly successfully with all other 802.11g and 802.11b devices, while standards-based 802.11a devices can interoperate with each other (but not with 802.11b or 802.11g devices). However, devices based on different interpretations of the 802.11n standard (which is in draft at this writing) often have problems connecting to devices from other manufacturers and have to drop down to disappointing data rates before they can establish a connection.

When evaluating wireless networking equipment, keep the following considerations in mind:

Price As with most hardware, a high price doesn't always guarantee high quality, but buying the cheapest devices available is seldom a wise move.

Range If you've used cordless phones, you won't be surprised that the maximum range listed for most wireless network cards turns out to be wildly optimistic or achievable only under atmospheric conditions and surroundings that can be recreated in laboratories but not real life. For example, some 802.11g devices claim to deliver 6Mbps at 1,800 feet—plenty far enough to work wirelessly on your laptop at your local coffee shop or bar, perhaps, while maintaining a connection to your home network. Typically, the ranges you'll experience in the real world are far less. Try to get a demonstration of a device's range before buying if at all possible.

External antenna attachment If you need to extend the range of wireless networking equipment, make sure the cards and access point you buy have a socket for attaching an external antenna.

Roaming Usually more of a consideration in offices than in home buildings, roaming is worth thinking about if you need wireless access from an area greater than a single access point can cover. First, make sure that the network interface cards and access points you buy can handle roaming, so that you'll be able to move from one access point's coverage to the next access point's without dropping your network connection. (If you just need to be able to establish a connection from the garden or the garage, you won't necessarily need roaming—you can disconnect from the network, go to the garden or garage, and establish a new connection with the nearest access point.) And, second, work out how many access points you need.

Number of access points From the range and the need for roaming, establish the number of access points you need to provide effective coverage for your building or area.

Placement of access points Whether you get one access point, two, or 10, you need to place them optimally in order to balance the widest possible coverage with the fastest possible connections. The nearer you are to an access point, the better your chances of getting the full data rate the hardware supports.

The Bottom Line

Understand the benefits of networking your home or home office Networking your computers lets you share files and resources (such as printers or an Internet connection) among the computers. You can transfer files from one computer to another, back up files, or play multiplayer games.

Know what network architectures and protocols are Most home and home-office networks are peer-to-peer networks, in which each computer shares resources with other computers. However, you may prefer a client/server network, in which all the shared resources are hosted by a single server. In a client/server network, you need keep only the server running in order to make the resources available, rather than keeping each sharing computer running. Most Windows networks use the TCP/IP protocol for communication. Windows Vista uses IPv6 when connecting to IPv6-capable servers and uses IPv4 when connecting to other servers.

Plan a network that's right for your needs   To plan a network, first choose your architecture: client/server or peer-to-peer. Then choose the means of connection: wired only, wireless only, or a combination of the two. For a wired network, you can choose among different networking technologies: Gigabit Ethernet (usually the best choice), Fast Ethernet, FireWire, phone-line, or power-line networking. You then need to decide where to keep your files: preferably in as few locations as possible (for ease of access and backup), perhaps on a server.

Choose hardware for a wired network   Each computer connected to a wired network will need a network adapter (if it doesn't have one built in). PCI is usually the best choice for a desktop computer, and PC Card for a laptop computer. USB 2.0 is also possible for both desktop computers and laptop computers, although it is not fast enough for full-speed Gigabit Ethernet connections. For an Ethernet network, you will need a switch with enough ports for all your current computers and any computers or devices you may add.

Choose hardware for a wireless network   You can create a wireless network with nothing more than a wireless network card for each computer, but you will normally get better results by building your network around an access point. Add a wireless network card to each computer that doesn't have it, using PCI or USB 2.0 for a desktop computer and PC Card or USB 2.0 for a laptop computer. Prefer equipment based on final networking standards to equipment based on draft standards, because the latter equipment may not be fully interoperable with equipment from other manufacturers.

Chapter 27

Building a Home or Home-Office Network

- ◆ Install a wired network
- ◆ Set up a wireless network
- ◆ Browse the network
- ◆ Map and disconnect network drives
- ◆ Connect Mac and Linux clients to the network

This chapter discusses how to build a network for your home or your home office. It assumes that you've read the previous chapter, decided on the network type you want to use, and purchased the necessary hardware for it.

Most likely, you'll want to set up a wired network, a wireless network, or a network that mixes wired and wireless. This chapter shows you how to do all three—and how to set up a network using FireWire cables, if that's your preferred technology.

Installing a Wired Network

To put your Ethernet network together, install your network hardware by following these basic steps:

1. Install a network interface card in each computer. If you bought your computer recently, chances are that it already has a network adapter built in.

2. If your network uses a switch or hub (for example, if you're creating Gigabit Ethernet, Fast Ethernet, or regular Ethernet network using a star configuration), position the switch or hub in a convenient central location. If you're using multiple switches or hubs, position them so that each is located conveniently for the computers that will connect to it, and then connect the switches or hubs via the uplink port on one and a regular port on the other.

3. Connect a network cable from the card to one of the ports on the switch or hub.

4. Power on the switch or hub.

5. Power on each computer in turn, and install a driver:

◆ Windows may install the driver for the computer's network card automatically, showing you no more than a pop-up message like that shown here.

◆ The Found New Hardware Wizard may launch and walk you through the process of finding a driver for the network interface card.

6. Once the network connection is working, Windows searches automatically for a DHCP server. If it finds one, Windows requests an IP address, and automatically configures TCP/IP settings to connect to the network.

7. When the computer is connected to the network, Windows prompts you to decide whether the network is public or private, and applies the corresponding security settings.

Reduced to their essentials, those steps for installing the network look straightforward enough—even friendly. But, as with many things in the physical world, the devil is in the details. The next sections discuss how to install network cards, how to cable an Ethernet network, and how to configure networking settings if you need to. There's also a sidebar on how to create a FireWire network.

Installing Network Cards

Installing a network card is typically straightforward as long as Windows supports the network card. If in doubt, check the Windows Catalog before buying a new network card.

◆ For a PCI card or an ISA card, shut down Windows, switch off the computer (if shutting down Windows didn't already switch it off), and unplug the power. Open the case, and then ground yourself to dissipate any static electricity by touching a metal part of the case. Locate an empty slot of the right type, install the card, and then close the case again. Plug the power back in and power up your computer again.

◆ For a PC Card or CardBus card, insert it while the computer is running.

◆ For a USB Ethernet connection, you normally install the software first, and then plug the connection in while the computer is running. If the instructions instruct you to plug in the connection before installing the software, do so.

Windows should detect the card automatically and display the Found New Hardware Wizard to walk you through the process of selecting and installing the appropriate driver for the card.

If Windows seems not to detect the card, follow these steps:

1. Press Windows Key+Break. Windows displays the System window.

2. In the left panel, click the Device Manager link, and then authenticate yourself to User Account Control. Windows displays the Device Manager window.

3. Expand the Network Adapters category, and see whether it contains an entry for your network card. If not, click the Scan for Hardware Changes button (the rightmost button) on the toolbar to force Device Manager to scan for hardware. The Found New Hardware Wizard should then launch.

Cabling an Ethernet Network

On a scale of difficulty from breaking an egg to building a house, cabling an Ethernet network falls well at the easier end of the scale—say, roughly the same difficulty as installing internal telephone cables. And as with installing telephone cables, you can use the quick-and-dirty approach or you can do the job properly.

SHOULD YOU DO IT YOURSELF (DIY) OR PAY A PROFESSIONAL?

If all your computers inhabit the same room, or if you're content to have the Ethernet cables trail across the floor from room to room, cabling can be as easy and swift as uncoiling the cables, plugging each into the appropriate sockets on the switch or hub and the computers and other network-enabled devices, and supplying power to the switch or hub. You can set up a quick-and-dirty network in minutes.

 Real World Scenario

INSTALLING TWO OR MORE NETWORK CARDS IN A COMPUTER

If you need to share a broadband connection from a computer without using a hardware router or residential gateway, or if you need to connect to two or more discrete networks, you'll need to install two or more network cards in the same computer. You may also need to install multiple network cards in the same computer if you need to bridge two networks (as discussed in the section "Connecting Two Networks via a Bridge" in Chapter 28).

Provided that both your network cards are compatible with Windows and that you have enough slots of the appropriate type available in your computer, installing two network cards should be little more difficult than installing just one. The most important thing is to avoid any confusion as to which card is which—in particular, to avoid creating two network connections named "Local Area Connection" and "Local Area Connection 2" and then having to figure out which is actually your broadband connection.

If the computer already has one of the network cards installed and configured, check the card's configuration and make sure that it's working as it should. If the connection is named Local Area Connection and the other connection will receive the same name, rename the connection to something more informative before installing the second network card and configuring its connection. Label the card so that you'll be able to tell easily which it is when you've installed the second card. Then go ahead and install the second card.

If you're installing both network cards from scratch, install them one at a time. Again, once you've got the first card and connection working, rename it to avoid any confusion with the second card. Then install the second card and configure it. Rename the resulting connection if necessary, and label the card.

At the other extreme, if you want your network cables to run almost invisibly from room to room and emerge tidily at wall plates into which you can plug patch cables when you need to connect, you'll need to invest some time and effort. You'll need to buy some tools (unless you already have all you need). Unless you're happy spelunking in drywall, ceilings, and basements, you might want to think about calling in a professional cabling contractor instead. A professional's rates may seem steep, but using a professional should get you a neat and effective cabling system that will add value to your property rather than detract from it. As usual when hiring someone for a task, see if your friends or colleagues can recommend anybody; ask for references; check how quickly they'll fix any problem that crops up; and make sure that the deal includes full documentation on the specifications, location, configuration, and upkeep of the cabling system.

If your property is cabling friendly—say, you're doing a major refit, or you're having a new house built—consider having it wired to the Residential Telecommunications Cabling Standard, also known as ANSI/TIA/EIA-507-A. This standard calls for one outlet in each bedroom, family room, and study, one outlet in the kitchen, and one outlet in any wall that has an unbroken space of 12 feet or more or in which a device would have to be 25 feet or more from an outlet (in other words, two or more outlets in big rooms). Under Grade 1 of this standard, each outlet is connected to one cable. Under Grade 2, each outlet is connected to two cables.

If that brief précis of ANSI/TIA/EIA-507-A raised your eyebrows, rest assured that you're not alone. For most homes, Grade 1 far surpasses the typical requirements, and Grade 2 seems like serious overkill. But as home-entertainment electronics and computers continue to grow into each other's roles, many people will need to be able to transfer data easily from one part of their home to another. For example, having two cables running to each room will let you share video from one room to another without swamping your computer network. Or you can integrate your telephone system with the network, so that you can make voice calls from any room. (Or you may buy an Internet-enabled fridge.) Besides, when you're installing cable, the hardware costs—the cable itself, the wall plates, the patch panel—tend to be far less than the labor costs, so it makes sense to go all out if you can afford it.

A GREAT RESOURCE FOR CABLING YOUR OWN NETWORK

If you're a DIY person, you may not like the idea of paying a cabling contractor to do work that you can do yourself. But at the very least, invest in a book on cabling such as *Cabling: The Complete Guide to Network Wiring, Third Edition* (by David Groth, Jim McBee, and David Barnett; Sybex, 2004) that will help you analyze your requirements and learn the most efficient and cost-effective ways of fulfilling them.

DOING IT YOURSELF

When installing network cables yourself, approach the job as focused and rational as possible. Assess your needs. Work out the best placement for the switch or hub (or switches or hubs). Measure the distances involved. Round up the equipment. And then install the network.

Choosing the Location for the Switch or Hub

If your computers are spread out through your home (or another building), choosing a location for the switch or hub becomes a key decision. Ideally, in a small area, you'll use a single switch or hub to keep your network simple. But you can use multiple switches or hubs if necessary to avoid running a large number of wires running along the same course. Figure 27.1 shows an example of a network layout using two switches.

Real World Scenario

CONNECT ONE COMPUTER AT A TIME RATHER THAN ALL IN A GRAND SLAM

It's tempting to try to set up your whole network in a grand slam—pull all the cables, punch them down into wall plates or a patch panel, attach the computers and other devices, and then power on the whole lot at once. If everything works, you'll feel a wonderful surge of techno-potency (and you may even deserve it). But if everything doesn't work, you'll be facing a much more complex troubleshooting task than you should.

So it's much better to start small: Connect two computers, make sure everything's working, and then build from there, adding one computer at a time. Doing so will let you identify any problems far more easily and quickly than the grand-slam approach.

Each switch or hub needs to be powered, so the location will need to be within striking distance of a power outlet. Alternatively, look for a switch or hub that can use Power over Ethernet (PoE), drawing power via the Ethernet cable from another device.

Most switches and hubs have an *uplink port* or *cascade port* to which you can connect a regular Ethernet cable from a standard port on another switch or hub. (On some switches and hubs, there's a button to toggle one of the ports between being a standard port and an uplink port.) If the switch or hub doesn't have an uplink port, you can connect it by using a crossover cable to a standard port.

FIGURE 27.1

To avoid running long cables, you can use multiple switches connected by the uplink port or cascade port to the central switch.

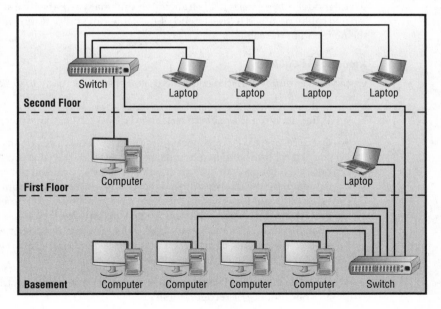

Measuring the Distances

Measure the distance that the cables will need to run from each computer to the hub. Be sure to include any vertical rises and drops that the cable run will need to include. Then, if you're cutting custom lengths of cable, allow a few feet extra on each cable to make sure they're long enough. (As with anything cut to length, you can always cut it shorter if necessary, but it's hard to make it longer.) If you're buying ready-made cable, buy the next longer length. You can always coil up any surplus length and stow it away discreetly.

Rounding Up the Equipment

Next, gather the equipment you need. At the minimum, you'll need a switch or hub and either ready-made patch cables of the appropriate lengths or a reel of cable, a cutting tool, and a cable stripper. If you're going to create your own patch cables, you'll need a crimping tool and an RJ-45 die for it. If you're going to bring the wires to a patch panel or wall plates, you'll need the panel or the plates and a matching punch-down tool for attaching the wires.

If you have to run cables through walls or between floors of a building, you'll need conventional builder's tools such as a drill and a Sheetrock saw.

For attaching cables to surfaces such as baseboards or floors, you'll need either a cable tacker (also known as a *cable stapler*) designed for the job and loaded with the right caliber of cable staples or a hammer and rigid cable clips (which you can get from a computer-supply store). For straight runs of cable, you may want to use *raceways* (wiring channels) and cable guards to hide the cables and give them some degree of protection. *Don't* use ordinary staples to secure cables, because it's very easy to drive them in too far and so damage the cable. (If you must use ordinary staples, do so with great care.)

For making sure the cables are working properly, a remote cable tester can save you a great deal of time and grief. A *remote cable tester* is a device into which you plug both ends of the cable you want to test and then send a signal through it to see if the wires are connected correctly. The most useful models have a detachable transmitter unit that you either use attached to the unit (for testing a patch cable) or attach to the far end of the cable run you're testing and then use the main unit on the near end of the cable.

Running the Cable

Once you've rounded up the equipment, you should be ready to get dirty. Here are basic tips for running cable:

◆ When securing the cable to baseboards, desks, floors, or other surfaces, do so carefully.

◆ Cat 5, 5e, or 6 UTP is reasonably resilient, but don't stress it any more than you must. When routing cable around baseboards, try not to bend it too sharply. If you end up pulling lengths of cable through wall or floor cavities yourself, be careful not to overstretch it, because that can degrade the quality of the signal or prevent the cable from working at all. You *can* get cable lubricant for greasing the cable's way around tight corners, but the lubricant means that not only does the cable tend to pick up any dirt it passes but it also sets into a facsimile of ancient crud in remarkably short order. You'll often do better to pull the cable in shorter stages (around one corner, then around a second) rather than longer stages (around both corners at once) to reduce the strain on the cable.

◆ When routing your cables, avoid electric wiring and any electrically noisy devices (such as air conditioning or refrigerators).

Connecting the Switch or Hub

Most switches and hubs have one or more lights for each port. At a minimum, most have a light to show whether the port is active. When you plug a cable into the switch or hub and into a functioning network card at the other end, the light should go on, showing that the cable is connected correctly.

Many dual- or triple-speed switches and hubs also have lights to show whether each port is running at 10Mbps, 100Mbps, or Gigabit (1,000Mbps) speed. Some switches and hubs also have lights to show whether the port is using full duplex or half duplex transmission. (Full duplex uses two pairs of wires to transmit data, while half duplex uses one pair.)

TROUBLESHOOTING: NO LIGHT ON SWITCH OR NETWORK CARD

If you don't get a light on the switch (or hub) or on the network card when you connect a computer or other device with a cable, the connection isn't working. Check the three candidates—the switch, the network card on the device, and the cabling—by taking the following steps:

1. Check that the switch is powered on. Chances are that it has a power light that will be on if it's getting power. If you've connected cables to other ports, those lights should be on.

2. Check that you're not using a crossover cable by mistake. Crossover cables can look exactly the same as regular patch cables, but they won't transmit data to a standard port. (Crossover cables can transmit data to an uplink port just fine. See the next section for a description of uplink ports.)

3. Check that you haven't plugged a standard patch cable into an uplink port.

4. Check the patch cable by using it to replace a patch cable that you know is good—for example, one that's connecting another computer to one of the ports on the switch. Replace the patch cable if it's bad.

5. If the patch cable works for the second computer, try connecting the first computer to a different port on the switch. If that works, you've got a bad port. If it doesn't work, you've got a bad network card. Replace the network card and try again.

6. If the switch, patch cable, and network card all check out okay, check your cabling, wall plates, and patch panel (if you have one). To test these most effectively, get a remote cable tester.

CONNECTING TWO COMPUTERS VIA A CROSSOVER CABLE

If you need to connect just two computers via Ethernet, you don't need a switch or hub. Instead, get a *crossover cable*—a cable that reverses the wires that send and receive signals so that connection doesn't need to pass through a switch or hub—and plug it into each network card, and you'll be done.

If the crossover cable isn't clearly marked as such, mark it before you forget, because otherwise crossover cables can be easy to confuse with regular Ethernet cables.

Configuring the Network Connections

Once you've connected a computer to the network, Windows tries to find a DHCP server on the network. The DHCP server can be a device such as a cable or DSL modem with built-in DHCP or a computer running Internet Connection Sharing.

If Windows finds a DHCP server, it requests an IP address from it; if it doesn't, it automatically allocates itself an IP address in the nonroutable 169.254.*n*.*n* subnet, and continues to look for a DHCP server at intervals to see if one has become available on the network.

Normally, you'll set up a DHCP server of some kind—for example, by adding a router or by sharing an Internet connection via ICS. You can also establish communication by configuring TCP/IP manually on your computers. See the section "Configuring TCP/IP Manually" in the next chapter for details.

CREATING A FIREWIRE NETWORK

By comparison with cabling an Ethernet network, cabling a FireWire network is simplicity itself: For two computers, you need only a cable, and for more computers, you need a FireWire hub and the appropriate number of cables. The length limit of FireWire cables (15 feet) further reduces the number of decisions you need to make.

If any of the computers you want to join to the network doesn't have a FireWire port, install a FireWire PCI card, PC Card, or CardBus card in it.

Then, with the computers running, connect each computer on the network to the next computer with one cable. Make sure that you don't connect any of the computers to any other computer with two cables.

Setting Up a Wireless Network

You have three main options when setting up a wireless network:

Ad hoc wireless network   If you have only a few computers, you can create an ad hoc wireless network—one without an access point. Ad hoc networks are suitable only for small numbers of computers. The following illustration shows an ad hoc network consisting of three computers, one of which is sharing an Internet connection with the other two.

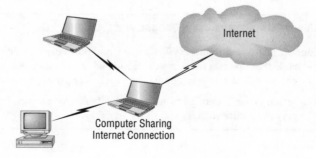

Internet

Computer Sharing
Internet Connection

Wireless-only network   If all your computers have wireless network adapters, you can make your entire network wireless, as in the following illustration, which shows a wireless network built around a DSL or cable router that includes a wireless access point. This type of network is also called an *infrastructure* network.

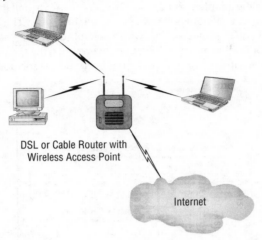

DSL or Cable Router with
Wireless Access Point

Internet

Wired and wireless network   For the best performance and flexibility, you can implement a wired network for those computers that don't need to move (or which you can reach easily with cables) and connect to that network a wireless network for the computers that need to move around (or which are in inaccessible locations). The following illustration shows two desktop computers connected through a switch to a cable or DSL router with a built-in wireless access point, to which two laptop computers connect wirelessly. Depending on the number of wired network ports you need, you may be able to simply use a router that has a switch built in as well.

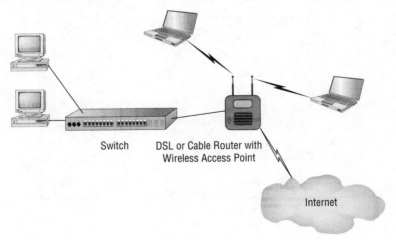

Switch   DSL or Cable Router with
Wireless Access Point

Internet

Setting Up an Ad Hoc Wireless Network

To set up an ad hoc wireless network, follow these steps:

1. Install a wireless network adapter in each computer that doesn't already have one. When Windows notices the adapter, you'll see a Driver Software Installation pop-up message above the notification area as Windows searches for a suitable driver. The Found New Hardware Wizard may prompt you to provide a disk with a suitable driver, as shown here. If so, follow through the process of finding and installing the driver. When the Found New Hardware Wizard tells you that to the software for the device has been successfully installed, click the Close button.

2. Choose Start ➤ Connect To. Windows launches the Connect to a Network Wizard, which displays a list of the available networks. If you're just starting to set up an ad hoc wireless network, you'll probably see the message "Windows cannot find any networks," as shown here.

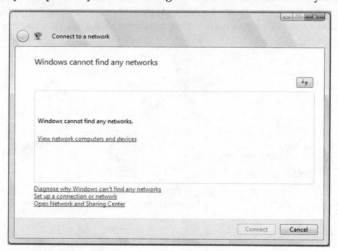

3. Click the Set Up a Connection or Network link near the bottom of the window. The wizard displays the Choose a Connection Option window, as shown here.

4. Click the Set Up a Wireless Ad Hoc (Computer-to-Computer) Network item in the list box, and then click the Next button. The wizard displays the Set Up a Wireless Ad Hoc Network window, as shown here.

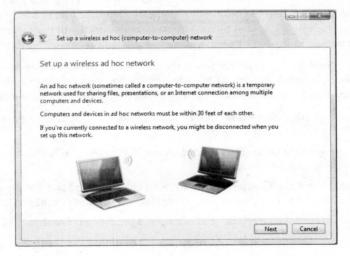

5. Click the Next button. The wizard displays the Give Your Network a Name and Choose Security Options window, as shown here.

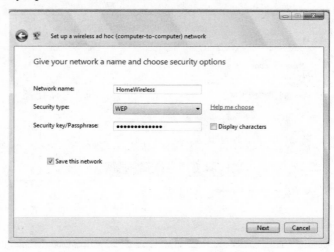

6. Type the name for the network in the Network Name text box. The name can be from 1 to 32 characters long, so you can make it descriptive.

7. In the Security Type drop-down list, select the WEP item. The alternative, No Authentication (Open), leaves your network wholly unsecured, which is never a good idea for a wireless network hosted by a computer. (Sometimes you may want to create open wireless networks hosted by access points—for example, for community use.)

8. In the Security Key/Passphrase text box, type the password that you will use to secure the network. Select the Display Characters check box if you want to make sure you're actually typing the characters you intend. The password can be any of the following:

5 case-sensitive characters For example, w1Rez. Five-character passwords are easy to break, so you shouldn't use them.

13 case-sensitive characters For example, RWirelessNet7. Thirteen-character passwords provide reasonable security.

10 hexadecimal characters Hexadecimal characters are the numbers 0–9 and the letters A–F. These characters are not case sensitive. For example, a1b2c3d4e5.

26 hexadecimal characters For example, a1b2c3d4e5f6ababac21863dae.

9. Select the Save This Network check box if you want to save this network for future use.

10. Click the Next button. The wizard sets up the network, and then displays a screen saying that the network is ready to use, as shown here.

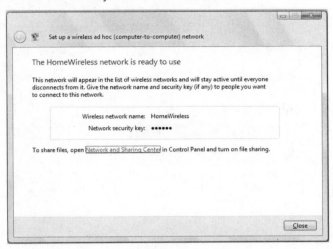

11. Click the Close button. The wizard closes.

Setting Up a Wireless-Only Network or a Wired-and-Wireless Network

To set up a wireless-only network or a wireless network that's attached to a wired network, begin by setting up the wireless access point. Once the access point is configured and operational, your next step will be to set up each of the computers that will connect to the wireless access point.

Most new and recent access points support USB flash drive configuration, which is usually the easiest way of configuring an access point and the computers that connect to it. Windows automates the process of defining the parameters for the network and saving them to a USB flash drive attached to the computer. You then plug the USB flash drive into the access point to load the network settings on the access point.

Other access points don't support USB flash drive configuration but do let you connect them directly to your computer via an Ethernet cable and configure them using the Set Up a Connection or Network Wizard. (The connection between the computer and the access must normally be direct, not through a switch or an existing network.) If your access point doesn't support USB flash drive configuration and requires custom setup, see the sidebar "Setting Up an Older Access Point."

To set up a wireless access point that supports USB flash drive configuration, follow these steps:

1. Click the Start button, right-click the Network item, and then choose Properties from the context menu. Windows displays a Network and Sharing Center window.

2. In the left panel, click the Set Up a Connection or Network link. Windows launches the Set Up a Connection or Network Wizard, which displays the Choose a Connection Option screen, as shown here.

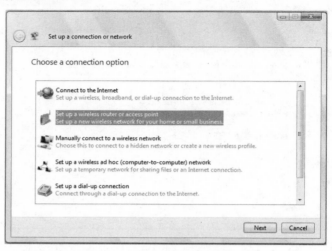

3. Select the Set Up a Wireless Router or Access Point item, and then click the Next button. The wizard displays the Set Up a Home or Small Business Network window, which provides information about what the wizard does.

4. Click the Next button, and then authenticate yourself to User Account Control. The wizard attempts to detect the wireless access point, as shown here.

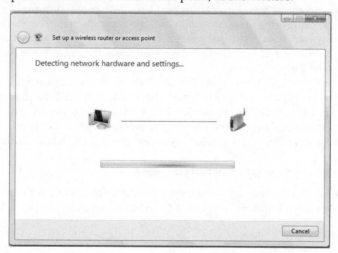

5. If you're using USB flash drive configuration and the wireless access point isn't connected to your computer, the wizard won't be able to find the access point, so it displays the Windows Did Not Detect Any Wireless Network Hardware window, as shown here.

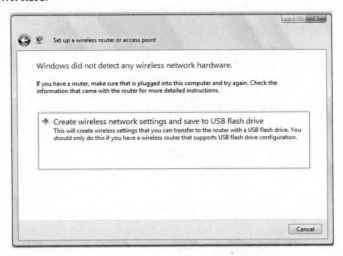

6. Click the Create Wireless Network Settings and Save to USB Flash Drive button. The wizard displays the Give Your Network a Name window, as shown here.

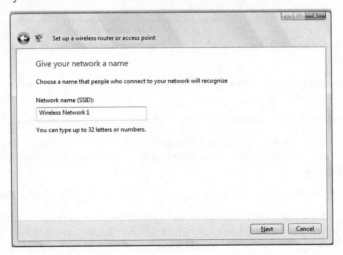

7. In the Network Name (SSID) text box, type a name for your network. Choose a name that you and other users will be able to identify easily but discreet enough that someone snooping the network from outside wouldn't necessarily be able to identify you or your dwelling from the name. (For example, if your name is Robertson and you live at 4455 Maple Street, calling your network Robertson4455Maple would be less than discreet.) You can use up to 32 characters in the network name.

8. Click the Next button. The wizard displays the Help Make Your Network More Secure with a Passphrase window, as shown here.

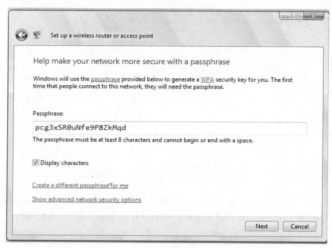

9. Examine the passphrase in the Passphrase text box and decide whether you want to use it or generate another:

   ◆ A random passphrase is more secure but harder to type than one composed of real words.

   ◆ The passphrase must be at least 8 characters long and can be up to 63 characters.

   ◆ The longer the passphrase, the more secure the network should be, but a passphrase of around 20 random characters should be plenty long enough for conventional purposes.

   ◆ To generate another passphrase, click the Create a Different Passphrase for Me link.

   ◆ If you want to choose a specific type of wireless network security, click the Show Advanced Network Security Options link. The wizard displays the Choose Advanced Network Security Options window, as shown next. Choose WPA-Personal, WPA2-Personal, WEP, or No Security in the Security Method drop-down list. WPA2-Personal is the most secure choice provided that your wireless network equipment supports it. Either accept the suggested passphrase in the Security Key or Passphrase text box, type a new passphrase if you are choosing, or click the Create a Different Security Key or Passphrase for Me link to have the wizard create another.

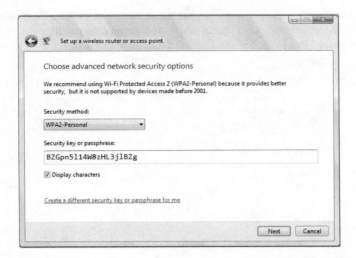

10. In either the Help Make Your Network More Secure with a Passphrase window or the Choose Advanced Network Security Options window, click the Next button. The wizard displays the Choose File and Printer Sharing Options window, as shown here.

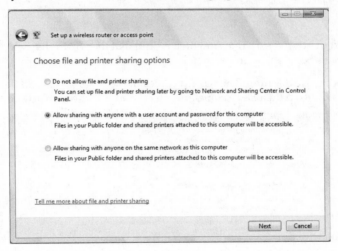

11. Choose whether to allow file and printer sharing on the network:

   Do Not Allow File and Printer Sharing   This option is the most secure. The computers on the network can connect to the Internet through the network but not to each other. You can set up file and printer sharing manually on each computer that needs it.

   Allow Sharing with Anyone with a User Account and Password for This Computer   This option lets you restrict sharing to those who can provide a correct user name and password for any computer they're trying to access from another computer.

Allow Sharing with Anyone on the Same Network as This Computer This option lets anyone logged onto a computer connected to the network access the contents of any other computer's Public folder and any shared printers.

12. Click the Next button. The wizard displays the Insert the USB Flash Drive into This Computer window, as shown here.

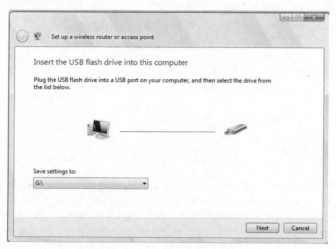

13. Insert the USB flash drive, and then ensure that the wizard has selected the correct drive in the Save Settings To drop-down list. If not, select the correct drive.

14. Click the Next button. The wizard copies the settings to the USB flash drive, and then displays the To Add a Device or Computer, Follow These Instructions screen, as shown here.

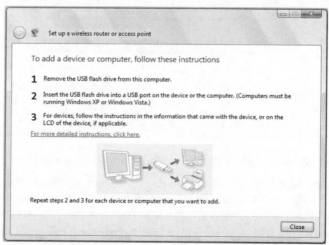

15. Click the Close button. The wizard closes.

16. Unplug the USB flash drive from the computer, and then plug it into the USB port on your wireless access point. Wait 30 seconds, or until the access point's lights flash three times (or gives another signal detailed in its manual), and then unplug it.

17. Plug the USB flash drive into each computer you want to add to the network, in turn:

- Windows displays the AutoPlay dialog box, as shown here.

- Click the Wireless Network Setup Wizard link. The wizard displays its first screen, as shown here.

- Click the OK button. The wizard adds the computer to the network, and then displays a message box to let you know it has done so, as shown here.

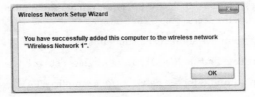

- Click the OK button. The wizard closes.
- Unplug the USB flash drive from the computer.

 **Real World Scenario**

SETTING UP AN OLDER ACCESS POINT

If you have an older wireless access point that doesn't support USB flash drive configuration, you'll need to use a different setup procedure than the one described in the main text. The procedure depends on the make and model, but these steps are fairly typical:

1. Unpack the access point and connect its power supply.

2. Connect one end of an Ethernet cable to the access point's Ethernet port and the other end to an Ethernet port on your computer. If your computer was connected to the Internet through the Ethernet port, you'll lose your Internet connection while you set up the access point.

3. Change your computer's TCP/IP setup for that Ethernet port to use the same subnet as the access point's preconfigured IP address, which you'll find in the documentation. For example:

   ◆ Click the Start button, right-click the Network item, and then choose Properties from the context menu. Windows displays a Network and Sharing Center window.

   ◆ Click the Manage Network Connections link in the left panel. Windows displays a Network Connections window.

   ◆ Right-click the Ethernet connection (for example, the Local Area Connection item), choose Properties from the context menu, and then authenticate yourself to User Account Control. Windows displays the Properties dialog box for the connection.

   ◆ In the This Connection Uses the Following Items list box on the Networking tab, double-click the Internet Protocol Version 4 (TCP/IPv4) item. Windows displays the Internet Protocol Version 4 (TCP/IPv4) Properties dialog box.

   ◆ Select the Use the Following IP Address option button, and then fill in the IP address, subnet mask, and default gateway required for connecting to the access point.

   ◆ Click the OK button to close each dialog box in turn.

4. Open a web browser, enter the access point's IP address in the Address bar, and then press Enter.

5. Log on to the access point using the credentials given in the documentation, and then use your web browser to configure the access point. For example:

   ◆ Set the access point's IP address and subnet mask.

   ◆ Set the service set identifier (SSID) for the wireless network.

   ◆ Choose security options for the network (for example, WPA).

   ◆ Set any routing information required.

◆ Choose whether the access point will run DHCP to allocate IP addresses to the computers that connect to the network. In a wireless-only network, or in a wireless-and-wired network in which the switch is integrated into the access point, you'll probably want the access point to handle DHCP. In a wireless-and-wired network that has other wired components, you may prefer to have another component (for example, a DSL router and switch) handle DHCP.

6. Restart the access point to write the new settings to its flash memory and put them into effect.

7. Disconnect the Ethernet connection from the access point.

8. Restore your computer's network connection and its TCP/IP setup.

9. Connect your computers to the wireless network using the manual technique described in the section "Adding a Wireless Network Manually," later in this chapter.

Connecting to a Wireless Network

To connect to a wireless network that is already running on another computer or access point, take the following steps:

1. Choose Start ➢ Connect To. (You can also click the network icon or the signal-strength icon in the notification area, and then click either the Wireless Networks Are Available notice in the pop-up window or the Connect to a Network link.) Windows launches the Connect to a Network Wizard, which displays the Select a Network to Connect To window, as shown here.

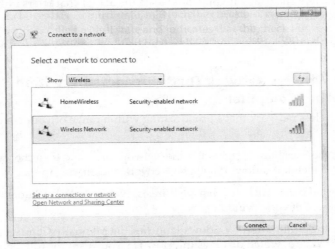

2. If necessary, choose Wireless in the Show drop-down list to restrict the display to only wireless networks. (If wireless networks are the only ones that are available, you may not need to do this.)

3. Select the network in the list, and then click the Connect button. The wizard displays the Type the Network Security Key or Passphrase window, as shown here.

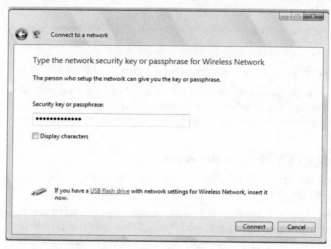

4. In the Security Key or Passphrase text box, type the password. Select the Display Characters check box if you want to see the actual characters rather than security-conscious dots.

5. Click the Connect button. The wizard establishes the connection to the network.

Adding a Wireless Network That's Broadcasting within Range of Your Computer

To add a wireless network that's broadcasting within range of your computer, follow these steps:

1. Click the Start button, right-click the Network item, and then choose Properties from the context menu. Windows displays a Network and Sharing Center window.

2. In the left panel, click the Manage Wireless Networks link. Windows displays the Manage Wireless Networks window.

3. Click the Add button. Windows launches the Manually Connect to a Wireless Network Wizard, which displays the How Do You Want to Add a Network? window, as shown here.

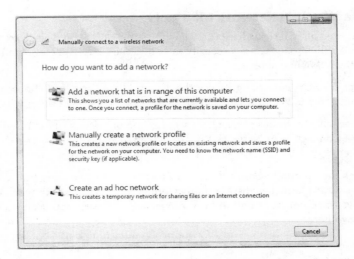

4. Click the Add a Network That Is in Range of This Computer button. The wizard displays the Select a Network to Connect To window, as shown here. You can choose Wireless in the Show drop-down list if you need to cut the list down to only wireless networks rather than all types of networks.

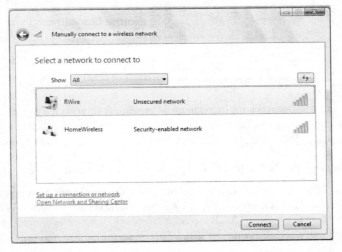

5. Click the desired network, and then click the Connect button. The wizard attempts to connect to the network, prompting you for a password if one is needed. After establishing the connection, the wizard displays a window telling you that the network is ready for use.

6. Click the Close button. The wizard closes, returning you to the Manage Wireless Networks window, in which the list of networks now includes the network you just added.

Adding a Wireless Network Manually

If you've turned off SSID broadcasts on the wireless network, you'll need to connect to it manually. (Turning off SSID broadcasts is a security measure. See Chapter 29 for details.) To connect manually, take the following steps:

1. Click the Start button, right-click the Network item, and then choose Properties from the context menu. Windows displays a Network and Sharing Center window.

2. In the left panel, click the Set Up a Connection or Network link. Windows launches the Set Up a Connection or Network Wizard, which displays the Choose a Connection Option screen.

3. Click the Manually Connect to a Wireless Network item, and then click the Next button. The wizard launches the Manually Connect to a Wireless Network Wizard, which displays the Enter Information for the Wireless Network You Want to Add window, as shown here.

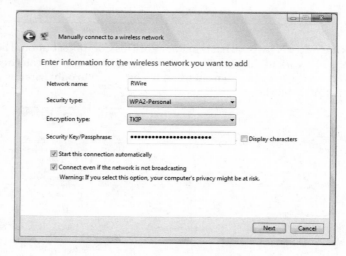

4. In the Network Name text box, type the network's name.

5. In the Security Type drop-down list, select the appropriate type of security: No Authentication (Open), WEP, WPA2-Personal, WPA-Personal, WPA2-Enterprise, WPA-Enterprise, or 802.1x. For a home network, your choices are most likely WPA2-Personal or WPA-Personal.

6. If the Encryption Type drop-down list is available, choose the appropriate encryption type. For example, for WPA2-Personal or for WPA-Personal, you can choose TKIP (Temporal Key Integrity Protocol) or AES (Advanced Encryption Standard). For WEP, there are no choices.

7. In the Security Key/Passphrase text box, type the passphrase (except for an open network). Select the Display Characters check box if you want to see the characters you're typing instead of dots.

8. Select the Start This Connection Automatically check box if you want Windows to connect automatically to this network when it's in range.

9. Select the Connect Even if the Network Is Not Broadcasting check box if you want to connect to the network even if it's not broadcasting its SSID. If you know that SSID broadcasting is turned off on the access point, select this check box—if you don't, you won't be able to connect to the network. The Warning that Windows gives about this option refers to the possibility that the data your computer sends in trying to connect to the network could be captured by someone who could use it to spoof the access point's identity, causing your computer to connect to a fake network instead of a real one.

10. Click the Next button. The wizard displays the Successfully Added *Network* window (where *Network* is the network's name), as shown here.

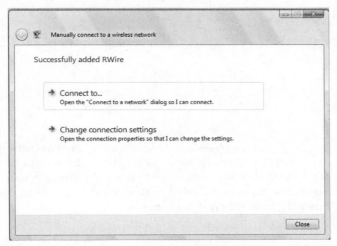

11. Click the appropriate button:

   ◆ Click the Connect To button if you want to open the Connect To window so that you connect to the network.

   ◆ Click the Change Connection Settings button if you want to display the Properties dialog box for the connection so that you can change some of the settings you just chose. You shouldn't normally need to do this; if you do, see the next section for details.

   ◆ Otherwise, click the Close button. The wizard closes.

Managing Your Wireless Networks

If your computer connects only to a single wireless network, you may be able to set it up and then use it without needing to change it. But if your computer connects to two or more networks, you'll need to choose the order in which to connect to them. You may also need to change the passphrase or security type required to connect to a network.

To make such changes, use the Manage Wireless Networks window. Take the following steps:

1. Click the Start button, right-click the Network item, and then choose Properties from the context menu. Windows displays a Network and Sharing Center window.

2. In the left panel, click the Manage Wireless Networks link. Windows displays the Manage Wireless Networks window, as shown here.

3. In the Networks You Can View and Modify list box, drag the networks into the order in which you want Windows to try to connect to them. Put your preferred network at the top of the list. You can also change the order by using the Move Up button and Move Down button on the toolbar or by right-clicking a network and then choosing Move Up or Move Down (as appropriate) from the context menu.

4. To add a network to the network list, follow these steps:

   ◆ Click the Add button. Windows launches the Manually Connect to a Wireless Network Wizard, which displays the How Do You Want to Add a Network? window.

   ◆ If you know the network is broadcasting its SSID, click the Add a Network That Is in Range of This Computer button. Follow the procedure described in the section "Adding a Wireless Network That's Broadcasting within Range of Your Computer," earlier in this chapter.

   ◆ If the network isn't broadcasting its SSID, click the Manually Create a Network Profile button. The wizard displays the Enter Information for the Wireless Network You Want to Add window. Follow the steps in the section "Adding a Wireless Network Manually," earlier in this chapter.

5. To remove a network from the list, click the network, and then click the Remove button. Windows displays the Manage Wireless Networks – Warning! dialog box, as shown next. Click the OK button if you're sure you want to remove the network.

6. To change the properties for an existing network (for example, if the network starts using a different security type or passphrase), follow these steps:

◆ In the Networks You Can View and Modify list box, right-click the network you want to change, and then choose Properties from the context menu. Windows displays the Wireless Network Properties dialog box for the network.

◆ On the Connection page (shown on the left in Figure 27.2), you can select or clear the Connect Automatically When This Network Is in Range check box, the Connect to a More Preferred Network if Available check box, and the Connect Even if the Network Is Not Broadcasting check box.

◆ On the Security page (shown on the right in Figure 27.2), you can choose the security type and encryption type, and enter a new network security key.

◆ When you've finished choosing settings, click the OK button. Windows closes the Wireless Network Properties dialog box for the network.

FIGURE 27.2
Use the Connection page (left) and the Security page (right) of the Wireless Network Properties dialog box to configure an existing wireless network.

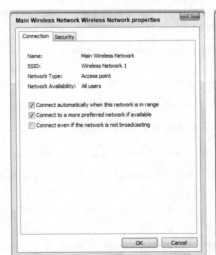 

7. By default, Windows makes each wireless network connection you create available to all users of your computer. Normally, this behavior is useful, because it means that Windows doesn't have to close down the network connection when you switch users. But sometimes you may need to prevent other users from using one of your wireless connections. When you do, take the following steps:

◆ In the Manage Wireless Networks window, click the Profile Types button on the toolbar. Windows displays the Wireless Network Profile Type dialog box, as shown here.

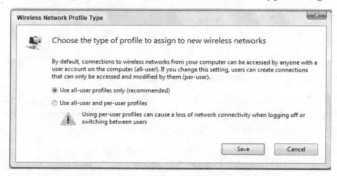

◆ Select the Use All-User and Per-User Profiles option button instead of the Use All-User Profiles Only option button.

◆ Click the Save button, and then authenticate yourself to User Account Control.

◆ From now on, when you create a wireless network connection, Windows includes two more option buttons in the controls for setting up the network. Select the Save This Network for Me Only option button if you want to keep the network to yourself. Select the Save This Network for All Users of this Computer option button if you want to make the network available to all users.

8. When you've finished managing your wireless networks, click the Close button (the × button).

 **Real World Scenario**

ADDING A PRINTER TO A WIRELESS-ONLY NETWORK

You can add a printer to a wireless network in any of the following ways:

◆ Get a printer that includes built-in wireless networking. You can then send print jobs to the printer directly over your wireless network.

◆ Get a wireless access point that includes a USB or Ethernet port to which you can connect the printer.

◆ Connect the printer to one of the computers participating in the network and share it from there. The printer will be available only when the computer is powered on and not sleeping.

◆ Connect the printer to a wireless print server and position it wherever best suits the needs of the users who will use it.

Browsing the Network

To browse the network that the Network Setup Wizard has created, choose Start ➢ Network. Windows displays a Network window showing the computers on the network, as in the example here.

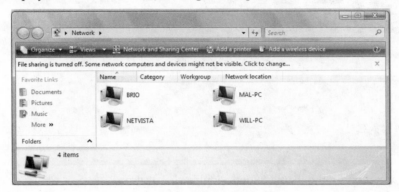

If the window includes an Information Bar below the toolbar telling you that "File sharing is turned off. Some network computers and devices might not be visible," you'll need to turn on Discovery and Sharing to see the rest of the network. To do so, click the Information Bar, choose Turn On Network Discovery and File Sharing from the pop-up menu, and then authenticate yourself to User Account Control.

Double-click a computer's icon to display the folders and resources that computer is sharing. If Windows displays a Connect To box, as shown here, type the username and password, select the Remember My Password check box if you want Windows to store the password, and then click the OK button.

ADDING THE NETWORK ITEM TO YOUR START MENU

If the Network item doesn't appear on your Start menu, you can add it by taking the following steps:

1. Right-click the Start button, and then choose Properties from the context menu. Windows displays the Start Menu page of the Taskbar and Start Menu Properties dialog box.

2. Click the upper Customize button. Windows displays the Customize Start Menu dialog box.

3. Select the Network check box.

4. Click the OK button to close each dialog box.

Once you've connected to the computer, the window shows the shared folders and resources (such as printers), as shown here.

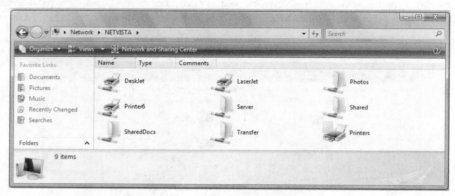

To access one of the shared folders, double-click its icon.

TROUBLESHOOTING: UNABLE TO BROWSE THE NETWORK

If you're unable to browse the network or access resources on it, take the following steps to troubleshoot it. This procedure assumes that your network is using TCP/IP version 4, Windows's standard networking protocol for local area networks.

1. Check that your switch or hub is powered on, that the necessary cables are connected, and that the lights for the relevant ports are lit. (If the lights aren't on, see the sidebar "Troubleshooting: No Light on Hub or Network Card," earlier in this chapter.)

2. Choose Start ➢ All Programs ➢ Accessories ➢ Command Prompt to open a command-prompt window, and then ping the loopback address for your network adapter to see if it's working: Type `ping 127.0.0.1`, and then press the Enter key. You should get four `Reply from 127.0.0.1` packets in response. If not, your network adapter isn't working. Press Windows Key+Break to open a System window, and then click the Device Manager item in the left pane and authenticate yourself to User Account Control. In the Device Manager window, expand the Network Adapters item, and ensure that Windows thinks the network adapter is working. If the adapter's icon has an exclamation point or a question mark, you may need to change the driver for the adapter, uninstall and reinstall the adapter, or (if Windows doesn't support the adapter) get a new adapter.

3. In the command-prompt window, type `ipconfig` and press the Enter key to get a readout of the IP addresses assigned to the network adapters on your computer.

4. Next, ping the IP address for your computer—for example, `ping 192.168.0.99` (and press the Enter key). Again, you should get four replies in the format `Reply from 192.168.0.99`. If not, the problem is with the network card on your computer.

5. If pinging your computer works, run the `ipconfig` command on another computer on the network to find out its IP address. Make sure that Discovery and Sharing is turned on for that computer, and then ping that IP address from the first computer. If that works, make sure that Discovery and Sharing is turned on for the first computer, and then ping the first computer from the second. If you can ping each computer from the other by IP address, but you can't connect by browsing from Explorer, open the System Properties dialog box and check on the Computer Name page that the computers belong to the same workgroup. If not, make the workgroups match. If you can't ping one computer from another, the problem lies in the physical network connection. Double-check the network connections, the cables, and the hub.

6. Ping the other computer by its hostname to test hostname resolution. Again, you should get four replies in the format "`Reply from.`" If you get the message "Ping request could not find host *hostname*" or "Unable to resolve target name system," the problem lies with your DNS server (for example, the DNS service supplied by Internet Connection Sharing).

Mapping and Disconnecting Network Drives

You can access a shared folder, as described in the previous section, by opening the Network folder, and then navigating through the computer down to the folder. But if you need to access the folder frequently or quickly, and especially if the folder is buried deep within the folder structure, you can save time and effort by mapping a network drive to the folder. By mapping the network drive, you essentially tell Windows that you want to refer to the folder as (say) `Z:` instead of (say) `\\COMPUTER1\Documents\Reading\Recommended\Plain Text\`. Mapping the drive makes it not only easier to connect but also faster, because Windows keeps a connection open to the shared folder (as long as the folder is available).

The two backslash characters at the beginning of that share name are part of the Universal Naming Convention (UNC for short). The two backslashes indicate the name of the server (the computer providing the shared service).

You can map as many network drives as you have free letters of the alphabet on your computer. Windows automatically starts mapping drives with the letter Z, then walks backward through the alphabet with each subsequent drive. But you can override Windows's choice of drive letter with one of your own if you prefer.

Mapping a Network Drive

To map a network drive, take the following steps:

1. Choose Start ➤ Computer. Windows displays a Computer window.

2. Click the Map Network Drive button on the toolbar. Windows displays the Map Network Drive dialog box, as shown here.

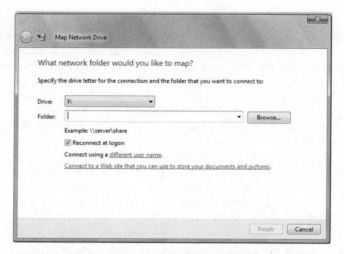

3. In the Drive drop-down list, select the drive letter you want to use. The list shows all currently unused letters. By default, Windows selects the last available letter.

4. Enter the path and folder name in the Folder text box.

◆ You can type in the path or (when you've mapped drives before) choose it from the drop-down list, but usually it's easier to click the Browse button, use the Browse for Folder dialog box (shown here) to select the folder, and then click the OK button.

◆ The Browse for Folder dialog box displays the Network tree. You can drill down through this tree to the local network, the computers on it, and the folders they contain. If a Windows Vista computer is sharing files, you'll see a Public folder under the computer's entry, as on MAL-PC here. If a Windows XP computer is sharing files, you'll see a `SharedDocs` folder under its entry, as on NETVISTA here. The `Printers` folder appears on any computer that's sharing one or more printers.

5. If you want Windows to try to reconnect the network drive each time you log on, select the Reconnect at Logon check box.

6. By default, Windows tries to log on to the network drive using the username and password (if any) under which you're currently logged on. To log on to the network drive under a different username, take the following steps:

   ◆ Click the Connect Using a Different User Name link. Windows displays the Connect As dialog box (shown here).

   ◆ Type the username in the User Name text box. If the network drive is in a different workgroup than the workgroup your computer is currently in, specify the network drive's workgroup and the appropriate username in it. For example, to use the username `Rikki` in the workgroup `Group2`, use `\\Group2\Rikki`.

   ◆ Type the password for the username in the Password text box.

   ◆ Click the OK button. Windows closes the Connect As dialog box, returning you to the Map Network Drive dialog box.

7. Click the Finish button. Windows connects the network drive to the specified folder and closes the Map Network Drive dialog box.

   ◆ If Windows can't find the folder you specified by typing in the Folder text box, it displays a Windows message box telling you the problem, as shown here. Click the OK button. Windows closes the message box and returns you to the Map Network Drive dialog box so that you can try again.

◆ If Windows can't connect the drive because the username is invalid or the password is wrong, it displays a Connect To dialog box telling you the problem, as shown here. Correct the username or password, and then click the OK button to try again.

MAPPING A NETWORK DRIVE TO A FOLDER YOU'VE FOUND BY BROWSING THE NETWORK

Instead of using the procedure described in these steps, you can browse through the network by using the Folders pane until you find the network drive or folder to which you want to connect. Then right-click the drive or folder and choose Map Network Drive from the context menu, as shown here.

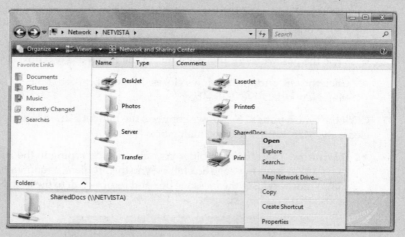

Windows displays the Map Network Drive dialog box with the computer's name and the folder's path entered already.

Reconnecting a Network Drive at Logon

If you selected the Reconnect at Logon check box in the Map Network Drive dialog box when mapping the drive, Windows tries to reestablish the network mapping each time you log on.

If Windows isn't able to connect a network drive, it displays a pop-up in the notification area telling you so. Click the pop-up to display a Computer window showing all the drives. Check which drives Windows wasn't able to reconnect, and reconnect them manually if they're available. (The usual reason for not being able to reconnect a network drive is that the computer it's on is currently not sharing it—for example, because someone has switched it off.)

Disconnecting a Network Drive

To disconnect a network drive you've mapped, take the following steps:

1. Choose Start ➢ Computer. Windows opens a Computer window showing the drives on your computer.

2. Right-click the network drive you want to disconnect, and then choose Disconnect from the context menu.

If you don't have any files or folders open on the drive you're disconnecting, Windows simply disconnects the drive and removes it from the Computer window. If you do have any files or folders open on the drive or drives, Windows displays an Error dialog box as shown here to warn you that you may lose data if you disconnect the drive while files are open. Click the Yes button if you want to proceed. Click the No button if you want to close the files before you disconnect the drive.

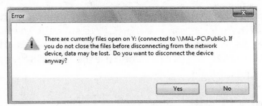

Connecting Mac and Linux Clients to the Network

This section gives brief details on connecting Mac and Linux clients to your Windows network.

Connecting Mac Clients

Mac OS X can connect directly to servers running the Server Message Block (SMB) protocol. (SMB is the native sharing protocol for Windows operating systems. Linux can provide SMB sharing as well if you use its Samba utility.) The easiest way to connect to a server is to follow these steps:

1. Click the Desktop to activate the Finder.

2. Choose Go ➢ Network. Mac OS X opens a Network window.

3. Click the group that contains the server—for example, your workgroup or the My Network item.

4. Navigate to the computer that's sharing the drive, and then click the Connect button.

5. Provide your username and password for the server when prompted, and then click the OK button.

You can then connect to the drive by using the Finder as you would for any other networked drive. To disconnect from the drive, either click its Eject button in a Finder window or simply drag it to the Trash.

USE NETWORK UTILITY'S PING TO TEST CONNECTIVITY

If your SMB connection seems not to be working, use the Mac OS X Network Utility to ping the IP address of the Windows (or Linux) computer to make sure it's accessible. You will need to turn on Discovery and Sharing on the Windows computer before a Mac or a computer running Linux can see it.

To share folders on your Mac with your Windows computers, take the following steps:

1. Click the Apple menu and choose System Preferences. Mac OS X displays the System Preferences window.

2. Click the Sharing icon. Mac OS X displays the Sharing page.

3. Select the Windows Sharing check box on the Services subpage. Mac OS X starts Windows sharing and displays the address at which you can access the shared folders.

4. Click the System Preferences menu and choose Quit System Preferences. Mac OS X closes the System Preferences window.

To give a Mac access to the Internet through Internet Connection Sharing (ICS), open the Network control panel in System Preferences, click the TCP/IP subtab, and select Using DHCP in the Configure IPv4 drop-down list. Alternatively, manually assign the Mac an IP address in the 192.168.0.*x* subnet (192.168.0.0 to 192.168.0.255). Don't use the 192.168.0.1 address, because the computer running ICS claims that for itself.

Connecting Linux Clients

To enable a Linux client to access shared folders on a Windows computer, you have several options:

◆ Use a mount -t smbfs command to mount a shared folder on the Windows computer to a mount point on the Linux client.

◆ Use a smbmount command to mount a shared folder on the Windows computer to a mount point on the Linux client. (Using smbmount is very similar to using mount -t smbfs, but smbmount sometimes works when mount -t smbfs won't work, so it's worth keeping in mind as an alternative.)

◆ Use smbclient to attach to a shared folder. smbclient has the advantage of being much less ticklish than the previous two options, so it almost always works, even when they don't. The disadvantage is that when you make a connection via smbclient, you're stuck with using FTP-like commands to manage files. For example, you can use get and mget to copy files from the Windows computer and put and mput to copy files to it.

So far, so good—but that's only one-way traffic. If you need the Windows computers to be able to access files on the Linux computer, set up Samba on the Linux computer. Some Linux distributions (for example, Xandros) have graphical Samba-configuration utilities that make it easy to set up sharing, but others require you to edit configuration files and that requires much more effort.

You can give a Linux computer access to the Internet through ICS in the same way as you can a Mac. Either configure it to use DHCP or manually assign it an IP address in the 192.168.0.*x* subnet (192.168.0.0 to 192.168.0.255). Again, don't use the 192.168.0.1 address, because the computer running ICS will be using it.

The Bottom Line

Install a wired network Install a network interface card in each computer that doesn't already have one. Position the switch in a convenient central location, and then connect each computer to a port on the switch using a network cable. Power on the switch, power on the computers, and install such drivers as are needed.

Set up a wireless network Choose among an ad hoc wireless network, a wireless-only network, and a combination wired and wireless network. For an ad hoc network, install a wireless network adapter in each computer that doesn't already have one, launch the Connect to a Network Wizard, and follow through the Set Up a Wireless Ad Hoc (Computer-to-Computer) Network procedure. For a wireless-only network or a combination network, set up the access point and then the computers. The easiest way to configure the network is to run the Set Up a Network or Connection Wizard, save the settings to a USB flash drive, and then transfer the settings to the access point, the computers, and any other USB-configurable wireless devices that will take part in the network.

Browse the network Choose Start ➢ Network to open a Network window showing the computers on the network. You may need to turn on Discover and Sharing to see all the networks.

Map and disconnect network drives To map a network drive, choose Start ➢ Computer, click the Map Network Drive button on the toolbar, specify the path and folder, and then click the Finish button. To disconnect a network drive, right-click it in the Computer window, and then choose Disconnect from the context menu.

Connect Mac and Linux clients to the network You can connect a Mac OS X computer to a shared folder by activating the Finder, clicking the Desktop, choosing Go ➢ Network, navigating to the computer, clicking the Connect button, and then providing your user name and password. To connect a Linux computer to a shared folder, use a `mount -t smbfs` command, a `smbmount` command, or use `smbclient`. Some Linux distributions come configured to connect to Windows networks right out of the box.

Chapter 28

Sharing Resources on Your Network

◆ Connect your network to the Internet

◆ Share files or folders with other network users

◆ Allow other network users to print to your printer

◆ Configure networks, network connections, and network components

In the previous chapter, you saw how to create a basic network configuration for sharing resources, including folders, printers, and an Internet connection. This chapter discusses how to share (and unshare) resources manually. So if you set up your network and connected it to the Internet in the previous chapter, and everything is fine, you can probably ignore this chapter for now.

But if you need (or want) to perform some manual configuration, here's what this chapter contains: First, it shows you how to share your Internet connection and how to use an Internet connection that another computer is sharing. Next, it moves on to sharing printers connected to your computer and using printers shared by other computers, mapping a drive by using the `net use` command, and configuring network components manually. It ends by discussing how to bridge two networks together or merge them into a single network.

Connecting Your Network to the Internet

If you have a home network that you haven't yet connected to the Internet, you'll probably want to connect it to the Internet through a shared Internet connection so that each of the computers can send e-mail, browse the Web, and enjoy instant messaging and the other delights of the wired.

This section discusses the pros and cons of connecting your network to the Internet, ways of doing so, and considerations to keep in mind. As you'll see, you need to answer several questions, and the answers to the questions are related. The next section discusses how to implement Windows's Internet Connection Sharing (ICS) feature, should you choose that as your way of connecting your network to the Internet.

Should You Connect Your Network to the Internet?

Instead of connecting the whole network through a single Internet connection, you can let individual computers connect through their own Internet connections. Doing so has the following advantages:

◆ If you can access the Internet only via dial-up, and you have multiple phone lines, you may prefer to have each computer connect separately so that each computer can enjoy as fast a connection speed as possible. Sharing, say, a 29.6Kbps connection among three or four computers will be no fun for anyone. (Alternatively, you can establish a multilink connection and share that connection—if your Internet service provider, or ISP, supports multilink.)

- Each computer that connects directly to the Internet can run programs that have difficulty running via a shared connection protected with a firewall—for example, some games.

- You can restrict use of the Internet to those computers that have a direct connection.

Having computers connect to the Internet individually has the following disadvantages:

- If the computers are trying to connect to the Internet by using the same phone line, only one will be able to connect at a time. If the computers are using separate phone lines, you'll need to pay for those phone lines. You'll probably also have to pay for multiple ISP accounts rather than just one account.

- Having more computers connect to the Internet increases the number of points at which your network can be attacked. (Chapter 29 discusses how to secure your network, but reducing the number of attack points is a good start.)

Should You Use Multiple IP Addresses or NAT?

If you do decide to connect your network to the Internet, your next decision is whether to use multiple public IP addresses—one for each computer on your network that connects to the Internet—or a single IP address with Network Address Translation (NAT).

See the sidebar "IP Addresses and How They Work" in Chapter 26 for a discussion of the differences between public and private IP addresses.

MULTIPLE IP ADDRESSES

Whether you *can* use multiple IP addresses depends on your connection. Typically, in order to use multiple IP addresses, you'll need an always-on connection such as a DSL or a cable connection that can be assigned a fixed IP address. You'll need to request *routed Internet service* from your ISP, who will assign you the appropriate number of fixed IP addresses. Some ISPs will provide a handful of IP addresses for the same price as your regular connection, whereas others consider supplying multiple IP addresses to be "business" service rather than "residential service" (which gets a single IP address) and charge accordingly.

Routed Internet service has a couple of advantages over NAT. First, because with routed Internet service each computer has a public IP address, all features in all Internet programs should work on each computer, because the computer is directly accessible from the Internet. Second, you can publish the IP address or the name of any given computer so that people can connect directly to it. If you get your ISP to implement what's called *inverse DNS* for your domain name, you can also allow people on the Internet to look up the name of your computer. (DNS is the abbreviation for Domain Name Service, the service that translates URLs, such as http://www.wiley.com, into IP addresses, such as 208.215.179.146.)

The disadvantages to routed Internet service are that it'll almost invariably cost you more than sharing an Internet connection using NAT and that it increases your exposure to security threats, because you'll need to protect each of the computers on the network against direct attack via the Internet. If you use inverse DNS, any website you access will be able to tell the name of the computer that accessed it, whereas when you access a website via NAT, the website can tell only the IP address of the computer or device running NAT.

Over software NAT devices (as opposed to hardware NAT devices), routed Internet service has another advantage: Because the service is implemented via a hardware device, you don't need to leave a host computer running the whole time you want any computer on the network to be able to access the Internet.

NETWORK ADDRESS TRANSLATION

In most cases, you'll do better to use Network Address Translation (NAT) for a network based on computers running Windows Vista Home. Network Address Translation, which is also known as *IP masquerading* (particularly in the Linux world), lets multiple computers connect through a single Internet connection using a single public IP address. So if you have an Internet connection on one of your PCs, you can easily share it with the other computers on the network. This sharing is more appealing for a high-speed connection than for a modest dial-up connection, but it works just as well for either. But there are a couple of catches, as you'll see later in this section.

The NAT host acts as an intermediary between the client (the PC connected to the network) and the server (the Internet server that is supplying information). Basically, NAT receives any packets sent by the client to destinations not on the local network, changes the source IP address on the packets so that they appear to come from the NAT host rather than from the client, assigns a source port to them that lets itself track reply packets, and sends the packets on to the destination. When the replies come back, NAT matches them to the original packets and forwards them to the client.

In NAT, the identity of the client submitting a request is hidden: Instead, the request appears to come from the host. This can be good and bad. NAT gives you more freedom in the IP addresses you assign within the network. Typically, you'll want to use nonroutable internal IP addresses within the network so that incoming packets can reach a computer only through the router, which gives you some protection against attacks. On the bad side, if someone on your network takes some illegal or offensive action (for example, posting libelous comments or downloading unsuitable material), the culprit will appear to be the host rather than the individual concerned. (If you had multiple IP addresses, only the specific IP address involved would appear to be guilty.)

As mentioned earlier, you need only one ISP account and one IP address (either static or dynamic) to connect your network to the Internet via NAT. This usually makes NAT the most economical option for connecting a network to the Internet. If you regularly have a half-dozen users using a broadband connection that's supposedly limited to a single user, your ISP will probably suspect that you have multiple users connected, but all the traffic *will* be coming from the single IP address they've assigned to you. Unless you're actually violating any terms of service you've subscribed to, the chances that they'll pull the plug on your connection are low. Most ISPs now expect a residential account to have multiple PCs connected, so this is less of a problem than it used to be.

The main disadvantage of NAT is that not every program works across NAT, depending on the NAT device used and on the needs of the program. Problems are most likely to arise when a computer connected to the Internet through your NAT device is trying to connect to a computer that itself connects to the Internet through another NAT device.

What usually happens with NAT is one of the computers inside the network originates the conversation with a computer on the Internet. For example, consider Figure 28.1. This shows two simple home networks, named West Network and East Network. Each network contains a computer that's connected to the Internet (West 1 and East 1) and running NAT so that it can provide Internet connectivity to the two other computers in its network (West 2, West 3, East 2, and East 3). In the middle of the figure is the Internet, represented by its traditional cloud. Below the cloud is the Sybex web server.

So far, so good. Now, here's the problem that used to occur with NAT. The computers that connect through the NAT devices have only internal IP addresses. That means they can originate a conversation with a computer on the Internet, but they can't take part in a conversation originated from beyond their NAT devices. For example, West 2 can access the Sybex web server with no problem. It sends its request to the NAT router on West 1, which recognizes that the address is on the Internet, and forwards the request out through its external connection. The Sybex web server responds to the request and sends back a response to West 1. The NAT router receives this response, matches it to the outgoing request, and passes the data on to West 2. And so it continues: West 2 (and the other internal computers) can access Internet sites provided that it starts the conversation.

But if West 3 wants to start a conversation with East 2, it can't, because it can't see East 2 through the NAT router on East 1. It can get as far as East 1, because that computer has an external IP address. But the computers beyond the NAT router are hidden from view. So other computers can't access those computers directly.

There are various workarounds for this problem, including the following:

◆ Both computers can sign into an online service that enables them to connect with each other. For example, if each computer establishes a connection to a chat service, neither computer needs to contact the other through the NAT device.

◆ The computer behind the NAT device can start the conversation. This workaround works when only one of the computers is behind a NAT device, and you're able to start the conversation from that computer rather than from the other computer.

◆ ICS lets you communicate across two NAT routers. This workaround is handy if you're using ICS as your NAT device, but if you're using a hardware NAT device, it doesn't help.

◆ You can configure your NAT device to forward all packets directed to a specified port to a particular internal IP address on the LAN. For example, you tell the NAT device to pass all incoming Half-Life packets along to your games PC and all incoming web-page requests to your web server.

FIGURE 28.1
Two networks using NAT to connect internal computers to the Internet

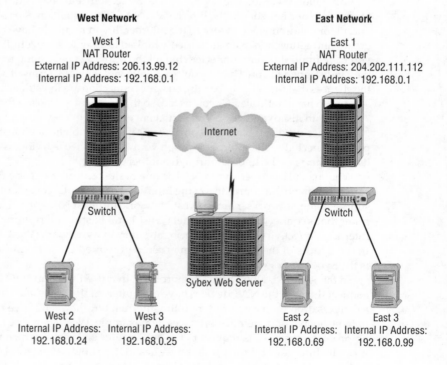

West Network

West 1
NAT Router
External IP Address: 206.13.99.12
Internal IP Address: 192.168.0.1

East Network

East 1
NAT Router
External IP Address: 204.202.111.112
Internal IP Address: 192.168.0.1

Internet

Switch

Switch

Sybex Web Server

West 2
Internal IP Address:
192.168.0.24

West 3
Internal IP Address:
192.168.0.25

East 2
Internal IP Address:
192.168.0.69

East 3
Internal IP Address:
192.168.0.99

Should the Connection Connect Automatically to the Internet?

If you do decide to connect your network to the Internet, and your means of connection is a dial-up connection rather than an always-on connection, your next decision is whether to have the connection be established automatically whenever one of the computers on the network tries to access the Internet or whether to require the connection to be established manually.

Because having the connection established automatically is by far the most convenient arrangement for most networks, you'll probably want to connect automatically unless you have a good reason not to. Such reasons include the following:

◆ You want to restrict Internet usage to certain times of day for whatever reason (for example, to avoid per-minute charges in the daytime, or to make sure that your children do their homework and don't spend the night online).

◆ Your dial-up connection shares your voice line, and you want to prevent the Internet connection from interrupting your voice calls.

◆ You want to make sure that no program is able to "call home" by establishing an Internet connection of its own accord. Many Trojan-horse programs and viruses do this, but many other programs may be configured to automatically establish a connection. For example, Windows Messenger and other instant-messaging programs are often set by default to sign you in as soon as you log on to Windows. If your network isn't connected to the Internet at the time, these programs establish the connection.

A dial-up modem connection tends to be the least satisfactory way of connecting a network to the Internet, because the time needed to establish a connection makes for a poor user experience on one of the networked computers. Because the user probably won't be able to hear the modem dialing as the computer sharing the modem tries to set up the connection at their demand, the connection will seem not to be working. So if you have a flat-rate dial-up connection, you may want to set it to redial automatically when the connection is dropped so as to keep the connection open as much of the time as possible. To do so, display the Options page of the Properties dialog box for the connection, select the Redial if Line Is Dropped check box, choose Never in the Idle Time Before Hanging Up drop-down list, and reduce the time specified in the Time Between Redial Attempts drop-down list to a sensibly small value.

Should You Use ICS or Another NAT?

If you've decided that NAT is the way to go, choose between using Windows' ICS and another NAT device (either hardware or software).

ICS has several strong points:

◆ ICS is included with Windows, so the price is right. By contrast, a hardware NAT device will typically set you back $30 to $100. However, if your NAT device is included in a DSL router or a wireless access point that you need to buy anyway, the cost may be irrelevant.

◆ ICS includes the various networking components that you need to share a network connection: NAT, a proxy server, a router, and a DHCP allocator (a minimalist DHCP server). ICS even gets around some of the problems of computers not being able to communicate with each other when each is behind a different NAT device.

◆ ICS is integrated with Windows Firewall. This integration lets you set up a shared and fairly well firewalled Internet connection easily. You can poke holes through Windows Firewall easily to enable programs that have specific connectivity needs.

◆ ICS and Windows Firewall are fully aware of Windows' features and Microsoft's add-on programs and are designed to work with them. For example, Windows Live Messenger knows how to automatically ask ICS and Windows Firewall to open the ports that it needs to communicate. Likewise, ICS and Windows Firewall open ports for remote-connection technologies such as Remote Assistance (discussed in Chapter 21) and Remote Desktop Connection (discussed in Chapter 30).

ICS has two significant limitations:

◆ You need to keep the ICS host computer running all the time so that it can handle the Internet connection and the sharing. This limitation is obvious, but it can be restrictive.

◆ Because of the way ICS is set up, you can share only one Internet connection at the same time on the same network by using ICS. To share two Internet connections, you'll need to set one up manually for sharing via another technology. (Alternatively, you can create two separate networks with an ICS connection in each, but doing so is usually much more work than setting up a second shared connection manually, because those two networks won't be able to talk to each other directly without ICS conflicts.) You can also use unshared Internet connections alongside your shared connections without any problems.

You can get around the limitation of needing to keep the host computer running by using a hardware NAT device—for example, a cable router, DSL router, or ISDN router—instead of ICS.

Almost all these routers have NAT built in, and most can run DHCP as well, so they provide an effective means of sharing an Internet connection. Some routers have firewalls built in as well, which you can use instead of or in addition to Windows Firewall.

Some models are designed to connect to a network switch or hub and have two ports: an internal port for connecting to the switch or hub and an external port for connecting to the cable modem or DSL splitter. Others have switches or hubs built in, so if you haven't yet bought the switch or hub for your network, you can solve all your connectivity needs with a single box.

If you do decide to get a hardware NAT device, install it according to the instructions supplied. If you decide to stick with ICS, and you haven't set it up yet, set it up and configure it as described in the following sections.

Configuring ICS Manually

If you haven't had the Network Setup Wizard set up Internet Connection Sharing for you, configure it manually by taking the following steps:

1. Choose Start ➢ Connect To. Windows displays the Select a Network to Connect to window.

2. Right-click the dial-up connection for which you want to implement ICS, choose Properties from the context menu, and then authenticate yourself to User Account Control. Windows displays the Properties dialog box for the connection.

3. Click the Sharing tab. Windows displays the Sharing page (shown in Figure 28.2).

4. Select the Allow Other Network Users to Connect through This Computer's Internet Connection check box.

FIGURE 28.2
Use the controls on the
Sharing page of the
Properties dialog
box for an Internet
connection to set
up ICS.

5. If you want other computers to be able to cause ICS to start up the network connection when it's not running, make sure the Establish a Dial-up Connection Whenever a Computer on My Network Attempts to Access the Internet check box is selected. Clear this check box if you want only the computer with the connection to be able to start the connection.

6. If you want users of the other computers on the network to be able to control the Internet connection, select the Allow Other Network Users to Control or Disable the Shared Internet Connection check box. Clear this check box if you don't want them to be able to manipulate the Internet connection directly.

7. If you want to set Windows Firewall to allow incoming requests for certain services across this connection, follow the steps shown in the next section. (Normally, you won't need to allow incoming requests across your Internet connection.)

8. Click the OK button. Windows displays a Network Connections dialog box (shown next) to make sure you understand the settings that the wizard will apply and that you still want to proceed.

9. Click the Yes button. Windows closes the Properties dialog box for the connection, changes the IP address of your network adapter to the static IP address 192.168.0.1, and starts telling the other computers to get their IP addresses from it (if there's no other DHCP server on the network).

At this point, ICS should be up and running. The shared connection appears in the Network Connections window with the word "Shared" next to it.

Most Internet-enabled programs on computers that connect to the Internet through the ICS host should now be working. ICS shares the details of the connection via UPnP, so the client computers learn of the ICS host automatically.

Other programs and services have special requirements for Internet connectivity and so run afoul of the protection provided by Windows Firewall. For example, if you've chosen to host a website on a computer that connects to the Internet through an ICS host, you'll need to configure Windows Firewall to pass on the requests to the web server, because otherwise Windows Firewall will treat the incoming requests as hostile and discard them automatically. For such programs and services, follow the instructions in the section "Configuring Windows Firewall Manually," a little later in this chapter.

ALLOWING INCOMING SERVICES TO TRAVERSE YOUR INTERNET CONNECTION

In general, incoming requests across your Internet connection are a threat to your computer—for example, unauthorized people trying to access your computers. So Windows Firewall comes configured to block such requests by default. But if you run a web server or an FTP (File Transfer Protocol) server inside your network, you may need to allow incoming services to traverse your Internet connection.

TROUBLESHOOTING: DEALING WITH AN IP ADDRESS CONFLICT WHEN YOU TURN ON ICS

If you have another computer on the network using the 192.168.0.1 IP address, Windows gives you a Network Error dialog box, as shown here, telling you to change the IP address on the other computer if you assigned the address manually.

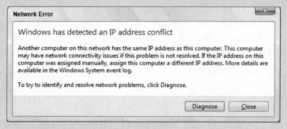

The most likely reason for this error is that you've already set up ICS on another computer. Alternatively, you may have another NAT device currently managing the network and using this address range. To deal with the problem, take one of these actions:

◆ If you have another NAT device, remove it.

◆ If you have another computer running ICS, display the Properties dialog box for its shared connection, clear the Allow Other Network Users to Connect Through This Computer's Internet Connection check box on the Sharing page, and then click the OK button.

◆ If the other computer isn't running ICS but has the 192.168.0.1 IP address set manually, either set a different address manually or switch to automatic addressing.

If you take one of these actions, click the Close button to close the Network Error dialog box. If none of the above applies to your network, click the Diagnose button. Windows attempts to diagnose the problems and then displays a Windows Network Diagnostics dialog box such as the one shown next.

Usually, your best bet here is to click the Reset the Network Adapter "Local Area Connection" button, authenticate yourself to User Account Control, and let Windows try to resolve the problem.

To allow incoming services to traverse your Internet connection, follow these steps:

1. On the Sharing page of the Properties dialog box for the Internet connection, click the Settings button. Windows displays the Advanced Settings dialog box (see Figure 28.3).

FIGURE 28.3
Use the Advanced Settings button to choose which services Internet users can access across your Internet connection. These services are connections coming into your network, not outgoing services.

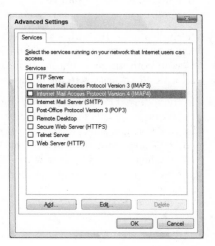

2. In the Services list box, select the check box for each service you want to allow. For example, if you're running an FTP server on one of your computers that you want Internet users to be able to access (or that you want to be able to access when you're elsewhere), select the FTP Server check box. To tell Windows which computer should receive the data, follow these steps:

◆ Select the service in the list, and then click the Edit button. Windows displays the Service Settings dialog box, as shown here:

◆ In the Name or IP Address of the Computer Hosting This Service on Your Network text box, type the computer's name or IP address. If you've assigned static IP addresses to your computers, using the IP address is clearest here. But if you're using DHCP to allocate IP addresses to the computers as needed, enter the computer name instead.

◆ Click the OK button. Windows closes the Service Settings dialog box.

3. To add a service, follow these steps:

◆ Click the Add button. Windows displays the Service Settings dialog box.

◆ Type a descriptive name in the Description of Service text box. This name is for your benefit, so make it whatever you want. Windows will add this name to the Services list box.

◆ In the Name or IP Address of the Computer Hosting This Service on Your Network text box, type the computer's name or IP address. If you've assigned static IP addresses to your computers, using the IP address is clearest here. But if you're using DHCP to allocate IP addresses to the computers as needed, enter the computer name instead.

◆ In the External Port Number for This Service text box, type the port number on which the requests for this service will arrive. Select the TCP option button if the requests will be TCP packets. Select the UDP option button if the requests will be UDP packets. (TCP and UDP are Transmission Control Protocol and User Datagram Protocol, respectively, two of the protocols that make up TCP/IP. See http://www.iana.org/assignments/port-numbers for a list of common port numbers.)

- ◆ In the Internal Port Number for This Service text box, type the port number that ICS should use when passing along the packets for the service.

- ◆ Click the OK button. Windows closes the Service Settings dialog box, adds the service to the Services list in the Advanced Settings dialog box, and selects its check box.

4. To delete a service you've created, select it and click the Delete button. Windows deletes the service from the list without confirmation.

5. Click the OK button. Windows closes the Advanced Settings dialog box.

SETTING THE IP ADDRESSES OF CONNECTED COMPUTERS

If your Windows computers are set to get IP addresses via DHCP, they should automatically get IP addresses from ICS within a few minutes of your implementing ICS. If you're configuring IP addresses manually, give each computer an IP address in the 192.168.0.2 to 192.168.0.254 range.

TURNING OFF ICS

To turn off ICS, clear the Allow Other Network Users to Connect Through This Computer's Internet Connection check box on the Sharing page of the Properties dialog box for the connection, and then click the OK button. Windows closes the Properties dialog box and changes your computer's IP address from using 192.168.0.1 to obtaining an IP address automatically.

If you have a DHCP server on your network, Windows grabs an IP address from it on the next go-around of network polling. If Windows doesn't find a DHCP server (which will be the case if ICS was handling DHCP for you before you turned it off), Windows falls back on its alternate TCP/IP configuration, which uses Automatic Private IP Addressing (APIPA) to automatically assign an IP address in the range 169.254.0.1 to 169.254.255.254.

Configuring Windows Firewall Manually

By default, Windows Firewall is configured to block any incoming traffic that it can't match to an outgoing request, not to log dropped packets or successful connections, and not to respond to Internet Control Message Protocol (ICMP) messages. You can change these settings as described in the following subsections.

To configure Windows Firewall, you work in the Windows Firewall dialog box. To display this dialog box, take the following steps:

1. Choose Start ➢ Control Panel. Windows displays Control Panel.

2. In Control Panel Home view, click the Security link. Windows displays the Security window.

3. Click the Windows Firewall link. Windows displays the Windows Firewall window (see Figure 28.4).

FIGURE 28.4
The Windows Firewall window lets you check the status and configuration of Windows Firewall, turn Windows Firewall on and off, or allow a program through Windows Firewall.

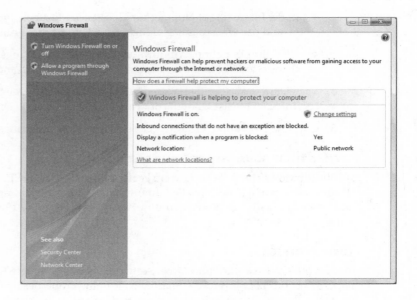

Configuring Windows Firewall to Pass Data for Programs and Services on All Connections

To configure Windows Firewall to pass data for specific programs and services through all network connections, click the Allow a Program Through Windows Firewall link in the left pane of the Windows Firewall window and then authenticate yourself to User Account Control. Windows displays the Exceptions page of the Windows Firewall Settings dialog box (see Figure 28.5).

FIGURE 28.5
On the Exceptions page of the Windows Firewall dialog box, specify which programs and services you want Internet users to be able to access.

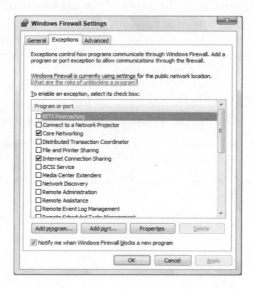

The list box on this page contains the services that come preconfigured with Windows, together with any services that Windows has added automatically on your behalf (for example, services related to Windows Live Messenger, Remote Desktop Connection, or Remote Assistance) and any services you've defined manually.

In the To Enable an Exception, Select Its Check Box list box, select the check boxes for the programs and services running on your network that you want Internet users to be able to access. Don't turn on a program or service unless you actually need it, because packets being redirected to a destination that's not ready to receive them opens a security hole into your network. It's much safer to gradually add exceptions as you find you need them than to add a swath of exceptions in case you might need them in the future.

ADDING A PROGRAM THAT CAN PIERCE THE FIREWALL

To add a program, take the following steps:

1. Click the Add Program button. Windows displays the Add a Program dialog box (see Figure 28.6).

2. If the program appears in the Programs list box, click it. If it doesn't, click the Browse button, use the Browse dialog box to select the program, and then click the Open button. Windows adds the program's name to the Path text box.

3. If you need to change the *scope* of the program (the context in which Window Firewall will pass data for it), follow these steps:

   ◆ Click the Change Scope button. Windows displays the Change Scope dialog box, as shown here.

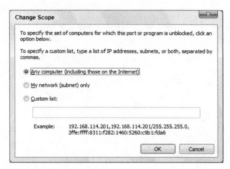

   ◆ Select the Any Computer (Including Those on the Internet) option button if you need to let any program connect. Select the My Network (Subnet) Only option button if only computers on your local network will need to connect; this option gives good security as long as users of your network are sensible and trustworthy. Select the Custom List option button if you know only certain computers with fixed IP addresses will need to connect. Type the addresses in the text box. Custom List lets you restrict the connection to a single computer if you want, reducing the security risk of letting the program through the firewall.

   ◆ Click the OK button. Windows closes the Change Scope dialog box and returns you to the Add a Program dialog box.

4. Click the OK button. Windows closes the Add a Program dialog box, adds the program to the list on the Exceptions page, and selects the check box for the program.

FIGURE 28.6
Use the Add a
Program dialog
box to allow a
program to receive
data through
Windows Firewall.

ADDING A PORT THAT CAN PIERCE THE FIREWALL

Instead of allowing a particular program to pierce the firewall, you can allow a particular port to pierce it. This capability is useful when you know that you will receive data on a particular port but you don't want to tie it to a single program. (For example, you might want to use different programs to deal with this traffic at different times.)

To allow a port to pierce the firewall, take the following steps:

1. Click the Add Port button. Windows displays the Add a Port dialog box (shown here).

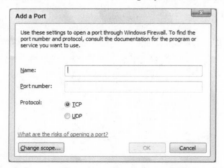

2. In the Name text box, type a name that describes the port and why you are choosing to let it pierce the firewall. This information is for your benefit and will appear in the To Enable an Exception, Select Its Check Box list on the Exceptions page of the Windows Firewall Settings dialog box.

3. In the Port Number text box, type the port number.

4. Below the Port Number text box, select the TCP option button (the default) or the UDP option button, as appropriate.

5. If you need to change the scope of the port, click the Change Scope button, and follow the instructions in step 3 of the previous list.

6. Click the OK button. Windows closes the Add a Port dialog box, adds the name to the list on the Exceptions page, and selects its check box.

CHANGING A PROGRAM OR PORT

Windows lets you change the details for a program or port you've added to the list on the Exceptions page of the Windows Firewall dialog box.

- To change a program or port, select it, click the Edit button, and then work in the resulting Edit a Program dialog box or Edit a Port dialog box. These dialog boxes have the same features as the Add a Program dialog box and the Add a Port dialog box, respectively.

- To delete a program or port, select it, click the Delete button, and then click the Yes button in the Delete a Port confirmation dialog box.

Windows protects the programs on its original list. To change one of these programs, you must use the Windows Firewall with Advanced Security window. See the section "Configuring Windows Firewall with Advanced Security" in the next chapter for details.

Using a Shared Internet Connection

Depending on how a shared Internet connection is configured, you can use it in much the same way as you can use a regular Internet connection on your computer. Choose Start ➤ Network, and you'll see the shared connection listed as a Residential Gateway Device in the Network window. Figure 28.7 shows an example.

If the connection is configured to start automatically on demand, you can start the connection by starting a program that attempts to access the Internet. For example, if you start Internet Explorer or Outlook Express, ICS automatically starts the connection.

If the connection is configured to let you control it, you can start it manually by right-clicking it and choosing Enable from the context menu.

FIGURE 28.7
A shared connection appears as a Residential Gateway Device in the Network window.

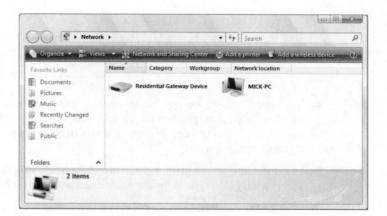

Sharing a File or Folder

As described in the section "Sharing Files and Folders" in Chapter 9, you can share a file or folder in two easy ways:

- Use the `Public` folder to share the file or folder with all other users of the computer and users of other computers on the same network.

- Change the permissions on a particular file or folder so that it's shared with one or more other users. You can decide exactly who you want to share the file or folder with.

Sharing a Printer

To get the most out of your printers, you can share them across your network with your other networked computers. Windows makes it easy to share printers and to connect to shared printers.

To share a printer that you've already set up on your computer, take the following steps:

1. Choose Start ➤ Control Panel. Windows displays a Control Panel window.

2. In Control Panel Home view, click the Printer link under the Hardware and Sound heading. Windows displays a Printers window.

3. Right-click the printer, and then choose Sharing from the context menu. Windows displays the Sharing page of the Properties dialog box for the printer. Figure 28.8 shows an example of the Sharing page.

FIGURE 28.8
Use the Sharing page of the Properties dialog box for a printer to set up sharing with other computers on your network.

4. Click the Change Sharing Options button, and then authenticate yourself to User Account Control. Windows removes the Change Sharing Options button and enables the other controls on the Sharing page. Windows also turns on Printer Sharing in Sharing and Discovery if it is currently turned off.

5. Select the Share This Printer check box. Windows activates the Share Name text box and enters a suggested name for the shared printer derived from the printer's existing name.

6. Change the name in the Share Name text box if you want:

   ◆ Keep the name down to eight or fewer characters if you need the printer to be accessible to computers running Windows 3.x or DOS.

   ◆ If all your computers use 32-bit or 64-bit versions of Windows, you can make the name longer and more descriptive. For example, you might want to include the computer's name or description so that when users print to the printer, they're clear as to where they'll find their printouts.

7. If you want to make each computer that uses the printer process its own print jobs rather than having the computer sharing the printer process them, select the Render Print Jobs on Client Computers check box. Selecting this check box is usually a good idea, because otherwise you may find the sharing computer slows down unexpectedly whenever other computers send print jobs to the printer.

8. If the computers with which you'll be sharing the printer use 64-bit versions of Windows or Itanium processors, click the Additional Drivers button. Windows displays the Additional Drivers dialog box (shown in Figure 28.9).

9. Select the appropriate check boxes in the Processor column. Itanium is Intel's advanced processor that has failed to take the computing world by storm. The x64 item is for 64-bit versions of Windows, which are promising but not widely used at this writing. The Installed column shows whether the drivers are installed; if they're not, you'll need to provide them in the next step.

10. Click the OK button. If Windows needs you to provide drivers for any of the operating systems you chose, it displays the Printer Drivers dialog box. Use the Browse button and the resulting Locate File dialog box to identify the drivers, and then click the Open button. Windows installs the drivers and closes the Additional Drivers dialog box, returning you to the Properties dialog box for the printer.

11. Click the Apply button, and then click the OK button. Windows closes the Properties dialog box and displays a shared icon for the printer (a printer with an inset picture of a couple of users).

Other computers can now connect to the shared printer as described in the next section.

FIGURE 28.9
If you'll be sharing this printer with computers running other versions of Windows, use the Additional Drivers dialog box to install drivers for them.

LETTING USERS KNOW WHEN THE SHARED PRINTER FINISHES THEIR PRINT JOBS

If you want remote users to receive a notification when their print jobs are printed, select the Show Informational Notifications for Network Printers check box on the Advanced page of the Print Server Properties dialog box. See the section "Configuring Your Print Server" in Chapter 12 for details.

Connecting to a Shared Printer

To connect to a printer shared by another computer, take the following steps:

1. Choose Start ➤ Control Panel. Windows displays a Control Panel window.

2. In Control Panel Home view, click the Printer link under the Hardware and Sound heading. Windows displays a Printers window.

3. On the toolbar, click the Add a Printer button. Windows starts the Add Printer Wizard, which displays its Choose a Local or Network Printer page.

4. Select the Add a Network, Wireless or Bluetooth Printer button. The Add Printer Wizard displays the next page, showing the shared printers it has found on the network. The list includes any printers your own computer is sharing.

5. If the printer appears in the list box, click it, and then go to step 7. Otherwise, click the The Printer That I Want Isn't Listed button. The wizard displays the Find a Printer by Name or TCP/IP Address page (see Figure 28.10).

6. Choose one of the following three ways of specifying the printer:

   ◆ To browse the network for the printer, select the Browse for a Printer option button, and then click the Next button. The wizard displays a window showing the computers on the network. Double-click the computer sharing the printer, provide a username and password if prompted, select the printer, and then click the Select button.

   ◆ If you know the printer's name and location, choose the Select a Shared Printer by Name option button, and then type the path and printer name in the text box. For example, if the computer Requiem is sharing a printer named Laser1, you would enter **\\Requiem\Laser1**. You can also click the Browse button, use the resulting window to select the printer, and then click the Select button.

FIGURE 28.10
The Find a Printer by Name or TCP/IP Address page of the Add Printer Wizard lets you find a printer by browsing, by providing the printer's name, or by providing the printer's TCP/IP address or hostname.

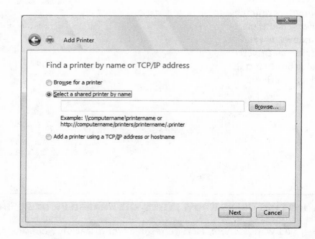

◆ If you know the IP address or hostname for the printer, select the Add a Printer Using a TCP/IP Address or Hostname option button, and then click the Next button. The wizard displays the Type a Printer Hostname or IP Address page (see Figure 28.11). Choose the device type—Autodetect, TCP/IP Device, or Web Services Device—in the Device Type drop-down list, type the hostname or IP address in the Hostname or IP Address text box, and then add the port in the Port Name text box. Select the Query the Printer and Automatically Select the Driver to Use check box if you want Windows to try to obtain the driver automatically (this is usually the easiest approach).

FIGURE 28.11

On the Type a Printer Hostname or IP Address page of the Add Printer Wizard, choose the printer type, specify the hostname or IP address, and type the port name.

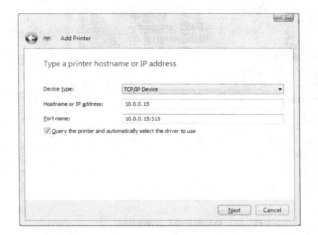

PRINTING ACROSS THE INTERNET WITH IPP

IPP is the Internet Printing Protocol, an HTTP-based protocol that lets you print to a shared printer across the Internet. IPP is appealing to business travelers and others who often need to print to a remote printer via an Internet connection. You might also want to use IPP to deliver a printed copy of, say, a proposal to a client rather than send them a (possibly editable) file to print out themselves. Or you might need to print certain jobs to a high-quality printer at a service bureau. (In both of the last two cases, an alternative is to send a print file or PDF to the recipient so that they can print it themselves. See the section "Printing to a File" in Chapter 12 for a discussion of how to create print files.)

If you need to print across the Internet with IPP, choose the Select a Shared Printer by Name option button on the Find a Printer by Name or TCP/IP Address page of the Add Printer Wizard, and then type the IP address, `printers`, and the printer name in the text box in the form `http://101.123.0.22/printers/.printer`.

Once you've installed an IPP printer on one of your computers that's running Windows, you can share it with other computers on your network. Doing so tends to be easier than installing the printer on each of them. If the IP address of the IPP printer changes, you need change it only on the computer that's sharing it, not on each of the other computers.

7. Click the Next button. The wizard displays the Type a Printer Name page (see Figure 28.12).

8. Either accept the default name for the printer, or change the name to suit yourself.

9. Click the Next button. The wizard displays a page saying that you've successfully added the printer. Click the Print a Test Page button if you want to print a test page—usually a good idea for making sure that the print driver was installed correctly.

10. Click the Finish button to close the Add Printer Wizard. The wizard closes and adds the printer to your Printers list. The icon for the printer has a network cable underneath it, indicating that the printer is connected via the network.

You can then use the printer as you would a local printer.

FIGURE 28.12
On the Type a Printer Name page of the Add Printer Wizard, name the printer and choose whether to use it as your computer's default printer.

Using a Print Server

As discussed in Chapter 12, one of the most appealing ways of making one or more printers available on your network is to add a print server to the network. Having a print server means that you don't need to keep the computer sharing the printer running in order for any of the computers connected to the network to be able to print. It also means that you can locate the print server and its printers anywhere on your network that has access to a network cable or a wireless connection rather than having to attach the printer directly to your computer.

Once you've bought and unpacked your print server, connect the printer or printers to it, and then connect it to the network and to its power supply (if it needs one). For some print servers, you may need to install TCP/IP redirection software that captures the print jobs and directs them to the print server.

So far, so easy. You then have to decide how to use the print server. If part of your motivation for getting the print server was to free up the computer that previously managed the printer or printers from its print-management duties, install the print software on all the computers that will need to print to the printers. That way, each can print independently, and each will be able to manage all print jobs on the printer. Alternatively, you can install the printer on one computer and share it from there, so that this computer will be able to manage all print jobs on the printer while other computers will be able to manage only their own print jobs—but the computer sharing the printer will need to be running all the time for the other computers to be able to print.

Connecting to an LPR Printer

Some printers are designed to be connected directly to a network (rather than to a computer or to a print server) and print using LPR/LPD, the Line Printer Remote/Line Printer Daemon printing protocol originally developed for Unix. Windows can print to LPR printers as long as you install LPR support, which isn't installed by default.

INSTALLING LPR SUPPORT

To install LPR support, take the following steps:

1. Choose Start ➤ Control Panel. Windows opens a Control Panel window.

2. In Control Panel Home view, click the Programs link. Windows displays a Programs window.

3. Under the Programs and Features heading, click the Turn Windows Features On or Off link, and then authenticate yourself to User Account Control. Windows displays the Windows Features window.

4. Expand the Print Services item, and then select the LPR Port Monitor check box. (Don't select the LPD Print Service item; this service makes printers attached to your computer appear to be LPD printers, so that Unix computers can print to them.)

5. Click the OK button. Windows closes the Windows Features window and installs the LPR Port Monitor feature.

ADDING AN LPR PRINTER

Once you've installed LPR support, you can add an LPR printer by running the Add Printer Wizard and making the following choices:

1. On the Choose a Local or Network Printer page of the wizard, click the Add a Local Printer button. The wizard displays the Choose a Printer Port page.

2. Select the Create a New Port option button, and then choose the LPR Port item in the Type of Port drop-down list.

3. Click the Next button. Windows displays the Add LPR Compatible Printer dialog box, as shown here.

4. In the Name or of Server Providing LPD text box, enter the host name or IP address of the server.

5. In the Name of Printer or Print Queue on that Server text box, enter the name of the printer or the print queue.

6. Click the OK button. The wizard displays the Printer Driver page. Choose the printer manufacturer and printer model, and then follow through the rest of the wizard to complete the installation.

Working with Networks, Network Connections, and Networking Components

Windows Vista automates as much network setup, configuration, and maintenance as possible. Even so, sometimes you'll find that a network connection has stopped working; if so, you'll need to diagnose the problem and repair it if possible. You may also need to map drives from the command line; install, remove, or configure networking components; and bridge or merge networks so that all your computers can see each other.

Diagnosing and Repairing a Network Connection

If a network connection seems not to be working or seems to be malfunctioning, you may need to repair it. To do so, take the following steps:

1. Click the Start button, right-click Network, and then choose Properties from the context menu. Windows displays a Network and Sharing Center window.

2. In the left pane, click the Manage Network Connections link. Windows displays a Network Connections window.

3. Right-click the connection that's giving problems, and then choose Diagnose from the shortcut menu. (Alternatively, click the Connection, and then click the Diagnose this Connection button on the toolbar.) Windows attempts to diagnose the problem, and then displays a Windows Network Diagnostics dialog box showing actions you can take. Figure 28.13 shows two examples of Windows Network Diagnostics dialog boxes.

4. Click the appropriate button. For example, click the Enable button to enable a connection that has been disabled, or click the Reset button to reset a connection with which Windows can't find a specific problem.

FIGURE 28.13
When you tell Windows to diagnose problems with a network connection, it may find an obvious problem (top). If it doesn't (bottom), you can try resetting the network adapter to resolve the problem.

EXPERT KNOWLEDGE: MAPPING DRIVES FROM THE COMMAND LINE VIA THE *NET USE* COMMAND

You can map a drive quickly from the command line by using the net use command. Choose Start ➤ All Programs ➤ Accessories ➤ Command Prompt to open a Command Prompt window, and then follow the instructions in this sidebar.

The basic syntax for the net use command is as follows:

```
net use drive path
```

Here, *drive* is the drive letter that you want to use to access the shared folder, and *path* is the path to the folder. For example, the following command connects the shared folder \\TBC\users as drive F:

```
net use f: \\TBC\users
```

If Windows is able to assign the share, it reports "The command completed successfully." If Windows isn't able to assign the share because it can't find the network drive, it returns a system error 53 and tells you "The network path was not found."

To make the mapping persistent use the /persistent parameter with the argument "yes". For example, the following command connects the shared folder \\TBC\users as drive F and will reconnect at each subsequent logon:

```
net use f: \\TBC\users /persistent:yes
```

If you want net use to use the next available drive letter for the share, enter an asterisk in the command instead of specifying the drive letter. For example,

```
net use * \\TBC\users
```

If you need to supply an account name and a password for the drive you're connecting to, specify them in this format:

```
net use drive path password /user:domain\username
```

Here, *password* is the password, and *domain\username* is the domain or workgroup name, a backslash, and the username. For example, the following command connects drive Z to the shared folder \\TBC\users using the password 1llumin8! and the username Jaq in the workgroup MSHome:

```
net use z: \\TBC\users 1llumin8! /user:MSHome\Jaq
```

You can also use the server's IP address instead of its name. This can be especially useful if you're connecting to the server across the Internet.

If you see the message *"The credentials supplied conflict with an existing set of credentials,"* usually accompanied by a system error 1219, it can mean either of two things. First, that you already have a connection to this share using a different username and (valid) password, and that net use doesn't approve of your trying to connect with another username or password. Or second, that the computer to which you're trying to connect has decided, on the basis of a failed connection attempt you've made, that you aren't authorized to access this connection.

In either case, use the net use *drive*: /d command to disconnect from the server, then try to connect again:

```
net use Z: /d
```

If you're in doubt as to which folders are connected to which drive, type **net use** at the command prompt without any arguments and press the Enter key. Windows displays a list of the local drives, the remote folders, and their status.

To see the status of a network drive, type **net use** *drive:,* where *drive* is the drive letter. You'll see a printout something like the following, giving the name of the remote folder, the resource type, the status, the number of files open, and the number of connections.

```
C:\>net use q:
Local name      Q:
Remote name     \\Donner\SharedDocs\Fun
Resource type   Disk
Status          OK
# Opens         3
# Connections   1
The command completed successfully.
```

Configuring Networking Components Manually

When you install Windows Vista Home Edition, the installation routine automatically installs and configures the network clients, network services, and network protocols normally needed for home or home-office networks. When you set up your network, Windows may install other network components needed for the type of network configuration it finds.

Sometimes, however, you may need to configure networking components manually. You may also need to install networking components—although, as Windows Vista installs all those a small network usually needs, this is not so likely. You can also remove some networking components if necessary—for example, for security reasons.

UNDERSTANDING WINDOWS VISTA'S STANDARD NETWORKING COMPONENTS

This section explains the networking components that Windows installs. The table at the end of the section shows you which networking components Windows uses for wired LAN connections, wireless connections, and dial-up connections.

CLIENT FOR MICROSOFT NETWORKS

The Client for Microsoft Networks enables your computer to access files and printers that other computers on the network are sharing. Normally, you won't need to configure Client for Microsoft Networks unless you're using Distributed Computing Environment (DCE) server or client kits, which is very unlikely.

QOS PACKET SCHEDULER

The QoS Packet Scheduler organizes the sending and receiving of *packets* (chunks of data packaged for transmission) so as to maintain quality of service (QoS).

QoS may sound esoteric (and the details are), but the principle is straightforward enough. Some data transmissions suffer more than others from a delay in the stream of packets. For example, when you transfer a data file from one computer to another, it doesn't much matter if there's a delay while the data is being delivered: After all the packets of data have arrived, the network card and network client software put the packets back into the correct order and reassemble them into a file that you can work with. By contrast, if you're listening to streaming audio or watching streaming video across a network connection, a delay in the stream of packets will produce a break in the audio or video, spoiling the experience. So the QoS Packet Scheduler gives priority to data that would suffer from being interrupted over data that's less sensitive to time lags.

QoS Packet Scheduler has no configurable properties.

FILE AND PRINTER SHARING FOR MICROSOFT NETWORKS

File and Printer Sharing for Microsoft Networks enables your computer to share files and printers with other computers on the network. If you turn on Sharing and Discovery, other computers can then access shared files and printers on your computer.

Make sure that your dial-up Internet connection isn't using the File and Printer Sharing for Microsoft Networks item, because this could expose your shared files and printers to everyone on the Internet.

File and Printer Sharing for Microsoft Networks has no configurable properties.

INTERNET PROTOCOL VERSION 6 (TCP/IPV6) AND INTERNET PROTOCOL VERSION 4 (TCP/IPV4)

TCP/IP is the protocol suite on which the Internet is based. Windows Vista uses TCP/IPv6 and TCP/IPv4 as its default network protocols, using TCP/IPv6 (the latest version) with servers that support TCP/IPv6 and using TCP/IPv4 with other servers.

TCP/IP has various properties that you can set in the Internet Protocol (TCP/IP) Properties dialog box. The section "Configuring TCP/IP Manually," later in this chapter, discusses how to set these properties.

LINK-LAYER TOPOLOGY DISCOVERY MAPPER I/O DRIVER AND LINK-LAYER TOPOLOGY
DISCOVERY RESPONDER

Link-Layer Topology Discovery (LLTD) is a protocol that figures out the topology of the network to which the computer is attached. Windows Vista uses LLTD to produce the network map that appears in Network and Sharing Center windows. The Mapper I/O Driver works out which computers and devices are on the network, creates a map, and estimates the network's bandwidth. (I/O is the abbreviation for input/output.) The Responder listens for LLTD requests and replies to them, allowing the Mapper to find out which computers and devices are present.

These two items have no configurable properties.

Table 28.1 shows you the networking components normally used for a wired LAN connection, a wireless network connection, and a dial-up connection.

TABLE 28.1: Windows Vista's Standard Networking Components and Which Connections Use Them

COMPONENT	WIRED LAN CONNECTION	WIRELESS NETWORK CONNECTION	DIAL-UP CONNECTION
Client for Microsoft Networks	Yes	Yes	No
QoS Packet Scheduler	Yes	Yes	Yes
File and Printer Sharing for Microsoft Networks	Yes	Yes	No

TABLE 28.1: Windows Vista's Standard Networking Components and Which Connections Use Them *(CONTINUED)*

COMPONENT	WIRED LAN CONNECTION	WIRELESS NETWORK CONNECTION	DIAL-UP CONNECTION
Internet Protocol Version 6 (TCP/IPv6)	Yes	Yes	Yes
Internet Protocol Version 4 (TCP/IPv4)	Yes	Yes	Yes
Link-Layer Topology Discovery Mapper I/O Driver	Yes	Yes	No
Link-Layer Topology Discovery Responder	Yes	Yes	No

UNDERSTANDING WINDOWS VISTA'S EXTRA NETWORKING COMPONENTS

Apart from the networking components discussed in the main text of this chapter, Windows Vista includes various networking components that are not normally needed for home or home-office networking. This sidebar briefly explains what these components are and when (if ever) you might need to use them. If you do need to install any of these components, take the following steps:

1. Choose Start ➢ Control Panel. Windows opens a Control Panel window.

2. In Control Panel Home view, click the Program link. Windows displays a Programs window.

3. Under the Programs and Features heading, click the Turn Windows Features On or Off link, and then authenticate yourself to User Account Control. Windows displays the Windows Features window.

4. Select the check box for each feature you want to install.

5. Click the OK button. Windows closes the Windows Features window and installs the features.

RIP Listener A tool that enables Windows to listen to Router Information Protocol (RIP) broadcast packets giving information about router availability and reconfigure its TCP/IP routing tables accordingly. You won't normally need RIP Listener on a small network.

Simple TCP/IP Services A group of TCP/IP services (including a Quote of the Day service and an Echo generator) that you're unlikely to need. Don't install them unless you're sure you need them, because they can be used in denial-of-service (DoS) attacks by malware that gets onto your computer. Worse yet, some personal firewall software packages don't monitor these services.

SNMP Feature Simple Network Management Protocol (SNMP) is used to manage larger networks (for example, remotely administering routers and switches). The WMI SNMP Provider lets Windows Management Interface (WMI) programs access SNMP information. You shouldn't need to use SNMP on a home network or a home-office network.

Telnet Client Telnet Client lets you connect to a remote computer using the text-based telnet protocol. You may need to install Telnet Client if you need to log on remotely to Unix-based computers.

Telnet Server   Telnet Server is the server component of telnet and lets other computers connect to your computer via telnet. While using telnet to access your own computer from a remote computer is viable, it is also much less secure than other methods and is best avoided.

TFTP Client   TFTP is the Trivial File Transfer Protocol, which is used for transferring files from one computer to another. You will seldom need to install TFTP on Windows Vista.

INSTALLING AND REMOVING NETWORKING COMPONENTS

Windows Vista installs all the components you'll need to create most kinds of home networks and to connect to public networks, so you'll seldom need to install other networking components. However, if you need to do so, follow these steps:

1. In the Network Connections window, right-click a connection, choose Properties from the context menu, and then authenticate yourself to User Account Control. Windows displays the Properties dialog box for the connection.

2. On the Networking page, click the Install button. Windows displays the Select Network Feature Type dialog box, as shown here.

3. In the list box, select the Client item, the Service item, or the Protocol item as appropriate.

4. Click the Add button. Windows displays the Select Network Client dialog box, the Select Network Service dialog box, or the Select Network Protocol dialog box as appropriate. Figure 28.14 shows the Select Network Protocol dialog box.

5. If the component you want to add appears in the list box, select it. If you have on disk a component that Windows doesn't provide, click the Have Disk button and use the resulting Install from Disk dialog box to specify the location of the file containing the component, and then select the component itself.

6. Click the OK button. Windows installs the component and returns you to the Properties dialog box for the connection.

FIGURE 28.14
In the Select Network
Protocol dialog box
(shown here), the
Select Network Client
dialog box, or the
Select Network
Service dialog box,
select the protocol,
client, or service to
install.

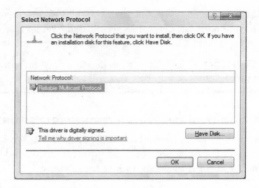

7. If the component has configurable properties that you want to configure, select it in the This Connection Uses the Following Items list box, and then click the Properties button. (If the component has no configurable properties, this button will be dimmed and unavailable.) Windows displays the Properties dialog box for the component. Choose properties as needed, and then click the OK button to close the Properties dialog box.

8. If Windows tells you that you need to restart your computer before the new settings will take effect, click the Yes button. Windows restarts your computer. When you log back on to Windows, the network connection will have the client, service, or protocol installed and available for use.

You'll seldom need to remove one of the standard networking components, because Windows needs them for most network connections, and removing a component from one connection removes it from all connections. Instead, you can clear the component's check box in the This Connection Uses the Following Items list on the Networking page of the Properties dialog box for the connection to prevent the connection from using the component.

However, if you install an extra networking component, you may need to uninstall it. To do so, select the component in the This Connection Uses the Following Items list on the Networking page of the Properties dialog box for the connection, click the Uninstall button, and then click the Yes button in the Uninstall confirmation dialog box (see the example shown here).

Depending on the component, you may need to shut down and restart your computer after removing the component.

Configuring TCP/IP Manually

For most home network or home-office network configurations, it's normally easier to use a DHCP server of some sort to assign IP addresses automatically when they're needed rather than set the addresses manually. For example, if you use ICS to share your Internet connection, Windows Home automatically configures the ICS host to use ICS's built-in DHCP allocator to supply IP addresses to the computers on your network. Similarly, many residential gateways and other shared Internet access devices offer built-in DHCP servers that automatically allocate IP addresses for computers connected to the same network.

Even so, sometimes you may need to configure TCP/IP manually to specify a fixed IP address and DNS server details. To do so, take the following steps:

1. Click the Start button, right-click Network, choose Properties from the context menu, and then authenticate yourself to User Account Control. Windows displays a Network and Sharing Center window.

2. In the left pane, click the Manage Network Connections link. Windows displays a Network Connections window.

3. Right-click the connection you want to affect (for example, your Local Area Connection item), and then choose Properties from the shortcut menu. Windows displays the Properties dialog box for the connection.

4. In the This Connection Uses the Following Items list box on the Networking page, double-click the Internet Protocol item you want to configure. (Alternatively, click the appropriate Internet Protocol item, and then click the Properties button.) This example uses the Internet Protocol Version 4 (TCP/IPv4) item, because TCP/IPv4 is more widely used than TCP/IPv6 at this writing. Windows displays the Internet Protocol Properties dialog box for that version of TCP/IP. Figure 28.15 shows the Internet Protocol Version 4 (TCP/IPv4) Properties dialog box.

5. Select the Use the Following IP Address option button. Windows hides the Alternate Configuration tab, because it's not relevant when you use a fixed IP address.

6. In the Use the Following IP Address group box, type the details of the IP address: the IP address itself (for example, 192.168.0.44), the subnet mask (for example, 255.255.255.0), and the default gateway (for example, 192.168.0.1).

7. In the Use the Following DNS Server Addresses group box, type the IP addresses of your preferred (or *primary*) DNS server and alternate (or *secondary*) DNS server.

FIGURE 28.15

If necessary, you can configure TCP/IP manually in the Internet Protocol Version 4 (TCP/IPv4) dialog box. When the computer is using DHCP to obtain an address, this dialog box contains a General page and an Alternate Configuration page. When the computer is using a fixed IP address, this dialog box contains only the General page.

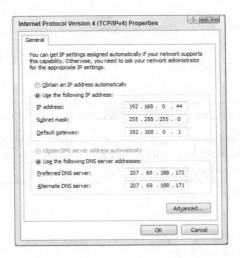

8. If you need to add further DNS servers, click the Advanced button. Windows displays the Advanced TCP/IP Settings dialog box.

9. Click the DNS tab. Windows displays the DNS page (see Figure 28.16).

10. In the DNS Server Addresses, in Order of Use list box, arrange the list of DNS servers into the order in which you want the servers queried:

   ◆ Use the Up and Down buttons to shuffle the listed servers into order.

   ◆ Use the Add button and the resulting TCP/IP DNS Server dialog box to add a server to the list.

   ◆ Use the Edit button and the resulting TCP/IP DNS Server dialog box to edit an existing server entry.

   ◆ Use the Remove button to remove a server.

11. Click the OK button. Windows closes the Advanced TCP/IP Settings dialog box.

12. Click the OK button. Windows closes the Internet Protocol Version 4 (TCP/IPv4) dialog box.

FIGURE 28.16
You can adjust your DNS configuration on the DNS page of the Advanced TCP/IP Properties dialog box.

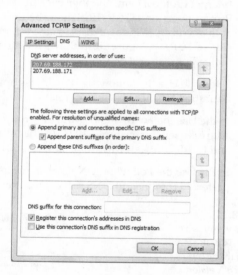

OTHER ADVANCED TCP/IP SETTINGS: IP SETTINGS AND WINS SETTINGS

You'll rarely need to change the settings on the IP Settings page and the WINS page of the Advanced TCP/IP Settings dialog box. WINS is the acronym for Windows Internet Name Service, a service that TCP/IP uses to resolve NetBIOS names.

Connecting and Merging Networks

If you set up your home network or home-office network in separate stages, or if you set up a home-office network and then set up a separate home network as well, you may end up with two separate networks that you need to join. You can join them in two ways: by bridging the networks together or by merging them into a single network.

CONNECTING TWO NETWORKS VIA A BRIDGE

Windows lets you *bridge* (connect) two separate networks so that they essentially function as a single network. For example, you might need to connect:

◆ A wireless network to a wired network

◆ A FireWire network to a wired Ethernet network

◆ A FireWire network to a wireless network

Windows can automatically set up bridging for your network if all your network connections are present and correct when you run the wizard. But you may also need to set up bridging manually as described in this section so that you have more control over the connections established.

The computer on which you implement the bridging must be connected to both networks, so it will have at least two network interfaces, one connected to each network.

To bridge the network connections, select them in the Network Connections window, right-click the selection, choose Bridge Connections from the context menu, and then authenticate yourself to User Account Control. Windows creates the bridge (as shown in the next illustration), applies it to the network connections, and displays an icon named Network Bridge. If you're likely to forget which connections are bridged, rename the Network Bridge icon to something more descriptive (for example, add the names of the connections that the bridge connects).

Once you've created a bridge, the bridged network adapters have the same IP address, and Windows forwards all data packets from each segment to the other network segment. To configure properties for the bridged network adapters, work with the bridge rather than with the individual network adapters: Right-click the bridge and choose Properties from the context menu to display its Properties dialog box, then make the changes there.

Apart from configuring the bridge's properties, you can manipulate it from the context menu as follows:

◆ To add a connection to the bridge, right-click it and choose Add to Bridge from the context menu.

◆ To remove a connection from the bridge, right-click it and choose Remove from Bridge from the context menu.

♦ To disable the bridge, right-click it and choose Disable from the context menu.

♦ To delete the bridge, right-click it and choose Delete from the context menu. Windows prompts you to confirm the deletion, and then removes the bridge.

MERGING TWO NETWORKS

To merge two networks together into a single network, follow these steps:

1. Click the Start button, right-click Network, choose Properties from the context menu, and then authenticate yourself to User Account Control. Windows displays a Network and Sharing Center window.

2. In the main part of the window, click the Customize link next to the listing for your main network connection. Windows displays the Customize Network Settings window.

3. Click the Merge or Delete Network Locations link near the bottom of the window, and then authenticate yourself to User Account Control. Windows displays the Merge or Delete Network Locations dialog box (see Figure 28.17).

4. Select the networks you want to merge, and then click the Merge button. Windows displays the Merge Network Locations dialog box, shown here.

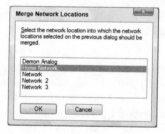

5. In the list box, select the network into which you want to merge the network locations—in other words, the network that you want to have once the merge is complete.

6. Click the OK button. Windows merges the networks.

FIGURE 28.17
In the Merge or Delete Network Locations dialog box, select the networks you want to merge, and then click the Merge button.

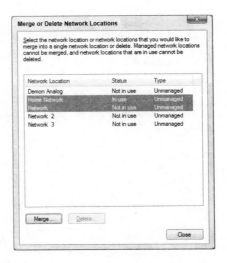

The Bottom Line

Connect your network to the Internet   Windows Vista encourages you to connect your network to the Internet from the start so that all computers on the network can access Internet resources. If your Internet connection is fast enough, you'll probably want to connect your entire network. In most cases, the best way to connect the network is by using a Network Address Translation (NAT) device, such as Windows' built-in Internet Connection Sharing (ICS) or a hardware device such as a router, which connects all the network's computers to the Internet while providing some protection from the Internet's dangers.

Share a file or folder with other network users   You can share a file or folder with other network users either by putting it in the Public folder or by changing the permissions on the file or folder so that other users can access it.

Allow other network users to print to your printer   To allow other network users to print to your printer, right-click the printer in the Printers window, and then choose Sharing from the context menu. Click the Change Sharing Options button, authenticate yourself to User Account Control, select the Share This Printer check box, and then name the printer.

Configure networks, network connections, and network components   If a network connection stops working, right-click it, choose Diagnose from the shortcut menu, and then choose an option from the Network Diagnostics dialog box that Windows presents. To install, configure, or remove networking components, work on the Networking page of the Properties dialog box for the connection. If you've created two separate networks but need them to act as a single network, you can either bridge them together temporarily or merge them into a single network.

Chapter 29

Securing Your Network

◆ Assess the threats to your network

◆ Secure your Internet connection with a firewall

◆ Learn to use the Windows Firewall with Advanced Security application

◆ Secure your software and limit user access to computers and files

◆ Back up data on your network

◆ Secure your wireless network

This chapter shows you how to secure your network against both external and internal threats. It discusses how to identify the points of weakness on a typical network and the best ways of securing them, and it provides in-depth coverage of how to secure wireless networks, which have additional security considerations.

Assessing the Threats to Your Network

Before deciding what measure you'll take to protect your network, assess the threats to the network and determine what you're trying to protect and the degree of protection it requires. This section suggests how you might approach these issues.

Why Would Anyone Attack Your Network?

For many home network and home-office network administrators, the main problem with network security is getting people—including perhaps you—to take it seriously. It's tempting to believe that your computer or your network is unlikely to be attacked and that therefore you don't really need to bother securing it. After all, if several hundred million computers are on the Internet, why should anyone pick on yours?

Similarly, you might choose not to pay for home insurance on the assumption that your home will probably not be broken into. But unlike your home, which is vulnerable only to thieves in the neighborhood, a computer or network connected to the Internet is vulnerable to everyone else who's online—and unlike thieves, hackers have automated tools with which they can scan millions of Internet addresses for unprotected computers and attack them automatically.

People who have secured their networks often find in their firewall logs frequent attempts to access their networks from IP addresses all over the world. And if an attacker is subtle rather than destructive, they can access your unprotected computer, read your files, and steal your secrets without you being any the wiser.

What Do You Have to Protect?

Only you know what secrets you keep on your computer (until someone hacks in to it, that is). But chances are that you have plenty of data you need to protect, from confidential documents and e-mail messages, personal details, online accounts, credit card data, bank records, tax files, and much more.

Beyond the risk of having your data stolen and your identity perhaps impersonated, you probably also want to guard against indirect attacks such as an outsider using your computer to perform unsavory or illegal acts—for example, sending spam, posting offensive material online, or attacking other computers.

How Much Security Do You Need?

Just as there's no sense in installing maximum security on an empty garden shed, you may well not need to turn your home network into a virtual Alcatraz. So when you're thinking about securing your network, it helps to have an idea of what you're trying to protect and what kinds of attacks you're trying to thwart.

Most likely, you'll want to prevent casual access to your network—for example, by someone looking for a free wireless connection—and put enough easy-to-implement security into place to deter all but determined attackers. But someone determined enough will probably be able to circumvent sensible security measures, and you may need to restore data from backup to recover from a destructive attack. Similarly, if you're protecting your house against break-ins, you probably secure your windows, doors, and other points of entry. But if a burglar brings a crane with a wrecking ball, or drops a bomb from a helicopter, your locks and bolts probably won't withstand the attack.

Understanding the Points of Weakness on Your Network

A house has certain obvious points of weakness for an attacker: the doors, the windows, the chimney (possibly), and any hole in the roof, walls, floors, or ceiling. An attacker could brazenly try to open a door or window. They could try to slip into the house undetected by weaseling through a mouse hole in the baseboard. They could simply smash their way in by using a bulldozer. Or they could try to persuade you (or your house) to open the door for them.

Similarly, stand-alone computer has obvious points of weakness, the usual suspects being the floppy drive, the CD or DVD drives, and any other removable drives, any of which can be used to load infected files or malware onto the computer. The computer may also be open to physical attacks, such as cutting off the power supply (either at the computer, at the wall socket or breaker box, or outside the building) or trying to open it with a sledgehammer.

As soon as you connect your computer to the Internet, you open another channel for attack or infection. In many cases, the Internet connection poses a far greater threat to the security of the computer than do the floppy, CD, and removable drives.

When two or more computers are connected in a network, each point of weakness on an individual computer becomes a threat to the other computers on the network. And when you connect the network to the Internet, each computer connected to the network becomes vulnerable to attack and infection through the Internet connection. Unless the Internet connection is tightly protected, an attacker can take control of a computer on the network and use it to attack or infect the other computers on the network.

To keep your network safe, you essentially want to make it the equivalent of a tightly controlled gated community surrounded by a high-risk area: Each computer attached to the network must be a known quantity, just as each house in a community must be (houses outside the community can't suddenly become part of the community). Users of networked computers have levels of access appropriate to their trustworthiness, just as community members do. For example, most community members will be allowed to access their own house but not other people's houses. Most users on the network will be allowed to use their own computer (or a computer they share with other people) but not other computers. Just as the road into the community from the outside needs to be guarded so that community members can come and go freely, but unauthorized traffic is kept out, so the Internet connection needs to be firewalled and policed to prevent unauthorized data from entering the network. And the community leaders (read: the Administrator users) supervise what's happening in the community, check periodically that the gatekeeper is doing its job (read: examine the firewall logs), and generally keep an eye on things.

Your home network is likely to have three main points of weakness:

◆ The network's Internet connection (or connections) can give an attacker access to your network; can bring in viruses, malware, or inappropriate material; and can send out your private data.

◆ The removable-media drives on the computers can be used to introduce dangerous material to your network or to copy your private data.

◆ The users of the computers on the network can delete files, steal files, install dangerous software, or introduce malware or inappropriate material to the network.

If your network is a home or home-office network, as this chapter assumes, your users probably pose less of a threat than do the users of a corporate, governmental, or military network. But don't discount them as a threat, because even well-intentioned actions can damage your valuable data. For example, if someone decides to, say, install Linux on the same partition as your data files, you'll find yourself giving your backup and disaster-recovery strategy an impromptu workout—together with your central nervous system, most likely.

Normal Methods of Securing a Home Network

The typical methods of securing a home or home-office network are as follows:

◆ Secure the Internet connection with a firewall and configure the connection to prevent file sharing across it.

◆ Scan all incoming files for viruses. Monitor each computer for unusual activity.

◆ Choose browser settings to minimize the dangers of hostile web pages, scripts, and infected files. Choose high-security settings for programs that allow the execution of macros, scripts, and user forms.

◆ Implement user accounts actively to control which computers users can log on to and which actions they can take on them.

◆ Use permissions to prevent users from accessing files you don't want them to access.

◆ Educate users about security risks and how to minimize them.

◆ Prevent untrustworthy users from physically accessing computers that contain sensitive or otherwise important data or that are mission-critical. For example, in a home setting, lock your office so that young children can't access your files.

◆ For each computer that contains important data files or delivers services to other computers, keep the hardware and software maintained so that no computer stops working unexpectedly. (You should maintain *all* your computers, of course, but if time is short, concentrate your efforts on those that contain important data.)

◆ To make sure that no unauthorized traffic can enter certain parts of your network, implement Windows Firewall rules on key computers.

◆ Back up any and all data that could possibly be damaged, stolen, deleted, or otherwise cause problems if it were to disappear.

Besides securing the network using these techniques, you need to have a disaster-recovery plan for when the network's security is compromised. As with a stand-alone PC, that means backing up all the data files that you can't easily re-create and knowing how to restore the files.

The rest of this chapter discusses these steps in more detail, referring you to features covered in other chapters where appropriate.

Securing Your Internet Connection with a Firewall

If your network is connected to the Internet, securing your Internet connection is a vital step in securing your network. To secure the Internet connection, you need to implement a firewall on it. (If your network has multiple Internet connections, you need to implement a firewall on each connection.)

If you use Internet Connection Sharing (ICS) to share the connection, you have an easy solution available: Windows Firewall is fully integrated with ICS. You should also use Windows Firewall on any other Internet connections that computers on your network have—for example, if your network connects via a shared broadband connection, but one or two computers have additional dial-up connections, you need to implement Windows Firewall on those dial-up connections as well as on the shared broadband connection. Windows also implements Windows Firewall on all internal network connections for additional security.

Windows enables Windows Firewall by default, so Windows Firewall should be running unless you've explicitly turned it off.

If you need tight security, or you don't entirely trust Windows Firewall, or both, you can add a hardware firewall to the network. You can either implement a hardware firewall on its own, or you can use it to harden a network protected by a software firewall such as Windows Firewall. See a book about firewalls for advice on choosing a hardware firewall. Check that the hardware firewall supports Universal Plug & Play (UPnP) if you want to be able to use programs such as Messenger across it.

Make sure you haven't bound File and Printer Sharing to the network adapter for your Internet connection. Display the Networking page of the Properties dialog box for the connection and verify that the File and Printer Sharing for Microsoft Networks check box in the This Connection Uses the Following Items list box is cleared. If not, clear it, then close the Properties dialog box and restart your Internet connection if it's currently connected.

Once your firewall is in place, check that it's working. One easy method is to run the free probe tools at the Gibson Research Corporation website (`http://www.grc.com`). This offers several free checks, including ShieldsUP!, PortProbe, and File Sharing Probe, designed to help you identify weaknesses in your security arrangements.

HOW ARE HIGH-SECURITY NETWORKS SECURED?

The security measures discussed so far in this section are adequate for most home and home-office networks. But what about networks that need really high security—corporate networks, governmental networks, and military networks? What do they use? This sidebar discusses some of the common techniques for securing networks. You could apply some of these measures to your home or home-office network if you felt the need—actually, you *could* just conceivably apply all of them. But as you'll see, that'd be extreme.

As mentioned earlier in this book, there's a foolproof way of making your computer truly secure from being hacked: Disconnect it from any network, unplug the modem, and seal the computer in a lead-lined room in a bunker deep underground. There you can compute in near-total security.

Most people don't find this approach practical. But many high-security installations do follow this approach to a certain extent: Vital networks and workstations are kept physically isolated and protected. This isolation may involve anything from a secure room or secure area of a building to a secure site protected by a patrolled and mined boundary fence.

For security, many networks aren't connected to the Internet at all. They may be completely isolated, or they may have secure connections to other high-security networks via private communication lines.

If the network has any Internet access, it'll be through at least one hardware firewall. Only users with a valid reason are allowed to access the Internet, and this access is likely to be through a proxy server, a computer that filters requests for web pages and retrieves those that are for permitted sites. A proxy server also stores the most frequently accessed web pages so that it can deliver them quickly when a user requests them.

Any publicly accessible servers and services are kept outside the firewall in what's called a demilitarized zone (DMZ) in a tribute to Kuwait, Korea, or Berlin, depending on your historical preference. The DMZ is created by placing the computers that need to be in it between the firewall and the Internet connection. Computers placed in the DMZ contain no sensitive data and are locked down tightly so that people who access them can manipulate them only in approved ways and cannot use them to attack computers located inside the firewall. The computers in the DMZ are checked frequently to make sure they haven't been cracked and taken over.

E-mail—again, only if it's used, and usually it'll be available only for some users—goes through an e-mail gateway that filters both incoming and outgoing messages to prevent messages from being sent to or arriving from forbidden addresses and to prevent inappropriate material from entering or leaving the network. For example, an e-mail gateway might check the content of incoming and outgoing messages, blocking or referring to an administrator any messages that fell afoul of its rules. Almost certainly, it would also scan all attachments for viruses and for content.

All files coming into the network—whether via an Internet connection, a network connection, or on physical media—are scanned for viruses and to make sure that their content is appropriate to its destination. Any executable files, and all new code, are tested in simulated environments to make sure they perform as they should before they're introduced to the working environment.

All personnel are closely evaluated for security before being employed. Access to the secure site or area requires an identity check. And personnel's actions at work are likely to be monitored or recorded.

As you can see, you *could* apply some of these measures to your home or home-office network. But in most cases you'll do best to stick with the simpler and less stringent measures outlined in the previous section.

Configuring Windows Firewall with Advanced Security

Earlier in this book, you saw how Windows Vista enables Windows Firewall by default and protects your network connections and Internet connections. On many computers, you'll want to leave Windows Firewall that way, simply enjoying the protection it gives without changing its settings.

On other computers, however, you may need to configure Windows Firewall manually, either to allow incoming traffic sent to certain programs or ports to pass to specific computers on your network (as described in Chapter 28) or to set up rules for outbound traffic or rules for connection security. You may also need to monitor the connections that Windows Firewall allows and those it blocks.

This section introduces you to configuring Windows Firewall. It's a big topic, and because Windows Firewall comes configured adequately for most purposes, you may not need to explore it at all.

Windows Firewall's Default Settings

Windows Firewall's default settings are as follows:

Outgoing Traffic Allow all traffic unless it matches a rule that tells Windows Firewall to do something with it (for example, to block it).

Incoming Traffic Allow traffic that is a response to a request (for example, your computer requests a web page, and the server sends it) or traffic that matches a rule. Otherwise, block all traffic.

Opening Windows Firewall with Advanced Security

To configure the advanced features of Windows Firewall, you use the Windows Firewall with Advanced Security program. To launch this program, take the following steps:

1. Choose Start ➤ Control Panel. Windows opens a Control Panel window.

2. In Control Panel Home view, click the System and Maintenance link. Windows opens a System and Maintenance window.

3. Click the Administrative Tools link. Windows displays the Administrative Tools window.

4. Double-click the Windows Firewall with Advanced Security item, and then authenticate yourself to User Account Control. Windows displays the Windows Firewall with Advanced Security window (see Figure 29.1).

If the Windows Firewall with Advanced Security item at the top of the left pane isn't selected, click it. Windows Firewall with Advanced Security displays its Overview pane.

Understanding the Domain Profile, Private Profile, and Private Profile

The Windows Firewall with Advanced Security overview shows you the status of your computer's three profiles and indicates which profile is active.

Domain Profile The domain profile applies only when your computer is connected to a domain-based Windows network, which Windows Vista Home Edition normally won't be. (By contrast, Windows Vista Business Edition computers will normally be connected to such a network, and Windows Vista Ultimate Edition computers often will be.)

Private Profile The private profile applies when your computer is connected to a private Windows network, such as your home network. A private network is one that's protected from the Internet to some extent—for example, the network is behind a router or gateway and a firewall. A private network normally contains computers that are known and trusted. For example, you'll normally control which computers are attached to a home network or home-office network.

FIGURE 29.1

The Windows Firewall with Advanced Security window lets you monitor what Windows Firewall is blocking and configure rules for inbound traffic, outbound traffic, and connection security. Use the tree in the left pane to select the item you want to configure.

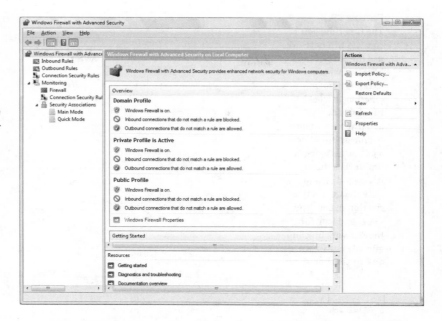

Public Profile   The public profile applies when your computer is connected to a public network, such as a citywide wireless network or a wireless network in a coffee shop. A public network is one that is directly connected to the Internet without protection.

The first time you connect to any particular network, Windows Vista displays the Set Network Location window (see Figure 29.2) to prompt you to decide which type of network it is. Follow these steps:

1. Choose the Home item or the Work item for a private network; the security level of each is the same, but having separate Home and Work items lets you distinguish between two different locations (for example, your home and your office) more easily. Choose the Public Location item for a public network.

2. Click the Customize the Name, Location Type, and Icon for the Network link. Windows displays the Customize Network Settings window (see Figure 29.3).

3. In the Network Name text box, type a descriptive name for the network.

4. In the Location type area, select the Public option button if the network is public. Otherwise, select the Private option button.

5. To change the icon Windows displays for the network, click the Change button. Windows displays the Change Network Icon dialog box. Select the icon you want, and then click the OK button. Windows closes the Change Network Icon dialog box and returns you to the Customize Network Settings window.

6. Click the Next button, and then authenticate yourself to User Account Control to apply the change. Windows displays the Successfully Set Network Settings window.

7. Click the Close button. Windows closes the window.

FIGURE 29.2
The first time you connect to a network, use the Set Network Location window to tell Windows whether to treat the network as a private network (Home or Work) or a public network (Public Location). It's a good idea to click the Customize the Name, Location Type, and Icon for the Network link and give the network a descriptive name.

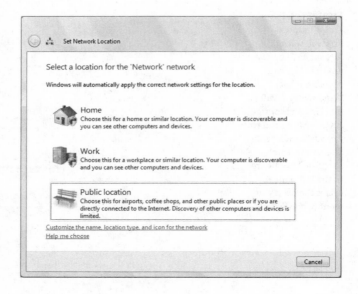

FIGURE 29.3
Normally, it's helpful to give each network a descriptive name—and perhaps a different icon—so that you can easily tell which network is which.

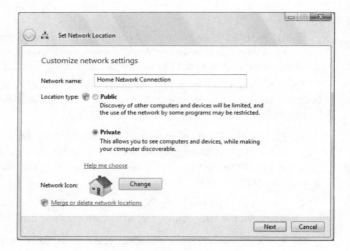

Configuring the Private Profile and Public Profile

To configure the private profile and the public profile, take the following steps:

1. In the left panel, right-click the Windows Firewall with Advanced Security item, and then choose Properties from the context menu. Windows displays the Windows Firewall with Advanced Security on Local Computer Properties dialog box. This dialog box contains four pages:

   ◆ The Domain Profile page, the Private Profile page, and the Public Profile page each contain the same set of controls, but apply to the three different profiles. Normally, you'll want to set the private profile and the public profile but not the domain profile.

   ◆ The IPSec Settings page contains IP Security (IPSec) settings.

2. Start by configuring the private profile. Click the Private Profile tab. Windows displays the Private Profile page (see Figure 29.4).

3. In the State group box, choose settings for the firewall's state:

   Firewall State   In this drop-down list, select On to turn the firewall on. Select Off if you need to turn the firewall off. (It's seldom advisable to turn the firewall off except temporarily while you're trying to resolve connectivity issues on your local network.)

   Inbound Connections   Choose Block (the default setting) to block all connections except those that you have told Windows Firewall to pass, Block All Connections to block all connections (for example, for extra protection), or Allow if you need to allow all connections. (Allow is a dangerous setting because it removes the protection that the firewall offers.)

   Outbound Connections   Choose Allow (the default setting) to allow all connections that aren't specifically blocked. Choose Block to block all outbound connections (for example, if you're trying to contain malware on your computer).

4. In the Settings group box, click the Customize button. Windows displays the Customize Settings for the Private Profile dialog box (see Figure 29.5), in which you can choose the following settings and then click the OK button:

   Firewall Settings   In the Display a Notification drop-down list, choose Yes or No to control whether Windows Firewall should display a notification to the user when it blocks a program from receiving incoming connections. Usually the notification is helpful, because it lets the user know why a program may not be working and gives him or her the choice of unblocking it. For some users, however, you may prefer to suppress the notification.

   Unicast Response   In the Allow Unicast Response drop-down list, choose Yes or No to control whether Windows Firewall should allow a unicast response to be received in response to multicast messages or broadcast messages that your computer sends. The default setting is Yes, but you may want to turn off receiving of unicast responses if your computer appears to be receiving too much incoming traffic when it sends multicast messages or broadcast messages.

   Rule Merging   The settings in this group box apply only to versions of Windows administered through Group Policy—for example, the Business and Ultimate versions of Windows Vista.

FIGURE 29.4

The Private Profile page of the Windows Firewall with Advanced Security on Local Computer Properties dialog box lets you configure Windows Firewall's behavior for when your computer is connected to a private network such as your home network.

FIGURE 29.5
The Customize Settings dialog box for a profile lets you suppress notification when Windows Firewall blocks a connection and choose whether to respond to multicast or broadcast network traffic.

5. To find out which packets Windows Firewall is discarding, you need to configure security logging. In the Logging group box, click the Customize button. Windows displays the Customize Logging Settings for the Private Profile dialog box (see Figure 29.6). Choose settings as described next, and then click the OK button.

   Name   Choose where to store your log file and what to name it. The default name is `pfirewall.log` in the `%windir%\system32\LogFiles\Firewall` folder (where `%windir%` is the environmental variable that returns the folder in which Windows is installed). Change the name or folder only if you want to keep your entire log files in a particular folder; otherwise, leave the default name and location. The log is a text file, so you can view it in any text editor (for example, Notepad).

   Size Limit (KB)   If you want, use the Size Limit text box to change the size limit for the security log file. The default setting is 4,096KB (which is 4MB), but you may want to increase it if you choose to log successful connections.

   Log Dropped Packets   Choose Yes if you want to log dropped data packets. These are the packets that Windows Firewall discards because it can't match them to an outgoing request. They may reveal attempts to scan your system for a security hole. They may also help you identify legitimate programs that are having problems communicating across the firewall. The default setting is No.

   Log Successful Connections   Choose Yes if you want to log successful inbound and outbound connections (for example, to see which Internet sites the computers on your network are connecting to and which computers are connecting to your network from the Internet). If you use your Internet connection actively, logging successful connections will rapidly fill up your firewall log. The default setting is No.

6. Click the Public Profile tab, and then repeat steps 3 through 5 to choose settings for the public profile.

FIGURE 29.6
Use the Customize Logging Settings dialog box to choose whether to log dropped packets and successful connections for this profile.

Choosing IPSec Settings

Windows Firewall uses IPSec (Internet Protocol Security) to help secure your computer. Windows Vista comes with preset IPSec settings that work well for most computers, so you don't need to configure the settings. Unless you're familiar with IPSec, you're best off leaving Windows Vista's default IPSec settings in place.

If, however, you need to use specific IPSec settings, or you want to exempt Internet Control Message Protocol (ICMP) packets from IPSec control so that you can troubleshoot network connectivity problems more easily, click the IPSec Settings tab in the Windows Firewall with Advanced Security on Local Computer dialog box. Windows displays the IPSec Settings page (see Figure 29.7).

To remove IPSec restrictions from ICMP packets, choose Yes in the Exempt ICMP from IPSec drop-down list. The default setting is No.

To customize the IPSec settings, click the Customize button. Windows displays the Customize IPSec Settings dialog box (see Figure 29.8), in which you can change the following settings:

Key Exchange   These settings control the encryption keys that Windows uses to establish IPSec on connections.

FIGURE 29.7
The IPSec Settings tab of the Windows Firewall with Advanced Security on Local Computer dialog box lets you exempt ICMP from IPSec or customize IPSec settings.

Data Protection These settings control the protocols that Windows uses for protecting data integrity (making sure it hasn't been altered during transmission) and encryption.

Authentication Method These settings control the protocol that Windows uses for authenticating computers and users.

When you've finished choosing IPSec settings, click the OK button. Windows closes the Customize IPSec Settings dialog box, returning you to the Windows Firewall with Advanced Security on Local Computer dialog box. Click the OK button. Windows closes the dialog box and applies your choices.

FIGURE 29.8

The Customize IPSec Settings dialog box lets you choose settings for key exchange, data protection, and authentication. Unless you're familiar with IPSec, you probably shouldn't change the default values, which work well for normal purposes.

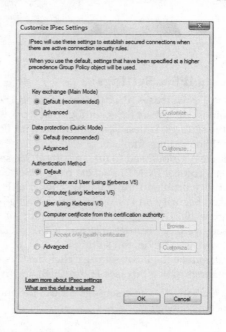

Creating an Inbound or Outbound Rule

To create a new inbound rule or a new outbound rule, take the following steps:

1. In the left pane, right-click the Inbound Rules item or the Outbound Rules item, and then choose New Rule from the properties menu. Windows launches the New Inbound Rule Wizard or the New Outbound Rule Wizard, which displays the Rule Type screen (see Figure 29.9). The screens in this example use the New Inbound Rule Wizard.

2. In the What Type of Rule Would You Like to Create? list, select the appropriate option button (see the following list). The Steps list on the left of the window changes to show the steps involved in the type of rule you chose. This example uses the Port option.

   Program Select this option button to create a rule that affects a particular program.

   Port Select this option button to create a rule that affects a particular TCP port or UDP port. (Internet traffic is typically sent to a particular port or a range of ports.) Transmission Control Protocol (TCP) and User Datagram Protocol (UDP) are two of the protocols in the TCP/IP protocol suite.

FIGURE 29.9
On the Rule Type
screen, choose the
type of rule you
want to create.
For example, you
can create a rule
that affects a
particular program
or a particular
TCP/IP port.

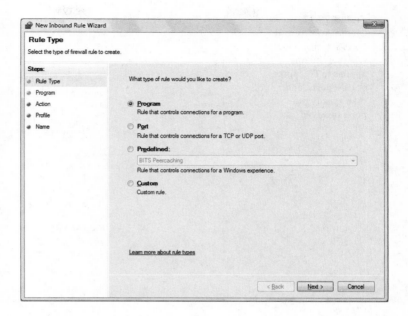

Predefined   Select this option button to create a rule that affects one of the Windows features that appears in the drop-down list—for example, Connect to a Network Projector, Remote Assistance, or Windows Media Player.

Custom   Select this option button when you need to create a rule manually—for example, because there are criteria that the Wizard doesn't let you set.

3. Click the Next button. The wizard displays the screen for the next step in the rule type you chose. For the Port rule type, the next step is the Protocol and Ports screen (see Figure 29.10).

4. In the Does This Rule Apply to TCP or UDP? area, select the TCP option button or the UDP option button, as appropriate.

5. In the Does This Rule Apply to All Local Ports or Specific Local Ports? area, select the All Local Ports option button or the Specific Local Ports option button, as appropriate. If you select the All Local Ports option button, type the port number in the text box. To make the rule apply to multiple ports, type the port numbers separated by commas: for example, **407 , 417**. The best place to get a list of TCP/IP port assignments is `http://www.iana.org/ assignments/port-numbers`.

6. Click the Next button. The wizard displays the next screen for the rule. For the Port rule type, the next step is the Action screen (see Figure 29.11).

7. Select the appropriate action button for the rule:

Allow the Connection   Select this option button to allow both secure and insecure connections.

FIGURE 29.10
On the Protocol and Ports screen, choose whether the rule applies to TCP ports or UDP ports, and then specify the ports involved.

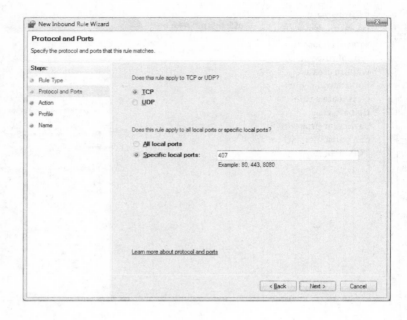

FIGURE 29.11
On the Action screen, choose the action Windows Firewall should take when a connection matches the conditions you've specified: allow the connection, allow the connection if it is secure, or block the connection.

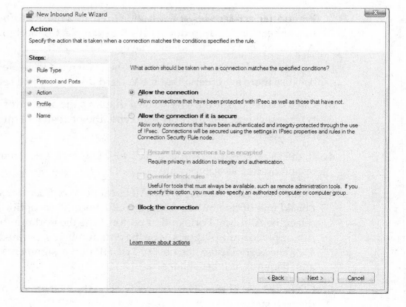

Allow the Connection If It Is Secure   Select this option button if you want to accept only connections secured with IPSec. If you select this option button, you can also select the Require the Connections to Be Encrypted check box to require encryption as well as authentication and data integrity, and the Override Block Rules check box if you want to make your new rule override any existing rules that might block it.

Block the Connection   Select this option button if you want to block the connection.

8. Click the Next button. The wizard displays the next screen for the rule. For the Port rule type, the next screen is the Profile screen (see Figure 29.12).

9. Select or clear the Domain check box, the Private check box, or the Private check box, as appropriate for the rule.

10. Click the Next button. The wizard displays the next screen for the rule. For the Port rule type, the next screen is the final screen, the Name screen (see Figure 29.13).

11. Type a descriptive name for the rule in the Name text box, and type a description in the Description text box. The description is optional, but it's almost always helpful.

12. Click the Finish button. The wizard creates the rule and closes itself.

FIGURE 29.12
On the Profile screen, select the check box for each profile to which the rule applies. Your choices are the domain profile, the private profile, and the public profile.

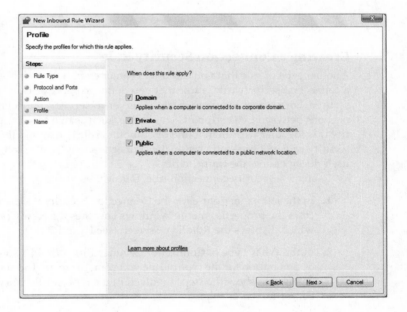

FIGURE 29.13
On the Name screen,
type a name for the
rule, and then add a
description of what
the rule does.

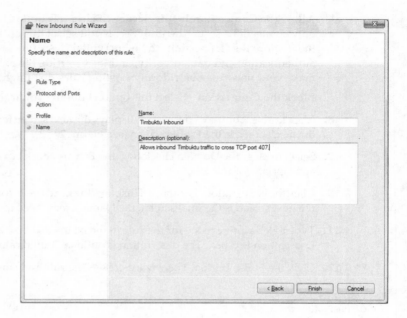

Creating a Connection Security Rule

Another type of rule that you can use in conjunction with an inbound rule or an outbound rule is a connection security rule, a rule that you define to specify how a particular connection should be secured. For example, you can create a "server-to-server" connection security rule that secures connections between two endpoints you define, such as two servers. You must use a connection security rule together with an inbound or outbound rule that allows the connection that the connection security rule will use—otherwise, the connection may be blocked, as the connection security rule itself doesn't allow the traffic to pass.

To create a security connection rule, follow these steps:

1. In the left pane, right-click the Connection Security Rules item, and then choose New Rule from the properties menu. Windows launches the New Connection Security Rule Wizard, which displays the Rule Type screen (see Figure 29.14).

2. In the What Type of Connection Security Rule Would You Like to Create? area, select the option button for the type of rule you want to create. The steps list on the left of the window changes to show the steps involved in the type of rule you chose. This example uses the Server-to-Server rule.

   Isolation   Select this option button if you want to restrict connections to a computer based on whether it is a member of a particular domain or it has had a recent system health check. This option is primarily useful for computers connected to domain-based Windows networks rather than home or home-office networks.

FIGURE 29.14
On the Rule Type screen of the New Connection Security Rule Wizard, select the type of rule you want to create: Isolation, Authentication Exemption, Server-to-Server, Tunnel, or Custom.

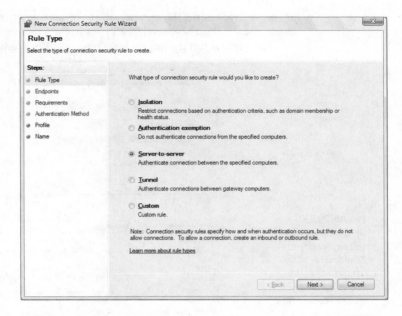

Authentication Exemption   Select this option button if you want to create a rule that exempts certain specified computers from authentication requirements. For example, you might want to exempt a computer that you fully trust from authentication.

Server-to-Server   Select this option button if you want to secure the connection between two particular computers.

Tunnel   Select this option button if you want to secure the connection across an encrypted tunnel through an insecure network.

Custom   Select this option button when you need to create a connection security rule manually—for example, because there are criteria that the wizard doesn't let you set.

3. Click the Next button. The wizard displays the next screen for the rule. For the Server-to-Server rule type, the next screen is the Endpoints screen (see Figure 29.15).

4. Specify the endpoints for the connection:

   ◆ In the Which Computers Are in Endpoint 1? area, select the Any IP Address option button or the These IP Addresses option button. Normally, you'll want to select the These IP Addresses option button to restrict the rule to certain computers. Click the Add button, and then use the IP Address dialog box (see Figure 29.16) to specify the IP addresses involved. You can add multiple IP addresses or sets of IP addresses if necessary.

   ◆ In the Which Computers Are in Endpoint 2? area, repeat the procedure described in the previous paragraph, but for the other endpoint of the connection.

◆ If you need to restrict the security rule to certain network interfaces, click the Customize button, select the These Interface Types in the Customize Interface Types dialog box (shown here), select the appropriate option buttons, and then click the OK button.

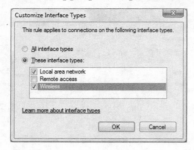

FIGURE 29.15
On the Endpoints screen, specify the IP addresses of the computers at the two endpoints of the secured connection.

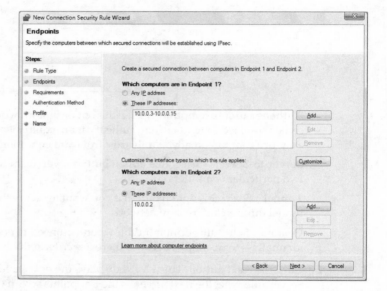

FIGURE 29.16
The IP Address dialog box lets you specify a particular IP address or subnet, a range of IP addresses (for example, 10.0.0.3–10.0.0.15), or a predefined set of computers (such as the local subnet or the default gateway).

5. Click the Next button. The wizard displays the next screen for the rule. For the Server-to-Server rule type, the next screen is the Requirements screen (see Figure 29.17).

6. Select the appropriate option button:

Request Authentication for Inbound and Outbound Connections   Select this option button if you're prepared to dispense with authentication for both inbound and outbound connections. This is the least secure of the three options.

Require Authentication for Inbound Connections and Request Authentication for Outbound Connections   Select this option button if you want to require inbound connections to be authenticated but are prepared to dispense with authentication for outbound connections. Inbound security tends to be more important than outbound security, so this is a reasonable compromise.

Require Authentication for Inbound and Outbound Connections   Select this option button if you want to ensure authentication on both inbound and outbound connections. This is the most secure setting.

7. Click the Next button. The wizard displays the next screen for the rule. For the Server-to-Server rule type, the next screen is the Authentication Method screen (see Figure 29.18).

8. Select the appropriate option button:

Computer Certificate   Select this option button if you want to use digital certificates issues by the same certification authority (CA) as the authentication method. Click the Browse button, select the certificate in the Select Certificate dialog box, and then click the OK button. For example, if both you and the people with whom you want to establish a secure connection have certificates from VeriSign, you might choose this method. In a corporate setting, you can select the Accept Health Certificates Only check box to use Network Access Protection certificates for authentication. (Such certificates are primarily used in corporate networks.)

FIGURE 29.17

On the Requirements screen, choose when to require authentication for the connection and when merely to request authentication.

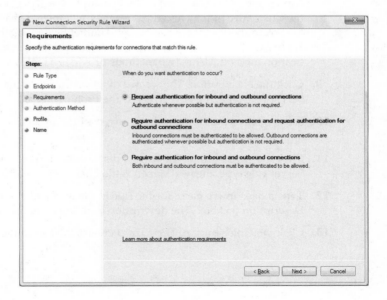

FIGURE 29.18
On the Authentication Method screen, choose whether to have the computers authenticate using a certificate, a preshared key, or an advanced method.

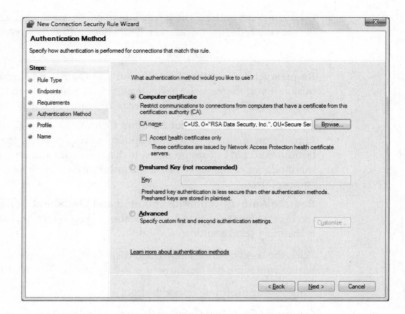

Preshared Key   Select this option button (and type the key in the text box) if you want to use a text key to authenticate the connection. Whoever is setting up the other end of the connection will need to enter the same key. Windows stores preshared keys in plain text (in other words, unencrypted), so this option offers weaker protection than the other two options. However, preshared keys are relatively easy to implement (for example, you can set them up over the phone) and may be adequate for moderate-security connections.

Advanced   Select this option if you want to specify custom authentication methods. Click the Customize button, and then use the Customize Advanced Authentication Methods dialog box to specify the first and second authentication methods. For example, you might use Kerberos V5 as the first authentication method and a digital certificate as the second authentication method. Using two methods provides a highly secure connection.

9. Click the Next button. The wizard displays the next screen for the rule. For the Server-to-Server rule type, the next screen is the Profile screen.

10. Select or clear the Domain check box, the Private check box, or the Public check box, as appropriate for the rule.

11. Click the Next button. The wizard displays the next screen for the rule. For the Server-to-Server rule type, the next screen is the final screen, the Name screen.

12. Type a descriptive name for the rule in the Name text box, and type a description in the Description text box. The description is optional, but it's almost always helpful.

13. Click the Finish button. The wizard creates the rule and closes itself.

Using Antivirus Software

To further secure your network, use antivirus software to scan all incoming files for viruses and to monitor each computer for unusual activity, such as programs being run remotely or Trojan horses coming to life.

To find a list of antivirus software compatible with Windows Vista, follow these steps:

1. Choose Start ➢ Control Panel. Windows opens a Control Panel window.

2. In Control Panel Home view, click the Check This Computer's Security Status link under the Security heading. Windows displays the Windows Security Center window.

3. Click the Malware Protection heading to expand its contents, as shown here. (If they're expanded already, you don't need to click.)

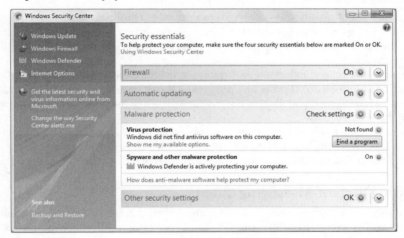

4. If you don't have an antivirus program installed, the Virus Protection readout will show Not Found. Click the Find a Program button. Windows opens an Internet Explorer window to a page on the Microsoft website that lists compatible antivirus programs, including trial versions.

Because each computer that gets infected can then infect other computers on the same network, it's vital to use antivirus software on all computers on your network. There's no sense in implementing Baked-Alaska security, in which your network is hard to attack on the outside but easy to attack on the inside. By the same token, educate the users about viruses and other threats to the network so that they can help keep the network secure rather than blithely compromising security by downloading Trojan-loaded screen savers and pirated software.

Securing Your Browsers and Programs

In theory, any program can compromise the security of your computer (or network), but in practice, the four leading contenders are web browsers, e-mail clients, instant-messaging clients, and programs that include programming or scripting languages. By choosing as high security as you can for these programs, you can limit the amount of damage they can cause.

Securing Your Web Browsers

Because they're designed to access a wide variety of different types of content on the Internet, web browsers are a prime source of danger and contagion across the Internet connection. To help keep your network secure, you'll want to limit the amount of harm that browsers can do while enabling your Internet users to surf as widely as they wish (or you wish them to).

If you're using Internet Explorer, see the sections "Choosing Security Options," "Choosing a Level of Privacy," "Blocking Pop-ups," "Handling Cookies," "Screening Out Objectionable Content," "Managing Add-ons," and the "Security Category" subsection in the "Advanced Options" section in Chapter 2 for a discussion of the security options that Internet Explorer offers. If you're using another browser, consult its documentation for details of its security options.

Securing E-mail Clients

Your e-mail client can also pose a considerable threat to the security of your computer or network, because it brings in messages and attachments from anyone who chooses to send them to you (or whose computer has caught an e-mail virus that automatically sends messages to people in the address book).

If your e-mail client includes a programming language or scripting language (as both Outlook Express and Outlook do), it poses an even greater threat, as an incoming e-mail message can include a script that runs when you display the message (or when the program automatically displays it to you in the preview pane).

If you're using Outlook Express, see the section "Security Page Options" and the sidebar "Expert Knowledge: Protecting Yourself Against Malicious Attachments" in Chapter 17 for a discussion of how to secure Outlook Express. If you're using a different e-mail client, investigate its security options.

Securing Instant-Messaging Clients

Instant messaging also exposes your computer to Internet-based threats, especially if you receive files from other users. If you're using Windows Live Messenger for instant messaging, see the section "Security Page Options" in Chapter 20 for coverage of Messenger's features for protecting your computer against threats.

Securing Programmable Programs

In much the same way that e-mail clients that include programming or scripting languages can host an attack on your computer, so can any program that includes a programming or scripting language. To counter this threat, choose high-security settings for programs that allow the execution of macros, scripts, and user forms.

Visual Basic for Applications (VBA) is a favorite tool of malicious hackers because it's used in a huge range of widely used programs—Word, Excel, PowerPoint, Access, Visio, WordPerfect, AutoCAD, and many others—it's easy to learn, and it's very powerful. Other programming languages (such as LotusScript, which is used by programs such as Lotus Notes) are equally powerful but tend to be seen as less attractive targets.

If you're using a VBA-enabled program, take the following steps to secure it:

1. Choose Tools ➤ Macro ➤ Security. The program displays the Security dialog box.

2. On the Security Level page, select the High option button if you don't use macros yourself or the Medium option button if you do.

3. On the Trusted Sources page, reduce the number of trusted sources to a minimum. (A trusted source is someone you trust to develop safe macros or code.)

4. If you have any doubts about the quality of macros or code in templates already installed on your computer, clear the Trust All Installed Add-ins and Templates check box.

5. Click the OK button. The program closes the Security dialog box and applies your changes.

Limiting User Access to Computers and Files

Next, you need to limit users' access to the computers and files on your network. Restrict each user as far as you reasonably can without preventing them from taking the actions they need to. For example:

◆ Create only those user accounts you need to. Don't create a user account for each member of the household on each computer unless each user will need to use each computer. (Alternatively, create the accounts but disable extra accounts until they're needed.)

◆ Create user accounts as Standard accounts rather than as Administrator accounts. That way, the users can do less damage if they're attacked by bad intentions or bad ideas.

◆ Leave User Account Control turned on. Having to click through User Account Control dialog boxes each time you make a system change is tedious, but User Account Control provides vital protection against malware surreptitiously installing itself on your computer.

◆ As well as your Administrator account, create a Standard account for yourself. Use the Standard account for day-to-day work, providing your Administrator credentials whenever User Account Control prevents you from making a system change.

◆ Use strong passwords on all user accounts. Discourage users from sharing their passwords with each other.

◆ Share as few files as possible. What a user can't reach, he or she can't harm.

◆ Lock away any computer that you can't afford to have other people in the house mess with. (Alternatively, get a removable hard drive and take it with you to prevent others from accessing your data. Or, for a small amount of data, a USB flash drive tends to be the handiest solution.)

Maintaining Your Hardware and Software

Maintain your hardware and software so that your computers don't quit unexpectedly on you. This advice is so obvious that far too many people ignore it. It goes almost without saying that you should maintain your hardware and software to keep your computers running. But the point is that in a network, the failure of even one of the less interesting computers can deny the other computers data or services that they need.

If you know you'll need to repair or upgrade a computer, plan the process ahead of time so that you can transfer your data files to another computer for the duration of the upgrade or repair.

Backing Up Data on Your Network

Having a network lets you back up all the important data from each computer on the network to a central location, whether you have a peer-to-peer network or a server-based network. And back the data up you must, because (as discussed earlier in this chapter) having a network also increases the number of threats to your data.

As with a stand-alone PC, you can back your network's data up to recordable CD, recordable DVD, or removable disk if that gives you enough capacity. Removable media have the advantage that you can implement an off-site backup by sending the media elsewhere. If your network contains too much data for such media, back up your data either to an internal hard drive or an external hard drive. External hard drives (for example, USB 2.0 or FireWire drives) have the advantage that you can easily move them to another computer, making them an attractive solution for speed and capacity. However, it's hard to implement off-site backups unless you can afford a large number of external hard drives.

Another possibility is to back data up to an Internet backup site. Unless you've got both the money to pay for plenty of storage and a broadband Internet connection that's fast upstream as well as downstream, you'll probably want to back up only a small amount of critical data online—and because online backups raise security concerns, encrypt the data before backing it up.

Backup procedures are essentially the same as described in Chapter 16. Connect the backup unit to (or install it on) a computer that will always be running when the other computers on the network need to back up data. This is particularly important if you schedule the backups to take place when no one is using the computers (but they're not powered down or in hibernation), as you'll probably want to do.

Securing Your Wireless Network

Wireless networks require more security measures than wired networks, because they're often easily accessible from outside the property they cover and because most wireless access points automatically broadcast the network name so that clients can easily connect to it. Some neighborhoods have used these capabilities positively to implement Wi-Fi area networks for sharing a high-speed Internet connection with people in the same group of houses or street. Less positively, in the same way, if you don't secure your wireless network, your neighbors will be able to access your network, use any Internet connection you've shared, and perhaps even dip into your files.

This section discusses the steps you can take to secure your wireless network. This section presents the steps separately, because you may want to implement only some of them, and discusses the significance, benefits, and drawbacks of each security step.

Keeping Your Expectations Realistic

Ideally, no one unauthorized would be able to access your wireless network. In practice, this is hard to achieve, simply because of the nature of wireless network technology. Similarly, you might like to ensure that nobody could ever break into your house—but the design of most houses, including openings such as doors and windows, makes this expensive and difficult to manage.

More realistically, your security measures are designed to make your house a less attractive target for an attacker rather than an impossible target. If your house has an alarm system and your neighbor's house doesn't, most would-be thieves would find your neighbor's house a more attractive target. (Other thieves might reckon you had more to protect.) Likewise, if your neighbor's wireless network is unprotected, while your wireless network uses some basic protective measures, anyone looking for a free wireless connection will probably try your neighbor's network rather than yours.

THE WORST OFFENDERS

Corporations are enthusiastic implementers of wireless networks, because it allows their employees to lug their laptops to meetings and squeeze in a little more work. But many corporations are amazingly lax in securing their wireless networks. Hackers report performing "war drives" in San Francisco and being able to access different corporate networks from anywhere on the downtown section of Market Street.

In many cases, the administrators have failed to secure the wireless networks they've implemented. In other cases, they've been undermined by users bringing in their own wireless equipment and setting up rogue wireless nodes on the network.

Even if your security measures are relatively easy to defeat, they will have served their purpose if an attacker chooses to go elsewhere.

Using WPA or WEP

The first step in securing your wireless network is to turn on Wi-Fi Protected Access (WPA) if your hardware supports it, or Wired Equivalent Privacy (WEP) if your hardware doesn't. WPA provides a good security base for your wireless network and is much more secure than WEP, so you should use WPA if you can. If your hardware supports only WEP, check the manufacturer's site for a firmware upgrade. If none is available, consider buying new wireless hardware that supports WPA.

WEP is supposed to provide wireless networks with security equivalent to that of a physical (wired) network cable. Unfortunately, the WEP algorithm is flawed, with problems that include weaknesses in the method of using a stream cipher to encrypt the packets of data sent over the wireless network. These problems mean that WEP traffic can be hacked into using a network sniffer and performing a series of computations. Worse, because many 802.11b networking cards use the same encryption key, they're also vulnerable to hacking. So if you need your wireless network traffic to be secure, you can't rely on WEP. The best solution is to use virtual private networking, which is discussed in detail in Chapter 30.

If you set up your wireless network using the Set Up a Network Wizard, it will already be using WPA or WEP (depending on the capabilities of your wireless network hardware and the settings you chose).

Effectiveness   WPA provides good protection against intrusion. Use a preshared key to set up the network (as Windows recommends). Make the key available only to trusted computers.

WEP provides only token protection against intrusion. Use a 13-character password to maximize the protection offered, but understand that any determined attacker can sniff the network traffic and crack the password with relative ease. Look to upgrade your wireless network to WPA as soon as possible.

Changing the SSID for the Wireless Network

Once you've turned on WPA or WEP, your next move toward securing your wireless network is to change the service set identifier (SSID) for the wireless network. The reason for changing the SSID is that many default SSIDs are easy to guess, which makes it easier for an attacker to contact the access point. Changing the SSID is not essential but a good step to securing your network. It has no disadvantage beyond requiring a small amount of effort on your part.

The procedure for changing the wireless network's SSID depends on the wireless network device. For example, most wireless access points use a browser-based configuration utility, usually accessed from a computer connecting to the access point's wired network port. If you've created an ad hoc wireless network using only wireless network adapters, you can change the SSID from within Windows.

Effectiveness Changing the SSID for the wireless network is only a mildly effective security measure. It protects your network from anyone looking for the default SSID, but if your access point broadcasts its new SSID, an attacker can easily identify the network.

Configuring Your Access Point Not to Broadcast Its SSID

The next step in securing your wireless network is to configure your access point not to broadcast its SSID. Most access points let you make this change, but the details depend on the access point's configuration mechanism. This change isn't essential, but it increases your wireless network's security, and you can perform it at the same time as the previous step, so you'll probably want to perform it.

While you're configuring your access point not to broadcast its SSID, change the access point's password as well if you haven't done so already. Many manufacturers use feeble passwords on their access points, and you should assume that hackers know these standard passwords by heart. Use a password that you've never used before—don't reuse one of your existing passwords or previous passwords.

If you followed the advice in the previous section to change the SSID of your wireless network, you'll see why you should turn off SSID broadcasting: By doing so, you make it much more difficult for an attacker to access your wireless network. Otherwise, they can just tune in on the Wi-Fi frequency, and the access point will obligingly tell them the SSID so that they can attack it.

The disadvantage to turning off SSID broadcasts is that you won't be able to browse the network for wireless connections either. Instead, you'll need to connect to the network manually.

Effectiveness Turning off the SSID for your wireless network may deter casual browsers looking for a wireless network connection they can borrow. For example, if both you and your neighbor have wireless networks, and hers is broadcasting its SSID while yours isn't, people are more likely to try to use your neighbor's network. But anyone armed with a packet sniffer can find out your access point's SSID by snooping any connection to the access point (for example, from one of your computers), so this measure doesn't provide effective protection.

Restricting the MAC Addresses Allowed to Access Your Wireless Network

A MAC address (written in uppercase to distinguish it from Mac computers) is the Media Access Control address for a piece of network hardware. Each MAC address is unique, so even if you have two apparently identical wireless network adapters from the same manufacturer, they will have different MAC addresses.

Most wireless access points allow you to create a "white list" of MAC addresses that are permitted to connect to the network. When a device asks to join the network, the access point allows it to join only if its MAC address appears on the white list.

Effectiveness Restricting MAC addresses is a basic security measure that can deter casual browsers but has little effect against a determined attacker. Where this security measure falls down is that MAC addresses can be spoofed: An attacker can snoop your network traffic, identify one or more MAC addresses of hardware devices that are used to connect, and then tell his or her wireless network adapter to give that MAC address (when the device that really has that address isn't connected to the network).

Using Password Protection on Your Files

To protect your files from anyone unauthorized who succeeds in accessing your network, implement password protection on all your data files. For example, in Microsoft Word, when saving a file, click the Tools menu in the Save As dialog box and choose Security Options from the menu, and then enter a password in the Password to Open text box on the Security tab of the Security dialog box.

Effectiveness   Password protection makes it harder for anyone who accesses your files to open them, but many password-cracking utilities are available on the Internet.

Using Virtual Private Networking to Secure the Data You're Transmitting

As mentioned earlier, WPA is pretty secure, but WEP isn't. Because the WEP algorithm is flawed, data transmitted across wireless networks secured with WEP can be decrypted relatively easily by determined hackers. For any data that you absolutely need to keep private, use virtual private networking to secure the data transmitted across the wireless network.

See the section "Creating and Using VPN Connections" in Chapter 30 for a discussion of what virtual private networking is and how to implement it.

Effectiveness   Securing your network traffic with virtual private networking provides effective protection against the data being snooped in transit. While a sniffer will still be able to capture the transmissions, the data will be unintelligible.

Repositioning Your Access Point for Security

Another step you can take is to position your access point so that it provides as little coverage outside your property as possible. Depending on the access point, you may also be able to turn down the signal strength if you don't need the signal to carry as far as possible within your property. Turning down the signal strength can also help to decrease interference with your neighbors' wireless networks.

Effectiveness   In theory, reducing the spread of your access point's coverage is a good move, because if you could confine the access point's coverage to the boundaries of your property, you could more easily prevent most unauthorized people from accessing your wireless network. Unfortunately, you won't be able to do this short of investing in lead-lined walls, floors, and roofs—even if your property covers a large area. By using booster antennae or parabolic dishes, hackers can pick up wireless network signals from distances of up to about 15–20 miles (even from over the horizon, with determination). So if anyone is targeting your wireless network in particular, repositioning the access point won't help.

Where repositioning does help is if you're trying to prevent casual access to your network. To check the spread of your network, take your wireless-enabled laptop or Pocket PC for a walk around your property and its immediate surroundings to see where your access point is accessible from. Relocate it if necessary, being careful not to lose access from the places you need it.

Trying to Hack into Your Own Network

Once you've taken the measures discussed above to secure your wireless network, try to hack into it yourself. Download a tool such as NetStumbler for Windows or MiniStumbler for Pocket PC (both from `http://www.netstumbler.com`) and take a quick look around your property to see what you can pick up. Change your security configuration as necessary depending on what you find—or warn your neighbors that you're picking up their wireless networks' SSIDs loud and clear.

The Bottom Line

Assess the threats to your network   Any network connected to the Internet is vulnerable to attack from any other Internet computer, so it's vital to secure your network. Consider what types of data you're trying to protect—private files, financial data, or personal details—and decide how much effort to expend in protecting them. Learn the points of weakness in your network so that you can either secure them or eliminate them.

Secure your Internet connection with a firewall   Windows Vista enables Windows Firewall by default, so unless you've turned Windows Firewall off, your computer should already be protected. You may want to use another hardware or software firewall as well. For example, many Internet access devices include firewalls.

Learn to use the Windows Firewall with Advanced Security application   Windows Firewall comes with suitable settings for many small networks, but if you want to configure security further, run the Windows Firewall with Advanced Security application. You can create custom rules for inbound traffic, outbound traffic, and connection security.

Secure your software and limit user access to computers and files   Use antivirus software on all the computers in your network to ensure that one unprotected computer can't infect the others. Choose secure settings for browsers, e-mail programs, instant messaging clients, and programmable programs (such as those that include VBA or a scripting language). Ensure that User Account Control is turned on for your Windows Vista computers; create only such user accounts as are necessary, make them Standard accounts rather than Administrator accounts, and use a strong password on each user account.

Back up data on your network   Protecting your network is a pyrrhic endeavor if you lose your data, so back up your data regularly and frequently. An external hard drive is usually the easiest solution for quantities of data too large for recordable CDs or DVDs. Online backup sites can be good storage for vital files, provided that you encrypt them.

Secure your wireless network as much as needed   Your primary protection for securing a wireless network should be WPA. Other measures, such as changing the network's SSID, suppressing SSID broadcasts, restricting MAC addresses, and repositioning your access point, can help deter casual browsers but do little against determined attackers. You can also use virtual private networking to prevent data being sniffed while in transit.

Chapter 30

Connecting to a Remote Computer or Network

♦ Take control of a remote computer using Remote Desktop Connection

♦ Connect to a remote network via a dial-up connection

♦ Connect to a remote network via a virtual private network connection

So far in this book, we've assumed that you're working locally at your computer—computing the normal way, as it were. But Windows also provides technologies for working remotely, both for remotely controlling a computer running Windows and for connecting remotely to a network.

♦ Remote Desktop Connection lets you use a computer running any version of Windows Vista to take control of a remote computer running Windows Vista Business Edition, Windows Vista Ultimate Edition, or Windows XP Professional Edition. For example, if your computer at work runs Windows Vista Business Edition and your computer at home runs Windows Vista Home Edition, you can connect from your home computer to your work computer. Once connected, you can work on the remote computer as if you were sitting at it (provided your Internet or network connection is fast enough—otherwise everything happens much more slowly).

♦ Dial-up networking lets you establish a dial-up connection to a server. For example, you might use dial-up networking to connect your home computer to a remote-access server on your company's network so that you can access files and resources from home.

♦ Virtual private network (VPN) connections let you connect to a network via a secure connection across an insecure medium. Usually the insecure medium is the Internet. You establish your Internet connection via your ISP as usual, and then create an encrypted "tunnel" to a VPN host on the destination network. Once you've connected to the VPN host, you can work as if your computer were directly attached to the network. For example, you might use a VPN connection to connect to your company's network so that you could upload or download files, or work with e-mail, from your home computer.

Using Remote Desktop Connection

Remote Desktop Connection lets you take control of another computer via a local area network connection or your Internet connection.

Remote Desktop Connection is designed to let you access and control one computer (say, your work computer) from another computer (say, your home computer or your laptop). It's great for catching up with the office when you're at home, or for grabbing the files that you forgot to load on your laptop before you dived into the taxi for the airport. Remote Desktop Connection isn't suitable for helping a friend or family member find their way out of a computing problem from a distance—for such tasks, use Remote Assistance instead (see Chapter 21).

SHARING A PROGRAM VIA REMOTE DESKTOP CONNECTION

Remote Desktop Connection is also great for sharing a program from other computers without needing to buy extra copies to install on them. For example, say you want to manipulate digital photos using a high-end graphics program. By installing the program on a computer that's running Windows Vista Business Edition or Windows Vista Ultimate Edition, you can connect with Remote Desktop Connection from other computers on your home or home-office network (one at a time) so that you can use the same copy of the program to manipulate photos as needed. That saves a lot of money compared with buying a copy of the program for each computer you have.

Remote Desktop Connection Terminology and Basics

Remote Desktop Connection uses the following terms:

◆ The *home computer* is the computer on which you're working. The home computer needs Remote Desktop Connection installed. Remote Desktop Connection is installed by default in Windows Vista Home Edition, so you shouldn't have to install it.

◆ The *remote computer* is the computer that you're accessing from the home computer. The remote computer must have Remote Desktop installed. Remote Desktop is separate from Remote Desktop Connection and is included in Windows Vista Business Edition, Windows Vista Ultimate Edition, Windows XP Professional Edition, and Windows Server 2003. Remote Desktop is not included in Windows Vista Home Edition.

So the typical user-level Remote Desktop Connection scenario is for the home computer to be running Windows Vista Home Edition and the remote computer to be running Windows Vista Business Edition or Windows Vista Ultimate Edition. You can also access a Business or Ultimate computer from another Business or Ultimate computer. You can also use any version of Windows Vista or Windows XP to control a Windows Server 2003 computer remotely.

RUNNING MULTIPLE REMOTE DESKTOP CONNECTION SESSIONS AT ONCE

You can access more than one remote computer at a time from the same home computer. This capability is handy when you're working with computers on the same network or computers connected with high-speed Internet connections. If you're using a slow connection (such as dial-up), using multiple connections at the same time gives very slow performance.

For you to be able to connect to another computer via Remote Desktop Connection, any active session on that computer must be disconnected. That active session can be either a local session (a user working directly at the computer) or another Remote Desktop Connection session. Both you and the other user receive warnings about this. If you choose to proceed, the remote computer displays the Welcome screen or the Log On to Windows dialog box (depending on how it is configured) while your Remote Desktop Connection session is going on. There's no easy way for anyone looking at that computer to tell that you're remotely connected to it.

If a user comes back and starts using the remote computer while your Remote Desktop Connection session is going on, Windows terminates your session.

In lay terms, Remote Desktop Connection works as follows:

◆ Keystrokes and mouse clicks are transmitted from the home computer to the remote computer via the display protocol. The remote computer registers these keystrokes and clicks as if they came from the keyboard attached to it.

◆ Programs run on the remote computer as usual. (Programs aren't run across the wire—that would be very slow.) Documents you create and save during a Remote Desktop Connection session are saved on the remote computer, just as if you were working at it, unless you specifically save them elsewhere (for example, on the home computer's local drives).

◆ Screen display information is passed to the home computer, again via the display protocol. This information appears on the display as if it came from the video adapter (only rather more slowly, and usually in a window). You can reduce the resolution, the colors, and the complexity of the Windows interface to improve performance over slower connections.

Sound can be passed to the home computer as well, so that you can hear what's happening at the remote computer. Transferring sound like this enhances the impression of controlling the remote computer, but sound takes so much bandwidth that transferring it isn't a good idea on slow connections. The default Remote Desktop Connection setting is to transfer sound, but you may well want to switch it off.

Setting the Remote Computer to Accept Incoming Connections

The first step in getting Remote Desktop Connection to work is to set the remote computer to accept incoming connections. This example shows a computer running Windows Vista Ultimate Edition, but the steps are similar in Windows XP Professional Edition.

To set your remote computer to accept incoming connections, take these steps:

1. Press Windows Key+Break to open a System window. Alternatively, click the Start button, right-click the Computer item, and then choose Properties from the context menu.

2. In the Tasks list, click the Remote Settings link, and then authenticate yourself to User Account Control. Windows displays the Remote page of the System Properties dialog box (see Figure 30.1).

FIGURE 30.1

To allow incoming connections, select the Allow Connections from Computers Running Any Version of Remote Desktop option button or the Allow Connections Only from Computers Running Remote Desktop with Network Level Authentication option button on the Remote page of the System Properties dialog box.

3. Choose the appropriate option button:

Don't Allow Connections to This Computer   Select this option button when you want to turn Remote Desktop off.

Allow Connections from Computers Running Any Version of Remote Desktop   Select this option button if you want to be able to connect to this computer by using any version of Remote Desktop Connection, including those in Windows XP and earlier versions of Windows.

Allow Connections Only from Computers Running Remote Desktop with Network Level Authentication   Select this option button if you want to restrict Remote Desktop connections to computers that have Network Level Authentication. Network Level Authentication gives greater security and better performance, but it means that only computers running Windows Vista and Windows 2003 Server will be able to connect. Computers running Windows XP and earlier versions of Windows will not be able to connect.

4. To specify which users may connect via Remote Desktop Connection, click the Select Users button. Windows displays the Remote Desktop Users dialog box, shown here. The list box shows any users currently allowed to connect to the computer. Below the list box is a note indicating that you (identified by your username) already have access. You have access because you are logged on to the computer.

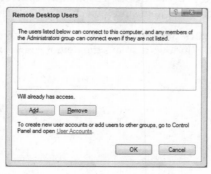

Real World Scenario

YOU MAY NEED TO CHANGE POWER SETTINGS ON THE REMOTE COMPUTER

When you select the Allow Connections from Computers Running Any Version of Remote Desktop option button or the Allow Connections Only from Computers Running Remote Desktop with Network Level Authentication option button, Windows checks your computer's power settings. If the computer is configured to go to sleep, Windows displays the Remote Desktop dialog box shown here to warn you of the problem.

Click the Power Options link. Windows displays the Power Options window, in which you can change your power plan or configure the settings for your current plan. For example, you might click the Change Settings link, and then choose Never in the Put the Computer to Sleep drop-down list. See Chapter 13 for instructions on choosing power settings.

FINDING OUT WHETHER YOUR COMPUTER SUPPORTS NETWORK LEVEL AUTHENTICATION

Any computer running Windows Vista supports Network Level Authentication, but Windows XP and earlier versions of Windows don't. If you're not sure whether your version of Windows supports Network Level Authentication, follow these steps to find out:

1. Choose Start ➢ All Programs ➢ Accessories ➢ Remote Desktop Connection. Windows displays the Remote Desktop Connection window.

2. Press Alt+spacebar or click the upper-left corner of the window, and then choose About from the menu. Windows displays the About Remote Desktop Connection dialog box.

3. If you see a readout saying "Network Level Authentication supported," your computer supports Network Level Authentication. Otherwise, it doesn't.

4. Click the OK button. Windows closes the About Remote Desktop Connection dialog box.

5. Click the Add button. Windows displays the Select Users dialog box, as shown here.

6. Type the user's or group's name in the Enter the Object Names to Select list box, and then click the OK button. Windows adds the user to the list in the Remote Desktop Users dialog box.

7. Add further users or groups as necessary.

8. To remove a user or a group, select them in the list box and click the Remove button.

9. Click the OK button. Windows closes the Remote Desktop Users dialog box.

10. Click the OK button in the System Properties dialog box. Windows closes the dialog box and applies your changes.

The remote computer is all set. Leave it up and running and return to the home computer.

SET A PASSWORD ON YOUR ACCOUNT (IF YOU DON'T ALREADY HAVE ONE)

Although the Remote Desktop Users dialog box indicates that your user account is already set up to use Remote Desktop Connection, you will not be able to connect unless your user account on the remote computer has a password. If your account doesn't have a password, add one by clicking the Start button, clicking your picture on the Start menu, and then clicking the Create a Password for Your Account link.

Choosing Settings for Remote Desktop Connection

Next, choose settings for Remote Desktop Connection on the home computer. Remote Desktop Connection has many settings, but many of them are set-and-forget. Even better, you can save sets of settings so that you can quickly apply them for accessing different remote computers (or the same remote computer under different circumstances, such as when the cable modem is working and when it's not).

To choose settings for Remote Desktop Connection, follow these steps:

1. Choose Start ➤ All Programs ➤ Accessories ➤ Remote Desktop Connection. Windows starts Remote Desktop Connection and displays the Remote Desktop Connection window in its reduced state, as shown here.

2. Click the Options button. Windows displays the rest of the Remote Desktop Connection window.

3. The General page of the Remote Desktop Connection window (shown in Figure 30.2) offers these options:

Computer In this drop-down list, type the name or the IP address of the computer to which you want to connect; select it from the drop-down list; or click the Browse for More item from the drop-down list to display the Browse for Computers dialog box, select the computer in the Available Computers list box, and then click the OK button.

User Name   If this text box is available, you can enter the username under which you want to connect to the remote computer.

Connection Settings   Once you've chosen settings for a connection, you can save the connection information by clicking the Save As button and specifying a name for the connection in the Save As dialog box that Windows displays. Windows saves Remote Desktop Connection connections as files of the file type Remote Desktop File, which by default is linked to the .RDP extension, in your Documents folder. You can open saved connections by clicking the Open button and using the resulting Open dialog box. To save changes to the connection you're currently using, click the Save button.

KEEPING DIFFERENT SETS OF REMOTE DESKTOP CONNECTION SETTINGS

When you start using Remote Desktop Connection, Windows saves your settings in a file named Default.rdp in your Documents folder. This file is hidden, so you won't see it unless you turn on the display of hidden files and folders. (To do so, choose Start ➤ Computer, and then choose Organize ➤ Folder and Search Options. Click the View tab of the Folder Options dialog box, select the Show Hidden Files and Folders option button, and then click the OK button.)

If you only connect to one computer via Remote Desktop Connection, you may find it convenient to save your current settings to the Default.rdp file. To do so, click the Save button on the General page of the Remote Desktop Connection dialog box. But if you connect to multiple computers, you'll do better to give each connection a different and more descriptive name. To do so, set up the connection, click the Save As button, and then specify the name.

FIGURE 30.2
The General page of the expanded Remote Desktop Connection window lets you save and reopen connections.

4. The Display page of the Remote Desktop Connection window (see Figure 30.3) offers three display options:

Remote Desktop Size   Drag the slider to specify the screen size you want to use for the remote Desktop. The default setting is Full Screen, but you may want to use a smaller size so that you can more easily access your home computer's Desktop. When you display the remote Desktop full screen, it takes over the whole of the local Desktop, so that you can't see your local Desktop. (To get to your local Desktop, you use the connection bar, discussed in a moment or two.)

Colors   In the drop-down list, select the color depth to use for the connection. Choose a low color depth (for example, 256 colors) if you're connecting over a low-speed connection, because reducing the number of colors decreases the amount of data that Windows needs to transfer in order to draw the screen on your computer. Your Colors choice will be overridden by the display setting on the remote computer if you ask for more colors than the remote computer is using.

Display the Connection Bar When in Full Screen Mode   Leave this check box selected (as it is by default) if you want Windows to display the connection bar when the remote Desktop is displayed full screen. The connection bar provides Minimize, Restore/Maximize, and Close buttons for the remote Desktop. (When the remote Desktop is displayed in a window, that window has the control buttons, so the connection bar isn't necessary.)

5. The Local Resources page of the Remote Desktop Connection window (see Figure 30.4) offers the following options:

Remote Computer Sound   In the drop-down list, specify what you want Windows to do with sounds that would normally be generated at the remote Desktop. The default setting is Bring to This Computer, which transfers the sounds to the home computer and plays them there. This setting helps sustain the illusion that you're working directly on the remote Desktop, but it's heavy on bandwidth, so don't use it over low-speed connections. Instead, choose the Do Not Play setting or the Leave at Remote Computer setting. The Leave at Remote Computer setting plays the sounds at the remote computer and is best reserved for occasions when you need to frighten somebody remotely or pretend to be in your office. You might also use this setting if the "remote" computer is actually in the same room as the home computer and you're using Remote Desktop Connection to reduce the number of monitors you need.

Keyboard   In the drop-down list, specify how you want Windows to handle Windows key combinations that you press (for example, Alt+Tab or Ctrl+Alt+Delete). Select the On the Local Computer item, the On the Remote Computer item, or the In Full Screen Mode Only item (the default) as suits your needs. In Full Screen Mode Only tends to be the most convenient option, because it's the closest to working normally in Windows—whichever Desktop you're viewing full screen receives the key combinations.

Local Devices   Select the Printers check box if you want to be able to print from the remote computer to a printer attached to your home computer. This capability is very useful, but print jobs can take a long time to transfer over a slow connection. Select the Clipboard check box if you want to be able to copy data between the remote computer and your home computer. This capability is also often useful.

More If you need to have drives, smart cards, or other devices on your home computer available to the remote computer, click the More button, and then choose the devices in the Remote Desktop Connection dialog box shown in Figure 30.5.

6. The Programs page of the Remote Desktop Connection window (see Figure 30.6) lets you set Windows to run a program when you connect via Remote Desktop Connection. Select the Start the Following Program on Connection check box, and then type the program path and name in the Program Path and File Name text box. If you need to specify the folder in which the program should start, type it in the Start in the Following Folder text box.

FIGURE 30.3

Choose display settings on the Display page of the Remote Desktop Connection window.

FIGURE 30.4

Choose how to handle sound, keystrokes, and local devices on the Local Resources page.

FIGURE 30.5

This dialog box lets you connect drives, smart cards, and devices on the local computer to the remote computer during the Remote Desktop Connection session.

FIGURE 30.6

On the Programs page of the Remote Desktop Connection window, specify any program to run automatically when you connect.

7. The Experience page of the Remote Desktop Connection window (see Figure 30.7) contains the following options:

Choose Your Connection Speed to Optimize Performance   In this drop-down list, select one of the four listed speeds to apply a preselected set of settings to the five check boxes in the Performance group box. The choices in the drop-down list are Modem (28.8Kbps), Modem (56Kbps), Broadband (128Kbps–1.5Mbps), LAN (10Mbps or Higher), and Custom. If you change a setting applied by one of the preset sets, Windows selects the Custom item for you.

Desktop Background   Select this check box if you want Remote Desktop Connection to transmit the Desktop background. Because Desktop backgrounds are graphical, transmitting them is sensible only at LAN speeds. (If you clear this check box, Remote Desktop Connection uses a blank Desktop background.)

FIGURE 30.7

On the Experience page of the Remote Desktop Connection window, choose which graphical information Remote Desktop Connection should transmit.

Font Smoothing   Select this check box if you want Remote Desktop Connection to transmit font-smoothing information. Unless you're using a LAN connection, it's best to clear this check box to reduce the amount of data that Remote Desktop Connection needs to transfer.

Desktop Composition   Select this check box if you want Remote Desktop Connection to mimic the look of the remote computer's desktop as closely as possible, transmitting the user interface and the style used for windows. Clear this check box if you're using a slow connection and can settle for basic window styles.

Show Contents of Window While Dragging   Select this check box if you want Remote Desktop Connection to transmit the contents of a window while you're dragging it, or only the window frame. Don't use this option over a modem connection, because the performance penalty outweighs any benefit you may derive from it. For most purposes, dragging the window frame is easy enough.

Menu and Window Animation   Select this check box if you want Remote Desktop Connection to transfer menu and window animations (for example, zooming a window you're maximizing or minimizing). Don't use this option over a modem connection—it's a waste of bandwidth.

Themes   Select this check box if you want Remote Desktop Connection to transmit theme information; clear the check box to use "classic" Windows–style windows and controls. Transmitting theme information takes a little bandwidth, so you can improve performance over a very slow connection by clearing the Themes check box. But bear in mind that Windows will look different enough to unsettle some inexperienced users.

Bitmap Caching   Select this check box if you want Remote Desktop Connection to use bitmap caching to improve performance by reducing the amount of data that needs to be sent across the network to display the screen remotely. Caching could prove a security threat, so you may want to turn it off for security reasons. But in most cases, you're better off using it.

Reconnect if Connection Is Dropped   Select this check box if you want Remote Desktop Connection to attempt to reconnect to the remote computer if the connection is severed.

8. The Advanced page of the Remote Desktop Connection window (see Figure 30.8) contains the following options:

Server Authentication   In this drop-down list, select the Always Connect, Even if Authentication Fails item, the Warn Me if Authentication Fails item, or the Do Not Connect if Authentication Fails item. This authentication is making sure that the computer to which you're connecting is the one to which you're intending to connect. Windows can authenticate only computers running Windows Vista or Windows Server 2003 with Service Pack 2 or a later version. If you're connecting to one of your own computers, choose the Always Connect, Even if Authentication Fails item, because you will be able to recognize a computer masquerading as your computer. If you're connecting to someone else's computer, choose the Warn Me if Authentication Fails item, so that you can decide whether to proceed if Windows cannot authenticate the computer.

Connect from Anywhere   If you need to connect to a computer on a corporate network, you may have to configure Remote Desktop Connection to use a Terminal Services gateway—a computer on the network that accepts Remote Desktop Connection requests and passes them along to the correct computer. (The gateway, which is directly accessible from the Internet, protects the other computers, which are not directly accessible.) Click the Settings button, and then choose settings in the Gateway Server Settings dialog box (see Figure 30.9). For most purposes, the Automatically Detect TS Gateway Server Settings option button works well, but you may need to select the Use These TS Gateway Server Settings option button and specify the server name and logon method. Select the Bypass TS Gateway Server for Local Addresses check box to make sure that Windows doesn't try to use the gateway server for addresses on the same network as your home computer.

9. If you want to save the settings you've chosen under a particular name so that you can reload them at will, click the Save As button on the General page of the Remote Desktop Connection window. Windows displays the Save As dialog box. Type a name in place of the default file name (`Default.rdp`), and then click the Save button.

FIGURE 30.8
The Advanced page of the Remote Desktop Connection dialog box lets you choose authentication options and configure Terminal Services Gateway settings.

FIGURE 30.9

When connecting to a corporate network, you may need to configure a Terminal Services Gateway server to forward Remote Desktop Connection requests to the computer you want to access.

Connecting via Remote Desktop Connection

Once you've chosen settings as outlined in the previous section, you're ready to connect. If you're connecting via the Internet (rather than a local network) and you have a dial-up connection, make sure it's up and running.

To connect via Remote Desktop Connection, follow these steps:

1. Click the Connect button in the Remote Desktop Connection window. Windows displays the Windows Security dialog box. The Windows Security dialog box may contain a username for the remote PC and a Use Another Account button, as shown here, or it may simply contain a blank User Name text box and a Password text box.

2. If your username appears, type your password in the Password text box; if you need to log on using another user's credentials, click the Use Another Account button, and then type the username and password. Otherwise, type your username and password in the text boxes. If you want to skip this step in the future for this connection, select the Remember My Credentials check box.

3. Click the OK button. If you chose to share local devices, Windows displays the Remote Desktop Connection: Do You Trust the Computer You Are Connecting To? dialog box (see Figure 30.10) to make sure you understand that supplying your credentials to the remote computer, and making any local devices (such as drives and the Clipboard) available to it may be a security risk.

FIGURE 30.10

The Remote Desktop Connection: Do You Trust the Computer You Are Connecting To? dialog box checks that you want to share your credentials and any connected devices you enabled with the remote computer. The default button for this dialog box is the No button, so you can't just press Enter to proceed.

4. If you decide you don't want to share your local drives, clear the Allow Access to Your Local Disk Drives check box. If you choose not to share your Clipboard, clear the Allow Access to Your Local Clipboard check box.

5. If you want to suppress the security warning in future, select the Don't Prompt Me Again for Connections to This Computer check box, and then click the Yes button. Otherwise, click the Yes button if you want to proceed with the connection. Windows tries to connect to the remote computer.

If Windows is able to connect to the computer, it logs you on, and you can start working. If you left a user session active on the computer, Remote Desktop Connection drops you straight into it, and you can pick up where you left off. Similarly, if you left a user session running but disconnected, and no other user session is active, you can resume that user session.

The next sections show you what happens if your credentials don't work, if another user is using the computer when you try to log on, or Windows can't connect to the remote computer.

SPECIFYING OTHER CREDENTIALS

If you don't enter your password in the Windows Security dialog box when you connect to the remote computer, or if your username or password are not accepted, Windows displays the Windows Security dialog box again. Either type your password again under your username, or click the Use Another Account button, type the username and password, and then click the OK button. As before, you can select the Remember My Credentials check box to make Remote Desktop Connection store your username and password for future use.

DECIDING WHAT TO DO WHEN ANOTHER USER IS ACTIVE

If another user is active on the remote computer when you submit a successful logon and password, Windows displays a Logon Message screen to tell you that another user is logged on and will have to disconnect if you continue. Click the Yes button if you want to proceed. Click the No button to withdraw stealthily.

If you click the Yes button, the active user gets a Remote Desktop Connection dialog box, as shown here, telling them that you (it specifies your name) are trying to connect to the computer and gives them 30 seconds to decide whether to disconnect (so that you can connect) or cancel your connection.

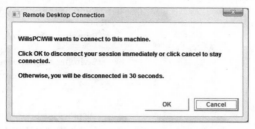

If the user clicks the OK button, or doesn't click either button within 30 seconds, Remote Desktop Connection disconnects their session and connects your session. If the user clicks the Cancel button, Remote Desktop Connection displays a screen on your local computer saying that the user "denied your disconnect request." Either click the OK button or simply wait a few seconds, and Remote Desktop Connection times out the connection and closes it, returning you to the Remote Desktop Connection window.

WHEN REMOTE DESKTOP CONNECTION CAN'T CONNECT

If Windows is unable to establish the connection with the remote computer, it displays a Remote Desktop Disconnected dialog box, as shown here. Click the OK button to close the dialog box and return to the Remote Desktop Connection dialog box, in which you can check that you've entered the correct computer name or IP address.

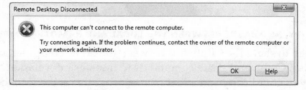

Working via Remote Desktop Connection

Once you've reached the remote Desktop, you can work more or less as if you were sitting at the computer. The few differences worth mentioning are discussed briefly in this section.

USING KEYBOARD SHORTCUTS

Most mouse actions are straightforward with Remote Desktop Connection: If the remote connection is shown full screen, or if mouse pointer is in the Remote Desktop Connection window, mouse clicks and movements go to the remote computer. Much the same happens with keystrokes, with the exception of the Windows keyboard shortcuts listed in Table 30.1, which you can use in Remote Desktop Connection windows. For full-screen Remote Desktop Connection sessions, use the normal keyboard shortcuts.

TABLE 30.1: Special Keyboard Shortcuts for Remote Desktop Connection Windows

REMOTE DESKTOP CONNECTION SHORTCUT	ACTION
Alt+Page Up	Switches between programs (as Alt+Tab does locally)
Alt+Page Down	Switches in reverse order (as Alt+Shift+Tab does locally)
Alt+Insert	Switches among programs in the order in which you started them (as opposed to the order in which they appear)
Alt+Home	Displays the Start menu when the Remote Desktop Connection session is in a window. When the Remote Desktop Connection session is full screen, you can press Windows key or Ctrl+Esc to display the Start menu.
Alt+Delete	Displays the control menu for the active window
Ctrl+Alt+− (minus on numeric keypad)	Copies the active window to the Clipboard (as Alt+PrintScreen does locally)
Ctrl+Alt++ (plus on numeric keypad)	Copies the remote Desktop to the Clipboard (as PrintScreen does locally)
Ctrl+Alt+End	Displays the Lock This Computer screen (as Ctrl+Alt+Delete does locally)

USING CUT, COPY, AND PASTE BETWEEN THE LOCAL AND REMOTE COMPUTERS

If you've chosen to share the Clipboard between the home computer and the remote computer, you can use Cut, Copy, and Paste commands to transfer information between the computers. For example, you could copy some text from a program on the local computer, and then paste it into a program on the remote computer. Or you could use the Ctrl+Alt+− (the minus key on the numeric keypad) keystroke to copy the active window to the Clipboard, and then paste it into a window on the local computer.

COPYING FROM REMOTE DRIVES TO LOCAL DRIVES

If you chose to make drives on the home computer available to the remote computer, you can copy from remote drives to local drives by working in Explorer. The drives on your local computer appear in Explorer windows on the remote computer as network drives named *Driveletter on COMPUTERNAME*, where *COMPUTERNAME* is the name of the local computer. Figure 30.11 shows an example.

The drives on the remote computer appear as regular drives. You can copy and move files from one drive to another as you would with local drives. Depending on the speed of your connection to the remote computer, copying large files from one computer to another may take a while.

FIGURE 30.11
When you've made drives on the home computer available to the remote computer, you can access all the drives through Explorer on the remote computer.

PRINTING TO A LOCAL PRINTER

You can print to a local printer from the remote Desktop by selecting the local printer in the Print dialog box just as you would any other printer.

Printer settings are communicated to the remote Desktop when you access it. If you add a local printer during the remote session, the remote Desktop won't be able to see it. To make the printer show up on the remote Desktop, log off the remote session and log back on.

Returning to Your Local Desktop

If you have the remote Desktop displayed in a window rather than full screen, you can return to the home computer's Desktop by clicking anywhere outside the Remote Desktop Connection window. But if the remote Desktop is displayed full screen, you need to use the connection bar to return to your home computer's Desktop.

If you chose to display the connection bar, it hovers briefly at the top of the screen, and then slides upward to vanish like a docked toolbar with its Autohide property enabled. To pin the connection bar in position, click the pin icon at its left end. (To unpin it, click the pin icon again.) To display the connection bar when it has hidden itself, move the mouse pointer to the top edge of the screen, just as you would do to display a docked toolbar hidden there.

The connection bar provides a Minimize button, a Restore/Maximize button, and a Close button. Use the Minimize and Restore buttons to reduce the remote Desktop from full screen to an icon or a partial screen so that you can access your local Desktop. Maximize the remote Desktop window to return to full-screen mode when you want to work with it again. Use the Close button as discussed in the next section to disconnect your remote session.

EXPERT KNOWLEDGE: REMOTE DESKTOP CONNECTION WRINKLES

This sidebar discusses some wrinkles of Remote Desktop Connection that you probably would like to know about before you run into them firsthand.

ACCOMMODATING DIFFERENT DISPLAY SETTINGS AND SPANNING DISPLAYS

The most pressing of these wrinkles concern the logistics of translating what's on the display or displays of the remote computer to the display on the local computer.

If the local computer is using a lower resolution than the remote computer, Windows reduces the size of program windows as necessary to make them fit on the screen.

If the remote computer has multiple monitors configured, Windows shows just the primary display, as you'd expect—it doesn't try to show both (or all) the displays, even if the local computer has the same number of monitors as the remote computer. If the Taskbar is displayed on a monitor other than the primary monitor, Windows moves it to the primary monitor so that you can see it. (This happens even if the Taskbar is locked.) Similarly, Windows moves all the open windows onto the primary monitor, which can make it absurdly crowded.

If the remote computer has a high-resolution monitor and your home computer has multiple monitors, you can span the Remote Desktop Connection display across the monitors. For this to work, the multiple monitors must use the same vertical resolution and should preferably be aligned horizontally (so that the parts of the picture match up). Start Remote Desktop Connection by pressing Windows Key+R, typing **mstsc /span** into the Run dialog box, and then pressing Enter. You can toggle full-screen spanned mode on and off by pressing Ctrl+Alt+Break.

It'd be helpful if Windows restored the remote Desktop to its previous condition when you disconnect a Remote Desktop Connection session—but it doesn't. So if you use Remote Desktop Connection a lot, it's a good idea to designate the monitor on which your Taskbar appears as the primary monitor. Otherwise, when you return to the remote computer, you'll find your Taskbar rearranged, and you'll need to unlock it (if you keep it locked) and move it back to where it belongs. Your program windows will be rearranged anyway, but there's not much you can do about this—Windows doesn't restore them to their previous size when you disconnect the Remote Desktop Connection session.

USING DIFFERENT KEYBOARD LAYOUTS

The keyboard setting on the remote computer decides how your keystrokes are interpreted—the keyboard setting on the local computer isn't used when you're working on the remote computer. For example, if you want to use a Dvorak keyboard layout on the remote computer, you need to apply that layout to the remote computer. You can't apply the layout to the local computer instead and have the layout apply to the remote computer.

DAISY-CHAINING REMOTE DESKTOP CONNECTION CONNECTIONS

Last, while you *can* connect via Remote Desktop Connection to one computer (let's call it remote computer A) and then use Remote Desktop Connection on that computer to access another computer (remote computer B), things tend to get confused when you try to control remote computer B from your local computer. You probably won't want to create such daisy chains. Instead, connect directly from the home computer to each remote computer that you want to control.

Disconnecting the Remote Session

You can disconnect the remote session in either of the two following ways:

◆ On the remote Desktop, choose Start ➤ Disconnect (the Disconnect button is the orange button bearing an X to the left of the Lock button). Windows disconnects the Remote Desktop Connection session with confirmation.

◆ Click the Close button on the connection bar (if the remote Desktop is displayed full screen) or on the Remote Desktop window (if the remote Desktop is not displayed full screen). Windows displays the Disconnect Windows Session dialog box, shown here. Click the OK button.

Remote Desktop Connection disconnects the remote session but leaves the programs running for the time being. You can then log on again and pick up where you left off.

Logging Off the Remote Session

To log off and end your user session, click the Start button on the remote Desktop, click the arrow button to the right of the Lock icon on the Start menu, and then choose Log Off. Remote Desktop Connection logs you off the remote computer, and then closes the Remote Desktop Connection session.

When someone else bumps you off the remote Desktop (by logging on locally or remotely), Windows displays a Remote Desktop Disconnected dialog box telling you that the remote session has ended, as shown here.

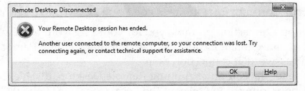

If the network connection between the home computer and the remote computer is broken, the home computer displays a message to let you know. If you've selected the Reconnect if Connection Is Dropped check box on the Experience page, Remote Desktop Connection attempts to reconnect, as shown here.

Shutting Down or Restarting the Remote Computer

You can also shut down or restart the remote computer from Remote Desktop Connection. To help you avoid turning off the remote computer by accident, Windows doesn't offer access to the Turn Off Computer command from the Start menu on the remote computer.

But sometimes you *will* need to shut down the remote computer—for example, say you've left it running so that you can retrieve files via Remote Desktop Connection, you've now retrieved them, and you don't need to access it anymore. Other times you'll need to restart the computer—for example, if it seems to be unstable, or if it has suffered memory leaks that have crippled its performance—so that you can connect to it again using Remote Desktop Connection.

To shut down or restart the remote computer, click the Start button, and then choose Windows Security. From the Windows Security screen, click the drop-down arrow on the power button, and then choose Shut Down or Restart.

If other users have disconnected sessions on the computer you're proposing to shut down (or restart), Windows warns you that you'll terminate these sessions.

Troubleshooting Remote Desktop Connection Connections

This section discusses an error message and a problem that you may run into when using Remote Desktop Connection, what causes them, and how to solve them.

"THE LOCAL POLICY OF THIS SYSTEM DOES NOT PERMIT YOU TO LOGON INTERACTIVELY" ERROR

If Remote Desktop Connection fails to connect with the error message "The local policy of this system does not permit you to logon interactively," it means you need to add your account to the Remote Desktop Users group. Log on as an Administrator user locally and then add your account to the group by following the steps in the section "Setting the Remote Computer to Accept Incoming Connections," earlier in this chapter.

REMOTE DESKTOP CONNECTION PROMPTS FOR YOUR PASSWORD EVEN WHEN YOU'VE SAVED IT

If Remote Desktop Connection prompts you for your password even when you've saved your password in the connection, it means that the computer running Remote Desktop is set to always prompt for the password at connection time.

If you administer the computer running Remote Desktop, disable the Always Prompt Client for Password upon Connection policy in the Local Computer Policy\Computer Configuration\Administrative Templates\Windows Components\Terminal Services\Encryption and Security item in Microsoft Management Console. If someone else administers the computer, ask them to do this.

Using a Dial-up Connection to a Remote Network

Rather than taking control of a remote computer as discussed in the previous section, you may need to connect directly to a remote network. You can do this in two ways:

Dial-up connection If the remote network has a remote access server, you can connect via a dial-up connection across a phone line. Normally, you'd use a dial-up connection to connect to a corporate network rather than a home network, but it is possible to install a remote access server on a home network too. Dial-up connections are effective but slow.

Virtual private network   If the remote network has a virtual private network (VPN) server, you can connect to the network via an Internet connection. A VPN connection takes place at the speed of your Internet connection, so it can be much faster than a dial-up connection. See the next section for details.

Getting the Information for the Connection

Creating a dial-up connection to a remote network is like creating an Internet connection, only with a few differences. Start by assembling the following information:

◆ Your username and password for the remote access server.

◆ The telephone number and area code of the remote access server.

◆ The modem type required (for example, V.92 or V.90), to make sure your modem is compatible.

◆ Whether the remote access server uses Dynamic Host Configuration Protocol (DHCP) to assign IP addresses or whether you need to specify a particular IP address. If you need a particular IP address, learn what it is.

◆ The protocol or protocols used on the remote network. In most cases, it'll be TCP/IP, but you may need to use IPX/SPX for some remote access servers.

◆ The names or IP addresses of any mail servers that you'll need to connect to.

Creating the Connection

To create the connection, take the following steps:

1. Choose Start ➢ Connect To. Windows launches the Connect to a Network Wizard. (If no Connect To item appears on the Start menu, choose Start ➢ Control Panel, click the Network and Internet link in Control Panel Home view, and then click the Connect to a Network link under the Network and Sharing Center heading.)

2. Click the Set Up a Connection or Network link near the bottom of the window. The wizard displays the Choose a Connection Option window (see Figure 30.12).

FIGURE 30.12
To set up a dial-up connection, select the Connect to a Workplace item in the Choose a Connection Option window.

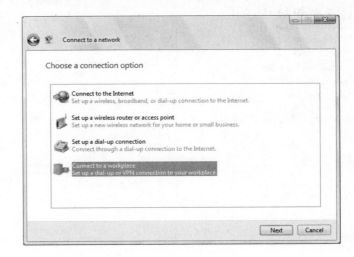

3. Click the Connect to a Workplace item, and then click the Next button. If the wizard displays the Do You Want to Use a Connection That You Already Have? window, select the No, Create a New Connection option button, and then click the Next button. Windows displays the How Do You Want to Connect? window (see Figure 30.13).

4. Click the Dial Directly item, and then click the Next button. If Windows prompts you to select which dial-up device to use, click the device, and then click the Next button. Windows displays the Type the Telephone Number to Connect To window (see Figure 30.14).

5. Type (or paste) the phone number, including any long-distance and area code necessary, in the Telephone Number box.

6. Type a descriptive name for the connection in the Destination Name text box. (This name is for your benefit and needn't have anything to do with the name of any company involved.)

FIGURE 30.13
In the How Do You Want to Connect? window, select the Dial Directly item.

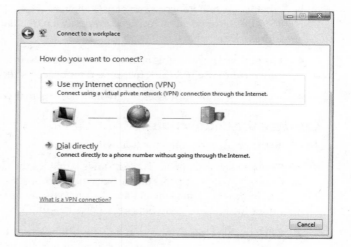

FIGURE 30.14
In the Type the Telephone Number to Connect To window, type the telephone number and give the connection a descriptive name.

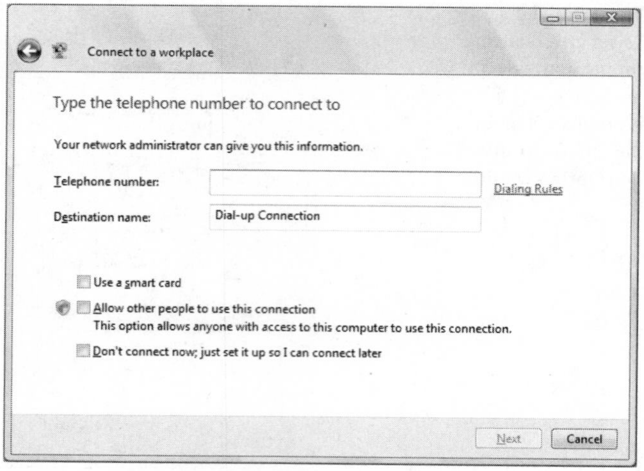

7. If you need to set up dialing rules for the connection, click the Dialing Rules link, and then work in the Phone and Modem Options dialog box. See the section "Using Dial-Up Networking from Multiple Locations" in Chapter 14 for details on dialing rules.

8. If you need to use a smart card to authenticate yourself for the connection, select the Use a Smart Card check box. Windows changes the Next button to a Create button.

9. If you want to share this connection with other users of your computer, select the Allow Other People to Use This Connection check box, and then authenticate yourself to User Account Control.

10. If you want to set up the connection now but not try it, select the Don't Connect Now; Just Set It Up So I Can Connect Later check box. Usually, it's best to test the connection as soon as you've set it up, so that you can be sure it works, but this feature can be useful when you're setting up a connection without a phone line available.

11. Click the Next button. Windows displays the Type Your User Name and Password window (see Figure 30.15). If you selected the Use a Smart Card check box, click the Create button that replaces the Next button. You'll need to provide the smart card to make the connection.

12. Type your username in the User Name text box and your password in the Password text box. If you want to see the characters in your password to make sure you enter it correctly, select the Show Characters check box.

13. If you want Windows to store the password for this connection, select the Remember This Password check box. Storing the password is convenient, especially if you're planning to share the connection with other users of your computer, but it reduces the security of the remote network.

14. If you need to supply a domain name in order to log on to the remote network, type the name in the Domain text box.

15. Click the Connect button. Windows dials the number you specified and establishes the connection.

FIGURE 30.15
In the Type Your User Name and Password window, you can choose whether to have Windows remember the password for the dial-up connection.

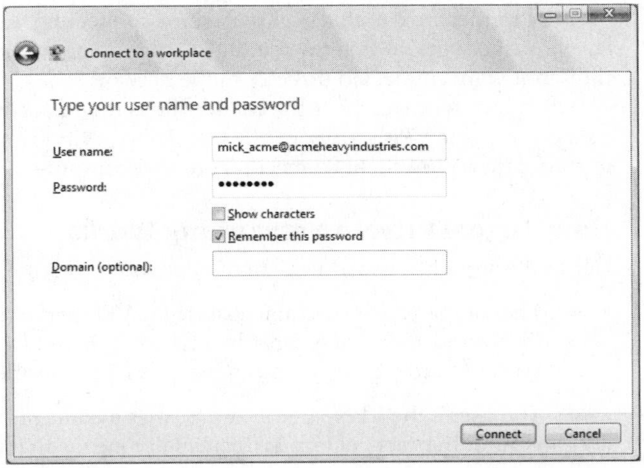

Using a Dial-up Connection You've Created

Once you've created a dial-up connection, you can use it as follows:

1. Choose Start ➢ Connect To. Windows displays the Select a Network to Connect To window.

2. Click the dial-up connection, and then click the Connect button. If the window contains many connections, choose Dial-Up and VPN in the Show drop-down list to restrict the display to dial-up connections and VPN connections.

Changing the Properties of a Dial-up Connection

To change the properties of a dial-up connection, follow these steps:

1. Choose Start ➢ Connect To. Windows displays the Select a Network to Connect To window.

2. Right-click the dial-up connection, and then choose Properties from the shortcut menu. Windows displays the Properties dialog box for the connection.

You can then use the options on the five pages of the Properties dialog box to adjust the connection. These properties are the same as those for a dial-up Internet connection, discussed in the section "Configuring the Connection Manually" in Chapter 2.

One difference is that a dial-up connection for a remote network will often need to have the Client for Microsoft Networks bound to it, whereas a dial-up Internet connection will not. Another difference is you will likely need different security settings for a connection to a remote network—particularly a connection to a corporate network—than to your ISP. Ask the network's administrator for specifics if they don't actively press them on you.

Creating and Using VPN Connections

Virtual private networking is a method of connecting two computers securely across an insecure network. In practice, the insecure network is usually the Internet, although in theory it can be any network, public or private, on which the prevailing level of security isn't adequate for the needs of the connection. For example, you might use a VPN connection to connect via a wireless network on which your network traffic might be snooped.

VPN connections are typically used for connecting a remote PC securely to a computer on a corporate network so that the remote PC can use network resources (files, printers, and so on) as though it were connected directly to the network.

The computer that makes the connection is the *VPN client*, while the computer that accepts the connection is the *VPN server* or *VPN host*. To use Windows Vista to call into a network, you'll need to configure a VPN client connection on your computer.

How Virtual Private Networking Works

Here's the straightforward version of how virtual private networking works:

◆ The company or individual hosting the VPN server connects the server to the Internet (either directly to an ISP or indirectly through a shared Internet connection) and configures the server to accept incoming connections from specified users.

◆ The user—the VPN client—establishes a connection to the insecure network as it usually would. In practical terms, this usually means that the remote user establishes an Internet connection through their ISP just as they normally would when accessing the Internet. When using a VPN over a LAN or wireless network, the user would establish a network connection as usual. (Typically, the user's computer would already be directly connected to the network.)

◆ The user then connects to the VPN server across the insecure network, providing such authentication as necessary—for example, a username and a password, a certificate, or a smart card. Once the user has authenticated, they can connect to the resources on the server—and, if the server is configured to permit them to do so, on the network—as if they were connected locally to it.

◆ The VPN client and server use the protocols of the insecure network to transfer data as usual—for example, if they're connecting across the Internet, they'll use TCP/IP, much as for any other Internet connection. But the client and server tunnel under those protocols to create a direct, secure connection between the two endpoints. The connection is secured by encrypting each packet (or frame, depending on the network protocol used) of data to be transmitted and encapsulating it in another packet (or frame) for transmission. The resulting packet (or frame) receives a new header for transmission. At the destination, the other computer removes the header, extracts and decrypts the packet (or frame), and reassembles the data in its unencrypted form.

Windows Vista supports the Point-to-Point Tunneling Protocol (PPTP) and the Layer 2 Tunneling Protocol (L2TP) for VPN connections. L2TP is much more secure than PPTP (which is sometimes referred to disparagingly by cryptographers as *kiddy crypto* because its encryption is reckoned easy to break). When connecting to a VPN server, Windows can use either PPTP or L2TP.

Advantages of VPN Connections

For remote access to a network, VPN connections have compelling advantages over direct dial-up connections for both users and network administrators.

VPN connections let users connect at the full speed of their broadband Internet connection (assuming they have broadband) rather than at dial-up speeds. Using broadband for such tasks can make a huge difference to the user's experience of remote networking. If the user doesn't have broadband, the dial-up connection to the ISP won't be any faster than a dial-up connection to a remote access server, but it should normally be a flat-rate local call rather than a metered call.

Meanwhile, the network administrator doesn't need to worry about buying (or building) and maintaining a remote access server with dozens of modems connected to a corresponding number of phone lines—nor paying for those phone lines or the metered (or long-distance) calls charged back to the company. All they need do is configure the VPN server carefully, connect it to the Internet, keep it running, and probably monitor who's logging on and what actions the users are performing remotely.

Creating a VPN Client Connection

To connect to a remote VPN server, create a VPN client connection by following these steps:

1. Choose Start ➢ Connect To. Windows launches the Connect to a Network Wizard, which displays the Select a Network to Connect To window.

2. Click the Set Up a Connection or Network link near the bottom of the window. The wizard displays the Choose a Connection Option window.

3. Click the Connect to a Workplace item, and then click the Next button. If Windows displays the Do You Want to Use a Connection That You Already Have? window, select the No, Create a New Connection option button, and then click the Next button. Windows displays the How Do You Want to Connect? window.

4. Click the Use My Internet Connection (VPN) item. Windows displays the Type the Internet Address to Connect To window (see Figure 30.16).

5. In the Internet Address text box, type the address of the VPN server. The address may take the form of a domain name (for example, `acmevirtualindustries.com`), an IPv4 address (for example, `158.152.0.44`), or an IPv6 address (for example, `3dce:ffff:0000:2f3b:02ba:00ff:fe28:9c5a`).

6. In the Destination Name text box, type a descriptive name for the connection. This name is for your benefit and doesn't have to include the name of the company.

7. If you need to use a smart card to authenticate yourself for the connection, select the Use a Smart Card check box. Windows changes the Next button to a Create button.

8. If you want to share this connection with other users of your computer, select the Allow Other People to Use This Connection check box, and then authenticate yourself to User Account Control.

9. If you want to set up the connection now but not try it, select the Don't Connect Now; Just Set It Up So I Can Connect Later check box. Usually, it's best to test the connection as soon as you've set it up, so that you can be sure it works, but this feature can be useful when you're setting up a connection when not connected to a network.

10. Click the Next button. Windows displays the Type Your User Name and Password window (see Figure 30.17). (If you selected the Use a Smart Card check box, click the Create button that replaces the Next button. You'll need to provide the smart card to make the connection.)

FIGURE 30.16
In the Type the Internet Address to Connect To window, type the domain name or IP address, and give the connection a descriptive name.

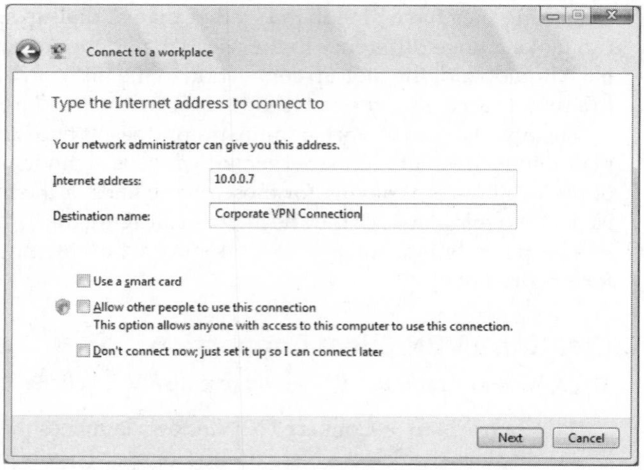

FIGURE 30.17
In the Type Your User Name and Password window, you can choose whether to have Windows remember the password for the VPN connection.

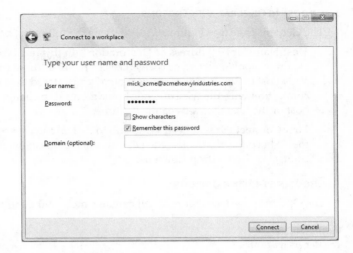

11. Type your username in the User Name text box and your password in the Password text box. If you want to see the characters in your password to make sure you enter it correctly, select the Show Characters check box.

12. If you want Windows to store the password for this connection, select the Remember This Password check box. Storing the password is convenient, especially if you're planning to share the connection with other users of your computer, but it reduces the security of the remote network.

13. If you need to supply a domain name in order to log on to the remote network, type the name in the Domain text box.

14. Click the Connect button. Windows attempts to connect to the VPN server at the domain or IP address you specified.

Configuring the VPN Client Connection

If you managed to establish a connection at the end of the setup process in the previous section, your VPN connection is probably ready for use. If you weren't able to connect, or if you need to provide further details, configure the connection further by using its Properties dialog box as discussed in this section.

To display the Properties dialog box for the connection, follow these steps:

1. Choose Start ➤ Connect To. Windows displays the Select a Network to Connect To window.

2. Right-click the VPN connection, choose Properties from the context menu, and then authenticate yourself to User Account Control. Windows displays the Properties dialog box.

CHOOSING GENERAL VPN OPTIONS

The General page (see Figure 30.18) contains the following options:

Host Name or IP Address of Destination In this text box, type or paste the host name (for example, vpnserver.mycompany.com) or the IP address (for example, 206.13.48.12) of the VPN host to which you're connecting. If you entered the name or address while setting up the connection with the wizard, you shouldn't need to change it unless the company changes the host or the host uses a dynamic IP address.

First Connect If you need Windows to dial an Internet connection before trying to establish the VPN connection, select the Dial Another Connection First check box, and then choose the connection in the drop-down list.

CHOOSING DIALING OPTIONS

The Options page (see Figure 30.19) contains most of the same options as for a dial-up connection.

FIGURE 30.18

The General page of the Properties dialog box for a VPN connection lets you tell Windows to dial an Internet connection before trying to connect to the VPN.

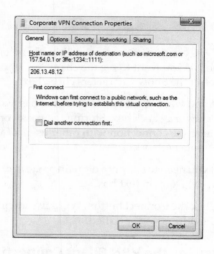

FIGURE 30.19

On the Options page of the Properties dialog box for a VPN connection, you can choose whether to display progress while connecting (which is usually helpful) and how many times to attempt redialing the connection.

CHOOSING SECURITY OPTIONS

The Security page (see Figure 30.20) lets you choose how to verify your identity. Normally, you'll want to select the Typical option button to make the upper set of controls available. In the Verify My Identity as Follows drop-down list, you can select Require Secured Password to use an encrypted password for verification, or select Use Smart Card to use a smart card. (The password is "secured" in that it's not transmitted unencrypted across the wire.)

If you need to use your Windows credentials to log on to the VPN, you can select the Automatically Use My Windows Logon Name and Password (and Domain, if Any) check box.

Normally, you should select the Require Data Encryption (Disconnect If None) check box to ensure that the data you send is encrypted. However, for some connections, you may need to clear this check box before you can connect.

If your network administrator has told you to use specific security settings, select the Advanced option button, and then click the Settings button. Windows displays the Advanced Security Settings dialog box (see Figure 30.21).

FIGURE 30.20
Depending on the remote network's security settings, you may need to change Windows Vista's default settings on the Security page for a VPN connection.

FIGURE 30.21
If your VPN host requires strong authentication (such as EAP or MS-CHAP v2), apply it to the VPN connection by using the Advanced Security Settings dialog box.

In the Data Encryption drop-down list, choose the encryption option you want:

No Encryption Allowed (Server Will Disconnect if It Requires Encryption) This setting prevents you from using encryption on the connection. You will seldom need this setting.

Optional Encryption (Connect Even if No Encryption) Select this setting if you want to be able to connect even if the server doesn't offer encryption. Usually, it's best to try the Require Encryption setting first, and then use this setting if the server doesn't offer encryption. (You then know that you're not using encryption rather than leaving the question open.)

Require Encryption (Disconnect if Server Declines) Use this setting to protect your connection with regular-strength encryption.

Maximum Strength Encryption (Disconnect if Server Declines) Use this setting to use the strongest possible encryption. From a security point of view, this setting is a good choice, but some servers support only regular-strength encryption.

In the Logon Security group box, you'll typically need to select the Use Extensible Authentication Protocol (EAP) option button, and then choose the EAP device in the drop-down list, which offers the choices Smart Card or Other Certificate and Protected EAP. (For example, if you have a smart card, select the Smart Card or Other Certificate item.) Otherwise, if your network administrator has told you to use specific protocols, select the Allow These Protocols option button, and then select the appropriate check boxes below it. For example, you might need to select the Microsoft CHAP Version 2 (MS-CHAP v2) check box if you've been told to use MS-CHAP v2. Don't select the Unencrypted Password (PAP) check box unless you've specifically been instructed to: Password Authentication Protocol sends passwords unencrypted, so anybody intercepting your Internet traffic can grab your password and then masquerade as you.

Whichever type of logon security you choose, you can select the When Connected, Prevent Sharing of This Connection with Other Users on This Computer check box to prevent others from using this connection while you're using it. Selecting this check box should give you better performance as well as greater security.

CHOOSING NETWORKING OPTIONS

At the top of the Networking page (see Figure 30.22) of the Properties dialog box is the Type of VPN drop-down list, which lets you select the type of VPN connection you want to establish:

Automatic Windows tries to connect via L2TP first, and then falls back to PPTP if it can't connect via L2TP.

L2TP IPSec VPN Using Layer 2 Tunneling Protocol and IPSec provides a more secure connection.

PPTP VPN Using Point-to-Point Tunneling Protocol provides a less secure connection but enables you to connect to servers that don't support L2TP.

FIGURE 30.22
The Networking page
of the Properties
dialog box for a VPN
connection lets you
choose which protocol
to use.

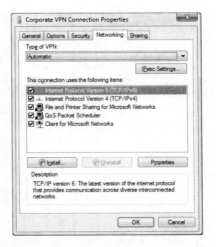

To choose IPSec settings for a VPN connection using L2TP, click the IPSec Settings button page. Windows displays the IPSec Settings dialog box (shown here), which lets you choose between authenticating using a preshared key (type the key in the Key text box) or using a certificate.

Choosing Sharing Options

The Sharing page (not shown) lets you choose whether to share the connection via Internet Connection Sharing. See the section "Configuring ICS Manually" in Chapter 28 for a discussion of the Internet Connection Sharing options.

ESTABLISHING A VPN CONNECTION

To establish a VPN connection, follow these steps:

1. Choose Start ➢ Connect To. Windows displays the Select a Network to Connect To window.

2. Click your VPN connection, and then click the Connect button. Windows displays the Connect dialog box for the connection (see Figure 30.23).

FIGURE 30.23
The Connect dialog box for a VPN connection lets you save the username and password for either yourself only or for other users as well.

3. If necessary, type your username, password, and domain.

4. If you want to save your credentials so you don't need to enter them again, select the Save This User Name and Password for the Following Users check box, and then select the Me Only option button or the Anyone Who Uses This Computer option button as appropriate.

5. If you're connecting to a VPN server that has a dynamic IP address rather than a fixed address or host name, click the Properties button in the Connect dialog box, authenticate yourself to User Account Control, and then enter the host's current IP address in the Host Name or IP Address of Destination text box on the General page of the Properties dialog box. Click the OK button to return to the Connect dialog box.

6. Click the Connect button to establish the connection. Normally, Windows simply establishes the connection, but you may also see a couple of other dialog boxes:

   ◆ If you've configured the connection to connect to an Internet connection before establishing the VPN connection, Windows displays the Initial Connection dialog box to prompt you to connect to the Internet. Select the Yes button or the No button as appropriate. If you want Windows to go ahead and dial without prompting you, or to refrain from prompting you, select the Don't Display This Reminder Again check box before dismissing the Initial Connection dialog box.

   ◆ If your username or password isn't recognized, or if you need to provide domain information, Windows prompts you for the information, as shown here.

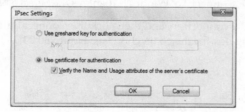

Working via the VPN Connection

When you've connected, you'll be able to access your usual network drives, printers, and other resources. The main difference is that the connection takes place at the speed of your Internet connection, which typically means that performance will be far slower than that of a LAN connection.

TROUBLESHOOTING: YOU CAN'T BROWSE THE NETWORK YOU'RE CONNECTED TO

If you can establish a VPN connection to the VPN host but you then can't browse the network, the most likely explanation is that your TCP/IP configuration is incorrect.

1. Choose Start ➢ Connect To. Windows displays the Select a Network to Connect To window.

2. Right-click the connection, and then choose Properties from the context menu. Windows displays the Properties dialog box for the connection.

3. On the Networking tab, click the Internet Protocol item for the version of TCP/IP you're using—most likely the Internet Protocol Version 4 (TCP/IPv4) item—and then click the Properties button. Windows opens the Internet Protocol Version dialog box for that version of TCP/IP. (Ask an administrator if you're not sure which version of TCP/IP the connection uses.)

4. Either specify the IP address and DNS server information supplied by the network's administrator or tell Windows to obtain the IP address and DNS server address manually.

5. Click the OK button to close each dialog box in turn, and then try the connection again.

TROUBLESHOOTING: USING YOUR VPN DISABLES YOUR OTHER INTERNET PROGRAMS

If using a VPN connection appears to disable your other Internet programs, make sure that Windows isn't trying to access the Internet via the VPN connection.

1. Choose Start ➢ Connect To. Windows launches the Connect to a Network Wizard, which displays the Select a Network to Connect To window.

2. Right-click the connection, and then choose Properties from the Context menu. Windows displays the Properties dialog box for the connection.

3. On the Networking tab, click the Internet Protocol item for the version of TCP/IP you're using—most likely the Internet Protocol Version 4 (TCP/IPv4) item—and then click the Properties button. Windows opens the Internet Protocol Version dialog box for that version of TCP/IP. (Ask an administrator if you're not sure which version of TCP/IP the connection uses.)

4. Click the Advanced button. Windows displays the Advanced TCP/IP Settings dialog box.

5. Clear the Use Default Gateway on Remote Network check box on the IP Settings page.

6. Click the OK button in all three dialog boxes to close them.

You may also need to flush the DNS cache. To do so, open a command-prompt window and issue an `ipconfig /flushdns` command.

The Bottom Line

Take control of a remote computer using Remote Desktop Connection   Remote Desktop Connection lets you take control of a remote computer via your Internet connection or a network connection. The remote computer must be running a version of Windows that includes Remote Desktop, such as a Windows Vista Business Edition, Windows Vista Ultimate Edition, or Windows XP Professional. Choose Start ➤ All Programs ➤ Accessories ➤ Remote Desktop Connection to launch Remote Desktop Connection. Once connected, the remote computer's display appears on your monitor, and you can work much as if you were sitting at the computer. You can also transfer files from the remote computer to your home computer or print from the remote computer to a printer attached to the home computer.

Connect to a remote network via a dial-up connection   When you need to make your computer part of a remote network, you can connect via dial-up to a remote access server. To create a dial-up connection, choose Start ➤ Connect To, click the Set Up a Connection or Network link, click the Connect to a Workplace item, and then click the Dial Directly item. Provide your username, password, and the telephone number for the remote access server.

Connect to a remote network via a virtual private network connection   A virtual private network connection lets you connect to a remote network securely across an insecure network, such as the Internet or a wireless network. To create a VPN connection, choose Start ➤ Connect To, click the Set Up a Connection or Network link, click the Connect to a Workplace item, and then click the Use My Internet Connection (VPN) item. Provide the domain name or IP address of the remote network, your username, and your password.

Appendix A

Windows Vista Basics

- ◆ Learn how to use the mouse
- ◆ Learn how to select items
- ◆ Use drag-and-drop to perform operations
- ◆ Work with windows and dialog boxes

This appendix presents the basic things you need to know about the Windows Vista graphical user interface (GUI) in order to get started with the main text of the book. If you've used Windows before and are comfortable with the GUI, you probably don't need to read this appendix, though you might want to skim through the sections about Windows controls to make sure you're clear on the terms involved.

Mouse Basics and Terminology

For navigating the Windows GUI, a pointing device is almost essential. You can get a bewildering variety of pointing devices that work with Windows—everything from a conventional mouse or trackball with two, three, or more buttons, to a set of foot pedals that provide mouse functionality, to a head-mounted infrared reflector that reflects a beam sent from a device mounted on your monitor to track your head movements and so move the mouse pointer. But the basic principle of all these devices is the same: You move the pointer around the screen to indicate one or more objects on which you want to take an action. You then click in one of the following ways to take the action:

Click   Press the primary mouse button once (and release the button). The primary mouse button on a conventional mouse is the left button, on which your right forefinger rests.

Double-click   Press the primary mouse button twice in quick succession.

Right-click   Press the secondary mouse button once.

Drag   Press the primary mouse button to select the object, keep holding the mouse button down, and move the mouse to drag the object to where you want it to appear. Release the mouse button.

Right-drag   Drag (as described in the previous paragraph) except using the secondary mouse button.

If you're using a Tablet PC with a stylus, you tap instead of clicking, double-tap instead of double-clicking, and press and hold for a right-click. See the section "Configuring Tablet PC and Pen and Input Settings" in Chapter 14 for details of how you can customize these settings.

Selection Basics

These are the basic moves for selecting objects in Windows:

◆ To select one object, click it with the primary mouse button. Alternatively, use the arrow keys to move the focus (the current selection) to the object, and then press the spacebar.

◆ To deselect a selected object, click in open space elsewhere in its window. With the keyboard, use the arrow keys to move the focus off the object.

◆ To select multiple objects that appear next to each other (for example, in a dialog box or in a Windows Explorer window), click the first object to select it as usual. Then hold down the Shift key and click the last object in the range. Release the Shift key.

◆ To select multiple objects that don't appear next to each other, click the first object to select it as usual. Then hold down the Ctrl key while you click each of the other objects in turn. Release the Ctrl key.

◆ To deselect some of multiple objects you've selected, hold down the Ctrl key and click each selected object that you want to deselect in turn. Release the Ctrl key.

◆ To select multiple objects that appear near each other on your Desktop or in a folder in Tiles view or Icons view, click in empty space outside one corner of the area occupied by the objects you want to select, and then drag to draw a dotted box around them. When you release the mouse button, Windows selects the objects.

◆ To select all the objects in a Windows Explorer window, choose Organize ➤ Select All. To toggle the selection (selecting the objects that weren't selected and deselecting those that were), press the Alt key to display the menu bar, and then choose Edit ➤ Invert Selection. For example, to select all but three objects in a Windows Explorer window, select those three objects and then press the Alt key and choose Edit ➤ Invert Selection.

Drag-and-Drop

Windows makes extensive use of functionality known as *drag-and-drop*, which lets you select an object on your Desktop or in a window, then drag it to a different location and drop it there.

Drag-and-drop has different effects depending on the object you're dragging, its source, and the location or object you drop it on. Here are some examples:

◆ Dragging a file and dropping it in a folder on the same drive moves the file from its source folder to the destination folder.

◆ Dragging a file and dropping it in a folder on a different drive copies the file from its source folder to the destination folder.

◆ Dragging a document and dropping it on the icon for a printer prints the document.

To use drag-and-drop, select an object by clicking it, keep holding down the mouse button, drag the object to its destination, and release the mouse button to drop it there.

Most drag-and-drop techniques use the primary mouse button, but some (usually less common) techniques use the secondary mouse button. The latter technique is referred to as *right-drag-and-drop*.

If you need to cancel a drag-and-drop operation you've started, press Esc.

Working with Windows and Dialog Boxes

When you're working in Windows, most of the action takes place in windows on the screen. A *window* is essentially a rectangular area on screen. For example, when you run a program, it typically opens one or more windows for you to work in. Figure A.1 shows two program windows—a Notepad window and a Computer window—open on the Windows Desktop.

Most applications also use *dialog boxes*—windows that typically contain controls but don't let you create documents.

The distinction between a window and a dialog box is highly fluid. In the past, generally speaking, windows were resizable, whereas dialog boxes were not. Windows Vista blurs the distinction between windows and dialog boxes by using windows instead of dialog boxes and having dialog boxes that are resizable.

FIGURE A.1

Two program windows open on the Windows Desktop

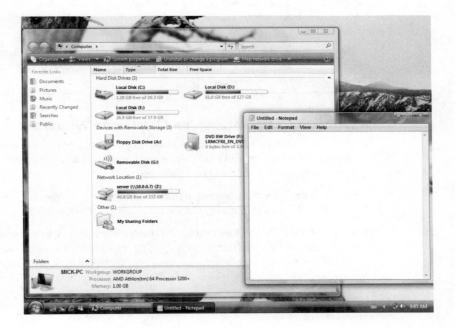

Dialog Box Modality

Most dialog boxes are *modal*. *Modal* means that when a dialog box is open, you cannot take any further action in the program that displayed the dialog box until you dismiss the dialog box. Modality is intended to focus your attention on what the dialog box is expecting you to do. For example, when you issue a Print command to print the document you're working on, Windows figures you shouldn't be able to edit or format the document until you've finished printing it.

The opposite of a modal dialog box is a *modeless* dialog box. A *modeless* dialog box does not prevent you from taking actions in its program while it's displayed. Most programs use few modeless dialog boxes, but other applications use them extensively. For instance, in Word for Windows, some dialog boxes are modeless. For example, when the Find and Replace dialog box is displayed, you can click in your document and continue working around the dialog box. But most dialog boxes in Word are modal. For example, when you display the Open dialog box or the Save As dialog box, you can't take any further action in the program until you dismiss the dialog box.

The problem with modeless dialog boxes is that, because you can continue working while a modeless dialog box is displayed on screen, you can in theory stack up an absurd number of modeless dialog boxes on screen while you continue to work. In practice, most people get annoyed enough by modeless dialog boxes that they close them smartly, provided that they can see them.

UNDERSTANDING APPLICATION MODALITY AND SYSTEM MODALITY

Technically, there are two types of modality: *application modality* and *system modality*. When a dialog box is application modal, you can take no further action in its application until you dismiss the dialog box. When a dialog box is system modal, you can take no further action *on your computer* until you dismiss the dialog box.

System modality is supposedly reserved for events of systemwide importance, such as Windows errors and crashes, but some applications display system-modal dialog boxes when they should display application-modal dialog boxes.

Maximizing, Minimizing, and Restoring Windows

Most windows have three buttons: a Minimize button, a Maximize button that swaps places with a Restore Down button, and a Close button. Figure A.2 illustrates these buttons.

These buttons are intuitive enough to use:

- Click the Maximize button to maximize its window. Windows expands the window to take up all the Desktop and replaces the Maximize button with a Restore Down button.

- Click the Restore Down button to restore the window to its former size. Windows replaces the Restore Down button with the Maximize button again. Once you've restored the window, it's in a *normal* state—in other words, neither maximized nor minimized.

FIGURE A.2
Most windows have three buttons for minimizing, maximizing or restoring, or closing the window.

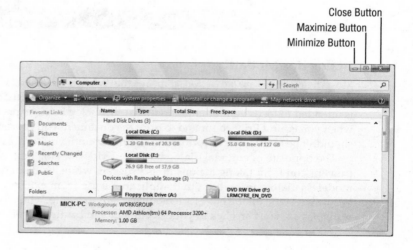

Close Button
Maximize Button
Minimize Button

◆ Click the Minimize button to minimize its window down to a Taskbar button. Click the Taskbar button to restore the window to its pre-minimized size.

◆ Click the Close button to close its window.

You can also maximize, minimize, and restore windows by using the control menu (see the next section).

Using the Control Menu on Windows and Dialog Boxes

At the left end of its title bar, each window and dialog box has a *control menu* that contains commands for moving, resizing, and closing the window or dialog box.

The control menu was a standard feature of earlier versions of Windows. Users grew so used to the control menu that Microsoft has carried it over to Windows Vista even though the Vista user interface doesn't really suit it. In Vista, some windows and dialog boxes don't display an icon in the control-menu area. Many windows and dialog boxes have an icon to indicate the control menu's presence, but Windows Explorer windows and many dialog boxes do not.

To display the control menu on a window and in some dialog boxes, click the icon at the upper-left corner of the window (or, if there is no icon, click just inside the upper-left corner of the window) or press Alt+spacebar. To display the control menu on a dialog box when clicking doesn't work, press Alt+spacebar. Figure A.3 shows the control menu on a dialog box that thinks it's a window.

FIGURE A.3

Use the control menu to move, resize, or close a window, or to move or close a dialog box.

The control menu for most dialog boxes offers just two commands: Move and Close. The control menu for most windows offers these commands: Restore, Move, Size, Minimize, Maximize, and Close.

The Restore, Minimize, Maximize, and Close commands do what they say. Either Restore or Maximize is available at any time: If the window is maximized, Restore is available; if the window is normal, Maximize is available.

Move is available if the window is in a normal state (because you cannot move a maximized window). To move the window by using the keyboard, select Move from the control menu, then use the arrow keys to move the window to where you want it, and press the Enter key. (You can also move the window with the mouse, but unless the window has somehow moved to a position off your monitor, it's easier simply to drag the title bar of the window with the mouse rather than display the context menu and issue the Move command.)

Similarly, Size is available only if the window is in a normal state. Use the arrow keys to resize the window, and then press the Enter key.

Double-click the control menu box or area to close a window. This is often a handy way to close a window if the Close button (the × button) is too far from where the mouse pointer is positioned.

Dialog Box Controls

Figure A.4 shows the main controls that you'll find in dialog boxes in Windows. The following sections discuss these controls.

FIGURE A.4

A dialog box with the most-used controls in Windows

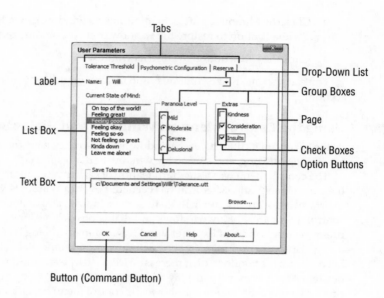

PAGE CONTROLS AND TABS

Some dialog boxes contain multiple *pages* of information. Each page typically contains a different set of controls. For example, in Figure A.4 the Psychometric Configuration page and the Reserve page would contain a different set of controls than the Tolerance Threshold page.

To access one of the pages, you click its *tab*—the visible protrusion at the top of the page. Some people (including Microsoft sometimes) refer to the pages as *tabs*, though this usage tends to be confusing.

The Windows convention is for the tab to be placed at the top of the page, though some programmers choose to place them at the bottom or at one of the sides of the pages for special effects.

LABEL CONTROLS

Labels are used to display text in dialog boxes. Typically, labels are static, though some dialog boxes use labels that you can change, either by clicking the label or by clicking a button associated with the label.

LIST BOX CONTROLS

A *list box* contains a number of items that typically are related. Most list boxes are configured so that you can choose only one of their items, but some list boxes are configured so that you can select multiple items.

DROP-DOWN LIST CONTROLS

A *drop-down list* control provides a number of preset values (presented via the list that you can access by clicking the down-arrow button). Some drop-down lists also let you enter a new value by typing into the text box.

The formal name for the latter type of drop-down list controls is *combo boxes* because they combine a text box and a list box.

GROUP BOX CONTROLS

The *group box* control is a visual aid for grouping other controls into logical sets. (The formal name for a group box control is *frame*.) For example, you'll find option buttons or check boxes arranged into group boxes to make clear that they belong together.

OPTION BUTTON CONTROLS

Option buttons (also called *radio buttons*) are groups of buttons of which only one can be chosen at any given time. (The name *radio button* comes from a physical radio with a number of preset stations. When you choose one preset button, it cancels the other buttons, because the radio can play only one station at a time.)

Selecting an option button clears all other option buttons in the set.

CHECK BOX CONTROLS

Check boxes are widely used controls for turning options on and off, or for indicating that (for multiple objects) the item specified by the check box is on for some and off for the others.

Most check boxes have two states: *selected* (with a check mark in them) and *cleared* (without a check mark in them). Clicking the check box toggles it from one state to the other. People use a variety of terms for describing what to do with check boxes, such as *put a check in the check box* or *click to remove the check from the check box*. For clarity, this book uses the phrases *select a check box* and *clear a check box*. If the check box in question is already in the state described, you don't need to do anything.

Some check boxes have a third state, in which the check box is selected but grayed out. This state, which technically is called a Null state and indicates that the check box contains no valid data, typically means that the option identified by the check box is on for part of the current selection. For example, in Microsoft Word, if you select three words, one of which has strikethrough formatting, and display the Font dialog box, the Strikethrough check box appears in a Null state, because it applies to part of the selection but not to all of it.

Some Windows applications use check boxes instead of option buttons. This is poor practice that sends programmers into conniptions and frustrates many users.

TEXT BOX CONTROLS

A *text box* is a control in which you can enter and edit text. Text boxes often contain a default value that you can change if necessary or simply accept if it seems suitable.

COMMAND BUTTON CONTROLS

A *command button* is a control that performs an action when you click it. For example, most dialog boxes contain a default action button (for example, a Print command button in a Print dialog box or an OK command button in many dialog boxes) to take the actions specified in the dialog box. Most dialog boxes contain a Cancel command button to cancel the actions specified in the dialog box and close the dialog box.

This book refers to command buttons as *buttons*.

CLOSING A DIALOG BOX

When you've made changes in a dialog box, you typically need to close it to apply them. To close a dialog box and apply the changes you've made, click the default command button (for example, an OK button, a Close button, or a Save button).

To close a dialog box without applying the changes you've made in it, click the Cancel button.

Some dialog boxes have an Apply button that you can click to apply your changes without closing the dialog box. This lets you make further changes before closing the dialog box.

Appendix B

Installing or Upgrading to Windows Vista

- ◆ Plan to install Windows Vista
- ◆ Determine whether your computer can run Windows Vista
- ◆ Choose a method of installing Windows Vista
- ◆ Upgrade Windows XP Home Edition to Windows Vista
- ◆ Perform a new installation or clean installation of Windows Vista
- ◆ Complete the setup process and create your user account
- ◆ Activate Windows Vista
- ◆ Transfer your files and settings

If you bought your computer with Windows Vista preinstalled on it, you're all set to use Windows Vista. However, you may need to transfer files and settings from your old computer to your new computer by using Windows Easy Transfer.

If you've bought a copy of Windows Vista at retail for a computer you already have, or one you're building from scratch, you'll need to install Windows. This chapter shows you how to install Windows Vista from scratch, how to upgrade from Windows XP to Windows Vista, and (where appropriate) how to decide between upgrading and performing a fresh installation.

Planning to Install Windows Vista

Here's how to go about installing Windows Vista successfully:

1. Make sure that your computer will be able to run Windows Vista. Start by comparing your system specifications with the minimum requirements, and see if you need to upgrade any components.

2. Assuming your computer has an operating system loaded already—load the Windows Vista DVD in your computer and run the Windows Vista Upgrade Advisor.

3. If you want to perform a new installation or a clean installation of Windows Vista rather than an upgrade, but you want your new installation or clean installation to pick up your current settings and some of your files, run Windows Easy Transfer to save the settings from your current version of Windows.

4. Perform the upgrade, new installation, or clean installation.

5. If you ran Windows Easy Transfer, run it again to apply your settings to Windows Vista and to make your files available.

Determining Whether Your Computer Can Run Windows Vista

First, make sure that your computer will be able to run Windows Vista. The following sections discuss the main requirements.

To run Windows Vista at all, you need a pretty recent PC with 512MB RAM or more and 16GB or more free hard disk space. To use the Vista Aero user interface with the Glass transparency effects, you need a modern graphics card with 128MB RAM or more. In general, to get the most out of Windows Vista, you need a fairly high-performance PC.

Understanding the Different Levels of Vista "Experience"

Microsoft breaks down the requirements into different levels of "experience" with Windows Vista into "good," "better," and "best" experience. This section explains these levels in reverse order to see how good the experience can be and what you lose at the lower levels. After that, the section looks at the hardware you need to get these levels.

BEST EXPERIENCE

In the "best" experience, you get the Vista Aero user interface, which has translucent elements (such as the title bars and frames of windows, as shown in most of the screens in this book) and transitional effects.

The translucence and transitional effects are pleasing on the eye but essentially useless. More useful are the thumbnail previews of windows for taskbar buttons, which help you to identify windows from the taskbar buttons, and 3D task switching, which displays thumbnails of windows in the task-switching box (when you press Alt+Tab to switch from one application to another).

If you have a high-resolution display, you'll probably appreciate another feature of the Vista Aero user interface: *Interface scaling* lets you change the number of dots per inch (dpi) that Windows uses to calculate the sizes of the objects it displays. By scaling the interface, you can make Windows easy to read at high resolution rather than having to suffer the awkwardness of tiny elements for the sake of a giant display. (While Windows XP and earlier versions of Windows let you change the size of desktop icons and fonts, they did not let you scale all of the user interface.)

BETTER EXPERIENCE

In the "better" experience, you get the Vista Basic user interface (with no transparency or drop shadows), what Microsoft calls "enhanced graphics stability," and better performance for running multiple applications at once. What's more compelling is that you can *hot-plug* monitors. That means you can plug in a monitor while your PC is running, and then start using the monitor without having to restart Windows. (You can also unplug a monitor without making Vista unhappy.)

In the "better" experience, you may see some artifacts or blockiness as Windows redraws the screen, but most people find this easy enough to ignore. You won't get thumbnail previews of windows for taskbar buttons or in the task-switching box.

GOOD EXPERIENCE

In the "good" experience, you get the Aero Basic user interface and desktop graphics that Microsoft describes as "comparable" to those on Windows XP. You may be able to hot-plug monitors, but doing so may cause errors or crashes.

 Real World Scenario

THE VISTA BASIC INTERFACE IS ALL YOU NEED FOR WORK

The Vista Aero UI with Glass transparency effects is great to look at, but it doesn't help you get your work done. If you don't need the graphical previews and are content with the Vista Basic UI, you can run Windows Vista on relatively modest hardware.

Choosing Hardware for Windows Vista

Choosing hardware for Windows Vista involves two main factors:

Compatibility All your hardware must be compatible with Windows Vista. Compatibility should be an issue only if you're upgrading an existing PC to Windows Vista or building your own PC. If you're planning to buy a new PC to run Windows Vista, you shouldn't need to worry about hardware compatibility, because any PC manufacturer selling Windows Vista PCs will design those PCs for Windows Vista. (You may still run into compatibility issues when adding your existing hardware to a Windows Vista PC.)

Power You must make sure your hardware is powerful enough to run Windows Vista well enough to deliver the level of experience you want. (See the previous section for details on the good, better, and best levels of experience.)

CHOOSING A PROCESSOR

Any current processor from Intel Corporation or Advanced Micro Devices, Inc. (AMD) will run Windows Vista at a decent speed. Intel and AMD constantly release faster processors and new technologies, so it's worth spending a little time researching the latest processors if you're planning to buy a computer.

Here are suggestions for approaching the task of choosing a processor (as of December 2006):

◆ For a high-performance desktop computer, consider an Intel Core 2 Duo processor or an AMD Athlon 64 processor.

◆ For a value desktop computer, consider an Intel Celeron processor or an AMD Sempron processor.

◆ For a high-performance laptop computer, consider an Intel Centrino Duo processor or an AMD Turion 64 processor.

◆ For a value laptop computer, consider an Intel Centrino (not Centrino Duo) processor or a Celeron processor.

◆ For an ultra-quiet PC, consider a VIA Technologies processor such as a VIA C7, VIA C7-M, or VIA Eden.

◆ Never buy the newest and fastest processor unless you simply must have the latest and greatest technology no matter how high the cost. The newest and fastest processors tend to be far more expensive than slightly slower processors, even though they offer only marginally better performance.

If you're installing Windows Vista as an upgrade to an existing computer, you're probably stuck with that computer's current processor. Windows Vista does run on old processors (for example, a 1999-vintage Celeron 600), but performance is poor. In practice, a Pentium 4 or low-end Athlon 64 processor will probably be usable, but you'll get better performance from a faster and more capable processor.

CHOOSING A GRAPHICS CARD

Windows Vista is a highly graphical operating system, so your PC's graphics card is a vital component.

PCs usually have one of three types of graphics hardware:

◆ **Unified Memory Architecture (UMA)** The motherboard includes a graphics chip that borrows some of the PC's main memory (the RAM) for video use. UMA is the least expensive graphics solution, so the lowest-cost PCs tend to use it. It also delivers the worst performance and reduces the amount of RAM available for non-video tasks.

◆ **Graphics chip on the motherboard** The motherboard includes a graphics chip that has video memory built into it. This is a neat and effective solution as long as you don't need extremely high graphics performance: The graphics chips used are usually not the most powerful, and in most cases you can't directly upgrade them (though you may be able to add a separate graphics card and disable the built-in graphics chip). Many laptops and desktops use this solution.

◆ **Graphics card** The graphics card is separate and fits into a slot on the motherboard. This is the most flexible solution, as you can fit any of a wide range of graphics cards, from the modest to the most powerful. This solution is typically used only in desktop computers, as laptop computers don't have enough space for a separate graphics card. This tends to be the most expensive solution.

FEW LAPTOP PCS HAVE UPGRADEABLE GRAPHICS CHIPS

If you have a laptop PC, you're usually stuck with the graphics chip that came with it. A few laptops have upgradeable memory chips, so it's worth checking if yours does. Otherwise, you can find third-party graphics solutions that use the PC Card slot, but these tend to be expensive and suitable for special purposes only, such as attaching two or more external displays to your laptop.

Choosing RAM

Windows Vista requires at least 512MB RAM and is happy to use up to 4GB on most standard PCs. Having more RAM greatly improves performance, so if you're buying a new PC, look for 1GB as a practical minimum for normal computer use and 2GB as suitable for heavy use.

Choosing a Hard Disk

To install a fresh copy of Windows Vista, you need approximately 16GB of free space on your hard disk. To upgrade Windows XP to Windows Vista, you need a little less—around 15GB. These figures are pretty much absolute minimums for Windows Vista itself and allow you hardly any space for your documents, music files, photos, video files, and other files. So normally you'll want to have far more free space than this. However, if your computer has two disks, you can install Windows Vista on a disk that has only around this amount of space free, and then store your files on the other disk.

Adding a Hard Disk to Resolve a Space Crunch

If your hard disk has only just enough free space for Windows Vista, you may want to add another hard disk to hold your files. For a desktop, this can be either an internal or an external hard disk. For a laptop, it can usually be only an external hard disk. (Some laptops can accept a second internal hard disk, usually at the expense of the optical drive or battery. A few monster laptops have space for a second hard disk without sacrificing any components.)

Consider these four factors when choosing a disk drive:

◆ **Interface type** Check which interface type—for example, Serial ATA (SATA) or ATA—your computer uses. For an external disk drive, your normal choice is USB 2.0. (Avoid USB 1.1 or USB 1.0, because their data transfer speed is too slow for hard disks.)

◆ **Size** Desktops typically use 3.5-inch disk drives, while laptops typically use 2.5-inch drives. Some extra-small laptops (such as subnotebooks) use even smaller hard disks or 2.5-inch hard disks with a low height (9 mm instead of 12.5 mm). Flash-memory disk drives are just becoming viable at this writing, but their capacities remain low and their prices excruciatingly high.

◆ **Speed** The speed at which a disk can transfer data largely depends on its rotation speed in revolutions per minute (rpm). For a desktop, look for a 7,200 rpm drive rather than a 5,400 rpm drive. For a laptop, get a 5,400 rpm drive or a 7,200 rpm drive. Faster drives consume more power, are noisier, and run hotter than slower drives. Power, noise, and heat tend to be more serious considerations in laptops than in desktops, but you can find extra-quiet 7200-rpm drives for desktops too.

◆ **Cache** This is memory built into the disk drive that lets it store frequently accessed data and deliver it faster than reading it from the disk. The more cache memory, the more data the drive can cache—but the more expensive it is.

DVD Drive

You will need a DVD drive on your computer to install Windows from the DVD. If you want to use Windows' DVD-burning features for backup or entertainment, buy a DVD+/–RW drive rather than a plain DVD drive.

Checking Whether Your Computer Is Suitable for Windows Vista

To check whether your Windows XP computer is suitable for Windows Vista, download the Windows Vista Upgrade Advisor program from `http://www.microsoft.com/windowsvista/ getready/upgradeadvisor/default.mspx`, and then install it. On the Installation Complete page, make sure the Launch Microsoft Windows Vista Upgrade Advisor check box is selected, and then click the Close button. Windows Vista Upgrade Advisor opens.

Make sure that you've plugged all the devices that you want to be able to use with Windows Vista into your computer and turned them on. For example, make sure your printer, scanner, and memory card reader are connected and powered on.

Click the Start Scan button. The Upgrade Advisor scans your system, during which time you can browse information on the features Windows Vista offers. When the Scan Complete screen appears, click the See Details button. The Advisor then displays a screen telling you the following:

Whether Your Computer Can Run Windows Vista The Upgrade Advisor recommends a version of Windows Vista that appears to suit you. For example, if your computer is running Windows XP Home Edition, the Upgrade Advisor normally recommends Windows Vista Home Premium. If your computer is running Windows XP Professional, the Upgrade Advisor normally recommends Windows Vista Business.

System Requirements Whether the Upgrade Advisor has detected any system issues that will prevent you from upgrading to Windows Vista. Click the See Details button to display the details. For example, the Upgrade Advisor tells you if you need to add memory, or if your computer's graphics adapter will not support the Vista Aero UI.

Devices Whether the Upgrade Advisor has discovered hardware devices that won't work with Windows Vista. Click the See Details button to display the details. Even if the Upgrade Advisor hasn't found any devices that won't work, it may have found devices for which it has no information—so you won't know if these devices will work until you upgrade to Windows Vista.

Programs Whether the Upgrade Advisor has discovered programs that won't work with Windows Vista. Click the See Details button to display the details. For example, some older programs won't run on Windows Vista. Be prepared to stop using these programs if you upgrade.

After reviewing the system requirements, devices, or programs, you can click the Task List button in the Report Details window to see list of the tasks you should perform before and after upgrading to Windows Vista.

Once you've finished reviewing the Upgrade Advisor's findings, click the Close button (the × button) to close the Advisor.

Choosing a Method of Installing Windows Vista

You can install Windows Vista in three different ways:

Upgrade If you have Windows XP Home Edition, you can perform an upgrade, replacing Windows XP with Windows Vista. Upgrading like this transfers all your files, settings, and programs to Windows Vista, so (in theory) you can pick up your work or play straightaway in Windows Vista where you left off in Windows XP.

New installation You can install Windows Vista alongside your current version of Windows. Windows Vista creates a dual-boot setup (or modifies an existing dual-boot setup to create a multiboot setup) so that you can run either operating system. Installing like this lets you compare Windows Vista with your previous version of Windows so that you can see whether Vista suits you. You can use Windows Easy Transfer to copy your files and settings from your previous version of Windows to Windows Vista. You'll need to install all the programs you want to use on Windows Vista.

Clean installation   You can install Windows Vista from scratch on your computer, setting it up as the only operating system but not upgrading from your current operating system. You can use Windows Easy Transfer to copy your files and settings from your previous version of Windows to Windows Vista. You'll need to install all the programs you want to use on Windows Vista.

The procedures for the new installation and the clean installation are almost the same, so this appendix discusses them together, pointing out the variations.

Preparing for Installation

Once you've established that your computer should be able to run Windows Vista, prepare for installation by taking those of the following steps that are applicable to the type of installation you're planning (upgrade, new installation, or clean installation).

Back Up All Your Data Files

If you're installing Windows Vista on a computer that already has an operating system installed, back up all your data files shortly before installation using your usual backup medium. For example, from Windows XP, use the Backup program (Start ➤ All Programs ➤ Accessories ➤ System Tools ➤ Backup) to back up your files to removable media.

Write Down Internet Connection Information

If you're planning a new installation or clean installation rather than an upgrade, and you use a dial-up Internet connection, write down the information you need to create the connection: your ISP account username, your password, your ISP's phone number, and your ISP's primary and secondary DNS servers.

Plug In and Switch On All Hardware

Make sure that all the hardware you intend to use with the computer is attached to it and powered on. For example, if you'll use a printer and scanner with the computer, make sure these devices are attached to the computer and powered on, so that Setup can detect them if it's smart enough.

If you're installing Windows Vista on a laptop, make sure it's plugged into an electric socket so that it won't run out of power or put itself to sleep during the installation.

Use Windows Easy Transfer to Start Transferring Your Files and Settings

Windows Vista includes a wizard for transferring files and settings from one computer or operating system to another. You don't need to use this wizard, which is called Windows Easy Transfer, if you're upgrading Windows XP to Windows Vista, because Windows automatically transfers all your settings when you perform an upgrade. But Windows Easy Transfer can save you a great deal of time when you want to transfer files and settings either to a new computer that's running Windows Vista or to a new installation of Windows Vista on the same computer on which you've kept your previous installation of Windows as a dual-boot. For example, if you choose to test Windows Vista on a new partition before committing yourself to it, you can use

Windows Easy Transfer to transfer your work environment to the new partition so that you can use your regular settings and files.

In earlier versions of Windows, the wizard is called the Files and Settings Transfer Wizard. It works in a similar way to the Windows Easy Transfer Wizard.

ESTABLISHING WHEN TO RUN WINDOWS EASY TRANSFER

When you need to run Windows Easy Transfer depends on how you're moving to Windows Vista:

Upgrading Windows XP to Windows Vista   You don't need to run Windows Easy Transfer: Windows automatically transfers your settings from Windows XP to Windows Vista, and your files remain in place.

Moving to Windows Vista on a new computer   Run Windows Easy Transfer once you've set up Windows Vista on the new computer. The easiest method is to connect your old computer to your new computer via a network or a USB Easy Transfer cable, but you can also copy your files to a CD, DVD, USB flash drive, or external hard disk, or to a network drive.

Installing Windows Vista as a dual-boot on the same computer   Before installing Windows Vista, run Windows Easy Transfer on your old OS, and save your files to a CD, DVD, USB flash drive, an external hard disk, or to a network drive. After installing Windows Vista, run Windows Easy Transfer on Windows Vista, and bring in the files from the medium to which you saved them.

Before you use Windows Easy Transfer, make sure you've connected any network drive you want to use, or that you have a removable disk or recordable CD or DVD ready. To transfer files and settings, you'll need plenty of storage. You can save settings files to a floppy drive, but most data files will be too big.

CHOOSING THE FILES AND SETTINGS TO TRANSFER

To use Windows Easy Transfer, follow these steps:

1. Insert the Windows Vista DVD. If your computer doesn't automatically start running the DVD, open an Explorer window, navigate to the DVD, right-click, and choose AutoPlay from the context menu. Windows displays the Install Windows window.

2. Click the Transfer Files and Settings from Another Computer link. Windows launches the Windows Easy Transfer Wizard, which displays the Welcome to Windows Easy Transfer screen.

3. Click the Next button. If the wizard displays the Close Programs screen, telling you that you need to close some programs you're running, click the Close All button.

4. The wizard displays the Choose How to Transfer Files and Settings to Your New Computer screen (see Figure B.1).

5. Click the appropriate button, and then make choices on the resulting screen (which depends on the button you click):

Use an Easy Transfer Cable   Click this button if you want to connect the two computers via a USB Easy Transfer cable. The wizard displays the Install the Easy Transfer Cable and Connect Your Computer screen. Connect the two computers via the cable. Windows Vista should automatically detect the cable, but you may need to load a driver for Windows XP or another earlier version of Windows. (Depending on the cable, you may need to load a driver for Windows Vista as well.)

Transfer Directly, Using a Network Connection   Click this button if you want either to connect two computers via a network or to save files from one computer or operating system to a network drive from which you can then load them on another computer or operating system. The wizard displays the Choose How to Transfer Files and Settings over a Network screen. Click the Use a Network Connection button if you want to establish a direct network connection. If the wizard prompts you to let Windows Easy Transfer unblock itself from the firewall, click the Yes button, and then follow through the process of obtaining and entering a Windows Easy Transfer key (a code that enables Windows Easy Transfer to establish a connection across the network). Click the Copy to and from a Network Location button if you want to save your files. The wizard displays the Choose a Network Location screen. Specify the folder to use (you can use a local drive if you want), and optionally create a password to protect your files from other people.

Use a CD, DVD, or Other Removable Media   Click this button if you want to save the files to a CD, DVD, USB flash drive, or external hard disk, or to a network drive. Windows displays the Choose How to Transfer Files and Program Settings screen. Click the CD button, the USB Flash Drive button, or the External Hard Disk or to a Network Location button, and then use the resulting screen and optionally to create a password to protect the files.

6. Once you've chosen your transfer method and supplied the connection or media, the wizard displays the What Do You Want to Transfer to Your New Computer? screen (see Figure B.2).

7. Click the appropriate button:

All User Accounts, Files, and Settings   Click this button if you're migrating all users from the old computer or operating system to the new one.

FIGURE B.1

The Choose How to Transfer Files and Settings to Your New Computer screen of the Windows Easy Transfer Wizard.

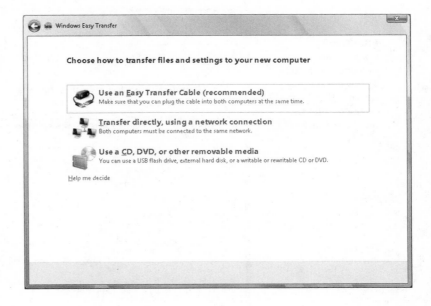

My User Account, Files, and Settings Only   Click this button if you're the only user from this computer who will be using the new computer or operating system. For example, you might be moving each user to a separate computer.

Advanced Options   Click this button if you want to transfer only specific files and settings. The wizard displays the Select User Accounts, Files, and Settings to Transfer screen (see Figure B.3). Use the check boxes and links to specify files to transfer, and then click the Next button.

FIGURE B.2

On the What Do You Want to Transfer to Your New Computer? screen of the wizard, choose whether to transfer all user accounts, files, and settings; just your own user account, files, and settings; or only the files you specify.

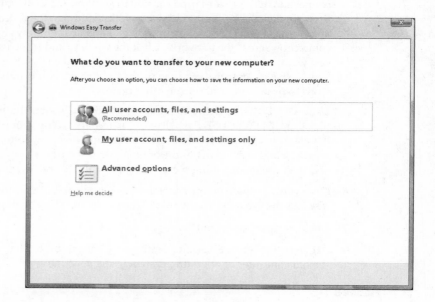

FIGURE B.3

On the Select User Accounts, Files, and Settings to Transfer screen of the wizard, choose the files and settings to transfer.

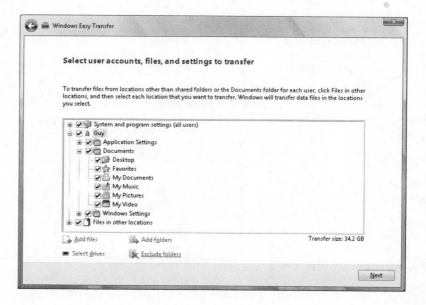

8. The wizard displays the Please Wait until the Transfer Is Complete screen as it transfers the files and settings you specified.

9. When the wizard has finished running, click the Close button.

For details of how to apply your saved files and settings to your new installation of Windows Vista, see "Transferring Your Files and Settings" later in this chapter.

Stop Any Antivirus Software, Disk Utilities, or Boot Managers

Stop any antivirus software or disk utilities before running the Windows installation, because the installation process needs direct access to your hardware. Disable or uninstall boot-manager software, or make sure that you know how to bypass it during the installation.

Upgrading Windows XP Home Edition to Windows Vista

This section discusses the procedure for upgrading your current installation of Windows XP Home Edition to Windows Vista. When you upgrade, the installation procedure copies the settings from your current version of Windows XP Home Edition and applies them to the installation of Windows Vista.

To upgrade Windows XP Home Edition to Windows Vista, take the following steps.

1. Close any programs you're running.

2. Insert the Windows Vista DVD, and then click the Install Now link on the introductory screen that appears. (If the introductory screen doesn't appear, choose Start ➢ My Computer, right-click the DVD drive, and then choose AutoPlay from the context menu.) Windows displays the Install Windows: Get Important Updates for Installation screen, as shown here.

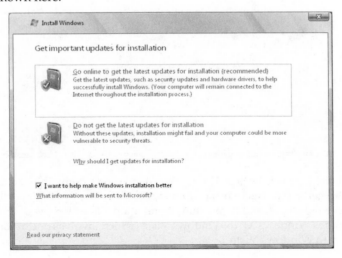

3. If you want to send general information about the upgrade process to Microsoft to help the company improve installation in future versions of Windows, select the I Want to Help Make Windows Installation Better check box.

4. If you have a fast Internet connection, click the Go Online to Get the Latest Updates for Installation button. Windows searches for updates and downloads them Otherwise, click the Do Not Get the Latest Updates for Installation button.

5. When Windows displays the Type Your Product Key for Activation screen, type the product key from the Windows packaging. Leave out the hyphens—Windows automatically inserts them for you. While Windows offers you the option of entering the key later, it's best to enter it right away.

6. If you want Windows to activate itself automatically as soon as your computer goes online, select the Automatically Activate Windows When I'm Online check box. You may prefer to clear this check box and then activate Windows manually when you've made sure that the upgrade has been successful.

7. Click the Next button. Windows displays the license agreement.

8. Read the terms, select the I Accept the License Terms check box if you can accept them, and then click the Next button. Windows displays the Which Type of Installation Do You Want? screen, as shown here.

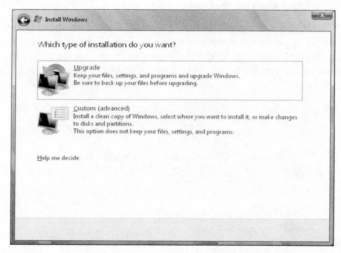

9. Click the Upgrade button. If Windows displays a Compatibility Report dialog box, as shown here, that lists issues you must resolve before upgrading, click the Close button, resolve the issues, and then restart installation. Otherwise, wait while Windows Setup upgrades Windows XP to Windows Vista (which involves one or more reboots), and then log on to Windows Vista.

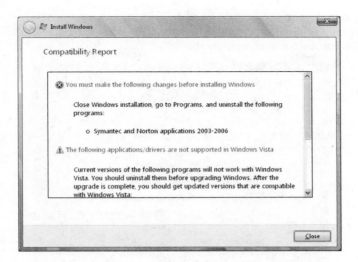

Performing a New Installation or Clean Installation of Windows Vista

This section shows you how to perform either a new installation of Windows Vista (creating a dual-boot setup of Windows Vista alongside your existing version of Windows or adding Windows Vista to an existing dual-boot setup) or a clean installation.

If you decide you want to perform a new or clean installation of Windows Vista, follow these steps:

1. Make enough space on your computer's hard disk to install Windows Vista on a separate partition of 16GB or more:

   ◆ If you have unused free space or an unused partition, you're all set.

   ◆ If you need to create a new partition by shrinking one or more existing partitions, use a tool such as PartitionMagic from Symantec (`http://www.symantec.com`).

   ◆ If you're performing a clean installation on a new hard disk, or if you'll overwrite the existing operating system, you just need to make sure the disk has a 16GB or larger partition.

2. For a new installation, back up your files in case anything goes wrong with creating the dual-boot or multiboot setup.

3. Set up your computer to include the optical drive in the boot sequence before the hard drive. The steps involved depend on your computer's BIOS (basic input/output system), but typically you press a particular key (such as Delete or F2 during bootup) to access the BIOS screens, and then use the arrow keys and the Page Up and Page Down keys to navigate among settings.

4. Insert the Windows Vista DVD, and then restart your computer. When your computer invites you to press the spacebar to boot from the DVD, press the spacebar. The Windows Vista installation routine launches itself, as shown here.

5. In the Language to Install drop-down list, choose your language—for example, English.

6. In the Time and Currency Format drop-down list, choose your location—for example, English (United States).

7. In the Keyboard or Input Method drop-down list, choose the keyboard layout you're using—for example, US.

8. Click the Next button. Windows displays a screen with an Install Now button, as shown here.

9. Click the Install Now button. Windows displays the Type Your Product Key for Activation screen.

10. Type the product key from the Windows packaging. Leave out the hyphens—Windows automatically inserts them for you. While Windows offers you the option of entering the key later, it's best to enter it right away.

11. If you want Windows to activate itself automatically as soon as your computer goes online, select the Automatically Activate Windows When I'm Online check box. You may prefer to clear this check box and then activate Windows manually when you've made sure that the installation has been successful.

12. Click the Next button. Windows displays the license agreement.

13. Read the terms, select the I Accept the License Terms check box if you can accept them, and then click the Next button. Windows displays the Which Type of Installation Do You Want? screen, as shown here. (When you boot from the DVD, the Upgrade item is disabled, as in this example. When you launch the installation from Windows XP, the Upgrade item is enabled.)

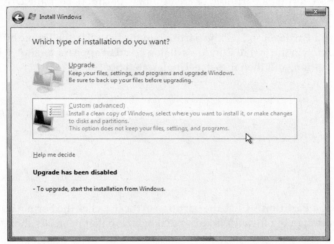

14. Click the Custom button. Windows displays the Where Do You Want to Install Windows? screen, which lists the disks and partitions available on your computer. Click the Drive Options (Advanced) link if you want to see the commands for manipulating partitions, as shown here.

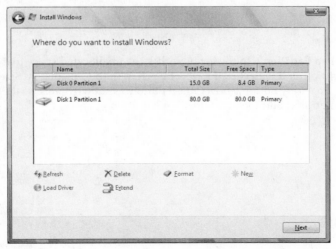

LOADING DRIVERS AND REFRESHING THE VIEW

If any of your drives or partitions don't appear in the list, click the Load Driver button to force Windows to scan the hardware again.

If Windows doesn't update the list of drives and partitions to reflect changes you make, click the Refresh button.

15. If you have already prepared a suitable partition, go to the next step. If you need to delete a partition, format a partition, or create a new partition, click the Drive Options (Advanced) link, and then work as follows.

Delete a Partition   Click the partition in the list, click the Delete button, and then click the OK button in the Install Windows dialog box that appears, as shown here. Windows deletes the partition, and then lists it as Unallocated Space.

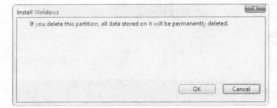

Format a Partition   Click the partition in the list, click the Format button, and then click the OK button in the Install Windows dialog box that appears, as shown here.

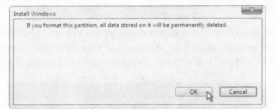

Create a Partition   In the list box, click the unallocated space that you want to turn into a partition, and then click the New button. Windows displays a Size box with spinner controls, an Apply button, and a Cancel button, as shown here. Use the Size box to specify the partition size, and then click the Apply button.

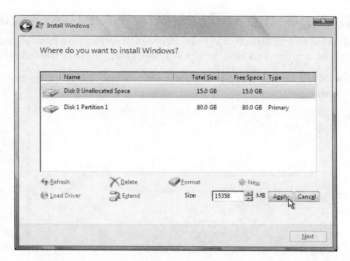

Extend a Partition   To extend an existing partition by adding unallocated space that appears after it, click the partition in the list box, click the Extend button, and then work with the controls that Windows displays. Windows allows you to extend a partition only once.

16. Select the partition in the list box, and then click the Next button. Windows copies files, expands them, and then installs the operating system, displaying a progress readout (as shown here) while it does so.

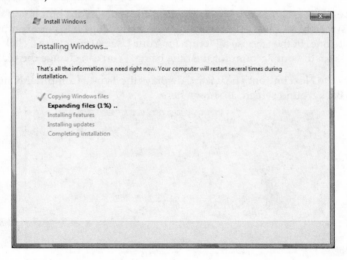

17. When Windows has finished installing, it reboots your computer, mulls its existence for a few minutes, and then displays the Set Up Windows Wizard (discussed in the next section).

Completing Setup and Creating Your User Account

When completing an installation of Windows, or when setting up a preinstalled version of Windows Vista for the first time, you use the Set Up Windows Wizard. Take the following steps:

1. The wizard first displays the Choose a User Name and Picture screen, shown here with information entered.

2. Type the username, a password (twice), and a password hint if you want to use one. The password hint is available to anyone who tries to log on to your computer, so it's best not to create one. In the Choose a Picture for Your User Account area, click the picture you want to assign to your account for the time being. (You can change the picture later.)

3. Click the Next button. The wizard displays the Type a Computer Name and Choose a Desktop Background screen, as shown here.

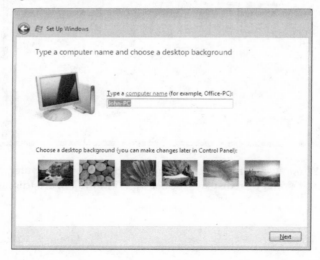

4. Type a name for the computer, using letters, numbers, and hyphens (or accept the suggested name based on the username you chose). Click one of the desktop backgrounds to use for the time being. (You can change the desktop background later too.)

5. Click the Next button. The wizard displays the Help Protect Windows Automatically screen, as shown here.

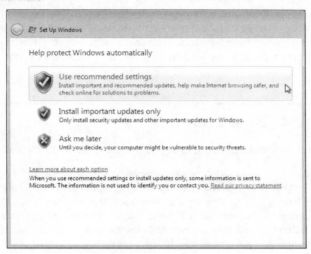

6. Click the appropriate button:

   Use Recommended Settings   Click this button if you want to install all important (critical) updates, recommended (noncritical) updates, turn on Internet safety features, and check online for solutions to Windows problems. If you have an always-on Internet connection, this is the best choice.

   Install Important Updates Only   Click this button if you want to install all critical updates but not recommended updates. You can check manually for other updates.

   Ask Me Later   Click this button if you want to postpone the decision. Because Windows doesn't install critical updates, your computer may remain open to recently developed malware or other security threats.

7. The wizard displays the Review Your Time and Date Settings screen.

8. Choose your time zone in the Time Zone drop-down list, and select the Automatically Adjust Clock for Daylight Saving Time check box if appropriate.

9. Use the date picker to change the date if necessary, and the time text box to change the time.

10. Click the Next button. The wizard displays the You're Ready to Start screen.

11. Click the Start button. Windows starts and displays the logon screen.

12. Click your username, type your password (if you assigned one), and then click the arrow button. Windows logs you on and displays the Welcome Center window, which displays brief details about your computer and provides links for getting started with Windows Vista and learning about Windows-related offers from Microsoft (such as downloading Windows Live Messenger or signing up for Windows Live OneCare antivirus software).

Activating Windows

Microsoft requires you to activate Windows Vista within 30 days of installation. Activation is a once-only procedure that you normally perform online, but there's also a phone-based backup system in case online activation is unavailable or you have an activation problem that the online system can't handle. If you don't activate Windows, it lapses into a "reduced-functionality mode" in which you can do little except go online to activate it.

Windows offers during installation to activate itself automatically, and it reminds you that you need to register, so there's little danger that you'll forget. To help you further, some computer manufacturers preactivate Windows Vista, so once you've completed setup, activation is complete.

 Real World Scenario

MAKE SURE ALL YOUR HARDWARE IS WORKING BEFORE YOU ACTIVATE WINDOWS

If you've upgraded to Windows Vista or performed a new installation or clean installation, don't activate Windows immediately. Instead, make sure that all your hardware works satisfactorily with Windows before activating it. If you've already activated Windows and then find you need to replace several of your computer's components to get Windows running well, you may have to jump through additional activation hurdles, as Windows' activation component monitors your computer's configuration to make sure you haven't surreptitiously moved an activated copy of Windows to another computer.

To see whether you need to activate Windows, and activate it if necessary, take the following steps:

1. Press Windows Key+Break. Windows displays a System window.

2. If the Windows Activation area doesn't say "Windows is activated," click the link for activation, and then follow through the resulting wizard.

Transferring Your Files and Settings

If you've upgraded from Windows XP to Windows Vista, you should be ready to start computing at this point. But if you've performed a new installation or a clean installation of Windows Vista, you may need to use Windows Easy Transfer to copy your files and settings from your old operating system or computer. To do so, take the following steps

1. If the Welcome Center window is open, double-click the Transfer Files and Settings icon in the Get Started with Windows area. Otherwise, choose Start ➢ All Programs ➢ Accessories ➢ System Tools ➢ Windows Easy Transfer. Either way, authenticate yourself to User Account Control. Windows launches the Windows Easy Transfer wizard, which displays the Welcome to Windows Easy Transfer screen.

2. Click the Next button. The wizard displays the Do You Want to Start a New Transfer or Continue One in Progress? screen. Follow through the appropriate one of the next three sections for the type of transfer you want to perform: via a USB cable; via a network; or via a CD, DVD, or removable drive.

Transferring via a USB Cable

To transfer files and settings via a USB Easy Transfer cable with Windows Easy Transfer, take the following steps:

1. Connect the USB Easy Transfer cable to each computer. If the Found New Hardware Wizard asks you to provide a driver for the cable, supply the driver that came with the cable. (The Windows Easy Transfer Wizard says that Windows Vista automatically detects USB Easy Transfer connections, but even so, you may need to install a driver for some cables.)

2. After installing any driver needed on each computer, unplug the cable again.

3. On the Do You Want to Start a New Transfer or Continue One in Progress? screen of the Windows Easy Transfer Wizard, click the Start a New Transfer button. The wizard displays the Which Computer Are You Using Now? screen.

4. Click the My New Computer button. The wizard displays the Do You Have an Easy Transfer Cable? screen.

5. Click the Yes, I Have an Easy Transfer Cable button. The wizard displays the Install the Easy Transfer Cable and Connect Your Computers screen.

6. Connect to the cable to a USB 2.0 port on each computer. When the wizard detects the connection, it displays the What Do You Want to Transfer to Your New Computer? screen.

7. Select the files and settings to transfer, as discussed in the section "Choosing the Files and Settings to Transfer," and then follow the wizard's instructions to complete the transfer.

8. The wizard displays the Please Wait until the Transfer Is Complete screen as it transfers the files and settings you specified.

9. When the wizard displays the The Transfer Is Complete screen, click the Close button.

Transferring via a Network

To transfer your files and settings via a network connection, take the following steps:

1. On the Do You Want to Start a New Transfer or Continue One in Progress? screen of the Windows Easy Transfer Wizard, click the Continue a Transfer in Progress button. The wizard displays the Are Your Computers Connected to a Network? screen.

2. Click the Yes, I'll Transfer Files and Settings over the Network button. If the wizard tells you that your firewall is blocking Windows Easy Transfer from using the network, as

shown here, click the Yes button. The wizard displays the Type Your Windows Easy Transfer Key screen.

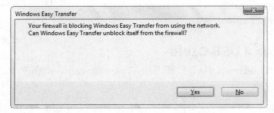

3. Type the key (the code) from your old computer, and then click the Next button. The wizard establishes a connection between the two computers, and then displays the Your Computers Are Now Connected screen.

4. Select the files and settings to transfer, as discussed in the section "Choosing the Files and Settings to Transfer," and then follow the wizard's instructions to complete the transfer.

5. The wizard displays the Please Wait until the Transfer Is Complete screen as it transfers the files and settings you specified.

6. When the wizard displays the The Transfer Is Complete screen, click the Close button.

Transferring via a CD, DVD, or Drive

To transfer your files or settings via a CD, DVD, USB flash drive, or network drive, take the following steps.

1. On the Do You Want to Start a New Transfer or Continue One in Progress? screen of the Windows Easy Transfer Wizard, click the Continue a Transfer in Progress button. The wizard displays the Are Your Computers Connected to a Network? screen.

1. Click the No, I've Copied Files and Settings to a CD, DVD or Other Removable Media button. The wizard displays the Where Did You Save the Files and Settings You Want to Transfer? screen.

2. Click the On a CD or DVD button, the On a USB Flash Drive button, or the On an External Hard Disk or Network Location button, as appropriate.

3. On the next screen (the name varies depending on the medium), tell the wizard where the disc or drive is, type the password (if there is one), and then click the Next button. Windows displays the Review Selected Files and Settings screen.

4. Double-check the list of files and settings, and then click the Transfer button.

5. Windows displays the Please Wait until the Transfer Is Complete screen as it transfers the files and settings you specified.

6. When the wizard displays the The Transfer Is Complete screen, click the Close button.

Real World Scenario

STARTING A TRANSFER FROM WINDOWS EXPLORER

If you've saved your files and settings to a file on a CD, DVD, or drive, you don't need to go through the preliminary stops of the Windows Easy Transfer Wizard. Instead, follow these steps:

1. Insert the disc or connect the drive.

2. Open a Windows Explorer window to the folder that contains the file.

3. Double-click the file, and then authenticate yourself to User Account Control. Windows launches the Windows Easy Transfer Wizard at the Review Selected Files and Settings screen, where you can simply click the Transfer button to start the transfer.

Logging Off (If Necessary)

If the Windows Easy Transfer Wizard prompts you to log off so that it can finish applying your files and settings, do so. When you log back on, you'll find the files and settings.

Index

Note to the Reader: Throughout this index **boldfaced** page numbers indicate primary discussions of a topic. *Italicized* page numbers indicate illustrations.

H

M

U